Encyclopedia of
Environmental Issues

Encyclopedia of
Environmental Issues

Third Edition

Volume 1

A to D

Editor
Richard Renneboog, MSc

SALEM PRESS
A Division of EBSCO Information Services, Inc.
Ipswich, Massachusetts

GREY HOUSE PUBLISHING

Publisher's Cataloging-In-Publication Data
(Prepared by The Donohue Group, Inc.)

Names: Renneboog, Richard, editor.
Title: Encyclopedia of environmental issues / editor, Richard M. Renneboog, MSc.
Description: Third edition. | Ipswich, Massachusetts : Salem Press, a division of EBSCO Information Services ; Amenia, NY : Grey House Publishing, [2019] | Includes bibliographical references and index.
Identifiers: ISBN 9781642650549 (set) | ISBN 9781642653533 (v. 1) | ISBN 9781642653540 (v. 2) | ISBN 9781642653557 (v. 3) | ISBN 9781642653564 (v. 4)
Subjects: LCSH: Environmental sciences–Encyclopedias. | Pollution–Encyclopedias.
Classification: LCC GE10 .E52 2019 | DDC 363.7003–dc23

FIRST PRINTING
PRINTED IN THE UNITED STATES OF AMERICA

■ Table of Contents

■ Publisher's Note

As we enter the third decade of the twenty-first century, environmental issues are at the top of the urgent concerns facing the world. In *Encyclopedia of Environmental Issues*, 3rd edition, the fundamental concepts, issues, and debates are considered. This 4-volume encyclopedia is a definitive reference to environmental issues from Acid deposition and acid rain to Zoos' involvement in wildlife conservation.

From fossil fuels to renewable resources, pollution to sustainability, from Edward Albee to Howard Clinton Zahniser, the *Encyclopedia of Environmental Issues* is a roundup of environment-related curricular disciplines, including agriculture, history, sociology, energy, public policy, science, climatology, engineering, and business. Especially targeted toward high-school students, this outstanding reference work is edited to tie into the high-school curriculum, making the content readily accessible as well as to patrons of public, academic, and university libraries. Pedagogical elements include a timeline, resource guides, glossary, and thorough index.

Scope of Coverage

This academic, multi-author reference work serves as a general and nontechnical resource for students and teachers to understand the importance of the many issues related to the environment, from agriculture and engineering to disasters and breakthroughs. The intent is to gain an appreciation for the dramatic impact our interactions with the environment, negative and positive, can have on nations around the world; to learn the history of environmental studies; and to initiate educational discussion brought forth by the specific social and topical articles presented in the work. Individuals who have made significant contributions are included as well as topics related to the field of environmentalism, including important legislation, treaties, governmental action, and industry.

Article Length and Format

Articles in the encyclopedia range in length from 500 to 3,500 words. Each is first presented with the category to which it belongs (for example, Agronomy; Anthropology; or History), a statement of the significance of the topic or identification of the individual, and an article summary.

The article body contains a thorough explanation and review of the topic or the work of the individual being profiled. Each article is then followed by a "Further Reading" section that includes bibliographic citations and, where appropriate, a "See Also" section that includes cross-references to other relevant articles in the set. Many articles are richly illustrated with photos and captions, and charts, graphs, and tables. Each article is signed by the contributor to the encyclopedia.

Frontmatter and Backmatter

Volume 1 of the *Encyclopedia of Environmental Issues* begins with an introduction to the set. The "List of Articles," repeated in all four volumes, features all the articles in alphabetical order with page numbers as they are listed in the encyclopedia. The "List of Contributors" presents all the writers for the encyclopedia.

The backmatter of the encyclopedia at the end of Volume 4 includes the following:

- Glossary
- Timeline of American Environmentalism
- Key Figures in Environmentalism
- U.S. Federal Laws Concerning the Environment
- Directory of U.S. National Parks
- Major World National Parks and Protected Areas
- Environmental Organizations
- Subject Index

■ Editor's Introduction

To paraphrase a famous movie title, our environment is a many-splendored thing. It surrounds us, supports us, and shelters us from the celestial storm. We breathe it, we swim through it, we walk on it, and we live within it. Yet most never realize the interconnected whole of our environment. To do that requires that people become inactive observers who look at some part of the environment that surrounds them, look at how that part interacts with the other parts of the immediate environment, and keep on looking until they see what lies far beyond. The atmosphere is a perfect example. We breathe the air that surrounds us and see it stretching away into the distance when we look outside. The wind blows, but where did that come from? Looking beyond, eventually we realize that the entire planet is surrounded by air. The nearest star, the Sun, shines through and heats the air. Heat transfer takes place, and the warmed air rises. But Earth's gravity and the realities of heat transfer limit the extent to which that heated air can rise. We see that air is a continuous fluid, and movement of some part of any continuous fluid results in movement of the rest of the fluid to replace the fluid that has moved first. So as the warmed air rises, cooler air moves in to take its place. Physics identifies this as a convection current, and in such a current the warmed air eventually cools, becomes denser, and sinks once more to the appropriate level. All of the air moves in the atmosphere, and the planet spins at a rate of one revolution per day within the atmosphere. Because of that, the air that rises doesn't stay over the same location, but moves sideways relative to the surface before cooling a descending. The planet is essentially spherical in shape, so the distance traveled relative to the surface in that once-a-day rotation varies drastically according to location on Earth's surface. The movement of the atmosphere as a whole is thus chaotic in nature, but over many millions of years, some static features have come into existence. There are the polar vortices bordered by the northern and southern jet streams, bands of wind that encircle the planet in the same way that that they do in the atmospheres of other planets with atmospheres. In the fluid layer that we call oceans, static currents have arisen in much the same way, affected by the movement of the air above, and by movement of the ground below. Seen in this longer perspective, our environment is a gigantic, slow, yet dynamic, dance performed on a planetary scale. This is the environment nature has gifted the human race, and all known life, as its home.

Like all homes, the environment must be tended with care and respect. Yet this has not been the human race's strong point throughout time. The environment of Earth is inextricably linked to the human population, and depends on human nature for its long-term sustainability. How humans have used this unique environment called Earth has in many ways been admirable. But in many other ways the human race has treated its environment abominably. The articles in this volume attempt to identify and address some of the important issues that have themselves become part of the human environment. While the environment of Earth spans the entire planet, the issues addressed in these articles are of necessity centered primarily about the North American continent, and specifically the United States of America. As the developed nation that has the highest rate of consumption in the entire world, it is easy to understand why the focus is on this part of the world. Consumption demands production of goods to be consumed, everything from basic staple foods to the most frivolous of 'toys' require that humans alter and affect change in their environment to produce those goods. In order to produce crops of food goods, natural habitats must be cleared of everything that would interfere with the production of that food. Accordingly, humans have created fields for vegetable crops and pasture lands for animal crops. Ecosystems are like that fluid atmosphere in the sense that the natural wildlife that was in those areas has been forced to move into other locations as the new domestic animals and vegetation moved in. This is an environmental issue of high importance, simply because the land and the ecosystems it contains are finite. There is only so much land that can be affected in this way, and unfortunately this has been all to the detriment of the natural environment and for the benefit of humans. In 2019, it is believed that some 60% of all species on Earth, both animal and plant, have been lost through the short-sightedness of human activities. It has become increasingly apparent that the human race in the developed nations has used Earth as its private dumping ground in ways that have polluted the waters, the air, and even the ground beneath our feet.

Air pollution, as the spewing of billions of tons of carbon dioxide and other gases into the atmosphere, now threatens to raise the average temperature of Earth in such a way that the entire environment is at risk. A sufficient rise in average temperature will result in an influx of water from melted glaciers and polar icecaps that will see ocean water levels rise to heights the human race has never seen in its entire existence, covering much of the current coastlines and destroying the cities there. This will affect not just North America, but the entire world.

Water pollution, as the spewing of billions of tons of refuse and waste into the waters of the oceans, has created large 'islands' of floating plastics and other materials in all of the major oceans. This has endangered much of the wildlife that lives in the oceans, as plastic items are mistaken as food in their appearance. To sea turtles that dine exclusively on jellyfish a plastic bag floating in the water looks like a tasty morsel rather than an indigestible thing that will block its digestive tract and cause it to starve. The same is true of whales, sharks and numerous other ocean carnivores that mistake a bit of floating junk for the fish that they normally feed on.

Land pollution, as the billions of tons of fertilizers and pesticides that have been routinely used in agricultural practices for decades; the millions of tons of chemical wastes that have been buried and forgotten only to resurface years later to cause terrible damage to the environment and the people who live in it; the forest lands stripped bare of trees, allowing erosion to have free reign; the lands either stripped or mined for mineral resources, releasing great amounts of toxic materials into the environment.

This list could go on and on, yet environmental issues are not all doom and gloom. Many have recognized the need to address the manner in which humans use the environment in which we all live. This has lead to the establishment of large wilderness areas as national parks, not just in the United States but in essentially all countries of the world. On a smaller scale, all states, provinces, cities and towns have similar greenspaces and parklands. These are seen as not only beneficial to the people in general, but to the protection and maintenance of the natural environment and biodiversity as well. It is unfortunate indeed that these changes have come too late for many species that have become extinct through human activities, but at the same time it is a hopeful step toward securing the future of the myriad species that remain in our shared environment. People generally have accepted coexistence with nature in the broad scheme of things rather than the subjugation of the natural world to the selfish desires of the human race. As a result, steps have been taken to undo the damage that human interference has done in the past. A prime example, however one that is still contentious to some, is the reintroduction of a grey wolf population into Yellowstone National Park in the 1990s. The indigenous grey wolf population there was purposefully eliminated in 1915, resulting in a complete imbalance down the entire trophic chain in the park. Herbivores and prey species were uncontrolled and ran rampant, quickly overpopulating and stripping native plant species that had played a vital role in the park ecosystem. With those plants gone from riparian spaces, stream and river banks were destabilized and allowed swamps and marsh areas to expand away from the natural watercourses. With the predator-prey balance restored, however, the herbivore populations have been controlled and even the geography of the park has been restored as waterways regained their proper structures.

Water continues to be an issue of concern as the human population and its attendant need for more and more food continue to grow. This has lead to advances in agricultural techniques that in turn produce more and better foods for health-conscious people. Efficiency in growing practices and decreasing reliance on drug-assisted growth and outdated factory farming methods is becoming more and more important as the population has become more aware of how these practices have affected the environment.

The quality of the air we breathe continues to be an environmental issue, especially in the face of climate change. This is perhaps the most contentious issue of the twentieth and twenty-first centuries, as it has in many ways been made into a political issue rather than an environmental issue, with one administration working to reduce the effects of carbon emissions and the next working to undo and eliminate those efforts. It is unfortunate that the people of the nation, who are not involved in the policy decisions of the administration, are caught between the two opposing political wills in such a way that the actual science on both sides of the climate change debate is neither understood nor appreciated. Nevertheless, the energy and transportation industries seem to have come to an appreciation of the fact that Earth's mineral resources are finite, and are actively seeking ways to maintain the standards of North American living without further damaging the environment. Accordingly, significant investments are being made in alternative energy sources and fuels that do not produce carbon emissions.

In places where the soil has been contaminated by irresponsible disposal methods for chemical and industrial wastes, significant and costly measures are being taken for the remediation of those sites. There are several examples of this failure and what remediation is costing. The old adage that 'an ounce of prevention is worth a pound of cure' having been ignored in the past, the present-day cures for past indiscretions are costing massive amounts of money. But they are being undertaken, and the environment we share is being repaired.

Taken all together, there will always be environmental issues that must be addressed, and the nature of those issues will no doubt change as the human population continues to grow, weather changes, natural disasters occur and life goes on. Our environment is a dynamic place, with a complex structure and a complicated network of anthropogenic and natural interactions, all of which affect each other in some way. The articles in this volume provide insight into some of the significant events and people that have been part of the cause-and-effect relations that have affected the human presence in this environment in the past and that will continue to affect it in future times.

Richard M. Renneboog, MSc

■ Contributor List

Richard Adler

Emily Alward

R. Baird Shuman

Anita Baker-Blocker

Elizabeth A. Barthelmes

Melissa A. Barton

Robert B. Bechtel

Raymond D. Benge Jr.

Alvin K. Benson

Massimo D. Bezoari

Cynthia A. Bily

Richard G. Botzler

Lakhdar Boukerrou

Pat Brereton

Victoria M. Breting-García

Howard Bromberg

Kenneth H. Brown

Bruce G. Brunton

Michael A. Buratovich

Byron Cannon

Glenn Canyon

Frederick B. Chary

Dennis W. Cheek

Nader N. Chokr

Thomas Clarkin

Kathryn A. Cochran

Daniel J. Connell

Mark Coyne

Ralph D. Cross

Anna M. Cruse

Robert L. Cullers

George Cvetkovich

Dennis R. DeVries

Joseph Dewey

Stephen B. Dobrow

Gary E. Dolph

Colleen M. Driscoll

Andrew P. Duncan

Sohini Dutt

Timothy C. Earle

Frank N. Egerton

Howard C. Ellis

C. R. de Freitas

Brian J. Gareau

Roberto Garza

Soraya Ghayourmanesh

Craig S. Gilman

Lissy Goralnik

D. R. Gossett

Daniel G. Graetzer

Hans G. Graetzer

Jerry E. Green

Phillip A. Greenberg

Wendy Halpin Hallows

Wendy C. Hamblet

Gerald K. Harrison

C. Alton Hassell

Thomas E. Hemmerly

Jane F. Hill

Laurent Hodges

John R. Holmes

Robert M. Hordon

Louise D. Hose

Ronald K. Huch

Patrick Norman Hunt

H. David Husic

Diane White Husic

Solomon A. Isiorho

Allan Jenkins

Bruce E. Johansen

Karen N. Kähler

Karen E. Kalumuck

Joseph Kantenbacher

Susan J. Karcher

Jamie Michael Kass

Robert W. Kingsolver

Samuel V. A. Kisseadoo

Grove Koger

Narayanan M. Komerath

Padma P. Komerath

Andrew Lambert

Nicholas Lancaster

Timothy Lane

Eugene Larson

Thomas T. Lewis

Josué Njock Libii

Michael Mooradian Lupro

Marianne M. Madsen

Louise Magoon

Nancy Farm Männikkö

Sergei A. Markov

Chogollah Maroufi

Steven B. McBride

Roman Meinhold

Randall L. Milstein

Richard F. Modlin

M. Marian Mustoe

Alice Myers

Peter Neushul

Beth Ann Parker

Gordon A. Parker

Julio César Pino

P. S. Ramsey

C. Mervyn Rasmussen

Donald F. Reaser

Claudia Reitinger

Raymond U. Roberts

James L. Robinson, PhD

Charles W. Rogers

Carol A. Rolf

Keith E. Rolfe

Robert M. Sanford

Elizabeth D. Schafer

Alexander Scott

Rose Secrest

Martha A. Sherwood

Roger Smith

Jane Marie Smith

Adam B. Smith

Daniel L. Smith-Christopher

Joan C. Stevenson

Toby Stewart

Dion Stewart

Theresa L. Stowell

Hubert B. Stroud

Rena Christina Tabata

John M. Theilmann

Nicholas C. Thomas

Joseph M. Wahome

John P. Watkins

Shawncey Webb

Robert J. Wells

Marcie L. Wingfield

Sam Wong

Lisa A. Wroble

Jay R. Yett

Ming Y. Zheng

■ Complete List of Articles

A

■ Abbey, Edward

FIELDS OF STUDY: Popular Culture, Media, Publishing; Authors, Writers; Ethics, Advocacy, Policy, Protest; Ecology, Environment, Environmentalism.
CATEGORIES: Activism and advocacy; preservation and wilderness issues
IDENTIFICATION: American environmental activist and author

The originality of Abbey's ideas regarding the preservation of nature, expressed with great eloquence in his writings, helped to increase awareness of environmental issues and inspired a radical environmental movement.

Over the course of his lifetime, Edward Abbey produced twenty-one volumes of fiction, essays, speeches, and letters expressing his love for the earth, his hatred of modern technological society, and his fervent belief that development was destroying the American West. When he was twenty-one years old, having spent some time in the military and in college, he left his home in Pennsylvania to see the American West. He hitchhiked, rode trains, and walked over the mountains and through the desert. He claimed the desert as his spiritual home and lived in or near it for most of the rest of his life. He completed a master's degree at the University of New Mexico and wrote his Ph.D. thesis on anarchism and the morality of violence. During his ten-year college career, which included two years as a Fulbright Fellow at the University of Edinburgh in Scotland, he began a number of writing projects and published his first novel, *Jonathan Troy* (1954).

For fifteen years, during his thirties and forties, Abbey worked as a part-time ranger at various national parks in the American Southwest. The two years in the late 1950's that he spent at Arches National Monument (now a national park) in Utah led to his first important book, *Desert Solitaire: A Season in the Wilderness* (1968). This book combines beautiful descriptive passages, an unflinching look at the violence in nature, and a strong call for the preservation of desert habitats. Reminiscent of Henry David Thoreau's *Walden* (1854) in its ideas and its use of the natural year for its structure, *Desert Solitaire* brought Abbey national attention as an environmental writer.

In 1975 Abbey published *The Monkey Wrench Gang*, a novel about four rebels who set out to destroy the roads, bridges, and power lines that they believe are defacing the southwestern desert. This work is loosely based on the exploits of a friend of Abbey who had committed some of the acts depicted in the novel. Despite the fact that Abbey consistently maintained that he intended the book primarily as humor, it helped inspire the radical environmental group Earth First!, a group that Abbey did come to support, praising its operations although never actually joining it. In fact, Abbey never joined any political or environmental organizations, although he participated in political actions, especially those that expressed disapproval of the military or land development.

Though most of his books are set in the wilderness of the Southwest and express his deep love for such spaces, Abbey disliked being called a "nature writer." In fact, students of his work have had difficulty attaching any label to Abbey and making it stick, so idiosyncratic are his ideas and connections. When Abbey died in 1989, he left instructions that he should be buried in the desert, unembalmed, in his sleeping bag. Although this kind of burial was illegal, his friends followed his wishes.

Cynthia A. Bily

Further Reading
Bishop, James, Jr. *Epitaph for a Desert Anarchist: The Life and Legacy of Edward Abbey.* Atheneum, 1994.
Cahalan, James M. *Edward Abbey: A Life.* University of Arizona Press, 2001.

Pozza, David M. *Bedrock and Paradox: The Literary Landscape of Edward Abbey.* Peter Lang, 2006.

See also: Earth First!; Monkeywrenching; Preservation.

■ Accounting for nature

FIELDS OF STUDY: Economics; Business Management; Ecosystem Management;

IDENTIFICATION: The expansion of economic principles and adaptation of financial decisions to take into consideration natural resources, ecosystem services, and values derived from human contact with the natural world

In comparisons of the costs and benefits of various actions in relation to the environment, the coordination of ecological and economic expertise can result in a balanced problem-solving approach.

Environmental decisions frequently set ecologists and economists on a collision course: Does society's demand for energy justify the environmental impacts of mining and burning coal? Is the increased economic efficiency of large corporate farms worth the loss of a rural lifestyle? How much should the public sacrifice to protect endangered birds or plants? These decisions are difficult because they force comparisons of "apples and oranges," pitting one set of values against another. Quantitative models (or accounting systems) that compare the costs and benefits of a course of action are frequently used to guide business and government decisions, but these have generally omitted environmental values. Accounting for nature in these models cannot produce completely objective solutions but can help coordinate ecological and economic expertise in a more balanced problem-solving approach.

Ecologist Edward O. Wilson has identified three kinds of national wealth: economic, cultural, and biological. He has observed that nations frequently create the illusion of a growing economy by consuming their biological or cultural "capital" to create short-term economic prosperity. For example, burning rain forests and replacing them with row crops may temporarily increase farm production in a

Photo of Dr. Paul R. Ehrlich, entomologist. By Ilka Hartmann (eBay).

developing nation, but tropical soils are often nutrient-poor and easily degraded by exposure to the sun and rain. If the biological basis of production is ignored, the population simply transfers wealth from one category to another, ensuring ecological disaster for its children in the process.

Developed nations have also neglected biological wealth in past cost-benefit analyses. Nations have justified the damming of wild rivers to make recreational lakes, for example, by counting the benefits of lumbering trees from the watershed but not the losses of aquatic and forest habitats. Recreational activities have been evaluated according to the money that people pay to participate in them; thus hikers and canoeists in a wilderness area are given less consideration than water-skiers or drivers of recreational vehicles in a developed area because hikers and canoeists spend less money on equipment, fuel, and supplies.

Ecologists Eugene P. Odum and Howard T. Odum addressed this issue by calculating the value of ecosystem services provided by intact biological communities. Their approach was to measure the beneficial work performed by living systems and place a value on that service based on the time and energy required to replicate the service. A living tree, they reasoned, may provide a few hundred dollars in lumber if cut; if left alive, however, the oxygen it produces, carbon dioxide it absorbs, wildlife it feeds and shelters, soil it builds, evaporative cooling it yields, and flood protection it provides are worth far more on an annual basis.

In 1972, economists William Nordhaus and James Tobin refined the concept of national wealth by developing an index of net economic welfare (NEW) to replace the more familiar measurements of economic health such as gross domestic product (GDP). Their criticism of the GDP was that it counts any expenditure as a positive contribution to national wealth, whether or not the spending improves people's lives. A toxic waste dump, for example, contributes to the GDP when the pollutants are produced, again when millions of dollars are spent to clean it, and yet again if medical costs rise because of pollution-related illness. Nordhaus and Tobin's NEW index subtracts pollution abatement and other environmental costs from the value of goods and services that actually improve living standards.

Economist E. F. Schumacher subsequently argued that environmental costs should be "internalized," or charged to the industries that create them. This idea, also called the "polluter pays principle," not only generates funds for environmental cleanup but also encourages businesses to make environmentally sound decisions. The price of recycled paper, for example, would be more competitive if the public costs of deforestation and pollution from pulp mills were added to the price of virgin wood fiber. Proposals for internalizing environmental costs have ranged from centrally planned models, such as a carbon tax on fossil fuels, to free market trading of pollution credits. Debt-for-nature swaps, through which developing nations receive financial benefits for preserving natural ecosystems, represent environmental cost accounting on the asset side of the ledger.

A fundamental difference between economic and ecological worldviews is the time scale under consideration. Business strategies may look five years ahead, but ecological processes can take centuries. Thus economic models that fail to take long-term issues into account are a frequent source of criticism by environmentalists. The U.S. decision to build nuclear fission reactors during the 1960's and 1970's is a case in point. Nuclear power appeared economically attractive over the thirty-five-year life span of a fission reactor, but the twenty-four-thousand-year half-life of radioactive plutonium 239 in spent fuel rods made skeptics wonder who would pay the costs of nuclear waste disposal for generations after the plants were closed.

Debates about growth are especially contentious. Traditional economists view the growth of populations, goods, and services as positive and necessary for economic progress and social stability. As early as 1798, however, economist Thomas Robert Malthus pointed out that on a finite Earth, an exponentially expanding human population would eventually run out of vital resources. In the closing decades of the twentieth century, Paul R. Ehrlich and Anne Ehrlich warned that unless population growth slowed soon, each person would have to consume less space, food, fuel, and other materials to avoid a global population crash. Whether one considers them economic pessimists or environmental realists, Malthus and the Ehrlichs demonstrate that taking a longer view is central to the task of accounting for nature. Sustainable development is the watchword for ecologists, economists, and political leaders attempting to create prosperity today while accounting for the welfare of future generations.

Robert W. Kingsolver

Further Reading

Anderson, Terry L., Laura E. Huggins, and Thomas Michael Power, eds. *Accounting for Mother Nature: Changing Demands for Her Bounty.* Stanford University Press, 2008.

Costanza, Robert, ed. *An Introduction to Ecological Economics.* St. Lucie Press, 1997.

Pearce, Joseph. *Small Is Still Beautiful: Economics As If Families Mattered.* ISI Books, 2006.

Schumacher, E. F. *Small Is Beautiful: Economics As If People Mattered.* 1973. Reprint. Point Roberts, Hartley & Marks, 1999.

Worldwatch Institute. *State of the World.* W. W. Norton, 2010.

■ Acid deposition and acid rain

FIELDS OF STUDY: Chemistry; Elements, Substances, Chemicals, Compounds; Pollution, Emissions, Toxic Waste, Hazardous Materials; Biology, Life Sciences, Ecosystems; Ecology, Environment, Environmentalism.

IDENTIFICATION: Deposition of acidic gases, particles, and precipitation (rain, fog, dew, snow, or sleet) on the surface of the earth

Electric utilities, industries, and automobiles emit sulfur dioxide and nitrogen oxides that are readily oxidized into sulfuric and nitric acids in the atmosphere. Long-range transport and dispersion of these air pollutants produce regional acid deposition, which alters aquatic and forest ecosystems and accelerates corrosion of buildings, monuments, and statuary.

In 1872 Robert Angus Smith used the term "acid rain" in his book *Air and Rain: The Beginnings of a Chemical Climatology* to describe precipitation affected by coal-burning industries. Acidity is created when sulfur dioxide (SO_2) and nitrogen oxides (NO_x) react with water and oxidants in the atmosphere to form water-soluble sulfuric and nitric acids. The normal acidity of rain is pH 5.6, which is caused by the formation of carbonic acid from water-dissolved carbon dioxide. The acidity of precipitation collected at monitoring stations around the world varies from pH 3.8 to 6.3 (pH 3.8 is three hundred times as acidic as pH 6.3). Ammonia, as well as soil constituents such as calcium and magnesium that are often present in suspended dust, neutralizes atmospheric acids, which helps explain the geographical variation of precipitation acidity.

Increasing Acidity

Between the mid-nineteenth century and World War II, the Industrial Revolution led to a tremendous increase in coal burning and metal ore processing in both Europe and North America. The combustion of coal, which contains an average of 1.5 percent sulfur by weight, and the smelting of metal sulfides released opaque plumes of smoke and SO_2 from short chimneys into the atmosphere.

Copper, nickel, and zinc smelters inundated nearby landscapes with SO_2 and heavy metals. One of the world's largest nickel smelters, located in Sudbury, Ontario, Canada, began operation in 1890 and

by 1960 was pouring 2.6 million tons of SO_2 per year into the atmosphere. By 1970 the environmental damage extended to 72,000 hectares (278 square miles) of injured vegetation, lakes, and soils surrounding the site; within this area 17,000 hectares (66 square miles) were barren. The land was devastated not only by acid deposition but also by the accumulation of toxic metals in the soil, the clear-cutting of forested areas for fuel, and soil erosion caused by wind, water, and frost heave. (The situation improved dramatically in the ensuing decades, but only after construction in 1972 of a tall "superstack" that dispersed emissions farther from the smelting facility, followed by an extensive tree-planting program and other major environmental reclamation efforts, as well as installation of industrial scrubber systems at the facility during the 1990's.)

In urban areas, high concentrations of sulfur corroded metal and accelerated the erosion of stone buildings and monuments. Historical structures such as the Acropolis in Greece suffered serious damage from elevated acidity. During the winter, added emissions from home heating and stagnant weather conditions caused severe air pollution episodes characterized by sulfuric acid fogs and thick, black soot. In 1952 a four-day air-pollution episode in London, England, killed an estimated four thousand people.

After World War II, large coal-burning utilities in Western Europe and the United States built their plants with particulate control devices and stacks higher than 100 meters (328 feet) to improve the local air quality. (By contrast, huge industrial facilities throughout Eastern Europe and the Soviet Union operated without air-pollution controls for most of the twentieth century.) The tall stacks increased the dispersion and transport of air pollutants from tens to hundreds of kilometers. While this measure eased localized impacts, it simultaneously made the problem more widespread. Worldwide emissions of SO_2 increased; in the United States emissions climbed from 18 million tons in 1940 to a peak of 28 million tons in 1970. Acid deposition evolved into an interstate and even an international problem.

In major cities, exhaust from automobiles combined with power plant and industrial emissions to create a choking, acrid smog of ozone mixed with nitric and organic acids formed by photochemical processes. The rapid deterioration of air quality in cities, with attendant health and environmental consequences, spurred the passage of environmental laws

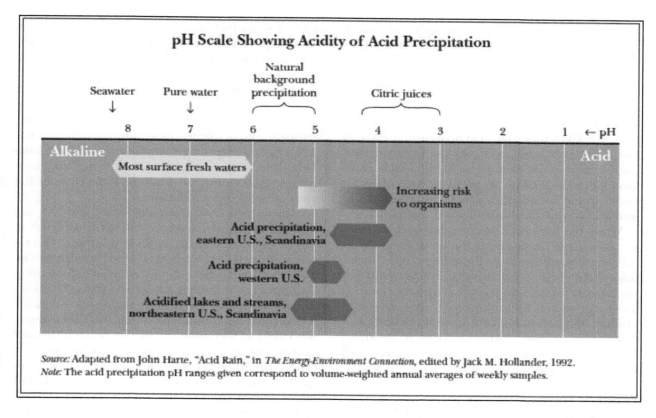

pH Scale Showing Acidity of Acid Precipitation

Source: Adapted from John Harte, "Acid Rain," in *The Energy-Environment Connection*, edited by Jack M. Hollander, 1992.
Note: The acid precipitation pH ranges given correspond to volume-weighted annual averages of weekly samples.

such as the U.S. Clean Air Act (CAA) of 1963, which was amended and expanded in 1970, 1977, and 1990. Each amendment to the CAA brought new requirements for air-pollution controls.

Effects on Aquatic Ecosystems

Landscapes rich in limestone or acid-buffering soils are less sensitive to acid deposition. Regions that are both sensitive and exposed to acid deposition include the eastern United States, southeastern Canada, the northern tip of South America, southern Sweden and Norway, central and Eastern Europe, the United Kingdom, southeastern China, northeastern India, Thailand, and the Republic of Korea (South Korea). Within these regions, acid rain disrupts aquatic ecosystems and contributes to forest decline.

A strong correlation has been found between fish extinction and lake and stream acidity. Researchers have also found that the diversity of not only fish but also phytoplankton, zooplankton, invertebrates, and amphibian species diminishes by more than 50 percent as surface water pH drops from 6.0 to 5.0. Below pH 5.6, aluminum released from bottom sediments

or leached from the surrounding soils interferes with gas and ion exchange in fish gills and can be toxic to aquatic life. At pH 5.0, most fish eggs cannot hatch; below pH 4.0, no fish survive.

In southern Norway, the virtual extinction of salmon in all the larger salmon rivers is attributed to acid rain. In 2008 it was found that twelve salmon stocks were endangered and another eighteen had been wiped out altogether. Records and long-term monitoring show that the decline of fish populations began during the early twentieth century, with dramatic losses during the 1950's. Between 1950 and 1990, fish mortality in the region became more widespread. In the three decades following 1980, pollution-control measures in Norway and the rest of Europe cut acid precipitation over Norway by roughly half. Aquatic animal and plant populations and ecosystems continue to recover from the damage.

In the United States the New York State Department of Environmental Conservation reported in 2008 that 26 percent of the state's lakes in the Adirondack Mountains were unable to neutralize incoming acids to concentrations that fish could tolerate. During certain times of year, up to 70 percent of the lakes had the potential to become intolerably acidic. Of forty-eight Adirondack lakes surveyed, sixteen had aluminum concentrations above levels that juvenile fish could withstand. Ecosystems in this region have been affected by plumes of air pollutants carried by prevailing winds from the Ohio River Valley. Like their Norwegian counterparts, the Adirondack lakes have low acid-neutralizing capacity. Fish declines that began during the early twentieth century and continued through the 1980's corresponded to reductions in pH. Fish kills often followed spring snowmelt, which filled the waterways with acid accumulated in winter precipitation.

While the CAA and its amendments have done much to reduce the acidity of the precipitation in the Adirondacks, and thus of the lakes, recovery takes time. Lake chemistry that is acidic year-round may take twenty-five to one hundred years to return to levels that aquatic life can tolerate, while seasonally acidic lake waters may take a few years or several decades. Once a lake regains its ability to neutralize acid, wildlife in the lake's ecosystem require additional time to become reestablished.

Effects on Forests and Cities
In areas exposed to acid rain, dead and dying trees stand as symbols of environmental change. In Germany the term *Waldsterben*, or forest death, was coined to describe the rapid declines of Norway spruce, Scotch pine, and silver fir trees during the early 1980's, followed by beech and oak trees during the late 1980's, especially at high elevations in the Black and Bavarian forests. At higher altitudes, clouds frequently shroud mountain peaks, bathing the forest canopy in a mist of heavy metals and sulfuric and nitric acids. Under drought conditions, invisible plumes of ozone from sources hundreds of kilometers distant intercepted the mountain slopes. Several forests within the United States have been likewise affected by both ozone and acidic deposition, including the pine forests in California's southern Sierra Nevada and high-elevation spruce-fir forests in the Northeast.

Intensive field and laboratory investigations of forest decline in North America and Europe have yielded contradictory results regarding the link between dead trees and acid deposition. Some laboratory experiments have found that acid rain has no effect, or even a fertilizing effect, on trees. Symptoms

of tree stress include changes in foliage color, size, and shape; destruction of fine roots and associated fungi; and stunted growth. Many researchers attribute these symptoms and forest decline to complex interactions among a variety of stressors, including acid precipitation, ozone, excessive nitrogen deposition, land management practices, climate change, drought, and pestilence. Acid rain generally does not kill trees directly; rather, it weakens them by damaging their leaves, impairing their leaves' functionality, stripping nutrients from the soil, and releasing toxic substances from the soil.

Ambient air concentrations of SO_2 and NO_x are typically higher in major cities owing to the high density of emission sources in these locations. The resulting haze may be carried by winds hundreds of kilometers from where it was generated, obscuring visibility even in remote wilderness areas. The acids formed accelerate the weathering of exposed stone, brick, concrete, glass, metal, and paint. For example, the calcite in limestone and marble reacts with water and sulfuric acid to form gypsum (calcium sulfate). The gypsum washes off stone with rain or, if eaves protect the stone, accumulates as a soot-darkened crust. Acid-induced weathering has obscured the details of elaborate carvings on medieval cathedrals, ancient Greek columns, and Mayan ruins at alarming rates.

Prevention Efforts
Discovery of the connection between sulfur emissions in continental Europe and lake acidification in Scandinavian countries ultimately led to the 1979 Convention on Long-Range Transboundary Air Pollution. This legally binding international agreement addresses air-pollution issues on a broad regional basis. Subsequent protocols to the convention deal specifically with sulfur emissions (1985 and 1994 protocols), NO_x emissions (1988 protocol), and acidification abatement (1999 protocol).

In the United States the Acidic Deposition Control Program, Title IV of the CAA amendments of 1990, directs the Environmental Protection Agency (EPA) to reduce the adverse effects of acid rain, specifically through a reduction in emissions of SO_2 and NO_x. The program sets an annual cap on SO_2 emissions from power plants and establishes allowable NO_x emission rates based on boiler type. Between 1990 and 2006, the program achieved a reduction of

SO$_2$ emissions by more than 6.3 million tons from 1990 levels. The program, in combination with other efforts to reduce emissions, also cut NO$_x$ emission by roughly 3 million tons, making 2006 emissions less than half what would have been expected without the program.

The National Acid Precipitation Assessment Program coordinates interagency acid deposition monitoring and research and assesses the cost, benefits, and effectiveness of acid deposition control strategies. Acid deposition reduction schemes in the United States target large electric utilities, which as of 2006 were responsible for about 67 percent of the country's SO$_2$ and 19 percent of the NO$_x$ emissions from anthropogenic sources. Utilities participate in a novel market-based emission allowance trading and banking system that permits great flexibility in controlling SO$_2$ emissions. For example, utilities may choose to remove sulfur from coal by cleaning it, to burn a cleaner fuel such as natural gas, or to install a gas desulfurization system to reduce emissions. They may also buy or sell emissions allowances. U.S. research efforts cost-shared between government and industry, such as the Clean Coal Power Initiative and similar programs before it, have developed technologies—for example, the catalytic conversion of NO$_x$ to inert nitrogen—that can radically decrease emissions of acid gases from coal-fired power plants.

Between 1990 and 2006 annual atmospheric concentrations of SO$_2$ in the United States decreased by 53 percent, while nitrogen dioxide concentrations fell by 30 percent. Emissions of SO$_2$ dropped during this period by 38 percent; NO$_x$ emissions declined 29 percent, with most of the decrease occurring after 1998. These reductions resulted in significant decreases in acid rain. Between 1985 and 2002, nitrate deposition declined in the New England states; however, in the western states, increasing oil and gas production and other factors caused nitrate deposition to rise. In the eastern states, sulfate concentrations in the air generally declined, affected regions decreased in size, and the magnitude of the highest concentrations dropped. During the periods from 1989 to 1991 and 2004 to 2006, sulfate deposition in the Northeast and the Midwest decreased by more than 30 percent. As a result, surface water quality improved.

Noreen D. Poor; updated by Karen N. Kähler

Further Reading

Brimblecombe, Peter, et al., eds. *Acid Rain: Deposition to Recovery.* Springer, 2007.

Finlayson-Pitts, Barbara J., and James N. Pitts. *Chemistry of the Upper and Lower Atmosphere: Theory, Experiments, and Applications.* Academic Press, 2000.

Hill, Marquita K. "Acidic Deposition." In *Understanding Environmental Pollution.* 3d ed. Cambridge University Press, 2010.

Lane, Carter N., ed. *Acid Rain: Overview and Abstracts.* Nova Science, 2003.

Little, Charles E. *The Dying of the Trees: The Pandemic in America's Forests.* Viking Press, 1995.

McGee, Elaine. *Acid Rain and Our Nation's Capital: A Guide to Effects on Buildings and Monuments.* U.S. Geological Survey, 1995.

Smith, Robert Angus. *Air and Rain: The Beginnings of a Chemical Climatology.* 1872. Reprint. Kessinger, 2007.

Visgilio, Gerald R., and Diana M. Whitelaw, eds. *Acid in the Environment: Lessons Learned and Future Prospects.* Springer, 2007.

See also: Air pollution; Automobile emissions; Clean Air Act and amendments; Coal-fired power plants; Convention on Long-Range Transboundary Air Pollution; Fish kills; London smog disaster; Nitrogen oxides; Power plants; Sudbury, Ontario, emissions; Sulfur oxides.

■ Acid mine drainage

Fields of Study: Biology, Life Sciences, Ecosystems; Elements, Substances, Chemicals, Compounds; Pollution, Emissions, Toxic Waste, Hazardous Materials; Ecology, Environment, Environmentalism.

Identification: The flow of acidified waters from mining operations and mine wastes

Acid mine drainage can pollute groundwater, surface water, and soils, producing adverse effects on plants and animals.

During mining, rock is broken and crushed, exposing fresh rock surfaces and minerals. Pyrite, or iron sulfide, is a common mineral encountered in metallic ore deposits. Rainwater, groundwater, or surface water that runs over the pyrite leaches out sulfur,

Acid mine drainage. By Office of Surface Mining.

which reacts with the water and oxygen to form sulfuric acid. In addition, if pyrite is present in the mining waste materials that are discarded at a mine site, some species of bacteria can directly oxidize the sulfur in the waste rock and tailings, forming sulfuric acid. In either case, the resulting sulfuric acid may run into groundwater and streams downhill from the mine or mine tailings.

Acid mine drainage (AMD) pollutes groundwater and adjacent streams and may eventually seep into other streams, lakes, and reservoirs to pollute the surface water. Groundwater problems are particularly troublesome because the reclamation of polluted groundwater is very difficult and expensive. Furthermore, AMD dissolves other minerals and heavy metals from surrounding rocks, producing lead, arsenic, mercury, and cyanide, which further degrade the water quality. Through this process, AMD has contributed to the pollution of many lakes.

AMD runoff can be devastating to the surrounding ecosystem. Physical changes and damage to the land,

soil, and water from AMD directly and indirectly affect the biological environment. Mine water immediately adjacent to mines that are rich in sulfide minerals may be as much as 100,000 to 1,000,000 times more acidic than normal stream water. AMD water poisons and leaches nutrients from the soil so that few, if any, plants can survive. Animals that eat those plants, as well as microorganisms in the leached soils, may also die. AMD is also lethal for many water-dwelling animals, including plankton, fish, and snails. Furthermore, people can be poisoned by drinking water that has been contaminated with heavy metals produced by AMD, and some people have developed skin cancer as a result of drinking groundwater contaminated with arsenic generated by AMD leaching.

Alterations in groundwater and surface-water availability and quality caused by AMD have also had indirect impacts on the environment by causing changes in nutrient cycling, total biomass, species diversity, and ecosystem stability. Additionally, the deposition of iron as a slimy orange precipitate produces an unsightly coating on rocks and shorelines.

AMD was so severe in the Tar Creek area of Oklahoma that the US Environmental Protection Agency designated the area as the nation's foremost hazardous waste site in 1982. The largest complex of toxic waste sites in the United States was produced by the mines and smelters in Butte and Anaconda, Montana, with much of the pollution attributed to direct and indirect effects of AMD. AMD is also a widespread problem in many coal fields in the eastern United States. In 2013, Earthworks, a nonprofit environmental organization, issued a report, based on its review of extensive government documents, revealing the size and scope of the problems created because of AMD. The forty hard-rock mines studied are projected to contaminate between 17 and 27 billion gallons of water. The Environmental Protection Agency has spent more than $210 billion cleaning up the damage caused by acid runoff from the Summitville Mine, Colorado, alone.

Alvin K. Benson

Further Reading

Bell, F. G. *Basic Environmental and Engineering Geology.* CRC, 2007.

Gestring, Bonnie, and Lisa Sumi. "Polluting the Future: How Mining Companies Are Polluting Our Nation's Waters in Perpetuity. *Earthworks.* Earthworks, 1 May 2013. PDF file.

Jacobs, James A., Jay H. Lehr, and Stephen M. Testa. *Acid Mine Drainage, Rock Drainage, and Acid Sulfate Soils: Causes, Assessment, Prediction, Prevention, and Remediation.* Wiley, 2014.

"Watershed Contamination from Hard Rock Mining." *USGS.* United States Geological Survey, 6 May 2014. Web. 29 Jan. 2015.

Younger, Paul L., Steven A. Banwart, and Robert S. Hedin. *Mine Water: Hydrology, Pollution, Remediation.* Kluwer Academic, 2002.

■ Adams, Ansel

FIELDS OF STUDY: Popular Culture, Media, Publishing; Photography, Imaging; Ecology, Environment, Environmentalism.

IDENTIFICATION: Activism and advocacy; preservation and wilderness issues

Through his spectacular photographs and advocacy, Adams helped to increase Americans' awareness of the beauty of the nation's wilderness areas and the importance of preserving that beauty.

Ansel Adams was the only son of Charles and Olive Bray Adams. Although a gifted child, he detested public schools and was educated primarily by tutors, graduating from a private school in 1917. His early interests centered on music and, after he acquired his first camera, photography. A visit to Yosemite National Park in California in 1916 sparked his interest in nature photography, and he made frequent return visits to Yosemite throughout his lifetime.

Adams was able to support himself with music and photography during his early working years. As his interest in photography increased, however, it became the dominant factor in his life. He traveled extensively throughout the American West, photographing landscapes. His first published photograph appeared in the *Sierra Club Bulletin* in 1927, and the first of his numerous photographic collections was published in the same year. In 1928 he married Virginia Rose Best in Yosemite and held his first one-person exhibit in San Francisco. The Adamses had two children: Michael, born in 1933, and Anne, born in 1935.

In 1934 Adams was elected to the board of directors of the Sierra Club, a position he held until 1971. He was a cofounder of Group f/64, an organization dedicated to the use of photography to emphasize and preserve the natural beauty of the American West.

Adams's photographs, almost exclusively in black and white, are renowned for their sharp contrast, detail, use of light and shadow, and ability to capture the beauty of their natural settings. During his lifetime, Adams often exhibited his work in museums and at universities that recognized his artistic talent. In addition to this artistry, he developed several innovative techniques for developing photographs to enhance their contrast and embellish their appearance. He published several how-to books on photography and taught workshops on how to utilize his techniques. In addition, he established his own studio to exhibit and sell his works.

Largely self-taught, Adams is recognized as one of the leaders in nature photography. He not only photographed nature but also realized the need for environmental activism and lobbied extensively for conservation measures. As early as 1936 he approached the U.S. Congress to promote the establishment of additional national parks in the western states. He was a member of President Lyndon B. Johnson's environmental task force and later met with both President Gerald Ford and President Ronald Reagan to discuss environmental issues.

Adams's work extended beyond nature photography to include architectural studies, portraits, and commercial photography. In 1943 he photographed the Manzanar Relocation Center, where Japanese Americans were interned by the U.S. government during World War II. In 1960 he was commissioned to photograph scenes from all nine campuses of the University of California. In his later years he received several honorary doctoral degrees and other awards, including one named in his honor by the Wilderness Society. During these years he traveled widely, giving lecturers and exhibiting his works.

Gordon A. Parker

Further Reading

Adams, Ansel. *Ansel Adams: Four Hundred Photographs.* Edited by Andrea G. Stillman. Little, Brown, 2007.

Alinder, Mary Street. *Ansel Adams: A Biography.* Henry Holt, 1996.

Lichtenstein, Therese. *Master of Light: Ansel Adams and His Influences.* New Line Books, 2006.

See also: National forests; National parks; Sierra Club; Wilderness Society; Yosemite Valley.

■ Aerosols and the environment

FIELDS OF STUDY: Chemistry; Elements, Substances, Chemicals, Compounds; Ecology, Environment, Environmentalism; Pollution, Emissions, Toxic Waste, Hazardous Materials; Industries, Commercial Products.

IDENTIFICATION: Aggregations of small particles, both liquid and solid, and the atmospheric gases in which they are suspended

Atmospheric aerosols are responsible for diminishing environmental air quality throughout much of the world.

An aerosol is a multiphasic system consisting of tiny liquid and solid particles and the gas in which they are suspended. In unpolluted areas such as New Zealand, aerosols contain impurities from natural sources; acidity comes from carbonic acid (H_2CO_3). In central Europe and other industrialized areas throughout the world, fossil-fuel combustion contributes large amounts of oxides of sulfur (SO_x) and oxides of nitrogen (NO_x) to the atmosphere, leading to the formation of sulfuric acid and nitric acid aerosols. In these polluted areas, acidity levels are much higher in fog than in rain, and dry deposition of sulfuric and nitric acid particulates from impactions of acid fog may be more damaging to buildings and the environment than acid rain. Forest canopies tend to scavenge acid aerosols; on conifer-covered mountains, cloud droplets are the major source of acid deposition. Dry deposition on canopies rapidly affects root systems and increases soil acidification over the long term. Soil acidification has been linked to a number of adverse effects on vegetation, especially tree dieback and forest decline in Europe.

Aerosols in industrialized areas often contain heavy metals—including chromium (Cr), iron (Fe), copper (Cu), cadmium (Cd), cobalt (Co), nickel (Ni), and lead (Pb)—latex, surfactants, and asbestos. When tetraethyl lead was used as a gasoline additive, inhalation of lead aerosols contributed a substantial fraction of the body burden of lead in urban dwellers. Recognition of this hazard led to a ban on leaded gasoline. Dry deposition of heavy metals in aerosols can have adverse effects on ecosystems; $CdSO_4$ and $CuSO_4$ are known to reduce root elongation in trees. Fluorides released by heavy industry contribute to tree dieback.

The adverse impact of aerosols on air quality has been noted by many writers since the time of John Evelyn, who, on January 24, 1684, recorded a marked decrease in atmospheric visibility and increased respiratory problems associated with London smog. During the late nineteenth and early twentieth centuries, the lethal effects of aerosols were evident in the greatly increased mortality that occurred during London smog episodes. A historic episode in 1952, during which smog in London reduced visibility to zero, caused an estimated four thousand excess deaths, doubling the normal death rate for children

Aerosols can both reflect and absorb solar radiation, making their role in the greenhouse effect particularly complex. (NOAA)

and for adults ages forty-five to sixty-four. This episode led to legislation regarding emissions controls, and by the late 1960's, the health effects related to coal burning were reduced to minimal levels.

Urban aerosols—with their mix of latex, soot, hydrocarbons, SO_x and NO_x, and other pollutants—have been implicated in the growing prevalence of asthma. In the United States, the National Institutes of Health (NIH) estimated that asthma prevalence rose 34 percent between 1983 and 1993. About 4.8 million children in the United States were estimated to suffer from asthma in 1993. Asthma deaths have rapidly increased in the United States, rising from 0.9 per 100,000 people in 1976 to 1.5 per 100,000 people in 1986. Deaths from asthma among African Americans of all ages rose from 1.5 per 100,000 in 1976 to 2.8 per 100,000 in 1986. African Americans between the ages of fifteen and twenty-four had an asthma death rate of 8.2 per one million in 1980; by 1993, the rate had increased to 18.8 per one million.

Aerosols also increase the absorption and scattering of light in the atmosphere, reducing visibility. When smoke particle concentrations exceed 80-100 milligrams per cubic meter (mg/m^3), visibility falls below 1 kilometer (0.62 miles). Smoke palls can travel considerable distances; for example, during the spring of 1998, agricultural burning in the Yucatán in Mexico created a pall that markedly diminished visibility in Dallas, Texas.

Particulates in aerosols serve as condensation nuclei and may enhance fog formation. Visibility reductions by hygroscopic (moisture-retaining) air pollutants are noticeable at relative humidities of about 50 percent. A number of multicar chain-reaction accidents have occurred downwind of industrial plants when hygroscopic plumes have passed over cooling ponds adjacent to highways, creating abrupt reductions in visibility. When drivers of cars and trucks moving at high speeds suddenly become engulfed in an area with visibility of only a few feet, they often respond erratically, causing accidents.

Extremely low air temperatures can lead to the formation of ice fogs—known as "arctic haze"—over cities; such fogs, which are entirely anthropogenic (caused by humans), are fed by moisture and by particles given off by combustion. They are composed of minute ice crystals that substantially reduce visibility to the point where air travel is restricted. Ice fogs last for several days at a time and are frequent during winters in Fairbanks, Alaska, and many Canadian cities. The Siberian city of Irkutsk reports an average of 103 days of fog yearly, all during winter.

Anita Baker-Blocker

Further Reading

Colbeck, Ian, ed. *Environmental Chemistry of Aerosols.* Blackwell, 2008.

Cotton, William R., and Roger A. Pielke, Sr. *Human Impacts on Weather and Climate.* 2nd ed. Cambridge University Press, 2007.

Katsouyanni, K., et al. "Short-Term Effects of Ambient Sulphur Dioxide and Particulate Matter on Mortality in Twelve European Cities: Results from Time Series Data from the APHEA Project." *British Medical Journal* 314 (June 7, 1997).

■ African elephant poaching

FIELDS OF STUDY: Biology, Life Sciences, Ecosystems; Animals, Zoology, Marine Biology; Ecology, Environment, Environmentalism.

IDENTIFICATION: Illegal killing of largest living land mammals, native to Africa

Owing primarily to habitat destruction and hunting, both legal and illegal, the population of African elephants has been reduced steadily over time. Although populations in protected areas have achieved some stability, poaching and progressive desertification continue to threaten the species.

Elephants of Africa's savanna regions belong to the taxonomic group *Loxodonta africana*. Debate continues over whether the lesser-known African bush elephant is a separate species (as *Loxodonta cyclotis*) or subspecies. Some biologists postulate that an extinct elephant species may have also previously existed in the Atlas Mountains of North Africa (*Loxodonta africana pharaonensis*), but if so it disappeared by the end of the Roman Empire owing to hunting and habitat change.

Elephants are the largest living land mammals known, with male African elephants often standing 3.7 meters (12 feet) tall at the shoulder and weighing up to 6 tons. Both male and female African elephants have tusks. They can live on average sixty to eighty years in the wild, and perhaps longer in captivity. Female elephants are highly social, living in groups led

AFRICAN ELEPHANTS
U.S. Fish and Wildlife Service / Miriam Westervelt

African elephants are the largest land mammal in the world, weighing several tons. They are intelligent, social animals. Elephants experienced a severe population decline in the late 1980s due to illegal killing (poaching) for their ivory tusks. (US Fish and Wildlife Service)

by the eldest female, to whom they are generally related, with the adult males usually living alone on the group perimeter, although bachelor herds also exist for periods of time.

Although the primary habitat of the largest group of African elephants is the great savanna, elephants have historically ranged across the entire African continent, south of the great Sahara. They were at one time ubiquitous in this geographic region, but African elephant populations have shrunk greatly in the past two centuries because of human activity, especially habitat loss—resulting from land mismanagement and climatic aridization—along with hunting and poaching, primarily for their ivory tusks. Estimated around 1980 as numbering up to 1.3 million (quite a few experts believe this number was inflated), by 2010 they numbered around 400,000. Where protected in nature preserves, this population is relatively stable, but outside these conservation areas African elephants are still considered to be an endangered species ("threatened" or "vulnerable" status). Habitat loss for African elephants owing to desertification and deforestation is also considered to be highly problematic for wild populations, especially if desertification continues at the rates seen since the late twentieth century.

Trade in ivory has been mostly banned since 1989 by the Convention on International Trade in Endangered Species (CITES), backed by the United Nations, but illicit trade continues in politically unstable parts of Africa. Some ivory exportation is allowed, although only a fraction of the revenue generated appears to have ever benefited Africans, according to Oxford University studies conducted in 2000. One of the most egregious single incidents of deliberate elephant poaching took place in southeastern Chad in 2006 just outside Zakouma National Park, where more than one hundred elephants were slaughtered for ivory. It is estimated that 96 percent of the 300,000 Chadian elephant population was lost between 1970 and 2010, when numbers were down to approximately 10,000 elephants in Zakouma National Park. In 2018, conservation officers found a similar kill site near a national park in Botswana. Some 97 elephants had been massacred *en masse* at that location, their tusks cut out with chain saws and the bodies left to rot where they lay. Some of the very young elephant calves survived and were taken to shelters.

Individuals and organizations such as Sir Richard Leakey and Sir Iain Douglas-Hamilton of Save the Elephants, both in Kenya, and J. Michael Fay of the Wildlife Conservation Society are strong advocates for African elephant preservation. Because elephants are migratory, following water and plant seasons, they can cover a territory of up to 3,600 square kilometers (about 1,400 square miles), which is problematic when they leave protected areas where hunting is forbidden.

Patrick Norman Hunt

Further Reading

Beard, Peter *The End of the Game* Chronicle Books, 1988.

Bradshaw, G. A. *Elephants on the Edge: What Animals Teach Us About Humanity.* Yale University Press, 2009.

Chadwick, Douglas H. *The Fate of the Elephant.* Sierra Club Books, 1992.

Christo, Cyril. *Walking Thunder: In the Footsteps of the African Elephant.* Merrell, 2009.

Meredith, Martin. "Ivory Wars." In *Elephant Destiny: Biography of an Endangered Species in Africa.* PublicAffairs, 2001.

Walker, John Frederick. *Ivory's Ghosts: The White Gold of History and the Fate of Elephants.* Grove/Atlantic, 2009.

■ Africa's ecosystem

FIELDS OF STUDY: Places, Peoples, Societies; Continents, Regions, Areas, Islands; Biology, Life Sciences, Ecosystems; Animals, Zoology, Marine Biology; Ecology, Environment, Environmentalism; Plants, Vegetation, Botany, Horticulture; Renewable Resources.

General Environmental Characteristics

The ecosystems of Africa range from the desolate expanses of the Sahara to the dense confines of equatorial rain forests. Threats to the plant and animal life found across the continent have placed Africa in the forefront of global environmentalist campaigns, some of which aim not only to save menaced species but also to conserve other natural resources, including soils and minerals.

The image of the African continent containing primarily dense tropical jungles holds true for limited regions only—those near the equator and subject to heavy seasonal rainfall. In fact, Africa has several different environmental regions. These correspond mainly, but not only, to relative latitudinal position north or south of the equator. Geographers generally separate the continent into five zones: North, South, East, West, and Central. The environmental conditions that are found in the zones vary widely.

In comparison to other continents, Africa possesses relatively few major mountain ranges. The most important tectonic upliftings are in South Africa—notably the Drakensberg range, which is 1,000 kilometers (620 miles) long, with elevations reaching in places nearly 3,500 meters (11,500 feet)—and in the northwestern and northeastern areas of the continent (the Aurès and Atlas mountains in Tunisia and Morocco, and the Simyen and Bale mountains in Ethiopia). The geology of the Ethiopian ranges, which boast peaks such as Ras Dashen in the Simyens,

more than 4,500 meters (14,800 feet) high, and many volcanic peaks, is closely connected with the tectonic phenomena that created the Great Rift Valley running north to south from the Red Sea to Malawi in Southern Africa.

Whereas these long ranges contribute to extensive regional environmental patterns—combining patterns of flora and fauna that determine the livelihoods of entire sections of Africa—other quite different mountains (mostly volcanic "monoliths") lend themselves to more localized environmental, and therefore human cultural, settings. Prototypical examples would be Mount Kenya and Mount Kilimanjaro in Tanzania (the latter being the highest mountain in Africa—reaching almost 6,000 meters, or 19,700 feet) and Mount Cameroon near the Gulf of Guinea coast in West Africa. Mount Kenya became the site of one of Africa's earliest national parks, founded in 1949. Each of these famous mountains is associated with indigenous legends tying them to local religious beliefs. High levels of rainfall close to such prominent peaks often combine with fertile volcanic soil to create not only lush natural vegetation but also fairly high levels of domestic and commercial agricultural productivity (both Kenya and Tanzania, for example, produce famous coffee strains).

Africa contains the most extensive and arid expanse in the world: the Sahara. This desert region, which covers most of North Africa, is bordered on the south by the Sahel, a region that forms a broad continental dividing line between North Africa (where basic environmental characteristics are shared among the five modern countries of Morocco, Algeria, Tunisia, Libya, and Egypt) and sub-Saharan Africa. Much of North Africa (except for Egypt's Nile River Valley, which runs south to north between desolate desert littorals, reaching to the Red Sea in the east and to Libya's Fezzan desert region to the west) is characterized by rain-fed coastal plains bordered by the higher altitudes of the Aures and Atlas mountain chains. Once the Sahara begins, however, vegetation is very scant or nonexistent, except in oasis areas, where subsurface water sources are available. The estimated average annual rainfall for the Sahara is approximately 25 millimeters (about 1 inch).

Another major desert in Africa is the Kalahari, which, in combination with the contiguous Namib Desert, covers much of the land area of South Africa

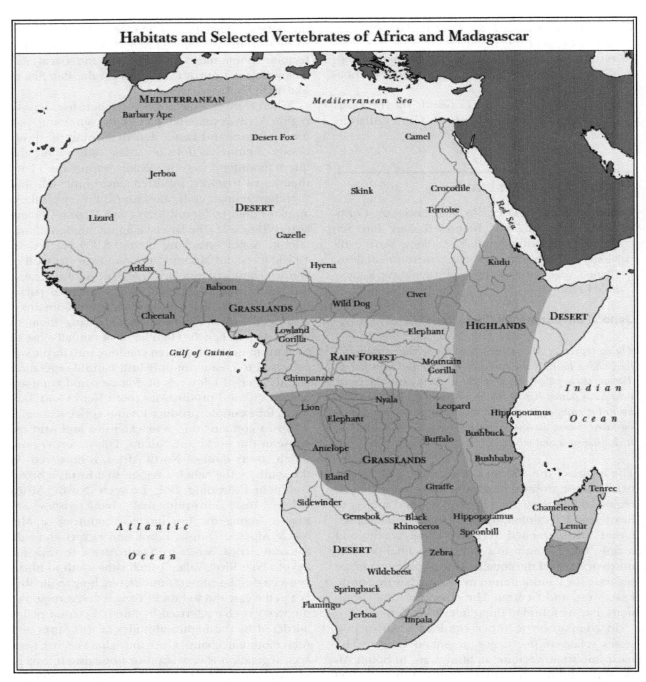

Habitats and Selected Vertebrates of Africa and Madagascar

from the Orange River into modern Angola and Namibia. The Kalahari is not nearly as arid as the Sahara, having widely dispersed thorny trees and bushes.

The greatest territorial expanses of Africa are characterized by semiarid savanna conditions; their ecology includes extensive grasslands with widely dispersed trees. Savannas, which receive quite limited and seasonally specific rainfall, are typically located between desert expanses and tropical zones near the equator. African savannas are found in the immediate sub-Saharan zones of Senegal, Mali, Niger, Chad, and Sudan, and in Central and Southern Africa stretching eastward to the Indian Ocean.

Because of their extensive grasslands, these zones form (or formed) the habitats of many of Africa's famous wild animal herds (especially in the Serengeti of Tanzania) and areas of Zambia, Zimbabwe, and South Africa. Rains totaling as much as 635 millimeters (25 inches) come from May into the summer, but then disappear by early fall.

Clearly, the major factor contributing to dense vegetation in Africa is rainfall, as the label "tropical rain forest" suggests. Regions close to the equator (including in Guinea, southern Côte d'Ivoire, and Ghana, but especially in Cameroon, Equatorial Guinea, Gabon, and the Congo) receive the highest rainfall, and their environments support extensive multitiered forests that are habitats for many animal species, including primates such as gorillas and chimpanzees. The extensive and complicated watershed of the Congo basin produces vegetation necessary to support both human and animal life and is the source of the Congo River. Another very long African river, the Niger, has its sources in the West African tropical zone of Guinea.

Africa's major inland lakes are found in different environmental settings. What was once the continent's largest lake, Lake Chad, is located in the middle of the dry interior of what was formerly part of French West Africa and French Equatorial Africa. This lake is probably the remnant of an ancient inland sea. Although it is still fed by the Chari River and its tributary the Logone (which carry water from equatorial Africa), its shores have receded considerably. This is part of the increasing desiccation of the African Sahel, which has caused major environmental problems for inhabitants of the region.

By contrast, many of the main lakes of East Africa—including Lake Tanganyika and Lake Malawi, also known as Lake Nyasa—are formed by water runoff from the high elevations surrounding the Great Rift Valley. The more centrally located Lake Victoria, also known as Victoria Nyanza, is an exception. Lake Malawi is the largest East African lake (covering nearly 70,000 square kilometers, or 27,000 square miles), and Lake Tanganyika (covering almost 34,000 square kilometers, or 13,000 square miles) is the longest and second-deepest lake in the world (some 680 kilometers, or 420 miles, long, with a maximum depth of almost 1,500 meters, or 5,000 feet). Although all major and lesser East African lakes provide natural habitat for cichlid fish populations,

Lake Malawi has a greater variety of such fish than any other place in the world, including many species that are unknown anywhere else.

In addition to the obvious environmental features of Africa's vast landmass and its lakes and rivers, the continent's natural resources are tied to its Mediterranean Sea, Atlantic Ocean, and Indian Ocean coastal waters and estuaries. Beyond their value for commercially viable fishing (and fishing for domestic consumption) some coastal regions of Africa offer features that began to attract particular attention during the late decades of the twentieth century.

Environmental Issues

Among the environmental issues affecting Africa are concerns about declining numbers and even extinctions of indigenous plant and animal species. The list of menaced African species ranges from the cichlid tropical fish populations in East Africa's freshwater lakes through the African elephant.

Various factors have caused a sharp decline in what was once a thriving habitat for more than five hundred species of cichlids in Lake Victoria. It is estimated that almost half of the cichlids have disappeared as the result of the decision to introduce Nile perch into the lake waters to increase local fishing harvests for food and commercial sale. The nonnative perch proved to be predatory and fed off the local cichlid populations.

There are many other examples of rising concerns among environmentalists who study declining numbers of animal species that were once very numerous in different areas of Africa. Those that have drawn the greatest attention are the large mammals, including mountain gorillas, elephants, and members of the "great cat" family (lions, leopards, and cheetahs). Questionable human actions—including poaching for food or trophies—are generally behind the threats to these species.

By the end of the twentieth century, organized conservation efforts were on the rise in Africa. The obvious importance of saving large game species led, for example, to "safari tourism" in protected parks. Among the best known of these parks is the Selous Game Reserve in Tanzania, which covers more than 54,000 square kilometers (21,000 square miles) and is home to an incredibly diverse array of animals, including elephants, black rhinoceroses, giraffes, and crocodiles.

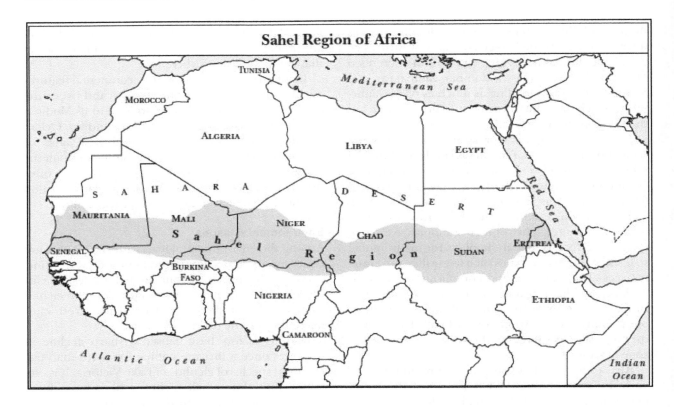

Sahel Region of Africa

Some environmental activists have attempted to create programs to promote the conservation of both animal and plant species. Some, such as Conserve Africa, a nonprofit organization based in the United Kingdom, support environmental conservation efforts that can benefit not only flora and fauna but also local African populations that depend directly on the environment for their livelihoods. The primary goal of Conserve Africa is to help develop skills among Africans that will benefit both the local environment and the Africans' material welfare. Examples include the development of apiculture (beekeeping), the training of Africans in the careful selection of tree and medicinal plant species for cultivation, and the promotion of ecotourism.

The African Conservation Foundation (ACF) coordinates the sharing of information among conservation groups working in Africa and posts alerts concerning alarming developments. A prime example of an ACF alert is one stating the organization's opposition to illicit mining (particularly in the violence-torn eastern Congo) of what the ACF calls the "Three T's"—tin, tantalum, and tungsten (all minerals in great demand because of their use in developed countries' high-technology industries).

In some cases, efforts to protect the environment in Africa are complicated by various political factors. For example, pressures toward economic development conflict with concerns about the environment in decisions regarding offshore petroleum drilling, particularly along the coasts of West Africa (extending from the Niger Delta through Cameroon, Equatorial Guinea, and Gabon). The potential threat that such drilling poses for marine life and vegetation, particularly in environmentally unique coastal mangrove ecosystems, may rank as high as inland deforestation and mineral extraction concerns as major African environmental issues in the twenty-first century.

Some areas of Africa face environmental concerns stemming from natural causes presumed to be tied to global warming. This is particularly the case in the Sahel region to the south of the Sahara. Beginning during the mid-1970's and intermittently since then, drought conditions have caused major crop shortages as well as widespread losses in animal herds that provide the only means of survival for many Sahel populations, as well as for inhabitants of other arid regions of Africa. As human migration out of such stricken zones rises, environmental problems are often seen in the areas receiving the migrants; these problems include urban sprawl, shortages of safe water supplies, and the spread of communicable animal and human diseases.

Byron Cannon

Further Reading

Doyle, Shane. *Crisis and Decline in Bunyoro.* British Institute in Eastern Africa, 2006.

Goldblatt, Peter, ed. *Biological Relationships Between Africa and South America.* Yale University Press, 1993.

Maddox, Gregory H. *Sub-Saharan Africa: An Environmental History.* ABC-CLIO, 2006.

Shorrocks, Bryan. *The Biology of African Savannahs.* Oxford University Press, 2007.

United Nations Environment Programme. *Africa: Environment Outlook.* Author, 2006.

■ Agenda 21

FIELDS OF STUDY: Government, Politics, International Relations; International Relations, Agreements, Treaties; Ecology, Environment, Environmentalism; Renewable Resources.

CATEGORIES: Treaties, laws, and court cases; ecology and ecosystems; resources and resource management

IDENTIFICATION: Plan of action adopted by 178 nations at the United Nations Conference on Environment and Development in Rio de Janeiro, Brazil

DATE: Adopted on June 13, 1992

Agenda 21 represents an important step by the international community in planning for the changes necessary to protect the environment, including reducing human consumption patterns and promoting sustainable development. It outlines the techniques that should be implemented to balance the needs of humans with the preservation of natural resources.

The opening paragraph of the Preamble to Agenda 21 presents an unusually stark statement of the challenges facing humanity at the beginning of the twenty-first century and the need for international cooperation to meet those challenges:

> *"Humanity stands at a defining moment in history. We are confronted with a perpetuation of disparities between and within nations, a worsening of poverty, hunger, ill health and illiteracy, and the continuing deterioration of the ecosystems on which we depend for our well-being. However, integration of environment and development concerns and greater attention to them will lead to the fulfilment of basic needs, improved living standards for all, better protected and managed ecosystems and a safer, more prosperous future. No nation can achieve this on its own; but together we can—in a global partnership for sustainable development."*

The 1992 United Nations Conference on Environment and Development, widely known as the Earth Summit, produced five documents: Agenda 21, the Rio Declaration on Environment and Development, the United Nations Framework Convention on Climate Change, and the United Nations Convention on Biological Diversity. Agenda 21 challenges governments to adopt practices that promote sustainable development. It encourages national governments to work with nongovernmental organizations (NGOs), local governments, and businesses to create change and to reduce wasteful actions that harm the earth. Although designed to be implemented by national governments, Agenda 21 also includes directives for the regional and local levels; these are commonly referred to as Local Agenda 21, or LA21, programs.

Agenda 21 addresses both current problems and foreseeable problems of the future. One theme is improvement of the economic situation for those living in poverty. Agenda 21 notes that conditions can improve if the less fortunate have access to the resources necessary to lead sustainable lives. As the world's less industrialized countries strive to achieve their maximum potential, they must approach development in ways that do not harm the environment. Agenda 21 proposes that since the more industrialized countries have produced more pollution than others, these countries should provide the funding necessary to help underdeveloped countries grow in a sustainable manner. The plan recognizes the roles that nontraditional groups—such as indigenous peoples, women, industries, young people, and NGOs—can play in such development.

Another theme of Agenda 21 is the need for proper management of natural resources. Along with acknowledging that progress must be made, the plan emphasizes the need to combat desertification and deforestation, to care for the atmosphere and the oceans, to protect biodiversity, and to encourage sustainable agriculture practices. It also seeks to prevent disputes over the high seas and to discourage practices that deplete the oceans' fish stocks. Agenda 21 calls for increasingly high standards of energy efficiency and encourages the development and use of clean technologies. It promotes the preservation of forests, the planting of new trees, and the elimination of slash-and-burn agriculture methods that destroy forests. Noting the scarcity of clean drinking water for many around the world, Agenda 21 challenges nations to provide safe water and sanitation for all citizens by the year 2025.

Kathryn A. Cochran

Further Reading

Porter, Gareth, Janet Welsh Brown, and Pamela Chasek. "The Emergence of Global Environmental Politics." In *Global Environmental Politics.* Westview Press, 2000.

Sitarz, Daniel, ed. *Agenda 21: The Earth Summit Strategy to Save Our Planet.* EarthPress, 1993.

Speth, James Gustave, and Peter M. Haas. "From Stockholm to Johannesburg: First Attempt at Global Environmental Governance." In *Global Environmental Governance.* Island Press, 2006.

See also: Convention on Biological Diversity; Earth Summit; Environmental law, international; Johannesburg Declaration on Sustainable Development; Rio Declaration on Environment and Development; Sustainable development; United Nations Commission on Sustainable Development; United Nations Environment Programme; United Nations Framework Convention on Climate Change.

■ Agent Orange (AO)

FIELDS OF STUDY: Chemistry; Elements, Substances, Chemicals, Compounds; Health, Medicine, Disease, Illness; Ecology, Environment, Environmentalism.

IDENTIFICATION: Powerful defoliant used extensively by the U.S. military during the Vietnam War

The spraying of Agent Orange resulted in the deforestation of large sections of Southeast Asia, and exposure to the herbicide has been linked to the development of serious health problems in both military personnel and civilians.

Between 1962 and 1971, some 19 million gallons of herbicides were sprayed by the U.S. military over South Vietnam and Laos by airplane, helicopter, boat, truck, and manual sprayers in an effort to reduce ground cover for enemy troops and to destroy enemy crops. About 11 million gallons of this total was sprayed in the form of Agent Orange, a fifty-fifty mixture of the herbicides 2,4-D and 2,4,5-T combined with a kerosene-diesel fuel for dispersal. The principal components of both 2,4-D and 2,4,5-T decompose within weeks after application; however, 2,4,5-T contains between 0.05 and 50 parts per million of dioxin, primarily 2,3,7,8-tetrachlorodibenzo-para-dioxin (TCDD), which is among the deadliest chemicals known and which has a half-life of decades. Approximately 368 pounds of dioxin were released during the spraying, with profound effects on both the ecology of the region and the subsequent health of U.S. military personnel, the residents of Vietnam and Laos, and their offspring.

Agent Orange constituted about 60 percent of total volume of herbicides sprayed by U.S. personnel in the region; other substances used included dinoxol, trinoxol, bromacil, diquat, tandex, monuran, diuron, and dalapon as well as compounds known by such code names as Agent White, Agent Blue, Agent Purple, Agent Green, Agent Pink, and Agent Orange II ("Super Orange"). In addition to 2,4-D and 2,4,5-T, various mixes included picloram (a growth regulator similar to 2,4-D and 2,4,5-T) and cacodylic acid, an arsenic-containing organic that dehydrated and killed plants. Unlike 2,4-D and 2,4,5-T, which acted on plant surfaces, mobile picloram penetrated soil to be absorbed by roots and induce systemic effects.

Military Background

The U.S. military developed weapon herbicides during World War II at Fort Detrick in Frederick, Maryland, and considered using them against Japanese food plots on Pacific islands. The British used herbicides in Malaya in the 1950's to destroy rebel food plots. Domestic tests of Agent Orange were conducted at Camp Drum, New York, and Eglin Air Force Base, Florida, in the 1950's. The first field tests were conducted in South Vietnam in 1961 and in Thailand in 1964 and 1965.

"Operation Ranch Hand" was the code name given to the U.S. Air Force program of herbicide application during the Vietnam War. The program

U.S. Huey helicopter spraying Agent Orange over Vietnam. U.S. Army Operations in Vietnam R.W. Trewyn, Ph.D. , (11) Huey Defoliation National Archives: 111-CC-59948, originally found in Box 1 Folder 9 of Admiral Elmo R. Zumwalt, Jr. Collection: Agent Orange Subject Files.

involved a total of thirty-six aircraft that sprayed roughly 10 percent of the area of South Vietnam. The spraying and defoliation targeted jungles, inland forests, camp edges, roads, trails, railroads, and canals to make enemy movement conspicuous and easier to attack. Because of the possible risk to the crops of the United States' South Vietnamese allies, spraying of enemy food plots was not as extensive. In addition, the Army Chemical Corps conducted truck, helicopter, and manual spraying (particularly around base camps and transportation routes); the U.S. Navy, using small riverboats, sprayed edges of rivers and canals; and Special Forces troops conducted covert spraying operations.

Environmental Damage in Vietnam

Many of the trees in the tropical mangrove forests near the southernmost coasts of South Vietnam were killed by a single spraying. It is estimated that it will take up to a century for the mangrove forests to recover without reseeding. Since these and adjacent waters served as breeding and nursery grounds for

wildlife, the area's ecology was catastrophically affected.

Inland forests were less sensitive to Agent Orange. They usually recovered after single or double sprayings with only temporary foliage loss. However, three or more sprayings eventually induced tree death and converted forests to grasslands. Wildfires burned seeds and seedlings of native trees, further delaying recovery. Erosion washed sediment into deltas near river outlets, compounding environmental damage. Since approximately one-third of sprayed land was sprayed more than once, and 52,600 hectares (130,000 acres) were sprayed more than four times, damage to Vietnam's ecology was extensive.

Elevated concentrations of toxins have continued to affect Vietnam's population and environment. Because of the persistent effects of dioxin, which is fat-soluble and bioaccumulates up the food chain, health problems related to the spraying have affected not only Vietnamese alive during the war but also their offspring. Malformations and birth defects are common in Vietnamese children, and other maladies are suspected to be linked to dioxin exposure.

It took more than two decades for a serious effort at characterizing and alleviating these problems to be begun, because it took years after the war for the problems to become recognized. In addition, Vietnam had other pressing economic, military, and rebuilding concerns. In the 1990's, the Vietnamese National Committee for the Investigation of the Consequences of the Chemicals Used During the Vietnam War, also known as the 10-80 Committee, solicited international help. In an effort to determine existing dioxin levels, from 1994 to 1998, Hatfield Consultants of West Vancouver, British

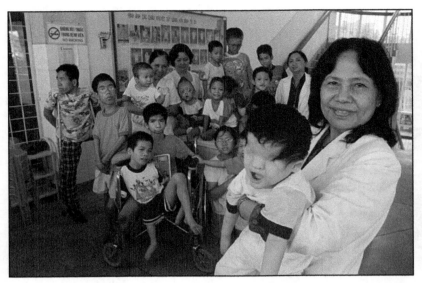

Professor Nguyen Thi Ngoc Phuong, at Tu Du Obstetrics and Gynecology Hospital in Ho Chi Minh, is pictured with a group of handicapped children, most victims of Agent Orange. By Alexis Duclos (Alexis Duclos)

Columbia, sampled soils, crops, fish, poultry, livestock, and human blood in the A Luoi Valley in central Vietnam near the old Ho Chi Minh Trail. The investigators also performed satellite characterization of topography changes in the Ma Da region of southern Vietnam caused by defoliation and sediment washing.

The Vietnamese Red Cross established a fund for Agent Orange victims in 1998; in April, 1998, Vietnam's prime minister ordered the first nationwide survey of Agent Orange-related problems. Vietnam also established several "peace villages," each of which could accommodate up to five hundred patients with health problems related to Agent Orange.

Health Effects in American Vietnam Veterans

Agent Orange and dioxin are now known to have caused comparable health problems in American veterans of the Vietnam War. Health problems linked to exposure include the cancers soft-tissue sarcoma, non-Hodgkin's lymphoma, and Hodgkin's disease and the skin diseases chloracne and porphyria cutanea tarda. There is a definite correlation between Agent Orange exposure and respiratory cancer, prostate cancer, multiple myeloma, acute and subacute peripheral neuropathy, and spina bifida (abnormal spine development in children of veterans). Other

suspected health effects include immune system disorders, reproductive difficulties and cancers, diabetes, endocrine and hormone imbalances, cancer in offspring, and malformations and defects (there is much stronger evidence linking birth defects to dioxin in Vietnamese). It appears that many of these health problems (including spina bifida, birth defects, immune system problems, and cancer propensity) can be passed on to the children and even the grandchildren of those initially exposed.

These issues were controversial for years after the war, but as evidence accumulated, the Department of Veterans Affairs (VA) eventually addressed the issue. Free medical examinations and care were offered to Vietnam veterans with suspected Agent Orange-induced problems in 1978. By 1981, the VA had established a program providing follow-up hospital care to veterans with any health problem of which the cause was unclear. The VA now provides monthly compensation for those with the ten diseases for which there is a proven cause-and-effect or positive correlation. Also, compensation, health care, and vocational rehabilitation are provided to children of veterans with spina bifida. The VA now presumes that all military personnel who served in the Vietnam theater were exposed to Agent Orange.

Other groups of people—including farmers, foresters, ranchers, chemical industry workers, incinerator workers, and paper mill workers—are often exposed to trace dioxin and related chemicals such as polychlorinated biphenyls (PCBs) at levels in excess of those experienced by the typical Vietnam veteran. Workers in these areas occasionally exhibit increased frequencies of diseases (for example, prostate cancer is especially common among farmers). Trace dioxins are commonly produced by the burning of chlorine-containing organics and other chemical processes. It is likely that nearly all persons in the industrialized world have some amount of dioxin in their bodies. However, because of many epidemiological and exposure variables, symptoms vary widely, and it is difficult to establish conclusive links between symptoms and particular chemicals or activities.

Defenders of the spraying program in Vietnam point out that the use of Agent Orange and related herbicides was highly successful in meeting the U.S. military's goals and, hence, likely saved the lives of many American servicemen. Moreover, although the resulting environmental and health effects might have been less severe if another chemical had been used rather than the dioxin-containing 2,4,5-T, dioxin's long-term effects were not known at the time. The long-term consequences of the use of Agent Orange in Vietnam thus drive home the lesson that unanticipated outcomes often result from the employment of new technologies.

Robert D. Engelken

Further Reading

Buckingham, William A., Jr. *Operation Ranch Hand: The Air Force and Herbicides in Southeast Asia, 1961-1971.* Office of Air Force History, U.S. Air Force, 1982.

Griffiths, Philip Jones. *Agent Orange: Collateral Damage in Vietnam.* Trolley, 2004.

Institute of Medicine. *Veterans and Agent Orange: Health Effects of Herbicides Used in Vietnam—Update 2008.* National Academy Press, 2009.

Young, Alvin Lee. *The History, Use, Disposition, and Environmental Fate of Agent Orange.* Springer, 2009.

■ Agricultural chemicals

FIELDS OF STUDY: Chemistry; Elements, Substances, Chemicals, Compounds; Pollution, Emissions, Toxic Waste, Hazardous Materials; Ecology, Environment, Environmentalism; Agriculture, Farming, Animal Husbandry.

IDENTIFICATION: Chemicals utilized by the agriculture industry to improve crop yield or the quality of produce

The chemical fertilizers and pesticides used by the agriculture industry have the potential to stay in soil and water for long periods, creating unintended environmental impacts.

To grow, plants require sunshine, water, carbon dioxide from the atmosphere, and mineral nutrients from the soil. Mineral nutrients may be subdivided into macronutrients (calcium, magnesium, sulfur, nitrogen, potassium, and phosphorus) and micronutrients (iron, copper, zinc, boron, manganese, chloride, and molybdenum). Plant growth, and thus crop yields, is reduced if any one of these nutrients is not present in sufficient amounts. Micronutrients are required in small quantities, and deficiencies do not occur frequently; therefore, the majority of agricultural fertilizers contain only macronutrients. Magnesium and calcium are utilized in large quantities, but most agricultural soils contain an abundance of these two elements, either derived from parent material or added as lime. Most soils also contain sufficient amounts of sulfur from the weathering of sulfur-containing minerals, the presence of sulfur in other fertilizers, and atmospheric pollutants. The remaining three macronutrients (nitrogen, potassium, and phosphorus) are readily depleted; these are referred to as fertilizer elements, as they must be added to most soils on a regular basis. Mixed fertilizers contain two or more nutrients. For example, a fertilizer labeled 10-10-10 contains 10 percent nitrogen, 10 percent phosphorus, and 10 percent potassium.

Fertilizers and Environmental Concerns

The application of fertilizer to agricultural soil is by no means new. Farmers have been applying manures to improve plant growth for more than four thousand years. For the most part, this practice had little environmental impact. Since the development of chemical fertilizers in the late nineteenth century, however, fertilizer usage has increased tremendously. During the second half of the twentieth century, the amount of fertilizer applied to the soil increased more than 450 percent. While this increase more than doubled the worldwide crop production, it also generated some environmental problems.

The production of fertilizer requires the use of a variety of natural resources, and some people have argued that the increased production of fertilizers has required the use of energy and mineral reserves that could have been used elsewhere. For every crop, there is a point at which the yield may continue to increase with the application of additional nutrients, but the increase will not offset the additional cost of the fertilizer. The economically feasible practice, therefore, is to apply the appropriate amount of fertilizer that produces maximum profit rather than maximum yield. Unfortunately, many farmers still tend to overfertilize, which wastes money and contributes to

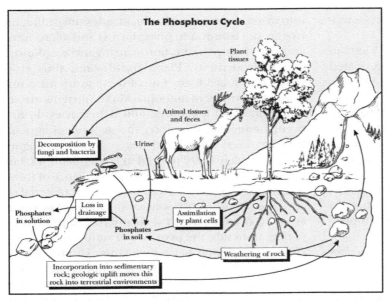

The Phosphorus Cycle

The biogeochemical phosphorus cycle is the movement of the essential element phosphorus through the earth's ecosystems.

environmental degradation. Excessive fertilization can result in adverse soil reactions that damage plant roots or produce undesired growth patterns; it can actually decrease yields, as some micronutrients, if applied in excessive amounts, are toxic to plants and will dramatically reduce their growth.

The most serious environmental problem associated with fertilizers is their contribution to water pollution. Excess fertilizer elements, particularly nitrogen and phosphorus, are carried from farm fields and cattle feedlots by water runoff and are eventually deposited in rivers and lakes, where they contribute to the pollution of aquatic ecosystems. High levels of plant nutrients in streams and lakes can result in increased growth of phytoplankton, a condition known as eutrophication. During the summer months, eutrophication can deplete oxygen levels in lower layers of ponds and lakes. Excess nutrients can also leach through the soil and contaminate underground water supplies. In areas where intense farming occurs, nitrate concentrations are often above recommended safe levels. Water that contains excessive amounts of plant nutrients poses health problems if consumed by humans and livestock, and it can be fatal if ingested by newborns.

Pesticides

Pesticides are chemicals designed to kill unwanted organisms that interfere, either directly or indirectly, with human activities. The major types of pesticides in common use are those designed to kill insects (insecticides), nematodes (nematocides), fungi (fungicides), weeds (herbicides), and rodents (rodenticides). Herbicides and insecticides make up the majority of the pesticides applied in the environment.

The application of chemicals to control pests is not new. Humans have been using sulfur and heavy metal compounds as insecticides for more than two thousand years. Residues of toxic metals such as arsenic, lead, and mercury continue to be accumulated in plants that are grown on soil where these materials have been used. The commercial introduction of Dichloro-Diphenyl-Trichloroethane (DDT) in 1942 opened the door for the synthesis of a host of synthetic organic compounds to be used as pesticides.

Chlorinated hydrocarbons such as DDT were eventually banned or severely restricted in the United States because of their low biodegradability and persistence in the environment. They were replaced by organophosphates, which biodegrade rapidly but are generally much more toxic to humans and other animals than chlorinated hydrocarbons. In addition, they are water-soluble and, therefore, more likely to contaminate water supplies. Carbamates have also been used in place of the chlorinated hydrocarbons, and while these compounds biodegrade rapidly and are less toxic to humans than organophosphates, they are also less effective in the killing of insects.

A large number of herbicides have also been developed. These chemicals are generally classified as one of three types: contact herbicides, systemic herbicides, and soil sterilants. Contact herbicides kill when they come in contact with the leaf surface. Systemic herbicides circulate throughout the plant after being absorbed and cause abnormal growth. Soil sterilants kill microorganisms necessary for plant growth and act as systemic herbicides.

Pesticides and Environmental Concerns

Approximately fifty-five thousand different pesticides are available in the United States, and Americans apply about 500 million kilograms (1.1 billion pounds) of pesticides each year. Fungicides account for 12 percent of all pesticides used by farmers, while insecticides account for 19 percent and herbicides account for 69 percent. Billions of pounds of pesticides are applied each year throughout the world. While most of these chemicals are applied in developed countries, the amount of pesticides used in underdeveloped countries is rapidly increasing.

There is no doubt that pesticides have had a beneficial impact on the lives of humans by increasing food production and reducing food costs. Alongside these benefits, however, the use of pesticides has caused some environmental problems, including the development of pesticide resistance. When a new pesticide is first utilized, it is effective in reducing the number of target pests, but within a few years, a number of species develop genetic resistance to the chemical and are no longer controlled with it, necessitating the development of another pesticide to replace the one that is no longer effective. The pests in turn develop resistance to the newer pesticides, and so on. As a result, many synthetic chemicals have been introduced into the environment, yet the pest problem is as great as it ever was.

Another problem with pesticides is that they do not go away after they have done their job; they can remain in the environment for varying lengths of time. For example, chlorinated hydrocarbons can persist in the environment for up to fifteen years. This can be beneficial from an economic standpoint because the pesticide has to be applied less frequently, but it can be detrimental from an environmental standpoint. When many pesticides are degraded, many of their breakdown products, which are often toxic to other organisms, may also persist in the environment for long periods of time.

A third problem with pesticides is their tendency to become more concentrated as they move up the food chain. A pesticide may not affect species at the base of the chain, but it may be toxic to organisms that feed at the apex because the concentration of the chemical increases at each higher level of the food chain. Many algal species, for example, can be sprayed with an insecticide without any apparent effect to the algae. However, the chemical can be detrimental to organisms such as birds that eat fish that have eaten insects that have fed on the algae.

A fourth problem is broad-spectrum poisoning. Few, if any, chemical pesticides are selective. They kill a wide range of organisms rather than just the target pests. Many insects are beneficial to the

environment, and more damage than good may be done by the use of insecticides that kill these organisms along with the harmful insects.

Many pesticides, particularly insecticides, are also toxic to humans. Thousands of people, many of them children, have died as the result of direct exposure to high concentrations of these chemicals. In addition, many workers in pesticide factories have been poisoned through job-related contact with the chemicals. Numerous agricultural laborers, particularly in countries that have no laws in place specifying stringent guidelines for the handling of pesticides, have also died as a result of direct exposure to these chemicals. Some pesticides have been classified as carcinogens by the U.S. Environmental Protection Agency.

D. R. Gossett

Further Reading

Akinyemi, Okoro M. *Agricultural Production: Organic and Conventional Systems.* Science Publishers, 2007.

Altieri, Miguel A. *The Scientific Basis of Alternative Agriculture.* Westview Press, 1987.

Carson, Rachel. *Silent Spring.* 40th anniversary ed. Houghton Mifflin, 2002.

Miller, G. Tyler, Jr., and Scott Spoolman. "Food, Soil, and Pest Management." In *Living in the Environment: Principles, Connections, and Solutions.* 16th ed. Brooks/Cole, 2009.

Montgomery, David R. *Dirt: The Erosion of Civilizations.* University of California Press, 2007.

Ohkawa, H., H. Miyagawa, and P. W. Lee, eds. *Pesticide Chemistry: Crop Protection, Public Health, Environmental Safety.* Wiley-VCH, 2007.

■ Agricultural revolution

FIELDS OF STUDY: Biology, Life Sciences, Ecosystems; Agriculture, Farming, Animal Husbandry; Ecology, Environment, Environmentalism; Food, Hunger.

IDENTIFICATION: Advances in agricultural technology during the twentieth century

The agricultural revolution led to a dramatic increase in the worldwide production of food and fiber crops, but this increase did not occur without negative environmental consequences.

Early agricultural centers were located near large rivers that helped maintain soil fertility through the deposition of new topsoil during each annual flooding cycle. Agriculture, however, eventually moved into other regions that lacked the annual flooding of large rivers, and humans began to utilize a technique known as slash-and-burn agriculture, in which they cleared the land by burning the existing vegetation and then used the ashes to fertilize their crops. This type of agriculture is still practiced in many developing nations and is one reason the tropical rain forests are disappearing at such a fast rate. During the nineteenth century, the Industrial Revolution led the way for the development of many different types of agricultural machinery, which resulted in the mechanization of most farms and ranches in industrialized nations.

The Green Revolution, as advances in agricultural science during the twentieth century came to be known, resulted in the development of new, higher-yielding varieties of numerous crops, particularly the seed grains that supply most of the calories necessary for maintenance of the world's growing population. While higher-yielding crops, along with improved farming methods, resulted in tremendous increases in the world's food supply, they also led to an increased reliance on monoculture, the practice of growing only one crop over a vast area of land. This practice decreased the genetic variability of many agricultural plants, increased the need for commercial fertilizers, and produced an increased susceptibility to damage from a host of biotic and abiotic factors.

The agricultural revolution has resulted in the development of an agricultural unit that requires relatively few employees, is highly mechanized, devotes large amounts of land to the production of a single crop, and is highly reliant on agricultural chemicals such as fertilizers and pesticides. While this has led to tremendous increases in agricultural productivity, it has also had significant impact on the environment. During the past one hundred years, the world has undergone a continual loss of good topsoil. Even under ideal conditions, the process of soil formation is very slow. Many agricultural techniques lead to the removal of trees and shrubs that provide windbreaks or to the depletion of soil fertility, which reduces the plant cover on the fields. The result of these practices has been the exposure of the soil to increased erosion from wind and moving water, to the extent that as much as one-third of the world's croplands are losing topsoil more quickly than it can be replaced.

Agriculture represents the largest single user of global water. Approximately 73 percent of all water withdrawn from freshwater supplies is used to irrigate crops. Some irrigation practices are actually detrimental. Overwatering can waterlog the soil, and irrigation of crops in dry climates can result in salinization of the soil, which occurs when irrigation water rapidly evaporates from the soil, leaving behind the mineral salts that were dissolved in the water. The salts accumulate and become detrimental to plant growth. It has been estimated that as much as one-third of the world's agricultural soils have been damaged by salinization. In addition, debate exists as to whether the increased usage of water for agriculture has decreased the supply of potable water fit for other human uses.

The nutrients most often depleted from agricultural soils are nitrogen, phosphorus, and potassium, and these nutrients must be applied to the soil regularly in order to maintain fertility. During the second half of the twentieth century, the amount of fertilizer applied to the soil increased more than 450 percent, causing environmental problems in some areas. Fertilizer elements, particularly nitrogen and phosphorus, are carried away by water runoff and are eventually deposited in rivers and lakes, where they contribute to the pollution of aquatic ecosystems. In addition, nitrates can accumulate in underground water supplies.

Agriculture is highly dependent on the use of pesticides to kill organisms such as insects, nematodes, weeds, and fungi that directly or indirectly interfere with crop production. The use of pesticides has dramatically improved crop yields, primarily because pesticides are designed to kill pests before significant damage can occur to the crop. Pesticides often kill nonpests as well, however, and evidence suggests that indiscriminate use of these chemicals can have detrimental effects on wildlife, the structure and function of ecosystems, and even human health. In addition, the overuse of pesticides can lead to the development of resistance in the target species, which can result in a resurgence of the very pest the pesticide was designed to control.

Modern agriculture also consumes large amounts of energy. The operation of farm machinery requires large supplies of liquid fossil fuels, and the production of fertilizers, pesticides, and other agricultural chemicals is another energy cost associated with agriculture. Energy used in food processing, distribution, storage, and cooking after a crop leaves the farm may be five times as much as the energy used to produce the crop. Most of the foods consumed in the United States require more calories of energy to produce, process, and distribute to the market than they provide when they are eaten.

D. R. Gossett

Further Reading

Carson, Rachel. *Silent Spring*. 40th anniversary ed. Houghton Mifflin, 2002.

Conkin, Paul K. *A Revolution Down on the Farm: The Transformation of American Agriculture Since 1929*. University Press of Kentucky, 2008.

Federico, Giovanni. *Feeding the World: An Economic History of Agriculture, 1800-2000*. Princeton University Press, 2005.

Miller, G. Tyler, Jr., and Scott Spoolman. *Environmental Science: Problems, Concepts, and Solutions*. 13th ed. Brooks/Cole, 2010.

Pierce, Christine, and Donald VanDeVeer. *People, Penguins, and Plastic Trees*. Wadsworth, 1995.

■ Agricultural runoff

FIELDS OF STUDY: Biology, Life Sciences, Ecosystems; Agriculture, Farming, Animal Husbandry; Ecology, Environment, Environmentalism; Oceans, Seas, Lakes, Bodies of Water; Pollution, Emissions, Toxic Waste, Hazardous Materials; Water Resources.

IDENTIFICATION: Water that flows into rivers, lakes, and other bodies of water from agricultural land and operations

Runoff from land used for agriculture, which often contains the residues of chemical and organic fertilizers and pesticides, is one of the major sources of water pollution around the world.

The water that flows into streams from farmland after rain or snowmelt carries the residue of the herbicides, fungicides, insecticides, and fertilizers that farmers have used on the land. Many of the wastes produced by cattle, hogs, sheep, and poultry that are raised on feedlots flow into nearby streams. The water that returns to nearby rivers and lakes after it is used to irrigate farmland may be polluted by salt,

agricultural pesticides, and toxic chemicals. These organic materials and chemicals that are carried with soil eroding from agricultural land and transported by water runoff degrade the quality of streams, rivers, lakes, and oceans.

Agricultural runoff enters rivers and lakes from farmland spread over large areas. Since such runoff is a nonpoint source of water pollution, it is more difficult to control than discharges from factories and sewage treatment plants. The chemicals in agricultural runoff have contaminated surface water in many areas of the United States. Rivers pick up sediments and dissolved salts from agricultural runoff as they flow to the oceans. Salt concentration in the Colorado River, for example, increases from about 40 parts per million to 800 parts per million as the river flows down from its headwaters to Mexico.

Nutrients such as potassium, phosphates, and nitrogen compounds from organic wastes and fertilizers are carried by agricultural runoff into rivers and lakes. In the process known as eutrophication, excessive nutrients in bodies of water stimulate the growth of plants such as pond weeds and duck weeds, plant-like organisms called algae, fish and other animals, and bacteria. As more of these organisms grow, more also die and decay. The decay process uses up the oxygen in the water, depriving the fish and other aquatic organisms of their natural supply of oxygen. Some types of game fish, such as salmon, trout, and whitefish, cannot live in water with reduced oxygen. Fish that need less oxygen, such as carp and catfish, will replace them. If all the oxygen in a body of water were to be used up, most forms of life in the water would die. Eutrophication that results from human activities, such as agriculture, is known as cultural eutrophication. In the late 1950s Lake Erie, 26,000 square kilometers (10,000 square miles) in area, was reported to be eutrophic. Thanks to stringent pollution-control measures, however, the lake has improved steadily since that time.

Mitigating Environmental Impacts

The 1987 amendments to the Clean Water Act represent the first comprehensive attempt by the US government to control pollution caused by agricultural activities. In 1991 the US Geological Survey began to implement the full-scale National Water-Quality Assessment (NAWQA) program. The long-term purposes of NAWQA are to describe the status and trends in the quality of the nation's water resources and to provide a scientific understanding of the factors affecting the quality of these resources. In October, 1997, an initiative intended to build on the environmental successes of the Clean Water Act was announced. It focused on runoff from farms and ranches, city streets, and other diffuse sources. The plan called for state and federal environmental agencies to conduct watershed assessments every two years.

Irrigation is necessary for survival in many developing countries. Governments struggle to build advanced agricultural systems, and developments in agriculture have improved food production around the world. However, the increasing reliance on fertilizers and other agricultural chemicals has contributed to the pollution of rivers and lakes. Therefore, interest has shifted to farming with reduced use of chemicals. Scientists have turned their attention to developing organic ways to grow food that require less fertilizer and fewer pesticides, and many farmers rotate their crops from year to year to reduce the need for chemical fertilizers. Instead of spraying their crops with harmful pesticides, some farmers combat damaging insects by releasing other insects or bacteria that prey upon the pests. Scientists have also developed genetically engineered plants that are resistant to certain pests. Other strategies for minimizing pollution caused by agricultural runoff include maintaining buffer zones between irrigated cropland and sites where wastes are disposed, restricting application of manure to areas away from waterways, avoiding application of manure on land subject to erosion, reusing water used to flush manure from paved surfaces for irrigation, constructing ditches and waterways above and around open feedlots to divert runoff, constructing lined water-retention facilities to contain rainfall and runoff, applying solid manure at a rate that optimizes the use of the nitrogen it contains for a given crop, and allowing excess wastewater to evaporate by applying it evenly to land.

Watersheds are areas of land that drain to streams or other bodies of water. Most nonpoint pollution-control projects focus their activities around watersheds because watersheds integrate the effects that land use, climate, hydrology, drainage, and vegetation have on water quality. In the United States, the National Monitoring Program was initiated in 1991 to evaluate the effects of improved land management in reducing water pollution in selected watersheds.

Federal agencies involved in this program include the Environmental Protection Agency (EPA), the Department of Agriculture, the US Geological Survey, and the US Army Corps of Engineers. A composite index was constructed and published to show which watersheds had the greatest potential for possible degradation of water quality from combinations of pesticides, nitrogen, and sediment runoff. The EPA sets criteria on water quality to help states set their own site-specific standards to control nutrient pollution and thus reduce nutrient loading to rivers and lakes.

G. Padmanabhan

Further Reading

Copeland, Claudia. *The Clean Water Initiative.* Congressional Research Service, Library of Congress, 1998.

Hill, Marquita K. "Water Pollution." In *Understanding Environmental Pollution.* 3rd ed. Cambridge University Press, 2010.

Hunt, Constance Elizabeth. *Thirsty Planet: Strategies for Sustainable Water Management.* Zed Books, 2004.

Sullivan, Patrick J., Franklin J. Agardy, and James J. J. Clark. "Water Pollution." In *The Environmental Science of Drinking Water.* Elsevier Butterworth-Heinemann, 2005.

■ Agriculture: history & overview

FIELDS OF STUDY: Agronomy; Anthropology; History;
IDENTIFICATION: The practice of raising vegetable and animal crops to supply food and support a social economic structure.

Agriculture is the ability to produce sufficient food and fiber to feed and shelter the population, the most important natural resource a nation can have. In modern urban societies, it is also the natural resource that is most often taken for granted.

The beginnings of agriculture predate written history. No one knows when the first crop was cultivated, but at some time in the distant past humans discovered that seeds from certain wild grasses could be collected and planted in land that could be controlled and the grasses later gathered for food. Most scholars believe this occurred at about the same time in both the Eastern and Western Hemispheres, some eight thousand to ten thousand years ago.

Early Agriculture

The earliest attempts to grow crops were primarily to supplement the food supply provided by hunting and gathering. However, as the ability to produce crops increased, people began to *domesticate* plants and animals, and their reliance on hunting and gathering decreased, allowing the development of permanent settlements in which humans could live. As far back as six thousand years ago, agriculture was firmly established in Asia, India, Mesopotamia, Egypt, Mexico, Central America, and South America.

The earliest agricultural centers were located near large rivers that helped maintain soil fertility by the deposition of new *topsoil* with each annual flooding cycle. As agriculture moved into regions that lacked the annual flooding of the large rivers, people began to utilize a technique known as *slash-and-burn agriculture*. In this type of agriculture, a farmer clears a field, burns the tress and brush, and farms the field. After a few years soil nutrients become depleted, so the farmer must repeat the process at a new location. This type of agriculture is still practiced in some developing countries and is one reason tropical rain forests are disappearing at a fast rate.

Until the nineteenth century, most farms and ranches were family-owned, and most farmers practiced *sustenance agriculture*. Each farmer produced a variety of crops sufficient to feed his or her family as well as a small excess which was sold for cash or bartered for other goods or services. Agricultural tools such as plows were made of wood, and almost all agricultural activities required human or animal labor. This situation placed a premium on large families to provide the help needed in the fields.

The arrival of the Industrial Revolution changed agriculture, just as it did almost all other industries. Eli Whitney invented the cotton gin in 1793. The mechanical reaper was invented by Cyrus McCormick, and John Lane and John Deere began the commercial manufacture of the steel plow in 1833 and 1837, respectively. These inventions led the way to the development of the many different types of agricultural machinery that resulted in the *mechanization* of most farms and ranches. By the early part of the twentieth century, most agricultural enterprises in the United States were mechanized. American society was transformed from an agrarian society into an urban

society. People involved in agricultural production left farms to go to cities to work in factories. At the same time, there was no longer a need for large numbers of people to produce crops. As a result, fewer people were required to produce the growing amounts of agricultural products that supplied an increasing number of consumers.

Modern Agriculture

As populations continued to grow, there was a need to select and produce crops with higher yields. The *Green Revolution* of the twentieth century helped to make these higher yields possible. Basic information supplied by biological scientists allowed agricultural scientists to develop new, higher-yielding varieties of numerous crops, particularly the *seed grains* which supply most of the calories necessary for maintenance of the world's population. These higher-yielding crop varieties, along with improved farming methods, resulted in tremendous increases in the world's food supply.

The new crop varieties also led to an increased reliance on *monoculture*. While the practice of growing only one crop over a vast number of acres has resulted in much higher yields, it has also decreased the genetic variability of many agricultural plants, increased the need for commercial fertilizers, and produced an increased susceptibility to damage from a host of biotic and abiotic factors. These latter two developments have resulted in a tremendous growth in the *agricultural chemical industry*. Today's modern agricultural unit requires relatively few employees, is highly mechanized, devotes large amounts of land to the production of only one crop, and is highly reliant on agricultural chemicals such as fertilizers and pesticides.

Agricultural Diversity

Modern agriculture is subdivided into many different specialties. Those agricultural industries that deal with plants include *agronomy*, the production of field crops; *forestry*, the growth and production of trees; and *horticulture*. Horticulture is subdivided into *pomology*, the growth and production of fruit crops such as oranges and apples; *olericulture*, the growth and production of vegetable crops (tomatoes, lettuce); *landscape horticulture*, the growth and production of trees and plants that are used in landscape design; and *floriculture*, the growth and production of flowering plants used in the floral industry.

The various agriculture industries produce a tremendous number of agricultural products. Agricultural products that are derived from plants can be subdivided into timber products (lumber, furniture), grain products (wheat, oats), fiber products (cotton, flax), fruit products (grapes, peaches), nut crops (pecans, hazelnuts), vegetable products (lettuce, cabbage), beverage products (tea, coffee), spice and drug crops (garlic, mustard, opium, quinine), ornamental crops (carnations, chrysanthemums), forage crops (alfalfa, clover), and other cash crops such as sugarcane, tobacco, artichokes, and rubber.

Impact on Soil Resources

While there have been tremendous increases in agricultural productivity through the use of modern agricultural practices, these practices have had a significant impact on some other natural resources. *Soil* is one of the most overlooked and misunderstood resources. Most people think of soil as an inert medium from which plants grow. In reality, *topsoil*—that upper 15 to 25 centimeters (6 to 10 inches) of the earth's terrestrial surface in which nearly all plants grow—is a complex mixture of weathered mineral materials from rocks, partially decomposed organic molecules, and a large number of living organisms.

The process of soil formation is very slow. Under ideal conditions, enough topsoil can form in one year to produce a layer of about 1 millimeter (0.04 inch) thick when spread over 1 hectare (2.5 acres). With proper management, topsoil can be kept fertile and productive indefinitely. Unfortunately, many agricultural techniques lead to the removal of trees and shrubs, which provide windbreaks, or to the depletion of soil fertility, which reduces the plant cover over the field. These practices expose the soil to increased erosion from wind and moving water. As a result, as much as one-third of the world's current croplands are losing topsoil faster than it can be replaced.

Water & Irrigation

Because plants require water in order to grow, agriculture represents the largest single use of global water. About 73 percent of all fresh water withdrawn from groundwater supplies, rivers, and lakes is used in the irrigation of crops. Almost 15 percent of the world's croplands are irrigated. Water use varies among countries. Some countries have abundant water supplies and irrigate liberally, while water is very scarce in other countries and must be used very carefully. Because as much as 80 percent of the water intended for irrigation is lost to evaporation before reaching the plants, the efficiency of water use in some countries can be very low.

There is no doubt that irrigation has dramatically increased crop production in many areas, but some irrigation practices have been detrimental. Overwatering can lead to a *waterlogging* of the soil. Waterlogging cuts off the supply of oxygen to the roots, and the plants die. Irrigation of crops in dry climates can often result in *salinization* of the soil. In these climates, the irrigation water rapidly evaporates from the soil, leaving behind mineral salts that were dissolved in the water. As the salts accumulate, they become lethal to most plants. Some experts estimate that as much as one-third of the world's agricultural soil has been damaged by salinization. There is also an argument as to whether the increased usage of water for agriculture has decreased the supply of potable water fit for other uses.

Fertilizers

Plants require sunshine, water either from rainfall or irrigation, carbon dioxide from the atmosphere, and thirteen mineral nutrients from the soil. Of these, calcium, magnesium, nitrogen, phosphorus, and potassium are required in the greatest amounts. Calcium and magnesium are plentiful in soils located in dry climates, but in wetter climates these nutrients are often *leached* through the soil. In these regions, calcium and magnesium are returned to the soil in the form of lime, which is also sometimes added to soil to raise its pH (increase its alkalinity). Nitrogen, phosphorus, and potassium are the nutrients which are most often depleted from agricultural soils, and these nutrients are often referred to as the *fertilizer elements*. Because these nutrients stimulate plant growth and can greatly increase crop yields, it is necessary to apply them to the soil regularly in order to maintain fertility.

The amount of fertilizer applied to the soil increased more than 450 percent in the second half of the twentieth century. While this increase in the use of fertilizers has more than doubled worldwide crop production, it has also caused some problems. The increased production of fertilizers has required the use of energy and mineral resources that could have been used elsewhere. In many cases, farmers tend to overfertilize. Overfertilization not only wastes money but also contributes to environmental degradation. Fertilizer elements, particularly nitrogen and phosphorus, are carried away by water runoff and are eventually deposited in the rivers and lakes, where they contribute to pollution of aquatic ecosystems. In addition, nitrates can accumulate in underground water supplies. These nitrates can be harmful if ingested by newborns.

Other Resources

Modern agriculture, as it is practiced in the United States, consumes large amounts of energy. Farm machinery used in planting, cultivating, harvesting, and transporting crops to processing plants or to market consumes large supplies of liquid fossil fuels such as gasoline or diesel. The energy required to produce fertilizers, pesticides, and other agricultural chemicals is the second largest energy cost associated with agriculture. The use of fuel required by pumps to irrigate crops is also a major energy consumer. Additional energy is used in food processing, distribution, storage, and cooking after the crop leaves the farm. The energy used for these activities may be five times as much as that used to produce the crop.

About 16 percent of the total energy used in the United States is consumed by systems devoted to feeding people, and most of the foods consumed in the United States require more calories of energy to produce, process, and distribute to the market than they provide when they are eaten. The next major development in agriculture will be the *biotechnical revolution*, in which scientists will be able to use molecular biological techniques to produce new crop varieties. In the future, agricultural scientists may be able to develop crop plants that can be produced, processed, and distributed with less impact on other resources.

Commercial Impact

While fewer than 1 percent of Americans are directly involved in agricultural production, agriculture in the United States employs about seventeen million people in some phase of the industry, from production to retail sales. This includes workers hired by agricultural chemical companies which produce or sell agricultural implements and machinery, processing and canning plants, and wholesale and retail

marketing firms such as grocery stores. In 1997 there were six thousand to eight thousand different agricultural products on the market. Agriculture is also big business, with assets of about one hundred billion dollars. This figure equals 88 percent of the combined capital assets of all the major U.S. corporations. American farmers now produce 76 percent more crops than the previous generation did on the same amount of land, and one-third of all American agricultural products are exported. This makes the United States the world's most agriculturally productive country and the largest exporter of agricultural products.

D. R. Gossett

Further Reading

Acquaah, George. *Principles of Crop Production: Theory, Techniques, and Technology.* Prentice Hall, 2001.

Grigg, David. *An Introduction to Agricultural Geography.* Routledge, 2005.

Janick, Jules. *Horticultural Science.* 4th ed. W. H. Freeman, 1986.

Smith, Bruce D. *The Emergence of Agriculture.* W. H. Freeman, 1994.

Zohary, Daniel, and Maria Hopf. *Domestication of Plants in the Old World: The Origin and Spread of Cultivated Plants in West Asia, Europe, and the Nile Valley.* 3rd ed. Oxford University Press, 2001.

Major Crops & Places of Original Cultivation

Crop	Region
Apples	Central Asia and the Middle East
Apricots	China
Asparagus	Mediterranean
Avocados	Central and South America
Bananas	India and Southeast Asia
Beans	Ethiopia
Bell peppers	Central and South America
Cantaloupes	Central Asia and the Middle East
Carrots	Central Asia and the Middle East
Cashews	Central and South America
Celery	Mediterranean

　　　　　　　　　　　　　　　Encyclopedia of Environmental Issues

Cherries	China
Coconuts	India and Southeast Asia
Coffee	Ethiopia
Corn	Central and South America
Cotton	Central Asia and the Middle East
Cucumbers	China
Eggplant	China
Figs	Central Asia and the Middle East
Garlic	Central Asia and the Middle East
Ginger	India and Southeast Asia
Grapes	Central Asia and the Middle East
Leeks	Central Asia and the Middle East
Lettuce	Mediterranean
Lima beans	Central and South America
Mangoes	India and Southeast Asia
Mustard	India and Southeast Asia
Oats	Central Asia and the Middle East
Okra	Ethiopia
Olives	Mediterranean
Onions	Mediterranean
Oranges	China, India, and Southeast Asia
Papayas	Central and South America
Parsnips	Mediterranean

Peaches	China
Peanuts	Central and South America
Pears	Central Asia and the Middle East
Peas	Ethiopia
Pineapples	Central and South America
Potatoes	Central and South America
Pumpkins	Central and South America
Radishes	India and Southeast Asia
Rhubarb	Mediterranean
Rice	India and Southeast Asia
Rye	Central Asia and the Middle East
Soybeans	China
Spinach	Central Asia and the Middle East
Sugarcane	China
Sweet potatoes	Central and South America
Tangerines	India and Southeast Asia
Tea	China
Tomatoes	Central and South America
Turnips	Central Asia, the Mediterranean, and the Middle East
Walnuts	China
Wheat	Central Asia and the Middle East
Yams	India and Southeast Asia

Source: Data are from Brian Capon, *Botany for Gardeners: An Introduction and Guide,* Timber Press, 1990), p. 81. Note: More recent research may indicate different or more specific points of origin for some crop species.

■ Agriculture: modern problems

FIELDS OF STUDY: Agricultural Management;
Agronomy; Animal Husbandry; Business
Management; Ecology; Ecosystem Management;

IDENTIFICATION: Environmental, ecological and business problems arising in the practice of raising vegetable and animal crops to supply food and support a social economic structure.

Many modern problems in agriculture are not new. Erosion and pollution, for example, have been around as long as agriculture. However, agriculture has changed drastically within its ten-thousand-year history, especially since the dawn of the Industrial Revolution in the eighteenth century. Erosion and pollution are bigger problems than before and have been joined by a host of other issues that are equally critical, but not all related to physical deterioration.

Monoculture

Modern agriculture emphasizes crop specialization, also known as monoculture. Farmers, especially in industrialized regions, often grow a single crop on much of their land. Problems associated with this practice are exacerbated when a single variety or cultivar of a species is grown. Such a strategy allows the farmer to reduce costs, but it also makes the crop, and thus the farm and community, susceptible to widespread crop failure. The corn blight of 1970 devastated more than 15 percent of the North American corn crop. The corn was particularly susceptible to harmful organisms because 70 percent of the crop being grown was of the same high-yield variety. Chemical antidotes can fight pests, but they increase pollution. Maintaining species diversity or varietal diversity—growing several different crops instead of one or two—allows for crop failures without jeopardizing the entire economy of a farm or region that specializes in a particular monoculture, such as tobacco, coffee, or bananas.

Genetic Engineering

Growing genetically modified (GM) crops is one potential way to replace post-infestation chemical treatments. Recombinant technologies used to splice genes into varieties of rice or potatoes from other organisms are becoming increasingly common. The benefits of such GM crops include more pest-resistant plants and higher crop yields. However, environmentalists fear new genes could trigger unknown side effects with more serious, long-term environmental and economic consequences than the problems they were used to solve. GM plants designed to resist herbicide applications could potentially pass the resistant gene to closely related wild weed species that would then become "super weeds." Also, just as pests can develop resistance to pesticides, they may also become resistant to defenses engineered into GM plants.

Erosion

An age-old problem, soil loss from erosion occurs all over the world. As soil becomes unproductive or erodes away, more land is plowed. The newly plowed lands usually are considered marginal, meaning they are too steep, nonporous or too sandy, or deficient in some other way. When natural vegetative cover blankets these soils, it protects them from erosive agents: water, wind, ice, or gravity. Plant cover "catches" rainwater that seeps downward into the soil rather than running off into rivers. As marginal land is plowed or cleared to grow crops, erosion increases.

Expansion of land under cultivation has not been the only factor contributing to erosion. Fragile grasslands in dry areas have also been used more intensively. Grazing more livestock than these pastures can handle decreases the amount of grass in the pasture and exposes more of the soil to wind, the primary erosive agent in dry regions. Overgrazing can affect pastureland in tropical regions, too. Thousands of acres of tropical forest have been cleared to establish cattle-grazing ranges in Latin America. Tropical soils, although thick, are not very fertile. After one or two growing seasons, crops grown in these soils will yield substantially less than before.

Tropical fields require fallow periods of about ten years to restore the soil after it is depleted. That is why tropical farmers using slash-and-burn agriculture move to new fields every few years in a cycle that returns them to the same place years later, after their particular lands have regenerated. Where there is heavy forest cover, soils are protected from exposure to the massive amounts of rainfall. Organic material for crops is present as long as the forest remains in place. When the forest is cleared, however, the resulting grassland cannot provide adequate protection, and erosion accelerates. Lands that are heavily grazed provide even less protection from heavy rains, and erosion accelerates even more.

The use of machines also promotes erosion, and modern agriculture relies on machinery such as tractors, harvesters, trucks, balers, and ditchers. Machinery is used intensely in industrialized nations, and its use has been on the rise in developing countries such as India, China, Mexico, and Indonesia, where traditional, nonmechanized farming methods were previously the norm. Farming machines, in gaining traction, loosen topsoil and inhibit vegetative cover growth, especially when farm implements designed to rid the soil of weeds are attached. The soil is then more prone to erosion.

Eco-fallow farming has become more popular in the United States and Europe as a way to reduce erosion. This method of agriculture, which leaves the crop residue in place over the fallow (nongrowing) season, does not root the soil in place as well as living plants do, so some erosion continues. Additionally, eco-fallow methods require the heavy use of chemicals, such as herbicides, to "burn down" weed growth at the start of the growing season. This contributes to increased erosion and pollution.

Pollution & Silt

Besides causing resistance among harmful bacteria, insects, and weeds, pesticides inevitably wash into surface and groundwater supplies, contaminating them. Pesticides are potentially harmful to human health; there has been concern that their seepage into land and water is linked to cancer.

An increasingly heavy silt load has been choking the life out of streams and rivers. Accelerated erosion from water runoff carries silt particles into streams, where they remain suspended and inhibit the growth of many forms of plant and animal life. The silt load in American streams has become so heavy that the Mississippi River delta has been growing faster than it once did. Heavy silt loads, combined with chemical residues, have been creating an expanded dead zone. By taxing the capabilities of ecosystems around the delta, sediments have been filtered out slowly, plant absorption of nutrients has decreased, and salinity levels for aquatic life have been unable to be stabilized. Most of the world's population lives in coastal zones, and 80 percent of the world's fish catch comes from coastal waters over continental shelves that are most susceptible to this form of pollution.

Pesticide Resistance

With the onset of the Green Revolution of the mid-twentieth century, the use of herbicides, insecticides, and other pesticides increased dramatically all over the world. An increasing awareness of problems caused by the overuse of pesticides followed, extending even to household antibacterial cleaning agents and other products. Mutations among the genes of bacteria and plants have allowed these organisms to resist the effects of chemicals that were toxic to their ancestors. The use of pesticides leads to a cycle wherein more or different combinations of chemicals are used, and more pests develop resistance to these toxins. Additionally, the development of herbicide-resistant crop plants enables greater use of herbicides to kill undesirable weeds on croplands.

Increasing interest in biopesticides (biological pesticides) may slow the cycle of pesticide resistance. Types of biopesticides include beneficial microbes, fungi, and insects such as ladybugs that can be released in infested areas to prey upon specific pests. Biopesticides may be naturally occurring or genetically modified organisms. Their use also avoids excessive reliance on chemical pesticides.

Fertilizers & Eutrophication

Increased use of fertilizers was another result of the Green Revolution. Particulate amounts of most fertilizers enter the hydrologic cycle through runoff. As a result, bodies of water become enriched by dissolved nutrients, such as nitrates and phosphates. The growth of aquatic plants in rivers and lakes is overstimulated, which results in the depletion of dissolved oxygen. This process of eutrophication can harm all aquatic life in these ecosystems.

Water Depletion

An increasing reliance on irrigation has contributed to the mismanagement and overtapping of groundwater resources. The rate of groundwater recharge is slow, usually between 0.1 and 0.3 percent per year. When the amount of water pumped out of the ground exceeds the recharge rate, it is referred to as aquifer overdraft. An aquifer is a water-bearing stratum of permeable rock, sand, or gravel.

In Tamil Nadu, India, groundwater levels dropped twenty-five to thirty meters during the 1970s due to excessive pumping for irrigation. In Tianjin, China, the groundwater level has declined 4.4 meters per year. In the United States, aquifer overdraft has averaged 25 percent over the replacement rate. The Ogallala aquifer—located under parts of South Dakota, Wyoming, Nebraska, Colorado, Kansas, Oklahoma, Texas, and New Mexico—represents an extreme example of overdraft: the rate of depletion has annually been three times faster than its rate of recharge. The capacity of the aquifer decreased by an estimated 33 percent between 1950 and 2004. At this rate, the Ogallala aquifer, which supplies water to countless communities and farms, has been projected to become nonproductive by 2030.

Soil Salinization

In addition, continued irrigation of arid regions can lead to soil problems. Soil salinization has been widespread in the small-grained soils of these regions, which have a high water absorption capacity and a low infiltration rate. Some irrigation practices add large amounts of salts into the soil, increasing its natural rate of salinization. This can also occur at the base of a hill slope. Soil salinization has been recognized as a major process of land degradation.

Although surface and groundwater resources cannot be enriched by technology, conservation and improved environmental management can make the use of precious freshwater more efficient. In agriculture, for example, drip irrigation can reduce water use by nearly 50 percent. In developing countries, though, equipment and installation costs often limit the availability of these more efficient technologies.

Urban Sprawl

With the increasing mechanization of farms, the need for farmers and farm workers has been drastically reduced. From a peak in 1935 of about 6.8 million farmers farming 1.1 billion acres in the United States, for example, the country at the end of the twentieth century counted fewer than two million farmers farming 950 million acres. In 2012, the number of farm operations was at 2.17 million, according to the U.S. Department of Agriculture, with only 914 million acres of land in use.

Urban sprawl converts a tremendous amount of cropland into parking lots, shopping malls, industrial parks, and suburban neighborhoods. If cities were located in marginal areas, then concern about the loss of farmland to commercial development would be nominal. However, the cities attracting the greatest numbers of people have too often replaced the best cropland. Taking the best cropland out of primary production imposes a severe economic penalty.

Energy & Technological Efficiency

The increasing mechanization of farms has led to major increases in the amounts of energy consumed by these farms, particularly those in industrialized nations. Farms use large quantities of energy for irrigation, to operate machinery, to heat and cool buildings, for food processing and shipment, to spray pesticides, and to fertilize crops. The latter two are products of fossil fuels. Raising livestock on grain also consumes large quantities of fossil fuel. Large-scale livestock farmers often feed their animals grains and protein byproducts rather than employing traditional methods of foraging and consuming crop waste. Grain and protein byproduct feeding requires less land and allows for the animals to grow to market weight quickly. However, this method of feeding can be inefficient, as animals convert only a fraction of their food energy into growth; for example, it has been estimated that seven kilograms of grain are needed to produce only one kilogram of beef.

Practices such as conservation tilling, which requires less working of the soil, have helped reduce energy use on farms. Another practice is drip irrigation, in which water drips slowly to the roots of plants, thus saving on both water and fertilizer. Farmers have also begun to plant genetically modified crops that do not need pesticide, which itself has become more sophisticated and therefore used in smaller quantities than before. Other farms have opted to grow organic (pesticide-free) food and to raise animals that are not given growth hormones and that are free-range, or not always confined in tight quarters. While these practices can be expensive, they can also save on energy costs and alleviate consumer concerns about ingesting potentially harmful chemicals.

Another way farmers have learned to save money on energy is to use renewable energy sources such as wind power, solar power, and biomass products (also called biofuel). By having electric wind turbines built on their farms, farmers can produce their own energy. Wind power can be used to power an entire farm or to power a specific area of the farm, such as pumping water for cattle. Solar energy can power a farm's lighting and heating (e.g., in greenhouses), pump water, and produce electricity. It can even be used to dry crops faster and more evenly than crops left prone to damage in the fields. Many farmers grow corn to make ethanol. Other crops have begun to be used for fuel as well, since there is virtually no limit to the type of plant and organic waste that can be used to produce energy. Agriculture creates a lot of waste; there is the potential for taking that waste and converting it into energy, thus saving on energy production costs, disposal costs, and pollution. Crops grown specifically for biofuel—for farms and other consumers—can be produced in large quantities and thus become profitable when sold.

Other technologies that have made farming become more efficient—and that have saved and made farmers money—are broadband Internet access, smartphones, and Global Positioning System (GPS) technology. Use of the Internet has helped farmers quickly exchange important data with each other and has helped farmers connect directly to their markets and consumers. GPS technology has helped farmers navigate their fields in a fraction of the time it took before this invention; equipment can be guided through fields, with no overlap or gaps, so that seeds can be planted and pesticides sprayed evenly. Smartphone applications (apps) for crop scouting can help farmers identify a problem and its specific source immediately, eliminating the need to apply pesticide, for example, to an entire field in the hopes of rectifying that one problem. There are numerous other mobile applications useful to farmers as well.

James Knotwell, Denise Knotwell, Bryan Ness, and Elizabeth Slocum

Further Reading

Campbell, Elizabeth. "Number of US Farms Fell to Six-Year Low in 2012, USDA Says." *Bloomberg*, 19 Feb. 2013, www.bloomberg.com/news/articles/2013–02–19/number-of-u-s-farms-fell-to-six-year-low-in-2012-usda-says-1-. Accessed 7 Apr. 2017.

Cockrall-King, Jennifer. *Food and the City: Urban Agriculture and the New Food Revolution.* Prometheus Books, 2012.

Hoag, Dana L. *Agricultural Crisis in America: A Reference Handbook.* ABC-CLIO, 1999.

Jackson, Wes. *New Roots for Agriculture.* 1980. U of Nebraska P, 1985.

Lægreid, M., et al. *Agriculture, Fertilizers, and the Environment.* Cabi, 1999.

Magdoff, Fred, and Brian Tokar, editors. *Agriculture and Food in Crisis: Conflict, Resistance, and Renewal.* Monthly Review Press, 2010.

McKee, Gregory J., et al., editors. *Pesticide Resistance, Population Dynamics, and Invasive Species Management.* Nova Science Publishers, 2010.

Paarlberg, Don, and Philip Paarlberg. *The Agricultural Revolution of the 20th Century.* Iowa State UP, 2000.

Pfeiffer, Dale A. *Eating Fossil Fuels: Oil, Food and the Coming Crisis in Agriculture.* Gabriola Island (BC: New Society Publishers, 2008. Print.

Pimentel, David, and Anne Wilson. "World Population, Agriculture, and Malnutrition." *World Watch*, Sept.–Oct. 2004, pp. 22–25. Accessed 7 Apr. 2017.

"Renewable Energy and Agriculture: A Natural Fit." *Union of Concerned Scientists*, 2003, www.ucsusa.org/clean_energy/smart-energy-solutions/increase-renewables/renewable-energy-and.html. Accessed 7 Apr. 2017.

Rissler, Jane, and Margaret Mellon. *The Ecological Risks of Engineered Crops.* MIT P, 1996.

"Unit 7: Agriculture // Section 8: Agriculture and Energy." *The Habitable Planet*, Annenberg Learner, www.learner.org/courses/envsci/unit/text.php?unit=7&secNum=8. Accessed 7 Apr. 2017.

■ Agriculture: traditional

FIELDS OF STUDY: Agricultural Management; Agronomy; Anthropology; History;

IDENTIFICATION: The older, non-technological practices used to supply food and support a very basic social structure.

Two agricultural practices that are widespread among the world's traditional cultures, slash-and-burn agriculture and nomadism, share several features. Both are ancient forms of agriculture, both involve farmers not remaining in a fixed location, and both can pose serious environmental threats if practiced in a nonsustainable fashion. The most significant difference between the two is that slash-and-burn is associated with raising field crops, while nomadism usually involves herding livestock.

Slash-and-Burn Agriculture

Farmers have practiced *slash-and-burn agriculture*, which is also referred to as *shifting cultivation* or *swidden agriculture*, in almost every region of the world where farming is possible. Although at the end of the twentieth century slash-and-burn agriculture was most commonly found in tropical areas such as the Amazon River basin in South America, swidden agriculture once dominated agriculture in more temperate regions, such as northern Europe. Swidden agriculture was, in fact, common in Finland and northern Russia well into the early decades of the twentieth century.

Slash-and-burn acquired its name from the practice of farmers who cleared land for planting crops by cutting down the trees or brush on the land and then burning the fallen timber on the site. The farmers literally slash and burn. The ashes of the burnt wood add minerals to the soil, which temporarily improves its fertility. Crops the first year following clearing and burning are generally the best crops the site will provide. Each year after that, the yield diminishes slightly as the fertility of the soil is depleted.

Farmers who practice slash-and-burn do not attempt to improve fertility by adding fertilizers such as animal manure to the soil. They instead rely on the soil to replenish itself over time. When the yield from one site drops below acceptable levels, farmers then clear another piece of land, burn the brush and other vegetation, and cultivate that site while leaving their previous field to lie fallow and its natural vegetation to return. This cycle will be repeated over and over, with some sites being allowed to lie fallow indefinitely, while others may be revisited and farmed again in five, ten, or twenty years.

Farmers who practice slash-and-burn do not always move their dwelling places as they cultivate different fields. In some geographic regions, farmers live in a central village and farm cooperatively, with fields being alternately allowed to remain fallow and farmed, making a gradual circuit around the central village. In other cases, the village itself may move as new fields are cultivated. Anthropologists studying indigenous peoples in Amazonia, for example, discovered that village garden sites were on a hundred-year cycle. Villagers farmed cooperatively to clear a garden site. That garden would be used for about five years; then a new site was cleared. When the fields in use became an inconvenient distance from the village—about once every twenty years—the entire village would move to be closer to the new fields. Over a period of approximately one hundred years, a village would make a circle through the forest, eventually ending up close to where it had been located long before any of the present villagers had been born.

In more temperate climates, farmers often owned and lived on the land on which they practiced swidden agriculture. Farmers in Finland, for example, would clear a portion of their land, burn the covering vegetation, grow grains for several years, and then allow that land to remain fallow for five to twenty years. The individual farmer rotated cultivation around the land in a fashion similar to that practiced by whole villages in other areas but did so as an individual rather than as part of a communal society.

Although slash-and-burn is frequently denounced as a cause of environmental degradation in tropical areas, the problem with it is not the practice itself but the length of the cycle. If the cycle of shifting cultivation is long enough, forests will grow back, the soil will regain its fertility, and minimal adverse effects will occur. In some regions, a piece of land may require as little as five years to regain its maximum fertility; in others, it may take one hundred years. Problems arise when growing populations put pressure on traditional farmers to return to fallow land too soon. Crops are smaller than needed, leading to a vicious cycle in which the next strip of land is also farmed too soon, and each site yields less and less. As a result, more and more land must be cleared.

Nomadism

Nomadic peoples have no permanent homes. They earn their living by raising herd animals, such as sheep, horses, or other cattle, and they spend their lives following their herds from pasture to pasture with the seasons, going wherever there is sufficient food for their animals. Most nomadic animals tend to be hardy breeds of goats, sheep, or cattle that can withstand hardship and live on marginal lands. Traditional nomads rely on natural pasturage to support their herds and grow no grains or hay for themselves. If a drought occurs or a traditional pasturing site is unavailable, they can lose most of their herds to starvation.

In many nomadic societies, the herd animal is almost the entire basis for sustaining the people. The animals are slaughtered for food, clothing is woven from the fibers of their hair, and cheese and yogurt may be made from milk. The animals may also be used for sustenance without being slaughtered. Nomads in Mongolia, for example, occasionally drink horses' blood, removing only a cup or two at a time from the animal.

In mountainous regions, nomads often spend the summers high up on mountain meadows, returning to lower altitudes in the autumn when snow begins to fall. In desert regions, they move from oasis to oasis, going to the places where sufficient natural water exists to allow brush and grass to grow, allowing their animals to graze for a few days, weeks, or months, then moving on. In some cases, the pressure to move on comes not from the depletion of food for the animals but from the depletion of a water source, such as a spring or well. At many desert oases, a natural water seep or spring provides only enough water to support a nomadic group for a few days at a time.

In addition to true nomads—people who never live in one place permanently—a number of cultures have practiced *seminomadic farming*. The temperate months of the year, spring through fall, are spent following the herds on a long loop, sometimes hundreds of miles long, through traditional grazing areas, then the winter is spent in a permanent village.

Nomadism has been practiced for millennia, but there is strong pressure from several sources to eliminate it. Pressures generated by industrialized society are increasingly threatening the traditional cultures of nomadic societies, such as the Bedouin of the Arabian Peninsula. Traditional grazing areas are being fenced off or developed for other purposes.

Environmentalists are also concerned about the ecological damage caused by nomadism. Nomads generally measure their wealth by the number of animals they own and will try to develop their herds to as large a size as possible, well beyond the numbers required for simple sustainability. The herd animals eat increasingly large amounts of vegetation, which then has no opportunity to regenerate. Desertification may occur as a result. Nomadism based on herding goats and sheep, for example, has been blamed for the expansion of the Sahara Desert in Africa. For this reason, many environmental policymakers have been attempting to persuade nomads to give up their traditional lifestyle and become sedentary farmers.

Nancy Farm Männikkö

Further Reading

Beckwith, Carol, and Marion Van Offelen. *Nomads of Niger.* Academic Press, 1987.

Colfer, Carol J., with Nancy Peluso and Chin See Chung. *Beyond Slash and Burn: Building on Indigenous Management of Borneo's Tropical Rain Forest.* New York Botanical Garden, 1994.

Goldstein, Melvyn C., and Cynthia M. Beall. *The Changing World of Mongolia's Nomads.* University of California Press, 1994.

Grigg, David. *An Introduction to Agricultural Geography.* Routledge, 2005.

Mortimore, Michael. *Roots in the African Dust: Sustaining the Sub-Saharan Drylands.* Cambridge University Press, 1998.

Schmink, Marianne, and Charles H. Wood. *Contested Frontiers in Amazonia.* Columbia University Press, 1992. This interdisciplinary analysis of the process of frontier change in one region of the Brazilian Amazon shows how deforestation and settlement patterns were outcomes of the competition for resources among various groups.

■ Air conditioning and air-cooling technology

FIELDS OF STUDY: Technology and Applied Science; Industries, Commercial Products; Inventions; Chemistry; Elements, Substances, Chemicals, Compounds; Ecology, Environment, Environmentalism.

IDENTIFICATION: Intentional modification of indoor air temperature, humidity, or other characteristics for the purpose of comfort, health, or protection of items sensitive to temperature or humidity

Air-conditioning benefits humankind in many ways, but it also has some negative environmental impacts. The refrigerants long used in air conditioners have proven to have adverse effects on ozone in the earth's stratosphere, and the use of air-conditioning accounts for a high percentage of energy consumption, particularly in regions with warm climates.

Since ancient times, human beings have tried to make the air inside buildings more comfortable. The Romans circulated cool water through buildings. Other cultures created fans or encouraged breezes to blow across pools of evaporating water to cool buildings. Cooling by evaporation of water, however, can

Air conditioning units for the Rackham Building at the University of Michigan. By Arbitrarily0 (Own work)

lower temperatures only by a few degrees and is not effective when the air is humid.

Most modern air conditioners are similar to that first proposed by Willis Carrier in 1902. Air conditioners work in much the same way as do electric refrigerators. Both kinds of devices make use of the thermodynamics of fluids. A fluid with a boiling point somewhat below room temperature is selected, and a compressor is used to compress the fluid. Under sufficiently high pressure, the fluid liquefies. This process produces heat, so, in a part of the system outside the area to be cooled, fans blow air over tubes containing the warm liquid to cool it. The liquid is then circulated into the part of the system within the area to be cooled, where it passes through tubes in which the pressure drops, allowing the fluid to evaporate. The evaporating fluid then cools to a temperature near its boiling point. A fan blows air over the cold tubes, cooling the air. Many early air conditioners used fluids such as ammonia, methyl chloride, or even propane. The problem with these materials is that they are health hazards, explosion or fire hazards, or both.

In 1928, Thomas Midgley Jr., developed chlorofluorocarbons (CFCs), a family of related chemicals that were nontoxic and nonexplosive and that had boiling temperatures and other properties making them suitable for use in air conditioners and refrigerators. It was unknown at the time that these nontoxic CFCs, when released into the atmosphere, break down ozone in the earth's stratosphere.

Because ozone in the stratosphere blocks ultraviolet light from the sun, maintenance of the ozone layer is important to life on earth. Without the ozone layer, the earth's surface would receive a lethal dosage of ultraviolet light. Some damage has already been done to stratospheric ozone by CFCs released from leaking air-conditioning systems. In addition to depleting stratospheric ozone, CFCs are greenhouse gases, which means that they contribute to global warming.

The international agreement known as the Montreal Protocol calls for the gradual reduction of the production of CFCs and other chemicals known to harm the ozone layer, and since the adoption of the protocol in 1987 the use of these substances has been greatly reduced around the world. Some non-CFC refrigerants have been developed that are less damaging to the environment; however, these newer refrigerants have slightly different properties and cannot simply be substituted for CFCs in older air-conditioning systems without modifications to the systems, some of which can be expensive.

In regions with warm climates, air conditioning accounts for the largest use of electricity in buildings. With electricity becoming increasingly expensive, many manufacturers of air conditioners emphasize energy efficiency in their marketing. The standard reference for air-conditioner energy efficiency is the seasonal energy-efficiency ratio (SEER), which is the thermal energy removed (measured in British thermal units) divided by the energy used (measured in watt-hours). The larger the SEER, the more energy-efficient the air conditioner.

Raymond D. Benge, Jr.

Further Reading

Achermann, Marsha E. *Cool Comfort: America's Romance with Air-Conditioning.* Smithsonian Institution Press, 2002.

Kwong, Qi Jie, Nor Mariah Adam, and B. B. Sahari. "Thermal Comfort Assessment and Potential for Energy Efficiency Enhancement in Modern Tropical Buildings: A Review." *Energy & Buildings* 68 (2014): 547–557. *Academic Search Complete.* Web. 14 Jan. 2015.

Miller, Rex, and Mark R. Miller. *Air Conditioning and Refrigeration.* McGraw-Hill, 2006.

Sivak, Michael. "Will AC Put a chill on the Global Energy Supply?" *Amer. Scientist.* 101.5 (2013): 330–333. *Academic Search Complete.* Web. 14 Jan. 2015.

Todorovic, Marija S., and Jeong Tai Kim. "In Search for Sustainable Globally Cost-Effective Energy Efficient Building Solar System—Heat Recovery Assisted Building Integrated PV Powered Heat Pump for Air-Conditioning, Water Heating and Water Saving." *Energy & Buildings* 85 (2014): 346–355. *Academic Search Complete.* Web. 14 Jan. 2015.

■ Air pollution policy to 2010

FIELDS OF STUDY: Government, Politics, International Relations; International Relations, Agreements, Treaties; Laws, Acts, Resolutions; Public Policy, Debates, Controversies; Regulation, Standards and Practices; Ecology, Environment, Environmentalism.

IDENTIFICATION: High-level governmental plan of action for establishing and maintaining acceptable air quality and regulating individual air pollutants

Laws and regulatory agencies establish air-pollution policy to control human-generated pollutants that can have negative impacts on human life and health, ecosystems, and global processes such as stratospheric ozone replenishment. Regulatory policy typically seeks to control pollutants by setting ambient air-quality standards, limiting allowable emissions, and requiring the use of specific pollution-control technologies.

The Clean Air Act, passed by the U.S. Congress in 1963, laid the foundation for what some consider to be the most progressive, wide-reaching, and complicated environmental cleanup legislation in the world. When the Clean Air Act and other early federal, state, and local clean air laws proved to be relatively ineffective, several sweeping amendments to the laws were enacted.

The groundbreaking 1970 amendments to the Clean Air Act resulted in emissions standards for automobiles and new industries in addition to establishing air-quality standards for urban areas. Devised through an exceptionally cooperative bipartisan effort, the 1970 amendments were proclaimed by President Richard M. Nixon to be a "historic piece of legislation" that put the United States "far down the road" toward achieving cleaner air. The amendments established specific maximum concentration levels for several hazardous substances, and the individual states were charged with developing comprehensive plans to implement and maintain these standards.

Tightly controlled scientific methodology was used for the first time to assess and determine acceptable levels for public and environmental health for six "priority air pollutants": carbon monoxide, sulfur dioxide, nitrogen dioxide, respirable particulate matter, ground-level ozone, and lead. Emission standards for air-pollution sources such as automobiles, factories, and power plants were established that also limited the discharge of air pollutants in geographical areas where air quality was already acceptable, thus preventing its deterioration.

The major Clean Air Act amendments of 1970 also stimulated many states to pass regional and local air-pollution legislation, with some areas eventually passing laws that later proved to be even more stringent than federally established guidelines. During this period, the newly created U.S. Environmental Protection Agency (EPA) began strongly suggesting the tightening of rules regulating the amount of lead that could be added to gasoline, a significant source of lead poisoning in urban children and young adults, thus laying the groundwork for the future elimination of all leaded gasolines. Many sectors of the business community challenged the wording of some of the 1970 amendments, arguing that the language was vague and required clarification, particularly regarding the deterioration of air quality in areas that were already meeting federal standards.

Milestones in Air-Pollution Policy

Year	Event
1963	The Clean Air Act sets aside $95 million to reduce air pollution in the United States.
1970	The Environmental Protection Agency is established to enforce environmental legislation.
1970	Clean Air Act amendments establish stricter air-quality standards.

1977	Additional Clean Air Act amendments extend compliance deadlines established by the 1970 amendments and allow the EPA to bring civil lawsuits against companies that do not meet air-quality standards.
1979	The United Nations sponsors the Convention on Long-Range Transboundary Air Pollution, which is designed to reduce acid rain and air pollution.
1987	The Montreal Protocol is signed by twenty-four nations pledging to reduce the output of ozone-depleting chlorofluorocarbons.
1990	Clean Air Act amendments increase regulations on emissions that cause acid rain and ozone depletion and also establish a system of pollution permits.
1997	The Environmental Protection Agency issues updated air-quality standards.
1998	California institutes tougher emission control standards for new cars; other states follow with similar laws.
2003	Proposed Clear Skies Act is designed to amend the Clean Air Act with a cap-and-trade system.
2005	EPA's Clean Air Interstate Rule (CAIR) begins a cap-and-trade program to keep air pollution generated in one state from rendering other states noncompliant with air-quality standards.
2008	A federal appeals court rules that CAIR exceeds the EPA's regulatory authority but later orders temporary reinstatement.
2009	The EPA officially finds that the greenhouse gases methane, carbon monoxide, nitrous oxide, hydrofluorocarbons, perfluorocarbons, and sulfur hexafluoride constitute a threat to the public health and welfare.
2010	The American Lung Association reports that about 58 percent of Americans endure unhealthy air-pollution levels.
2010	The EPA replaces CAIR with the Transport Rule, requiring eastern states to decrease power plant emissions severely by 2014.

1977 Amendments

The 1977 amendments to the Clean Air Act were stimulated by growing public and government awareness of the necessity for further clarification of standards and the increased knowledge that came from a decade of scientific pollution-control research. Industrial areas that were in violation of air-quality standards, called nonattainment areas, were allowed to expand their factories or build new ones only if the new sources achieved the lowest possible emission rates. Additionally, other sources of pollution under the same ownership in the same state were required to comply with pollution-control provisions, and unavoidable emissions had to be offset by pollution reductions by other companies within the same region. These emissions-offset policies forced new industries within geographical regions to make formal requests that existing local companies reduce their pollution production; such situations often resulted in new companies paying the considerable expense of new emissions-control devices for existing companies.

Protection of air quality in regions that were already meeting federal standards sparked congressional debate, as many environmentalists asserted that existing air-quality standards gave some industries a theoretical license to pollute the air up to permitted levels. Rules for the "prevention of significant deterioration" within areas that already met clean air standards were set for sulfur oxides and particulates in 1977, and many individual experts and organizations lobbied for the inclusion of other pollutants, such as ozone, the chief component of smog.

A final major change mandated by the 1977 amendments was the strengthening of the authority of the EPA to enforce laws by allowing the agency to use civil lawsuits in addition to the criminal lawsuits that were previously required. Civil lawsuits have the advantage of not carrying the burden-of-proof requirements needed for criminal convictions; this legal dilemma previously motivated violating companies to take part in lengthy legal battles, as the legal costs were lower than the costs of purchasing and maintaining the necessary pollution-control devices. The EPA was also empowered to levy noncompliance penalties without having to file lawsuits, using the argument that violators have an unfair business advantage over competitors that are currently complying with established legislation. Additionally, several "right-to-know" laws went into effect beginning in

National Ambient Air Quality Standards for Criteria Pollutants

POLLUTANT	AVERAGING TIME	POLLUTANT LEVEL	EFFECTS ON HEALTH
Carbon monoxide: colorless, odorless, tasteless gas; it is primarily the result of incomplete combustion; in urban areas the major sources are motor vehicle emissions and wood burning.	1-hour 8-hour	35 ppm 9 ppm	The body is deprived of oxygen; central nervous system affected; decreased exercise capacity; headaches; individuals suffering from angina, other cardiovascular disease; those with pulmonary disease, anemic persons, pregnant women and their unborn children are especially susceptible.
Ozone: highly reactive gas, the main component of smog.	1-hour 8-hour	0.120 ppm 0.080 ppm	Impaired mechanical function of the lungs; may induce respiratory symptoms in individuals with asthma, emphysema, or reduced lung function; decreased athletic performance; headache; potentially reduced immune system capacity; irritant to mucous membranes of eyes and throat.
Particulate matter < 10 microns (PM10): tiny particles of solid or semisolid material found in the atmosphere.	24-hour Annual arithmetic mean	$150\,\mu g/m^3$ $50\,\mu g/m^3$	Reduced lung function; aggravation of respiratory ailments; long-term risk of increased cancer rates or development of respiratory problems.
Particulate matter < 2.5 microns (PM2.5): fine particles of solid or semisolid material found in the atmosphere.	24-hour Annual arithmetic mean	$65\,\mu g/m^3$ $15\,\mu g/m^3$	Same as PM10 above.
Lead: attached to inhalable particulate matter; primary source is motor vehicles that burn unleaded gasoline and re-entrainment of contaminated soil.	Calendar quarter	$1.5\,\mu g/m^3$	Impaired production of hemoglobin; intestinal cramps; peripheral nerve paralysis; anemia; severe fatigue.
Sulfur dioxide: colorless gas with a pungent odor.	3-hour 24-hour Annual arithmetic mean	0.5 ppm 0.14 ppm 0.03 ppm	Aggravation of respiratory tract and impairment of pulmonary functions; increased risk of asthma attacks.
Nitrogen dioxide: gas contributing to photochemical smog production and emitted from combustion sources.	Annual arithmetic mean	0.053 ppm	Increased respiratory problems; mild symptomatic effects in asthmatics; increased susceptibility to respiratory infections.

Notes: ppm equals parts per million and $\mu g/m^3$ equals micrograms per cubic meter.
Source: United States Environmental Protection Agency (EPA); URL http://www.epa.gov.

1985 that required manufacturing plant managers to make health and safety information regarding toxic materials available to current and prospective employees, business partners, and sponsors.

1990 Amendments

In 1990 the Clean Air Act was further amended to address inadequacies in previous amendments, with major changes including the establishment of standards and attainment deadlines for 190 toxic chemicals. The amendments were approved through the same kind of bipartisan effort as the one that resulted in the 1970 amendments, prompting President George H. W. Bush to state that the new legislation moved society much closer toward the clean air environment that "every American expects and deserves."

The 1990 amendments established a market-based measure for pollution taxes on toxic chemical emissions, thus enhancing the incentive for businesses to comply as quickly as possible. Emissions standards were tightened for automobiles, and mileage standards for new vehicles were raised; these provisions attacked the pollution problem at its center by prompting numerous significant steps toward improved fuel efficiency. Notable results of these measures included significant reductions in vehicular emissions of sulfur dioxide and nitrogen oxide (50 percent), carbon monoxide (70 percent), and other harmful substances (20 percent).

The 1990 amendments also established market-based incentives to reduce nitrogen and sulfur oxides because of their role in the growing controversy regarding acid deposition within rainwater. The EPA was empowered to create tradable permits that stipulated permissible emissions levels for nitrogen and sulfur oxides. The permits were issued to U.S. companies that had emission rates lower than those set by current requirements for the improvement of air quality. This landmark legislation enabled companies that implemented innovative and cost-effective means to reduce air pollution to sell their unused credits to other companies.

Other significant legislation passed within or assisted by the 1990 amendments included the beginning of the phasing out of numerous ozone-depleting chemicals and the implementation of strategies that would help sustain the environment. Discovery of a seasonal "ozone hole" over Antarctica in 1985 had sparked international concern regarding the state of

the earth's ozone layer and its ability to continue to shield the planet's surface from harmful ultraviolet radiation. Many businesses complained that the considerable additional expenses associated with implementing these new laws created unnecessary burdens for industry that in many cases outweighed the potential environmental benefits. In some cases, this economic pressure merely transferred environmental problems elsewhere, with many businesses choosing to operate outside the United States, in countries with less stringent environmental requirements.

Another important clause in the 1990 amendments required the EPA to regulate emissions coming from solid waste incinerators, including incinerators used for disposal of medical waste. Medical waste incinerators are among the largest sources of airborne dioxin and mercury, which are widely believed to contribute to serious health problems.

Subsequent Developments

President Bill Clinton continued tightening acceptable levels of smog and soot in the United States but did begin allowing flexible methods for reaching these improved goals over a ten-year period. This marked a significant change from the earlier administration of President Ronald Reagan, which proposed a relaxation of environmental standards to favor industrial and technological interests. Clinton is credited with associating the problem of controlling fossil-fuel emissions with the threat of global warming, an issue that would undergo considerable debate within the United Nations and elsewhere for years to come. A 1990 amendment requiring the use of gasoline containing 2 percent oxygen by weight in regions classified as being in severe or extreme nonattainment for the federal ozone standard was followed by several state-level requirements.

The clean air changes of 1990 led the California Air Resources Board (CARB) to introduce the country's most stringent vehicle emissions quality controls to date later that year. Under the state's ambitious program, 2 percent of all new cars sold in California in 1998 were to have pollution-control devices that released no environmentally harmful emissions at all, and the figure was required to rise to 10 percent by 2003. These monumental state laws also dictated that the hydrocarbon emissions of all new cars sold in California be at least 70 percent less than those sold in 1993 by the year 2003. Thirteen northeastern states later passed similar, but somewhat less rigorous, laws; only New York retained the 2 percent goal.

Given 1990's technology, the CARB standards were in effect a mandate for the automobile industry to develop battery-powered electric vehicles. Automakers failed to mass-produce cost-effective, high-performance, battery-powered electric vehicles soon enough to meet regulatory requirements, however. When California adjusted its requirements in response to this slow progress, the result was a lowering of pressure on the auto industry to meet regulatory demands through innovation. By the early years of the twenty-first century, zero-emission vehicles had yet to become an industry standard, but low-emission vehicles such as hybrids had become commonplace, bringing the industry closer to realizing those goals.

During President George W. Bush's administration, the Clear Skies Act of 2003 sought to amend the Clean Air Act with a cap-and-trade system. The controversial bill was never enacted, but measures from it were included in the EPA's 2005 Clean Air Interstate Rule (CAIR), a cap-and-trade program to keep air pollution generated in one state from rendering another state noncompliant with air-quality standards.

In July, 2008, a federal appeals court ruled that CAIR exceeded the EPA's regulatory authority, but five months later the court ordered a temporary reinstatement until the EPA could develop a satisfactory replacement rule. A proposed replacement, known as the Transport Rule, was issued in July, 2010. The Transport Rule is intended to improve air quality in the eastern United States through a decrease in power plant emissions in thirty-one states and the District of Columbia. It requires that, by 2014, power plants reduce their sulfur dioxide emissions by 71 percent and their nitrogen oxides emissions by 52 percent. Each state must meet firm emissions requirements by 2014, which leaves room for only limited trading of pollution credits. The EPA estimates that the rule, if implemented, could prevent 14,000 to 36,000 premature deaths per year, as well as hundreds of thousands of cases of upper respiratory illness.

In late 2009 the EPA issued findings that current and projected atmospheric concentrations of the greenhouse gases (GHGs) methane, carbon monoxide, nitrous oxide, hydrofluorocarbons, perfluorocarbons, and sulfur hexafluoride constitute a threat to the public health and welfare. While this EPA action did not impose regulatory requirements, it paved the way for the agency to finalize GHG emissions standards for new motor vehicles, which contribute to atmospheric GHG concentrations. The EPA also proposed GHG emissions thresholds that would define whether Clean Air Act permits for such emissions are required. These thresholds would target the nation's largest stationary sources, such as power plants, refineries, and cement production facilities, but would not affect small businesses and farms. This proposed rule became the focus of a host of legal challenges.

Indoor Air Quality

Indoor air pollution began to receive serious public attention in the United States in the wake of the 1970's energy crisis. Interest in conserving energy drove changes in the construction of new buildings, and the retrofitting of old ones, aimed at retaining desired indoor temperatures. Making structures more airtight meant that air contaminants were also retained indoors. By the late 1980's, enough cases had emerged of people experiencing discomfort or various debilitating health problems—chronic respiratory issues, sinus infections, sore throats, headaches, and more—as a result of time spent in particular buildings that the phenomenon had been dubbed Sick building syndrome (SBS). The U.S. Occupational Safety and Health Administration has estimated that 30 to 70 million American workers are affected by SBS, although the vast majority do not suffer serious health problems as a result of exposure.

With most Americans spending more than 90 percent of their lives working, learning, and spending leisure time indoors, indoor air quality has the potential to have profound impacts on the population's health. Despite this fact, no comprehensive federal legislation has addressed indoor air quality in the United States; rather, various federal and state regulatory standards address indoor air quality by focusing on specific pollutants, activities, and types of structures.

Common indoor air pollutants include radon (a natural breakdown product of uranium in soil or rock), tobacco smoke, asbestos, formaldehyde, biological contaminants (such as mold and mildew), combustion products (such as carbon monoxide), cleansers and other household products, and pesticides. A number of federal and state laws address asbestos, including the 1976 Toxic Substances Control Act (TSCA), which gives the EPA broad authority to control the production, distribution, and disposal of potentially hazardous chemicals. Under TSCA, federal standards have also been established for the amount of formaldehyde (a chemical present in many adhesives, resins, and solvents) allowable in composite wood-based products

Other legislation, such as the 1976 Consumer Product Safety Act, has granted federal and state authority over consumer products that are potentially dangerous to public health and the environment, with many products that generate indoor air pollution falling under that jurisdiction. For example, carbon monoxide and other hazardous combustion products can be emitted by stoves, and formaldehyde can outgas from plywood and textiles.

Developing countries have different problems related to indoor air pollution than do the United States and other developed nations. In comparison with developed nations, developing nations generally have fewer and less restrictive environmental regulations in place, and indoor air pollution in these nations is less likely to be caused by the airtightness of buildings than by the use of substances indoors that can be harmful. For example, wood, dung, and crop residues are primary sources of cooking and heating fuels in many developing nations, and these can generate unhealthful air pollutants when burned. The United Nations is involved in various efforts to address the problem of indoor air pollution in developing nations.

Air Quality

In July, 1997, the EPA issued updated air-quality standards following the most complete scientific review process in the history of the organization. Based on the findings of this review, which was conducted by hundreds of internationally recognized scientists, industry experts, and public health officials, major steps were taken toward the improvement of environmental and public health through the revision of ozone standards for the first time in twenty years. In addition, annual exposure standards for fine particulate matter were introduced. (Short-term standards for coarse and fine particulates had been in place for a decade. Short-term standards that applied specifically to fine particulates were not introduced until 2006.) The EPA's 1997 study concluded that many previously imposed standards were not resulting in

enough protection for the environment and public health. Data indicated that repeated exposure to pollutants at levels previously considered to be acceptable could cause permanent lung damage in children and in adults who regularly exercise and work outdoors in many urban environments.

The EPA regularly reviews national air-quality standards for the Clean Air Act's six priority air pollutants. Between 1990 and 2008 the Clean Air Act and its supporting legislation enabled national emissions reductions of 78 percent for lead, 14 percent for ozone, 68 percent for carbon monoxide, 35 percent for nitrogen dioxide, 59 percent for sulfur dioxide, and 31 percent for respirable particulates. According to one study, between 1980 and 2000 the reduction in particle pollution alone increased life expectancy in fifty-one cities in the United States by an average of five months. Thanks to control programs for chemical plants, dry cleaners, coke ovens, incinerators, and mobile sources, total emissions of toxic air pollutants decreased by approximately 40 percent between 1990 and 2005. Haze and acid precipitation were also on the decline.

Despite the progress that has been made, air pollution remains a critical environmental risk in the United States. In 2008 thirty-one areas in the United States failed to meet ambient air-quality standards for ozone, eighteen areas failed to meet standards for particulates, and two failed to meet the standard for lead. In 2010 the American Lung Association reported that approximately 58 percent of the nation's population was continuing to experience unhealthy air-pollution levels. According to the U.S. Centers for Disease Control and Prevention, chronic lower respiratory diseases were the fourth leading cause of death in the United States in 2007; the asthma death rate for children under nineteen years old increased by nearly 80 percent between 1980 and 2001.

On the international level, a 1987 United Nations conference held in Canada saw twenty-four nations agree to guidelines established to protect the ozone layer through the Montreal Protocol on Substances That Deplete the Ozone Layer. The Montreal Protocol, which by 2010 had been ratified by 196 countries and amended several times, provides a framework for the phaseout of certain ozone-depleting compounds and includes a mechanism through which developed nations can aid developing countries in making this transition. The United States has also accepted several of the protocols of the 1979 Geneva Convention on Long-Range Transboundary Air Pollution, an international agreement that addresses the impacts of air-pollution migration across political boundaries. These protocols include those concerning reduction strategies for emissions of nitrogen oxides, cadmium, lead, mercury, sulfur, volatile organic compounds, and ammonia.

Daniel G. Graetzer;
Updated by Karen N. Kähler

Further Reading

Bailey, Christopher J. *Congress and Air Pollution: Environmental Politics in the US.* Manchester University Press, 1998.

Ferrey, Steven. "Air Quality Regulation." In *Environmental Law: Examples and Explanations.* 5th ed. Aspen, 2010.

Godish, Thad. "Regulation and Public Policy." In *Air Quality.* 4th ed. Lewis, 2004.

Kessel, Anthony. *Air, the Environment, and Public Health.* Cambridge University Press, 2006.

Melnick, R. Shep. *Regulation and the Courts: The Case of the Clean Air Act.* Brookings Institution Press, 1983.

Rushefsky, Mark E. "Environmental Policy: Challenges and Opportunities." In *Public Policy in the United States: At the Dawn of the Twenty-first Century.* 4th ed. M. E. Sharpe, 2008.

U.S. Environmental Protection Agency. *The Plain English Guide to the Clean Air Act.* Office of Air Quality Planning and Standards, 2007.

■ Air Quality Index (AQI)

FIELDS OF STUDY: Mathematics, Measurement, Mapping, Logic; Statistics, Modeling, Projection; Pollution, Emissions, Toxic Waste, Hazardous Materials.

IDENTIFICATION: The U.S. Environmental Protection Agency's tool for indicating the health risks posed by ambient air quality in given areas at particular times

Graph of Environment Canada Air Quality Index data, including proper delineations for categories. By Breadborder (Created with Environment Canada AQI data)

With air pollution a growing problem the world over, the Air Quality Index and equivalent tools in other nations have become an indispensable part of the efforts of regional and federal governments to convey information about ambient air quality to the general public.

Nations around the world employ a number of variations on the Air Quality Index (AQI) developed by the U.S. Environmental Protection Agency (EPA), but the basic methodology used to assess air quality is the same. The concentrations of various air pollutants in a testing area are measured regularly, and, based on this information, the area is assigned a number. This number fits into a color-coded rating system in which different tiers correspond to the severity of the health threat the air quality poses; the higher the number, the more severe the threat.

Although a host of air pollutants have the potential to cause adverse health effects, only a handful of criteria contaminants are generally used in the assessment of basic air quality. Individual criteria differ from place to place, but the most common pollutants monitored are suspended particulate matter, airborne lead, ground-level ozone, nitrogen dioxide, sulfur dioxide, and carbon monoxide. These hazardous compounds are capable of causing severe respiratory irritation, heart and circulatory problems, and other negative health effects.

Monitoring sites are typically limited to cities and towns, where pollution levels and population densities are both high. Different levels of pollution may fall into different tiers based on the stringency of a particular agency's approach to measuring air quality. For example, Hong Kong's Air Pollution Index has come under heavy criticism for its relatively lax standards, as the air quality it rates as safe sometimes contains pollutants at levels several times higher than those considered acceptable by the World Health Organization.

Bernard Jacobson

■ Airborne particulates

FIELDS OF STUDY: Chemistry; Elements, Substances, Chemicals, Compounds; Pollution, Emissions, Toxic Waste, Hazardous Materials.

IDENTIFICATION: Tiny particles found in the air

Airborne particulate matter (PM) represents a complex mixture of organic and inorganic substances and varies in size, composition, and origin. Primary particles, are emitted directly from sources such as construction sites, unpaved roads, fields, smokestacks, and fires. Secondary particles are formed by reactions of gases, such as sulfur dioxide and nitrogen oxides, that are emitted from power plants, industrial plants, and automobiles, and make up most of the fine-particle pollution in the United States. Some airborne particulates, such as dust, dirt, soot, and smoke, are large enough to be visible to the naked eye, while others require electron microscopes for their detection. Inhalation of particulates can have serious adverse effects on respiratory and cardiovascular health.

Particulate pollution contains microscopic solids or liquid droplets that are small enough to travel deep into the lungs and cause serious health problems. Breathing such pollution can lead to respiratory symptoms such as coughing and difficult breathing; it can decrease lung function and aggravate existing asthma. Also associated with exposure to particle pollution are chronic obstructive pulmonary disease and emphysema, chronic bronchitis, irregular heartbeat, nonfatal heart attacks, and premature death in people with heart or lung disease.

The size of airborne particulates is directly linked to their potential for causing health problems. The US Environmental Protection Agency (EPA) has established air-quality standards concerning two sizes (or fractions) of particles: PM10 and PM2.5. PM10 particles (coarse particles) are those with a diameter of 10 micrometers or smaller (10 micrometers is equal to 0.004 inch, or one-seventh the width of a human hair); they include both coarse and fine particles. PM10 particles smaller than 10 micrometers can settle in the bronchi and lungs and cause health problems. PM2.5 particles (fine particles) are 2.5 micrometers in diameter or smaller. Particles in this fraction tend to penetrate further, reaching the gas exchange regions of the lung, and even smaller particles (0.1 micrometer or smaller) may pass through the lungs into the bloodstream and affect other organs, particularly the cardiovascular system. These particles can also adsorb harmful gases or other components (such as iron, carcinogens, or ozone) and release them within lung cells. Particles emitted from modern diesel engines are typically 0.1 micrometer or smaller. PM2.5 inhalation can lead to high plaque

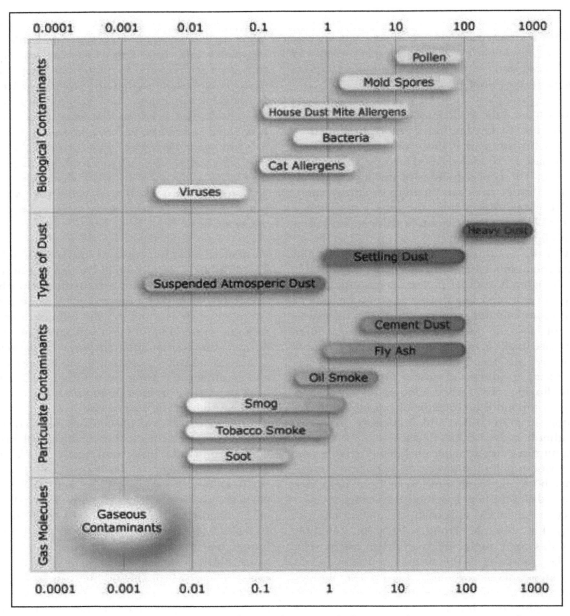

Airborne particles are commonly either biological contaminants, particulate contaminants, gaseous contaminants, or dust. This diagram shows the size distribution in micrometres (µm) of various types of airborne particles. By Jisaac9 (Own work)

deposits in the arteries, causing vascular inflammation and atherosclerosis (hardening of the arteries that reduces elasticity and can lead to heart attacks).

The federal Clean Air Act requires the EPA to review the latest scientific information every five years and promulgate the National Ambient Air Quality Standards for six pollutants, among them PM. US

air-quality standards for PM were first established in 1971 and were not significantly revised until 1987, when the EPA changed the indicator of the standards specifically to regulate PM10 levels. Ten years later, the agency set a separate standard for PM2.5 particles based on new research findings regarding their link to serious health problems. The 1997 standards also retained but slightly revised the PM10 standards, which were intended to regulate inhalable coarse particles ranging from 2.5 to 10 micrometers in diameter. The EPA revised the air-quality standards for airborne particle pollution in 2006, lowering the acceptable level of PM2.5 over a 24-hour period from 65 micrograms per cubic meter to 35 micrograms per cubic meter (1 cubic meter is roughly equivalent to 35 cubic feet). It retained the 24-hour PM10 standard of 150 micrograms per cubic meter. In 2012 the standard for acceptable levels of PM2.5 exposure averaged over the course of a year (annual mean) was set at 12 micrograms per cubic meter.

Daniel J. Connell

Further Reading

Hilgenkamp, Kathryn. "Air." In *Environmental Health: Ecological Perspectives.* Jones and Bartlett, 2006.

National Research Council. *Research Priorities for Airborne Particulate Matter, IV: Continuing Research Progress.* National Academies Press, 2004.

"Particulate Matter (PM) Pollution." *Environmental Protection Agency,* 21 Aug. 2017, www.epa.gov/pm-pollution. Accessed 28 Mar. 2018.

Peters, Annette, and C. Arden Pope III. "Cardiopulmonary Mortality and Air Pollution." *The Lancet* 360 (October 19, 2002): 1184-1185.

Rasmussen, Niels, and Henrik Knudsen. *Particulate Matter: Sources, Emission Rates, and Health Effects.* Nova Science, 2012. *eBook Collection (EBSCOhost).* Web. 14 Jan. 2015.

Vallero, Daniel A. *Fundamentals of Air Pollution.* Elsevier, 2014. *eBook Collection (EBSCOhost).* Web. 14 Jan. 2015.

■ Alar and carcinogen controversy

FIELDS OF STUDY: Chemistry; Biochemistry; Industries, Commercial Products; Agriculture, Farming, Animal Husbandry.

IDENTIFICATION: Brand name for the chemical daminozide, used as a plant growth regulator

The use of Alar to improve the quality and appearance of apples became controversial in the late 1980's, when a debate arose over the chemical's carcinogenic properties.

Alar is a growth-regulating chemical manufactured by Uniroyal Chemical Company. In the late 1960's,

apple farmers began using the product to improve the quality and appearance of their fruit. The use of Alar by apple growers to preserve crispness as the fruit was sent to market was a common practice for more than twenty years. In 1989, however, a controversy erupted regarding the potential harmful effects of the chemical, and Alar was accused—erroneously, according to many experts—of being the most potent carcinogen in the food supply.

The first questions about the chemical were raised in the 1970's by Dr. Bela Toth of the University of Nebraska, whose research appeared to indicate that Alar created tumors in mice but not in rats. Reports of Toth's discovery did not stress the fact that the rodents were fed massive amounts of the chemical, far exceeding the maximum tolerated dose used in cancer testing.

At the time, the U.S. Environmental Protection Agency (EPA) disregarded the study. In 1983, however, under attack by environmental and media groups critical of the environmental policies of Ronald Reagan's presidential administration, the EPA began its questioning of Alar. Steve Schatzow, a lawyer, was appointed to lead the Office of Pesticide Programs (OPP), and in conjunction with other organizations, including the Natural Resources Defense Council (NRDC) and the American Council on Science and Health (ACSH), the OPP began the fight against Alar, proclaiming it to be the most potent cancer-causing substance in the food industry.

The effect of OPP's announcement was dramatic. Consumers poured apple juice down drains, stores pulled apple products from their shelves, and farmers suffered losses estimated in the hundreds of millions of dollars. The anti-Alar campaign became more aggressive when such celebrities as *Sixty Minutes* newsman Ed Bradley, consumer activist Ralph Nader, and actor Meryl Streep—who set up a group called Mothers and Others for Pesticide Limits—expressed fears about the chemical.

Despite the anti-Alar fanfare, subsequent studies on the consumption of traces of the chemical, whether in apple juice or any other form of apples, proved to be negative. After 1990, no mainstream, peer-reviewed research demonstrated any linkage between the chemical or its breakdown product, UMDH, and cancer. For example, Dr. Jose R. P. Cabral, an investigator with the International Agency for Research on Cancer, declared that Alar is safe to use and that his group's experiments had not found tumors in rodents that had consumed reasonable quantities of the chemical. In the wake of such findings, the U.S. Food and Drug Administration issued a statement affirming that eating apples that have been treated with Alar poses no health threat.

Soraya Ghayourmanesh

Further Reading

Blay-Palmer, Alison. *Food Fears.* Ashgate, 2008.

Ohkawa, H., H. Miyagawa, and P. W. Lee, eds. *Pesticide Chemistry: Crop Protection, Public Health, Environmental Safety.* Wiley-VCH, 2007.

■ Alaska Highway

FIELDS OF STUDY: Places, Peoples, Societies; Continents, Regions, Areas, Islands; Ecology, Environment, Environmentalism.

CATEGORIES: Places; land and land use

IDENTIFICATION: Important transportation and tourist corridor through northwest Canada and Alaska

DATE: Completed in 1943

The presence of the Alaska Highway has caused environmental change in the regions through which it passes, in conjunction with the land-use development associated with transportation and tourism.

In the early 1940's, during World War II, fear that Japan would invade Alaska prompted the construction of the Alaska Highway for military use. Begun in 1942 and completed in 1943, the Alaska Highway was an all-weather gravel road that connected Dawson Creek in British Columbia, Canada, with Fairbanks, Alaska. The highway was initially a military road only and, as such, was designed for military transport; little attention was given to environmental considerations in deference to the war effort. The road had to be constructed for ease and speed of movement of military goods, and engineering efforts were aimed at meeting these needs. Grades, road cuts, and stream crossings were made quickly, without much consideration of the environmental impact of constructing a highway through some 2,400 kilometers (1,500 miles) of previously untraversed wilderness.

For a few years following World War II, civilian travel on the Alaska Highway, also known as the Alcan Highway, was limited and carefully controlled. With the removal of travel restrictions in 1947, however,

traffic increased, and environmental degradation inevitably followed. While early travelers had to attend to most of their needs themselves, the flow of traffic proved an incentive for the provision of services. Gas stations, restaurants, and lodging facilities all grew to meet the needs of the traveling public on the Alaska Highway. In turn, the presence of a well-maintained highway and available public facilities fostered additional growth, and the new facilities themselves created a need for waste removal, storage areas, and underground fuel tanks. Interest in and use of the highway—which passes through wilderness areas, historically important settings such as the Klondike, and active mining areas—have continued to grow.

Regular improvements have been made to the highway. It has been upgraded from a gravel to a paved surface, curves have been straightened, and grades have been improved. These changes themselves have imposed additional imprints on the adjacent environment. Successive efforts to widen and straighten the highway have increased the direct physical impact on the surrounding landscape.

Jerry E. Green

Further Reading

Brown, Tricia. *The World-Famous Alaska Highway: A Guide to the Alcan and Other Wilderness Roads of the North.* 2nd ed. Alaska Northwest Books, 2005.

Nelson, Daniel. *Northern Landscapes: The Struggle for Wilderness Alaska.* Resources for the Future, 2004.

See also: Conservation; Road systems and freeways; Trans-Alaska Pipeline.

■ Alaska National Interest Lands Conservation Act (ANILCA)

FIELDS OF STUDY: Government, Politics, International Relations; Laws, Acts, Resolutions; Parks, Monuments, Reserves; Ecology, Environment, Environmentalism.

THE LAW: U.S. law intended to resolve conflicts regarding landownership in Alaska among Native Alaskans and the federal and state governments

DATE: Enacted on December 2, 1980

The Alaska National Interest Lands Conservation Act more than tripled the amount of land protected as wilderness in the United States, but it did not lead to the resolution of all conflicts over Alaska land use.

The 1959 Alaska Statehood Act allowed the state government to choose 41.5 million hectares (102.5 million acres) of federal land from that part of the public domain not reserved for parks or other designated use. The land-selection process proceeded slowly, complicated by such issues as Native Alaskan claims, which were not clarified in the statehood bill. The discovery of oil fields in northern Alaska prompted

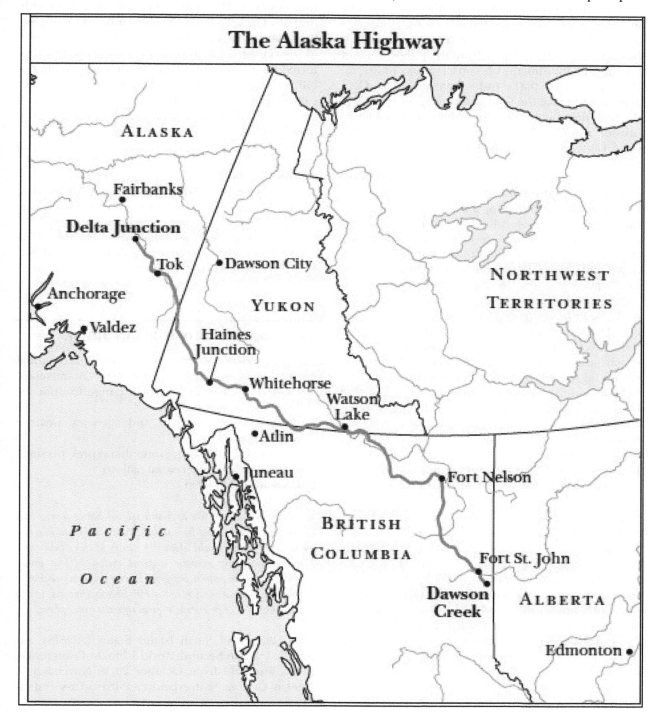

The Alaska Highway

passage of the 1971 Alaska Native Claims Settlement Act (ANCSA), which extinguished Native Alaskan land claims and allowed for construction of the Trans-Alaska Pipeline. To secure support for the ANCSA from conservation groups, the U.S. Congress included a provision in the bill that allowed the secretary of the interior to withdraw up to 32.4 million hectares (80 million acres) from the public domain for the establishment of conservation units, including national parks and wilderness areas. Congress would make the final determination regarding the final disposition of withdrawn lands. In order to provide a forum for cooperative planning on the issue, Congress created the Joint Federal-State Land Use Planning Commission.

An intense political battle ensued. Federal agencies, including the Forest Service and the National Park Service, competed for the authority to manage the withdrawn lands. Environmentalists favored agencies that would limit development, while Alaska state officials threw their support behind agencies that might prove willing to allow multiple use and the exploitation of natural resources for economic gain. After years of contentious debate, in 1979 the House of Representatives passed a bill establishing 51.4 million hectares (127 million acres) of conservation units, 26.3 million hectares (65 million acres) of which were designated wilderness areas. The Senate version of the bill significantly reduced the amount of land, and the legislation did not become law. The following year, the election of Ronald Reagan to the U.S. presidency and a Republican majority to the Senate convinced House members that they had no alternative but to accept the Senate version of the bill, which passed in 1980 and became known as the Alaska National Interest Lands Conservation Act (ANILCA).

ANILCA set aside 42.1 million hectares (104 million acres) of land as conservation units, with 23 million hectares (57 million acres) of wilderness. The National Park Service received 17.8 million hectares (44 million acres), the Fish and Wildlife Service 20.2 million hectares (50 million acres), and the Forest Service 1 million hectares (2.5 million acres). The Bureau of Land Management, the federal agency most amenable to development, received a patchwork of marginal lands that no other agency desired.

The act more than tripled the amount of land protected as wilderness in the United States, and its provisions placed 75 percent of national park land in Alaska. It did not solve the conflicts over Alaska land use, however. The state contested some land withdrawals. The act allowed for the construction of pipelines and roadways through conservation units. Moreover, ANILCA contained no measures that protected the habitats of migratory animals. Finally, the bill included provisions that allowed for the future exploitation of mineral resources, including oil, should both the Congress and the president deem it necessary.

Thomas Clarkin

Further Reading

Haycox, Stephen W. *Frigid Embrace: Politics, Economics, and Environment in Alaska.* Oregon State University Press, 2002.

Nelson, Daniel. *Northern Landscapes: The Struggle for Wilderness Alaska.* Resources for the Future, 2004.

Ross, Ken. *Pioneering Conservation in Alaska.* University Press of Colorado, 2006.

■ Alliance of Small Island States

FIELDS OF STUDY: Government, Politics, International Relations; Organizations, Agencies, Commissions, Centers; Climate and Climate Change; Continents, Regions, Areas, Islands.

CATEGORIES: Organizations and agencies; weather and climate

IDENTIFICATION: Lobbying group that represents small island and low-lying coastal nations

DATE: Founded in 1990

Members of the Alliance of Small Island States worry that global warming caused by human activity will lead to a rise in sea levels that could obliterate much of their land and cause increasingly extreme tropical cyclones. The group quickly developed into a powerful force for the promotion of international treaties such as the 1997 Kyoto Protocol, which limits emissions of greenhouse gases into the atmosphere.

The Alliance of Small Island States (AOSIS) was founded at the Second World Climate Conference, which was held from October 29 to November 7, 1990, in Geneva, Switzerland. AOSIS is an association

Millennium Island, part of Kiribati, a member of the Alliance of Small Island States, as seen from the International Space Station. The island, no part of which is more than 6 meters (20 feet) above the ocean, has been identified by the United Nations as being at significant risk from rises in sea level. (NASA)

of its member states' ambassadors to the United Nations; it does not have a charter, a budget, or its own secretariat. By 2010 AOSIS had thirty-nine member nations and four observers.

Because global warming is expected to raise seawater levels as glaciers melt at both of Earth's poles, the member nations of AOSIS fear future inundation by rising seas. Moreover, they fear that the rising salt water could contaminate their freshwater resources and erode their coasts, and that global warming could bleach their coral reefs and cause increasingly severe storms that could wreck their lands and their coastlines.

Most of the founding AOSIS member nations are small islands or coastal states in the Caribbean Sea, the Indian Ocean, and the Pacific Ocean. Given that their own emissions of greenhouse gases have generally been very low, owing to the small size and developing nature of their economies, the member states expressed unhappiness at having to carry the burden of global warming caused by others—namely, the developed and large developing nations. This led to AOSIS's consistent demand for money transfers from the countries emitting the majority of greenhouse gases to the AOSIS nations, to help them mitigate the expected effects of global warming on their endangered islands and coastlines.

From 1991 to 1994, under its first chair, Suriname-born activist Robert Van Lierop, who represented the Pacific Island nation of Vanuatu at the United Nations from 1981 to 1994, AOSIS worked proactively to shape global climate policy at the United Nations. AOSIS members were initial signatories to the United Nations Framework Convention on Climate Change (UNFCCC) in June, 1992. Next, AOSIS proposed and helped to draft the text of the 1997 Kyoto Protocol, which committed those nations that signed it to controlling, limiting, and reducing their greenhouse gas emissions.

AOSIS also works very closely with the Small Island Developing States group at the United Nations and has been active at each of the annual Conferences of the Parties of the UNFCCC. At the fifteenth Conference of the Parties in Copenhagen, Denmark, on December 10, 2009, AOSIS submitted an ambitious proposal to limit human-made global warming to absolutely no more than 1.5 degrees Celsius (2.7 degrees Fahrenheit) instead of the previous limit of 2 degrees Celsius (3.6 degrees Fahrenheit). However, in an atmosphere of increased skepticism about the science behind the models of human-caused global warming and a lingering global economic crisis, other nations did not take up this proposal. Some scientists argued that at that time, many of the problems of the small island and low-level coastal states had been caused by coastal mismanagement and population growth, and that these were a greater threat than future global warming.

R. C. Lutz

Further Reading

Ashe, John W., Robert Lierop, and Anilla Cherian. "The Role of the Alliance of Small Island States (AOSIS) in the Negotiation of the United Nations Framework Convention on Climate Change." *Natural Resources Forum* 23, no. 3 (1999): 209-220.

Barnett, Jon, and John Campbell. *Climate Change and Small Island States: Power, Knowledge, and the South Pacific.* Earthscan, 2010.

Kasa, Sjur, Anne Gullberg, and Gørild Heggelund. "The Group of 77 in the International Climate Negotiations: Recent Developments and Future

Directions." *International Environmental Agreements: Politics, Law, and Economics* 8, no. 2 (2008): 113-127.

Risse, Mathias. "The Right to Relocation: Disappearing Island Nations and Common Ownership of the Earth." *Ethics and International Affairs* 23, no. 3 (2009): 281-300.

See also: Climate change and oceans; Climate change skeptics; Climate models; Climatology; Coral reefs; Glacial melting; Global warming; Intergovernmental Panel on Climate Change; Kyoto Protocol; Maldive Islands; Pacific Islands; Sea-level changes; United Nations Framework Convention on Climate Change.

■ Alternative energy sources

FIELDS OF STUDY: Technology and Applied Science; Ecology, Environment, Environmentalism; Energy and Energy Resources; Renewable Resources.

IDENTIFICATION: Sources of energy other than the dominant fossil and mineral fuels

Energy sources that offer alternatives to the burning of fossil fuels such as coal and petroleum are urgently needed to address rising demand for energy in ways that will not contribute to air pollution and climate change. The ideal alternative energy source is renewable or inexhaustible and causes no lasting environmental damage.

Both the extraction and the burning of fossil fuels have caused severe and growing damage to the environment, contributing to such problems as air pollution, the release of greenhouse gases (which retain heat and contribute to climate change), and sulfuric acid in rainfall. Nuclear energy sources are very limited in supply and expensive, require extreme amounts of processing, and produce long-lasting radioactive waste. In the long term, energy release from nuclear fusion has been proposed as a limitless supply of power, but industrial-scale production of fusion power continues to pose large and uncertain obstacles and hazards.

Solar Power

The sun powers winds, ocean currents, rain, and all biomass growth on the earth's surface. Because the availability and extraction means for each of these secondary sources of solar power are diverse, each forms a different field of alternative energy technology. Where solar power is extracted and converted to energy directly, the capture can be by means of flat-plate receivers that collect at the incident intensity but can operate in diffuse light, or by means of concentrators that can achieve intensities of several hundred suns but work poorly in diffuse light.

In solar photovoltaic power (PV) technology, solar radiation is directly converted to useful power through PV cell arrays, which require semiconductor mass-production plants. PV cell technologies have evolved from using single-crystal silicon to using thinner polycrystalline silicon, gallium arsenide, thin-film amorphous silicon, cadmium telluride, and copper indium selenide. The needed materials are believed to be abundant enough to meet projected global growth. The process of purifying silicon requires large inputs of energy, however, and it generates toxic chemical waste. Regeneration of the energy required to manufacture a solar cell requires about three years of productive cell operation.

Solar cell technology continues to evolve and new materials for use in PV cells that are more efficient is an ongoing area of research. Broadband solar cell technologies have the potential to make cells sensitive to as much as 80 percent of the energy in the solar spectrum, up from about 60 percent. High-intensity solar cells could enable operation at several hundred times the intensity of sunlight, reducing the cell area required when used with concentrator mirrors and enabling high thermal efficiency.

Direct solar conversion is another option. Laboratory tests have shown 39 percent conversion from broadband sunlight to infrared laser beams using neodymium-chromium fiber lasers. Direct conversion of broadband sunlight to alternating-current electricity or beamed power through the use of optical antennae is projected to achieve 80 to 90 percent conversion. Such technologies offer hope for broadband solar power to be converted to narrowband power in space and then beamed to Earth by satellites.

Another way of harnessing solar power is through solar thermal technology. Solar concentrators are used with focal-point towers to achieve temperatures of thousands of kelvins and high thermal efficiency, limited by containment materials. The resulting

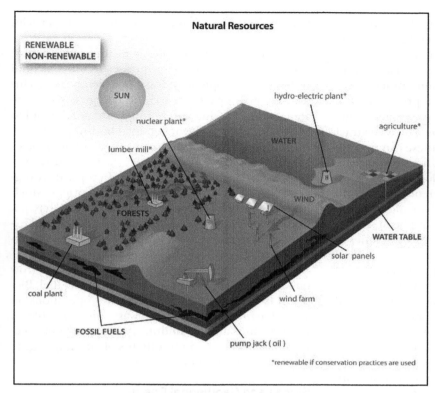

Natural Resources

RENEWABLE
NON-RENEWABLE

SUN

hydro-electric plant*

nuclear plant*

agriculture*

lumber mill*

WATER

coal plant

FORESTS

WIND

WATER TABLE

solar panels

FOSSIL FUELS

wind farm

pump jack (oil)

*renewable if conservation practices are used

The earth has many natural resources, some are renewable and others are not. Conservation practices will ensure that resources do not become depleted. © EBSCO

high-temperature electrolysis of water vapor generates hydrogen and oxygen in an efficient manner, and this technology has demonstrated direct solar decomposition of carbon dioxide (CO_2) to carbon monoxide (CO) and oxygen.

Wind Power

Winds are driven by temperature and pressure gradients, ultimately caused by solar heating. Wind energy is typically extracted through the operation of turbines. Power extraction is proportional to the cube of wind speed, but wind-generated forces are proportional to the square of wind speed. Wind turbines thus can operate safely only within a limited range of wind speed, and most of the power generation occurs during periods of moderately strong winds. Turbine efficiency is strongly dependent on turbine size and is limited by material strength. The largest wind turbines have reached eight megawatts in capacity. Denmark, the Netherlands, and India have established large wind turbine farms on flat coastal land,

and Germany and the United Kingdom have opted for large off-shore wind farms. In the United States, wind farms are found in the Dakotas, Minnesota, and California, as well as on Colorado and New Mexico mountain slopes and off the coasts of Texas and Massachusetts.

Because of wind fluctuations and the cubic power relation, wind power is highly unsteady, and means must be established for storing and diverting the power generated before it is connected to a power grid. In addition, offshore and coastal wind farms must plan for severe storms. Smaller wind turbines are sometimes used for power generation on farms and even for some private homes in open areas, but these tend to be inefficient and have high installation costs per unit power. They are mainly useful for pumping irrigation water or for charging small electrical devices.

Environmentalists have raised some concerns about large wind turbines. The machinery on wind farms causes objectionable noise levels, and many assert that the wind turbine towers themselves constitute a form of visual pollution. Disturbances to wildlife, particularly deaths and injuries among bird populations, are another area of concern. In addition, the construction of wind farms often requires the building of roads through previously pristine areas to enable transportation of the turbines' large components.

Hydroelectric Power and Tidal Power

Large dams provide height differences that enable the extraction of power from flowing water using turbines. Hydroelectric power generated by dams forms a substantial percentage of the power resources in several nations with rivers and mountains. However, the building of large dams raises numerous technical, social, and public policy issues, as damming rivers may displace human inhabitants from fertile lands and may result in the flooding of pristine eco-systems, sometimes the habitats of endangered species. Increased incidence of earthquakes has also been associated with the existence of very large dams.

In some of the world's remote communities, micro hydroelectric (or micro hydel) plants provide power, generating electricity in the 1–30 megawatt range. Very small-scale systems, known as pico hydel, extract a few kilowatts from small streams; these can provide viable energy sources for individual homes and small villages, but the extraction technology has to be refined to bring down the cost per unit of power.

Although tidal power is abundant along coastlines, the harnessing of that power has been slow to gain acceptance, in part because of the difficulties of building plants that can survive ocean storms. Tidal power is extracted in two principal ways. In one method, semipermeable barrages are built across estuaries with high tidal ranges, and the water collected in the barrages is emptied through turbines to generate power. In the second, offshore tidal streams and currents are harnessed through the use of underwater equivalents of wind turbines.

Tidal power plants typically use pistons that are driven up and down by alternating water levels or the action of waves on turbines. A rule of thumb is that a tidal range of 7 meters (23 feet) is required to produce enough hydraulic head for economical operation. One drawback is that the 12.5-hour cycle of tidal operation is out of synchronization with daily peak electricity demand times, and hence some local means of storing the power generated is desirable. In many cases, impellers or pistons are used to pump water to high levels for use when power demand is higher.

China, Russia, France, South Korea, Canada, and Northern Ireland all have operational tidal power stations. The first US tidal power station became operational in 2012 in Cobscook Bay, near Eastport, Maine.

Biomass Power

Biomass, which consists of any material that is derived from plant life, is composed primarily of hydrocarbons and water, so it offers several ways of usage in power generation. Combustion of biomass is considered to be carbon-neutral in regard to greenhouse gas emissions, but it may generate smoke particles and other pollution.

One large use of biomass is in the conversion of corn, sugarcane, and other grasses to ethyl alcohol (ethanol) to supplement fossil petroleum fuels. This use is controversial because the energy costs associated with producing and refining ethanol are said to be greater than the savings gained by using such fuel. It is argued that subsidies and other public policies and rising energy prices entice farmers to devote land to the production of ethanol crops, thus triggering shortages and increases in food prices, which hurt the poorest people the most. Brazil has advanced profitable and sustainable use of ethanol extracted from sugarcane to replace a substantial portion of the nation's transportation fossil-fuel use.

Jatropha plants, as well as certain algae that grow on water surfaces, offer sources of biodiesel fuel. Biodiesel from jatropha is used to power operations on several segments of India's railways, and vegetable oil from peanuts and groundnuts, and even from coconuts, has been used in test flights of aircraft ranging from strategic bombers to jetliners.

Biogas and Geothermal Energy

Hydrocarbon gases from decaying vegetation form large underground deposits that have been exploited as sources of energy for many years. Technology similar to that used in extracting energy from these natural deposits, which are not considered a renewable energy source, can be used to tap the smaller but widely distributed emissions of methane-rich waste gases from compost pits and landfills. Creating the necessary infrastructure to capture these gases over large areas poses a difficult engineering challenge, however. In addition, care must be taken to avoid the release of methane from these deposits into the atmosphere, as methane is considered to be twenty times as harmful as carbon dioxide as a greenhouse gas.

Geothermal energy comes from heat released by radioactive decay inside the earth's core, perhaps augmented by gravitational pressure. Where such heat is released gradually through vents in the earth's surface, rather than in volcanic eruptions, it forms an abundant and steady, reliable, long-term source of thermal power. Hot springs and geothermal steam generation are used on a large scale in Iceland, and geothermal power is used in some American communities and military bases.

Narayanan M. Komerath and Padma P. Komerath

Further Reading

Charlier, R. H., and C. W. Finkl. *Ocean Energy: Tide and Tidal Power*. Springer, 2009.

Edwards, Brian K. *The Economics of Hydroelectric Power*. Edward Elgar, 2003.

Klass, Donald L. *Biomass for Renewable Energy, Fuels, and Chemicals*. Academic Press, 1998.

"Largest WTG Yet Makes Its Debut." *Modern Power Systems* 34.3 (2014): 39–40. *Energy & Power Source*. Web. 15 Jan. 2015.

Pollan, Michael. *The Omnivore's Dilemma: A Natural History of Four Meals*. Penguin Press, 2007.

"Tidal Power." *Chemical Business* 28.10 (2014): 53. *MasterFILE Premier*. Web. 15 Jan. 2015.

Traynor, Ann J., and Reed J. Jensen. "Direct Solar Reduction of CO_2 to Fuel: First Prototype Results." *Industrial and Engineering Chemistry Research* 41, no. 8 (2002): 1935-1939.

Vaitheeswaran, Vijay. *Power to the People: How the Coming Energy Revolution Will Transform an Industry, Change Our Lives, and Maybe Even Save the Planet*. Farrar, Straus and Giroux, 2003.

Walker, John F., and Nicholas Jenkins. *Wind Energy Technology*. John Wiley & Sons, 1997.

Wenisch, A., R. Kromp, and D. Reinberger. *Science or Fiction: Is There a Future for Nuclear?* Austrian Ecology Institute, 2007.

■ Alternative fuels

FIELDS OF STUDY: Biohemical Engineering; Biochemistry; Chemical Engineering; Chemistry;

IDENTIFICATION: Materials or substances that can be safely substituted for commonly used fossil fuels

The development of alternatives to fossil fuels (gasoline, diesel, natural gas, and coal) has been spurred by growing awareness of the environmental damage associated with the burning of fossil fuels, as well as by the knowledge that at some time in the future Earth's supply of fossil fuels will be exhausted.

With the exception of nuclear-powered seagoing vessels, most vehicles are powered by internal combustion engines that use either gasoline or diesel fuel.

Gasoline and diesel release significant amounts of greenhouse gases into the atmosphere when burned; these gases include water vapor, carbon dioxide, ozone, nitrous oxide, and methane. These gases absorb and emit radiation in the infrared range; thus they increase the earth's temperature. In addition to the fact that the internal combustion engine burns an environment-polluting fossil fuel, it also is an inefficient method for transferring the energy stored in the fuel into propulsion. Most of the stored energy is lost in heat, which escapes through the exhaust pipe. In addition, the pistons within the engine accelerate up, stop, accelerate down, and stop with each revolution. This rapid cycle of acceleration and deceleration wastes energy. Many of the alternative fuels available are used to power internal combustion engines and thus have the same limitations as fossil fuels in this regard. Using an alternative fuel such as stored electricity does not have these limitations because it produces an insignificant amount heat in propelling an electric motor, which rotates continuously (no starting and stopping with each cycle).

Comparisons of the costs and levels of pollutant production of nonfossil fuel sources must take into account the costs associated with production of the fuels. An example is the use of corn for the production of ethanol. Raising the crop requires energy for production, such as fuel for tractors, harvesters and other powered equipment. The corn must then be fermented (yeast converts the sugar in the corn into ethanol), and the fermented product must be distilled (boiled to release the alcohol), which requires fuel to heat the still. The process increases the cost of ethanol and also produces pollution. The electricity that charges an electric vehicle may have been produced by a fossil-fuel source such as a diesel generator. Another problem with alternative fuels lies in the difficulty consumers may have in replenishing their supplies. Facilities distributing gasoline and diesel are prevalent throughout most developed nations; in contrast, sources of alternative fuels such as hydrogen and ammonia are not readily available. The ideal alternative fuel is one that is nonpolluting, cheap to produce, and easy to replenish.

Biofuels

Biofuels are derived from plant sources such as corn, sugarcane, and sugar beets; in some cases, they are blended with a fossil fuel, usually gasoline. Alcohol,

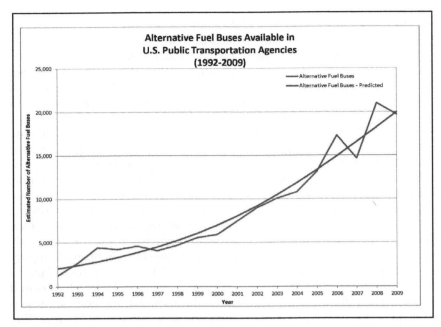

Predicted and Actual Alternative Fuel Bus Graph (APTA): 1992-2009. By Nesse069 (Own work).

methanol, butanol, biodiesel, biogas, and wood gas are all examples of biofuels.

Alcohol was initially used as a fuel in the Ford Model T automobile, which was first produced in 1908. The carburetor (a device that mixes fuel with air prior to entry into the engine) of the Model T could be adjusted to burn gasoline, ethanol, or a mixture. Many modern-day vehicles can run on a mixture of 10–15 percent ethanol and gasoline (E10, or gasohol, is 10 percent alcohol). The fuel known as E85 is a mixture of 85 percent ethanol and 15 percent gasoline; this fuel can be used only in flexible-fuel vehicles (FFVs). FFVs are designed to run on gasoline, E85, or any other gasoline-ethanol mixture. A disadvantage of ethanol is that it has approximately 34 percent less energy per volume than gasoline. Because ethanol has a high octane rating, ethanol-only engines may have relatively high compression ratios, which increases efficiency. In developed nations such as the United States, ethanol blends are available in many areas. Critics of ethanol as an alternative fuel note that it requires a large amount of agricultural land, which is diverted from producing crops used for food and the use of crops such as corn for ethanol production drives up food prices.

Methanol can be used as an alternative fuel, but automakers have not yet produced any vehicles that can run on it. Butanol and certain other compounds that can be produced from wood are more similar to gasoline than ethanol and can be used in some engines designed for use with gasoline without modification.

Biodiesel can be manufactured from vegetable oils and animal fats, including recycled restaurant grease. It is slightly more expensive than diesel, although research into more efficient conversion methods is reducing the cost of production. Biodiesel from vegetable oils and animal fats is produced by cleaving the long-chain fatty acids from the component triglycerides that make up the oils and fats. This produces large quantities of glycerol, however, which is difficult to separate from the fatty acid product and has no value. Complete removal of the glycerol from the biodiesel product is essential, otherwise any engine burning glycerol-contaminated biodiesel would be severely damaged. However, the pure biodiesel is a safe, biodegradable fuel that produces fewer pollutants than petroleum-based diesel and is carbon-neutral. Diesel engines are more efficient than gasoline engines (44 percent versus 25–30 percent efficiency); thus they have better fuel economy than gasoline engines. Some diesel engines can run on 100 percent biodiesel with only minor modifications. Biodiesel can be combined with regular diesel in various concentrations (for example, B2 is 2 percent biodiesel, B5 is 5 percent biodiesel, and B20 is 20 percent biodiesel).

Biogas is produced by the biological breakdown of organic materials such as rotting vegetables, plant wastes, and manure, and the energy produced varies depending on the source. Biogas can replace compressed natural gas for fueling internal combustion engines. Wood gas is another biofuel that can power an internal combustion engine. It is produced by the incomplete burning of sawdust, wood chips, coal, charcoal, or rubber. Depending on the source, the gas produced varies in energy content and contaminants. Contaminants in wood gas can foul an engine.

Electric Vehicles

At the beginning of the twentieth century, automobiles powered by steam, gasoline, and electricity were available. Electric vehicles were popular into the early 1920s, but then the automotive industry became dominated by gasoline-powered vehicles. The decline in electric-powered vehicles occurred for several reasons: road improvement allowed travel over longer distances, and the range of electric vehicles was limited; fossil fuels became cheap and plentiful; the electric starter replaced the hand crank on gasoline engines, which rendered starting such engines both easier and safer; and mass production of automobiles by Henry Ford's company made gasoline-powered vehicles much less expensive than electric-powered vehicles ($650 versus $1,750 average price at that time). By the end of the twentieth century, a growing emphasis on environmentally friendly energy sources encouraged the reemergence of electric vehicles and the development of hybrid vehicles powered by both gasoline (or diesel) and electricity.

A hybrid vehicle contains an electric motor that can both propel the vehicle and recharge the battery. Hybrid vehicles have achieved greater popularity than electric-only vehicles, as electric-only vehicles continue to have some of the same basic problems as earlier electric cars: limited range and higher cost than gasoline-powered or hybrid vehicles. Public recharging facilities for electric vehicles are not as common as gasoline stations, and recharging takes more time than a 'fill-up' at a gasoline station. Most electric cars owners are recharge their car overnight with a plug-in adapter, and modern 'rapid charge' outlets can fully recharge an electric vehicle in just 20 minutes, about the time it takes to enjoy a cup of coffee. The latest electric and hybrid vehicles use lithium-ion batteries rather than the lead-acid batteries used by earlier versions (and still used in gasoline and diesel vehicles). Lithium-ion batteries are much lighter than lead-acid batteries and can be molded into a variety of shapes to fit available areas. One criticism of electric vehicles, including hybrids, is that many are small and lightweight and thus less safe for passengers in collisions, than are larger gasoline-powered vehicles.

Other Fuels Derived from Nonfossil Sources

Ammonia has been evaluated for use as an alternative fuel. It can run in either a spark-ignited engine (that is, a gasoline engine) or a diesel engine in which the fuel-air mixture ignites upon compression in the cylinder. Modern gasoline and diesel engines can be readily converted to run on ammonia. Although ammonia is a toxic substance, it is considered no more dangerous than gasoline or liquefied petroleum gas (LPG). Ammonia can be produced by electrical energy and has half the density of gasoline or diesel; thus it can be placed in a vehicle fuel tank in sufficient quantities to allow the vehicle to travel reasonable distances. A disadvantage of ammonia is that it typically produces harmful nitrogen oxide emissions during combustion, in addition to nitrogen and water. Only under extremely well-regulated conditions that exclude excess oxygen in the combustion process, would only nitrogen gas and water vapor be produced. The technical requirements for such regulation, as well as for capture and sequestration of nitrogen oxides produced in combustion, mitigate against the use of ammonia as a combustion fuel.

Compressed-air engines are piston engines that use compressed air as fuel. Air-engine-powered vehicles have been produced that have a range comparable to gasoline-powered vehicles. Compressed air is much less expensive than fossil fuels. Ambient heat (normal heat in the environment) naturally warms and expands the cold compressed air upon the air's release from the storage tank, increasing its efficiency. The only exhaust is cold air, which can be used to cool the interior of the vehicle. An inherent problem with the use of fuels such as compressed or liquefied air or nitrogen gas is that heat exchange quickly lowers the temperature of the engine material to the point that it is ineffective at heating and expanding the fuel. In internal combustion engines, heat is constantly produced by the combustion of the fuel. This does not occur in 'decompression engines'.

Hydrogen vehicles can be powered by the combustion of hydrogen in the engine much as the typical gasoline engine operates. Fuel cell conversion is another method of using hydrogen by using the hydrogen to produce electricity. The most efficient use of hydrogen to power motor vehicles involves the use of fuel cells and electric motors. Hydrogen reacts with oxygen inside the fuel cells, which produces electricity to power the motors. With either method no harmful emissions are produced, as the electricity-generating reaction between hydrogen and oxygen produces only water. Hydrogen is much more expensive to produce than fossil fuels, and it contains significantly less energy on a per-volume basis, meaning that the vehicle's range is reduced. Experimental fuel cell vehicles have been produced, but such vehicles remain far too expensive for the average consumer.

Liquid nitrogen (LN_2) contains stored energy. Energy is used to liquefy air, then LN_2 is produced by evaporation. When LN_2 warms, nitrogen gas is produced; this gas can power a piston or turbine engine. Nitrogen-powered vehicles have been produced that have ranges comparable to gasoline-powered vehicles; these vehicles can be refueled in a matter of minutes. Nitrogen is an inert gas and makes up about 80 percent of air. It is virtually nonpolluting. Furthermore, it produces more energy than does compressed air. However, as mentioned above, heat exchange between liquid nitrogen (temperature = -77°C) and the engine components demands a secondary source of heat to maintain operation.

Oxyhydrogen is a mixture of hydrogen and oxygen gases, usually in a 2:1 ratio, the same proportion as water. Oxyhydrogen can fuel internal combustion engines, and, as in hydrogen-fueled engines, no harmful emissions are produced. The gas mixture is extremely dangerous, however, and can explode if any opportunity for ignition exists.

Steam was a common method of propulsion for vehicles during the early twentieth century, but, like electricity, it fell into disfavor with the advent of the electric starter, cheap gasoline, and mass production of Ford automobiles. A disadvantage of steam-powered vehicles is the time required to produce the steam. A steam engine is an external combustion engine—that is, the power is produced outside rather than inside the engine. Steam engines are less energy-efficient than gasoline engines. Fuel for steam engines can be derived from fossil fuels or from non-fossil fuel sources. William Lear attempted, unsuccessfully, to bring steam-powered engines back into the mainstream in the last quarter of the twentieth century, by producing a small, but powerful, closed-circuit steam engine. However, his design could not compete with internal combustion 'muscle car' engines that were increasingly popular at that time, and

his experiment ultimately failed to perform reliably in application.

Alternative Fossil Fuels

Some fossil fuels are less polluting than gasoline or diesel, and some are in plentiful supply. Natural gas vehicles use compressed natural gas (CNG) or, less commonly, liquefied natural gas (LNG). Internal combustion engines can be readily converted to burn natural gas. Natural gas is 60–90 percent less polluting than gasoline or diesel and produces 30–40 percent less greenhouse gases. Furthermore, it is less expensive than gasoline. Limitations of natural gas vehicles include a lack of available fueling stations and limited space for fuel, given that natural gas must be stored in cylinders, which are commonly located in the vehicle's trunk.

Liquefied petroleum gas is suitable for fueling internal combustion engines. Like natural gas, LPG is less polluting than gasoline, with 20 percent less carbon dioxide emissions; it is also less expensive. LPG is added to a vehicle's fuel tank through the use of a specialized filling apparatus; a limitation to LPG is the lack of fueling stations.

Robin L. Wulffson

Further Reading

DeGunther, Rik. *Alternative Energy for Dummies.* John Wiley & Sons, 2009.

Gibilisco, Stan. *Alternative Energy Demystified.* McGraw-Hill, 2007.

Hordeski, Michael F. *Alternative Fuels: The Future of Hydrogen.* 2nd ed. Fairmont Press, 2008.

Lee, Sunggyu, James G. Speight, and Sudarshan K. Loyalka. *Handbook of Alternative Fuel Technologies.* CRC Press, 2007.

Nersesian, Roy L. *Energy for the Twenty-first Century: A Comprehensive Guide to Conventional and Alternative Sources.* M. E. Sharpe, 2007.

■ Alternatively fueled vehicles

FIELDS OF STUDY: Technology and Applied Science; Industries, Commercial Products; Inventions; Energy and Energy Resources; Ecology, Environment, Environmentalism.

IDENTIFICATION: Vehicles fueled, wholly or partially, by energy derived from sources other than petroleum

The development of vehicles that operate efficiently using little or no petroleum-based fuel is an important part of efforts to address the problems of declining petroleum resources and the pollution caused by emissions from petroleum-based fuels.

Almost all of the fuel used for transportation in the United States is derived from petroleum. In California, a huge consumer of fuel to run its millions of vehicles, a mere one-fourth of 1 percent of those vehicles used alternative fuel sources in 2010. As the world's oil fields become depleted and petroleum reserves shrink, and as awareness grows regarding the harm to the environment caused by the burning of fossil fuels, the pressure to develop alternative fuels and vehicles that can operate using them has become intense. Since the late twentieth century, significant progress has been made in this area: Between 1970 and 2010, advances in automotive technologies decreased toxic vehicle emissions by an estimated 90 percent. These advances included the development of vehicles powered by non-petroleum-based fuels.

Auto manufacturers long resisted producing vehicles that would not be dependent on petroleum-based energy sources; for many years, they rejected alternative technologies in favor of the entrenched gasoline-burning internal combustion engine. Significant gasoline shortages in 1973 and 1979, however, clearly demonstrated the need for mass production of vehicles that could be powered by renewable resources. Whereas automobile companies and the petroleum industry had previously discouraged technologies related to the development of practical electric vehicles, many such corporations came to recognize the need to explore and encourage the production of alternative fuel sources.

Hybrid and Electric Vehicles

By the late twentieth century, automobile manufacturers, first in Japan but later in the United States and Europe, turned their attention to producing reasonably priced, fuel-efficient, nonpolluting vehicles. The most popular of such vehicles are hybrid vehicles; by 2010, nearly twenty versions of such vehicles were available commercially.

Hybrids such as Toyota's Prius and Honda's Insight are powered by gasoline-fueled internal combustion engines in combination with electric motors. These motors, which receive their electricity from batteries, provide power for the automobiles, but when they run down, small internal combustion engines take over. The batteries in hybrid vehicles are also recharged by capturing electrical energy when the brakes are applied. The ranges of such vehicles—that is, the distances that they can be driven between refuelings—are comparable to those of conventional vehicles.

Plug-in electric vehicles have a much more limited range than do hybrids; most can be driven only about 160 kilometers (100 miles) before they require recharging. Such vehicles are useful for service within limited areas, where they can be driven for short periods and recharged when not in use. Recharging a plug-in electric vehicle's batteries fully can take four to eight hours at the normal charge stations, or just twenty minutes at a 'rapid charge' station.

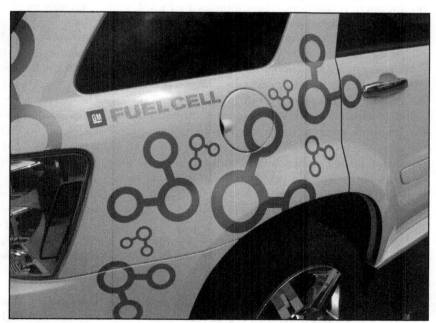

An environmentally friendly hydrogen station is located in the Del Mar area of Camp Pendleton, Calif. The station is compliant with a presidential directive mandating alternative-fueled vehicles. *By English: Pfc. Damien Gutierrez.*

Anticipated improvements in electric vehicle technology include enhancement of battery life to extend the vehicles' range and enhanced 'brake recharge' methods.

Other Fuels for Internal Combustion Engines

The conventional internal combustion engines found in most vehicles can often be run on nonpetroleum fuels or on mixtures of petroleum-based and other fuels. One frequently used alternative fuel is ethanol, an alcohol derived from plants that can be mixed with conventional gasoline. Such mixtures usually consist of 5 percent ethanol and 95 percent conventional gasoline, however, so the gasoline savings are negligible.

Another nonpetroleum fuel is hydrogen, which can be used to fuel slightly modified existing vehicles. As of 2010, more than one hundred buses fueled by hydrogen were operating in the United States, Canada, Mexico, Brazil, Japan, Egypt, Iceland, and India. Hydrogen has the advantage of producing water as its sole emission, so it does not contribute to air pollution. The major problem with using hydrogen is that it is not readily available to consumers. Proponents of hydrogen as a motor vehicle fuel assert that successful solution of the problem of distribution might revolutionize how vehicles are fueled.

Although hydrogen is the most plentiful element in the universe, it is not available merely for the taking. Because it bonds readily with other elements, such as oxygen, it is a carrier of energy rather than a source of energy like petroleum or coal. To power a vehicle, hydrogen must pass through onboard fuel cells in which a chemical reaction combines hydrogen and oxygen to produce water, with the transfer of electrical charge as electricity used to power the vehicle. When hydrogen is used in its gaseous state, leakage is a problem. Hydrogen can be liquefied and can also exist in powder form. Its most efficient use in fueling vehicles is usually in its gaseous or liquefied form.

Liquefied natural gas, which is less expensive to produce than gasoline, is used to fuel some fleets of taxicabs and other commercial vehicles. Liquefied petroleum gas, or propane, is also used to provide the power for many commercial fleets. It is less expensive and less polluting than regular gasoline.

R. Baird Shuman

Further Reading

Chan, C. C., and K. T. Chau. *Modern Electric Vehicle Technology.* Oxford University Press, 2001.

Ehsani, Mehrdad, et al. *Modern Electric, Hybrid Electric, and Fuel Cell Vehicles: Fundamentals, Theory, and Design.* CRC Press, 2005.

Erjavec, Jack, and Jeff Arias. *Hybrid, Electric, and Fuel-Cell Vehicles.* Thomson Delmar Learning, 2007.

Halderman, James D., and Tony Martin. *Hybrid and Alternative Fuel Vehicles.* Pearson/Prentice Hall, 2009.

Hanselman, Duane C. *Brushless Permanent-Magnet Motor Design.* McGraw-Hill, 1994.

King, Nicole Bezic, ed. *Renewable Energy Resources.* Smart Apple Media, 2004.

Lee, Sunggyu, James G. Speight, and Sudarshan K. Loyalka. *Handbook of Alternative Fuel Technologies.* CRC Press, 2007.

■ Amazon River basin

FIELDS OF STUDY: Places, Peoples, Societies; Agriculture, Farming, Animal Husbandry; Continents, Regions, Areas, Islands; Biology, Life Sciences, Ecosystems; Animals, Zoology, Marine Biology; Ecology, Environment, Environmentalism; Forests, Forestry.

IDENTIFICATION: River basin in South America bounded by the Guiana Highlands to the north and the Brazilian Highlands to the south

The Amazon River basin contains the world's largest rain forest, in which one-tenth of the known species in the world are found. Because of the unique biodiversity and geography of the region, it has been the subject of mass efforts by international conservation groups and an ongoing topic in discussions regarding global environmental protection and sustainability. Environmentalists and human rights advocates argue that the destruction of habitat in the basin will result in losses not only in biodiversity but also in human lives, as many indigenous peoples still live in the forest and rigidly continue their ways of life, refusing to integrate into modern society.

The Amazon River basin is best known for two characteristics: its high biodiversity and its enormous vegetative productivity. These characteristics give the basin a special significance to the biological world. The rain forest itself produces an estimated 20

Habitats and Selected Vertebrates of South America

The Amazon River basin is known for its high biodiversity and its enormous vegetative productivity. (©Paura/Dreamstime.com)

percent of Earth's atmospheric oxygen. The Amazon River, which is some 6,400 kilometers (4,000 miles) long, has the largest drainage basin in the world, accounting for nearly one-fifth of total global river flow. Further, this basin harbors the largest concentration of animal and plant species on the planet. In addition to the self-evident reasons to protect the non-human species of the basin from extinction, the basin holds great economic potential for the discovery of important medicines and plant-based products.

Many people live in the Amazon basin, including farmers and loggers with South American national ties and groups of indigenous peoples. Most of the area's original indigenous population was wiped out by disease and conflict during and after the European invasion; from an estimated pre-Columbian population of several millions, the numbers have been reduced to roughly two hundred thousand. Many of these natives have cultures and languages that are still alive and vibrant, but they remain under threat as their land and resources are coveted by outsiders, both South American nationals and prospectors from abroad.

Ecological Diversity

Much of the Amazon basin remains unexplored and therefore certainly uncataloged, and only estimates exist for total species numbers. However, more than four hundred species of mammals, twelve hundred

species of birds, three thousand species of fish, four hundred species of amphibians, three hundred species of reptiles, two and one-half million species of insects, and forty thousand species of plants have been described or projected. The density, inaccessibility, and harshness of the terrain all make species cataloging difficult, but efforts are ongoing, and the numbers continue to grow.

Flagship species include the Brazilian tapir, a large forest ungulate with a prehensile snout; the jaguar, a cousin of the leopard; the golden lion tamarin, a small and charismatic monkey with striking orange hair; the scarlet macaw, a multicolored large parrot; the quetzal, a brilliantly green frugivorous (fruit-eating) bird; the poison dart frog, the toxins of which are used by some indigenous groups to tip the darts they shoot through blowguns; the anaconda, a very large constricting snake that can grow to up to 9 meters (30 feet) long; and the howler monkey, which makes vocalizations that can be heard through the forest for up to 5 kilometers (3 miles). Nearly all these species are under threat of extinction, but a plenitude of other lesser known species suffer the same threat, and many of those unknown to science must be under similar circumstances. The dangers to Amazon species include habitat destruction, poaching and the pet trade, hunting for food and medicine, and the impending yet unclear effects of climate change.

Cultural Diversity

The human population of the Amazon River basin prior to the arrival of Europeans in the sixteenth century was somewhere on the order of five million, with around five thousand tribes. Nearly five hundred years later and after exploitation, disease, and violence, about half a million individuals remain living in the basin in traditional ways, with approximately five hundred tribes, seventy-five of which are seldom, if ever, contacted and live in voluntary isolation. Great linguistic diversity exists in the basin, where more than thirty language families are recognized. With the advent of industrial logging and oil extraction, conflicts between prospectors and indigenous Amazonians began to rise, and many still go unreported in extremely remote areas.

Groups such as the U.S.-based Amazon Watch fight for the legal rights of the indigenous peoples to own their land and to dictate who may and may not enter and extract resources. This movement is separate from the ecological conservation movement and is better characterized as an environmental justice movement, but the two necessarily go hand in hand as the indigenous peoples depend on forest resources to continue their ways of life. Certainly, not all indigenous Amazonians live in the forest; many have moved to cities and have chosen modern lifestyles. People with indigenous blood make up significant portions of the populations of most South American countries.

Habitat Destruction

In the Amazon River basin, habitat destruction usually takes the form of deforestation. Between 1991 and 2000, the total area of forest lost rose from 415,000 to 587,000 square kilometers (160,000 to 227,000 square miles), nearly six times the size of Portugal. Although the logging and oil industries are responsible for much of the degradation of the landscape, a large percentage is the result of the conversion of forest to pasture and farmland by local people. Most of the formerly forested land is used for livestock pasture, as grass grows well even in poor Amazonian soils and raising livestock has relatively high returns for minimal effort. Long-term, large-scale farming is usually ineffective because of the paucity of nutrients in the soil, and therefore slash-and-burn agriculture is widely practiced. This involves logging all the trees in an area, setting a fire and letting it burn through the remaining tree and other plant growth, then planting crops in the resulting ash, which provides temporary nutrients. The ability to grow crops on the land lasts for only a short time, so a slash-and-burn farmer must move to a new spot every few years, thus accelerating deforestation.

Another important contributor to deforestation has been the Trans-Amazonian Highway, which cuts straight through the rain forest from Brazil to Peru and opens up much of the surrounding regions to farming and resource extraction. It has been projected that if the rates of deforestation seen in the early twenty-first century continue, in two decades the extent of the Amazon rain forest will have decreased by 40 percent. Many innovative projects have been developed to oppose unsustainable use of the forest, one of the most notable of which is the ecovillage of Gaviotas in Colombia, which was founded in 1971 as part of an effort to build and develop a sustainable model for a modern Amazonian village.

Jamie Michael Kass

Further Reading

Benjamin, Alison. "More than Half of the Amazon Will Be Lost by 2030, Report Warns." *Guardian*, December 6, 2007.

London, Mark, and Brian Kelly. *The Last Forest: The Amazon in the Age of Globalization*. Random House, 2007.

Sheil, Douglas, and Sven Wunder. "The Value of Tropical Forest to Local Communities: Complications, Caveats, and Cautions." *Conservation Ecology* 6, no. 2 (2002): 9-24.

Slater, Candace. *Entangled Edens: Visions of the Amazon*. University of California Press, 2002.

Smith, Nigel J. H. *The Amazon River Forest: A Natural History of Plants, Animals, and People*. Oxford University Press, 1999.

See also: Biodiversity; Logging and clear-cutting; Rain forests; Rainforest Action Network; Slash-and-burn agriculture; South America; Sustainable forestry.

■ American alligator and conservation efforts

FIELDS OF STUDY: Biology, Life Sciences, Ecosystems; Animals, Zoology, Marine Biology; Ecology, Environment, Environmentalism.

IDENTIFICATION: Crocodilian species native to the southeastern United States

Once an endangered species, the American alligator made a striking comeback in the last few decades of the twentieth century, thanks to conservation efforts.

The American alligator (*Alligator mississippensis*) is a surviving member of the crocodilians—a family of reptiles that roamed Earth along with dinosaurs 230 million years ago. Ranging between 2.5 and 4.6 meters (8 to 15 feet) in length and weighing up to 450

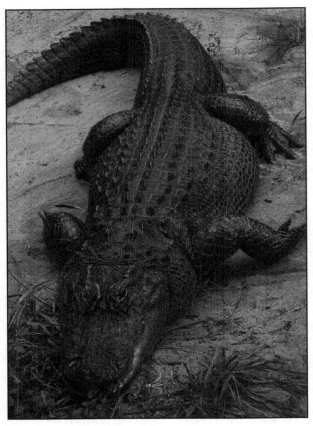

An American Alligator in captivity at the Columbus Zoo, Powell, Ohio.

kilograms (1,000 pounds), it is the largest reptile in North America.

The American alligator inhabits coastal areas, swamps, ponds, and marshes of the southeastern United States, from North Carolina to Florida and along the Gulf Coast to Texas. Spanish explorers were the first Europeans to come across the American alligator, which they named _el lagarto_ ("the lizard"), an expression Americans later turned into "alligator." Various descriptions of alligators by eighteenth century trappers, explorers, adventurers, and naturalists quickly earned the reptile a place in legend and folklore. Americans and Europeans alike became fascinated with false, but entertaining, portrayals of the reptile as an almost mythological, smoke-breathing dragon.

Although white southerners and Native Americans hunted the alligator for centuries, the reptile faced no serious, widespread threat as a species until the 1870's, when a worldwide demand arose for its soft hides, which were turned into belts, hats, shoes, and handbags. Their value grew in the following decades, and by the 1940's alligator populations were so dangerously reduced that southern states outlawed the hunting and trapping of the reptiles. These actions, however, stimulated illegal poaching during the 1960s and drove the alligator to the brink of extinction.

In 1973 the U.S. government put the alligator—along with its cousin, the American crocodile (_Crocodylus acutus_)—on the endangered species list and banned the trafficking of its hides. The protection worked so well that alligators were removed from the endangered list in 1987, and as of 2018 are still considered a species of least concern. Open hunting of alligators is still illegal, though Florida and Louisiana allow permitted hunts to control alligator populations and protect fur-bearing animals.

New problems, however, confront the American alligator. Land development continues to destroy its natural habitat, but human activity also creates new artificial living spaces for alligators in canals and drainage ditches. These new environs often put alligators in close proximity to humans. As a result, alligators commonly appear in the swimming pools or yards of private homes, on docks, at highway toll booths, and even at schools and shopping centers, and their encounters with humans are on the rise. Though alligators feed mainly on fish, snails, crabs, amphibians, and small mammals, they also occasionally consume dogs, cats, and even calves. Attacks on humans, especially small children, are rare—only twenty-four people were killed by alligators from 1948 to 2017—but have increased somewhat as humans encounter alligators more frequently.

Pollution also threatens alligators. In 1996, researchers from the University of Florida reported serious reproductive problems among alligators in Lake Apopka, Florida's third-largest lake. The researchers suspected that the fertility problems were the result of a 1980 chemical spill and agricultural pesticide runoff into the lake. According to one University of Florida study, Lake Apopka lost 90 percent of its alligator population in a recent twenty-year period. More research is needed to determine whether the Lake Apopka situation is an isolated case or an indicator of a wider problem that could again put alligators in grave danger.

John M. Dunn

Further Reading

Alligator Bites on People in Florida. Florida Fish and Wildlife Conservation Commission, 2017, myfwc.com/media/310203/Alligator-GatorBites.pdf. Accessed 28 Mar. 2018.

Fujisaki, Ikuko, et al. "Possible Generational Effects of Habitat Degradation on Alligator Reproduction." *Journal of Wildlife Management* 71 (September, 2007): 2284-2289.

Izadi Elahe. "We Saved the Alligators from Extinction—Then Moved into Their Territory." *The Washington Post,* 17 June 2016, www.washingtonpost.com/news/animalia/wp/2016/06/17/we-saved-the-alligators-from-extinction-then-moved-into-their-territory/. Accessed 28 Mar. 2018.

Lockwood, C. C. *The Alligator Book.* Louisiana State University Press, 2002.

■ American bison

FIELDS OF STUDY: Biology, Life Sciences, Ecosystems; Animals, Zoology, Marine Biology; Ecology, Environment, Environmentalism.

IDENTIFICATION: Large, oxen-like animal native to North America

The American bison was nearly exterminated during the late nineteenth century, but efforts to protect the species—first undertaken in 1870—became one of the first North American environmental success stories.

The American bison (often commonly called the American buffalo) is a large, oxen-like animal with a large head, well-developed front quarters, pronounced hump, and thin rear quarters. The ancestors of the American bison originated in the colder climates of Eurasia and made their way from Siberia to Alaska across the Bering land bridge during the ice ages three hundred thousand to six hundred thousand years ago. They underwent several changes to evolve into the modern species about five thousand years ago and to become one of the most abundant land animals of all time. By 1500, some thirty million were in North America, mostly on the plains between the Mississippi River and the Rocky Mountains, from Canada to Mexico. The species owed its success to its abilities to subsist on the grasses of the plains, to survive often bitterly cold and snowy winters, and to outrun predators, including human beings.

After 1500, with the arrival of the horse in North America, humans could better keep up with these fleet and unpredictable animals, and by the late nineteenth century, three new technologies contributed to their wholesale slaughter. The first was an effective weapon, the Sharps 50-caliber rifle, which permitted long-range killing. The second was the transcontinental railroad (completed in 1869), which provided cheap transportation of the bisons' heavy hides to market. The third was the development of a new tanning process that made the bison hides malleable for processing into leather, which was used primarily for industrial machine belts. In addition, the extermination of bison was promoted as a way of controlling

The Far West–Shooting buffalo on the line of the Kansas-Pacific Railroad. (Library of Congress)

the American Indian tribes that depended on bison meat and hides for survival. By 1883, the American bison was no longer viable as a commercially exploitable species and was nearly biologically extinct.

As early as 1870, attempts were made to protect and preserve the American bison, but few federal or state laws were adopted or enforced. Although 200 bison were living in Yellowstone National Park when it was established in 1872, their numbers had dwindled to 25 from poaching by 1894. At that time, the Lacey Yellowstone Protection Act was enacted, finally providing public protection to the surviving wild bison. Meanwhile, a few people, motivated by their own interest in the animals and by plans to sell them to zoos and others, developed herds in Texas, Kansas, Nebraska, South Dakota, and Montana.

During the early twentieth century, efforts to provide public protection for bison were successful. Foremost in this endeavor was the American Bison Society, one of the first environmental organizations in the United States, founded in 1905 and consisting primarily of eastern industrialists. The society succeeded in getting the US Congress to set aside four additional areas for bison preservation: the National Bison Range in Montana, Wichita Mountain in Oklahoma, Fort Niobrara in Nebraska, and Wind Cave National Park in South Dakota. The society then purchased the animals to stock these preserves primarily from private holdings, although the Bronx Zoo donated 15 animals to Wichita Mountain in 1907. A census in 1929 counted 3,385 bison, and the species had been rescued from extinction.

As of 2010 the population of American bison in the United States and Canada was estimated at 500,000. More than 90 percent were in private holdings, farmed like livestock and subject to genetic selection to make them more useful to humans and less unpredictable. Such breeding practices have the effect of reducing the animals' wild features, and some commentators have noted that it would be unfortunate for the species to survive physical extinction only to face genetic obliteration. Those bison managed in the public domain have the chance to remain the majestic, wild animals that long dominated North America. Because most public preserves are small, a Great Plains Park has been proposed (perhaps on both sides of the US-Canadian border) to provide habitat for large, nomadic herds of bison such as those that once roamed the middle of the continent.

James L. Robinson

Further Reading

Hodgson, Bryan. "Buffalo Back Home on the Range." *National Geographic,* November, 1994, 64-89.

Lott, Dale F. *American Bison: A Natural History.* University of California Press, 2002.

Zontek, Ken. *Buffalo Nation: American Indian Efforts to Restore the Bison.* University of Nebraska Press, 2007.

■ Amoco Cadiz oil spill

FIELDS OF STUDY: Biology; Ecology; Ecosystem Management; Environmental Management; Environmental Studies; Fisheries; History; Oceans; Transportation Management;

THE EVENT: Grounding of the tanker *Amoco Cadiz* off the coast of Brittany, France, resulting in the spilling of its cargo of crude oil into the sea

DATE: March 16, 1978

The Amoco Cadiz oil spill resulted in the deaths of thousands of fish and seabirds and the pollution of coastal waters important to France for the harvest of marine life and for the tourism industry.

The AMOCO CADIZ ran aground off the coast of Brittany, France on March 16, 1978, spilling 68.7 million gallons of oil. It currently is #6 on the list of the largest oil spills of all time.

The four-year-old very large crude carrier (VLCC) *Amoco Cadiz* had been built in Spain. At 331 meters (1,086 feet) long and 68.6 meters (225 feet) wide, and with a draft of 19.8 meters (65 feet), it was one of the largest ships afloat. The vessel was American owned (by Standard Oil of Indiana), Liberian flagged, and crewed by Italians.

The *Amoco Cadiz* was in the final stages of its voyage from the Persian Gulf to Rotterdam in the Netherlands with 223,000 tons of mixed Kuwaiti and Iraqi crude oil. The vessel was northbound along the coast of Brittany, France, at about 10:00 AM when a steering failure occurred. The ship was about 24 kilometers (15 miles) off the French coast. Within two hours, the tugboat *Pacific* was alongside the *Amoco Cadiz* connecting a towline. The tug ran out about 914 meters (3,000 feet) of steel towing wire in an attempt to keep the large tanker off the rocks, but after only two hours of towing, the towline broke. During this time, shipboard engineers had attempted to fix the tanker's damaged rudder, but the system was beyond repair. The ship was 10.5 kilometers (6.5 miles) off the coast of France.

By 9:00 PM, the tug had reattached a towline to the stern of the *Amoco Cadiz*, but shortly thereafter the large tanker grounded on the Roches de Portsall. It immediately began leaking its cargo of crude oil over the coast of Brittany. This area accounts for almost 40 percent of the marine life and 7 percent of the oysters harvested in France. Within three days, the oil slick had spread almost 80 kilometers (50 miles) to the north of the ship and 32 kilometers (20 miles) to the south. The French government implemented its oil-spill cleanup plan. Within six days of the spill, all of the vessel's tanks were open to the sea, and the slick measured 129 kilometers (80 miles) by 29 kilometers (18 miles). The French were unable to pump oil off the grounded vessel because of both poor weather and poor charts of the area.

Ten days after the ship grounded, the highest tide of the period occurred, and beach cleaning began in earnest. By the beginning of April, the French had mustered almost six thousand military personnel, three thousand civilians, twenty-eight boats, and more than one thousand vehicles for the cleanup operation. By the end of May, 206,000 tons of material had been cleaned off the shores of Brittany. Only 25,000 tons of this was actually oil—the rest was sand, rock, seaweed, and other plant life. Those involved in

rescue efforts found some ten thousand dead fish and twenty-two thousand dead seabirds.

The cleanup effort was declared a success even though many criticized the French government for a slow response and fragmented efforts. The bulk of the oil cleanup was attributed to the sea itself. The relatively deep water and fast current along the shore helped the sea to disperse and dissipate the 223,000 tons of crude oil that had spilled into it over a six-day period.

Robert J. Stewart

Further Reading

Clark, R. B. *Marine Pollution*. 5th ed. Oxford University Press, 2001.
Fairhall, David, and Philip Jordan. *The Wreck of the Amoco Cadiz*. Stein and Day, 1980.
Fingas, Merv. *The Basics of Oil Spill Cleanup*. 2nd ed. CRC Press, 2001.

■ Amory, Cleveland

FIELDS OF STUDY: Ethics, Advocacy, Policy, Protest; Authors, Writers; Animals, Zoology, Marine Biology.

IDENTIFICATION: Activism and advocacy; animals and endangered species

Amory's decades of activism for animal rights and animal protection saved thousands of animals from extermination and helped bring the issue of cruelty to animals into the public spotlight.

As an author, Cleveland Amory is perhaps best known for his best-selling books featuring his cat, Polar Bear: *The Cat Who Came for Christmas* (1987), *The Cat and the Curmudgeon* (1990), and *The Best Cat Ever* (1993). He also published a number of social history studies, and in 1974 he published *Man Kind? Our Incredible War on Wildlife*, a work that has been credited with influencing the antihunting movement in the United States.

From the time he was a young child, Amory harbored a dream to create a sanctuary for animals where they would be protected from harm and allowed to roam free. To this end, he established the Fund for Animals, a nonprofit organization, in 1967. In 1977, the Fund for Animals initiated its first major rescue of animals when the U.S. Park Service scheduled the extermination, by shooting, of all the wild burros living in the Grand Canyon in Arizona. Over the next two years, Amory's organization orchestrated a helicopter airlift of 577 burros from the floor of the Grand Canyon, some seven thousand feet below its rim. An intensive, nationwide adoption campaign was conducted for the burros; those animals not adopted found homes at the Black Beauty Ranch, an animal sanctuary founded by Amory in Murchison, Texas, in 1979. Two years later, the Fund for Animals rescued another 5,000 burros that had been earmarked for destruction at Death Valley National Monument and the Naval Weapons Center at China Lake, both in California.

In the early 1980's the organization rescued more than sixty wild Spanish Andalusian goats from San Clemente Island off the coast of California after the U.S. Navy had decided to eradicate the island's population of the animals, saying that the move was mandated by the Endangered Species Act (1973) because the goats were eating the native, endangered species of vegetation on the island. The Navy intended to allow hunters to kill the animals for a fee. The Fund for Animals arranged a helicopter airlift of the animals to temporary quarters in San Diego, California, and another adoption campaign was successfully conducted.

Black Beauty Ranch, which was renamed Cleveland Amory Black Beauty Ranch in 2004 to honor its founder, has been home to thousands of domestic and exotic animals rescued from neglectful or abusive situations. Among the animals given sanctuary at the ranch since its founding have been chimpanzees, kangaroos, wild horses, buffalo, and elephants.

Through his work with the Fund for Animals, Amory developed the resources to conduct high-profile rescues of large numbers of animals, and the organization's continuing efforts have received much national and international publicity. This publicity has helped raise the public's consciousness about issues of cruelty and neglect toward animals.

Karen E. Kalumuck

Further Reading

Greenwald, Marilyn S. *Cleveland Amory: Media Curmudgeon and Animal Rights Crusader.* University Press of New England, 2009.

Marshall, Julie Hoffman. *Making Burros Fly: Cleveland Amory, Animal Rescue Pioneer.* Johnson Books, 2006.

See also: Animal rights; Animal rights movement; People for the Ethical Treatment of Animals; Pets and the pet trade; Wild horses and burros.

■ Amphibians and habitat destruction

FIELDS OF STUDY: Biology; Ecology; Ecosystem Management; Environmental Studies;

IDENTIFICATION: Class of vertebrate animals with thin, permeable skin and generally characterized by an aquatic larval stage and a more or less terrestrial adult stage

Amphibian populations have been suffering worldwide declines as a consequence of habitat destruction and alteration, parasites and diseases, and pollution, to which their permeable skin renders them particularly vulnerable.

Amphibians include frogs and toads, salamanders, and caecilians (rarely encountered legless tropical forms). Because nearly all amphibians lead double lives, they are affected by habitat alterations and environmental contaminants in both aquatic environments (as larvae, such as tadpoles) and terrestrial environments (as adults). Also, because amphibians breathe primarily through their skin, they are very sensitive to chemicals and to poor water quality. Like the proverbial canary in the coal mine, amphibians serve as environmental monitors. Consequently, declining amphibian populations are of concern not only because amphibians are important components of many ecosystems but also because the declines may signal the onset of deteriorating conditions that will soon affect other forms of life, including humans.

About 32 percent of the world's amphibian species are known to be threatened or extinct, and insufficient data are available to allow determination of the threat status of another 25 percent. At least 38 amphibian species are known to be extinct and at least another 120 species have not been found in recent years and could be extinct. At least 42 percent of all amphibian species are declining, suggesting that the number of threatened species will rise in the future.

Most of the declines are attributable to habitat alterations and destruction. Especially in the Tropics, deforestation has affected a number of species, and the cool, wet mountaintop habitats favored by many amphibians are particularly vulnerable to global climate change. Complicating the issue is the rapid worldwide spread of the chytrid fungus, which has devastated amphibian populations. The fungus invades the thin skin of amphibians and kills them by disrupting their ability to regulate the movement of water and oxygen in their bodies. The fungus spreads in water and through direct body contact. A few resistant species, such as bullfrogs, clawed frogs, and cane toads, serve as vectors, transmitting the disease to sensitive species. Chytrid thrives in the same cool, wet conditions favored by most amphibians.

Deformed frogs with missing or extra limbs were brought to the attention of the world when they were discovered by schoolchildren in Minnesota in 1995. At first, chemical pollutants were thought to be the cause, but it became apparent that parasitic flatworms (trematodes) were responsible. However, experts believe that, like chytrid, stress imposed by deteriorating habitats and a changing climate may well be aggravating the problem in a synergistic fashion.

Another environmental concern associated with amphibians is not related to declines but is, in fact, caused by too many frogs in the wrong places. A few very hardy species have been transported by humans to places far from their native ranges. These invasive species upset biotic communities by competing with or eating native species. Large and voracious cane toads, introduced widely to control insect pests in sugarcane fields, have been implicated in the decline or extinction of native frogs in places as far from one another as Florida and Australia. Equally large and voracious bullfrogs, intentionally imported around the world for food, are responsible for declines of native frogs in the western United States, Latin America, and even Europe. Coquís, small tree frogs native to Puerto Rico, pose a threat to unique Hawaiian insects. Cuban tree frogs, introduced into Florida, have hitchhiked on tropical plants shipped around the world, and in their new habitats they eat other frogs and even small lizards.

Robert Powell

Further Reading

Collins, James P., and Martha L. Crump. *Extinction in Our Times: Global Amphibian Decline.* Oxford University Press, 2009.
Heatwole, Harold, and John W. Wilkinson, eds. *Amphibian Decline: Diseases, Parasites, Maladies, and Pollution.* Surrey Beatty & Sons, 2009.
Lannoo, Michael, ed. *Amphibian Declines: The Conservation Status of United States Species.* University of California Press, 2005.
Stuart, S. N., et al., eds. *Threatened Amphibians of the World.* Conservation International, 2008.

■ Animal rights movement

FIELDS OF STUDY: Ethics, Advocacy, Policy, Protest; Public Policy, Debates, Controversies; Animals, Zoology, Marine Biology; Agriculture, Farming, Animal Husbandry.

IDENTIFICATION: Social movement involving groups and individuals concerned with the basic rights and welfare of animals

The animal rights movement has brought about a number of changes in laws as well as in public perceptions of issues involving animals, but debates continue concerning the extent of the rights to which animals are entitled.

People involved in the animal rights movement share philosophical beliefs based on the idea that all animals are entitled to an equal claim on life and liberty and possess the same rights to existence as humans. Animal rights activists oppose those who believe that animals exist for human use as objects of study, testing, and experimentation, as food, as beasts of burden, or as objects of amusement and recreation.

The philosophical concept of animal rights arose during the seventeenth and eighteenth centuries along with the development of biological science. The growing interest in biology gave rise to a sort of sideshow in which living, conscious dogs were cut open so that the animals' internal organs could be displayed to crowds of onlookers. A variety of blood sports were popular as well, including bullbaiting and bearbaiting. In these, a bull or a bear was chained in a ring along with one or more dogs that were trained to attack the larger animals. Dogfighting, in which various terrier breeds were encouraged to attack each other, was also popular. Although illegal, incidents of dogfighting still occur in the present day, typically involving high stakes gambling.

Major Animal Rights Organizations

ORGANIZATION	FOUNDED
American Society for the Prevention of Cruelty to Animals	1866
American Anti-Vivisection Society	1883
Animal Defense League	1934
Friends of Animals	1957
Fund for Animals	1967
Actors and Others for Animals	1971
American Fund for Alternatives to Animal Research	1977
People for the Ethical Treatment of Animals	1980
Alliance for Animals	1988

Birth of Animal Rights

Legislation directed at preventing animal cruelty was first overseen in 1824 the Royal Society for the Prevention of Cruelty to Animals (RSPCA) was founded in Great Britain to enforce new anticruelty laws. However, the laws and their enforcement had little, if any, effect in rural areas, which were far from the watchful eyes of the police or RSPCA agents. On many farms, animals were still kept in filthy conditions and beaten if they balked at hauling overloaded wagons. The slaughter of animals for market was carried out as simply and quickly as possible. A series of laws were enacted in the United States, beginning with the Animal Welfare Act of 1966, that limited the use of animals in scientific or other research.

Biomedical research, especially in human anatomy and physiology, advanced rapidly in Europe during the early to mid-nineteenth century. While anatomical study could be satisfied with human corpses, physiologists required living material, and animals became their targets. Although many of the animals used in medical research were rats and mice, dogs were also frequently used. Many of the animals were stolen pets, while others were strays that were found roaming on the streets. The treatment that dogs received in medical laboratories varied, but, for the purposes of good science, the animals had to be maintained and treated in clean, sanitary, and relatively stress-free environments. Many dogs died at the hands of medical researchers, and opposition to the practice quickly grew. Objections came from members of the general public, who had heard stories of both real and imagined horrors suffered by animals in the experiments.

The British government sought to quiet the complaints by passing the Cruelty to Animals Act of 1876.

The act did not prohibit the practice of experimenting on live animals; rather, it set regulatory procedures that had to be followed in the laboratories. Animal rights were no less an issue in the United States at that time. The first documented humane society in the United States was the American Society for the Prevention of Cruelty to Animals (ASPCA), incorporated in 1866. Another pioneer group, the American Antivivisection Society (AAS), was founded in 1883.

The animal rights movement in the United States was relatively quiet until the first Earth Day in 1970, after which it rapidly expanded with the help of various environmental organizations. Among the dozens of animal rights and animal welfare organizations in the United States are such diverse associations as Actors and Others for Animals, the League of Humane Voters, and the American Fund for Alternatives to Animal Research. The list also includes several confrontational groups that use direct action tactics, such as Greenpeace, People for the Ethical Treatment of Animals (PETA), Sea Shepherd Conservation Society, and the Animal Liberation Front (ALF).

Animal Rights Issues

One issue that quickly attracted animal rights proponents was the plight of the whales. For centuries whaling was conducted from sailing ships with handheld harpoons in the manner made famous in Herman Melville's novel *Moby Dick* (1851). By the 1800s the whaling industry was thriving, and whales, primarily sperm whales, were hunted and killed for their blubber, which was the source of prized whale oil. Even with such crude equipment and methodology, whalers significantly reduced the whale population in the Atlantic Ocean and then turned their attention to the Pacific Ocean. In the late nineteenth century, steam (and, later, diesel) vessels and cannonfired harpoons increased the whalers' efficiency. The methods of the whalers aroused the ire of many people. Frequently, a harpooned whale was forced to tow the steel "catcher" ship for hours until the animal succumbed to the injuries from the explosive-headed harpoon. Another whaling technique was to harpoon and kill a whale calf. The mother and other adults hovered around the injured or killed calf and were in turn harpooned.

Economics rather than animal rights brought about the formation of the International Whaling Commission (IWC) in 1946. The commission was established to manage and increase whale stocks. It had no regulatory authority, however, and Norway, Iceland, and Japan continued to hunt whales despite the recommendations of the IWC. These nations have defended their activities as a sustainable use of a natural resource. Opponents view whaling as an archaic activity and a violation of animal rights. In 1971, several environmental groups, including the Animal Welfare Institute, launched the Save the Whales Campaign in an effort to significantly reduce harvesting of whales. In 1972 the US government passed the Marine Mammal Protection Act (MMPA) as a move to protect the whales.

Dolphins are at risk from indirect human exploitation. In the eastern tropical Pacific Ocean, yellowfin tuna frequently swim below pods of dolphins, and commercial fishermen learned to set their nets around schools of dolphins in order to capture the tuna. As the fish are netted, the trapped dolphins drown. The killing of tens of thousands of dolphins each year in this manner led to protests by animal rights groups that included a nationwide boycott of canned tuna. In response to the public outcry, the US government instituted regulations that required both domestic and foreign fishers to follow practices that release the dolphins from their nets and still retain most of the tuna. Within a few years, the accidental catch and kill of dolphins was reduced by 25 percent. Animal rights groups remained concerned that dolphins were still being chased and encircled by fishermen in search of tuna, so in 1992, the International Dolphin Conservation Program Act was passed, which allowed only "dolphin-safe tuna" (only tuna that had been caught without chasing, encircling, or killing dolphins) to be sold in the United States. Critics of the act accused tuna manufacturers of using the dolphin-safe label as a marketing tool and that the term was no guarantee that dolphins had in fact been protected. Regulations were strengthened in 2004 and again in 2013 to further protect dolphins. The National Oceanic and Atmospheric Administration (NOAA) estimated in 2013 that the number of dolphins unintentionally caught in tuna nets had been reduced to 1,000 annually worldwide.

The animal rights movement has also brought increased scrutiny to the fur trade and to circuses, zoos, theme parks, and any other activity in which live animals are used. For example, Ringling Brothers and Barnum & Bailey Circus, a storied American traveling circus dating to the mid-nineteenth century, finally went out of business in 2017, due in part to recurring legal battles with animal rights groups such as PETA and the Humane Society.

Albert C. Jensen

Further Reading

Baker, Lawrence W. *Animal Rights and Welfare: A Documentary and Reference Guide.* ABC-CLIO, 2015.

Beers, Diane L. *For the Prevention of Cruelty: The History and Legacy of Animal Rights Activism in the United States.* Swallow Press/Ohio University Press, 2006.

Fellenz, Marc R. *The Moral Menagerie: Philosophy and Animal Rights.* University of Illinois Press, 2007.

Franklin, Julian H. *Animal Rights and Moral Philosophy.* Columbia University Press, 2005.

Garner, Robert. *The Political Theory of Animal Rights.* Manchester University Press, 2005.

Goodale, Greg, and Jason Edward Black. *Arguments about Animal Ethics.* Lexington, 2014. Print.

Harnack, Andrew, ed. *Animal Rights: Opposing Viewpoints.* Greenhaven Press, 1996.

Lin, Doris. "Historical Timeline of the Animal Rights Movement." *ThoughtCo.*, 10 June 2017, www.thoughtco.com/historical-timeline-of-animal-rights-movement-127594. Accessed 29 Mar. 2018.

Sunstein, Cass R., and Martha C. Nussbaum, eds. *Animal Rights: Current Debates and New Directions.* Oxford University Press, 2006.

Whisker, James B. *The Right to Hunt.* 2nd ed. Merril Press, 1999.

■ Animal testing

FIELDS OF STUDY: Technology and Applied Science; Scientific Equipment, Tools, Techniques, and Methods; Animals, Zoology, Marine Biology; Health, Medicine, Disease, Illness.

IDENTIFICATION: Use of nonhuman animals for research purposes, particularly medical research

Animal testing is an integral component of modern science, product testing, and education. Most significant developments in medicine directly or indirectly rely on animal

testing. Public debate about the moral and legal status of animals in society has resulted in numerous regulations on animal testing, yet it continues to be a controversial subject.

Animal testing, also known as animal experimentation, animal research, in vivo testing, and vivisection, is used to advance pure and applied research. Behavior, development, evolution, reproductive cloning, and genetic engineering research are all forms of pure research involving animals. Applied research includes medical research, defense research, and toxicology studies for drugs, food additives, pesticides, and cosmetics. The use of animals in medical education and training is typically considered to be a form of animal testing as well.

Rationale, Scope, and Regulations

The underlying rationale for the use of animal testing is that living organisms provide interactive, dynamic systems that scientists can observe and manipulate in order to understand normal and pathological functioning as well as the effectiveness of medical interventions. The vast majority of animal testing is for human benefit and relies on the physiological and anatomical similarities between humans and other animals. The term "animal model" refers to the use of live animals to study particular biological processes with the end of extrapolating that information to other animals, particularly humans.

Many species are used in animal testing. Nematode worms and fruit flies are commonly used invertebrates. Zebra fish and mice are commonly used vertebrates. While it is difficult to ascertain the exact number of animals used in research worldwide, the US Department of Agriculture (USDA) Animal and Plant Health Inspection Service (APHIS) reported that 820,812 laboratory animals were used for research, testing, and educational purposes in 2016. This represented an almost 7 percent increase over the 2015 figure of 767,622 animals, which was the lowest number on record after years of decline. These statistics, however, do not include animals not protected by the 1966 Animal Welfare Act (AWA), a federal law that has been amended numerous times and regulates the treatment of animals in exhibition, research, and transport. Many rats, mice, and fish are not protected by the act, and it is impossible to know exactly how many are used in the United States for testing.

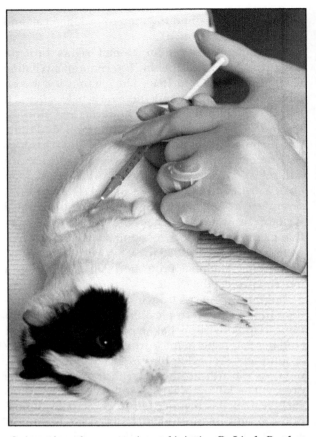

Guinea pig getting an experimental injection. By Linda Bartlett.

In 2013, the European Union (EU) provided 2011 statistics in its seventh report on the number of animals used for scientific purposes. The report stated that over 85 percent of research animals in the EU were rats, mice, fish, and cold-blooded species such as reptiles. In 2015, the European Commission voted to strike down a proposed ban to stop laboratory experiments on animals, although animal testing of cosmetics was banned in the EU in 2004. Individual EU member states regularly report their animal testing statistics. The United Kingdom, for example, reported that 2.02 million experimental procedures involving animals were conducted in 2016, with 60 percent using mice, 14 percent using fish, 12 percent using rats, and 7 percent using birds.

A chief moral concern raised in regard to animal testing is the pain and suffering it involves. Sentience, or subjective awareness, particularly of pain and pleasure, is common to all vertebrates. Evidence for sentience in invertebrates is generally absent, however, and for this reason research on invertebrates is largely unregulated. Cephalopods (the class of animals that includes octopi and squid) are notable exceptions and are covered by regulations in several countries owing to evidence of their sentience. Animal welfare regulations require those who use animals for research or educational purposes to report whether the animal experiences pain and whether pain-relieving medication was provided during procedures. Reporting on mice and rats is not required.

A societal consensus exists that animal testing for the advancement of science and medicine is justified, provided that there are no alternatives, the use of animals is kept to a minimum, and that animal pain and distress is minimized. Supporters of animal testing commonly cite the number of major medical advances that have resulted from the practice.

Animal testing is heavily regulated in many countries. Regulations have changed significantly since the mid-twentieth century, and they differ in the numbers of species covered, the kinds of animal welfare protections offered, and the regulatory approaches taken. In the United States, animal testing is governed by two federal statutes: the Animal Welfare Act (AWA) of 1966 and the Health Research Extension Act of 1985, the provisions of which are carried out in the Public Health Service Policy on Humane Care and Use of Laboratory Animals (PHS Policy). AWA establishes the minimum acceptable standards of care and treatment for certain animals in research, testing, experimentation, exhibition purposes, and use as pets. AWA covers all warm-blooded animals yet specifically excludes birds, mice, and rats bred for research purposes, as well as animals used for food, fiber, or many forms of agricultural research. PHS Policy, which applies to all research funded by the National Institutes of Health (NIH), applies to all live vertebrates used for research purposes.

Opposition and Alternatives

Opposition to animal testing is diverse and the pros and cons of the use of animals for scientific testing are heavily debated. Disagreement with the practice is based on both scientific and ethical grounds, and it varies according to species and to purpose. Research using primates, monkeys, cats, and dogs is particularly controversial.

The testing of cosmetics on animals is especially controversial because many consider the benefit of

yet another cosmetic product to be of dubious value when weighed against animals' interests. Cosmetics testing on animals remains legal in the United States, but in June of 2014, the California Senate passed Joint Resolution 22, which urged the US Congress to pass federal legislation banning the use of all animals in cosmetics testing. Cosmetics testing on animals has been outlawed in several countries, including Israel, the United Kingdom, and the European Union. In July of 2014, China removed a requirement for "ordinary cosmetics," such as hair products and fragrances, to be tested on animals. The country still required, however, that imported and special-use products such as sunblock be animal tested. The next year, South Korea followed in the European Union's footsteps by proposing a five-year plan to phase out the use of cosmetics testing on animals, starting with the prohibition of the use of animals to test finished cosmetic products. New Zealand banned animal testing in cosmetics in 2015. The US Humane Cosmetics Act was introduced to Congress in the summer of 2015, but did not pass.

Since federal laws, for the most part, do not protect farm animals from mistreatment in agricultural research experiments, the US Meat Animal Research Center came under fire in early 2015 as a *New York Times* article exposed alleged animal cruelty in studies being conducted on animals such as cows and lambs in an effort to increase the meat industry's bottom line. This investigation led to a review by the USDA, which funds the program, and the subsequent appointment of the USDA's Agricultural Research Service's first animal welfare ombudsman.

Those opposed to animal testing on scientific grounds cite the unreliability of predicting effects in humans based on animal models. Some argue that animal testing is not cost-effective; they assert that, given the substantial costs of conducting animal tests, which often last years and cost millions of dollars, the goal of improving human health would be more fully and efficiently realized through a reallocation of funding to implement existing medical technologies more widely. Some argue that much animal testing is immoral because the animal suffering caused is greater than the expected benefits to humans. The stronger animal rights view is that each animal has inherent moral worth, which prohibits humans from using them as experimental subjects for any reason.

First articulated by scientists William M. Russell and Rex L. Burch, the three Rs—replacement, reduction, and refinement—are influential guiding principles for the humane use of animals in research. Replacement involves seeking to increase alternatives to animal testing that generate the desired research data without the use of sentient animals. Examples of replacement include the use of computer models, epidemiological data, tissue cultures, isolated organs, and nonsentient animals. Reduction is the effort to obtain comparable data using fewer animals or to obtain more data using the same number of animals. Refinement involves favoring research protocols that alleviate or minimize animal pain and distress through the use of analgesics, veterinary care, improved living quarters, and enrichment. Further development and increased implementation of alternatives to and refinement of animal testing is an area of common ground between animal advocates and animal researchers.

Joel P. MacClellan

Further Reading

"Animal Research Numbers Continue Downward Trend According to Newly-Released Report." *National Anti-Vivisection Society*. Natl. Anti-Vivisection Soc., 6 July 2015. Web. 9 July 2015.

Aubrey, Allison. "Outrage Over Government's Animal Experiments Leads to USDA Review." *NPR*. NPR, 6 Feb. 2015. Web. 9 July 2015.

Bayne, Kathryn A. L., et al. *Laboratory Animal Welfare*. Academic Press, 2014.

Carbone, Larry. *What Animals Want: Expertise and Advocacy in Laboratory Animal Welfare Policy*. Oxford University Press, 2004.

"Ending Cosmetics Testing on Animals." *Cruelty Free International*. Cruelty Free International, n.d. Web. 14 June 2016.

Engebretson, Monica. "Will South Korea Be the Next Country to Beat the United States in Ending Cosmetics Testing on Animals?" *Huffington Post*. HuffingtonPost.com, 6 Jan. 2015. Web. 9 July 2015.

Fisher, Elizabeth. "Why We Should Accept Animal Testing." *Huffington Post*. AOL (UK), 17 July 2013. Web. 14 Aug. 2014.

Goodman, Justin R., et al. "Mounting Opposition to Vivisection." *Contexts* 11.2 (2012): 68–69. Print.

Guerrini, Anita. *Experimenting with Humans and Animals: From Galen to Animal Rights*. Johns Hopkins University Press, 2003.

"Here's How China Is Moving Away From Animal Testing." *Bloomberg*, 16 Jan. 2018, www.bloomberg.com/news/articles/2018-01-16/ending-china-animal-tests-is-salve-for-big-beauty-quicktake-q-a. Accessed 27 Mar. 2018.

Liebsch, Manfred, et al. "Alternatives to Animal Testing: Current Status and Future Perspectives." *Archives of Toxicology* 85 (2011): 841–58. Print.

Monamy, Vaughan. *Animal Experimentation: A Guide to the Issues*. 2nd ed. Cambridge University Press, 2009.

Newton, David E. *The Animal Experimentation Debate*. ABC-CLIO, 2013. Print.

"Opening the Doors on Animal Testing." *BBD*. BBC, 15 May 2014. Web. 15 June 2016.

Paul, Ellen Frankel, and Jeffrey Paul, eds. *Why Animal Experimentation Matters: The Use of Animals in Medical Research*. Transaction, 2001.

Wolfensohn, Sarah, and Maggie Lloyd. *Handbook of Laboratory Animal Management and Welfare*. 4th ed. Wiley, 2013.

■ Antarctic and Southern Ocean Coalition (ASOC)

FIELDS OF STUDY: Government, Politics, International Relations; Organizations, Agencies, Commissions, Centers; Biology, Life Sciences, Ecosystems; Continents, Regions, Areas, Islands; Ecology, Environment, Environmentalism.

IDENTIFICATION: Global coalition of nongovernmental organizations with a common commitment to preserve the lands of the Antarctic region and the southern oceans in perpetuity as a wilderness area

DATE: Founded in 1978

The Antarctic and Southern Ocean Coalition is the only nongovernmental organization that serves to advocate for environmental protection and reform for the Antarctic region. It plays an important role in support of the region by monitoring the Atlantic Treaty System.

The Antarctic and Southern Ocean Coalition (ASOC) was established by the Friends of the Earth International, the World Wildlife Fund office of New Zealand, and other environmental organizations to monitor the Atlantic Treaty System, to implement its environmental protocols, and to provide expert witness in Antarctic affairs. ASOC seeks to advance the preservation and protection of the fragile ecosystems of the Antarctic continent and its surrounding waters. It reports regularly to key international organizations serving mandates to protect the Antarctic environment and its ecosystems from illegal hunting and fishing practices and to advocate for sustainable resource management, including waste disposal and habitat protection.

World Wildlife Fund founder Sir Peter Scott visited Antarctica in 1966 in the wake of successive international expeditions to the South Pole in the twentieth century, notably during the International Geophysical Year of 1957-1958. Prior to that time the southern Antarctic region and its complex relationship to global ecosystems were poorly understood. Despite regularly coordinated International Polar

Year efforts, data systems were not sufficient to bring into clear focus the singular contributions of the southern oceans and icy landmasses of the Antarctic continent to the health of planetary biodiversity and the cosmography of global temperatures and climate. The critical roles of the Antarctic Convergence and the Antarctic Circumpolar Current in maintaining powerful hydraulic and chemical processes within the Pacific, Atlantic, and Indian oceans are of particular interest to international climatologists concerned with the possible consequences of global warming on sea levels and acidification.

Several international protocols are in place to preserve the Antarctic region in perpetuity as a pristine wilderness and global commons for international research. As an outcome of the International Geophysical Year of 1957-1958, twelve nations established research stations in the Antarctic, and on December 1, 1959, they signed the Antarctic Treaty proposed by the United States. By 2010, forty-seven international participants had agreed to honor the treaty's commitment to collaborative research and environmental protection while proscribing military operations on the continent. Twenty-eight nations serve as consultative parties with authority to make decisions on behalf of the treaty.

ASOC works closely with the Antarctic Treaty Secretariat and attends meetings sponsored by other international organizations, including the International Maritime Organization and the International Whaling Commission, as well as the bodies overseeing the Convention on the Conservation of Antarctic Marine Living Resources and the Agreement on the Conservation of Albatrosses and Petrels. Major ASOC campaigns have included the Antarctic Krill Conservation Project, the Southern Ocean Whale Sanctuary, and protection for the Ross Sea.

As an outcome of the 2007-2008 International Polar Year, the Scientific Committee on Antarctic Research (SCAR) developed a network of databases cataloging the extraordinary biodiversity of the South Pole region. The brainchild of Claude De Broyer and Bruno Danis at the Royal Belgian Institute of Natural Sciences, the Marine Biodiversity Information Network (SCAR-MarBIN) is a collaborative effort by hundreds of scientists worldwide to establish the Register of Antarctic Marine Species, the first complete online resource of its kind. This system collates data from more than one hundred international databases to create detailed mappings of the delicate ecology of Antarctica. These images provide valuable information for scientists seeking to understand and analyze the biological equilibrium of the region and the implications of global climate change on life-forms unique to its lands and waters.

Victoria M. Breting-García

Further Reading

Bargagli, R. *Antarctic Ecosystems: Environmental Contamination, Climate Change, and Human Impact.* Springer, 2005.

Joyner, Christopher C. *Governing the Frozen Commons: The Antarctic Regime and Environmental Protection.* University of South Carolina Press, 1998.

Steig, Eric J., et al. "Warming of the Antarctic Ice-Sheet Surface Since the 1957 International Geophysical Year." *Nature* 457 (January 22, 2009): 459-462.

Triggs, Gillian D., ed. *The Antarctic Treaty Regime: Law, Environment, and Resources.* 1987. Reprint. Cambridge University Press, 2009.

Turner, John, et al., eds. *Antarctic Climate Change and the Environment.* Scientific Committee on Antarctic Research, 2009.

■ Antarctic Treaty

FIELDS OF STUDY: Government, Politics, International Relations; International Relations, Agreements, Treaties; Biology, Life Sciences, Ecosystems; Continents, Regions, Areas, Islands; Ecology, Environment, Environmentalism.

CATEGORIES: Treaties, laws, and court cases; preservation and wilderness issues; ecology and ecosystems

THE TREATY: International agreement in which signatory nations have committed to setting aside the Antarctic region for scientific and peaceful pursuits

DATE: Opened for signature on December 1, 1959

The Antarctic Treaty preserves the continent of Antarctica for peaceful use and protects it from environmental exploitation and degradation; the agreement has in turn led to further international agreements concerning the protection of wildlife.

Articles I to III and V of the Antarctic Treaty lay out the major goals and objectives of the agreement and the positive obligations of its signatories.

Article I

1. Antarctica shall be used for peaceful purposes only. There shall be prohibited, inter alia, any measure of a military nature, such as the establishment of military bases and fortifications, the carrying out of military manoeuvres, as well as the testing of any type of weapon.
2. The present Treaty shall not prevent the use of military personnel or equipment for scientific research or for any other peaceful purpose.

Article II

Freedom of scientific investigation in Antarctica and cooperation toward that end, as applied during the

International Geophysical Year, shall continue, subject to the provisions of the present Treaty.

Article III

1. In order to promote international cooperation in scientific investigation in Antarctica, as provided for in Article II of the present Treaty, the Contracting Parties agree that, to the greatest extent feasible and practicable:

   a. information regarding plans for scientific programs in Antarctica shall be exchanged to permit maximum economy of and efficiency of operations;

   b. scientific personnel shall be exchanged in Antarctica between expeditions and stations;

   c. scientific observations and results from Antarctica shall be exchanged and made freely available.

2. In implementing this Article, every encouragement shall be given to the establishment of cooperative working relations with those Specialized Agencies of the United Nations and other technical organizations having a scientific or technical interest in Antarctica....

Article V

1. Any nuclear explosions in Antarctica and the disposal there of radioactive waste material shall be prohibited.

2. In the event of the conclusion of international agreements concerning the use of nuclear energy, including nuclear explosions and the disposal of radioactive waste material, to which all of the Contracting Parties whose representatives are entitled to participate in the meetings provided for under Article IX are parties, the rules established under such agreements shall apply in Antarctica.

Antarctica, the large body of land and ice that surrounds the South Pole, is among the earth's most unique and wild places. The only continent with no indigenous human population, Antarctica exceeds 12 million square kilometers (5 million square miles) in size, almost 1.5 times larger than the continental United States. An ice layer averaging more than 1.6 kilometers (1 mile) in thickness covers approximately 95 percent of the land area. Although very

few terrestrial species are found on the continent, the surrounding waters are rich in marine life and support large populations of marine mammals, birds, fish, and smaller creatures, some of which are found nowhere else in the world. Antarctica and its surrounding waters play a key but not yet fully understood role in the planet's weather and climate cycles.

In the early twentieth century, seven nations asserted territorial claims on Antarctica, and these claims persisted unresolved for decades. International scientific cooperation among twelve countries during the 1957 International Geophysical Year (IGY) led to the establishment of sixty research stations on the continent. As the IGY drew to a close, the scientific community argued that Antarctica should remain open for continuing scientific investigation and should be unfettered by national rivalries over territory. This led to the negotiation of the Antarctic Treaty, which entered into force in 1961.

The treaty prohibits military activity on the continent and promotes scientific cooperation among the parties. Signatory nations agree to freeze existing territorial claims and make no new ones. Initially, twelve nations signed and became consultative parties, agreeing to hold regular consultative meetings to discuss implementation of the treaty. Sixteen more countries have since been granted consultative party status. Twenty additional nations have acceded to the treaty but are not full parties and participate as observers only. The Antarctic Treaty was also the first major arms-control agreement among the nuclear weapons states and provided a model for several subsequent agreements, including the Limited Test Ban Treaty (1963). The Antarctic Treaty specifically prohibits nuclear test explosions in Antarctica.

Consultative meetings have resulted in more than two hundred implementation recommendations to national governments and have led to two additional treaties: the 1972 Convention for the Conservation of Antarctic Seals and the 1982 Convention on the Conservation of Antarctic Marine Living Resources (CCAMLR), which addresses fishery management. An unusual feature of the latter is that the applicable territory is defined by ecosystem criteria rather than by political boundaries. The Antarctic Treaty and all related agreements and recommendations form what is known as the Antarctic Treaty System.

Mineral discoveries in Antarctica in the 1970's led some nations and private companies to contemplate plans to exploit mineral resources there, but environmental advocates and the scientific community, sharing a concern about potential impacts, led a long fight to prevent such activities. In 1991 the historic Protocol on Environmental Protection was finally adopted; this agreement bans mineral and oil exploration in Antarctica for a minimum of fifty years. Annexes to the protocol contain legally binding provisions regarding environmental assessments, protection of indigenous plants and animals, waste disposal, marine pollution, and designation of protected areas. The protocol entered into force in January, 1998, after ratification by all consultative parties. Environmental issues that still posed challenges to the protection of Antarctica in the late 1990's included threats of overexploitation of Antarctic fisheries, impacts of expanding tourism, and the need for an agreement among the treaty parties regarding liability for environmental damages.

In 1978 several environmental organizations interested in Antarctica formed the Antarctic and Southern Ocean Coalition (ASOC), which by 2010 included more than one hundred member organizations from fifty countries. ASOC has been accorded status as an expert observer to the Antarctic Treaty System and represents member group interests. Environmentalists who have endorsed the concept of Antarctica as a "world park" lobbied for and strongly support the environmental protocol.

Phillip A. Greenberg

Further Reading

Cioc, Mark. *The Game of Conservation: International Treaties to Protect the World's Migratory Animals.* Ohio University Press, 2009.

Triggs, Gillian D., ed. *The Antarctic Treaty Regime: Law, Environment, and Resources.* 1987. Reprint. Cambridge University Press, 2009.

See also: Antarctic and Southern Ocean Coalition; Limited Test Ban Treaty.

■ Anthropocentrism

FIELDS OF STUDY: Anthropology; Biology; Environmental Sciences; Environmental Studies; Ethics; Sociology;

IDENTIFICATION: The view that human beings are of central importance in the universe

Some environmentalists believe that anthropocentric attitudes are largely responsible for human actions that have led to environmental calamities such as air and water pollution, species extinction, and global climate change.

For anthropocentrists human lives have greater value than do the lives of any other species. Anthropocentrists often point out that humans are the only beings that possess certain capacities. They note that, unlike other animals, humans are typically intelligent, self-aware, autonomous, language users, and moral agents; humans engage in play and make art, among other complex cognitive tasks. For anthropocentrists only humans are intrinsically valuable. The rest of nature (including all plant and animal species) has only instrumental value—that is, nature serves only as a means to human ends. From the anthropocentric point of view, biodiversity should be preserved only if it is in the interest of humans to preserve it—any duties that human beings have to preserve biodiversity are owed to other humans, not to any other species.

Anthropocentrism is deeply rooted in most human cultures, but this viewpoint has come under increasing challenges by environmental activists, animal rights advocates, and others. Among the major arguments against anthropocentrism is that it is invidiously perfectionist—that is, logically, those humans who do not display all the characteristics that anthropocentrists assert are uniquely human (intelligence, self-awareness, autonomy, and so on) should be viewed as less valuable than those who do. Some environmental philosophers believe that humans must eradicate both anthropocentrism and the related viewpoint of speciesism, replacing them with deep ecology, biocentrism, sentientism (the view that all sentient beings have moral worth), and ecocentrism. The search for a convincing nonanthropocentric foundation for what is valuable in nature is at the center of environmental philosophy.

Julia Tanner

Further Reading

Crist, Eileen, and Helen Kopnina. "Unsettling Anthropocentrism" *Dialectical Anthropology* 38.4 (2014): 387–396. *Humanities International Complete.* Web. 14 Jan. 2015.

Liu, Alexander, and Sara Jill Unsworth. "Cross-Cultural Differences in Core Concepts of Humans as a Biological Species." *Journal of Cognition & Culture* 14.3/4 (2014): 171–185. *Academic Search Complete.* Web. 14 Jan. 2015.

McIntyre-Mills, Janet Judy. "Anthropocentrism and Well-Being: A Way Out of the Lobster Pot?" *Systems Research & Behavioral Science* 30.2 (2013): 136–155. *Business Source Complete.* Web. 14 Jan. 2015.

Nolt, John. "Anthropocentrism and Egoism." *Environmental Values* 22.4 (2013): 441–459. *Environment Complete.* Web. 14 Jan. 2015.

Oriel, Elizabeth. "Whom Would Animals Designate as Persons? On Avoiding Anthropocentrism and Including Others." *Journal of Evolution & Technology* 24.3 (2014): 44–49. *Academic Search Complete.* Web. 14 Jan. 2015.

■ Antibiotics as environmental waste

FIELDS OF STUDY: Chemistry; Elements, Substances, Chemicals, Compounds; Ecology, Environment, Environmentalism; Health, Medicine, Disease, Illness.

IDENTIFICATION: Molecules that kill or inhibit the growth of bacteria

Antibiotics are used routinely in health care, industry, and agriculture to treat and prevent bacterial infections. Antibiotics released into the environment as waste can generate bacteria that are resistant to the antibiotics through the process of selective pressure. These antibiotic-resistant bacteria can enter the food chain and can indirectly or directly promote the generation of antibiotic-resistant bacteria pathogens.

Antibiotics are defined as bacteriostatic or bactericidal substances that can inhibit the growth of or kill bacteria, respectively. It is important to note that bacteria are animal species; viruses and fungi are entirely different from bacteria in nature and are not affected by antibiotics. Thus, any illness caused by a virus, such as influenza and the common cold, or by a fungus typically cannot be cured by treatment with antibiotics. Antibiotics can range from those isolated as natural compounds, such as aminoglycosides, to those that are completely synthetic, such as quinolones. The first modern antibiotic was penicillin, discovered by scientist Alexander Fleming in 1928; Fleming was later awarded the Nobel Prize for his contributions to medical science. Antibiotics work by inhibiting essential biochemical processes in cells, leading to the inhibition of growth or death of the target bacterium. For example, the bactericidal beta-lactam antibiotics such as penicillin work by inhibiting transpeptidase enzymes, which play an important role in synthesis of the protective peptidoglycan layer of the bacterial cell envelope. The bacteriostatic agent chloramphenicol inhibits protein synthesis by binding to the 50S subunit of the ribosome and interfering with peptide bond formation.

While various in vitro microbiological techniques may indicate whether or not a particular antibiotic is bacteriostatic or bactericidal, the antibiotic's clinical

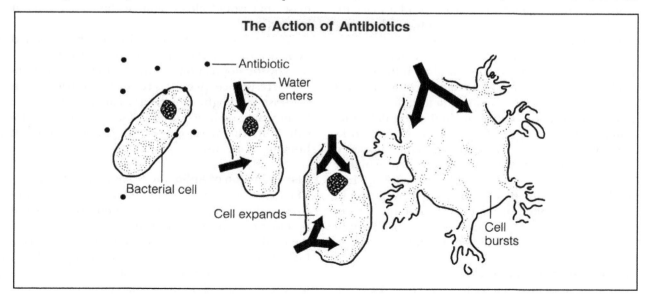

The Action of Antibiotics

Antibiotic

Water enters

Bacterial cell

Cell expands

Cell bursts

An antibiotic destroys a bacterium by causing its cell walls to deteriorate; water will then enter the bacterium unchecked until it bursts.

usefulness is dependent on other factors. These include the antibiotic's pharmacokinetic and pharmacodynamic characteristics as well as the host's state of health and immune system defense mechanisms. Antibiotics can generally be categorized as either narrow-spectrum or broad-spectrum. Narrow-spectrum antibiotics target certain families of bacteria, whereas broad-spectrum antibiotics can treat a wide variety of pathogens and also affect environmental bacteria.

Antibiotics have their origin in nature as molecules that are secreted by one type of bacteria to inhibit the growth of a competitor. It is believed that antibiotic-producing bacteria are the origin of antibiotic resistance genes, since these organisms must have the capacity to resist the effects of the antibiotics they produce.

Antibiotics and the Environment

Antibiotics are widely used by humans in clinical settings and to treat or prevent bacterial infections in companion and food animals. The Animal Health Institute and the Union of Concerned Scientists have estimated that in the United States alone, several million pounds of antibiotics are consumed per year in the treatment of humans and livestock. Antibiotics, especially nonbiodegradable antibiotics, can enter aquatic and terrestrial environments through avenues such as farms, wastewater, and animal manure containing these drugs. For example, a Norwegian study that investigated the release of pharmaceuticals in the wastewater effluent from two Oslo hospitals found that detectable levels of several antibiotics were present in both hospitals' wastewater. Furthermore, the same study showed that influent and sludge samples from a wastewater treatment works that serves the region contained detectable amounts of most of the antibiotics found in the hospital wastewater. Effluent samples from the treatment works contained reduced amounts of antibiotics; however, the levels of the antibiotic trimethoprim were higher in the effluent than in the influent samples. High levels of the antibiotic ciprofloxacin were found in the sludge samples. Antibiotics released into the environment have the potential to generate harmful and possibly deadly antibiotic-resistant bacteria.

Antibiotic-Resistant Bacteria

Antibiotic resistance in a bacterium can be the result of a random mutation in the target molecule or the transfer of antibiotic resistance genes from one bacterium to another. A random mutation can result in the positive selection of bacterial mutants resistant to the antibiotic. Another route whereby bacteria can gain resistance is through horizontal gene transfer (HGT). During HGT, a bacterium can gain an antibiotic resistance gene through transformation, transduction, or conjugation. In most bacteria, the major route of transmission of antibiotic resistance genes is through the conjugation of plasmids, which are extra chromosomal pieces of deoxyribonucleic acid (DNA) that are capable of autonomous replication. It is important to note that HGT can occur almost anywhere that bacteria exist, including the environment and the human gastrointestinal tract.

One example of an antibiotic resistance gene is the *bla* gene, which codes for the TEM-1 beta-lactamase enzyme. Beta-lactamases such as TEM-1 can cleave the beta-lactam ring in the molecular structure of beta-lactam antibiotics such as ampicillin. This cleavage results in the inactivation of the antibiotic. In an effort to increase the efficacy of some antibiotic drugs, some manufacturers add to antibiotic preparations other compounds that play a role in deactivating the biochemical mechanism in the resistant bacteria that degrades the antibiotic. For example, the drug Augmentin is a mixture of amoxicillin (a beta-lactam-containing antibiotic) and potassium clavulanate. The clavulanate is a beta-lactamase inhibitor—that is, it inhibits the beta-lactamase that would cleave amoxicillin and render it ineffective.

Any type of resistance to antibiotics that is gained by a bacterial population as a result of selective pressure by the population's natural habitat is called intrinsic resistance. Acquired resistance by bacteria, in contrast, is brought about as a result of antibiotic use by humans; such acquired resistance has been involved in the development of antibiotic-resistant human pathogens.

Dissemination of Antibiotic-Resistant Bacteria

The dissemination of antimicrobial resistance is not restricted by geographic, phylogenetic, or ecological boundaries, especially given the global economy of the modern world. The use of antibiotics in one ecological niche, such as in agriculture or aquaculture, may give rise to antimicrobial resistance in other ecological niches, such as the human environment. The spread of resistance can be indirect, such as through the horizontal transfer of resistance genes through plasmids, or direct, where antibiotic-resistant bacteria are transferred by direct contact with humans. An example of indirect transfer comes from a study that showed that a plasmid encoding for cephalothin resistance was transferable to *Escherichia coli* (*E. coli*), a bacteria in the human gut, from *Vibrio* strains found in a shrimp pond. Direct transfer can include the intake of harmful antibiotic-resistant bacteria from contaminated drinking water, food animal sources (such as chickens and turkeys), and vegetables.

Infections caused by antibiotic-resistant bacteria present a special challenge to physicians, especially in health care settings. Poor hygiene practices in hospitals (such as failure to decontaminate surgical or respiratory equipment), nursing homes, and dialysis centers have led to the spread and promotion of multidrug-resistant (MDR) bacteria, which usually have resistance to three or more antibiotics. One study on burn patients who had been hospitalized for a long period of time in an intensive care unit showed that the patients carried significantly more MDR bacteria than they had on admission. Methicillin-resistant *Staphylococcus aureus* (or MRSA) is resistant to a wide variety of beta-lactam antibiotics and has become a highly adaptable, drug-resistant pathogen that kills about seventeen thousand hospital patients per year. Antibiotic resistance increases morbidity and mortality from infectious diseases as well as the costs of treating such diseases. With the lack of many new antibiotics on the horizon, antibiotic resistance poses a serious public health dilemma.

Sandra S. Szegedi

Further Reading

Heuer, Ole E., et al. "Human Health Consequences of Use of Antimicrobial Agents in Aquaculture." *Clinical Infectious Diseases* 49 (2009): 1248-1253.

Keen, Edward F., III, et al. "Prevalence of Multidrug-Resistant Organisms Recovered at a Military Burn Center." *Burns: Journal of the International Society for Burn Injuries* (January, 2010).

Martinez, Jose L. "The Role of Natural Environments in the Evolution of Resistance Traits in Pathogenic Bacteria." *Proceedings of the Royal Society B* 276 (2009): 2521-2530.

Rice, Louis B. "The Clinical Consequences of Antimicrobial Resistance." *Current Opinion in Microbiology* 12 (2009): 476-481.

Sachs, Jessica Snyder. *Good Germs, Bad Germs: Health and Survival in a Bacterial World.* New York: Hill & Wang, 2007.

Thomas, Kevin V., et al. "Source to Sink Tracking of Selected Human Pharmaceuticals from Two Oslo City Hospitals and a Wastewater Treatment Works." *Journal of Environmental Monitoring* 9 (2007): 1410-1418.

Walsh, Christopher. *Antibiotics: Actions, Origins, Resistance.* ASM Press, 2003.

■ Antienvironmentalism

FIELDS OF STUDY: Ethics, Advocacy, Policy, Protest; Ecology, Environment, Environmentalism; Public Policy, Debates, Controversies.

IDENTIFICATION: Philosophy that holds that human beings' immediate economic and lifestyle needs are more important than concerns about the fate of other species and the general environment

The long-standing debates that continue between antienvironmentalists and environmentalists have important influence on both legislators and policy makers as they address environment-related issues.

In the early twentieth century, environmentalism in the United States was largely fostered by wealthy sportsmen who saw the need to protect the outdoors in order to maintain satisfactory areas for their pursuits of hunting, fishing, and camping. The movement got a populist boost in 1962 from the publication of Rachel Carson's *Silent Spring*, which presents an easily understood account of the dangers of toxic substances in the environment. For the first time, the American public began to demand that laws be enacted to protect the environment and clean up land, water, and air that had already been polluted.

Growth of the Environmental Movement

For several years the environmental movement gathered strength as the public voted into office politicians with environmental orientations. Public outcry surged against polluting companies, leading to boycotts of products. Grassroots, citizen-led efforts such as recycling programs and litter patrols gained support as the public became more educated and concerned about environmental issues. Among the

Air Pollution Source

issues that pitted environmentalists against the government and industry were toxic waste incineration, habitat destruction by logging and mining companies, and use of public lands, including national parks.

Two oil crises during the 1970s served to focus awareness on energy conservation and the need to develop alternatives to energy derived from fossil fuels. Many feared that oil supplies were dwindling, while others wished to end US reliance on oil-exporting nations in the Middle East. One important result was a general reduction in the size of motor vehicles. This, along with other technological advances, helped lead to the development of cars that were more fuel-efficient. The research required to accomplish these changes, however, was very costly to automakers.

The 1970s were also characterized by landmark legislation that imposed strict limits on pollution output and resource use and also provided for the remediation of polluted land and water. Large fines were imposed for violations of the new laws, which

were enforced by the newly formed US Environmental Protection Agency (EPA). One of the most important and pivotal developments was the passage of the Comprehensive Environmental Response, Compensation, and Liability Act, or Superfund, which provided vast sums of public money for the cleanup of designated industrial and military waste dumps and other degraded sites. Signed into law by the US Congress in 1980, Superfund's provisions allowed the government to bring lawsuits against the responsible parties, requiring them to help pay cleanup costs. In order to avoid fines, many industries were forced to develop and implement costly waste-processing technologies.

The political and economic situation began to change in the late 1970s as industry mounted a counteroffensive against environmental laws. Businesses contended with the burgeoning number of environmental regulations by finding and exploiting loopholes in legislation. A growing number of industries used stalling tactics and countersuits to delay or eliminate the need to implement required changes. Meanwhile, in the western United States, a coalition of loggers, miners, cattle ranchers, farmers, and developers demanded that the federal government transfer control of large tracts of federally owned land to individual states. Members of the so-called Sagebrush Rebellion felt that state ownership would give them more power to exploit the natural resources on the land.

Antienvironmentalist Backlash

A severe backlash against environmentalism began to occur when Ronald Reagan replaced Jimmy Carter as president of the United States in early 1981. Many environmental laws and regulations, which the new presidential administration viewed as barriers to economic progress, were weakened or abolished. A large number of federal judges who had started their careers during the 1960s retired, and they were replaced by politically conservative judges who began to interpret existing laws in favor of industry. The office of the EPA was weakened, and funding for environmental enforcement and remediation was slashed. Secretary of the Interior James Watt, who had been a leader of the Sagebrush Rebellion, promoted legislation to open previously protected areas to mining and oil exploration. The general public, experiencing growth and prosperity for the first time in many years, began to favor short-term economic gains and turned a blind eye to news of the weakening environmental movement.

The late 1980s saw the birth of the wise-use movement, which appeals to the pragmatic and optimistic aspects of human nature by asserting that some optimal balance of resource use and restoration is practicable and that technology, given time and funding, will develop workable solutions to existing environmental problems. This position assumes that human beings can understand the complex ecosystems involved well enough to know what these balances should be. Advocates of wise use believe that all public lands, including national parks, should be opened to mining and drilling. Like the Sagebrush Rebels, they also promote the strengthening of the rights of states and property owners to exploit resources with minimal federal regulation.

According to the tenets of wise use, the harvesting of timber from ancient forests would be followed by the planting of an equivalent acreage of saplings. Logging would be timed according to growth rates, and technology would produce fast-growing varieties of trees that would furnish adequate ecosystems for wildlife in the new forests. Environmentalists, in contrast, argue that ancient forests represent complex, irreplaceable ecosystems that cannot be substituted with new forests planted by logging companies. Similar disagreement exists regarding coastal wetlands, which provide vital habitat to numerous species and contain a high degree of biodiversity. Wetlands are frequently located in areas that are desired by real estate developers wishing to build vacation homes or resorts. Environmental protection laws based on the tenets of wise use mandate that destroyed wetlands must be replaced by new wetlands of equivalent size. Again, environmentalists worry that too many threatened species would be lost in the process of destroying and replacing wetland areas.

Scientific Controversy

Another significant trend in antienvironmentalism toward the end of the twentieth century and into the twenty-first involved public confusion over scientific debates concerning such topics as the hole in the ozone layer and global warming. Industry and government scientists often questioned and condemned dire predictions advanced by other scientists. The government frequently responded by requesting additional research before requiring vast, expensive reductions of known pollutants. Rather than believe the frightening scenarios painted by some scientists, many people sided with scientists who questioned the validity of these and other threats to the global environment.

Mainstream environmental organizations that had evolved from small groups of fervent individuals were now led by full-time professional lobbyists based in Washington, DC. Details of new legislation were negotiated among industry, government, and environmental leaders. National environmental organizations grew increasingly cumbersome and expensive to run. Many began accepting large donations from the same industries they were trying to monitor, which created serious conflicts of interest. Top industry executives became members of the boards of directors for environmental organizations. At the same time, these corporations also made large donations to elected officials and thus gained access and influence in government. As the 1990s progressed, membership in large environmental groups began to decline as "donor fatigue" set in, questions persisted about the true urgency of various environmental issues, and cynicism arose about the possibility of environmental progress under such circumstances.

A relaxation of concern about environmental problems came about in the late 1990s in the wake of encouraging news about improvements of environmental indicators such as air-pollution levels of certain gases in the aftermath of implementation of cleaner energy production. For example, atmospheric levels of sulfur dioxide, which leads to acid rain, decreased in the United States and Europe after cleaner coal- and oil-burning technologies were implemented. The air-quality goals of many cities were met through a combination of fuel efficiency and "scrubber" smokestacks. While environmentalists warned such progress did not indicate the end of environmental threats, the general public became less tuned to these issues once their direct negative effects were relieved.

A controversial strategy advanced by a coalition of industry, government, and environmental leaders involves tradable pollution permits. According to the plan, the government assigns utilities a certain number of pollution units per year. An especially clean-running plant will not need all of its units and will be able to sell them to plants that exceed their allotments. This system has been criticized by many environmentalists, who contend that some utilities are able to buy their way out of the need to reduce pollution. The position thought to be antienvironmentalist in this context would maintain that the plan is a realistic method of controlling overall levels of pollution without putting older utilities out of business while they endeavor to upgrade their performance.

The revelation that environmental degradation can, in certain cases, be reversed over a fairly short span of time led to the argument on the part of antienvironmentalists that nature is surprisingly resilient, and therefore environmental protection does not need to be so stringent, costly, and regressive. Environmentalists counter such arguments with a call to remain vigilant and to include the health of the environment in national and global visions of the future.

Political Considerations

The relative popularity and success of antienvironmentalism versus environmentalism often depends on the political climate. In the United States, political conservatism has tended to be more accepting of antienvironmentalism, elements of which came to often feature in Republican platforms. This alignment largely began during the Reagan administration, and grew stronger into the twenty-first century. For example, the Republican administration of President George W. Bush was noted for supporting policies seen as antienvironmental, such as oil drilling in the Arctic. However, having antienvironmentalists in power also helped motivate a surge in grassroots environmentalist organization, with greater public attention drawn to issues such as climate change in the 2000s.

The opposite effect was seen with the election of Democratic president Barack Obama in 2008. His administration was largely seen as pro-environmentalism, and strongly voiced support for climate change mitigation and other green policies, despite some environmentalists arguing it did not go far enough. In response, conservatives allied even more deeply with antienvironmentalist industries and other groups. The movement attacking mainstream climate science and other environmental science

became more powerful, finding great success in sowing doubt in the general public.

A culmination of this attitude was seen in the election of business tycoon Donald Trump in the controversial 2016 presidential election, after he expressed radically antienvironmentalist views on the campaign trail. His cabinet eventually included several noted antienvironmentalists and climate change skeptics, bringing the movement an unprecedented level of power and visibility. The Trump administration took steps not only to block new environmental legislation, but also to undo existing protections and regulations and severely weaken the EPA. However, this rise in antienvironmentalism did appear to again incite a public backlash. Environmentalist activist groups mounted an increasingly organized resistance, staging events such as a March for Science in Washington, DC, on Earth Day 2017.

Wendy Halpin Hallows

Further Reading

Dowie, Mark. *Losing Ground: American Environmentalism at the Close of the Twentieth Century*. MIT Press, 1995.

Easterbrook, Gregg. *A Moment on the Earth: The Coming Age of Environmental Optimism*. Penguin Books, 1995.

Helvarg, David. *The War Against the Greens: The "Wise-Use" Movement, the New Right, and the Browning of America*. Rev. ed. Johnson Books, 2004.

Hirt, Paul W. *A Conspiracy of Optimism: Management of the National Forests Since World War Two*. University of Nebraska Press, 1994.

Jacques, Peter J. *Environmental Skepticism: Ecology, Power, and Public Life*. Ashgate, 2009.

McKibben, Bill. *The End of Nature*. 1989. Reprint. Random House, 2006.

Sellers, Christopher. "How Republicans Came to Embrace Anti-Environmentalism." *Vox*, 7 June 2017, www.vox.com/2017/4/22/15377964/republicans-environmentalism. Accessed 27 Mar. 2018.

Shabecoff, Philip. *A Fierce Green Fire: The American Environmental Movement*. Rev. ed. Island Press, 2003.

Young, John. *Sustaining the Earth: The Story of the Environmental Movement—Its Past Efforts and Future Challenges*. Harvard University Press, 1990.

■ Antinuclear movement

FIELDS OF STUDY: Ethics, Advocacy, Policy, Protest; Ecology, Environment, Environmentalism; Public Policy, Debates, Controversies; Energy and Energy Resources; Nuclear Power, Nuclear Weapons, Radioactive Waste.

IDENTIFICATION: Social movement comprising a loose collection of organizations and individuals opposed to nuclear weapons and nuclear power

The antinuclear movement, which emerged during the 1950's and gained momentum during the 1960's, initially focused its attention on the proliferation of nuclear weapons and the threat of nuclear warfare. It later broadened its scope to include opposition to nuclear power plants and nuclear waste facilities. Antinuclear activists have had some success in raising public awareness of the dangers of nuclear proliferation and in using safety regulations and environmental law to slow the development of nuclear power, particularly in the United States.

Antinuclear activists generally believe that if nuclear weapons are available, these weapons will eventually be used; they therefore seek to rid the earth of all such armaments. By organizing seminars, rallies, protests, and public outreach campaigns, activists seek to stimulate public debate on issues previously left to insiders, and they help shape the political climate. For example, activists from the environmental organization Greenpeace drew international attention to French resumption of nuclear weapons testing in 1995. The outrage that this publicity fueled may have contributed to the French government's decision to conduct fewer tests than planned.

Antinuclear activists have often been successful in capturing favorable media coverage and mobilizing hundreds of thousands of citizens to protests. However, translating this success into practical results has often proved elusive. At a conference on abolishing nuclear weapons held at Boston College in October 1997, American Friends Service Committee staffer David McCauley offered a possible explanation. He suggested that the movement is fundamentally anarchistic and that distrust of people in power stifles activists' ability to cooperate with established political practices.

Nuclear Freeze and Disarmament Goals

In the multilateral Nuclear Non-Proliferation Treaty (NNPT), which was signed in 1968 entered into force in 1970, five recognized nuclear-weapons states—the United States, the United Kingdom, France, China, and the Soviet Union—agreed not to transfer nuclear weapons to states without such weapons. With the treaty, signatory nations committed to work toward nuclear disarmament, yet the arms race continued. Antinuclear activists claimed that arms negotiators were allowing themselves to be defeated by complexities and suggested a mutual and verifiable freeze by the United States and the Soviet Union on the testing, production, and deployment of all nuclear weapons. The campaign attracted sympathetic media coverage and gained momentum, so that by the late 1970s hundreds of thousands of people were attending massive rallies in the United States and Europe to protest the planned deployment of the ground-launched cruise missile (GLCM) and the Pershing II missile.

Leaders of the North Atlantic Treaty Organization (NATO), however, dared not ignore the complexities inherent in nuclear negotiations. In 1976 the Soviet Union began updating its forces by deploying

Against Nuclear Movement

SS-20 missiles. NATO viewed this as a destabilization of the balance of power because the SS-20s were mobile, more accurate, equipped with three warheads each, and able to fly 1,500 to 3,000 kilometers (930 to 1,860 miles) farther than the missiles they replaced. After all attempts at diplomatic negotiations with the Soviets failed, NATO responded in 1983 by deploying Pershing IIs and GLCMs, which were more accurate than the SS-20s but had less than one-half their range.

NATO and the Soviet Union eventually agreed to intrusive, on-site verification procedures. In late 1987, the two nations signed the Intermediate-Range Nuclear Forces Treaty, which completely eliminated an entire class of weapons: SS-20s, Pershing IIs, GLCMs, and all other ground-launched nuclear missiles with ranges between 500 and 5,500 kilometers (310 and 3,420 miles), along with their launchers, support facilities, and bases. The treaty also banned flight testing and production of these missiles. The antinuclear movement deserves credit for helping educate the public and adding to the pressure that pushed politicians to the bargaining table. However, based on history, it seems unlikely that the treaty would have come about had NATO not deployed its own weapons.

In 1995, the year the NNPT was extended indefinitely, an antinuclear initiative called Abolition 2000 was proposed. Within a few years, more than twelve hundred nongovernmental organizations on six continents had voiced support for it; by 2010 it had grown to a network of more than two thousand organizations in more than ninety countries. Abolition 2000 called for movement toward "clean, safe, renewable forms of energy production that do not provide the materials for weapons of mass destruction and do not poison the environment for thousands of centuries." It also called for negotiations on a nuclear weapons abolition convention that would establish a timetable for phasing out all nuclear weapons and include provisions for effective verification and enforcement.

At its 2003 annual meeting, Abolition 2000 launched a collaborative effort with Mayors for Peace, an international program established in 1982 in which the heads of city governments around the globe work to encourage city-by-city support of the abolition of nuclear weapons. By August 6, 2010 (on the sixty-fifth anniversary of the first use of the atomic bomb), 4,069 cities in 144 countries and regions around the world had become members of the Conference of Mayors for Peace and were calling for complete nuclear disarmament by 2020. Other Abolition 2000 projects have included an Economic Dimensions of Nuclearism working group established in 2012, the Peace and Planet organizational network founded in 2014, and the Missiles and Space program begun in 2016 to model regulation of missile systems and prevent space-based nuclear weapons.

Nuclear Power in the United States

Many members of the antinuclear movement are also against the development and expansion of nuclear power generation. They believe that nuclear technology is too dangerous and see reactor accidents caused by natural disasters, equipment failures, or human errors as inevitable. They do not believe that radioactive waste can be safely disposed of, and they see such waste as an unfair burden to pass on to future generations. Furthermore, many argue that terrorists or nations without their own nuclear arsenals could divert reactor materials to make nuclear weapons.

During the 1960s the antinuclear movement became concerned with the possible effects of low-level radiation from nuclear power plants. Scientists are divided as to whether low levels of radiation can cause increased incidence of cancer in communities located near nuclear power plants; whereas some studies point to significant risk, others report considerable evidence that the human body is able to repair damage caused by sufficiently low levels of radiation.

The antinuclear movement has been somewhat successful in using safety regulations and environmental law to effect change. By lobbying for stricter regulations and suing to force nuclear plants to follow safety regulations that they previously had been allowed to bypass, activists have contributed to making nuclear plants safer. These actions have also added to the costs of nuclear power plants and to delays in plant licensing. Using the courts to delay construction of nuclear plants has been a powerful tool for the movement. In 1967 construction time for a nuclear power plant in the United States averaged 5.5 years; by 1980 it had reached 12 years.

The price of electricity from nuclear plants has increased over time with lengthening construction time, the addition of safety features, and the tendency of nuclear power companies to try new designs instead of settling on a standard design. In 1976 the price of electricity from coal-fired and nuclear plants was nearly the same, but by 1990 nuclear power was twice as expensive as coal power in the United States. One goal of the antinuclear movement was reached in the United States: with economics against them, as well as public opinion after the Three Mile Island incident in 1979, planners ceased construction of new nuclear power plants for years.

The US Nuclear Regulatory Commission (NRC) eventually combined the construction and operating licensing procedures to minimize delays. Also, the industry significantly reduced operating costs. These factors, combined with mounting concerns about the finite nature of fossil-fuel supplies and the potential of the burning of such fuels to affect global climate, made nuclear power a more attractive prospect by the early twenty-first century. Some previously antinuclear environmentalists reconsidered their stance on nuclear power and came out in favor of it as an alternative to fuels that produce greenhouse gas emissions. However, even after a wave of new nuclear plant projects was announced in the 2010s, factors such as the declining price of natural gas and concerns following the 2011 Fukushima nuclear disaster in Japan conspired to see several projects abandoned and others delayed.

Nuclear Power in Asia and Europe

According to the International Atomic Energy Agency (IAEA), the nuclear share of electricity generation in 2016 was 19.7 percent of the electricity in the United States, 13.1 percent in Germany, 40.0 percent in Sweden, and 72.3 percent in France. Countries that must import much of their fuel find nuclear power particularly attractive.

Antinuclear sentiment led Sweden to announce a phaseout of nuclear power beginning in 1998. The shutdown was delayed, however, for several reasons, including lack of replacement power, fears by workers and industry that the shutdown would lead to higher energy prices and exacerbate unemployment, and a lawsuit by a nuclear plant's owners seeking indemnification. In 2009, citing climate concerns, the Swedish government officially abolished its phaseout scheme. Some 52 percent of the Swedes who responded to a 2010 survey favored keeping nuclear power and replacing old reactors with new ones.

As part of the price of forming a ruling coalition with Germany's Social Democratic Party, the environmentalist Green Party extracted a promise that Germany's nuclear power reactors would eventually be eliminated. Shutdown plans were made official in 2002. Germany's government faced problems similar to Sweden's in trying to phase out nuclear power and felt additional pronuclear pressure from England and France, which held contracts worth $6.5 billion to reprocess German nuclear fuel. By 2008 concerns about power availability, costs, and carbon dioxide emission reduction goals had prompted Germany to explore how to keep its existing nuclear power plants online, even as thousands of protesters turned out in opposition to the shipment of nuclear reactor waste from France to a German storage site in Gorleben. Major antinuclear protests were held in Germany in 2011 following the Fukushima incident, helping to prompt the government that it would fully phase out nuclear power by 2022.

As a significant generator of nuclear power, Japan historically saw less of a dedicated antinuclear movement than the United States or Europe from the 1950s through the 1980s. Several power plant accidents and scandals in the 1990s and early 2000s began to bring more public debate over the issue, however. The 2011 Fukushima disaster saw the Japanese antinuclear movement develop considerably, with major protests and marches occurring throughout the country. In 2012 the Japanese government responded to public pressure by announcing it would phase out nuclear power by the 2030s, focusing instead on green renewable resources such as solar and wind power. However, this course was reversed again when the administration of Japanese prime minister Shinzo Abe took up support of nuclear power.

Scientific Groups

A few scientific groups have been especially influential in the area of nuclear arms control. Many scientists who developed the atomic bomb were against leaving decisions about its uses to a few elite government and military officials. Immediately after World War II, some of them formed the Atomic Scientists of Chicago and began publication of the *Bulletin of the Atomic Scientists*. Another group formed the Federation of Atomic Scientists. The efforts of these scientists contributed to the founding in 1946 of the Atomic Energy Commission, a civilian agency that took control of the materials, facilities, production, research, and information relating to nuclear fission from the military.

In response to the escalating arms race, in 1955 the physicist Albert Einstein and the philosopher, mathematician, and social critic Bertrand Russell published a manifesto in which they called upon scientists to assemble and appraise the perils of nuclear weapons. Cyrus Eaton, a wealthy industrialist and admirer of Russell, invited twenty-two scientists from both sides of the Iron Curtain to a conference in July 1957 that was held in Eaton's summer home in the small village of Pugwash, Nova Scotia. The scientists were able to function as icebreakers between governments; in fact, some were government advisers. More Pugwash conferences followed, providing invaluable contacts, networks, and facts for those involved in arms control. The antinuclear movement in general and scientific organizations in particular were instrumental in bringing about several treaties, including the Limited Test Ban Treaty of 1963, in which signatory nations agreed to end aboveground nuclear testing.

The Union of Concerned Scientists (UCS) was formed in 1969 by faculty and students at the Massachusetts Institute of Technology who felt that too much emphasis was being placed on research with military applications and not enough on research that could address environmental and social concerns. The UCS subsequently grew to become a coalition of scientists and citizens across the United States and expanded its focus to include renewable energy and other environmental issues. The UCS combated the establishment of an antiballistic missile defense system in the United States and played a key role in defeating a scheme to rotate two hundred MX missiles among 4,600 protective silos. The plan would have cost $37 billion and would have swallowed vast tracts of the western desert of the United States.

The UCS has also waged campaigns calling for US support of the 1996 Comprehensive Nuclear-Test-Ban Treaty, which prohibits all nuclear explosions (the United States signed the treaty in 1996 but has not ratified it). The UCS has worked in support of other nuclear disarmament treaties as well, including a series of agreements between the United States and the Soviet Union (later the Russian Federation) limiting the number of nuclear warheads and delivery vehicles that these nations may deploy: the 1991 Strategic Arms Reduction Treaty (START), the 2002 Strategic Offensive Reductions Treaty (SORT), and the 2010 New START.

Alternative Energy Sources

One of the great challenges facing the antinuclear movement is that of finding alternative sources of energy. Many nonnuclear power plants have serious environmental effects of their own. By some estimates, cardiopulmonary illness linked to air pollution accounts for tens of thousands of deaths in the United States each year. Power plants are major contributors to such pollution, with older, coal-fired plants being among the worst offenders. Burning coal not only produces copious amounts of carbon dioxide but also releases particulates, sulfur compounds, lead, arsenic, mercury, naturally occurring radioactive elements, and other harmful elements. Pollution-control equipment increases the construction and operating costs of new coal-fired plants. Further, running this equipment expends energy, and the equipment can only reduce pollution, not eliminate it. Many segments of the antinuclear movement actively support the development of alternative energy sources, such as solar, geothermal, wind, and biomass power.

Charles W. Rogers;
Updated by Karen N. Kähler

Further Reading

Bodansky, David. *Nuclear Energy: Principles, Practices, and Prospects.* 2nd ed. Springer, 2004.

Coburn, Jon. "How Anti-Nuclear Movements Can Really Make a Difference." *The Conversation*, 10 Feb. 2017, theconversation.com/how-anti-nuclear-movements-can-really-make-a-difference-71959. Accessed 27 Mar. 2018.

Cooke, Stephanie. *In Mortal Hands: A Cautionary History of the Nuclear Age.* Bloomsbury, 2009.

Cortright, David, and Raimo Väyrynen. *Towards Nuclear Zero.* Routledge, 2010.

Evangelista, Matthew. *Unarmed Forces: The Transnational Movement to End the Cold War.* 1999. Reprint. Cornell University Press, 2002.

Giugni, Marco. *Social Protest and Policy Change: Ecology, Antinuclear, and Peace Movements in Comparative Perspective.* Rowman & Littlefield, 2004.

Gusterson, Hugh. *Nuclear Rites: A Weapons Laboratory at the End of the Cold War.* University of California Press, 1996.

"Nuclear Share of Electricity Generation in 2016." *International Atomic Energy Agency*, 26 Mar. 2018, www.iaea.org/PRIS/WorldStatistics/NuclearShareofElectricityGeneration.aspx. Accessed 27 Mar. 2018.

Peterson, Christian. *Ronald Reagan and Antinuclear Movements in the United States and Western Europe, 1981–1987*. Edwin Mellen Press, 2003.

Plumer, Brad. "The Rise and Fall of Nuclear Power, in 6 Charts." *Vox*. Vox Media, 1 Aug. 2014. Web. 15 Jan. 2015.

Price, Jerome. *The Antinuclear Movement*. Rev. ed. Twayne Publishers, 1990.

Wittner, Lawrence S. *Confronting the Bomb: A Short History of the World Nuclear Disarmament Movement*. Stanford University Press, 2009.

Wittner, Lawrence S. *Toward Nuclear Abolition: A History of the World Nuclear Disarmament Movement, 1971 to the Present*. Stanford University Press, 2003.

■ Antiquities Act

FIELDS OF STUDY: Government, Politics, International Relations; Laws, Acts, Resolutions; Parks, Monuments, Reserves.

CATEGORIES: Treaties, laws, and court cases; preservation and wilderness issues

THE LAW: U.S. federal law empowering the president to set aside as national monuments public lands deemed to be of historic or scientific importance

DATE: Enacted on June 8, 1906

The Antiquities Act was one of the earliest pieces of U.S. federal legislation aimed at historic and cultural preservation. Since passage of the act, U.S. presidents have used it more than one hundred times to protect natural phenomena as well as human-built sites of cultural interest.

The original impetus for the Antiquities Act of 1906 was public reaction to the widespread looting of prehistoric Native American ruins in the Southwest during the late nineteenth century. One of the individuals seeking some form of federal protection for these sites was anthropologist Edgar Lee Hewett, and Congressman John F. Lacey, a Republican from Iowa, joined in the effort during the early part of the century. President Theodore Roosevelt signed the resulting legislation into law in June of 1906, and three

months later he used the act for the first time to establish the Devils Tower National Monument in Wyoming.

All subsequent U.S. presidents have exercised the powers given them by the law to establish a wide variety of protected sites, from natural phenomena such as the Grand Canyon in Arizona and the Muir Woods in California to historic sites such as the Statue of Liberty and the birthplace of George Washington. The environmental significance of the act was expanded during the presidency of Jimmy Carter when it was used (in 1978) to establish a series of fifteen national monuments preserving a total of 22.7 million hectares (56 million acres) of wilderness land in Alaska, protecting the land from oil drilling and other forms of commercial development.

Nader N. Chokr

See also: Carter, Jimmy; Grand Canyon; National parks; Preservation; Roosevelt, Theodore; Wilderness areas; Wildlife refuges.

■ Appropriate technology (AT) movement

FIELDS OF STUDY: Technology and Applied Science; Ethics, Advocacy, Policy, Protest; Ecology, Environment, Environmentalism.

IDENTIFICATION: Technology that is developed with the needs of the intended users and potential impacts on the environment taken into account

The rise of the appropriate technology movement during the 1970's was a response to a growing appreciation of the idea that the people most qualified to find technological solutions to their societies' needs are the people who live in the societies and understand how various technologies will affect their environment.

The beginning of what would become the appropriate technology (AT) movement is commonly credited to Mohandas Gandhi, who helped lead India to independence from Great Britain during the 1930's and 1940's. Gandhi advocated the use of small, local, and mostly community-based technological solutions as a way to help people become self-reliant and independent. He rejected the common belief that modern, industrialized technological development

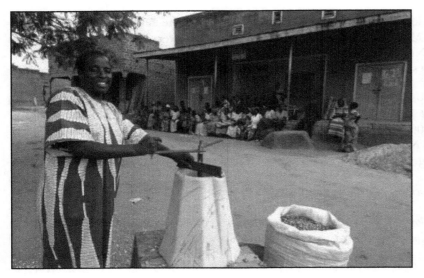

always amounts to progress. Instead, he thought that technology is best produced in a decentralized manner and best used in ways that benefit the people as much as possible. Gandhi believed in a radical revolution of production; he rejected the factory model of industrialization, which values the product and production over the individual worker.

Intermediate Technology

Gandhi's ideas had a great influence on E. F. Schumacher, who is best known for his 1973 book *Small Is Beautiful: Economics As If People Mattered* and for coining the phrase "intermediate technology" (IT) and later creating the Intermediate Technology Development Group (ITDG). Intermediate technologies, in Schumacher's usage, are technologies and tools that are more effective and expensive than traditional or indigenous methods and techniques but ultimately much cheaper than technologies of the developed world. Intermediate technologies, whether hard or soft, can presumably be acquired and used by poor people and can lead to increased productivity with minimal social and environmental costs. They are usually labor-intensive, rather than capital-intensive, and make use of local skills and materials. They are conducive to decentralization and empowerment of the people, compatible with ecological considerations, and better able to serve the interests of the poor than more advanced technologies. More important, they do not contribute to making the people who use them dependent and

subservient to machines over which they have no control.

Schumacher's formulation of an alternative approach came at a time of world energy crisis and a time of growing disenchantment with the broad social, political, and ecological implications of advanced technology; in particular, awareness was growing of the undesirable consequences of the wholesale transfer of such technologies to the less developed countries (LDCs). This may explain why, despite its problematic nature, it had a very substantial impact on the thinking of administrators and planners within aid agencies, as well as officials within the LDCs themselves. Later years witnessed a rapid expansion in the scale and scope of activities undertaken by ITDG (which in 2005 was renamed Practical Action) and the creation of similar organizations in many parts of the world.

Beginnings of AT

Around the time that Schumacher's concept of intermediate technology was catching on, the closely related concept of appropriate technology became enshrined in the operating principles of such agencies as the United Nations Environment Programme and the United Nations Industrial Development Organization, as well as other development organizations. The AT movement had taken off.

The concept of AT is not solely applicable to the nonmodern (as opposed to the modern) sectors of LDCs. In the developed countries, technological and engineering solutions that have minimal impacts on the environment and society are referred to as AT as well, in the sense that they are considered to be sustainable. Although Schumacher's proposal had an unquestionable impact, critics have been keen to point out that his construal of IT or AT excludes from consideration a whole range of issues relating to the interplay of political, social, and economic factors with technology. They have objected to his characterization of the dual economies of LDCs, in which the modern and nonmodern sectors are regarded as separate entities, such that activities designed to alleviate poverty in the latter are unaffected by the nature of the former, or of the forces giving rise to an apparently dual economy in the first place. Some observers have also questioned the underlying conception of technology at work in Schumacher's proposal, namely, that technology can somehow be regarded as a wholly independent variable in the development process, determining social, economic, and political relations, but in no sense being determined by them.

Some have even undermined Schumacher's position by turning it against itself. If the choice of industry is governed, according to Schumacher, by powerful forces that include entrepreneurial interests, why is it that these forces cease to operate somehow when the question of technology arises? Clearly, they cannot. By assuming otherwise, Schumacher is led into the contradictory position of arguing that radical social change in the form of alleviation of mass poverty in the LDCs can, by implication, be brought about without prior change or alteration of other elements in the political, economic, and social contexts within which it arises.

Resolving Contradictions

Despite efforts made over the years to reformulate Schumacher's view, proponents of AT have never really managed to escape fully from the contradiction of his original argument. The problem is both determined by and reflected in the way in which the concept of AT has taken over from its intermediate predecessor, assuming in the process a rather rigid set of connotations. It is difficult to locate the precise point in time at which AT replaced IT, and some would even argue that a valid distinction can still be drawn between the concepts. In general usage, however, the two terms have come to be virtually interchangeable, and the root of the problem may be traceable back to Schumacher himself and the clear impression he gives that IT is *the* appropriate solution for LDCs to pursue.

All these problems notwithstanding, some observers have argued, a renewed and strengthened effort can and must be made to reconceptualize the notion of appropriate, progressive, and sustainable technology and set it on new foundations. Proponents of this view assert that, given the morally outrageous and avoidable poverty plaguing the world, not to mention the dwindling supplies of some natural resources and the looming ecological catastrophe caused by runaway industrialization and technological explosion, such a task is a moral imperative. They argue that greater attention needs to be paid to questions of how technology is created, adapted, and modified in specific physical, social, cultural, political, and economic contexts, and by whom.

Scott Wright

Further Reading

Darrow, Ken, and Mike Saxenian. *Appropriate Technology Sourcebook: A Guide to Practical Books for Village and Small Community Technology.* Rev. ed. Appropriate Technology Project, Volunteers in Asia Press, 1993.

Howes, Michael. "Appropriate Technology: A Critical Evaluation of the Concept and the Movement." *Development and Change* 10 (1979): 115-124.

Jequier, Nicholas. *Appropriate Technology: Problems and Promises.* Paris: OECD, 1976.

Schumacher, E. F. *Small Is Beautiful: Economics As If People Mattered.* 1973. Reprint. Hartley & Marks, 1999.

■ Aquaculture

FIELDS OF STUDY: Biology, Life Sciences, Ecosystems; Agriculture, Farming, Animal Husbandry; Animals, Zoology, Marine Biology; Ecology, Environment, Environmentalism; Food, Hunger.

IDENTIFICATION: Production of marine and freshwater food sources in controlled, farmlike environments in ponds, canals, lakes, and confined coastal areas

Although aquaculture provides a good source of protein for the demands of a growing world population, as well as an economic endeavor for some, like many forms of farming it is not without its negative environmental impacts. Residues from fish wastes, pollution, coastal erosion, and impacts on adjacent species are some of the challenges to sustainable forms of aquaculture.

Aquaculture is one of the fastest-growing forms of food production in the world. It includes the processes of propagating, raising, and processing marine and freshwater food sources such as fish, shellfish, and even kelp. In some cases by-products of the production of these commodities produce fertilizers and feeds for other animals. Ornamental products such

U.S. Aquaculture Production, 2006

	THOUSANDS OF POUNDS	METRIC TONS	THOUSANDS OF DOLLARS
Finfish			
Baitfish	—	—	38,018
Catfish	566,131	256,795	498,820
Salmon	20,726	9,401	37,439
Striped bass	11,925	5,409	30,063
Tilapia	18,738	8,500	32,263
Trout	61,534	27,912	67,745
Shellfish			
Clams	12,564	5,699	72,783
Crawfish	80,000	36,288	96,000
Mussels	962	436	4,990
Oysters	13,711	6,219	92,602
Shrimp	8,037	3,646	18,684
Miscellaneous	—	—	254,738
Totals	**794,328**	**360,305**	**1,244,145**

Source: Data from the National Oceanic and Atmospheric Administration, National Marine Fisheries Association.

Note: Miscellaneous includes ornamental and tropical fish, alligators, algae, aquatic plants, eels, scallops, crabs, and others.

as cultured pearls are also produced within aquacultural systems.

The practice of aquaculture is not new. Fish farming has been a part of the cultures of Pacific islanders and Southeast Asian peoples for centuries. Early forms of aquaculture were quite rudimentary compared with modern techniques, however; they provided foods and other products on a limited scale, mostly for local villages. In the twenty-first century, sophisticated aquaculture systems control the complete life cycles of the fish and other animals under cultivation. In many of these modern facilities, automated feeding and harvesting systems alleviate the need for labor-intensive practices, reducing the costs of production. In some cases, however, because of the nature of the commodities, intensive human labor is still required. Oysters, for example, are

harvested from beds and then must be opened by hand, a process known as shucking, so that the integrity of the shells is maintained for the seeding of a future crop.

One of the elements that has spurred the development of aquaculture is the decline in production in fisheries in the open oceans owing to overfishing. According to the United Nations Food and Agriculture Organization (FAO), all major fishing regions in the world are now being fished intensely. The needs of the growing world population for protein and water pollution affecting natural sources of seafoods have also contributed to the growth of aquaculture.

Industry Growth

Commercial aquaculture ventures have been established in nations throughout the world. The majority of these operations utilize naturally existing water sources in coastal regions, canals, or rivers; others are built at sites where traditional agriculture could not take place. An ideal aquaculture site has certain conditions that are favorable to the healthful management of the stocks of fish and other animals produced. These include clean water, appropriate water temperatures and levels of dissolved gases, good site topography, and food sources.

In the United States aquaculture operations are found in coastal regions and in dry interior areas, where ponds or rivers are used. Clams and oysters are harvested from beds in the marine environment of Washington State's Puget Sound, for example, while in the eastern interior of the state, the Columbia River provides a freshwater source for the raising of salmon, trout, and steelhead, all for commercial uses. In dry west Texas, gravel pits filled with saline waters were some of the first ponds used to cultivate shrimp, an industry that now supplies millions of pounds annually from ponds filled with natural saline water. The state of Virginia has developed a large aquaculture industry, growing clams and oysters in hatcheries.

Crawfish, tilapia, trout, shrimp, cod, clams, oysters, frogs, and catfish are just some of the products found in aquacultural operations in the United

States. According to the U.S. National Oceanic and Atmospheric Administration, shellfish account for two-thirds of the total output of the U.S. aquaculture industry; salmon accounts for 25 percent, and shrimp for about 10 percent. Catfish is one of the most popular farmed fish in the United States.

The monetary value of worldwide aquaculture production is some $70 billion per year. FAO has estimated that almost half of the fish eaten in the world, nearly 45 billon tons of fish, is produced in aquacultural environments rather than caught in the open seas. According to FAO, the top ten aquaculture-producing nations are, in descending order, China, India, Vietnam, Thailand, Indonesia, Bangladesh, Japan, Chile, Norway, and the United States. Even with its tenth-place ranking, the U.S. aquaculture industry contributes about $1 billion annually to the nation's domestic economy.

Environmental Concerns

Aquaculture operations have a number of negative environmental impacts. Among these is that they generally require the installation of a considerable amount of technology, and thus disturb existing habitats, and they use large amounts of energy. Feed must be supplied to penned fish, and waste from the fish must somehow be managed. Diseases must be controlled, not only within the fish and other seafood stocks but also with respect to the possible spread of disease to adjacent native fish and other organisms outside the aquaculture pens or ponds. A particularly controversial element of aquaculture involves the genetic modification of many forms of fish stocks to enhance their ability to grow quickly under confined conditions. Critics of these practices question the safety of eating such fish and have also voiced concerns that if genetically modified species escape their aquaculture pens they may introduce unforeseeable problems into natural fish populations.

In many aquacultural settings, self-contained ecosystems are set up to supply nutrients for fish stocks. In some cases sewage and even commercial fertilizers have been used in such ecosystems to stimulate the production of phytoplankton, which in turn is eaten by zooplankton and bottom dwellers. These are then eaten by fish stocks within the pen or pond. Unless a consistent flow of water can be maintained through the pen area where the fish stock is raised, the bottom can become silted up with waste. In confined

estuaries this condition can have negative effects on fish outside the aquacultural operation. It has been suggested that the decay of fecal matter at the bottom of aquaculture pens and in areas where concentrated fish-rearing operations are conducted can contribute to the depletion of oxygen levels in the water near the bottom. This is especially the case if water currents are not efficient enough to purge the buildup of waste at the bottoms of these ponds and pens.

Shrimp, a major commodity from aquaculture, is a good example of some other environmental concerns. Aquaculture operations sometimes use antibiotics to control the diseases that shrimp are prone to acquire when they are being raised in confined areas. During the early part of 2000, the European Union banned shipments of shrimp containing chloramphenicol, an antibiotic used on shrimp that has been found to be dangerous for human health. In addition, fishing communities and coastal residents have been critical of shrimp aquaculture, asserting that it reduces fish catches because it has negative impacts on coastal habitats and because it uses wild fish as food for the shrimp being raised.

Additional concerns about the negative environmental impacts of aquaculture have to do with the use of pesticides and other chemicals in the management of unwanted organisms in aquacultural waters. To control infestations of fish lice, for example, aquaculture operations often disperse pesticides into the water. Other chemicals are often used to cut down on algae growth on the nets and floats used in pen operations.

Within food webs or trophic levels, energy flows from lower to higher levels. If a larger fish eats a smaller fish, not all of the energy available from the smaller fish is passed on to the larger. This transference of energy is known as ecological efficiency. Aquaculture can exhibit very low levels of ecological efficiency. For example, farm-raised salmon are reared on food made from other fish, which are caught and ground up before being fed to the salmon as pellets or in meal form. It has been estimated that it takes 10 grams (0.35 ounce) of feed to produce 1 gram (0.035 ounce) of salmon. Considering the pressure already existing on wild fish stocks, it has been argued that this low level of ecological efficiency is a considerable detriment for the economy of aquaculture. In contrast, some kinds of aquaculture operations, such as catfish farms, are relatively ecologically efficient, and catfish, which are herbivorous, require no fish-based foods.

Aquaculture operations are also sometimes negatively affected by environmental conditions that come from outside their confines. Along coastlines and in low-lying areas, for example, pollution from agricultural irrigation runoff can cause fish kills such as those that have taken place in aquaculture installations in Indonesia, Malaysia, and the Philippines. Washington State enacted a law to control the flow of manure effluent from dairy farms into the Nooksack River. Prior to the control of this pollution, coastal clam beds managed by the Lummi Nation were decimated; this aquacultural operation recovered after passage of the law.

M. Marian Mustoe

Further Reading

Jahncke, Michael L., et al., eds. *Public, Animal, and Environmental Aquaculture Health Issues.* John Wiley & Sons, 2002.

Mathias, Jack A., Anthony T. Charles, and Hu Baotong, eds. *Integrated Fish Farming.* CRC Press 1997.

Miller, G. Tyler, Jr., and Scott Spoolman. "Food, Soil, and Pest Management." In *Living in the Environment: Principles, Connections, and Solutions.* 16th ed. Brooks/Cole, 2009.

Pilay, T. V. R., and M. N. Kutty. *Aquaculture: Principles and Practices.* 2nd ed. Blackwell, 2005.

Stickney, Robert R. *Aquaculture: An Introductory Text.* 2nd ed. CABI, 2009.

■ Aquaponics

FIELDS OF STUDY: Technology and Applied Science; Biology, Life Sciences, Ecosystems; Agriculture, Farming, Animal Husbandry.

IDENTIFICATION: Combination of aquaculture and hydroponics that employs engineered aquatic ecosystems to grow edible plants and animals

Aquaponics is a method of food production that has few of the negative impacts on the environment seen with traditional agriculture. Aquaponics can efficiently produce food for local consumption without the use of pesticides or fertilizers, without degrading soils, and without altering land use on a major scale.

The production of food to meet the needs of the world's rapidly growing population has many effects on the environment. More than 35 percent of ice-free land is used to grow food for human consumption, and agricultural practices account for over 70 percent of water use, 30 percent of global warming potential, 85 percent of the six million tons of pesticides used annually, and nearly all of the 170 million tons of nitrogen, 50 million tons of phosphate, and 50 million tons of potash used annually. It has been estimated that in the United States, food travels about 3,219 kilometers (2,000 miles) before it reaches the consumer's plate, and about half of the food produced gets discarded before it can be consumed. High-production agricultural practices contribute to habitat loss and degradation, water pollution, salinization of soils, and the overdrawing of groundwater. Aquaponics, in contrast, is a technology that can efficiently produce food for local consumption without the use of pesticides or fertilizers, without degrading soils, and without altering land use on a major scale.

Aquaponics combines the time-tested practices of aquatic animal farming (aquaculture) and the growing of plants without soil (hydroponics) in ways that recirculate water and capitalize on the beneficial ecosystem services of both practices. In aquaponic systems, water from the aquaculture subsystem, which contains waste from the animals, is pumped into the hydroponics subsystem, where the nutrient-rich water fertilizes edible vegetation and the vegetation purifies the water, which then flows back to the aquaponics subsystem.

All aquaponic systems include basic components such as tanks, pumps, and vegetable beds, but the design configurations of these components are limited only by the creativity of their makers. Some aquaponic systems are as much art as they are food-generating systems. The materials used to construct aquaponic systems are often salvaged from discarded materials; this tendency to employ recycling further reduces the environmental and economic impacts of aquaponics. For example, aquaponic systems are often built from inexpensive repurposed barrels, tubs, pools, pumps, and plumbing. Whether new or recycled items are used to make aquaponic systems, those operating the systems must take care to ensure that toxins and other harmful substances are not allowed to leach into the systems.

The catfish in this tank feed the plants above, which feed the worms below, and which then feed the catfish. By Ryan Somma

Because aquaponics uses little water and space, it can be a source of food production practically anywhere in the world, even in places where traditional farming is impractical. Aquaponic systems range in size from tabletop 37.8-liter (10-gallon) fish tanks with small beds of vegetables to large industrial greenhouses with tanks holding more than 37.8 kiloliters (10,000 gallons) of water and floating racks of lettuce.

Aquaponics is a central component in the operation of Growing Power, a nonprofit organization headquartered in Milwaukee, Wisconsin, that is dedicated to growing fresh, healthy food with community involvement. Growing Power, which was founded in 1993 by former professional basketball player Will Allen, has farms in Milwaukee and Madison, Wisconsin, as well as Chicago, Illinois. It uses a variety of sustainable agricultural practices, including aquaponics, to grow food year-round in greenhouses. In a 1.2-hectare (3-acre) greenhouse, Growing Power uses aquaponics to raise approximately one million pounds of produce and ten thousand fish every year. Growing Power has demonstrated that food can be grown year-round even in an environment as cold as Milwaukee.

Greg Cronin

Further Reading

"Aquaponics." *United States Department of Agriculture,* n.d. Retrieved from https://www.nal.usda.gov/afsic/aquaponics.

Bridgewood, Les. *Hydroponics: Soilless Gardening Explained.* Marlborough, Crowood Press, 2003.

Dembkowski, Daniel J., Landon L. Pierce, and Craig P. Paukert. "In Response: The Use of Aquaponics in the Classroom." *Fisheries* 39.11 (2014): 530. Print.

Hart, Emily R., James B. Webb, and Andy J. Danylchuk. "Implementation of Aquaponics in Education: An Assessment of Challenges and Solutions." Science Education International 24.4 (2013): 460–80. Print.

Nelson, Rebecca L. "Ten Aquaponic Systems Around the World." *Aquaponics Journal,* no. 46 (2007).

Roberto, Keith. *How-to Hydroponics.* 4th ed. Farmingdale, N.Y.: Futuregarden Press, 2005.

Simpson, Randy. *Aquaponics Gardening for Beginners: Step-by-Step Guide to Getting Started on Raising Fish and Growing Vegetables in an Aquaponic Garden.* CreateSpace, 2014.

Stickney, Robert R. *Aquaculture: An Introductory Text.* 2nd ed. CABI, 2009.

■ Aqueducts

FIELDS OF STUDY: Technology and Applied Science; Architecture, Construction; Engineering, Materials Science; Water Resources.

IDENTIFICATION: Artificial waterways constructed to move water from one area to another

Human beings' redirection of water from one area to another through aqueducts can have numerous environmental effects. Ecosystems on both ends of an aqueduct are influenced by the reduction or increase in available water, and the building of aqueducts often involves the disturbance of what was formerly pristine land.

Sufficient water is an absolute necessity for all forms of life on earth (both plants and animals); this fact dictates that life-forms in areas that receive insufficient precipitation or that are not near lakes or rivers must either migrate to more favored regions to survive or develop techniques to bring water in from more favored areas. Certain xerophytic plants (such

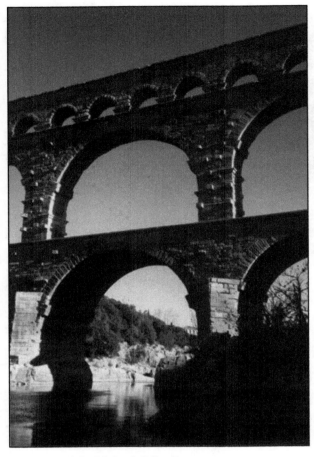

Pont du Gard. By Michael.chlistalla

as cactus) and animals (such as the kangaroo rat and the jackrabbit) manage to survive on minimal amounts of water, but they are exceptions; most species need abundant supplies of water. Over time, human societies have either adopted the migration alternative or developed techniques to import water into drier areas by building conveyance devices. The artificial waterways known as aqueducts date back several thousand years; they have allowed human settlement and agriculture to flourish in several regions.

Ancient Water Delivery Systems

The Minoan civilization, with its capital of Knossus on the Greek island of Crete in the Mediterranean Sea, represents the earliest known record of the development of water-supply infrastructure. Aqueducts were used to bring water into the city about five thousand years ago, until a major earthquake sometime

around 1450 BCE destroyed the region. The next major development in the building of aqueducts occurred circa 1000 BCE, when underground tunnels called *qanats* were used in the Middle East and North Africa to bring water from upland sources to villages and local farms. Modern-day Iran has the largest number of *qanats* in the region (more than twenty-two thousand), with lengths that vary from 40 to 45 kilometers (25 to 28 miles) and depths approaching 122 meters (400 feet).

The ancient Romans were renowned for their extensive system of elevated stone aqueducts beginning about 312 BCE. By 300 BCE, Rome had fourteen major aqueducts in service, bringing to the city about 150 million liters (roughly 40 million gallons) of water per day. Major water-supply systems were also built in those parts of Europe that were within the Roman Empire at that time, including what are now Italy, France, Spain, the Netherlands, and England. In Segovia, Spain, an aqueduct that was presumably built in the first century CE by the Romans is still being used.

In North America in the ninth century CE the Hohokam built canals that were 9-18 meters (30-60 feet) wide to transfer water from the Salt River, near present-day Phoenix, Arizona, to local farms for irrigation. In the tenth century the Anasazi developed a similar type of irrigation scheme in what is now southwest Colorado. During the fifteenth century, the Aztecs used rock aqueducts to supply both drinking water and water for irrigation to the area of present-day Mexico City.

Modern Aqueduct Systems

As might be expected, modern water-delivery systems use some of the same techniques that were used successfully in ancient times. For example, modern systems, like ancient ones, make use of gravity to move water along as much as possible. Increased populations and the accompanying increased demand for water, however, require modern designers of aqueducts to employ additional techniques. Modern aqueducts must often transport water over great distances from the sources to the consuming populations, and conflicts sometimes arise when water is withdrawn from one area to serve another. Electricity or turbines are used to power huge pumps that can move water long distances. In some areas, the use of underground conduits is necessary to avoid interference with street traffic.

In 1825 the completion of the Erie Canal between Buffalo, New York, and New York City encouraged the export of agricultural products from the American Midwest to Europe and led to an increase in population for New York City. Since the Hudson River was too salty to use as a supply source, the city started work on a reservoir and aqueduct in the Croton River watershed in Westchester and Putnam counties. The project was finished in 1842 with a capacity of 341,000 cubic meters (90 million gallons) per day, an amount that the planners thought would be sufficient for a future city population of one million. New York continued to grow, however, necessitating expansion during the early twentieth century into the Catskill and Delaware watersheds and the construction of six new reservoirs and connecting aqueducts. The overall system now serves some nine million people with an average daily consumption of 4.5 million cubic meters (1.2 billion gallons) per day.

In contrast to New York, which receives average annual precipitation of 1,067 millimeters (42 inches), the Los Angeles metropolitan area receives about 381 millimeters (15 inches) of precipitation per year. The first project to bring in outside water to Los Angeles began in 1907 with the construction of an aqueduct 375 kilometers (200 miles) long, from the Owens Valley in east-central California, a project that was met initially with stiff resistance from Owens Valley residents. The next major undertaking for Los Angeles was the Colorado River Aqueduct Project, which was started in 1928 under the sponsorship of thirteen cities in Southern California that formed the Metropolitan Water District (MWD). By 2010 the MWD consisted of twenty-six water districts and cities and was responsible for supplying drinking water to an estimated population of eighteen million, with an average delivery of 7 million cubic meters (1.8 billion gallons) of water per day.

Other major projects to transfer water in arid to semiarid regions of the United States include the Central Arizona Project, which was authorized in 1968 by the U.S. Bureau of Reclamation. Construction started in 1973 to convey water from the Colorado River at Lake Havasu on the Arizona-California border to central and southern Arizona. The delivery system is 540 kilometers (336 miles) long and includes fourteen pumping plants and three tunnels.

This is one prominent instance where huge amounts of power are required to overcome gravity, as the elevations at Lake Havasu, Phoenix, and Tucson are 136 meters (447 feet), 458 meters (1,503 feet), and 875 meters (2,870 feet), respectively.

Robert M. Hordon

Further Reading

Cech, Thomas V. *Principles of Water Resources: History, Development, Management, and Policy.* 3rd ed. John Wiley & Sons, 2010.

Hillel, Daniel. *Rivers of Eden: The Struggle for Water and the Quest for Peace in the Middle East.* Oxford University Press, 1994.

Koeppel, Gerald T. *Water for Gotham: A History.* Princeton University Press, 2000.

Powell, James L. *Dead Pool: Lake Powell, Global Warming, and the Future of Water in the West.* University of California Press, 2008.

Strahler, Alan. *Introducing Physical Geography.* 5th ed. John Wiley & Sons, 2011.

■ Aquifers

FIELDS OF STUDY: Biology, Life Sciences, Ecosystems; Water Resources; Pollution, Emissions, Toxic Waste, Hazardous Materials; Ecology, Environment, Environmentalism; Geology, Geosciences

IDENTIFICATION: Water-bearing geological formations that can store and transmit significant amounts of groundwater to wells and springs

Aquifers are important because groundwater supplies a substantial amount of the water available in many localities. The contamination of aquifers is thus a matter of concern, and so a variety of aquifer restoration techniques have been developed.

All rock layers found on or below Earth's surface can be categorized as either aquifers or confining beds. An aquifer is a rock unit that is sufficiently permeable to allow the transportation of water in usable amounts to a well or spring. (In geologic usage, the term "rock" also includes unconsolidated sediments such as sand, silt, and clay.) A confining bed is a rock unit that has such low hydraulic conductivity (or poor permeability) that it restricts the flow of groundwater into or out of nearby aquifers.

There are two major types of groundwater occurrence in aquifers. The first type includes those aquifers that are only partially filled with water. In those cases, the upper surface (or water table) of the saturated zone rises or declines in response to variations in precipitation, evaporation, and pumping from wells. The water in these formations is then classified as unconfined, and such aquifers are called unconfined or water-table aquifers. The second type occurs when water completely fills an aquifer that is located beneath a confining bed. In this case, the water is classified as confined, and the aquifers are called confined or artesian aquifers. In some fractured rock formations, such as those that occur in the west-central portions of New Jersey and eastern Pennsylvania, local geologic conditions result in semiconfined aquifers, which, as the name indicates, have hydrogeologic characteristics of both unconfined and confined aquifers.

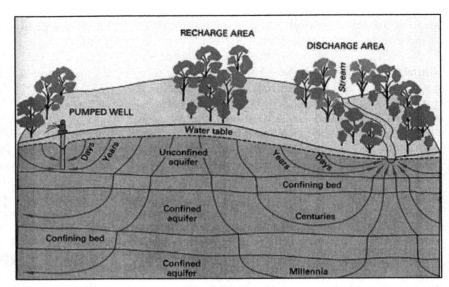

A standard aquifer system, featuring the flow times of different paths. (USGS)

Wells that are drilled into water-table aquifers are simply called water-table wells. The water level in these wells indicates the depth of the water table, which is the top of the saturated zone, below the ground level surface. Wells that are drilled into confined aquifers are called artesian wells. The water level in artesian wells is generally located at a height above the top of the confined aquifer but not necessarily above the land surface. Flowing artesian wells occur when the water level stands above the land surface. The water level in tightly cased wells in artesian aquifers is called the potentiometric surface of the aquifer.

Water flows very slowly in aquifers, from recharge areas in interstream zones at higher elevations along watershed boundaries to discharge areas along streams and adjacent floodplains at lower elevations. Aquifers thus function as pipelines filled with various types of earth material. Darcy's law governing groundwater flow was developed in 1856 by Henry Darcy, a French engineer. In brief, Darcy's law states that the amount of water moving through an aquifer per unit of time is dependent on the hydraulic conductivity (or permeability) of the aquifer, the cross-sectional area (which is at a right angle to the direction of flow), and the hydraulic gradient. The hydraulic conductivity depends on the size and interconnectedness of the pores and fractures in an aquifer. It ranges through an astonishing twelve orders of magnitude. Very few other physical parameters exhibit such a wide range of values. For example, the hydraulic conductivity ranges from an extremely low 10^7 to 10^8 meters per day in unfractured igneous rock such as diabase and basalt to as much as 10^3 to 10^4 meters per day in cavernous limestone and coarse gravel. Typical low-permeability earth materials include unfractured shale, clay, and glacial till. High-permeability earth materials include lava flows, coarse sand, and gravel.

In addition to this wide range of values, hydraulic conductivity varies widely in place and directionality within the same aquifer. Aquifers are isotropic if the hydraulic conductivity is about the same in all directions and anisotropic if the hydraulic conductivity is different in different directions. As a result of all of these factors, groundwater yield is extremely variable both within the same aquifer and from one aquifer to another when they are composed of different rock structures.

Because groundwater flows slowly in comparison with surface water, any contaminant that gets into the groundwater could remain for a long time, perhaps hundreds or thousands of years. It is thus simpler and much more cost-effective to prevent groundwater contamination than it is to try to correct a problem that has been in existence for years.

Restoration of a contaminated aquifer may be accomplished, albeit at a price, through one or more of the following procedures: inground treatment or containment, aboveground treatment, or removal or isolation of the source of contamination. The first approach involves natural treatment based on physical, chemical, or biological means, such as adding nutrients to existing subsurface bacteria to help them break down hazardous organic compounds into nonhazardous materials. The second approach uses engineered systems such as pumping wells or subsurface structures, which create hydraulic gradients that make the contaminated water stay in a specified location, facilitating removal for later treatment. Regardless of the restoration method selected, the source that is continuing to contaminate the aquifer must be removed, isolated, or treated.

Robert M. Hordon

Further Reading

Ahmed, Shakeel, R. Jayakumar, and Abdin Salih. *Groundwater Dynamics in Hard Rock Aquifers: Sustainable Management and Optimal Monitoring Network Design.* Springer, 2008.

Fetter, Charles W. *Applied Hydrogeology.* 4th ed. Prentice Hall, 2001.

Kuo, Jeff. *Practical Design Calculations for Groundwater and Soil Remediation.* CRC Press, 1998.

Nonner, Johannes C. *Introduction to Hydrogeology.* 2nd ed. CRC Press, 2010.

Todd, David K. *Groundwater Hydrology.* 3rd ed. John Wiley & Sons, 2005.

See also: Drinking water; Groundwater pollution; Water pollution; Water quality; Wells.

■ Aral Sea destruction

FIELDS OF STUDY: Places, Peoples, Societies; Disasters; Ecology, Environment, Environmentalism; Health, Medicine, Disease, Illness; Oceans, Seas, Lakes, Bodies of Water; Biology, Life Sciences, Ecosystems; Water Resources.

THE EVENT: The decades-long, human-induced decimation of one of the world's largest freshwater lakes, located in the central Asian republics of Kazakhstan and Uzbekistan

DATE: Begun in the 1950's

Increased diversion of water from Aral Sea by the government of the former Soviet Union, beginning during the 1950's, unleashed a host of drastic social, economic, and environmental changes in the region. Destruction of the Aral Sea is regarded as one of the greatest human-made catastrophes of the twentieth century.

Prior to 1960, the Aral Sea was a freshwater lake, the fourth largest in the world, covering 67,300 square kilometers (26,000 square miles). For thousands of years the Aral was fed by two rivers, the Amu Darya and the Syr Darya, which annually carried fresh water more than 2,400 kilometers (1,500 miles) across largely desert terrain. The Aral has no natural outlet; its water balance was maintained by extremely high losses to evaporation.

During the 1950's the government of the Soviet Union undertook a massive project to greatly increase the amount of land under cultivation for cotton in Central Asia. To accomplish this, the project diverted large amounts of water from the Amu and Syr into irrigation canals. Construction on the largest of these, the 845-kilometer (525-mile) Karakum Canal, was begun in 1954 and completed in 1975. After the development of the canal system, inflow to the Aral dropped dramatically. The deltaic wetlands of both rivers largely disappeared, and the bed of the Amu was left essentially dry where it finally reached the Aral Sea.

During the late 1980's, the depleted lake separated into two bodies of water, the "Small Aral" to the north and the "Large Aral" to the south. By the mid-1990's, as a result of water diversion, the Aral Sea had been reduced in surface area by more than 50 percent and in volume by more than 70 percent (an amount equal to one and one-half times that of Lake Erie). In addition, the water level had dropped by more than 18 meters (60 feet). Towns that were once ports at the water's edge became landlocked many miles from the sea, leaving stranded fishing vessels to rust in the sand. Continuing water loss caused the Large Aral to form separate east and west basins in 2003. By 2007, the Aral Sea was down to 10 percent of

The Shrinking Aral Sea

its original surface area. By 2009, the eastern basin of the Large Aral had largely dried up. What was once lake bed had become the Aralkum—the Aral Desert.

Consequences

The shrinking of the Aral Sea has had a number of serious social, economic, and environmental consequences. The Aral was once the site of a major fishing industry with twenty-four native species of fish. All disappeared, victims of water salinity that had increased to three times greater than that of the oceans. A saltwater species, the Black Sea flounder, was introduced during the 1970's, but by 2003 elevated salinity in the southern lakes had killed it off. The island of Muynak, which once lay within the delta of the Amu Darya, was eventually more than 150 kilometers (93 miles) from the sea. The thriving cannery industry that existed in Muynak persisted for a few years by processing frozen fish imported from the Baltic Sea and the North Atlantic, but with the breakup of the Soviet Union in 1991, other former Soviet republics ceased shipping their fish to Muynak, and the industry died.

The region surrounding the Aral Sea has become the site of one of the world's most dramatic examples of environmentally induced disease. The vast area of exposed former lake bed—54,000 square kilometers

(20,850 square miles) as of April, 2008—is covered with precipitated natural salts. Deposits of toxic substances such as pesticides and fertilizers from agricultural runoff are also found on the lake bed. Each year millions of tons of dust, dried salts, and pollutants are picked up by the winds and carried as massive dust storms. This wind-borne dust has caused high incidences of emphysema, pulmonary tuberculosis, and chronic bronchitis among persons living in the region. Arthritic diseases have increased sixtyfold. Other health problems that have shown dramatic increases in the region are kidney disease, thyroid dysfunction, and throat, intestinal, and liver cancers. The region around the Aral Sea has the highest maternal mortality (120 in every 100,000 mothers) and infant mortality (75 per 1,000 live births) levels in the former Soviet Union. It is estimated that up to 99 percent of the women of the Karakalpakstan region suffer from anemia. Pesticides are found in mothers' milk, and high levels of heavy metals, salts, and pesticides occur in the drinking water.

Vozrozhdeniye Island may constitute an additional health hazard. Formerly a remote location in the center of the lake, the island was the site of a secret bioweapons facility between 1948 and 1992. Pathogens such as anthrax, tularemia, brucellosis, plague, typhus, smallpox, and botulinum toxin were tested there on laboratory animals and livestock. When receding water levels connected the abandoned island base to the mainland in 2001, the possibility of civilian exposure to remaining biohazardous materials increased. A 2002 joint remediation effort between the United States and Uzbekistan decontaminated ten anthrax burial sites and dismantled the abandoned laboratory complex. It is unclear whether viable pathogenic agents remain in Vozrozhdeniye's soil.

Although the diversion of river water for irrigation initially resulted in a tripling of cotton production, the wind-deposited salts from the drying lake have gradually accumulated in the soils, causing a decline in productivity. Cattle have died in large numbers from eating salt-poisoned vegetation. In addition to containing high levels of salt, the soils are waterlogged, the result of poor drainage.

High evaporation rates over the Aral Sea had, in the past, formed a column of humid air that had deflected and diverted the hot, dry desert winds in the summer and the cold Siberian winds in the winter. This no longer occurs. Summer temperatures in the region are hotter and winter temperatures are colder. Both seasons show marked decreases in precipitation, and the summer growing season has shortened. The water evaporated from the Aral no longer falls as precipitation on the mountains to the south, the source of the river water; thus the local hydrologic cycle has been disrupted.

Mitigation Measures

A Soviet plan to restore the Aral Sea with waters from distant Siberian rivers was never carried out because of economic limitations and environmental concerns. With the dissolution of the Soviet Union, the newly independent states of Kazakhstan and Uzbekistan were left to compete for the lake's resources. During the early 1990's, all five of the states that occupy the Aral Sea watershed—Kazakhstan, Uzbekistan, Turkmenistan, Tajikistan, and Kyrgyzstan— agreed to contribute to the improvement of the situation in the Aral Sea basin. As these states had conflicting goals, however, and funding was insufficient, no unified water strategy was developed, and environmental concerns continued to have a lower priority than short-term economic gains.

Kazakhstan attempted a partial restoration of the Small Aral. With funding from the World Bank, the Syr Darya was reengineered to improve the river's flow, and a dam was constructed between the Small and Large Arals. After the dam's completion in 2005, the water level in the Small Aral rose by 2 meters (6.5 feet) over an eight-month period. The lake's salinity was sufficiently reduced to support fish populations, making commercial fishing possible once again. Bird, reptile, and plant species also began to reappear. A sluice in the dam is periodically opened to allow water to flow into the depleted lakes to the south. In addition, the Small Aral restoration has affected the region's microclimate, and rain has become more plentiful.

The Large Aral to the south lies in the poorer republic of Uzbekistan. While groundwater has been found to contribute more to the lake's recharge than was previously believed, the Large Aral would still require more inflow to thrive. Uzbekistan's economy depends heavily on cotton, however, and the republic has been more eager to divert water from the Amu Darya for crop irrigation than for Aral restoration. An international consortium of Uzbek, Russian, Korean, Chinese, and Malaysian interests was formed in 2005 to explore and develop oil and gas fields in the exposed lake bed, a venture that is unlikely to have positive environmental impacts.

Donald J. Thompson;
Updated by Karen N. Kähler

Further Reading

Ellis, William S. "The Aral: A Soviet Sea Lies Dying." *National Geographic*, February, 1990, 73-93.

Ferguson, Robert W. *The Devil and the Disappearing Sea: A True Story About the Aral Sea Catastrophe.* Raincoast Books, 2003.

Glantz, Michael H., ed. *Creeping Environmental Problems and Sustainable Development in the Aral Sea Basin.* Cambridge University Press, 2008.

Hinrichsen, Don. "Requiem for a Dying Sea." *People and the Planet* 4, no. 2 (1995).

Kostianoy, Andrey G., and Aleksey N. Kosarev, eds. *The Aral Sea Environment.* Springer, 2009.

Micklin, Philip P. "Destruction of the Aral Sea." In *Our Changing Planet: The View from Space*, edited by Michael D. King et al. New York: Cambridge University Press, 2007.

Pearce, Fred. *When the Rivers Run Dry: Water, the Defining Crisis of the Twenty-first Century.* Boston: Beacon Press, 2006.

United Nations Environment Programme. *Global*

International Waters Assessment, Regional Assessment 24: Aral Sea. Kalmar, Sweden: University of Kalmar, 2005.

Zonn, Igor S., et al. *The Aral Sea Encyclopedia.* New York: Springer, 2009.

■ Arctic National Wildlife Refuge

FIELDS OF STUDY: Places, Peoples, Societies; Continents, Regions, Areas, Islands; Parks, Monuments, Reserves; Biology, Life Sciences, Ecosystems; Animals, Zoology, Marine Biology; Ecology, Environment, Environmentalism.

CATEGORIES: Places; animals and endangered species

IDENTIFICATION: Large area of land in northeastern Alaska set aside by the U.S. government for the preservation and protection of wildlife

DATES: Established in 1960; expanded in 1980

The Arctic National Wildlife Refuge provides a home for a great many species of marine mammals, birds, and terrestrial animals. Its isolation, biodiversity, and protected status make it an important sanctuary for threatened species such as the polar bear. The possibility that oil exploration could be undertaken in a section of the refuge is a topic of ongoing debate.

Even before Alaska gained statehood in 1959, a movement was under way in the National Park Service and among conservationists to protect a small part of northeastern Alaska permanently from development and commercial interests. The Arctic National Wildlife Range was established as a federally protected area in 1960 by the U.S. secretary of the interior, Fred A. Seaton, in order to preserve the uniqueness of the wilderness and its wildlife. In 1980 passage of the Alaska National Interest Lands Conservation Act(ANILCA) expanded the protected area from less than 3.6 million hectares (9 million acres) to approximately 7.3 million hectares (18 million acres) and renamed it the Alaska National Wildlife Refuge (ANWR).

The remoteness and protected status of the refuge have limited the human impact on the environment there. It provides important habitat for marine life, which includes seals and whales as well as fish and seabirds, and terrestrial animals such as caribou, wolves, and the three North American species of bear. The refuge is home to many animals that flourish during the short Arctic summer, such as a variety of insects, and a safe haven where migratory birds can rest while moving south each year. The refuge has been a subject of controversy since the 1970's, and supporters of the area's protected status have fought off many attempts to open it up to oil and gas development.

Geography and Wildlife

The Arctic National Wildlife Refuge, sometimes called the Arctic Refuge, has greater species diversity than any other protected area in the Arctic Circle. The northern boundary of the refuge is the coastline of the Beaufort Sea and has habitats typical of coastal regions, such as river deltas, barrier islands, and salt marshes. These support wildlife that includes migratory seabirds and varieties of fish; in the summer caribou herds travel there to give birth and raise their young. Also during the summer, in addition to the many insects that thrive there, tens of thousands of migratory birds feed and rest on the coastal plain before traveling south. During the winter months, polar bears create birthing dens and hunt seals on the sea ice that grows along the coast.

Further inland, the coastal habitats give way to a plain, dotted with small lakes and braided rivers, that gradually moves upland to the Brooks Range. The Brooks Range region is made up of the foothills, valleys, and mountains north and south of the mountains and provides habitat for, among others, wolves, ducks, and birds of prey such as falcons and eagles. The region of the refuge on the south side of the Brooks Range consists mainly of the boreal forest characteristic of inland Alaska. Year-round residents of this forest include grizzly bears, lynx, wolverines, and moose; caribou herds spend the winter there, and migratory birds breed there during the spring and summer. On this side of the Brooks Range, the rivers that flow south to the Yukon River, the wetlands of the region, and the forest canopy provide a wide variety of habitats and food for many different species, from fish to mammals to birds.

Protection and Controversy

In 1968 the discovery of oil in Alaska's Prudhoe Bay, which is only sixty miles west of the western border of ANWR, began a political controversy that has not abated. When the Alaska National Interest Lands Conservation Act enlarged the refuge in 1980, it also left open the possibility of oil and gas exploration

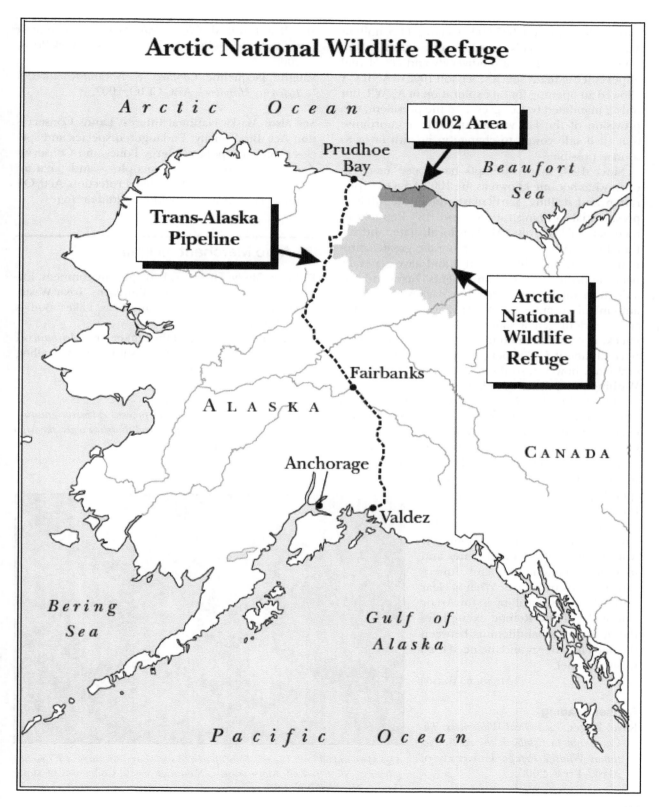

Arctic National Wildlife Refuge

and exploitation on 607,000 hectares (1.5 million acres) of the refuge's coastline and coastal plain, which are areas of great biodiversity and are of vital importance to many species. Section 1002 of ANILCA allowed an opening for oil exploration in ANWR, but only if mandated by Congress and the president; this provision of the law was an unhappy compromise that each side vowed to change in its own favor as soon as possible.

Since 1980 many attempts have been made to open what became known as the 1002 Area to exploration and drilling, particularly under Republican presidential administrations and by Republican members of Congress. Alaskan local, state, and national politicians have been among the greatest proponents of drilling in the refuge and have generally been supported by their constituents. Taxes and royalties from oil drilling in Prudhoe Bay provide a large amount of revenue for Alaska annually, and each state resident gets a share in the form of a yearly check; in 2000 the amount of this payment was reportedly about $1,900 per person. The refuge is federal land, however, so the issue must be decided in Washington, D.C., not in Alaska.

During President George W. Bush's two terms in office, moves to open the refuge to oil drilling occurred repeatedly in the Republican-controlled Congress, at first in specific proposals to allow drilling and then, when that approach failed, through attachments to major bills, such as defense-spending and energy bills, or additions to federal budgets. Whether enough oil actually exists in the 1002 Area to make drilling economically worthwhile to the United States and morally acceptable to many Americans remains unknown. What is clear is that the issue of drilling in the Arctic National Wildlife Refuge exemplifies the modern global dilemma between the need for energy and the need for a healthy planet.

Megan E. Watson

Further Reading

Kaye, Roger. *Last Great Wilderness: The Campaign to Establish the Arctic National Wildlife Refuge.* University of Alaska Press, 2006.

Standlea, David M. *Oil, Globalization, and the War for the Arctic Refuge.* State University of New York Press, 2006.

Vaughn, Jacqueline. *Conflicts over Natural Resources: A Reference Handbook.* ABC-CLIO, 2007.

See also: Alaska National Interest Lands Conservation Act; Biodiversity; Endangered species and species protection policy; Energy Policy and Conservation Act; Indigenous peoples and nature preservation; Marine Mammal Protection Act; Oil drilling; Trans-Alaska Pipeline; Wildlife refuges.

■ Argo Merchant oil spill

Fields of Study: Disasters; Ecology, Environment, Environmentalism; Pollution, Emissions, Toxic Waste, Hazardous Materials; Oceans, Seas, Lakes, Bodies of Water.

The Event: Grounding of the tanker *Argo Merchant* off the coast of Rhode Island, resulting in the spilling of heavy fuel oil into the sea

Date: December 15, 1976

A northwesterly wind helped to prevent extensive environmental damage to the New England shoreline when the Argo Merchant grounded.

Argo Merchant oil spill. The ship broke apart and spilled its entire cargo of 7.7 million gallons of No. 6 fuel oil. Massachusetts, Nantucket Shoals. Collection of Doug Helton, NOAA/NOS/ORR

The *Argo Merchant* was built as the *Arcturus* in Hamburg, Germany, in 1953 and renamed the *Permina Samudia III* in 1968. It was then renamed the *Vari* in 1970 and finally the *Argo Merchant* in 1973. Regardless of the name or the owners, the ship had a long history of accidents. The *Argo Merchant* was not an extremely large vessel. It was 195 meters (641 feet) in length and 25.6 meters (84 feet) wide and had a draft of 10.7 meters (35 feet). It was owned by the Thebes Shipping Company of Greece, was chartered to Texaco, and carried a crew of Greek officers and Filipino crewmen under the Liberian flag.

The vessel departed Puerto la Cruz in Venezuela bound for Salem, Massachusetts, with a cargo of 7.6 million gallons of heavy fuel oil in its thirty cargo tanks. The *Argo Merchant*'s problems began the evening before the grounding, as the onboard gyrocompass had broken, and the officers were unable to determine the ship's position.

At 6:00 A.M. on December 15, 1976, the *Argo Merchant* grounded on the southern end of Fish Rap Shoal in 5.5 meters (18 feet) of water. The ship was 48 kilometers (30 miles) north of the Nantucket lightship station, 24 kilometers (15 miles) outside the normal shipping lanes, and 39 kilometers (24 miles) off its charted track line. When the crew of the *Argo Merchant* called the U.S. Coast Guard to report the grounding, they had no idea of their position; the position they gave turned out to be 48 kilometers (30 miles) from where the tanker was located.

The Coast Guard, however, responded quickly and soon located the grounded vessel. Attempts were made to float the ship and to tow it, but neither method worked. The sea continued to batter the grounded ship, which began to bend and twist on the reef until oil started leaking from the cargo tanks. Within one week the *Argo Merchant* had broken in half and was leaking large amounts of oil. As in the case of the 1967 *Torrey Canyon* oil spill in the English Channel, attempts were made to ignite the oil, but no attempt was made to destroy the oil remaining in the ship's tanks.

Within ten days of the grounding, the oil slick from the *Argo Merchant* extended 160 kilometers (100 miles). Although the weather was rainy and windy, which made oil transfer and salvage operations difficult, the wind blew predominantly from the northwest, and this drove the oil offshore, so that very little oil came ashore in the rich fishing and shellfish areas

along the coast of New England. The northwesterly wind did drive the slick across Georges Bank, which is one of the richest fishing areas in the Atlantic Ocean, but the short-term effects of the windblown oil were marginal, and only a limited number of birds and marine mammals were killed. The long-term effects of the oil spill in the water column and the oil's impact on bottom-dwelling creatures have not been documented.

Robert J. Stewart

Further Reading

Clark, R. B. *Marine Pollution.* 5th ed. Oxford University Press, 2001.

Fingas, Merv. *The Basics of Oil Spill Cleanup.* 2nd ed. CRC Press, 2001.

Wang, Zhendi, and Scott A. Stout. *Oil Spill Environmental Forensics: Fingerprinting and Source Identification.* Academic Press, 2007.

■ Arsenic in water supplies

FIELDS OF STUDY: Chemistry; Elements, Substances, Chemicals, Compounds; Pollution, Emissions, Toxic Waste, Hazardous Materials; Ecology, Environment, Environmentalism; Health, Medicine, Disease, Illness.

IDENTIFICATION: Poisonous, crystalline metallic element

Ubiquitous in nature, arsenic represents a major health threat to human water supplies and foods, especially in the world's poorest countries.

Arsenic is naturally brittle, reactive element and is relatively soluble in water. It is found activated in the environment owing to a combination of natural processes (weathering, biological activity, and volcanic eruptions) and human activities. In some cases arsenic is naturally present in aquifers. It is also associated with geothermal waters, and its presence has been reported in several areas with hot springs. Human beings have played a significant role in increasing the rate of natural mobilization of arsenic through activities such as mining, combustion of fossil fuels, and the use of arsenic in pesticides, herbicides, crop desiccants, and food additives. Industrial effluents add to the environmental availability of arsenic. Even though human use of arsenic has been significantly reduced since the mid-twentieth century, the impacts of arsenic on the environment are likely to continue for some time.

Arsenic is found in various forms and is a major constituent of more than two hundred different minerals. Some of the elements with which arsenic often forms compounds are oxygen, chlorine, tungsten, tin, molybdenum, cadmium, sulphur, lead, silver, iron, and even gold. Arsenic is widely found in ores such as arsenopyrite.

Contamination of drinking water is one of the most significant ways in which arsenic threatens human health. Commonly four types of arsenic compounds exist in water: arsenite and arsenate ions, from inorganic mineral salts of arsenous and arsenic acids, and as methyl arsenic acid and dimethyl arsenic acid, which are organic forms of arsenic acid. The amount of arsenic present in drinking water varies among different local water sources, which include surface water (rivers, lakes, reservoirs, and ponds), groundwater (aquifers), and rainwater. Of these, groundwater contains the highest concentrations.

Long-term exposure to this element results in chronic arsenic poisoning, or arsenicosis. Prolonged exposure to arsenic causes various types of cancer; other common health effects include diabetes mellitus, hypertension, and respiratory diseases. Particularly in the world's poorest nations, people suffering from arsenicosis often withdraw from society, as the disease causes a deformation of the skin that is difficult to differentiate from leprosy. Arsenicosis caused by contaminated drinking water affects the poor more often than it affects the rich.

Because arsenic is carcinogenic, the World Health Organization has set a standard for the amount that is permissible in drinking water that is deemed to be safe. The original standard was 50 micrograms per liter, but the amount was reduced in 1993 to 10 micrograms per liter. In most developing countries that are plagued by the problem of arsenic contamination, however, the higher level is still allowed, in part because of a lack of testing facilities and water purification technologies that can remove the arsenic from drinking water.

Arsenic contamination of water supplies is relatively site-specific and affects a limited number of people who are in proximity to the contaminated water. A number of aquifers across the world have been identified as having arsenic concentrations greater than 50 micrograms per liter; these include aquifers in India, Bangladesh, Taiwan, China, Hungary, Mexico, Chile, Argentina, Thailand, Ghana, Austria, Japan, France, Argentina, New Zealand, and the United States. For a long time, arsenic was not among the list of elements tested by water-quality testing laboratories; thus scientists have not yet identified all of the world's regions that are vulnerable to arsenic contamination of drinking water.

The concentration of arsenic in natural waters is controlled by solid-solution interaction. The importance of oxides in reducing arsenic concentration in natural waters has been well recognized. Clays can also be used to adsorb arsenic, and iron, aluminum, and manganese salts are often used in the removal of arsenic from water. The extent of adsorption is strongly related to arsenic speciation, arsenic concentration, pH, and the concentration of opposing anions.

Sohini Dutt

Further Reading

Henke, Kevin R. *Arsenic: Environmental Chemistry, Health Threats, and Waste Treatment.* John Wiley & Sons, 2009.

Hill, Marquita K. "Drinking-Water Pollution." In *Understanding Environmental Pollution.* 3rd ed. Cambridge University Press, 2010.

Miller, G. Tyler, Jr., and Scott Spoolman. "Water Pollution." In *Living in the Environment: Principles, Connections, and Solutions.* 16th ed. Brooks/Cole, 2009.

Ravenscroft, Peter, Hugh Brammer, and Keith Richards. *Arsenic Pollution: A Global Synthesis.* Blackwell, 2009.

■ Asbestos as carcinogenic material

FIELDS OF STUDY: Biology, Life Sciences, Ecosystems; Ecology, Environment, Environmentalism; Health, Medicine, Disease, Illness; Pollution, Emissions, Toxic Waste, Hazardous Materials; Elements, Substances, Chemicals, Compounds; Industries, Commercial Products.

IDENTIFICATION: Industrial term for certain silicate minerals that occur in the form of long, thin fibers

The adverse health effects of breathing high concentrations of asbestos over prolonged periods have been known since the

early 1970's. The federal Clean Air Act of 1963 classified asbestos as a carcinogenic material, and in 1990 the U.S. Environmental Protection Agency established a broad ban on the manufacture, processing, importation, and distribution of asbestos products.

Asbestos-form minerals are natural substances that are common in many types of igneous and metamorphic rocks found over large areas of Earth. Erosion continually releases these fibers into the environment, and most people typically inhale thousands of fibers each day, or more than 100 million over a lifetime. Asbestos fibers also enter the body through drinking water. Drinking-water supplies in the United States typically contain almost 1 million fibers per quart, but water in some areas may have as many as 100 million or more fibers per quart.

Properties

Many silicate minerals occur in fibrous form, but only six have been commercially produced as asbestos. In order of decreasing commercial importance, these are chrysotile (white asbestos), crocidolite (blue asbestos), amosite (brown asbestos), anthophyllite, tremolite, and actinolite. All these minerals except chrysotile are members of the amphibole group of minerals, which have a chainlike arrangement of atoms in their molecular structures, like parallel threads running on one direction. In contrast, chrysotile, as a member of the serpentine family, has atoms arranged in a sheetlike fashion, in which the parallel threads form two-dimensional array.

Although the individual properties of these minerals differ greatly from one another, they share several characteristics that make them useful and cost-effective. These include great resistance to heat, flame, and acid attack; high tensile strength and flexibility; low electrical conductivity; resistance to friction; and a fibrous form, which allows them to be used for the manufacture of fabrics such as those used in fire- and heat-protective clothing. Asbestos thus was widely used until the 1970's in a great variety

U.S. End Uses of Asbestos, 1977 vs. 2003

END USE	METRIC TONS	
	1977	2003
Cement pipe	145,000	—
Cement sheet	139,500	—
Coatings and compounds	32,500	1,170
Flooring products	140,000	—
Friction products	83,100	—
Insulation: electrical	3,360	—
Insulation: thermal	15,000	—
Packing and gaskets	25,100	—
Paper products	22,100	—
Plastics	7,260	—
Roofing products	57,500	2,800
Textiles	8,800	—
Other	30,200	677

Source: Data from the U.S. Geological Survey.
Note: U.S. mining of asbestos ended in 2002.

of building and industrial products. Such common materials as vinyl floor tiles, appliance insulation, patching and joint compounds, automobile brake pads, hair dryers, and ironing board covers all might have contained asbestos. Most such products now contain one or more of several substitutes for asbestos instead of asbestos itself. However, many of the substitutes may not be hazard-free, a fact that is starting to be recognized by legislators. For example, in 1993 the World Health Organization (WHO) stated that all substitute fibers must be tested to determine their carcinogenicity. Germany now classifies glass, rock, and mineral wools as probable carcinogens.

Health Effects

The U.S. Department of Health and Human Services classifies asbestos as a carcinogen. Studies leading to this determination were mostly based on asbestos workers who had been exposed to extremely high levels of fibers for many years. These studies concluded that the asbestos workers had increased chances of developing two types of cancer: mesothelioma (a cancer of the thin membrane surrounding the lungs) and cancer of the lung tissue itself. These workers were also at increased risk of developing asbestosis, an accumulation of scarlike tissue in the lungs that can cause great difficulty in breathing and permanent disability. None of these diseases develops immediately; all have long latency periods, typically fifteen to forty years. Contrary to common misconception, exposure to asbestos does not cause muscle soreness, headaches, or any other immediate symptoms. The effects of asbestos exposure typically are not noticed for many years.

It is generally agreed that the risk of developing disease after asbestos exposure depends on the number of fibers in the person's body, how long the fibers have been in the body, and whether or not the person is a smoker, since smoking greatly increases the risk of developing disease. There is no agreement on the risks associated with low-level, nonoccupational exposure. The U.S. Environmental Protection Agency (EPA) has concluded that there is no safe level of exposure to asbestos fibers, but the Occupational Safety and Health Administration (OSHA) allows up to 0.1 fiber per cubic centimeter of air during an eight-hour workday.

Other Controversies

Another area of controversy stems from scientific studies showing that all forms of asbestos are not equally dangerous. Evidence has shown that the amphibole forms of asbestos, and particularly crocidolite, are hazardous, but the serpentine mineral chrysotile—accounting for 95 percent of all asbestos used in the past and 99 percent of current production—is not. For example, one case study involved a school that was located next to a 150,000-ton rock dump containing chrysotile. Thousands of children played on the rocks over a one-hundred-year period, but not a single case of asbestos-related disease developed in any of the children. The difference seems to be in how the human body responds to amphibole compared to chrysotile. The immune system can eliminate chrysotile fibers much more readily than

amphibole, and there is also evidence that chrysotile in the lungs dissolves and is excreted. This remains a controversial area, and most governments still treat all forms of asbestos with the same regard. This is not true of some European governments.

The risk of developing any type of disease from exposure to normal levels of asbestos fibers in outdoor air or the air in closed buildings is extremely low. The calculations of Melvin Benarde in *Asbestos: The Hazardous Fiber* (1990) show that the risk of dying from nonoccupational exposure to asbestos is one-third the risk of being killed by lightning. The Health Effects Institute made similar calculations in 1991 and found that the risk of dying from asbestos is less than 1 percent the risk of dying from exposure to secondary tobacco smoke.

Gene D. Robinson

Further Reading

Bartrip, Peter. *Beyond the Factory Gates: Asbestos and Health in Twentieth Century America.* Continuum, 2006.

Carroll, Stephen, et al. *Asbestos Litigation.* RAND, 2005.

Castleman, Barry. *Asbestos: Medical and Legal Aspects.* 5th ed. Aspen, 2005.

Chatterjee, Kaulir Kisor. "Asbestos." In *Uses of Industrial Minerals, Rocks, and Freshwater.* Nova Science, 2009.

Craighead, John E., and Allen R. Gibbs, ed. *Asbestos and Its Diseases.* Oxford University Press, 2008.

Deffeyes, Kenneth S. "Asbestos." In *Nanoscale: Visualizing an Invisible World.* Illustrations by Stephen E. Deffeyes. MIT Press, 2009.

Dodson, Ronald, and Samuel Hammar, eds. *Asbestos: Assessment, Epidemiology, and Health Effects.* CRC Press, 2005.

McCulloch, Jock, and Geoffrey Tweedale. *Defending the Indefensible: The Global Asbestos Industry and Its Fight for Survival.* Oxford University Press, 2008.

Maines, Rachel. *Asbestos and Fire: Technological Trade-Offs and the Body at Risk.* Rutgers University Press, 2005.

■ Asbestos releases in Silver Bay, Minnesota

FIELDS OF STUDY: Biology, Life Sciences, Ecosystems; Ecology, Environment, Environmentalism; Health, Medicine, Disease, Illness; Oceans, Seas, Lakes, Bodies of Water; Pollution, Emissions, Toxic Waste, Hazardous Materials; Water Resources; Geology, Geosciences; Mineral Resources.

THE EVENT: The dumping of mining wastes into Lake Superior by the Reserve Mining Company

DATE: Begun in 1947

Mining wastes deposited directly into Lake Superior were found to be the source of asbestos fibers in the drinking-water supply of Duluth, Minnesota, and other nearby communities.

Taconite is a low-grade iron ore used in the making of steel products. Rocks are crushed and the ore is magnetically removed; the residual materials, or tailings, are industrial waste. In 1947 the state of Minnesota, in an attempt to revive mining in the region known as the Iron Range, granted the Reserve Mining Company of Silver Bay, Minnesota, permission to dump the tailings from its taconite processing plant directly into Lake Superior. The company began depositing the tailings into a large chasm in the lake at the rate of 67,000 tons per day.

On June 14, 1973, the U.S. Environmental Protection Agency (EPA) announced that high concentrations of asbestos fibers had been found in the drinking water of Duluth, Minnesota. The fibers were identified by Irving Selikoff, director of an environmental sciences laboratory in New York, as amosite, the same asbestos fibers that, when inhaled, are known to cause lung, stomach, and colon cancers after an incubation period of twenty to thirty years. Duluth's drinking water was coming directly from Lake Superior, which was thought to have the purest lake water in the world.

State and U.S. government experts charged that the Reserve Mining Company's tailings were the source of these fibers and that lake currents had brought them into the water supply of Duluth and surrounding communities. At the time of the EPA warning, court action was under way to force Reserve to cease dumping its slurry into Lake Superior. Company executives protested that the fibers had come into the lake naturally from eroding rocks located in tributary streams. They also contended that the "water scare" was a ploy to influence the court's decision.

With Reserve threatening to close down its mining operation if it were to be forced to find another dump site, Silver Bay residents, nearly all of whom owed their jobs to Reserve, strongly defended the company. Duluth's residents, while wanting Reserve to stop its dumping, generally reacted with equanimity when confronted with the EPA report, many noting that they had been drinking Lake Superior water for more than thirty years without ill effects. As no filtration system existed that could remove the asbestos fibers from the water, most Duluthians had no option except to continue to drink the water. Moreover, it was unclear whether ingesting the fibers might have the same effect as inhaling them.

Numerous mortality studies were initiated by Selikoff and other scientists in 1973 to evaluate the impact of the fibers on Duluth's population. These studies failed to confirm that the water posed any serious threat to those who drank it. By 1975 the water scare had dissipated, and soon thereafter the fibers in the water ceased to be an issue. After years of litigation, Reserve agreed to stop dumping tailings in the lake and instead dispose of them on land. The company constructed a basin about 11 kilometers (7 miles) inland from Silver Bay to contain the tailings. In 1990 Reserve announced that it was bankrupt, and the company closed. Subsequently, another mining company reopened the Silver Bay taconite plant and continued to use the tailings basin built by Reserve.

Ronald K. Huch

Further Reading

Bartrip, Peter. *Beyond the Factory Gates: Asbestos and Health in Twentieth Century America.* Continuum, 2006.

Farber, Daniel A. "Economics Versus Politics." In *Ecopragmatism: Making Sensible Environmental Decisions in an Uncertain World.* University of Chicago Press, 1999.

■ Asbestosis

FIELDS OF STUDY: Biology, Life Sciences, Ecosystems; Ecology, Environment, Environmentalism; Health, Medicine, Disease, Illness; Pollution, Emissions, Toxic Waste, Hazardous Materials; Elements, Substances, Chemicals, Compounds; Industries, Commercial Products.

IDENTIFICATION: Disease of the lungs caused by repeated exposure to asbestos

The realization that exposure to asbestos could result in serious lung disease led to the banning of this material for many uses, as well as greater awareness of the concept of environmental illness.

The generic term "asbestos" is applied to such minerals as amosite, anthophyllite, chrysotile, and crocidolite. These silicates, first used extensively in the 1940s, have remarkable qualities that initially made them desirable as both thermal and electrical insulators. After the insulating properties of asbestos were recognized, such substances were commonly used in the building trades, notably to insulate pipes and boilers. Some cements and floor tiles contained substantial quantities of asbestos, which was used as a fireproof filler. Forms of asbestos were also used to make blankets designed to smother fires and in the manufacture of safety garments for firefighters. The substance is still used in the manufacture of automotive brake and clutch linings, where its insulating qualities are particularly valuable.

Asbestosis, a disease of the lungs, occurs in people who have been exposed to this silicate, but the onset of symptoms may occur years after exposure. Even those whose exposure to asbestos has been moderate may contract the disease, an early symptom of which is perpetual shortness of breath, especially following strenuous physical activity. This symptom is often accompanied by a persistent, hacking cough. Asbestosis is a progressive disease that characteristically begins in the lower lung and spreads to the middle and upper lungs, with disabling, sometimes fatal, results as the air spaces in the lungs narrow. Little aggressive treatment exists for the disease. Asbestosis victims are urged not to smoke and are usually treated with oxygen to improve their breathing.

Direct exposure to asbestos, especially when it occurs over extended periods, often results in asbestosis. The disease has been found in those who have worked in asbestos mines as well as in persons who have worked as pipe fitters, boilermakers, automotive mechanics working with brake and clutch linings, and demolition workers who have razed buildings in which asbestos was used for insulation.

Indirect exposure can also result in asbestosis. The disease has been reported among people who have regularly laundered work clothes that have been directly exposed to asbestos as well as among those who live or work in buildings where asbestos has been used as an insulator. Widespread community exposure has been noted in situations where steel girders in large buildings were sprayed with asbestos as a fire precaution. Cases occurred in a London neighborhood near an asbestos plant among persons who had no direct contact with the plant. South Africa had outbreaks among the general population near its asbestos mines.

After 1975 and with the implementation of the

High magnification micrograph of asbestosis of the lung, with characteristic ferruginous bodies and interstitial fibrosis. Lung biopsy. H&E stain. By Nephron (Own work)

asbestos-ban program, the use of asbestos declined substantially as it was replaced by other mineral fibers. By the end of the twentieth century, persons working with asbestos in the United States, particularly demolition workers, began receiving special training to help them avoid exposure that could lead to the onset of the disease. Environmental laws in most jurisdictions now prohibit the use of asbestos as an insulating material in new buildings, and many laws protect workers from exposure. Persons who were exposed in the past through work-related activities and currently suffer from the disease are usually eligible to receive workers' compensation payments.

R. Baird Shuman

Further Reading

Bartrip, Peter. *Beyond the Factory Gates: Asbestos and Health in Twentieth Century America.* Continuum, 2006. Print.

Castleman, Barry. *Asbestos: Medical and Legal Aspects.* 5th ed. Aspen, 2005.

Dodson, Ronald F., and Samuel P. Hammar, eds. *Asbestos: Risk Assessment, Epidemiology, and Health Effects.* CRC Press, 2006.

Maines, Rachel. *Asbestos and Fire: Technological Trade-Offs and the Body at Risk.* Rutgers University Press, 2013.

Oury, Tim D. *Pathology of Asbestos-Associated Diseases.* 3rd ed. Springer. 2014.

■ Asia

FIELDS OF STUDY: Places, Peoples, Societies; Continents, Regions, Areas, Islands; Biology, Life Sciences, Ecosystems; Animals, Zoology, Marine Biology; Ecology, Environment, Environmentalism; Plants, Vegetation, Botany, Horticulture; Renewable Resources; Pollution, Emissions, Toxic Waste, Hazardous Materials.

IDENTIFICATION: Places; population issues; ecology and ecosystems; resources and resource management; preservation and wilderness issues

Population growth, economic development, rising consumption, and unsustainable exploitation of natural resources have exerted severe stress on the environments of most Asian nations. The region faces the challenge of moving toward environmentally sustainable growth while reversing major environmental damage, including deforestation, habitat destruction, and air, water, and soil pollution.

Great progress in reducing poverty through economic growth has come at the expense of the environment in many Asian countries, particularly from the 1970's onward. Whereas 60 percent of all Asians lived in poverty in 1970, that number was almost halved, to 33 percent, by 2000. However, by 2005 about 670 million Asians still lived on less than the equivalent of one U.S. dollar per day (adjusted for purchasing-power effects), a situation that led to the undernourishment of more than 500 million people out of a total Asian population that reached just over 4 billion in 2010. The continent was subject to ongoing pressures on the environment owing particularly to unsustainable economic growth that depleted and degraded many natural resources.

Intensive Agricultural Development

In Asia, the twin pressures of population growth and poverty reduction have often led to severe environmental degradation. A negative process often begins with land conversion, when forests, wetlands, and other natural habitats are cleared for agricultural and industrial use or for human settlement. As Asia became home to about 60 percent of the world's human population by 2010 but encompassed only 30 percent of the earth's land, some of which, such as the Gobi Desert, is inhospitable to human population, the pressures on arable and potentially arable land increased. By 2005, Asian arable land per capita was only 80 percent of the global average.

Primarily through deforestation, cropland in Asia (excluding the Middle East and Asian Russia) increased from 210 million hectares (520 million acres) in 1900 to 453 million hectares (1.12 billion acres) by 1994. From the 1970's onward, high-yield strains of staple crops such as rice and wheat were planted and supported with chemical fertilizers, pesticides, and herbicides. In addition, Asian countries such as the People's Republic of China, India, and the nations of Southeast Asia developed 90 percent of the world's aquaculture, focusing on fish, shrimp, and shellfish. Unsustainably intense agriculture—involving irrigation of as much as 30 percent of the cropland in Asia and heavy use of agrochemicals—eroded soils and depleted and contaminated freshwater sources, threatening freshwater ecosystems and fisheries.

By the early twenty-first century, Asian nations were managing to extract more and more food from their land and coastal areas, both for domestic consumption and for interregional and intercontinental export. However, water pollution, soil erosion, and nutrient depletion led to general land degradation and loss of arable land. It was predicted that if unsustainable levels of agricultural use and development were not halted, the continent would eventually face a food crisis. Some observers advocated the use of genetically modified foods, which would lessen reliance on unsupportable levels of agrochemicals, but this alternative remained controversial. Promising developments, however, included the introduction of new, less environmentally destructive approaches to farming, such as conservation tillage practices and agroecology.

Economic Development

Whereas Japan began its industrialization with the Meiji Restoration after 1868, and beginnings of Chinese industry were seen at the end of the nineteenth century, most Asian nations did not begin to see full industrialization and above-world-average economic growth until the 1960's and 1970's. In 2004, Asia led all other global regions in economic growth. From 1995 to 2002, manufacturing in developing Asian nations grew by 40 percent. This rapid industrialization demanded land and energy and led to rapidly increasing emissions of pollutants into air, water, and ground. High levels of air pollution caused respiratory illnesses and acid rain that damaged lakes and forests; degraded soil, rivers, and aquifers; and harmed coastal ecosystems.

Initially, many developing Asian countries placed very little emphasis on technical means of pollution control and enforcement of antipollution laws. Power plants and factories were allowed to discharge their emissions into air and water, sometimes without even the most basic treatment. To fuel its industry and provide power and heat to its people, Asia used coal abundantly; by 2003, coal accounted for 41 percent of the energy consumed in Asia, particularly in China, India, and the Republic of Korea (South Korea). Another 39 percent of the energy came from oil, most of which came from the Middle East.

Burning this amount of fossil fuel, often with at most rudimentary pollution-control devices in place and operational in many Asian countries, led to severe air pollution and contributed to greenhouse gas emissions linked to global warming. Experts project that one result of global warming could be a rise in sea levels that would submerge island nations of South Asia and the Pacific and inundate heavily populated Asian coastal regions.

Air pollution became especially severe in Asian cities in China and India and in large urban agglomerations such as Bangkok, Thailand, and Hanoi, Vietnam. By 2006, the world's ten most polluted cities were all Chinese. From the late 1990's onward, China made fighting air pollution a national priority, and significant progress was achieved. Air pollution actually decreased as the economy grew, even though actual levels of reduction (for example, a 0.6 percent reduction of sulfur dioxide emissions in 2007) were still small. Emphasis was placed on increasing China's notoriously inefficient generation and use of energy; the nation's stated goal was to increase energy efficiency by 30 percent from 2006 to 2010. However, China's project devoted to calculating the true economic cost caused by environmental pollution and degradation (its "green gross domestic product") was stopped in 2007 when its negative figures exceeded even worst-case scenarios.

Very ambitious Asian projects to increase the share of cleaner hydroelectric power through construction of massive dams, such as the Three Gorges Dam on the Yangtze River, remained controversial. These megaprojects came with significant environmental problems of their own, including the destruction of river ecosystems, riverbank erosion, and resettlement of human populations on the scale of millions. Critics argued that better alternatives would be a series of smaller dams and increased energy efficiency. Another controversial approach to the reduction of pollution, undertaken in China and India, was the washing of coal to decrease its sulfur content; those opposing this practice noted that it depletes water resources. These cases show that no easy or quick solutions are available for the environmental problems caused by economic growth in Asia; the problems require a more holistic approach aimed toward sustainable economic development instead of rapacious resource depletion and environmental degradation.

Urbanization and Consumerism

In 2010 about half of Asia's people, approximately 2 billion persons, still lived in rural areas and drew their livelihoods from farming, fishing, or forestry. In South Asia, 73 percent of all land was used for agriculture. As Asian economies had developed throughout the region, however, urbanization had increased tremendously. From 1970 to 2000, 560 million people moved from the countryside into Asian cities, increasing urban populations by 260 percent. Urbanization continued to rise in the twenty-first century, with average Asian city growth rates of more than 3 percent annually.

The rapid growth of Asian cities severely taxed the environment. Poor land management led to habitat destruction that threatened many kinds of animals, from elephants to birds. Urban sprawl initiated the conversion of forests, wetlands, and agricultural land. The growing numbers of people in cities caused groundwater depletion and shortages of potable water. Municipal solid and liquid wastes polluted water supplies, and waste incineration polluted the air. Increases in motor vehicle use caused traffic congestion and air pollution. Growing suburbs required more roads as the residents depended on private vehicles in the absence of efficient public transport systems. Poor planning and ineffective law enforcement led to the rapid growth of crowded slum areas, where poor infrastructure failed to meet the needs of inhabitants, leading them to add to environmental degradation with untreated waste disposal that resulted in threats to public health.

Significantly rising living standards for many people in most Asian countries led to greater consumerism, which also affected the environment negatively, as the consumption of energy and natural resources increased along with waste production. All this taxed an environment strained already by intensive agriculture, new industry and manufacturing, and power generation. Many Asian nations were unable or unwilling to devote significant financial resources to addressing environmental degradation seriously and effectively when they were faced with the costs of serving increasing numbers of people desiring better living standards. It was not until the quality of daily life began to deteriorate visibly in Asian cities because of environmental degradation, and health and life expectancies of people began to decline owing to pollution-related illnesses, that

previously neglectful governments began to take environmental issues seriously.

Environmental Challenges and Opportunities

Asia enjoys tremendous biodiversity, but the pressures of population growth and economic development obliterated, degraded, or fragmented significant areas of natural land that had served as habitat for wild animals and plants. Asia's biodiversity became severely threatened as natural areas from lowland forests to grasslands and coastal estuaries, with their rivers and bays, were destroyed or degraded as the result of unregulated urban sprawl, legal and illegal logging, and land clearance for agricultural, industrial, or settlement use, with generally little regard for wildlife, plant life, and ecosystems. In addition, many species of animals were exploited legally and illegally for capture and sale to the pet trade or for use as food or in traditional medicines.

By 2010, approximately 7,500 Asian animal and plant species were considered to be threatened, half of them in Southeast and South Asia. About one-third of Southeast Asia's rain forests were fragmented, and two-thirds of Asia's wildlife habitat had been destroyed. Legal and illegal burning of forests in Indonesia had not only destroyed much wildlife habitat but also, together with industrial pollution, caused the annual emergence, beginning in 2001, of a huge brown cloud of polluted haze over South, Southeast, and East Asia. The severity of this problem led to the founding of the Reducing Emissions from Deforestation and Forest Degradation (REDD) initiative, a program sponsored by the United Nations. It was begun in September, 2008, and was reaffirmed in the Copenhagen Accord of December 18, 2009. The goal of REDD is to reward emissions reductions through financial incentives for regional governments and people.

Conservationists, scientists, and environmental activists all agree that Asia's poor overall record on nature preservation must be tackled with bold and effective conservation mechanisms, with a major shift toward environmental sustainability. Efforts have been made to place wildlife sanctuaries, nature reserves, and other open spaces under effective protection from development, with wildlife protected from poaching. The Asian tiger is just one of the species that has suffered greatly from habitat destruction and poaching; its numbers declined from about one hundred thousand in 1900 to a mere five thousand in 2000. One Asian success story has been China's protection of the giant panda in well-monitored preserves; any person caught poaching pandas is subject to a sentence of life in prison.

Asia enjoys biologically rich oceans and coastal regions. Most of these are threatened by unsustainable fishing practices and by high levels of pollution caused by extraordinary population growth and rampant urban, agricultural, and industrial development. The region's coral reefs are in particular danger; 88 percent of these reefs were considered at risk in 2010. The destruction of mangrove forests, more than 50 percent of which were gone by 2000, magnified human losses caused by the tsunami of December, 2004, which killed the most people where protective mangrove forests had been decimated.

The solutions to Asia's significant environmental problems cannot be imposed from the outside; they must come from within the Asian nations. If Asian leaders and policy makers begin to emphasize environmental sustainability as their nations pursue economic development, and if laws protecting the environment are put in place and enforced, the degradation of Asia's environment can be halted and slowly reversed. Such a major turnaround occurred in Japan during the 1970's, after a series of highly publicized human-made environmental disasters, including the mercury poisoning of Minamata Bay, led to a dramatic increase in environmental protection laws and their effective enforcement.

R. C. Lutz

Further Reading

Fayzieva, Dilorom, ed. *Environmental Health in Central Asia: The Present and Future.* WIT Press, 2004.

Hill, Christopher V. *South Asia: An Environmental History.* ABC-CLIO, 2008.

Hillstrom, Kevin, and Laurie Collier Hillstrom. *Asia: A Continental Overview of Environmental Issues.* ABC-CLIO, 2003.

Jha, Raghbendra. "Alleviating Environmental Degradation in the Asia Pacific Region: International Co-operation and the Role of Issue Linkage." In *Regional Integration in the Asia Pacific,* edited by Organization for Economic Co-operation and Development. OECD, 2005.

Kaup, Katherine Palmer. *Understanding Asia Pacific.* Lynne Rienner, 2007.

See also: Air pollution; Aquaculture; Ashio, Japan, copper mine; Bhopal disaster; Coal-fired power plants; Coral reefs; Deforestation; Fossil fuels; Ganges River; Greenhouse gases; Habitat destruction; Minamata Bay mercury poisoning; Population growth; Rain forests; Sustainable development; Water pollution.

■ Aswan High Dam

FIELDS OF STUDY: Biology, Life Sciences, Ecosystems; Water Resources; Energy and Energy Resources; Ecology, Environment, Environmentalism.
IDENTIFICATION: Dam on the Nile River in Egypt
DATE: Completed in 1970

The Aswan High Dam supplies electricity and has helped control seasonal flooding, but it has had several negative environmental effects, including loss of fertility on down-river floodplains, increased erosion, and increased incidence of earthquakes.

The Aswan High Dam was built with the aid of Soviet engineers on the Nile River approximately 960 kilometers (600 miles) south of Cairo, Egypt, between 1960 and 1970 at a cost of US$1 billion. The dam lies 7 kilometers (4.5 miles) south of the city of Aswan and several kilometers from a smaller dam constructed by British engineers between 1898 and 1902. The building of the High Dam followed the signing of the Nile Water Agreement between Egypt and Sudan in November of 1959.

The High Dam is a rock-fill structure with a core of impermeable clay. It measures 3,829 meters (12,562 feet) long, 111 meters (364 feet) high, 980 meters (3,215 feet) wide at the base, and 40 meters (131 feet) wide at the crest. The volume of material contained in the structure, 1.6 million cubic meters (56.5 million cubic feet), would be enough to construct seventeen Great Pyramids. The flow of the river's waters through the dam is via six tunnels, each controlled by a 230-ton gate.

The reservoir impounded by the High Dam is Lake Nasser, named for Egyptian president Gamal Abdel Nasser, who died the year the dam was completed. The portion of the reservoir that lies within Sudan, about 30 percent, is referred to as Lake Nubia. In total, the reservoir measures 499

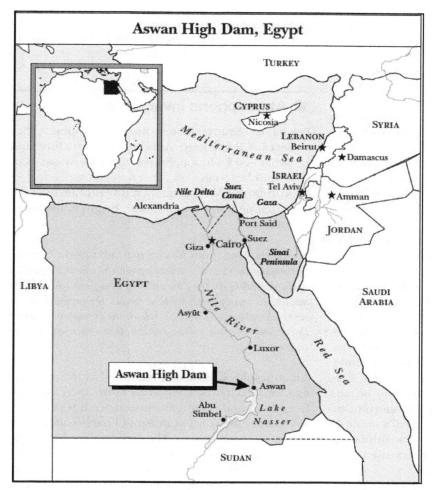

Aswan High Dam, Egypt

kilometers (310 miles) in length and has a surface area of approximately 5,996 square kilometers (2,315 square miles) and 9,053 kilometers (5,625 miles) of shoreline. It averages 9.7 kilometers (6 miles) wide, with a maximum width of 16 kilometers (10 miles). Mean water depth is 70 meters (230 feet), maximum depth is 110 meters (360 feet), and the annual vertical fluctuation is 25 meters (82 feet). The reservoir contains enough water to irrigate more than 2.8 million hectares (7 million acres).

Environmental Impacts

The filling of Lake Nasser came with a high cost. Thousands of people were displaced, and natural habitats were significantly altered. A number of ancient temples and monuments, which abound in the region, were to be submerged beneath the rising waters of the reservoir, but some of these were saved—they were cut into large blocks and reassembled at higher locations. High evaporation rates and water loss to infiltration into the underlying permeable Nubian sandstone caused the filling of the reservoir to take much longer than anticipated. A significant amount of water-storage capacity has also been lost as sediment that has been carried in occupies a part of the reservoir's volume.

The benefits derived from the High Dam are principally hydro-electric power generation and the regulation of water flow along the lower Nile for flood control. Twelve turboelectric generators capable of producing 10 billion kilowatt-hours provide 40 percent of Egypt's electrical power. The storage of water in Lake Nasser not only provides flood control but also allows for the irrigation of additional land and the ability to grow multiple crops over the course of a year. Since the filling of the reservoir, a fishing industry has also developed.

The yearly floods of the Nile are the result of late-summer rains that fall in the plateau region to the south in Ethiopia. At peak floods, river volume may increase by as much as sixteen times. More than 100 million tons of soil are carried with the water each year. While the impoundment of water in Lake Nasser has probably saved the lower Nile Valley from disastrous floods and alleviated the effects of regional droughts, the loss of yearly increments of silt—with its associated nutrients—on the floodplain has led to a decline in the floodplain's fertility. Without this natural fertilization, the Egyptians have had to rely on increasing use of artificial fertilizer. The floodwaters also provided a cleansing and draining action for the soil, preventing the accumulation of salts. Further, the floodwaters reduced the numbers of rats and disease-bearing snails. With the decline in flooding, the incidence of disease has been on the increase.

Historically, the influx of sediment to the Nile Delta has replenished sediment lost to wave and current erosion at the Delta's margins. Since the construction of the Aswan High Dam, the front of the Delta is being eroded at a rate of 1.8 meters (6 feet) per year. As on the floodplain, the soil of the Delta, a region that has been farmed for more than seven thousand years, also shows evidence of declining fertility.

Since the High Dam traps 98 percent of the Nile sediment, water passing through the dam has an enhanced ability to erode. Consequently, downstream erosion has become a significant problem, scouring the riverbed and undermining riverbanks and bridge piers. In some instances, the increased erosion has also affected the delicate balance of water irrigation systems.

The effects of trapped sediment are not confined to the floodplain and the Nile Delta. Prior to construction of the dam, the river brought sediment and nutrients into the normally nutrient-poor eastern Mediterranean Sea. This provided for blooms of phytoplankton that formed the base of a food pyramid that included sardines and other commercial varieties of fish. When construction of the dam began, the sardine fishing industry in the Mediterranean declined significantly. From the late 1980's onward, however, a resurgence occurred in sardine fishing, as the filling of Lake Nasser allowed for increased river discharge and nutrient enhancement.

One other environmental consequence of the construction of the High Dam has been the occurrence of earthquakes in the region. These are related to stress that is placed on the earth's crust by the weight of the water impounded in Lake Nasser. A large shock of magnitude 5.6, for example, occurred on November 14, 1981. This was followed by aftershocks for a period of seven months.

Donald J. Thompson

Further Reading

Caputo, Robert. "Journey up the Nile." *National Geographic*, May, 1985.

Collins, Robert O. *The Nile*. Yale University Press, 2002.

Johnson, Irving, and Electra Johnson."Yankee Cruises the Storied Nile." *National Geographic*, May, 1965.

Smith, Scot E. "The Aswan High Dam at Thirty: An Environmental Impact Assessment." In *Conservation, Ecology, and Management of African Fresh Waters*, edited by Thomas L. Crisman et al. University Press of Florida, 2003.

■ Atmospheric inversions

FIELDS OF STUDY: Meteorology, Atmospheric Sciences, Climatology; Atmospheric Structure and Dynamics; Pollution, Emissions, Toxic Waste, Hazardous Materials.

IDENTIFICATION: Vertical temperature profiles in which air temperature increases with height in the atmosphere

Temperature inversions play an important role in trapping anthropogenic (human-caused) pollutants near the earth's surface, leading to the formation of smog and reduced air quality in many metropolitan areas. Temperature inversions also play an important role in the formation of severe thunderstorms and mixed precipitation (such as freezing rain and sleet).

An atmospheric inversion is defined in meteorology as a scenario in which air temperature increases with height. To understand its importance it is necessary to consider the concept in light of the broader structure of the atmosphere. The vertical structure of the atmosphere is characterized by four broad regions; in order of increasing altitude, these are the troposphere, stratosphere, mesosphere, and thermosphere. On average, temperatures decrease with height in the troposphere and mesosphere, and increase with height in the stratosphere and thermosphere. The atmosphere's vertical temperature profile is important because it affects the ability of air to move vertically (that is, to rise and fall) in the atmosphere. Vertical motions are generally permitted in regions where air temperatures decrease with height, and they are suppressed in regions where air temperatures increase with height. The latter condition, known as a temperature inversion, creates a layer in the atmosphere that has the ability to limit, or cap, vertical mixing. The stratospheric inversion is a prime example; it caps vertical motions associated with storms in the troposphere.

Smaller-scale temperature inversions that occur within the troposphere may have significant impacts on air quality at urban and regional levels because they trap polluted air masses close to the ground. A

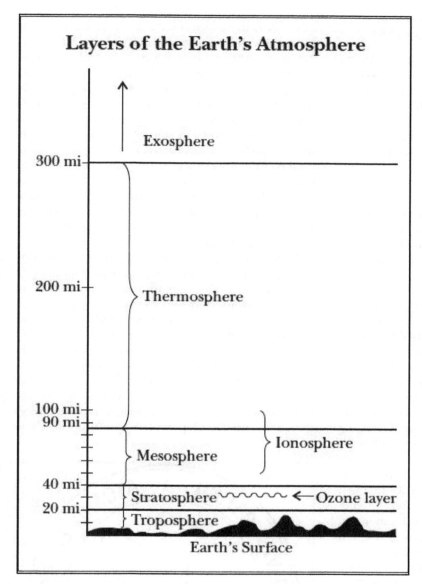

Layers of the Earth's Atmosphere

Exosphere

300 mi

Thermosphere

200 mi

100 mi
90 mi

Ionosphere

Mesosphere

40 mi

Stratosphere ∿∿∿ ← Ozone layer

20 mi

Troposphere

Earth's Surface

when solar radiation raises temperatures near the surface.

A larger-scale subsidence inversion forms when a high-pressure system causes air to subside and warm adiabatically (without gaining or losing heat) over a broad region. Different rates of subsidence between air near the surface and air aloft allow the air aloft to warm to a greater degree, setting up a large-scale temperature inversion. In contrast to radiation inversions, subsidence inversions have the potential to persist for long periods of time. This scenario is common in many metropolitan areas that are known for poor air quality, particularly Los Angeles, California. In Los Angeles, the impact of temperature inversions is magnified by the fact that the city is surrounded on three sides by mountains, which limit horizontal mixing and promote higher concentrations of air pollutants in the region.

The pollutants that build up in urban areas as the result of temperature inversions have important long-term health implications and, at times, can prove to be serious short-term threats. For example, in 1948 toxic air conditions that resulted from subsidence inversion in the western Pennsylvania town of Donora caused the deaths of twenty residents. A similar incident known as the London smog disaster killed nearly four thousand residents of London, England, in 1952.

Jeffrey C. Brunskill

common example of this is a radiation inversion, which often develops during winter months on days with limited wind and low humidity. These conditions allow the ground to cool quickly, thereby causing the air immediately above the ground to cool more than the air aloft. The warmer air aloft forms a stable layer, or cap, over the atmosphere below it. Radiation inversions are an air-quality concern because they often set up during the evening traffic rush hour and trap associated pollutants close to the surface. In general, radiation inversions affect small geographic regions and dissipate during the early morning,

Further Reading

Aguado, Edward, and James E. Burt. *Understanding Weather and Climate.* 5th ed. Pearson Education, 2010.

Ahrens, C. Donald. *Meteorology Today: An Introduction to Weather, Climate, and the Environment.* Brooks/Cole Cengage Learning, 2009.

■ Atomic Energy Commission (AEC)

FIELDS OF STUDY: Government, Politics, International Relations; Organizations, Agencies, Commissions, Centers; Public Policy, Debates, Controversies; Regulation, Standards and Practices; Nuclear Power, Nuclear Weapons, Radioactive Waste.

IDENTIFICATION: Agency established by the US Congress to promote and monitor the use of nuclear energy

DATES: 1946–1974

Because the Atomic Energy Commission was responsible for both the promotion of nuclear power and the safety regulation of nuclear facilities, many critics asserted that the commission was not as diligent as it should be in its regulatory duties.

In 1946, the U.S. Congress passed the Atomic Energy Act, which created the Atomic Energy Commission (AEC) to promote, monitor, and control the development and use of nuclear energy for civilian and military use. Not only was a buildup of nuclear weapons for defense expected, but also the development of nuclear science for peaceful uses. For security reasons, all nuclear production facilities and reactors were owned by the US government, but the information from research was to be controlled by the AEC. The Manhattan Project facilities, where scientists had developed the first atomic bombs during World War II, were taken over by the AEC. In 1954, Congress passed the Atomic Energy Act Amendments, which made possible the development of commercial nuclear power. The AEC was assigned the responsibility of promoting commercial nuclear power at the same time it was charged with developing safety regulations and controls for nuclear power plants.

The work of the AEC encompassed all areas of nuclear science. The AEC studied the production of nuclear weapons, improved and increased nuclear facilities, and oversaw the development of new weapons, such as the thermonuclear device, a fusion bomb, and nuclear propulsion for warships, especially submarines. The study of nuclear reactors led to improved energy-producing reactors and a new type of reactor, the breeder reactor, that produced new fuel while producing energy. Commercial production of nuclear energy became a reality. Regional research centers were established—at the Argonne National Laboratory near Chicago; at Oak Ridge, Tennessee; at Brookhaven, New York; and at the University of California Radiation Laboratory in Berkeley—where scientists could work on projects in nuclear or radiation science. The AEC also contracted with industrial and university researchers to conduct nuclear-related studies in all areas of scientific research, including medical diagnosis using nuclear techniques, disease treatment by radiation, and treatment for radiation exposure. Other areas of study included the effects of radiation, production of new isotopes, uses of new isotopes, and radiation safety. Reactors to produce energy for satellites were developed and sent into space.

Many observers were critical of the AEC's double role as promoter of nuclear power and monitor of radiation safety, saying that this was a conflict of interest. Many asserted that the AEC was promoting nuclear energy at the expense of regulation and that the safety regulations for reactors especially, but also for materials production, location of plants, and environmental protection, were inadequate.

The AEC was abolished in 1974, and its former two roles were split. The promotion of nuclear science in the United States was assigned to the Energy Research and Development Administration; these

The Atomic Energy Act of 1946 established the Atomic Energy Commission, which predated today's US Department of Energy. By Idaho

duties later became the responsibility of the Department of Energy. Responsibility for the safety monitoring of nuclear facilities went to the Nuclear Regulatory Commission.

C. Alton Hassell

Further Reading

Cooke, Stephanie. *In Mortal Hands: A Cautionary History of the Nuclear Age.* Bloomsbury, 2009.

Hewlett, Richard G., and Oscar E. Anderson. *A History of the United States Atomic Energy Commission.* 1962. Reprint. University of California Press, 1990.

Walker, J. Samuel. *A Short History of Nuclear Regulation, 1946–1999.* US Nuclear Regulatory Commission, 2000.

■ Automobile emissions

FIELDS OF STUDY: Chemistry; Elements, Substances, Chemicals, Compounds; Pollution, Emissions, Toxic Waste, Hazardous Materials; Industries, Commercial Products; Ecology, Environment, Environmentalism.

IDENTIFICATION: Combination of vehicular exhaust from incomplete combustion of gasoline or diesel fuel and hydrocarbons that escape these fuels through evaporation

Collectively, the emissions produced by the millions of vehicles on the roads of the world's major metropolitan areas have serious impacts on air quality and human health. They also represent a significant contribution to greenhouse gas emissions. The U.S. Environmental Protection Agency has described driving a private car as "probably a typical citizen's most 'polluting' daily activity."

Automobile emissions create ongoing and potentially dangerous environmental problems when gases and particulates are released into the atmosphere at a rate that exceeds the capacity of the atmosphere to dissipate or dispose of them. Motor vehicle emissions are a major component of the smog that blankets such urban areas as Los Angeles, California, and Denver, Colorado. The emissions produced by a motor vehicle consist of exhaust (the by-products of incomplete gasoline or diesel fuel combustion) and fuel that evaporates from the vehicle's fuel tank, engine, and exhaust system during operation, cooldown, and fueling.

Vehicle exhaust contains several problematic compounds. Carbon monoxide, produced by incomplete combustion, reduces the flow of oxygen in the bloodstream. Hydrocarbons, another product of imperfect combustion, are often toxic or carcinogenic. Nitrogen oxides, which are formed when combusting fuel reacts with oxygen in the air, contribute to the formation of acid rain and fine particles that can harm the lungs when breathed in. Together, hydrocarbons and nitrogen oxides react with the heat of sunlight to produce a hazy brown mixture of secondary pollutants. Notable among these pollutants is ground-level ozone, which irritates the eyes and causes damage to the respiratory system. (Nitrogen oxides also readily create ozone by reacting with naturally occurring hydrocarbons produced by trees.) Other secondary pollutants formed by photochemical reactions include the toxic compounds formaldehyde and peroxyacetyl nitrate. Carbon dioxide, a product of complete combustion, is not directly hazardous to human health in normal atmospheric concentrations, but it is chief among the anthropogenic (human-generated) greenhouse gases commonly believed to be affecting Earth's climate.

Impacts on Health and Environment

Environmental problems associated with automobile emissions include deleterious effects on many forms of agriculture and natural forests, reduction in visibility, and damage to metals, building materials such as stone and concrete, rubber, paint, textiles, and plastics. Automobile emissions cause lung and eye irritation, coughing, chest pain, shallow breathing, and headaches. Automobile-produced air pollution is also a factor contributing to allergies, asthma, emphysema, bronchitis, lung cancer, heart disease, and negative psychological states. Carbon monoxide quickly combines with blood hemoglobin and impairs oxygen delivery to the tissues, particularly in children and the elderly, causing heart and lung problems. Vehicular emissions and other sources of air pollution cost Americans billions of dollars each year in health care and related expenses.

The increased rate and depth of breathing during physical exertion exposes delicate lung tissues to more polluted air. Research indicates that exercise near a busy freeway may be more harmful than

Costs of Rural and Urban Air Quality Degradation by Motor Vehicles, 2000

POLLUTANT	IMPACT	RURAL EMISSIONS ($)	URBAN EMISSIONS ($)
Particulate matter	Mortality	12,695	21,558
Particulate matter	Nonfatal illness	3,683	6,232
Sulfur dioxide, nitrogen dioxide, carbon monoxide	Nonfatal illness	0	51
Ozone	Nonfatal illness	28	16
Total		16,406	27,857

Source: Federal Highway Administration, United States Department of Transportation.
Note: Costs of human illnesses, in millions of 1990 dollars. Costs of crop damage, reduced visibility, and other physical effects on the environment are not included.

beneficial to the body. At the 1984 Summer Olympics in Los Angeles, the evening rush-hour start of the men's marathon coincided with a stage 2 California health advisory alert, drawing criticism that the organizers of the event were more interested in commercial revenues than in the safety of the athletes and spectators. Later Olympic events were postponed during heavy air-pollution episodes. China faced similar, but more severe, challenges when heavily polluted Beijing hosted the 2008 Summer Olympics. Emergency measures that the city took to improve air quality in time for the games included allowing drivers to use their motor vehicles only every other day, which effectively took more than 1.5 million vehicles off the road daily.

Automobile emissions have been shown to exert their negative effects a considerable distance from the source, depending on atmospheric changes in wind and temperature. Suburbs often exhibit higher levels of pollution than the downtown areas where the emissions are produced. Remote national parks and wilderness areas have had their scenic vistas obscured by haze from distant cities. Fallout of tetraethyl lead from urban automobiles running on leaded gasoline has been observed in oceans and on the Greenland ice sheet. Automobile emissions may also have an impact on a global scale, as they are a significant source of greenhouse gases. Transportation contributed some 13.1 percent of the world's total anthropogenic greenhouse gas emissions in 2004.

Efforts to Reduce Emissions

Studies in cities such as London, England, have shown that major improvements in air quality can be achieved in less than ten years in urban areas with favorable climatic conditions through the use of more combustion-efficient engines and cleaner-burning fuels . In the United States, the 1970 amendments to the 1963 Clean Air Act (CAA) introduced automobile emissions standards for hydrocarbons, carbon oxides, and nitrogen oxides and ambient air-quality standards for six pollutants—carbon monoxide, sulfur oxides, nitrogen oxides, particulates, ozone, and lead—to protect human health and the environment. Through the CAA and its amendments of 1970, 1977, and 1990, the Environmental Protection Agency (EPA) has established increasingly stringent emissions-control policies for motor vehicles.

Although the EPA sets pollution standards for vehicles, vehicle manufacturers determine how they will meet those standards. Improved engine design, recirculation of exhaust gas to reduce nitrogen oxides, improved evaporative emissions controls, and computerized diagnostic systems have all led to a decline in polluting emissions. One of the most important milestones in the reduction of hydrocarbon and carbon monoxide emissions was the advent of the catalytic converter in 1975. Because lead impedes the catalyst that reduces emissions, unleaded gasoline became widely available at the same time. Ultimately, leaded gasoline was phased out in the United States and in many other countries, with the result that lead concentrations in ambient air have been lowered significantly.

Although the vehicle emissions controls implemented in the United States since 1970 have been effective, much of their success has been offset by the increasing numbers of vehicles on the roads and the greater distances driven, as many Americans travel farther from their homes to reach workplaces, schools, and shopping and recreation centers. Motor vehicle use has also become more widespread in developing countries, where air-quality standards are often more lax than in developed nations.

In the United States, the pollutant associated with vehicle emissions that has been reduced the most has been lead. Ambient concentrations of carbon monoxide and nitrogen oxides have also decreased; however, while they are low in relation to national standards, they remain a matter of concern because of the role they play in producing ozone and particulates and in impairing visibility. Ground-level ozone, toxic hydrocarbons, and particulates continue to be problems—as does carbon dioxide. In May, 2009, the EPA and the U.S. Department of Transportation agreed to establish national standards for greenhouse gas emissions and fuel economy for new cars and trucks sold in the United States.

Daniel G. Graetzer;
Updated by Karen N. Kähler

Further Reading

Godish, Thad. *Air Quality.* 4th ed. Lewis, 2004.

Griffin, Roger D. *Principles of Air Quality Management.* 2nd ed. CRC Press, 2007.

Hilgenkamp, Kathryn. "Air." In *Environmental Health: Ecological Perspectives.* Jones and Bartlett, 2006.

Jacobson, Mark Z. *Atmospheric Pollution: History, Science, and Regulation.* Cambridge University Press, 2002.

McCarthy, Tom. *Auto Mania: Cars, Consumers, and the Environment.* Yale University Press, 2007.

Rajan, Sudhir Chella. *The Enigma of Automobility: Democratic Politics and Pollution Control.* University of Pittsburgh Press, 1996.

U.S. Environmental Protection Agency. *The Plain English Guide to the Clean Air Act.* Office of Air Quality Planning and Standards, 2007.

B

■ Bacillus thuringiensis

FIELDS OF STUDY: Agriculture, Farming, Animal Husbandry; Biology, Life Sciences, Ecosystems; Ecology, Environment, Environmentalism; Science

DEFINITION: Natural microbial pesticide used for biological control of insects

Bacillus thuringiensis provides an environmentally neutral alternative to chemical pesticides, which can leave pollutants in soil and water.

Chemical control of plant parasites using pesticides, while often effective, has generally been found to create its own problems in areas of environmental pollution. The use of microbial pesticides has often proven as effective at pest management, without the problems of polluting soil and water. In addition, since many of these organisms are species-specific, targeting only select insects, neither plants nor more desirable insects (such as ladybugs) are at risk.

Bacillus thuringiensis (*B.t.*) is one of several bacteria species that have been used as biopesticides for control of insects. The bacterium produces a proteinaceous parasporal crystal within the cell when it sporulates (that is, forms spores) that is toxic only for a specific insect host. The crystalline protein is harmless in its natural state, becoming toxic only when it is cleaved by specific proteases. Once the bacterium has been ingested by the target insect, the alkaline secretions within the midgut of the insect activate the toxic character of the crystalline body. The toxin binds the intestinal cells, resulting in formation of pores and leakage of nutrients from the gut, and the insect dies within three to five days. The ability of the bacterium to sporulate also provides a means to disseminate the organism as a spray. Some commercial treatments utilize the crystalline body itself, which is sprayed onto the plants.

Though commercial application of *B.t.* began in the 1960s, widespread use began only decades later with the decline in use of chemical pesticides for protecting food crops and other types of plants. Various strains of *B.t.* have been developed for use against numerous types of insects. The *israelensis* variety is used commercially for control of mosquitos and blackfly larvae. The variety *kurstaki* has been used effectively against both the gypsy moth and cabbage loopers. More recently developed strains of *B.t.* have been shown to be effective in controlling insects that feed

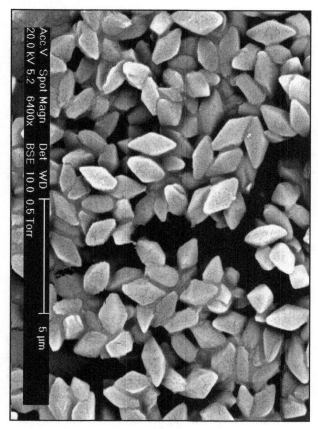

Crystals of Bt-toxin from Bacillus thuringiensis serovar morrisoni strain T08025. Microscopy by Jim Buckman

on fruit crops such as oranges and grapes. Varieties of *B.t.* are used commercially against some 150 different insect species, including cabbage worms, caterpillars, and other insects that feed on vegetable crops. The targeting of specific insects while using certain strains of *B.t.* also reduces the chance that desirable populations of organisms may be adversely affected.

Attempts have also been made through genetic engineering to introduce the gene that encodes the crystalline body directly into the plant genome. Since the protein is toxic only to insects, such an approach may result in naturally insect-resistant plants without further need for spraying. The procedure has proven effective in controlled experiments using tobacco plants, and more widespread testing in other plants has also been undertaken. The controversial nature of introducing such potentially toxic genes may preclude their use in food crops for some time, but such genetic experiments may prove useful in natural protection of ornamental trees and other plants.

Richard Adler

Further Reading

Letourneau, Deborah K., and Beth Elpern Burrows, eds. *Genetically Engineered Organisms: Assessing Environmental and Human Health Effects.* Boca Raton: CRC, 2002. Print.

Metz, Matthew, ed. *Bacillus Thuringiensis: A Cornerstone of Modern Agriculture.* Binghamton: Haworth, 2003. Print.

■ Back-to-the-land movement

FIELDS OF STUDY: Ecology, Environment, Environmentalism; Ethics, Advocacy, Policy, Protest; Social/Economic

Identification: Social movement based on the values of self-sufficiency and human harmony with nature

Dates: 1960's-1970's

The back-to-the-land movement exemplified a practice that sought to give greater meaning to everyday life through adherence to values of self-sufficiency, simplicity, freedom, and, most important, anticonsumerism.

The expression "back to the land" is commonly used in reference to a North American social and counItercultural phenomenon that started during the mid-1960's and continued well into the 1970's. The historical roots of the movement can be traced to Thomas Jefferson's agrarian vision and to the practice of self-reliance espoused by nineteenth century philosophers and essayists Ralph Waldo Emerson and Henry David Thoreau. Those who took part in the so-called back-to-the-land movement migrated from cities to rural areas because they had become increasingly disenchanted with the growing urban and industrial culture; they were attracted to a simple sort of daily life based on a set of values and choices that they saw as being in tune with an agrarian way of life and thus in greater harmony with the natural world.

Among the activities undertaken by those who joined the movement were building homes with natural materials; setting up systems to generate alternative forms of energy, such as solar and wind power; and growing their own food. They also faced choices regarding what types of livelihoods they should pursue and whether to work at home or outside the home; in addition, they somehow had to reconcile their desire to give up the rampant consumerism in society with their need to make a living. Members of the movement were arguably more interested in "making a life" for themselves than they were in "making a living," and many chose to live very simply, at the mercy of nature, and endure some of the inconveniences this may occasionally entail rather than indulge in what they viewed as the rampant and alienating consumerism of North American society at large.

By the end of the 1970's the movement evolved into one that took up the causes of the growing environmental movement, as people became more concerned with sustainable and holistic living. It has been estimated that by this time well over 1 million people had moved from the cities to rural areas. In the 1980's, however, a significant decline was noted in the number of people interested in leaving consumer culture for a simpler life in the countryside. This is explained in part by the booming and widespread prosperity of that decade. According to some observers of these trends, the 1990's saw a return to more environmentally conscious lifestyles among many North Americans, particularly in view of increasing awareness of global ecological crises.

Nader N. Chokr

Further Reading

Agnew, Eleanor. *Back from the Land: How Young Americans Went to Nature in the 1970's, and Why They Came Back.* Chicago: Ivan R. Dee, 2004.

Jacob, Jeffrey C. *New Pioneers: The Back-to-the-Land Movement and the Search for a Sustainable Future.* 1997. Reprint. University Park: Pennsylvania State University Press, 2006.

Nearing, Helen, and Scott Nearing. *Living the Good Life: How to Live Sanely and Simply in a Troubled World.* 1954. Reprint. New York: Schocken Books, 1987.

■ Bacterial resistance & public health

FIELDS OF STUDY: Animal Husbandry; Biochemistry; Biology; Medicine; Microbiology; Pharmacology; Veterinary Medicine;

Identification: The ability of bacteria to withstand antibiotics and other antimicrobial substances

Inappropriate use of antimicrobials such as antibiotics, antibacterial soaps, and hand sanitizers has caused some bacteria to develop resistance against the most common antibiotics, and many previously controlled infectious pathogens have become resistant to multiple drugs. Such multiresistant bacteria pose an increasing threat to public health and safety.

Overview

Bacteria are the most adaptable living organisms on earth and are found in virtually all environments—from the lowest ocean depths to the highest mountains. Bacteria resist extremes of heat, cold, acidity, alkalinity, heavy metals, and radiation that would kill most other organisms. *Deinococcus radiodurans,* for example, grow within nuclear power reactors, and *Thiobacillus thiooxidans* can grow in toxic acid mine drainage.

The terms "super bacteria" and "superbug" are often used to refer to bacteria that have either intrinsic (naturally occurring) or acquired resistance to multiple antibiotics. For example, two soil organisms—*Pseudomonas aeruginosa* and *Burkholderia* (*Pseudomonas*) *cepacia*—are intrinsically resistant to many antibiotics. Because many of the bacteria that acquire resistance are pathogens that were previously controlled by antibiotics, the development of antibiotic resistance represents a serious public health crisis, particularly for those individuals suffering from compromised immune systems.

History of Antibiotic Use

The history of antimicrobial compounds reaches into the early twentieth century, when German chemist Paul Ehrlich received worldwide fame for discovering Salvarsan, the first relatively specific chemical prophylactic agent against the microorganisms that causes syphilis. Salvarsan had serious undesirable side effects, as arsenic was its active ingredient. In addition, despite advances in antiseptic surgery, secondary infections resulting from hospitalization were a leading cause of death in the early twentieth century. Consequently, when Scottish bacteriologist Alexander Fleming reported his discovery of a soluble antimicrobial compound called penicillin, produced by the fungus *Penicillium,* the news attracted worldwide attention.

Antibiotics such as penicillin are low-molecular-weight compounds excreted by bacteria and fungi. Antibiotic-producing microorganisms most often belong to a group of soil bacteria called actinomycetes. *Streptomyces* are good examples of antibiotic-producing actinomycetes, and most of the commercially important antibiotics are isolated from *Streptomyces.* It is not entirely clear what ecological role the antibiotics play in natural environments. Microorganisms produce the antibiotics in a late, stationary growth phase, rather than during an early, active growth phase, which suggests that their chief function is not to inhibit the growth of competing microorganisms. The results of some studies suggest that, in natural ecosystems, antibiotics are types of signaling molecules that play a role in intercellular communication, while antibiotic resistance genes influence metabolism.

Fleming's discovery was not of much clinical importance until two English scientists, Howard Florey and Ernst Chain, took Fleming's fungus and produced purified penicillin just in time for World War II. The success of penicillin as a therapeutic agent with almost miraculous effects on infection prompted other microbiologists to look for naturally occurring antimicrobial compounds. In 1943 Selman Waksman, an American biochemist born in Ukraine, discovered the antibiotic streptomycin, the first truly effective agent to control *Mycobacterium tuberculosis,* the bacterium that causes tuberculosis. Widespread antibiotic

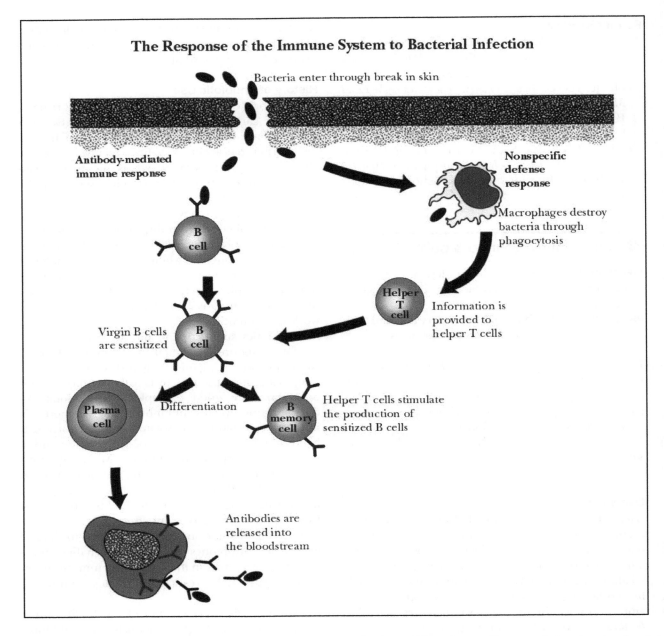

The Response of the Immune System to Bacterial Infection

Bacteria enter through break in skin

Antibody-mediated immune response

Nonspecific defense response

Macrophages destroy bacteria through phagocytosis

B cell

Virgin B cells are sensitized

B cell

Helper T cell

Information is provided to helper T cells

Plasma cell

Differentiation

B memory cell

Helper T cells stimulate the production of sensitized B cells

Antibodies are released into the bloodstream

use began shortly after World War II and was regarded as one of the great medical advances in the fight against infectious disease. By the late 1950's and early 1960's, pharmaceutical companies had devoted extensive research and development programs to isolating and producing new antibiotics.

Antibiotics were so effective, and their production ultimately so efficient, that they became inexpensive enough to be routinely prescribed for all types of infections, particularly to treat upper respiratory tract infections. When it was discovered that low levels of antibiotics also promote increased growth in domesticated animals, antibiotics began to be used routinely as feed supplements. Antibiotic use became ubiquitous among humans and livestock, to the degree that downstream from intense urbanization or livestock production, water sources commonly contain detectable levels of nonmetabolized, excreted antibiotics.

Development of Antibiotic Resistance

The widespread use and, ultimately, misuse of antibiotics inevitably caused antibiotic-resistant bacteria to emerge as microorganisms adapted to this new selective pressure. The prevalence of antimicrobial consumer products such as antibacterial soaps and hand sanitizers resulted in additional selective pressure. Eventually, many strains of pathogenic organisms developed on which antibiotics have little or no effect. Relatively recently discovered pathogens, such as the *Helicobacter pylori* bacterium associated with peptic ulcers, have rapidly developed resistance to the antibiotics used to treat them.

Streptococcal infections are a major bacterial cause of morbidity and mortality. In the mid-1970's *Streptococcus pneumonia* was uniformly susceptible to penicillin. However, penicillin-resistant streptococci strains were being isolated as early as 1967. A study in Denver, Colorado, showed that penicillin-resistant *S. pneumonia* strains increased from 1 percent of the isolates in 1980 to 13 percent of the isolates in 1995. One-half of the resistant strains were also resistant to another antibiotic, cephalosporin. It was apparent from the Denver study that a high correlation existed between antibiotic resistance in an individual and whether a member of the individual's family attended day care. Children attending day care are frequently exposed to preventive antibiotics, and these may have assisted in selecting for resistant bacteria. By 1996 penicillin-resistant *S. pneumoniae* represented between 33 and 58 percent of the clinical isolates around the world. In another U.S. study, conducted during the 1990's in middle Tennessee, non-penicillin-susceptible *S. pneumoniae* isolates increased over a nine-year period from 10 percent to 70 percent.

The disease tuberculosis (TB) was once the leading cause of death in young adults in industrialized countries. The disease was so common and feared that it was known as the White Plague. Before 1990 multidrug-resistant *M. tuberculosis* was uncommon, but by the mid-1990's increasing outbreaks were seen in hospitals and prisons, with death rates ranging from 50 to 80 percent. In a 2008 global report on anti-TB drug resistance, the World Health Organization noted that in 2006 the number of multidrug-resistant TB cases (those resistant to isoniazid and rifampicin, two of the first-line drugs used to treat the disease) had reached a record high of 489,139. Cases of the disease that were also resistant to second-line drugs were reported in 45 countries.

Likewise, multiple drug resistance in *Streptococcus pyogenes*, the so-called flesh-eating streptococci, was once rare, but erythromycin- and clindimycin-resistant strains have developed. In Italy, for example, antibiotic resistance in *S. pyogenes* increased from about 5 percent to more than 40 percent in some areas between 1993 and 1995.

Many old pathogens have become major clinical problems because of increased antibiotic resistance. *Salmonella* serotypes, for example, including those causing typhoid fever, have been discovered with resistance to at least five antibiotics, including ampicillin, chloramphenicol, streptomycin, sulfanilamide, and tetracycline. The number of these resistant isolates in England rose from 1.5 percent in 1989 to more than 34 percent in 1995. A Danish study found that persons suffering from resistant *Salmonella* infections had a higher mortality rate than those with drug-susceptible forms.

Gonorrhea, caused by *Neisseria gonorrhoeae*, is one of the most common sexually transmitted diseases. Physicians began using a class of broad-spectrum antibiotics called fluoroquinolones when *N. gonorrhoeae* developed resistance to penicillin, tetracycline, and streptomycin. By the late 1990's, however, resistance to the fluoroquinolone ciprofloxacin had developed in Hawaii and on the West Coast of the United States. By 2004 elevated resistance to ciprofloxacin was seen among men who had sex with men. Two years later, resistance was present in all regions of the country, including the heterosexual population. The U.S. Centers for Disease Control stopped recommending fluoroquinolones for the treatment of gonorrhea in 2007 and began monitoring gonorrhea patients being treated with the cephalosporin class of drugs for signs of treatment failure due to resistance.

Some antibiotic resistance appears to be linked to antimicrobial use in farm animals. Shortly after antibiotics appeared, it was discovered that subtherapeutic levels could promote growth in animals and treat acute infections in such settings as aquaculture. One antimicrobial drug, avoparcin, is a glycopeptide (a compound containing sugars and proteins) that is used as a feed additive. Vancomycin-resistant enterococci such as *Enterococcus faecium* were first isolated in 1988 and appeared to be linked to drug use in animals. Antibiotic resistance in enterococci was found to be more prevalent in farm animals exposed to antimicrobial drugs, and prolonged exposure to oral glycoproteins in tests led to vancomycin-resistant enterococci in 64 percent of the subjects. In 1997 the European Union banned the use of avoparcin, which is similar to vancomycin, as an animal feed additive. In June, 2010, the U.S. Food and Drug Administration issued draft guidelines to promote more prudent use of medically important antimicrobials in food-producing animals.

How Antibiotic Resistance Occurs

Antibiotic resistance occurs because the antibiotics exert a selective pressure on the bacterial pathogens. The selective pressure eliminates all but a few bacteria that can persist through evasion or mutation. One reason that the duration of antibiotic treatments is often several weeks is to ensure that bacteria that have evaded the initial exposure are killed. The rare bacteria that are resistant can persist and grow regardless of continued antibiotic exposure. Terminating antibiotic treatment early, once symptoms disappear, has the unfortunate effect of stimulating antibiotic resistance without completely eliminating the original cause of infection.

Mutations that promote resistance occur with different frequencies. For example, spontaneous resistance of *M. tuberculosis* to cycloserine and viomycin may occur in 1 in 1,000 cells, resistance to kanamycin may occur in only 1 in 1 million cells, and resistance to rifampicin may occur in only 1 in 100 million cells. Consequently, 1 billion bacterial cells will contain several individuals resistant to at least one antibiotic. Using multiple antibiotics further reduces the likelihood that an individual cell will be resistant to all antibiotics. However, it can cause multiple antibiotic resistance to develop in bacteria that already have resistance to some of the antibiotics.

Bacterial pathogens may not need to mutate spontaneously to acquire antibiotic resistance. There are several mechanisms by which bacteria can acquire the genes for antibiotic resistance from microorganisms that are already antibiotic-resistant. These mechanisms include conjugation (the exchange of genetic information through direct cell-to-cell contact), transduction (the exchange of genetic information from one cell to another by means of a virus), transformation (the acquisition of genetic information through the taking up of deoxyribonucleic acid, or DNA, directly from the environment), and transfer of plasmids, small circular pieces of DNA that

frequently carry genes for antibiotic resistance. Exchange of genes for antibiotic resistance on plasmids is one of the most common means of developing or acquiring resistance in hospitals because of the heavy antibiotic use in these settings.

The genes for antibiotic resistance take many forms. They may make the bacteria impermeable to the antibiotic. They may subtly alter the target of the antibiotic within the cell so that it is no longer affected. The genes may code for production of an enzyme in the bacteria that specifically destroys the antibiotic. For example, fluoroquinolone antibiotics inhibit DNA replication in pathogens by binding to the enzyme required for replication. Resistant bacteria have mutations in the amino acid sequences of this enzyme that prevent the antibiotic from binding to this region. Some resistant pathogens produce an enzyme called penicillinase, which degrades the antibiotic penicillin before it can prevent cell wall formation.

New Strategies

The heavy use of antibiotics has led to increases in morbidity, mortality caused by previously controlled infectious diseases, and health costs. Some of the recommended ways of dealing with this public health problem include changing antibiotic prescription patterns, changing both doctor and patient attitudes about the necessity for antibiotics, increasing the worldwide surveillance of drug-resistant bacteria, improving techniques for susceptibility testing, and investing in the research and development of new antimicrobial agents.

Gene therapy, which remains an experimental technique, is regarded as one promising solution to antibiotic resistance. In gene therapy, the genes expressing part of a pathogen's cell are injected into the patient to stimulate a heightened immune response. Some old technologies are also being revisited. There is increasing interest in using serum treatments, in which antibodies raised against a pathogen are injected into a patient to cause an immediate immune response. Previous serum treatment techniques have yielded mixed results, but with the advent of monoclonal antibodies and the techniques for producing them, serum treatments in future can be made much more specific and the antibodies delivered in much higher concentrations.

Another experimental treatment technique involves manipulating viruses genetically to make them target specific pathogens. Once injected into a patient, the reprogrammed viruses begin a focused attack on the pathogen. Viruses attack all living organisms, including bacteria, but are extremely specific. For this therapeutic technique, certain genes are removed to prevent the virus from causing disease or degrading anything other than the target pathogenic organism.

Mark Coyne; updated by Karen N. Kähler

Further Reading

Biddle, Wayne. *A Field Guide to Germs.* 3rd ed. Anchor Books, 2010.

Fong, Ignatius W., and Karl Drlica, eds. *Antimicrobial Resistance and Implications for the Twenty-first Century.* Springer, 2008.

Lashley, Felissa R., and Jerry D. Durham, eds. *Emerging Infectious Diseases: Trends and Issues.* 2nd ed. Springer, 2007.

Levy, Stuart B. *The Antibiotic Paradox: How the Misuse of Antibiotics Destroys Their Curative Power.* 2nd ed. Perseus, 2002.

Shnayerson, Michael, and Mark J. Plotkin. *The Killers Within: The Deadly Rise of Drug-Resistant Bacteria.* Little, Brown, 2002.

■ Balance of nature

FIELDS OF STUDY: Biology; Ecology; Ecosystem Management; Environmental Studies;

Identification: Ecological concept that nature, in its undisturbed state, achieves constant equilibrium

The concept of the balance of nature has never been legitimated in science as either a hypothesis or a theory, but it persists as a designation for a healthy environment.

Overview

Greek natural philosophers in the fifth and sixth centuries BCE attempted to explain in naturalistic terms how nature works rather than depending upon myths. The atomistic theory of Leucippus and Democritus stated that matter can be transformed but is never created or destroyed. The Pythagoreans heard musical harmony in the universe. Hippocratic medicine taught that the balance of 'humors' within the body produces health and an imbalance produces disease, and Greek physicians believed in the healing

power of nature. Within this worldview, ecological balance would have been a compelling expectation.

Herodotus, the father of history, wrote about not only the human histories of Greece, Persia, and Egypt but also their geographies and natural histories. He was influenced by ideas in natural philosophy, and he was concerned with concrete examples that might illustrate generalities. In organizing his information on the lions, snakes, and hares of Arabia, he asked why predatory species do not eat up all of their prey. His answer was that a superintending "Providence" had created the different species with different capacities for reproduction. Predatory species, such as lions and snakes, produce fewer offspring than species that they eat, such as hares. From Egypt, Herodotus obtained a report about a mutually beneficial relationship between Nile crocodiles and plovers: Crocodiles allow plovers to sit on their teeth and eat the leeches that infest their mouths.

Plato lived after the natural philosophers and Herodotus, but he lacked their trust in sensory data, and therefore he explained nature with naturalistic myths. In a dialogue called *Prōtagoras* (c. 390 BCE; English translation, 1804), Plato asked Herodotus's question about why some species do not eat up the others, but he asked it more abstractly and not for its own sake. The point of this creation myth was to explain why humans do not have specialized traits such as wings or claws. The gods assigned to Epimetheus the task of creating each species with traits that would enable it to survive. He had given out all the specialized traits before he got around to creating humans, and his brother Prometheus had to save humanity by giving it reason and fire. The secondary point of the myth supplements what Herodotus had concluded about differences in reproduction with a conclusion about differential traits that ensure survival.

In the writings of Aristotle and his colleagues in Athens, full-fledged science emerged. These scholars realized the importance of both collecting data and ordering it so as to allow the drawing of conclusions. These scholars, however, focused on physiology and anatomy and neglected to look for what modern-day persons call ecological explanations of how nature works. For example, they explained that the greater number of offspring in hares than in lions is because of their size. Since hares are smaller, it is easier for more of them to grow within a female than for multiple larger lion cubs to grow in their mother. The

Balance of nature statue near VUDA Park in Visakhapatnam, Andhra Pradesh. By Adityamadhav83 (Own work).

balance-of-nature concept was not distinct enough to require either defending or refuting.

Scientific Revolution

The ancient Romans excelled in engineering, not science. They were mostly content with abbreviated Latin versions of Greek science. Roman writings are still worth mentioning, however, because of their influence on later European naturalists. Aelianus compiled a popular natural history book that, among other things, explained that jackdaws are friends to the farmer because jackdaws eat the eggs and young of locusts that would eat the farmer's produce. The philosopher Cicero wrote an influential book, *De natura deorum* (44 BCE; *On the Nature of the Gods*, 1683), in which he saw the work of Providence in endowing plants with the capacity to feed humans and animals and still be able to have seeds left over to ensure their own reproduction. Another philosopher, Plotinus, pondered the evil of suffering when predators kill animals for food. He decided that the existence of predation allows a greater diversity of life to exist than would be possible if all animals ate plants. These miscellaneous observations were insufficient for a theory, but they kept alive the notion of a balance of nature.

During the scientific revolution, fresh observations and conclusions appeared. Most significant, John Graunt, a merchant, analyzed London's baptismal and death records in 1662 and discovered the balance in the sex ratio and the regularity of most causes of death (excluding epidemics). England's chief justice, Sir Matthew Hale, was interested in Graunt's discoveries, but he nevertheless decided that the human population, in contrast to animal populations, must have steadily increased throughout history. He surveyed the known causes of animal mortality and in 1677 published the earliest explicit account of the balance of nature.

English scientist Robert Hooke studied fossils and in 1665 concluded that they represented the remains of plants and animals, some of which were probably extinct. John Ray, a clergyman and naturalist, argued in response that the extinction of species would contradict the wisdom of the ages, by which he seems to have meant the balance of nature. Ray also studied the hydrologic cycle, which is a kind of environmental balance of water. In the late seventeenth century, Antoni van Leeuwenhoek, one of the first investigators to make biological studies with a microscope, discovered that parasites are more prevalent than anyone had suspected and that they are often detrimental or even fatal to their hosts. Before that, it was commonly assumed that the relationship between host and parasite was mutually beneficial.

Richard Bradley, a botanist and popularizer of natural history, pointed out in 1718 that each species of plant has its own kind of insect and that there are even different insects that eat the leaves and bark of a tree. His book *A Philosophical Account of the Works of Nature* (1721) explored aspects of the balance of nature more thoroughly than had been done before. Ray's and Bradley's books may have inspired the comment in Alexander Pope's *An Essay on Man* (1733-1734) that all the species are so closely interdependent that the extinction of one would lead to the destruction of all living nature.

Toward a Science of Ecology

Swedish naturalist Carolus Linnaeus was an important protoecologist. In his essay *Oeconomia Naturae* (1749; *The Economy of Nature*, 1749) he attempted to organize the aspect of natural history dealing with the balance of nature, but he realized that one must study not only ways that plants and animals interact but also their habitats. He knew that while balance had to exist, there occurred over time a succession of plants, beginning with a bare field and ending with a forest. In *Politia Naturae* (1760; *Governing Nature*, 1760) he discussed the checks on populations that prevent some species from becoming so numerous that they eliminate others. He noticed the competition among different species of plants in a meadow and concluded that feeding insects kept them in check. French naturalist Comte de Buffon developed a dynamical perspective on the balance of nature from his studies of rodents and their predators. Rodents can increase in numbers to plague proportions, but then predators and climate reduce their numbers. Buffon also suspected that humans had exterminated some large mammals, such as mammoths and mastodons.

However, a later Frenchman, Jean-Baptiste Lamarck, published a book on evolution called *Philosophie zoologique* (1809; *Zoological Philosophy*, 1914), which cast doubt on extinction by arguing that fossils represent only early forms of living species: Mammoths and mastodons evolved into African and Indian elephants. In developing this idea, he minimized the importance of competition in nature. An English opponent, the geologist Charles Lyell, argued in 1833 that species do become extinct, primarily because of competition among species. Charles Darwin was inspired by his own investigations during a long voyage around the world and by his reading of the works of Linnaeus and Lyell. In his revolutionary book *On the Origin of Species by Means of Natural Selection: Or, The Preservation of Favoured Races in the Struggle for Life* (1859), Darwin argued an intermediate position between those of Lamarck and

Lyell: Species do evolve into different species, but in the process, some species do indeed become extinct.

Darwin's theory of evolution might have brought an end to the balance-of-nature concept, but it did not. Instead, American zoologist Stephen A. Forbes developed an evolutionary concept of the balance of nature in his essay "The Lake as a Microcosm" (1887), in which he observes that although the reproductive rate of aquatic species is enormous and the struggle for existence among them is severe, "the little community secluded here is as prosperous as if its state were one of profound and perpetual peace." Forbes emphasized the stabilizing effects of natural selection.

Ecology

The science of ecology became formally organized in the period from the 1890's through the 1910's. One of its important organizing concepts was that of "biotic communities." Frederic E. Clements, an American plant ecologist, wrote a large monograph titled *Plant Succession* (1916), in which he drew a morphological and developmental analogy between organisms and plant communities. Both the individual and the community have a life history during which each changes its anatomy and physiology. This superorganismic concept was an extreme version of the balance of nature that seemed plausible as long as one believed that a biotic community was a real entity rather than a convenient approximation of what one sees in a pond, a meadow, or a forest. However, the studies of Henry A. Gleason in 1917 and later indicated that plant species merely compete with one another in similar environments; he concluded that Clements's superorganism was poetry, not science.

While the balance-of-nature concept was giving way to ecological hypotheses and theories, Rachel Carson decided that she could not argue her case in *Silent Spring* (1962) without it. She admitted, "The balance of nature is not a *status quo*; it is fluid, ever shifting, in a constant state of adjustment." Nevertheless, for Carson the concept represented a healthy environment, which humans could upset. Her usage of the phrase has persisted within the environmental movement.

In 1972 English medical chemist James Lovelock developed a new balance-of-nature idea, which he called Gaia, named for a Greek earth goddess. His reasoning owed virtually nothing to previous balance-of-nature notions, which focused on the interactions of plants and animals. His concept emphasized the chemical cycles that flow from the earth to the waters, atmosphere, and living organisms. Lovelock soon had the assistance of a zoologist named Lynn Margulis, and the studies they conducted together convinced them that biogeochemical cycles are not random; rather, they exhibit homeostasis, just as some animals exhibit homeostasis in body heat and blood concentrations of various substances. Lovelock and Margulis argued that living beings, rather than inanimate forces, mainly control the earth's environment. In 1988 three scientific organizations sponsored a conference to evaluate their ideas; the conference was attended by 150 scientists from all over the world. Although science more or less understands how homeostasis works when a brain within an animal controls it, no one has succeeded in satisfactorily explaining how homeostasis can work in a world "system" that lacks a brain. The Gaia hypothesis is as untestable as were earlier balance-of-nature concepts.

Frank N. Egerton

Further Reading

Egerton, Frank N. "Changing Concepts of the Balance of Nature." *Quarterly Review of Biology* 48 (June, 1973): 322-350.

_____. "The History and Present Entanglements of Some General Ecological Perspectives." In *Humans as Components of Ecosystems,* edited by Mark J. McDonnell and S. T. A. Pickett. Springer, 1993.

Judd, Richard W. *The Untilled Garden: Natural History and the Spirit of Conservation in America, 1740-1840.* Cambridge University Press, 2009.

Kirchner, James W. "The Gaia Hypotheses: Are They Testable? Are They Useful?" In *Scientists on Gaia,* edited by Stephen H. Schneider and Penelope J. Boston. MIT Press, 1991.

Kricher, John C. *The Balance of Nature: Ecology's Enduring Myth.* Princeton University Press, 2009.

Milne, Lorus J., and Margery Milne. *The Balance of Nature.* 1960. Reprint. Alfred A. Knopf, 1970.

■ Basel Convention & movement of hazardous waste

FIELDS OF STUDY: Government, Politics, International Relations; History/Biography; International Relations, Agreements, Treaties; Pollution, Emissions, Toxic Waste, Hazardous Materials

THE CONVENTION: International agreement designed to limit the movement of hazardous wastes across national boundaries

DATE: Opened for signature on March 22, 1989

The Basel Convention has been effective in raising public awareness of the transporting of hazardous wastes, and it has somewhat slowed the movement of such wastes from country to country. The convention is not always strictly enforced, however, and some nations continue to transport hazardous wastes across national boundaries illegally.

Spurred by interest generated by several incidents during the 1980's in which ships carrying waste materials sailed from port to port in unsuccessful efforts to be allowed to unload their cargoes, the international community, under the auspices of the United Nations Environment Programme, negotiated an agreement designed to limit the export of hazardous waste from one country to another. The Basel Convention on the Control of Transboundary Movements of Hazardous Wastes defines hazardous waste as used oils, biomedical wastes, persistent organic pollutants such as pesticides, polychlorinated biphenyls, and various other chemicals. The terms of the convention require that prior informed consent be obtained from a country before such wastes can be exported to that country. The goal of the Basel Convention is to minimize the movement of such wastes across national boundaries.

Since it entered into force in May, 1992, the Basel Convention has enabled countries to deal with attempts to move hazardous wastes across their borders. It was soon recognized that the industrialized nations are the major exporters of hazardous waste and that the less industrialized countries of Africa, Latin America, and Asia had been the primary recipients of such materials. In 1995, at the second meeting of the convention's signatory member states, agreement was reached to prohibit the movement of hazardous wastes from industrialized countries to less industrialized countries; this amendment is commonly referred to as the Basel Ban. Although many

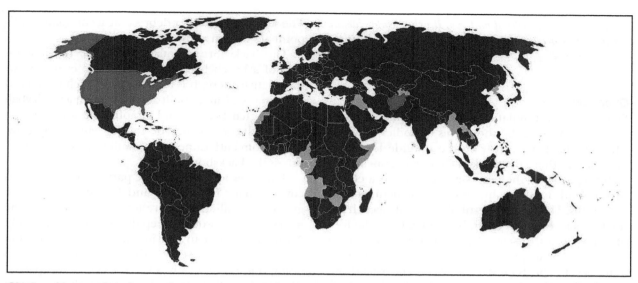

Blank world map, coloured as per the signatories and ratification of the Basel Convention. Blue = Signed and ratified Red = Signed, but not ratified Grey = Not a signatory. By Super cyclist

industrialized countries abide by the Basel Ban, it has not yet been ratified. Several countries, including the United States, that ratified the original agreement have yet to ratify the Basel Ban.

The Basel Convention and the Basel Ban have been effective in slowing the migration of hazardous wastes (which some estimate to be more than 8.5 million tons of waste per year) from industrialized to developing countries. Nonetheless, some critics of the convention argue for the use of developing countries as dumping grounds for industrialized countries, noting that such exchanges have economic benefits for both parties. This attitude ignores the economic costs associated with dealing with hazardous waste in developing countries, such as the health care costs that arise when illnesses are caused by contact with hazardous materials.

Even with the adoption of the Basel Convention, some parties still seek to dispose of hazardous wastes in cheap fashion. Several suspicious shipwrecks have occurred in the Mediterranean involving ships later found to have been carrying cargoes—such as radioactive materials—that would have been subject to the convention. In some cases these wrecks have led to fishing bans, as occurred along the coast of Italy in 2007.

Although the Basel Convention has been effective in raising public awareness of the transporting of hazardous wastes, it has not always been stringently enforced. The movement of hazardous wastes has been somewhat limited by the convention, but until tougher measures are adopted to reduce or somehow safely dispose of hazardous wastes at their points of origin, such wastes will continue to be exported, often illegally, from industrialized countries. Some of these wastes will arrive at developing countries, imposing costs on them; other wastes will be disposed of at sea, imposing costs on everyone.

John M. Theilmann

Further Reading

Mukerjee, Madhusree. "Poisoned Shipments." *Scientific American*, February, 2010, 14-15.

Pellow, David Naguib. *Resisting Global Toxics.* Cambridge, Mass.: MIT Press, 2007.

United Nations Environment Programme. *Minimizing Hazardous Wastes: A Simplified Guide to the Basel Convention.* Geneva: Author, 2002.

■ Beach erosion

FIELDS OF STUDY: Ecology; Environmental Studies; Fluid Dynamics; Limnology; Oceanography; Physical Geography;

IDENTIFICATION: Sandy or rocky areas on the shores of bodies of water

Beaches have significant value for recreational purposes, and important industries, such as those related to swim-

ming and surfing, depend on them. Beaches worldwide are threatened by accelerating erosion, as well as by a projected rise in sea level.

Overview

Beaches are accumulations of loose sedimentary material found along the shorelines of bodies of water. They extend landward from the low-tide level to a place where there is a marked change in appearance or topography of the land surface, such as a cliff, a row of sand dunes, or human-made structures such as seawalls. The two major subdivisions of a beach are the backshore, which extends seaward from the foot of a cliff, dunes, or seawall; and the foreshore, which usually has a steeper slope that continues down to water level. The boundary between the backshore and the foreshore is generally marked by a change in slope or by a small scarp excavated by wave activity.

Beach erosion coastal erosion. By Hillebrand Steve, US Fish and Wildlife Service.

The seaweed and other debris that accumulate at this point are known as the wrack.

The backshore is considered to be the inactive part of a beach because there is little evidence for wave activity here. It is the part of a beach most used by humans. Human-built additions such as volleyball nets, lifeguard stands, and campfire pits are found on the backshore; grasses or trailing vines may grow down from cliff, dunes, or seawall to extend partway across the backshore.

The foreshore is the active part of the beach. It is covered daily by the rise and fall of the tides; no grasses or trailing vines are found here because the waves and tides would sweep them away immediately. All traces of human activity, such as footprints and lost toys, are removed by the waves as well. Upon going out, the tide leaves the surface of this part of the beach perfectly smooth, broken only at its lower end by a slight dip known as the low-tide step. This is a gentle trough excavated by the breakers at low tide. Waves grind up shells and pebbles here in a so-called wave mill, and the resulting fragments become new materials for the beach. They grow finer-grained as the wind and waves carry them upward toward the dunes.

The widths of beaches vary greatly around the world. Beaches at the foot of cliffs or seawalls may be just a few feet wide, whereas those on low-relief coasts can extend seaward for many miles.

Accelerating Beach Erosion

Oceanographers calculate that 70 percent of the world's beaches are being cut back by erosion, 10 percent are growing forward, and the rest remain unchanged. Erosion of a beach occurs when it loses more sediment than it gains from the sources that feed it. Losses may take place when beach materials are carried inland during storm surges, when they are carried seaward as big waves cut back the coast during severe storms, or when they are carried along the shoreline by the longshore current. This current is present along coasts whenever waves strike the shoreline at an acute angle rather than coming in directly.

During severe storms the loss of beach materials can be rapid; evidence for this is seen in collapsed seawalls and cliffed dunes on the backshore or in salt marsh deposits and tree stumps uncovered on the foreshore as the beach moves inland over a previously vegetated area. Aerial photographs are generally used to determine how much material has been removed from beaches, with recent photographs compared to photographs taken previously.

Beach erosion accelerated in the early twenty-first century because of several factors: the active removal of materials by waves, wind, and currents; rising sea level, which resulted in the migration of shorelines inland; and increasing human modification of the coasts. Human-caused changes to coastlines that affect beach erosion include both the construction of seawalls, groins, offshore breakwaters, and jetties and the bringing in of new sand in a procedure known as beach nourishment. Seawalls are built at the backs of beaches to prevent erosion, but they may reflect the storm waves, causing them to carry sediment seaward. Groins, which are rock ribs extending seaward along the foreshore to trap sand on their up-drift sides, cause erosion on their down-drift sides, resulting in alternating scallops of erosion and deposition along the coast. Breakwaters, which are offshore structures built parallel to the coast, and jetties, which are walls extending seaward to stabilize inlets, both trap migrating sand, resulting in erosion on their down-drift sides. Even beach nourishment, a highly popular practice, has its negative effects. Because the sand that is added to beaches is dredged from offshore or trucked in from the land, it rarely has the same texture and composition of the original beach sand. The result is that this new sand usually erodes faster than the original sand that it replaces.

Donald W. Lovejoy

Further Reading

Bird, Eric. *Coastal Geomorphology: An Introduction.* 2nd ed. John Wiley & Sons, 2008.

Bird, Eric, and Nick Lewis. "Responses to Beach Erosion." *Beach Renourishment.* Springer International, 2015. 29–39.

"Coastal Change Hazards: Hurricanes and Extreme Storms." *United States Geological Survey,* 8 June, 2015. Retrieved from http://coastal.er.usgs.gov/hurricanes/coastal-change/beach-erosion.php.

Davis, Richard A., Jr., and Duncan M. FitzGerald. *Beaches and Coasts.* Blackwell, 2004.

Neal, William J., Orrin H. Pilkey, and Joseph T. Kelley. *Atlantic Coastal Beaches: A Guide to the Ripples, Dunes, and Other Natural Features of the Seashore.* Mountain Press, 2007.

Pilkey, Orrin H., and J. Andrew G. Cooper. *The Last Beach.* Duke University Press, 2014.

■ Bees & other pollinators

FIELDS OF STUDY: Apiculture; Agriculture; Agronomy; Biology;

IDENTIFICATION: Flying insects and other biological agents that facilitate plant reproduction by moving pollen among seed plants

Pollinators such as bees are extremely important to the health of the planet because without them most plant species would disappear. Pollinating species are in decline around the world, a trend that threatens biodiversity and food supplies for many animals, including humans.

Overview

Bees are the best-known group of pollinators; however, other insects such as butterflies, wasps, beetles, and ants are pollinators, too, along with some species of bats and birds. Plants and their pollinators co-evolved, forming symbiotic relationships in which plants provide food for the pollinators, which in turn aid the plants' reproduction. Many other species evolved over time to take advantage of this fundamental relationship between plant and pollinator, including humans and other animals that eat the results of the fertilized plants, such as nuts, seeds, and berries. Pollinators also contribute to the web of life by ensuring the continued survival of plants through the process of pollination; the loss of pollinators can affect the biodiversity and well-being of a whole ecosystem. By the early twenty-first century, declines in pollinator populations around the world led environmental groups and government agencies to include pollinators in their conservation efforts.

Pollinator Decline

The decline of pollinating species has many causes, all for the most part related to human activity. One cause is the use (and misuse) of pesticides meant to kill other insects, such as mosquitoes; such pesticides also indiscriminately kill off other insect populations, many of them pollinator species. Another cause of pollinator decline is the large-scale transport of pollinators around the world for agricultural purposes; this practice also results in the large-scale transport

Bee. By Mark Winterbourne from Leeds, West Yorkshire, United Kingdom

of parasites and diseases that affect them, as well as the introduction of invasive species that can compete with or destroy native pollinator populations.

Human expansion into previously wild or relatively untouched spaces contributes to pollinator decline through habitat loss and degradation, as development brings with it pollution, hive destruction, and fragmentation of traditional "nectar corridors." Wild pollinators have fewer places to nest, mate, and roost safely, and their historic ranges have been destroyed or partitioned in such a way that it is far more difficult for them to find the nectar they need to survive. Many pollinators are already on endangered or threatened species lists, including more than one hundred avian species and dozens of mammals.

Climate change has also affected pollinators. A 2015 study found that warming temperatures had caused bumblebees' range to shrink by as much as 300 kilometers (190 miles) since the 1970s, with the bees staying farther and farther north as the climates in the southern parts of Europe and North America became less hospitable.

The Importance of Bees

The thousands of species of bees in the world are widely known for pollination and for their making of honey and beeswax. Bees are the primary pollinators of flowers around the world and are also responsible for the pollination of approximately one-third of the human food supply. Many agricultural crops, ranging from watermelons to cashews, rely on pollination by bees. European honeybees, in particular, are extremely important to agriculture because of humans' ability to manage the species.

Pollination management, also called contract pollination, entails transporting honeybees in their hives to crops that are in need of pollination. Modern monoculture farming has created a situation in which the normal pollinators of some kinds of crops cannot pollinate them, either because of the huge size of the fields or because the pollinators have declined or died off. Honeybees, however, can be put in the fields in such large numbers that they make up for the fact that they are often less efficient pollinators than the native species that previously would have pollinated a particular crop. The economic viability of monoculture agriculture often depends entirely on pollination management, and most professional beekeepers in the twenty-first century focus on contract pollination rather than honey as their primary source of revenue.

The same factors that have caused declines in other pollinator populations since the late twentieth century have affected honeybees as well, causing a widespread honeybee population decline. In addition, across North America and Western Europe since at least 2006, honeybees have disappeared in what is called honeybee colony collapse disorder (CCD), the cause of which remains a mystery. CCD is characterized by the worker bees flying off and never returning to the hive or colony, leaving behind a healthy queen, an unhatched brood, and food supplies.

Given the importance of honeybees to agriculture around the world, scientists have investigated many possible causes for CCD; possibilities include a parasitic mite, insect diseases, and the use or misuse of insecticides. Some researchers have reported evidence that it may be viral. These possibilities are aggravated by other factors negatively affecting honeybee populations, such as poor diet related to monoculture, which can lead to malnutrition or impaired immune system, and migratory beekeeping, which spreads parasites and diseases among populations. One such disease, known as deformed wing virus after its chief symptom, became a serious threat to honeybee and bumblebee populations in the 2010s; a 2016 study found that the trade in pollinators was directly responsible for spreading the virus around the world.

Many pollinators are very small, but their importance to terrestrial life is great. Pollinators are a major part of the web of life, and what happens to them can affect every other creature in an ecosystem. Plants, whether they are cacti in the desert of Mexico or blueberries in Scotland, need their pollinators to survive—without pollinators a plant cannot reproduce and its species will go extinct. If this occurs, the pollinators adapted to that plant will no longer have a food supply and will either starve to death or switch to another source of nectar, inevitably intruding on another animal's food supply. As the plants disappear for lack of pollinators, animals such as birds, small mammals, and lizards that eat the fruit, nuts, and seeds produced by pollinated plants will also begin to starve. This effect will ripple through the food web until it reaches larger animals, including human beings.

Megan E. Watson

Further Reading

Buchmann, Stephen L., and Gary Paul Nabhan. *The Forgotten Pollinators*. Island, 1996.

Carswell, Cally. "Bumblebees Being Crushed by Climate Change." *Science News*. AAAS, 9 July 2015. Web. 1 Oct. 2015.

Fischer, David, and Thomas Moriarty. *Pesticide Risk Assessment for Pollinators*. Wiley, 2014.

Grimm, V., et al. "Ecological Modeling for Pesticide Risk Assessment for Honey Bees and Other Pollinators." *Pesticide Risk Assessment for Pollinators* (2014): 149–62.

James, Rosalind R., and Theresa L. Pitts-Singer, eds. *Bee Pollination in Agricultural Ecosystems*. Oxford University Press, 2008.

Kennedy, Merrit. "Report: More Pollinator Species in Jeopardy, Threatening World Food Supply." *NPR*. NPR, 26 Feb. 2016. Web. 2 Mar. 2016.

Miller-Struttmann, Nicole E., et al. "Functional Mismatch in a Bumble Bee Pollination Mutualism under Climate Change." *Science* 25 Sept. 2015: 1541–544.

"Pollinators." *US Fish & Wildlife Service*. Dept. of the Interior, 1 Mar. 2016. Web. 2 Mar. 2016.

St. Fleur, Nicholas. "Climate Change Is Shrinking Where Bumblebees Range, Research Finds." *New York Times*. New York Times, 9 July 2015. Web. 1 Oct. 2015.

Waser, Nickolas M., and Jeff Ollerton, eds. *Plant-Pollinator Interactions: From Specialization to Generalization*. University of Chicago Press, 2006.

Wilfert, Lena, et al. "Deformed Wing Virus Is a Recent Global Epidemic in Honeybees Driven by *Varroa* Mites." *Science* 351.6,273 (2016): 594–7.

■ Benefit-cost analysis

FIELDS OF STUDY: Ecology, Environment, Environmentalism; Economics, Business, Production, Commerce; Scientific Equipment, Tools, Techniques, and Methods; Social/Economic; Statistics, Modeling, Projection

DEFINITION: Method of determining the benefit of undertaking a program or project based on its costs

Benefit-cost analysis is used to determine the value of many types of projects and their impacts, including environmental management projects and the impacts of such projects as airport construction.

Benefit-cost analysis (also called cost-benefit analysis) is an idea that can be traced back to an article by nineteenth century French economist Jules Dupuit. Early use of the concept in the United States is seen in the water development projects of the U.S. Army Corps of Engineers, where it was used to prioritize projects concerning the nation's waterways. The term arose in the context of the environment and natural resources in the Flood Control Act of 1936, which states that the "federal government should improve or participate in the improvement of navigable waters or their tributaries, including watersheds thereof, for flood control purposes if the benefits to whomever they may accrue are in excess of the estimated costs." Hence the term "benefit-cost analysis" was established; it was later embraced by economists during the 1950's. Two important concepts in economics, the Pareto principle and Kaldor-Hicks efficiency, are related to benefit-cost analysis.

In benefit-cost analysis, the monetary measure of all expected benefits of proposed projects or activities is compared with the costs of undertaking those projects or activities. This typically involves using the "time value of money" formula, which converts the future expected streams of costs and benefits to a present value amount. This tool helps planners and policy makers to determine whether a project is

The French economist Jules Dupuit (1804-1866), credited with the creation of cost-benefit analysis.

worth undertaking by weighing the advantages and the disadvantages in monetary terms.

The kinds of projects for which benefit-cost analyses may be conducted include highways, training programs, and health care systems. Benefit-cost analyses can provide answers to questions about whether environmental management projects—such as constructing a new airport terminal, installing wind turbines on the Scottish coast, or building a new dam on a particular river—will provide benefits that outweigh the respective costs to the environment.

In conducting benefit-cost analysis, the analyst finds, quantifies, and adds up the values of the benefits of a course of action. The analyst then identifies, quantifies, and subtracts all the costs associated with the activities or project. The difference between the two indicates whether the planned action or project should or should not be undertaken. To conduct such an analysis well, the analyst must not only make sure all the costs and benefits are included and properly quantified but also avoid double counting.

One key problem in undertaking an environmental benefit-cost analysis lies in trying to assign monetary values to intangibles associated with the project. For example, a functioning ecosystem is of economic value to society, but its aesthetic functions, which may be lost because of a project and its future effects, fall outside the market system; such functions are often excluded from decision-making tools such as benefit-cost analysis. The construction of a dam or reclamation of land has benefits of water, energy, and fish supply. These benefits can be traded on the market, and a market price can be used to represent their economic value. Where benefits exist that cannot be traded on the market, shadow pricing may be used to place economic values on the benefits; this process is subjective, however.

In spite of its shortcomings for environment-related applications, benefit-cost analysis provides planners and policy makers with a method for putting all relevant benefits and costs of proposed projects on a common temporal footing so that they can make informed decisions. It also provides all parties concerned with greater understanding of the economic costs of their decisions and thus allows for arguments to be made both for and against a change based on benefit-cost considerations.

Josephus J. Brimah

Further Reading

Boardman, Anthony E., et al. *Cost-Benefit Analysis.* 4th ed. Upper Saddle River, N.J.: Prentice Hall, 2010.

Brent, Robert J. *Cost-Benefit Analysis for Developing Countries.* Northampton, Mass.: Edward Elgar, 2000.

Pearce, David. "The Limits of Cost-Benefit Analysis as a Guide to Environmental Policy." In *Economics and Environment: Essays on Ecological Economics and Sustainable Development.* Northampton, Mass.: Edward Elgar, 1998.

Puttaswamaiah, K., ed. *Cost-Benefit Analysis: Environmental and Ecological Perspectives.* New Brunswick, N.J.: Transaction, 2002.

■ Best available technologies to reduce pollution

FIELDS OF STUDY: Ecology, Environment, Environmentalism; Industries, Commercial Products; Pollution, Emissions, Toxic Waste, Hazardous Materials; Social/Economic; Technology and Applied Science

DEFINITION: The most efficient control and treatment techniques that are economically achievable by various industries to limit adverse environmental impacts

As concerns regarding all forms of pollution have increased around the world, many governments—including those of the United States and many European nations—have responded with environmental laws requiring industries to employ the best available techniques to reduce polluting emissions and discharges.

Major U.S. industries receiving national permits, usually from the Environmental Protection Agency (EPA), for new or modified emissions and point source discharges regulated by the Clean Air Act and the Clean Water Act are required to use the best available technologies to reduce environmental pollution. Best available technologies, also known as best available control technologies and best available techniques, include state-of-the-art controls on emissions and discharges into environmental media such as air, water, and soil. The term "available" means that the technology exists or is capable of being developed. A best available technology, however, must be affordable based on a cost-benefit analysis.

In addition to best available technology standards, the environmental laws in the United States include requirements for best conventional technologies. The best available technology mandates generally apply to pollutants that are considered to be toxic or are labeled as nonconventional because no determination has yet been made concerning their toxicity. However, once the EPA determines that a pollutant is toxic, an industry has three years to meet the best available technology standards that apply to that pollutant. Conventional pollutants, such as agricultural chemicals that have the ability to accumulate in body fat but have not been deemed toxic, are governed by the best conventional technology standards.

The permitting agency reviews each major industrial application for a stationary source permit to allow emissions into the air or discharges into the water on a case-by-case basis. Environmental, energy, and economic impacts are all considered in determining which processes and techniques an industry can afford while still protecting the environment. A variance from a best available technology standard may be granted as part of the permitting process to an industry that has agreed to use the best technology that is financially achievable, even if the technology is not the latest available. The technology used, however, must not create further pollution. For example, an industry will not receive a waiver to the best available technology requirements under the Clean Water Act unless it can show that the discharge controls and techniques it will utilize will not interfere with the quality of public water supplies, recreational activities, or wildlife, fish, and shellfish populations.

Under the Clean Air Act some of the best available technology standards include production and treatment techniques and fuel cleaning and combustion systems for various regulated air pollutants. Under the Clean Water Act effluent guidelines are based on best available technologies to achieve the goal of eliminating the discharge of all pollutants into the waters of the United States. Some of the factors considered in the cost-benefit analysis to determine if the effluent technologies are economically feasible include assessment of existing equipment, facilities, and techniques used in effluence reduction; the cost to achieve further effluent reduction; and other environmental impacts that are not related to water

Recycle logo. By Offiikart (Own work)

quality but that may occur if new technologies are employed, such as increased energy requirements. In addition to effluent guidelines, the Clean Water Act requires the use of best available technologies to minimize environmental impacts for cooling water intake structures that might be used in industries that produce heated water, such as nuclear power plants and food and beverage manufacturing facilities employing pasteurization.

Carol A. Rolf

Further Reading

Malone, Linda A. *Emanuel Law Outlines: Environmental Law.* 2d ed. Frederick, Md.: Aspen, 2007.

Morag-Levine, Noga. *Chasing the Wind: Regulating Air Pollution in the Common Law State.* Princeton, N.J.: Princeton University Press, 2005.

Revesz, Richard L. *Environmental Law and Policy: Statutory and Regulatory Supplement.* 2009-2010 ed. New York: Foundation Press, 2009.

■ Bhopal disaster

FIELDS OF STUDY: Disasters; Ecology, Environment, Environmentalism; Elements, Substances, Chemicals, Compounds; Health, Medicine, Disease, Illness; History/Biography; Industries, Commercial Products; Pollution, Emissions, Toxic Waste, Hazardous Materials

CATEGORIES: Disasters; pollutants and toxins

THE EVENT: Release of a highly toxic gas from a pesticide production plant that killed thousands of people and impaired the health of hundreds of thousands

DATES: December 2-3, 1984

The escape of methyl isocyanate from a pesticide production plant in Bhopal, India, resulted in the world's worst chemical disaster. The abandoned plant site, which was not properly remediated, continues to pose an environmental threat to nearby residents by contaminating their drinking-water source.

Union Carbide India, which was jointly owned by Union Carbide and the Indian public, ran a pesticide production plant in Bhopal, a city in central India with a population of approximately one million people. A heavily populated shantytown surrounded the plant. Methyl isocyanate (MIC), a very reactive and toxic chemical used in the production of pesticides, was stored at the plant.

As a cost-cutting measure the facility was understaffed, and the plant workers were poorly trained. The plant's signage and manuals were in English, but many of the workers were not English speakers. In 1982, U.S. engineers who conducted a safety audit of the plant noted sixty-one hazards in the unkempt facility. Thirty were deemed critical hazards; of these, eleven were found in the MIC/phosgene units. The audit warned that a major toxic release could result.

On the evening of December 2, 1984, the plant was closed for inventory reduction and routine maintenance. Around 11:30 P.M., workers realized when their eyes started to tear and burn that an MIC leak had occurred. They reported the leak to their supervisor and located a section of open piping that they believed to be the source. They took action to contain this presumed source, and the supervisor went on break. By 12:15 A.M., the pressure and temperature in the MIC storage tank had risen to dangerous levels.

When MIC comes into contact with water, a spontaneous reaction results, releasing heat. In the presence of a variety of catalysts, including iron ions, three molecules of MIC will join together to form a trimer. This reaction also releases heat. It is thought that both of these reactions occurred in the MIC storage tank. The heat released during the chemical reactions raised the temperature of the MIC, which increased the rates of the MIC reactions, releasing even more heat. MIC has a low boiling point, and this heat of reaction caused the MIC to vaporize into a gas. The gas expanded, increasing the pressure inside the storage tank until it burst a rupture disk on the line leading to the pressure release valve. When that safety valve was forced open, the gases from the tank began to escape and formed a lethal cloud that moved across Bhopal.

Some people were killed in their sleep by the toxic gas, while others awoke gasping for breath with their eyes and throats burning. The gas cloud quickly spread over an area of 65 square kilometers (25 square miles), engulfing panicked residents who were trying to flee. In a matter of minutes people began to collapse and die. Pregnant women caught in the cloud spontaneously miscarried.

According to the Indian Council of Medical Research, roughly three thousand people were initially killed, and another fifteen thousand later died from chemical-related illnesses. Approximately fifty thousand would suffer permanent disability. All told, the release affected the health of some half a million survivors. Their children would represent a second generation of victims, as many would be born with birth defects.

As a result of the Bhopal disaster, India significantly strengthened its regulation of hazardous industries. One of the most important actions the government took was the passage of its Environmental Protection Act of 1986.

A Series of Failed Safeguards

Culpability for the toxic release was found to extend from high levels of management at Union Carbide to workers at the plant. Four months after the disaster, Union Carbide released a report detailing failings that led to the MIC escape. Warren Anderson, the chairman of Union Carbide, acknowledged that conditions at the plant were so poor that it should not have been in operation. The report recounted that sometime before midnight on December 2, 1984, a considerable quantity of water entered the tank and started the heat-releasing reactions. Union Carbide claimed that a disgruntled employee had intentionally introduced the water. Plant workers said it occurred accidentally when water being used to clean pipes leaked into the tank. The tank was equipped with a refrigeration system designed to keep the contents at a low temperature, but it had been shut down months before to cut costs. At the higher storage temperature, the MIC reacted more rapidly with the water.

An alarm that should have sounded when the tank temperature started to rise failed to go off because it had not been reset for the higher storage temperature resulting from the lack of refrigeration. Union Carbide officials hypothesized that the water and high temperature in the tank caused rapid corrosion of its stainless-steel walls. This led to iron contamination that would have catalyzed the heat-releasing trimerization reaction. The temperature in the tank probably rose to at least 200 degrees Celsius (392 degrees Fahrenheit). A control-room operator manually started a sodium hydroxide vent scrubber designed to neutralize leaking MIC, but the sodium hydroxide failed to circulate. The gas rushed to the flare tower, where any MIC escaping the scrubber should have been burned off. This was the last safety control, but it was also out of service. A basic design fault of the plant was that the safety systems were designed to deal with only minor leaks, so even if they had been operative, the volume of gas released would have overwhelmed them.

Although the release started about 12:30 A.M., the plant's public alarm was not sounded until 2:00 A.M. So many small leaks had triggered it in previous months that the plant had shut it off to avoid disrupting the neighborhood. The local police were informed of the leak only after it had been stopped and after the alarm had been sounded.

An Ongoing Tragedy

The Indian government sued Union Carbide for $3.3 billion but accepted a settlement in February, 1989, that awarded $470 million to the victims. The next of kin of those killed were each awarded $2,000. Each injured survivor received roughly $500, an amount quickly consumed by medical costs. The tens of thousands who could not navigate the process of filing settlement claims or who were too ill to stand in line for hours to register their claims got nothing.

The settlement did not address environmental damages.

A lack of clear, continuing corporate liability, combined with negligence on the part of the Indian government, exacerbated the plight of Bhopal residents. Union Carbide and another company that took over the facility in 1994 performed some cleanup but did not fully remediate the 4.5-hectare (11-acre) site. When the state government took over the property in 1998, hundreds of tons of abandoned toxics remained on-site. In addition to toxic wastes dumped at and around the plant, hundreds of tons of pesticides and other chemicals had been left behind in the abandoned facility. The derelict buildings provided insufficient protection against the elements, allowing rainwater to mix with the chemicals and wash them into the soil. Eventually, the contaminants migrated into the groundwater and thus into the water supplies on which residents relied for drinking and washing needs.

In 2001 Dow Chemical acquired Union Carbide. Because Dow had not operated the plant or caused the accident, it would not acknowledge any responsibility to the affected population. Bhopal residents insisted that Dow had purchased not only Union Carbide's assets but also its liabilities, and they remained unmoved by the contention that Union Carbide's liability ended with the 1989 settlement.

Bhopal citizens have continued to demand that the American-based Dow remediate the site and address the problems that the abandoned facility has created: poisoned cattle, damaged crops, and an array of human health problems including cancers, neurological disorders, mental illness, and birth defects. The victims have also continued to demand action from their government, which they believe has placed greater priority on India's economic advancement and positive relations with multinational corporations than on justice. In 2009 Bhopal victims' groups commemorated the twenty-fifth anniversary of the lethal gas release with vigils and demonstrations.

Francis P. Mac Kay; updated by Karen N. Kähler

Further Reading

Amnesty International. *Clouds of Injustice: Bhopal Disaster 20 Years On.* London: Author, 2004.

D'Silva, Themistocles. *The Black Box of Bhopal: A Closer Look at the World's Deadliest Industrial Disaster.* Victoria, B.C.: Trafford, 2006.

Fortun, Kim. *Advocacy After Bhopal: Environmentalism, Disaster, New Global Orders.* Chicago: University of Chicago Press, 2001.

Hanna, Bridget, Ward Morehouse, and Satinath Sarangi, eds. *The Bhopal Reader: Remembering Twenty Years of the World's Worst Industrial Disaster.* New York: Apex Press, 2005.

See also: Environmental illnesses; Environmental justice and environmental racism; Environmental law, international; Hazardous and toxic substance regulation; Italian dioxin release; Pesticides and herbicides; Shantytowns

■ Bikini Atoll bombing

FIELDS OF STUDY: Disasters; Ecology, Environment, Environmentalism; History/Biography; Nuclear Power, Nuclear Weapons, Radioactive Waste

THE EVENT: Hydrogen bomb test conducted by the United States at the Bikini Atoll in the Marshall Islands

DATE: March 1, 1954

The hydrogen bomb test at the Bikini Atoll produced an explosion that was more powerful than had been anticipated, *and an unexpected shift in the wind resulted in radioactive fallout landing in populated regions of the Marshall Islands, on ships participating in the test, and on a Japanese fishing boat.*

The hydrogen bomb that the United States tested at the Bikini Atoll was code-named *Bravo.* It had an explosive force of approximately fifteen megatons. However, because of its new design, it used only about the same amount of the rare isotope uranium 235 as was used in the bomb dropped in 1945 on Hiroshima, Japan, which had an explosive yield one thousand times weaker. Although the residents of Bikini had been relocated before the test, the radiation spread to two inhabited islands, Rongelap and Utrick, located about 160 kilometers (100 miles) and 480 kilometers (300 miles) from Bikini, respectively. U.S. military personnel on Rongerik Atoll were also exposed to radiation, as was the crew of a U.S. Navy gasoline tanker en route from the Marshall Islands to Hawaii.

The crew of a Japanese tuna fishing boat, the *Lucky Dragon,* received the most serious radiation exposure. At the time of the explosion, the boat was located about 160 kilometers (100 miles) from Bikini, apparently outside the "danger zone" established by U.S. authorities. For about three hours following the

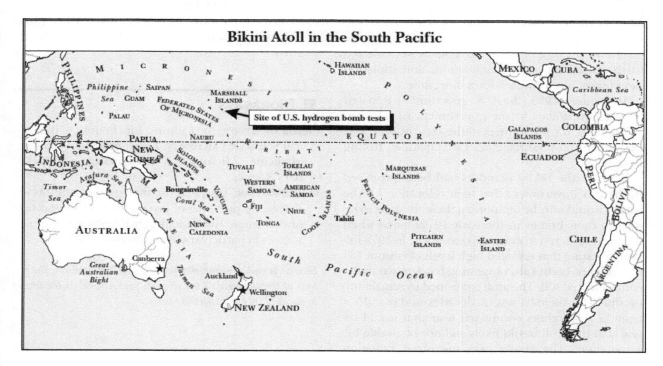

Bikini Atoll in the South Pacific

Site of U.S. hydrogen bomb tests

blast, the crew observed white, sandy dust falling onto the deck of their boat. Most of the twenty-three members of the *Lucky Dragon* crew later indicated they had suffered from skin inflammation and nausea over the next few days. On March 14, when the boat returned to port in Japan, the crew members were hospitalized and treated for radiation exposure. Medical tests indicated that they had suffered bone marrow damage, resulting in anemia, as well as temporary sterility. The exposed areas of their skin were also damaged.

The radiotelegraph operator of the *Lucky Dragon* died in September 1954. The cause of his death has been disputed. There were claims that he died as a direct result of radiation exposure, but U.S. officials said his death was caused by hepatitis contracted from the blood transfusions he received to treat the radiation exposure. The other crew members of the *Lucky Dragon* all recovered.

By the time the crew's radiation exposure was discovered, tuna from boats that had been fishing in the region of the bomb test had been shipped to the markets. Tests indicated that some of this tuna was radioactive. By the time officials realized this, some radioactive tuna had already been sold. About one hundred people in Japan consumed this contaminated fish before it was removed from the marketplace. No adverse health effects were reported, but when word of the contamination spread, many consumers simply stopped buying fish. Tuna canneries on the West Coast of the United States were alerted to the possibility of contamination, and radiation monitoring was instituted for a short time.

In January 1955, the U.S. government donated two million dollars to the government of Japan to compensate for the injuries to the crew of the *Lucky Dragon* and for damage to the Japanese fishing industry.

Though the Bikini islanders had been promised by the U.S. government that their relocation for the testing would only be temporary, their attempts to return to their homes in the early 1970s failed when they were ordered to evacuate once more in 1978 following testing that revealed high levels of cesium 137 in residents' bodies after ingesting food grown in the contaminated soil. The atoll continued to remain unoccupied for the next several decades, and in 2015, a team of researchers conducted tests that would reveal that the atoll would likely still not be livable for some time. The researchers measured radiation levels on three of the atolls in the Marshall Islands, comparing their findings to a control island that had been free of impact. While atolls such as , which had been the site of dedicated cleanup missions over the years, had levels below the U.S. safety standard of 100 millirems, the measurement on Bikini Atoll was still reading an average of 184 millirems; certain locations on the atoll measured at 640 millirems. Marshall Island residents as well as the president have argued that the United States owed more toward rectifying the lasting damages associated with the nuclear tests.

George J. Flynn

Further Reading

"Bikini Atoll Nuclear Test: 60 Years Later and Islands Still Unliveable." *Guardian.* Guardian News Media, 1 Mar. 2014. Web. 1 Sept. 2016.

International Atomic Energy Agency. *Radiological Conditions at Bikini Atoll: Prospects for Resettlement.* Vienna: Intl. Atomic Energy Agency, 1998. Print.

Mosbergen, Dominique. "70 Years Later, Bikini Atoll May Still Be Too Radioactive for Resettlement." *Huffington Post.* TheHuffingtonPost.com, 8 June 2016. Web. 1 Sept. 2016.

Niedenthal, Jack. *For the Good of Mankind: A History of the People of Bikini and Their Islands.* 2nd ed. Majuro: Bravo, 2002. Print.

Zak, Dan. "A Ground Zero Forgotten." *Washington Post.* Washington Post, 27 Nov. 2015. Web. 1 Sept. 2016.

■ Bioassays

FIELDS OF STUDY: Agriculture; Biochemistry; Biological Sciences; Chemistry; Environmental Sciences; Medicine; Microbiology; Pharmacology; Veterinary Science;

IDENTIFICATION: Tests that use biological organisms to detect the presence of given chemical substances or determine the biological activity of known substances in particular environments

Bioassays enable environmental scientists to evaluate the effects of the chemicals used in pesticides as well as the resistance of plants to particular pests.

Biologists are seining for fish to be used in bioassays. EPA Gulf Breeze Laboratory

Overview

In many instances, a scientist may suspect that a certain chemical is present in a given environment but may not have access to a specific piece of equipment designed to measure the presence of the chemical. In some cases, an experimental protocol for the detection of the chemical may not exist. In either of these cases, the scientist may be able to detect the presence of the chemical by using a biological organism that responds in a specific manner when exposed to that particular chemical agent. At other times, a scientist may know that a certain chemical is present but not know how a particular organism will respond when exposed to the agent. In this case, the scientist will expose the test organism to the chemical and measure a particular physiological response.

Bioassays are utilized in many different areas of the biological sciences, including environmental studies. Some bioassay methods work better than others. A good bioassay meets two basic criteria. First, it is specific for a given physiological response. For example, if a given chemical is responsible for inhibiting the feeding response of a particular insect, then the bioassay for that chemical should measure only the inhibition of feeding of that insect and not some other physiological response to the chemical. Second, a good bioassay measures the same response in the laboratory that is observed in the field. Again,

if a particular chemical inhibits the feeding response in the field, then the laboratory bioassay for that chemical should also inhibit feeding. An ongoing need exists for the development of accurate bioassay methods as well as the improvement of existing techniques.

Many different bioassays are used in environmental studies. One of the most common is the measure of the median lethal dose (LD_{50})—the concentration or dose of a chemical that will result in the deaths of one-half of a population of organisms—of a new pesticide on species of pest and nonpest organisms. To conduct this bioassay, the test species is exposed to a wide range of different concentrations of the chemical. The concentration of the pesticide that kills one-half of the test organisms represents the LD_{50}.

Another common environmental bioassay is the measure of resistance of plants to a particular insect pest. In order to reduce the dependence on chemical insecticides, plant breeders are continually trying to develop insect-resistant plants, either through traditional breeding programs or by using biotechnology to transfer resistance genes to susceptible crop strains. Bioassays are used to measure the degree of success of these attempts. In these bioassays, the same numbers of susceptible and resistant plants are subjected to infestation by equal numbers of the insect pest for which the breeder is trying to develop resistance. The two groups of plants are observed, and the degree of resistance, if any, is recorded.

D. R. Gossett

Further Reading

Ohkawa, H., H. Miyagawa, and P. W. Lee, eds. *Pesticide Chemistry: Crop Protection, Public Health, Environmental Safety.* Wiley-VCH, 2007.

Rand, Gary M., ed. *Fundamentals of Aquatic Toxicology: Effects, Environmental Fate, and Risk Assessment.* 3rd ed. CRC Press, 2008.

■ Biocentrism

FIELDS OF STUDY: Anthropology; Biology; Ethics; Law; Sociology;

IDENTIFICATION: Life-centered stance that rejects the view that only human beings and their interests matter, while recognizing the moral standing of all living creatures

Biocentrism has played a key role in the development of environmental ethics since that discipline was founded during the 1970s and had already been influential among important earlier thinkers, including Albert Schweitzer and Mahatma Gandhi. The principle of the sacred nature of all forms of life is a central feature of Jain, a Hindu religion.

Overview

Biocentrists hold that all living creatures have goods of their own and that their flourishing, or attaining their goods, is intrinsically valuable. This value should thus be taken into consideration whenever decisions affecting the flourishing of any creatures are being made. During the 1970s, Norwegian philosopher Arne Naess wanted to include living systems (such as habitats and ecosystems) within the scope of biocentrism as intrinsically valuable entities, but this view is now classified as "ecocentrism," and subsequent biocentrists have restricted moral standing to individual living creatures.

The most widespread kind of biocentrism was presented during the early 1980s by Paul Taylor, who advocated a life-centered ethic of respect for nature. In this ethic, the realization of the good of every living creature is intrinsically valuable and to be pursued for its own sake. In Taylor's version of biocentrism, not only is human superiority denied but also all living things are held to be equally worthy of respect, irrespective of differences of capacities, and to have the same moral importance. Taylor recommends defensible policies of conservation and social justice, but he has difficulty deriving them from these principles.

Another kind of biocentrism, not committed to equal respect for all living creatures, was proposed in 1981 by Robin Attfield and later by Gary E. Varner, who both defend the intrinsic value of the good of

every creature, whether sentient or nonsentient. Unlike Taylor, however, Attfield upholds Peter Singer's principle of equal consideration for equal interests, applying it to the entire realm of life; thus the satisfaction of greater interests takes priority over that of lesser ones when they conflict. (The capacities of living creatures for health and for being harmed are held to distinguish them from artifacts, which have no goods of their own.) Attfield integrates this account of intrinsic value into a consequentialist recognition of beneficial practices, general compliance with which makes actions right through generating or preserving greater value than would otherwise prevail.

More recently, James Sterba has defended a Taylor-like commitment to species equality through species-neutral principles authorizing resort to self-defense in certain circumstances (whether greater capacities are at stake or not). These principles are held to be defensible not by enhancing value but as part of a deontological ethical system. Simultaneously Sterba rejects the extension of biocentrism to ecosystems, holding that biotic communities have no clear goods of their own; individual living creatures constitute the limits of ethical egalitarianism.

Biocentrism in any form supports more radical policies to preserve habitats and curtail global warming than do anthropocentric stances. The biocentric viewpoint remains influential in debates about both normative principles and practical decision making.

Robin Attfield

Further Reading

Attfield, Robin. *Environmental Ethics*. Blackwell, 2003.

Attfield, Robin, ed. *The Ethics of the Environment*. Ashgate, 2008.

Sterba, James. "A Biocentrist Strikes Back." *Environmental Ethics* 20, no. 4 (Winter, 1998): 361-376.

Taylor, Paul. *Respect for Nature: A Theory of Environmental Ethics*. Princeton University Press, 1986.

Varner, Gary E. "Biocentric Individualism." In *Environmental Ethics: What Really Matters, What Really Works*, edited by David Schmidtz and Elizabeth Willott. Oxford University Press, 2002.

■ Biodiversity

FIELDS OF STUDY: Biology, Life Sciences, Ecosystems; Animals, Zoology, Marine Biology; Ecology, Environment, Environmentalism; Forests, Forestry; Plants, Vegetation, Botany, Horticulture.
DEFINITION: Biological variety in a given environment

Biodiversity—including diversity among species, among ecosystems, and among individuals within species—is generally assumed to enhance ecological stability

In 1993 the Wildlife Society defined biodiversity as "the richness, abundance, and variability of plant and animal species and communities and the ecological processes that link them with one another and with soil, air, and water." Included in this concept is the recognition that life on earth exists in great variety and at various levels of organization. Many kinds of specialists—including organismic biologists, population and evolutionary biologists, geneticists, and ecologists—investigate biological processes that are encompassed by the concept of biodiversity. Conservation biologists are concerned with the totality of biodiversity, including the process of speciation that forms new species, the measurement of biodiversity, and factors involved in the extinction process. The primary thrust of their efforts, however, is the development of strategies to preserve biodiversity.

The biodiversity paradigm connects classical taxonomic and morphological studies of organisms with modern techniques employed by those working at the molecular level. It is generally accepted that biodiversity can be approached at three levels of organization, commonly identified as species diversity, ecosystem diversity, and genetic diversity. Some also recognize biological phenomena diversity.

Species Diversity

No one knows how many species inhabit the earth. Estimates range from five million to several times that number. Each species consists of individuals that are somewhat similar and capable of interbreeding with other members of their species but are typically not able to interbreed with individuals of other species. The species that occupy a particular ecosystem are a subset of the species as a whole. Ecosystems are generally considered to be local units of nature; ponds, forests, and prairies are common examples.

Conservation biologists measure the species diversity of a given ecosystem by first conducting a careful, quantitative inventory. From such data, scientists may determine the "richness" of the ecosystem, which is simply a reflection of the number of species present. An island with three hundred species would thus be considered to be 50 percent richer than another with only two hundred species. Some ecosystems, especially tropical rain forests and coral reefs, are much richer than others. Among the least rich are tundra regions and deserts.

A second aspect of species diversity is "evenness," defined as the degree to which all of the various elements are present in similar percentages of the total species. As an example, consider two forests, each of which has a total of twenty species of trees. Suppose that the first forest has a few tree species represented by rather high percentages and the remainder by low percentages. A second forest with species more evenly distributed would rate higher on a scale of evenness.

Species diversity, therefore, is a value that combines both species richness and species evenness measures. Values obtained from a diversity index are used in comparing species diversity among ecosystems of both the same and different types. They also have implications for the preservation of ecosystems; other things being equal, it would be preferable to preserve ecosystems with high diversity indexes, thus protecting a larger number of species.

Considerable effort has been expended to predict species diversity as determined by the nature of the area involved. For example, island biogeography theory suggests that islands that are larger, are nearer to other islands or continents, and have more heterogeneous landscapes would be expected to have higher species diversity than those possessing alternate traits. Such predictions apply not only to literal islands but also to other discontinuous ecosystems; examples would be alpine tundra of isolated mountaintops and ponds several miles apart.

The application of island biogeography theory to designing nature preserves was proposed by Jared Diamond in 1975. His suggestion began the "single larger or several smaller," or SLOSS, area controversy. Although island biogeography theory would, in many instances, suggest selecting one large area for a nature preserve, it is often the case that several smaller areas, if carefully selected, could preserve more species.

The species diversity of a particular ecosystem is subject to change over time. Pollution, deforestation, and other types of habitat degradation invariably reduce diversity. Conversely, during the extended process of ecological succession that follows disturbances, species diversity typically increases until a permanent, climax ecosystem with a large index of diversity results. Ecologists generally assume that more diverse ecosystems are more stable than those with less diversity. Certainly, the more species present, the greater the opportunity for various interactions, both with other species and with the environment. Examples of interspecific reactions include mutualism, predation, and parasitism. Such interactions apparently help to integrate a community into a whole, thus increasing its stability.

Ecosystem Diversity

Ecology can be defined as the study of ecosystems. From a conservation standpoint, ecosystems are important because they sustain their particular assemblages of living species. Conservation biologists also consider ecosystems to have intrinsic value beyond the species they harbor; therefore, it would be ideal if representative global ecosystems could be preserved. This is far from realization, however. Just deciding where to draw the line between interfacing ecosystems can be a problem. For example, the water level of a stream running through a forest is subject to seasonal fluctuation, causing a transitional zone characterized by the biota (that is, the flora and fauna) from both adjoining ecosystems. Such ubiquitous zones negate the view that ecosystems are discrete units with easily recognized boundaries.

The protection of diverse ecosystems is of utmost importance to the maintenance of biodiversity, but ecosystems throughout the world are threatened by global warming, air and water pollution, acid deposition, ozone depletion, and other destructive forces. At the local level, deforestation, thermal pollution, urbanization, and poor agricultural practices are among the problems affecting ecosystems and therefore reducing biodiversity. Both global and local environmental problems are amplified by rapidly increasing world population pressures.

In the process of determining which ecosystems are most in need of protection, many scientists have recognized that the creation of a system for naming and classifying ecosystems is highly desirable, if not imperative. Efforts are being made to establish a

system similar to the hierarchical system applied to species that was developed by Swedish botanist Carolus Linnaeus during the eighteenth century. A comprehensive classification system for ecosystems is far from complete, but freshwater, marine, and terrestrial ecosystems are recognized as main categories, with each further divided into particular types. Though tentative, the system that has been established thus far has made possible the identification and preservation of a wide range of representative threatened ecosystems.

In 1995 conservation biologist Reed F. Noss of Oregon State University and his colleagues identified more than 126 types of ecosystems in the United States that are threatened or critically endangered. The following list illustrates their diversity: southern Appalachian spruce-fir forests; eastern grasslands, savannas, and barrens; California native grasslands; Hawaiian dry forests; caves and karst systems; old-growth forests of the Pacific Northwest; and southern forested wetlands.

Not all ecosystems can be saved. Establishing priorities involves many considerations, some of which are economic and political. Ideally, choices would be made on merit, taking into consideration the rarity, size, and number of endangered species that ecosystems include as well as other objective, scientific criteria.

Genetic and Biological Phenomena Diversity

Most of the variations among individuals of the same species are caused by the different genotypes (combinations of genes) the individuals possess. Such genetic diversity is readily apparent in cultivated or domesticated species such as cats, dogs, and corn, but it also exists, though usually to a lesser degree, in wild species. Genetic diversity can be measured only through the use of exacting molecular laboratory procedures. Such tests detect the amount of variation in the deoxyribonucleic acid (DNA) or isoenzymes (chemically distinct enzymes) possessed by various individuals of the species in question.

A significant degree of genetic diversity within a population or species confers a great advantage. This diversity is the raw material that allows evolutionary processes to occur. When a local population becomes too small, it is subject to a serious decline in vigor from increased inbreeding. This leads, in turn, to a downward, self-perpetuating spiral in genetic diversity and further reduction in population size.

Extinction may be imminent. In the grand scheme of nature, this is a catastrophic event; never again will that particular genome (set of genes) exist anywhere on the earth. Extinction is the process by which global biodiversity is reduced.

The term "biological phenomena diversity" refers to the numerous unique biological events that occur in natural areas throughout the world. Examples include the congregation of thousands of monarch butterflies on tree limbs at Point Pelee in Ontario, Canada, as they await favorable conditions before continuing their migration, and the return of hundreds of loggerhead sea turtles each April to Padre Island in the Gulf of Mexico in order to lay their eggs.

Although biologists have been concerned with protecting plant and animal species for decades, only recently has conservation biology emerged as an identifiable discipline. Conceived in a perceived crisis of biological extinctions, conservation biology differs from related disciplines, such as ecology, in that it is advocative in nature, insisting that the maintenance of biodiversity is intrinsically good. Conservation biology is a value-laden science, and some critics consider it akin to a religion with an accepted dogma.

The prospect of preserving global ecosystems and the life processes they make possible, all necessary for maintaining global diversity, is not promising. Western culture does not give environmental concerns a high priority. Among those who do, greater concern is often expressed about the immediate health effects of environmental degradation than about the loss of biodiversity. The impetus necessary to save ecosystems and all their inhabitants—including humans—will develop only when education in basic biology and ecology at all levels is extended to include an awareness of the importance of biodiversity.

Thomas E. Hemmerly

Further Reading

Chivian, Eric, and Aaron Bernstein, eds. *Sustaining Life: How Human Health Depends on Biodiversity.* Oxford University Press, 2008.
Ehrlich, Paul R., and Anne H. Ehrlich. *Extinction: The Causes and Consequences of the Disappearance of Species.* Ballantine Books, 1981.
Hunter, Malcolm L., Jr. *Fundamentals of Conservation Biology.* 3rd ed. Wiley-Blackwell, 2006.
Novacek, Michael J., ed. *The Biodiversity Crisis: Losing What Counts.* New Press, 2001.
Primack, Richard B. *Essentials of Conservation Biology.* 5th ed. Sinauer Associates, 2010.
Ray, Justina C., et al., eds. *Large Carnivores and the Conservation of Biodiversity.* Island Press, 2005.
Wilson, Edward O. *Biophilia.* 1984. Reprint. Harvard University Press, 2003.
_____. *The Diversity of Life.* New ed. W. W. Norton, 1999.
Zeigler, David. *Understanding Biodiversity.* Praeger, 2007.

See also: Biodiversity action plans; Convention on Biological Diversity; Ecology as a concept; Ecosystems; Extinctions and species loss; Global Biodiversity Assessment; Rain forests.

■ Biodiversity action plans

FIELDS OF STUDY: Government, Politics, International Relations; International Relations, Agreements, Treaties; Biology, Life Sciences, Ecosystems; Animals, Zoology, Marine Biology; Ecology, Environment, Environmentalism.

IDENTIFICATION: Government-devised plans for protecting and restoring threatened ecological systems and biological species

Biodiversity action plans are important tools that governments use in protecting and restoring threatened ecosystems. These plans seek to implement the 1992 United Nations Convention on Biological Diversity, which demonstrates worldwide recognition that biodiversity is intrinsically valuable and deserves to be protected or restored through careful planning.

The schemes for protecting and restoring threatened species of plants and animals and their ecosystems known as biodiversity action plans (BAPs; also known as national biodiversity strategies and action plans, or NBSAPs) gained worldwide recognition with the signing of the United Nations Convention on Biological Diversity (CBD) at the Earth Summit in Rio de Janeiro, Brazil, in 1992. BAPs represent the steps that nations are taking to implement the provisions of the convention. However, although most of the world's nations have ratified the CBD, only a handful have actually developed substantive BAPs.

A Biodiversity Action Plan habitat in the United Kingdom. By Hugh Venables.

Among those that have are the United States, Australia, the United Kingdom, Tanzania, and Uzbekistan.

A well-conceived BAP includes several components: plans for the carrying out of inventories and documentation of selected species and specific habitats, with particular emphasis placed on population distribution and conservation status within certain ecosystems; realistic targets or indicators for conservation and restoration; plans covering funding and time lines for achievement of specific goals; and plans for the establishment of partnerships among private and public institutions and agencies that will work together to achieve the goals set.

Obstacles and Criticisms

To implement a BAP effectively, a nation must overcome a number of obstacles; the difficulty of the process may explain in part why so few countries have attempted to develop such plans. In some parts of the world, for example, undertaking complete inventories of plant and animal species is not realistic. Scientists have estimated that only about 10 percent of the world's species have been characterized and documented; most of those still unknown include plants and lower animals such as insects. An ideal BAP includes the assessment of species population estimates over time so that the variability and degree of vulnerability of species can be determined; it also includes descriptions of species' ranges, habitats, behaviors,

breeding practices, and interactions with other species. The collection of such fundamental information can be a daunting task. Another factor preventing some nations from developing BAPs is the cost involved. Depending on the size of the country, the cost of preparing a solid BAP can easily come to the equivalent of millions of U.S. dollars, with about 10 percent of the initial cost factored in for annual maintenance. It is therefore not surprising that the call for BAPs has been criticized by some developing countries.

In addition to the difficulty and expense involved in the implementation of BAPs, many developing countries are unwilling to create such plans because, they argue, the plans obviously favor the consideration of wildlife and plant protection over food production and industrial growth; in some cases, BAPs may even represent impediments to population growth. Most of the Middle Eastern countries and many African nations have shown little interest in participating in a substantive way in such plans. Others have simply opted to create pro forma plans that expend little on research and even less on the management of natural resources. In contrast, the European Union has chosen to divert the purpose of BAPs, instead implementing the CBD through a set of economic development policies while paying special attention to the protection of certain ecosystems.

It has become increasingly clear that what is at stake is the very definition of "biodiversity" itself. According to the CBD, biodiversity is the variation of life-forms within a given ecosystem; it is a combination of ecosystem structure and function as well as components (species, habitat, and genetic resources). The CBD states:

> In addressing the boundless complexity of biological diversity, it has become conventional to think in hierarchical terms, from the genetic material within individual cells, building through individual organisms, populations, species, and communities of species, to biosphere overall. . . . At the same time, in seeking to make management interventions as efficient as possible, it is essential to take a holistic view of biodiversity and

address the interactions that species have with each other and their nonliving environment, i.e., to work from an ecological perspective.

At the World Summit on Sustainable Development in 2002, delegates adopted the objectives of the CBD and designated 2010 the Year of Biodiversity.

Nader N. Chokr

Further Reading

Chivian, Eric, and Aaron Bernstein, eds. *Sustaining Life: How Human Health Depends on Biodiversity.* Oxford University Press, 2008.

O'Riordan, Tim, and Susanne Stoll-Kleemann, eds. *Biodiversity, Sustainability, and Human Communities: Protecting Beyond the Protected.* Cambridge University Press, 2002.

Ray, Justina C., et al., eds. *Large Carnivores and the Conservation of Biodiversity.* Island Press, 2005.

Wilson, Edward O. *The Diversity of Life.* New ed. W. W. Norton, 1999.

Zeigler, David. *Understanding Biodiversity.* Praeger, 2007.

■ Biodiversity: Why Preserve Biodiversity?

FIELDS OF STUDY: Agronomy; Bioethics; Biology; Ecology; Environmental Studies; Ethics; Law; Religious Studies;

Biodiversity is defined as the total number of species within an ecosystem, and also as the resulting complexity of interactions among them. It measures the "richness" of an ecological community.

Among an estimated 8 to 10 million unique and irreplaceable species existing on Earth, fewer than 1.6 million have been named. A tiny fraction of this number has been studied. Over thousands of years, organisms in a community have been molded by forces of natural selection exerted by other living species as well as by the nonliving environment that surrounds them. The result is a highly complex web of interdependent species whose interactions sustain one another and provide the basis for the very existence of human life as well.

Loss of biodiversity poses a serious challenge to the sustenance of many communities and ecosystems. For example, the destruction of tropical rain forests by clear-cut logging produces high rates of extinction of many species. Most of these species have never been named, and many never even discovered. As species are eliminated, the communities of which they were a part may change and become unstable and more vulnerable to damage by diseases or adverse environmental conditions. Aside from the disruption of natural food webs, potential sources of medicine, food, and raw materials for industry are also lost. As Harvard professor Edward O. Wilson once said, "The loss of species is the folly our descendants are least likely to forgive us."

Thomas E. Hemmerly

■ Biofertilizers

FIELDS OF STUDY: Agriculture, Farming, Animal Husbandry; Biology, Life Sciences, Ecosystems; Ecology, Environment, Environmentalism; Science

DEFINITION: Fertilizers consisting of either naturally occurring or genetically modified microorganisms

Biofertilizers provide a means by which biological systems can be utilized to supply plant nutrients such as nitrogen to agricultural crops. The use of biofertilizers could reduce the dependence on chemical fertilizers, which are often detrimental to the environment.

Plants require adequate supplies of the thirteen mineral nutrients necessary for normal growth and reproduction. These nutrients, which must be supplied by the soil, include both macronutrients (those nutrients required in large quantities) and micronutrients (those nutrients required in smaller quantities). As plants grow and develop, they remove these essential mineral nutrients from the soil. Since normal crop production usually requires the removal of plants or plant parts, the nutrients are continuously removed from the soil. Therefore, the long-term agricultural utilization of any soil requires periodic fertilization to replace lost nutrients.

Nitrogen is the plant nutrient that is most often depleted in agricultural soils, and most crops respond to the addition of nitrogen fertilizer by increasing their growth and yield; therefore, more nitrogen fertilizer is applied to cropland than any other

Cyanobacteria cultured in specific media. Cyanobacteria can be helpful in agriculture as they have the capability to fix atmospheric nitrogen to soil. This nitrogen is helpful to the crops. Cyanobacteria is used as a bio-fertilizer. By Joydeep (Own work)

fertilizer. In the past, nitrogen fertilizers have been limited to either manures, which have low levels of nitrogen, or chemical fertilizers, which usually have high levels of nitrogen. The excess nitrogen in chemical fertilizers often runs off into nearby waterways, causing a variety of environmental problems.

Biofertilizers offer a potential alternative: They supply sufficient amounts of nitrogen for maximum yields yet have a positive impact on the environment. Biofertilizers generally consist of either naturally occurring or genetically modified microorganisms that improve the physical condition of soil, aid plant growth, or increase crop yield. Such fertilizers provide an environmentally friendly way to increase plant health and yields with reduced input costs, new products and additional revenues for the agricultural biotechnology industry, and cheaper products for consumers.

While biofertilizers could potentially be used to supply a number of different nutrients, most of the interest thus far has focused on enhancing nitrogen fertilization. The relatively small amounts of nitrogen found in soil come from a variety of sources. Some nitrogen is present in all organic matter in soil; as this organic matter is degraded by microorganisms, it can be used by plants. A second source of nitrogen is nitrogen fixation, the chemical or biological process of taking nitrogen from the atmosphere and converting it to a form that can be utilized by plants. Bacteria such as *Rhizobia* can live symbiotically with certain

plants, such as legumes, which house nitrogen-fixing bacteria in their roots. The *Rhizobia* and plant root tissue form root nodules that house the nitrogen-fixing bacteria; once inside the nodules, the bacteria use energy supplied by the plant to convert atmospheric nitrogen to ammonia, which nourishes the plant. Natural nitrogen can also be supplied by free-living microorganisms, which can fix nitrogen without forming a symbiotic relationship with plants. The primary objective of biofertilizers is to enhance any one or all of these processes.

One of the major goals in the genetic engineering of biofertilizers is to transfer the ability to form nodules and establish effective symbiosis to nonlegume plants. The formation of nodules in which the *Rhizobia* live requires plant cells to synthesize many new proteins, and many of the genes required for the expression of these proteins are not found in the root cells of plants outside the legume family. Many research programs have been devoted to efforts to transfer such genes to nonlegume plants so that they can interact symbiotically with nitrogen-fixing bacteria. If this is accomplished, *Rhizobia* could be used as a biofertilizer for a variety of plants.

There is also much interest in using the free-living, soil-borne organisms that fix atmospheric nitrogen as biofertilizers. These organisms live in the rhizosphere (the region of soil in immediate contact with plant roots) or thrive on the surface of the soil. Since the exudates from these microorganisms contain nitrogen that can be utilized by plants, increasing their abundance in the soil could reduce dependence on chemical fertilizers. Numerous research efforts have been designed to identify and enhance the abundance of nitrogen-fixing bacteria in the rhizosphere. Soil microorganisms primarily depend on soluble root exudates and decomposed organic matter to supply the energy necessary for fixing nitrogen; hence there is also an interest in enhancing the biodegradation of organic matter in the soil. This research has largely centered on inoculating the soil with cellulose-degrading fungi and nitrogen-fixing bacteria or applying organic matter to the soil, such as straw that has been treated with a combination of the fungi and bacteria.

D. R. Gossett

Further Reading

Akinyemi, Okoro M. *Agricultural Production: Organic and Conventional Systems.* Enfield, N.H.: Science Publishers, 2007.

Black, C. A. *Soil-Plant Relationships.* New York: John Wiley & Sons, 1988.

Crispeels, M. J., and D. E. Sadava. *Plants, Genes, and Agriculture.* Sudbury, Mass.: Jones and Bartlett, 1994.

Lynch, J. M. *Soil Biotechnology: Microbiological Factors in Crop Production.* Malden, Mass.: Blackwell, 1983.

Salisbury, F. B., and C. W. Ross. *Plant Physiology.* Pacific Grove, Calif.: Brooks/Cole, 1985.

Yadav, A. K., S. Ray Chaudhuri, and M. R. Motsara, eds. *Recent Advances in Biofertilizer Technology.* New Delhi: Society for Promotion and Utilisation of Resources and Technology, 2001.

■ Biogeochemical cycles

FIELDS OF STUDY: Chemistry; Climate and Climate Change; Elements, Substances, Chemicals, Compounds; Geology, Geosciences; Meteorology, Atmospheric Sciences, Climatology; Science

DEFINITION: Movements of chemical elements among parts of the earth, including the atmosphere, the earth's crust, oceans, and living things

The movement and location of chemical elements among the various systems that make up the earth affect the planet's climate, the diversity and range of species, the impact and intensity of geological events, and a host of other matters related to the earth as a whole and subsystems within it.

Modern geoscientists consider the earth to comprise a set of interacting open systems: the atmosphere (the layers of air that envelop the earth), the biosphere (the areas that support and are filled with living things), the lithosphere (the earth's crust), and the hydrosphere (the water found on the earth). These various spheres contain within them important chemical elements. The six most abundant elements are carbon, nitrogen, oxygen, hydrogen, phosphorus, and sulfur; these elements, alone or in combination with others, serve as critical macronutrients to living things. Other important macronutrients are potassium, calcium, iron, and magnesium. So-called micronutrients are present in smaller amounts and play critical roles in sustaining life on

earth: boron (used by green plants), copper (critical to the functioning of some enzymes), and molybdenum (vital for the functioning of nitrogen-fixing bacteria). Other chemical elements, such as ammonia, also are involved in biogeochemical cycles.

The atmosphere and the oceans serve as important reservoirs where the key gas elements (carbon, nitrogen, oxygen, and hydrogen) are mainly stored. Soils and sedimentary rocks serve as principal reservoirs for the storage of phosphorus and sulfur. Throughout the earth these various chemicals are moved about by different physical, chemical, and human-induced processes that alter the respective amounts of elements in various places and within both living and nonliving things.

An example of a biogeochemical cycle is the hydrologic (water) cycle that moves oxygen and hydrogen, along with other chemicals, from reservoir to reservoir, principally at or near the surface of the earth. This includes the proportionally large amounts of water residing within living things as well as the water found in the oceans, the atmosphere, surface water, groundwater, glaciers, and soils. During various periods of the planet's history the relative percentages of oxygen, hydrogen, and other chemical elements found in the hydrosphere have changed dramatically. These changes have in turn affected the overall temperature and climate of the earth and the types of environments available for living things; they have also sometimes caused physical changes to the other spheres (atmosphere, biosphere, and lithosphere).

Another biogeochemical cycle is the carbon cycle. Most of the original carbon in the earth's systems came out of the earth's mantle in the form of carbon dioxide gas released by volcanoes. The carbon dioxide in the atmosphere is taken up by various means, including dissolution in seawater in the form of bicarbonate ions and absorption by photosynthetic organisms such as algae and plants that convert it into sugar and other organic chemicals. As this carbon enters the food chain it ultimately finds its way into the tissues of animals. It is estimated that some 63 billion tons of carbon move every year worldwide from the atmosphere into life-forms. In this sense the carbon that has been so transformed has moved from the reservoir of the atmosphere into the reservoir of the biosphere.

Human beings' burning of fuels that are rich in carbon has resulted in increases in the amounts of

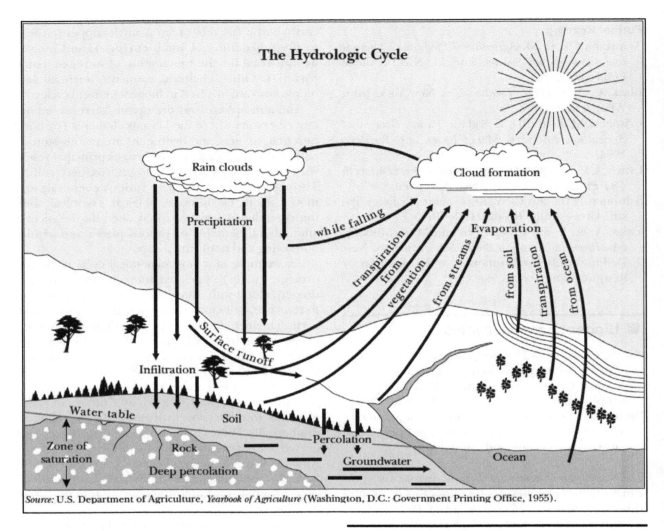

The Hydrologic Cycle

Source: U.S. Department of Agriculture, *Yearbook of Agriculture* (Washington, D.C.: Government Printing Office, 1955).

carbon dioxide and other greenhouse gases in the earth's atmosphere, beyond the rate that would have occurred via natural processes. Most climatologists and atmospheric scientists believe that these greenhouse gases contribute to increasing the earth's overall atmospheric temperature and that the resulting net global warming has the potential to produce catastrophic effects over time.

Dennis W. Cheek

Further Reading

Bashkin, Vladimir N., with Robert W. Howarth. *Modern Biogeochemistry.* Norwell: Kluwer Academic, 2003. Print.

Libes, Susan M. *Introduction to Marine Biogeochemistry.* 2nd ed. New York: Academic, 2009. Print.

■ Biogeography

FIELDS OF STUDY: Biology; Ecology; Environmental Studies; Physical Geography;

KEY CONCEPTS

ALIEN: a species of plant or animal that is not native to a particular place, but is found to have successfully colonized it, especially one that has been introduced as a result of human activity

ALLOPATRIC: of animals or plants, occupying separate, non-overlapping distribution areas; of speciation, occurring as a result of such geographic separation

BIOTA: the totality of the flora, fauna, and microbes that inhabit a particular region, habitat type, or time period

COLONIZATION: the long-term establishment of a successfully reproducing population of a particular species of plant or animal, in a habitat where it was not previously found

COSMOPOLITAN: of animals or plants, occupying distribution areas that span the entire or almost the entire globe

DISJUNCT: of animals or plants, having a fragmented distribution area that includes two or more, geographically separate, regions

DISPERSAL: for any given species, the movement out of its distribution area of the minimum number of individuals it will take to colonize a new area

distribution area: the geographic range of a particular group of organisms at any level of classification, such as species, genus, family, or class

ecogeographic rule: a principle describing correlations between the morphology of birds and mammals and the climatic or latitudinal gradients at which they are found

ENDEMIC: of animals or plants, being restricted to a particular region of the world

LATITUDINAL GRADIENT: of plant or animal species, an increase in overall numbers found when moving from higher to lower latitudes

SPECIATION: the process by which new species arise or populations of the same species become reproductively isolated from each other, either by geographical separation or some other mechanism

Biogeography is an interdisciplinary science that applies concepts and methodologies from biology, geography, systems ecology, evolutionary theory, conservation, statistics, and paleontology, among other fields, to study the features of the physical environment that affect the distribution of living organisms across space and time.

Distribution Areas & Species Distributions

The fundamental question that drives biogeographical study is: How is life distributed over the earth? This is a question that can be answered at many different levels. For example, any given taxon, or group of living organisms at a particular level of classification (such as a species, genus, family, or class), has a geographic range within which it is likely to be found. The plant *Yucca brevifolia*, a species of yucca also known as the Joshua tree, is only found growing in the dry desert soils, open plains, and mesas of the

southwestern United States. This is what biogeographers refer to as the tree's distribution area. A species like *Yucca brevifolia* is said to have an endemic distribution area, meaning one that is restricted to a particular region of the world. In contrast, *Drosophila melanogaster* (the common fruit fly), which is found in virtually all types of habitats across almost the entire globe, is said to have a cosmopolitan distribution area.

Many taxons have what are known as disjunct distribution areas; this occurs when very closely related species are found in widely geographically separated habitats. For example, many similar species of mosses, small mammals, and butterflies are found both in the mountain ranges of the far northerly Arctic, and in the more southerly mountain ranges of Europe, such as the Alps—but nowhere in between. There are several scientific hypotheses regarding historical reasons for the existence of disjunct biogeographic distribution areas.

Under the vicariance hypothesis, environmental events cause the range of a particular taxon to split into parts. For example, changes in the distribution of land can cause impassable fractures to form in what was once a continuous habitat. Plate tectonic shifts, continental drift, and the formation of mountains all have the potential to break apart a formerly intact habitat region. When this happens, allopatric speciation can occur. This is the evolution of new and distinct species of animals or plants as a result of a single species being separated into more than one non-overlapping distribution area. (Another form of vicariance occurs when individual members of a family that was once spread out over a large, continuous geographic range, go extinct. This, too, can cause fragmentation in the distribution area.) In contrast, some disjunct biogeographic distributions are believed to have been caused by dispersal, or the successful migration of species across an existing geographic barrier. For example, birds are capable of crossing oceans in order to colonize new habitats; other non-motile species, such as plants, may be transported along with them as seeds.

Besides studying how organisms range across the globe, biogeographers are interested in examining how individual organisms within a species are spatially arranged within the area where they are found. This is a concept known as species distribution. Three major types of species distribution are identified: clumped, random, and uniform. In a clumped species distribution, multiple groups of individuals tend to form; this is a common behavioral pattern found, for instance, in herding animals like deer or cattle. For such species, a clumped distribution is beneficial because it offers protection from predators. In a random species distribution, individuals are found in scattered locations with no particular organization or method—such as wildflowers whose seeds have been dispersed by the wind over a field, and which grow wherever they fall. In a uniform species distribution, individuals are spread out at a roughly even distance from each other. Many desert plants, for instance, are found in a uniform distribution because this is the pattern that enables each of them to absorb the most water from the arid environment.

Ecogeographic Rules

When biogeographic principles are used to look at the distribution of living organisms on a macroscopic scale, many striking principles emerge regarding the relative degree of biodiversity that can be found in different regions of the earth. One of the most significant of these "ecogeographic rules" is the latitudinal gradient in species diversity, or species richness. This term describes a striking, though as yet not fully understood pattern in global biodiversity: the tremendous increase in the number of unique species that can be found when traveling from high latitudes (colder regions) to low latitudes (warmer regions). In other words, the equatorial tropics are home to a far greater diversity of life than the poles. This pattern applies across nearly every possible form of life, including birds, mammals, freshwater fish, marine invertebrates, insects, and flowering plants and trees. For example, more than two hundred different species of ants are known in Brazil; Alaska has fewer than ten. The 50,000 square kilometers (approximately 19,305 square miles) of land in the Malaysian peninsular is home to nearly 1,500 different species of trees and shrubs; the same area in the southeastern part of Russia holds fewer than 50 different species.

Paleobiogeographic data—data derived from analyzing the relationships between fossilized animals and plants and the locations upon the earth where those fossils were found—indicates that species richness latitude gradients are not a recent phenomenon. It has been shown, for instance, that during the Triassic (a period spanning about 245 million to 208 million years ago), ammonoids (a now-extinct group of mollusks) were more diverse at lower latitudes than at higher ones, and that the same was true of brachiopods, another group of marine invertebrates, during the Paleozoic ice age (about 570 million to 245 million years ago).

Dozens of competing hypotheses have been put forth regarding the potential mechanism or mechanisms responsible for the existence of species richness latitude gradients. Among them are the time and area hypothesis, the diversification rate hypothesis, and the hypothesis of effective evolutionary time. The time and area hypothesis argues that the tropical regions of the earth are both older and larger than the polar regions, giving them a longer span of evolutionary time in which speciation could have occurred and a greater amount of available habitat—both of which could have resulted in the higher degree of species richness that is observed at lower latitudes. (The time and area hypothesis does not account for certain anomalies, such as why the South East Asian sea—which is not as large as other bodies of water in the Indo-Pacific region—has the greatest degree of species richness.) The diversification rate hypothesis argues that speciation occurs faster and more frequently in tropical regions than in polar regions, either because of lower extinction rates or other factors, such as the increased likelihood of achieving reproductive isolation. The hypothesis of effective evolutionary time takes into consideration the longer amount of time ecosystems are believed to have existed in the tropics, but also gives weight to the effects of temperature on the rate at which evolution can occur. At higher temperatures, such as those associated with lower latitudes, genetic mutation rates, among other factors influencing speciation, are higher. To date, no single hypothesis about the cause of species richness latitude gradients has gained widespread acceptance within the scientific community.

Another important ecogeographic principle related to latitudes is Bergmann's rule. The nineteenth-century biologist Carl Bergmann noted that when the same species (or closely related species) of mammals and other warm-blooded animals were found in different parts of the earth, those that lived closer to the equator were comparatively smaller than those that lived at higher latitudes. For example, polar bears are much more massive than related bear species in the tropics. Bergmann's rule is often explained as a result of the direct relationship between body size and heat. Larger animals generate a greater amount of heat as a result of cell metabolic activities, and they also lose less heat to their surroundings, since the ratio of their surface area to overall mass is comparatively low. These adaptations make them well suited to living in colder, high-latitude environments.

Biogeographic Divisions

Biogeographers use a series of imaginary lines to divide the earth into six major divisions, or realms. A distinct biota, or group of plants, animals, and microbes, inhabits each zone. The most famous of these imaginary divides runs between the islands of Borneo and Sulawesi in the Indonesian archipelago, and is known as Wallace's line, after Alfred Russel Wallace. Wallace was a nineteenth-century British naturalist— a contemporary of Charles Darwin's who also developed a theory of evolution based on natural selection. It was Wallace who first noticed the sharp distinction between birds and animals on the western side of the line—which mostly came from taxons common in Asia—and those on the eastern side of the line—which mostly came from taxons common in Australia.

To the west of the Wallace line, for instance, one would find woodpeckers, pheasants, primates, squirrels, and big cats; to the east, cockatoos, bats, eucalyptus trees, and marsupials. The Wallace line is the most well known of the world's biogeographical divisions not only because of the extreme contrasts between the zones on either side of it, but also because the entire region surrounding it is considered to be a very significant biodiversity hot spot. A biodiversity hot spot is a region characterized by a high density of species richness that is under threat of extinction due to human activity. Many of the species found in the region known as Wallacea have endemic distribution areas, including the caerulean paradise flycatcher (*Eutrichomyias rowleyi*) and the pig-like mammal known as the babirusa (*Babyrousa babyrussa*). Logging, mining, and agricultural development have all had a dramatic negative impact on the Wallacea ecosystem.

Biomes are another way in which biographers organize the earth's living communities. A biome is a large, naturally occurring ecosystem; the particular grouping of plants and animals that inhabit it are determined by its climate (especially temperature and precipitation) and geography. Different scientists classify biomes in different ways, but five of the most common terms used to describe biomes are aquatic (freshwater and marine habitats), desert (arid habitats), forest (densely wooded habitats), grassland (open plain habitats dominated by grasses), and tundra (open plain habitats with a permanently frozen layer of subsoil).

Theory of Island Biogeography

The theory of island biogeography was developed in the late 1960s by the ecologists E. O. Wilson, of Harvard University, and Robert MacArthur, of Princeton University, as a way of organizing and explaining the factors contributing to the relative richness of species biodiversity that occurs in the world's islands. In its most basic form, MacArthur and Wilson's theory states that the number of unique living species on any given island is primarily shaped by two competing forces: the rate at which new species move to the island and establish successful breeding populations there (the rate of immigration), and the rate at which existing populations of successfully breeding species disappear from the island (the rate of extinction).

Various other factors are responsible for determining the rate of immigration and extinction. For example, an island's rate of immigration is closely related to the distance of the island from other ecosystems from which potential colonizers could travel, such as other islands or a mainland. The theory predicts that the more geographically isolated an island is, the lower its rate of colonization will be; this pattern is known as the distance effect. Similarly, an island's rate of extinction is related to the size of the island is, the number of species that already inhabit it, and the availability of resources on it. According to the theory, a larger island will have more habitable area and more resources, like food, available—and will thus be able to support a greater number of species, lowering the extinction rate. As the number of existing species on an island increases, competition between these species for habitat and food will also cause its extinction rate to rise. By comparison, islands that have a variety of habitats (for example, mountainous regions as well as flat forested regions) will be able to support a larger number of different species.

Assuming that these factors remain unchanged, MacArthur and Wilson's theory predicts that for any newly created island, the rate of immigration will start high and drop over time, while the rate of extinction will start at zero and rise over time. Eventually, the number of unique species that exist on a newly created island will become stable, as a balance, or equilibrium, is reached between the rate of immigration and the rate of extinction. (Even after equilibrium has been reached, the specific composition of the island's flora and fauna will be dynamic, rather than static, as different species continue to replace each other.) For example, the 1883 volcanic eruption on the tiny island of Krakatoa in Indonesia caused the total extinction of all its plant and animal species. Observations over the following hundred years showed that the rates of immigration and extinction on what was now effectively a "new" island followed the pattern predicted by MacArthur and Wallace: Between 1883 and 1934, thirty-four new species moved to and colonized the island, five of which went extinct. But between 1934 and 1985, an additional fourteen species began to successfully breed on the island (a lower immigration rate than in the previous period) and an additional eight became extinct (a higher extinction rate than in the previous period).

The theory of island biogeography has since been expanded in scope; it is now used to estimate the probable degree of species richness in any isolated habitat area, such as a river or lake surrounded by desert, or a wetland region surrounded by dry woodlands. It is a particularly useful tool for predicting the effects of habitat fragmentation due to human activity. For example, much of the once continuous deciduous forest of the eastern United States has been cut up into smaller, geographically separated, patches of trees, with roads, farms, and cities taking up the spaces in between. The distance effect predicts that these isolated patches of forest will have a relatively low rate of immigration, since it is difficult for plants and animals to move across the gaps between them. In addition, their small size will reduce the available habitat area and resources they contain, raising the rate of extinction. Overall, the theory of island biogeography predicts that habitat fragmentation will reduce the level of species richness in fragmented

areas. Studies of avian populations in forest preserves surrounded by human development support this prediction.

Further Reading

Kruckeberg, Arthur R. *Geology and Plant Life: The Effects of Landforms and Rock Types on Plants.* University of Washington Press, 2004.

Lieberman, Bruce S. *Paleobiogeography: Using Fossils to Study Global Change, Plate Tectonics, and Evolution.* Kluwer Academic, 2000.

Lomolino, Mark V., Dov F. Sax, and James H Brown. *Foundations of Biogeography: Classic Papers with Commentary.* University of Chicago Press, 2004.

Losos, Jonathan B., Robert E. Ricklefs, and Robert H. MacArthur, eds. *The Theory of Island Geography Revisited.* Princeton University Press, 2010.

Morrone, Juan J. *Evolutionary Biogeography: An Integrative Approach with Case Studies.* Columbia University Press, 2009.

Newton, Ian. *Speciation and Biogeography of Birds.* Academic Press, 2003.

Shugart, H. H. *How the Earthquake Bird Got Its Name and Other Tales of an Unbalanced Nature.* Yale University Press, 2007.

■ Biomagnification

FIELDS OF STUDY: Biochemistry; Biology; Ecology; Ecosystem Management; Environmental Studies;

DEFINITION: Accumulation of toxic contaminants in organisms as they move up through the food chain

Recognition of the detrimental environmental effects of biomagnification led to the adoption of several procedures to prevent the accumulation of toxic materials in higher organisms along the food chain. Some pesticides were banned outright, and others were modified to prevent their accumulation in the environment.

Overview

As members of each level of the food chain are progressively eaten by those organisms found in higher levels of the chain, the potential grows for increased concentrations of toxic chemicals to accumulate within the tissues of the higher organisms. Not all chemicals, potentially toxic or not, are equally likely to undergo this accumulation, known as biomagnification. However, molecules susceptible to biomagnification have certain characteristics in common. They are resistant to natural microbial and biochemical degradation and therefore persist in the environment. They are also lipophilic—that is, they tend to accumulate in the fatty tissue of organisms. In addition, chemicals must be biologically active in order to have effects on the organisms in which they are found. Such compounds are likely to be absorbed from food or water in the environment and stored within the membranes or fatty tissues.

The process of biomagnification usually begins with the spraying of pesticides for the purpose of controlling insect populations. Industrial contamination, including the release of heavy metals, can be an additional cause of such pollution. Biomagnification results when these chemicals contaminate the water supply and are absorbed into the lipid membranes of microbial organisms. This process, often referred to as bioaccumulation, results in the initial concentration of the chemical in the organisms in a form that is not naturally excreted with normal waste material. The levels of the chemical in the organisms may reach anywhere from one to three times the level found in the surrounding environment. Since the nature of the chemical is such that it is neither degraded nor excreted, it remains within the organisms.

As the organisms on the bottom of the food chain are eaten and digested by members of the next level in the chain, the concentration of the accumulated material significantly increases; at each subsequent level, the concentration may reach one order of magnitude (a tenfold increase) higher. Consequently, the concentrations of the pollutant at the top of the environmental food chain, such as in fish or carnivorous birds, and potentially even humans, may be as much as one million times as high as the original, presumably safe, levels in the environment. For example, studies of Dichloro-diphenyl-trichloroethane (DDT) levels in the 1960's found that zooplankton at the bottom of the food chain had accumulated nearly one thousand times the level of the pollutant in the surrounding water. Ingestion of the plankton by fish resulted in concentration by another factor of several hundred. By the time the fish were eaten by predatory birds, the level of DDT was concentrated by a factor of more than two hundred thousand.

Pollutants Subject to Biomagnification

DDT is characteristic of most pollutants subject to potential biomagnification. It is relatively stable in the environment, persisting for decades. It is soluble in lipids and readily incorporated into the membranes of organisms. While DDT represents the classic example of biomagnification of a toxic chemical, it is by no means the only representative of potential environmental pollutants. Other pesticides with similar characteristics include aldrin, chlordane, parathion, and toxaphene. In addition, cyanide, polychlorinated biphenyls (PCBs), and heavy metals such as selenium, mercury, copper, lead and zinc have been found to bioaccumulate within the food chain.

Some heavy metals are inherently toxic or may undergo microbial modification that increases their toxic potential. For example, mercury does not naturally accumulate in membranes and was therefore not originally viewed as a significant danger to the environment. However, some microorganisms are capable of adding a methyl group to the metal, producing methylmercury, a highly toxic material that does accumulate in fatty tissue and membranes.

Since pesticides are, by their nature, biologically active compounds, which reflects their ability to control insects, they are of particular concern if subject to biomagnification. DDT remains the classic example of how bioaccumulation and biomagnification may have effects on the environment. Initially introduced as a pesticide for control of insects and insect-borne disease, DDT was not thought to be particularly toxic. However, biomagnification of the chemical was found to result in the deaths of birds and other wildlife. In addition, DDT contamination was found to result in the formation of thin eggshells in birds, which greatly reduced the numbers of birds successfully hatched. Before the use of DDT was banned in the 1960's, the population levels of predatory birds such as eagles and falcons had fallen to a fraction of the levels found prior to use of the insecticide. Though it was unclear whether there was any direct effect on the human population in the United States, the discovery of elevated levels of DDT in human tissue contributed to the decision to ban the use of the chemical.

Several procedures have been adopted since the 1960's to prevent the biomagnification of toxic materials. In addition to outright bans, pesticides are often modified to prevent their accumulation in the environment. The chemical structures of most synthetic pesticides are easily degraded by microorganisms found in the environment. Ideally, a pesticide should survive no longer than a single growing season before being rendered harmless by the environmental flora. Often such chemical changes require only simple modification of a compound's basic structure.

Richard Adler

Further Reading

Atlas, Ronald, and Richard Bartha. *Microbial Ecology.* 4th ed. Benjamin Cummings, 1998.

Carson, Rachel. *Silent Spring.* 40th anniversary ed. Houghton Mifflin, 2002.

Colborn, Theo, Dianne Dumanoski, and John P. Myers. *Our Stolen Future: Are We Threatening Our Fertility, Intelligence, and Survival?* Plume, 1996.

Karasov, William H., and Carlos Martínez del Rio. *Physiological Ecology: How Animals Process Energy, Nutrients, and Toxins.* Princeton University Press, 2007.

Primack, Richard B. *Essentials of Conservation Biology.* 5th ed. Sinauer Associates, 2010.

Willmer, Pat, Graham Stone, and Ian Johnston. *Environmental Physiology of Animals.* Blackwell Science, 2000.

■ Biomass conversion

FIELDS OF STUDY: Energy and Energy Resources; Industries, Commercial Products; Science; Technology and Applied Science

DEFINITION: Process of converting biological organic material, such as plant material and animal waste, into fuels

The conversion of biomass into fuels provides alternatives to the use of fossil fuels and thus can contribute to the reduction of air pollution. Biomass conversion also serves to reduce the amount of wastes that must be disposed of in other ways.

Plants and algae use solar energy and transform carbon dioxide (CO_2) from the atmosphere into their biomass (also called primary biomass). Human beings have converted biomass into energy for centuries. For example, burning biomass in the form of wood is the oldest form of such conversion. Biomass can also be converted into other energy sources or fuels—for example, through fermentation to alcohols (ethanol or butanol) or biogas and through gasification to a substitute for natural gas. In addition, biomass such as plant oil can be transformed by the chemical reaction of transesterification into biodiesel, a diesel fuel substitute. The processing of primary biomass by organisms creates secondary biomass sources, such as animal manure and other wastes. Several countries around the world use incinerators to convert this kind of biomass into electricity. Biomass is produced naturally (for example, in forests) and agriculturally (for example, agricultural residues and dung).

The processes used to convert biomass into fuels can have both positive and negative environmental impacts, but the positive influences on the environment outweigh the negative ones. It is widely recognized that the use of fossil fuels is the leading cause of global climate change due to carbon dioxide release. Biomass conversion does not result in net CO_2 emissions because it releases only the amount of CO_2 absorbed in the biomass during plant growth. Biomass conversion into energy is thus a favorable option for reducing CO_2 emissions.

Biomass conversion also offers a means of reducing wastes, such as agricultural residues and human wastes. A great number of wastes result from the cultivation of crops such as corn, and these wastes can be turn into ethanol, which is used as a transportation fuel. Conversion of biomass from landfills produces biogas, which is two-thirds methane. Methane is a very powerful greenhouse gas, and thus a contributor to global warming, but it is also a very good fuel. It can be burned in electrical generators to produce electricity, and it can be used as a fuel for vehicles. To prevent the methane produced by landfills from being released into the atmosphere, some municipalities have installed "gas wells" in landfills to tap the methane for use as fuel.

Biogas can also be generated from wastewater and from animal waste. In 2006 the city of San Francisco contemplated a plan to extend its recycling program to include conversion of dog feces into methane to produce electricity and to heat homes; given the city's dog population of 120,000, this initiative was seen to have the potential to generate significant amounts of fuel while reducing waste. The plan was never initiated, however, as the city opted to focus on other recycling programs.

Sergei A. Markov

Further Reading

Bourne, Joel K. "Green Dreams." *National Geographic*, October, 2007, 38-59.

Hall, David O., and Joanna I. House. "Biomass: A Modern and Environmentally Acceptable Fuel." *Solar Energy Materials and Solar Cells* 38 (1995): 521-542.

Wright, Richard T. *Environmental Science: Toward a Sustainable Future*. 10th ed. Upper Saddle River, N.J.: Prentice Hall, 2008.

■ Biomes & environmental issues

DEFINITION: Major ecological zones shaped primarily by climate and characterized by the types of plant and animal life they support

The complexity of biomes exposes them to varying and sometimes cascading changes from both natural and human-initiated events. The consequences for the larger environment can range from minimal to catastrophic.

Overview

Each of the earth's biomes has a typical ecological pattern, with its flora and fauna sharing similar characteristics, such as leaf forms and survival strategies. A study of any biome, on any continent, will show multiple ways its species carry out the essential tasks of life. Biomes are large and complex, with species forming intricate networks of life within subsets of the biomes.

Land-based major biomes include the following: tropical rain forest, tropical dry forest, savanna (tropical grassland), desert, temperate grassland, Mediterranean scrub or chaparral, temperate deciduous forest, temperate mixed and coniferous forest, boreal forest(taiga), and Arctic tundra. Marine biomes are basically characterized as oceanic or freshwater, although the lack of vegetation-climate links and the gradients between coastal and deep-sea habitats make the simplicity of this scheme problematic. Finally, human activities have so transformed large portions of the earth that some biologists treat anthropogenic (resulting from human activities) biomes as a

separate concept. These biomes range from dense settlement patterns in urban landscapes to cropland, rangeland, and forest.

Influences on Biomes

Biomes are sometimes viewed as giant ecosystems. Because of the size and complexity of biomes, however, both scientists and lay observers find it more useful to view them as made up of many different ecosystems and habitats.

Land-based biomes are shaped largely by their climates. The most important climatic factors are latitude and humidity (total precipitation, seasonal rainfall patterns, ambient moisture); sometimes elevation is important also. Cross-cutting these climatic factors—though influenced by them—are such features as terrain, soil type and nutrient status, and prevailing winds. All these affect the kinds of vegetation that can flourish in a region, thus determining the types and amounts of animal life the plant cover will support.

Generally biomes closer to the equator support more biodiversity, in the form of different species. An estimated 50 percent of all life-forms on earth are native to tropical forests. Tropical rain forests also have many layers of life systems, from the canopy ecosystems with their monkeys, marmosets, and tropical birds, such as macaws, down through several canopy-gap layers that shelter opossums and woodpeckers, to the forest floor, the base station for jaguars and frogs, among other jungle dwellers. What the tropical forests do not have is a rich nutrient base. They have poor soil quality, and most of the available nutrients are held within the trees themselves rather than fixed in the soil.

In contrast, temperate deciduous forests lack the great variety of species, and of levels, found in tropical rain forests. The life processes in temperate deciduous forests are highly regulated by seasonal temperature changes. As leaves fall to the ground, they carry calcium and other minerals to the forest floor; this litter turns into humus and becomes the nutrient-rich soil on which broad-leaved trees thrive.

Another mix of resources and life strategies is found in desert biomes. Most deserts do get some water and support some life, but anything growing there must adapt to little moisture and hot, unshaded land that is poor in nutrients. Desert plants store nutrients in underground organs such as their root

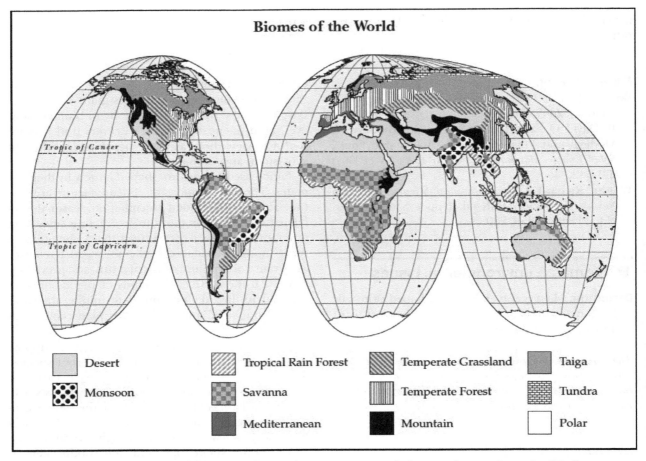

Biomes of the World

Tropic of Cancer

Tropic of Capricorn

Desert	Tropical Rain Forest	Temperate Grassland	Taiga
Monsoon	Savanna	Temperate Forest	Tundra
Mediterranean	Mountain		Polar

systems, and cacti have expandable stems for storing water from sudden but infrequent downpours. Desert dwellers such as the kangaroo rat get their moisture from eating seeds. Their underground burrows retain three times as much humidity as exists aboveground.

Environmental Issues and Biomes

For the nonhuman organisms living in any given biome, the environmental features of that biome are essential to life. Human beings, in contrast, interact with biomes by finding ways to use the biomes' natural resources to sustain them. Human technologies and large numbers of humans, however, can upset a delicately balanced biome far beyond its ability to recover. Even in the ancient world, large-scale grazing and firewood collection apparently turned

once-wooded coastal areas into the Mediterranean scrub that bears that region's name.

Throughout history, humans have cleared forests or modified grasslands for use in agriculture. Sometimes the environmental damage done by such processes is limited. For example, the prairie grasslands of the American Great Plains were originally roamed by bison, and the cattle herds that replaced the bison filled the same ecological niche. Other human-caused changes have brought near disaster to entire biomes.

Human activities have altered every one of the earth's biomes. Among the most dire changes has been the destruction of tropical forests caused by timber harvesting and by the clearing of trees and other plant life to make way for ranching or industry. The damage caused when a biome is altered is not confined to the loss of diverse natural resources within that biome; rather, such change threatens the entire biosphere because it interferes with the role the biome plays in balancing the earth's systems. Loss of rain forest, for example, damages the atmosphere because of the accompanying loss of oxygen renewal that was provided by the trees.

The ocean biome is central to regulating heat and rainfall around the world, and, through its plankton, is the source of most photosynthesis on the earth. The crumbling of coral reefs and the huge trash vortex reported in the North Pacific in the late 1990's are early warning signals about the environmental threats to this biome's future. Freshwater bodies are susceptible to damage from industrial and fertilizer runoff. Other natural biomes face their own unique threats of rapid environmental degradation.

Anthropogenic biomes are by definition shaped by human activity, but humans can make conscious decisions that can reduce the negative impacts of such activity on the environment. Within cities, for example, humans can counter the effects of vast, heat-retaining stretches of pavement by creating rooftop gardens, rain gardens, and other green spaces.

Emily Alward

Further Reading

Butz, Stephen D. *Science of Earth Systems.* 2nd ed. Thomson Delmar Learning, 2008.

Whitfield, Philip, Peter D. Moore, and Barry Cox. *Biomes and Habitats.* Macmillan, 2002.

Woodward, Susan L. *Biomes of Earth: Terrestrial, Aquatic, and Human-Dominated.* Greenwood Press, 2003.

_____. *Introduction to Biomes.* Greenwood Press, 2009.

■ Biopesticides & the environment

Fields of Study: Biochemistry; Biology; Chemistry; Ecology; Microbiology;

IDENTIFICATION: Biological agents that are used to control insect and weed pests

Biopesticides have significant advantages over commercial pesticides in that they appear to be environmentally safer, given that they do not accumulate in the food chain and they have only slight effects on ecological balances.

Overview

Pests are any unwanted animals, plants, or microorganisms. When the environment has no natural resistance to a pest and when no natural antagonists are present, pests can run rampant. For example, the fungus *Endothia parasitica*, which entered New York State in 1904, caused the nearly complete destruction of the American chestnut tree because no natural control was present.

Biopesticides represent the biological, rather than the chemical, control of pests. Many plants and animals are protected from pests by passive means. For example, plant rotation is a traditional method of insect and disease protection in which the host plant is removed for a period long enough to reduce pathogen and pest populations.

Biopesticides have several significant advantages over commercial pesticides. They appear to be ecologically safer than commercial pesticides because they do not accumulate in the food chain. Some biopesticides also provide persistent control, because pests require more than a single mutation to adapt to them and because they can become an integral part of a pest's life cycle. In addition, biopesticides have only slight effects on ecological balances because they do not affect nontarget species. Finally, biopesticides are compatible with other control agents. The major drawbacks to using biopesticides are that, in comparison with chemical pesticides, biopesticides work less efficiently and take more time to kill their targets.

Viruses, bacteria, fungi, protozoa, mites, and flowers have all been used as biopesticides. Viruses have been developed against insect pests such as *Lepidoptera*, *Hymenoptera*, and *Dipterans*. These viruses cause hyperparasitism. Gypsy moths and tent caterpillars, for example, periodically suffer from epidemic virus infestations.

Many saprophytic microorganisms that occur on plant roots and leaves can protect plants against microbial pests. *Bacillus cereus* has been used as an inoculum on soybean seeds to prevent infection by the fungal pathogen *Cercospora*. Some microorganisms used as biopesticides produce antibiotics, but the major mechanism for protection is probably competitive exclusion of a pest from sites on which the pest must grow. For example, *Agrobacterium radiobacter* antagonizes *Agrobacterium tumefaciens*, which causes crown gall disease. Two bacteria—*Bacillus* and

Comparison of the Properties of *Bacillus Thuringiensis* and *Bacillus Popilliae* as Microbial Biocontrol Agents

	BACILLUS THURINGIENSIS	*BACILLUS POPILLIAE*
Pest controlled	Lepidoptera (many)	Coleoptera (few)
Pathogenicity	low	high
Response time	immediate	slow
Formulation	spores and toxin crystals	spores
Production	in vitro	in vivo
Persistence	low	high
Resistance in pests	developing	reported

Source: Data adapted from J. W. Deacon, *Microbial Control of Plant Pests and Diseases* (1983).

Streptomyces—added as biopesticides to soil help control the damping off disease of cucumbers, peas, and lettuces caused by *Rhizoctonia solani. Bacillus subtilis* added to plant tissue also controls stem rot and wilt rot caused by the fungus *Fusarium. Mycobacteria* produce cellulose-degrading enzymes, and their addition to young seedlings helps control fungal infection by *Pythium, Rhizoctonia,* and *Fusarium. Bacillus* and *Pseudomonas* are bacteria that produce enzymes that dissolve fungal cell walls.

The best examples of microbial insecticides are *Bacillus thuringiensis* (*B.t.*) toxins, which were first used in 1901. They have had widespread commercial production and use since the 1960s and have been successfully tested on 140 insect species, including mosquitoes. *B.t.* produces insecticidal endotoxins during sporulation and also produces exotoxins contained in crystalline parasporal protein bodies. These protein crystals are insoluble in water but readily dissolve in an insect's gut. Once dissolved, the proteolytic enzymes paralyze the gut. *Bacillus* spores that have also been consumed germinate and kill the insect. *Bacillus popilliae* is a related bacterium that produces an insecticidal spore that has been used to control Japanese beetles, a pest of corn.

Saprophytic fungi can compete with pathogenic fungi. Among the fungi used as biopesticides are *Gliocladium virens, Trichoderma hamatum, Trichoderma harzianum, Trichoderma viride,* and *Talaromyces flavus.* For example, *Trichoderma* competes with the pathogens *Verticillium* and *Fusarium*

Peniophora gigantea antagonizes the pine pathogen *Heterobasidion annosum* through three mechanisms: It prevents the pathogen from colonizing stumps and traveling down into the root zone, it prevents the pathogen from traveling between infected and uninfected trees along interconnected roots, and it prevents the pathogen from growing up to stump surfaces and sporulating.

Nematodes are pests that interfere with commercial button mushroom (*Agaricus bisporus*) production. Several types of nematode-trapping fungi can be used as biopesticides to trap, kill, and digest the nematode pests. The fungi produce structures such as constricting and nonconstricting rings, sticky appendages, and spores, which attach to the nematodes. The most common nematode-trapping fungi are *Arthrobotrys oligospora, Arthrobotrys conoides, Dactylaria candida,* and *Meria coniospora.*

Protozoa have occasionally been used as biopesticide agents, but their use has suffered because of such difficulties as slow growth and complex culture conditions associated with their commercial production. Predaceous mites are used as a biopesticide to protect cotton from other insect pests such as the boll weevil.

Dalmatian and Persian insect powders contain pyrethrins, which are toxic insecticidal compounds produced in *Chrysanthemum* flowers. Synthetic versions of these naturally occurring compounds are found in products used to control head lice. Molecular genetics has also been used to insert the gene for the *B.t.* toxin into cotton and corn. *B.t.* cotton and *B.t.* corn both express the gene in their roots, which provides them with protection from root worms. Ecologists and environmentalists have expressed concern that constantly exposing pests to the toxin will cause insect resistance to develop rapidly and thus reduce the effectiveness of traditionally applied *B.t.*

Mark Coyne

Further Reading

Churchill, B. W. *Biological Control of Weeds with Plant Pathogens.* Edited by R. Charudattan and H. Walker. Wiley, 1982.

Deacon, J. W. *Microbial Control of Plant Pests and Diseases.* Instrumentation Systems & Automation, 1983.

Metz, Matthew, ed. *Bacillus Thuringiensis: A Cornerstone of Modern Agriculture.* Haworth, 2003.

Ohkawa, H., H. Miyagawa, and P. W. Lee, eds. *Pesticide Chemistry: Crop Protection, Public Health, Environmental Safety.* Wiley, 2007.

■ Biophilia

FIELDS OF STUDY: Ecology, Environment, Environmentalism; Ethics, Advocacy, Policy, Protest; Philosophy and History of Science; Social/Economic

DEFINITION: A philosophical hypothesis that addresses the relationship between human beings and other organisms

The biophilia hypothesis may be viewed as a bridge between the sciences and the humanities. It has been employed in the sciences, philosophy, and literature regarding investigations of biodiversity, habitat conservation, and ecosystem studies.

The word "biophilia," first coined by the German psychologist Erich Fromm, is a neologism combining two Greek terms (*bio,* meaning "life" and *philias,* meaning "friendly love"); it refers to the natural human inclination to focus on life and lifelike operations. Biophilia became a key concept in environmental studies in 1984 when Harvard entomologist Edward O. Wilson published a book titled *Biophilia.* In this volume, Wilson argues that human sympathy toward living things can be explained in terms of evolutionary developments in human physiology and psychology. Taking this natural affinity for life into account, Wilson asserts that conservation of species and their habitat is valuable to human beings not merely in the instrumental sense of resource management and profit but in an intrinsic sense as well, insofar as the diversity of life is essential to the human psyche.

Because of its focus on life and lifelike processes, biophilia is most often associated with biocentric views in environmental ethics, since it holds that land is valuable insofar as diversity in ecosystems is a requirement for diversity of life. However, the results of biophilia—particularly when viewed in light of co-evolutionary data (to which Wilson appeals)—reveal that ecosystem health depends on equilibrium in biodiversity. In this way, biophilia may be said to fall in line with more ecocentric views, such as the deep ecology and land ethic perspectives.

At the core of the biophilia hypothesis is the belief that the value human beings place on life, both human and nonhuman, will increase in proportion to the amount of understanding humans glean from studying other organisms. Without such understanding, it is argued, phobias regarding nature will endure. With this deeper understanding, phobias will be replaced by philias. Taking up the metaphor of historian Leo Marx, Wilson attributes this tension between biophobia and biophilia to a dilemma known as "the machine in the garden," wherein human beings cannot survive in the wild without technologies that have the potential to destroy wilderness. Thus he and other conservationists have embraced biophilia in calling for a more intelligent, limited use of technologies that have the potential to harm habitats.

Because it brings together biology and psychology in these ways, biophilia may be viewed philosophically as a bridge between the sciences and the humanities. While the sciences tend to aim at discovery of fact and the humanities at the transmission of value, both may be needed for the deep understanding of nature that biophilia pursues. In this way, the implications of biophilia may go beyond a mere division of labor between the sciences and the humanities toward a view of *Homo sapiens* as the "poetic species." Accordingly, the love for living things that brings together those human capacities for art and for science is found in human beings' biology and in their relationship to other organisms.

Christopher C. Kirby

Further Reading

Kellert, Stephen R., and Edward O. Wilson, eds. *The Biophilia Hypothesis*. Washington, D.C.: Island Press, 1993.

Wilson, Edward O. *Biophilia*. 1984. Reprint. Cambridge, Mass.: Harvard University Press, 2003.

_____. *The Diversity of Life*. New ed. New York: W. W. Norton, 1999.

■ Biopiracy & bioprospecting

FIELDS OF STUDY: Biology; Ecology; Ecosystem Management;

DEFINITION: Extraction of biological resources from areas of biodiversity

The practice of extracting biological resources from regions of the world known for their great biological diversity, often carried out by scientists working for corporations or educational institutions, is the subject of ongoing debate. Many environmentalists and indigenous peoples see such resource extraction as a form of exploitation.

Overview

With the signing of the United Nations Convention on Biological Diversity at the Earth Summit in Rio de Janeiro, Brazil, in 1992, participatory nations agreed to no longer consider biological resources the "common heritage of mankind" but conceded the rights to distribute such resources to the individual nations that housed them. Around the same time, the terms "biopiracy" and "bioprospecting" began to

be used to describe the acquisition of these newly protected resources. The two terms refer to essentially the same thing, the extraction of biological resources from areas of biodiversity, but they have decidedly different tones, the former having been coined by opponents of such activity and the latter being preferred by the practitioners of this type of resource extraction.

Biological resources include whole organisms such as crops or livestock, chemical compounds that can be purified from specific organisms that produce them, and even the genetic material taken from organisms that can then be used to produce desired proteins, usually in conjunction with some form of genetic engineering. These resources hold value in that they can be used to improve agricultural yields, perform certain industrial processes, or serve various pharmaceutical applications. The debate over the appropriate acquisition of these resources led to the split in the terms used to describe the same activity. "Biopiracy" brings to mind a swashbuckler who pillages resources without regard to the victims; "bioprospecting," in contrast, conveys the image of a gold miner staking out a claim and then working it, with no guarantee of ultimate success.

Bioprospecting

The image of the gold-rush prospector is perhaps most appropriate for one particular type of resource collection: the biodiversity-driven, or random-collection, approach. Scientists taking this approach sample large amounts of organisms for a desired chemical activity or genetic attribute without prior knowledge of precisely where to look. The screened organisms are typically plants, microorganisms, insects, or marine invertebrates. This is called the biodiversity-driven approach because mass sampling is best done in areas with wide ranges of different organisms living in close proximity.

Just as modern mining methods include scientific means for discovering deposits of minerals, however, bioprospecting often makes use of prior knowledge to narrow the pool of organisms being tested. This knowledge falls into three main categories: chemotaxonomic, ecological, and ethnobotanical/ethnopharmacological. The use of chemotaxonomic knowledge involves the sampling of organisms that belong to the same taxonomic class as an organism that is already known to have a desired property. An example would be screening a number of bacteria

Black turmeric (Curcuma caesia) *is a kind of turmeric with bluish-black rhizome, famous for its unique medicinal properties. It is a perennial herb, belonging to Zingibera-ceae (Ginger) family, native to North-East and Central India. Presently Black turmeric is on the verge of extinction due to biopiracy.* By Ramesh Raju (Own work).

Biopiracy

Much of the world's biodiversity lies in the tropical regions, often in developing countries that have historically experienced oppression by wealthier nations. It is not surprising, therefore, that indigenous peoples in these regions tend to be wary of the academic institutions and multinational corporations that engage in what these entities may view as simple bioprospecting. Often, indigenous peoples have concerns regarding the entire practice of treating biodiversity as a biological resource, including the patenting of living organisms and profiting from biological materials that for many years previously were exchanged freely among those who reaped the benefits. Even if these concerns are allayed, questions often remain about who should be compensated for traditional knowledge that leads to a "discovery," as well as what would constitute a fair level of compensation.

from the class Actinobacteria, the taxonomic group known to be responsible for the production of strep-tomycin, for antibiotic properties. Ecological knowledge is knowledge that can be gained from field observations of the interactions between particular organisms. Certain plants and animals, for example, produce chemical compounds called secondary metabolites that they use to defend themselves against predator attack. A scientist taking an ecological approach to bioprospecting may detect such interactions and choose species for further testing based on these observations.

The use of ethnobotanical/ethnopharmacological knowledge is the most controversial approach, as it seeks to capitalize on the medical practices of indigenous peoples who inhabit the areas of interest. Ethnobotanical knowledge focuses on plants that have traditionally been used for healing purposes by indigenous peoples, whereas ethnopharmacological knowledge is broader, encompassing all traditional drugs as well as their biological activities. Using such knowledge, scientists can screen specific organisms for desired properties with a much higher degree of success than is seen with randomly sampled collections.

Although no entity has been prosecuted officially for biopiracy under the Convention on Biological Diversity, many allegations of biopiracy have been made, and a number of planned bioprospecting projects have been abandoned after information about them became public and protests ensued. It may be partially because of such controversies that bioprospecting activities actually decreased in the decades following the convention's signing, as many companies turned away from using natural resources and instead developed synthetic processes, such as combinatorial chemistry to produce lead compounds that could be screened for a desired activity.

James S. Godde

Further Reading

Godde, James S. "Genetic Resources." In *Encyclopedia of Global Resources*, edited by Craig W. Allin. Salem Press, 2010.

Hamilton, Chris. "Biodiversity, Biopiracy, and Benefits: What Allegations of Biopiracy Tell Us About Intellectual Property." *Developing World Bioethics* 6 (2006): 158-173.

Soejarto, D. D., et al. "Ethnobotany/Ethnopharma-
cology and Mass Bioprospecting: Issues on Intel-
lectual Property and Benefit-Sharing." *Journal of
Ethnopharmacology* 100, nos. 1-2 (August, 2005):
15-22.
Tan, G., C. Gyllenhaal, and D. D. Soejarto. "Biodiver-
sity as a Source of Anticancer Drugs." *Current Drug
Targets* 7, no. 3 (March, 2006): 265-277.
Tedlock, Barbara. "Indigenous Heritage and Biopi-
racy in the Age of Intellectual Property Rights."
Explore: The Journal of Science and Healing 2, no. 3
(May, 2006): 256-259.

■ Bioregionalism

IDENTIFICATION: Environmental movement that holds
that local populations should be self-sustaining
based on the resources of their surrounding bioregions and largely self-governing

*Bioregionalists are concerned with reversing the alienation
from the land that is evident in the modern global economy,
with protecting the environment from unsustainable human
exploitation, and with ensuring that natural resources remain abundant and diverse for future generations.*

Overview

Bioregionalism rests on two basic ex-
istential principles: that humanity is
but one component of the "web of
life" (that is, the ecosystem) and that
humans best pursue their own welfare by living in balance with the
local environment. Bioregionalism
began as a philosophical offshoot of
the environmental movement
during the 1970's. Among its early
proponents were environmental activist Peter Berg, ecologist Raymond
F. Dasmann, and poet Gary Snyder.
They particularly worried that technology, consumerism, postmodern
culture, and global economics were
producing a rootless population es-
tranged from a sense of home and
community. Bioregionalism is one

of the "relocalization" movements seeking to reverse
this trend.

A bioregion is an area defined by natural rather
than political boundaries. It most commonly com-
prises a particular watershed, the plants, animals, climate, hydrology, and ecology of which give it a distinctive character. In 1978 Berg and Dasmann argued
that people must concentrate on "living-in-place,"
which entails satisfying the necessities of life and en-
joying life's pleasures as they are available in a particular area, as well as ensuring their long-term availability. The approach is pragmatic: It assumes that
people who live long in one place come to know it
thoroughly, come to care about it, and want to take
care of it.

Bioregionalism is an eclectic movement. It fosters
an awareness of local economic and cultural assets by
applying lessons from physical geography, ecology,
ecosystem management, sustainable agriculture, economics, literature, and political theory. For example,
the bioregionalist approach to architecture involves
the use of local materials and labor, as well as designs
that reflect both regional traditions and the surrounding landscape while satisfying the requirements of present-day life. Bioregionalist political
theory stresses participatory democracy and the resolution of social problems through the efforts of voluntary, nonprofit groups. Bioregionalist economics

*A map showing the two definitions of the proposed "Republic of Cascadia." Green shows
the American states of Oregon and Washington; and the Canadian province of British
Columbia (which make up the standard definition). The black-dotted line marks the
border of the Cascadia bioregion (which is also mentioned as a border).
By NuclearVacuum (Own work).*

is centered on locally produced goods and services in place of imports and encourages recycling.

Bioregionalism is neither essentially hostile to technology nor divorced from global civilization. It acknowledges that bioregions are parts of larger economic, political, and cultural contexts but emphasizes local resources, both physical and intellectual. Moreover, bioregionalism is not doctrinaire. A variety of philosophical approaches and different kinds of activism—not all of them congruent—participate in or derive from bioregionalism. Among the organizations and movements it has fostered are grassroots environmental efforts to preserve natural features (such as Oregon's Friends of Trees), watershed conservancy, the "locavore" effort (a movement devoted to the promotion of eating only locally produced food), coordinated resource management plans, farmers' markets, Green political parties, community-based alternative energy projects, and educational and research institutions, such as the Bioregional Congress.

Critics contend that bioregionalism is utopian and impractical, at least for large populations. Nonetheless, the movement attracted increasing interest during the late twentieth and early twenty-first centuries among persons interested in establishing self-sufficient economies, in preserving wildlife, and in safeguarding air and water against pollution.

Roger Smith

Further Reading

McGinnis, Michael Vincent. *Bioregionalism.* Routledge, 1999.

Sale, Kirkpatrick. *Dwellers in the Land: The Bioregional Vision.* University of Georgia Press, 2000.

Thayer, Robert L., Jr. *LifePlace: Bioregional Thought and Practice.* University of California Press, 2003.

■ Bioremediation

FIELDS OF STUDY: Biology; Biochemistry; Botany; Chemistry; Ecology; Ecosystem Management; Environmental Sciences; Environmental Studies; Microbiology;

DENTIFICATION: Waste management technology that employs naturally occurring plants, microorganisms, and enzymes or genetically engineered organisms to clean contaminated environments

The environmentally beneficial and inexpensive waste management strategy of bioremediation enables the degradation of toxic organic and inorganic compounds into environmentally harmless products.

Overview

Bioremediation uses biological agents to degrade or decompose toxic environmental compounds into less toxic forms. It is a beneficial and inexpensive strategy for waste management that is environmentally friendly in comparison with other remediation technologies. The products of waste decomposition are usually simple inorganic nutrients or gases.

Bioremediation works because, as a general rule, all naturally occurring compounds in the environment are ultimately degraded by biological activity. Toxic and industrial wastes, and even some chemically synthesized compounds that do not naturally occur, can also be decomposed because parts of their structures resemble naturally occurring compounds that are sources of carbon and energy for biological systems. Wastes are either metabolized, in which case they are used as a source of carbon and energy, or cometabolized, in which case they are simply modified so that they lose their toxicity or are bound to organic material in the environment and rendered unavailable.

Bioremediation can occur 'in situ' (Latin: 'in place') at the contaminated site or 'ex situ' (Latin: 'out of place'), in which case contaminated soil or water is removed to a treatment facility where bioremediation takes place under controlled environmental conditions. Bioremediation can use organisms that naturally occur at a site, or it can be stimulated through the addition of organisms, sometimes genetically engineered organisms, to the contaminated site in a process known as "seeding." The first organism ever patented was a genetically engineered bacterium that had been designed to degrade the components of oil.

Techniques

Numerous approaches to bioremediation have been developed. One of the simplest is to fertilize a contaminated site to optimal nutrient levels and allow naturally occurring biodegrading populations to increase and become active. Organic contaminants have been mixed with decomposed and partially decomposed organic material and composted as a bioremediation process. In a method analogous to the activated sludge process in wastewater treatment, contaminants are mixed in slurries and aerated to promote their decomposition. It is possible to obtain biosolids that are specially adapted for slurry systems because they have previously been exposed to similar organic wastes.

In situ restoration of contaminated groundwater is often accomplished through the injection of nutrients and oxygen into the aquifers to promote the population and activity of indigenous microorganisms. Trichloroethylene (TCE), for example, is cometabolized by methane-oxidizing bacteria and can be bioremediated through the injection of oxygen and methane into contaminated aquifers to stimulate the activity of these bacteria. Nitrate-contaminated aquifers have been successfully treated through the pumping of readily available carbon-containing methanol or ethanol into the aquifers to stimulate denitrifying bacteria, which subsequently convert the nitrate to harmless nitrogen gas.

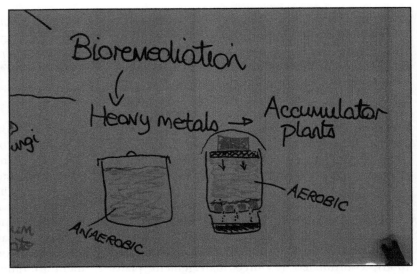

Lecture drawings by Aranya, from a Permaculture Design Course in Sweden, July 2011, showing bioremediation of heavy metals.

Bioreactors have been used in which the contaminant is mixed with a solid carrier, or the organisms are immobilized to a solid surface and continuously exposed to the contaminant. This has been used with both bacteria and fungi. For example, *Phanerochaete chysosporium*, which produces an extracellular peroxidase and hydrogen peroxide (H_2O_2), has been used to cleave various organic contaminants such as dichloro-diphenyl-trichloroethane (DDT) in bioreactors.

Highly chlorinated organic contaminants such as TCE and polychlorinated biphenyls (PCBs) resist degradation aerobically, but the contaminants can be dechlorinated by anaerobic bacteria, which decreases their toxicity and makes them easier to decompose. High concentrations of PCBs in the Hudson River in New York have been dechlorinated to less toxic forms by anaerobic bacteria. Methanogens—anaerobic bacteria that produce methane—have been observed to dechlorinate TCE in anaerobic bioreactors.

One of the problems with some wastes is that they are mixed with radioactive materials that are highly toxic to living organisms. One solution to this problem has been the genetic engineering of radiation-resistant bacteria so that they also have the ability to bioremediate. For example, *Deinococcus radiodurans*, a bacterium that can survive in nuclear reactors, has been genetically engineered to contain genes for the metabolism of toluene, which will enable it to be used in the bioremediation of radiation- and organic waste-contaminated sites.

Phytoremediation

Phytoremediation is a special type of bioremediation in which plants—grasses, shrubs, trees, and algae—are used to biodegrade or immobilize environmental contaminants, usually metals. Types of phytoremediation include phytoextraction, in which the contaminant is extracted from soil by plant roots; phytostabilization, in which the contaminant is immobilized in the vicinity of plant roots; phytostimulation, in which the plant root exudates stimulate rhizosphere microorganisms that bioremediate the contaminant; phytovolatilization, in which the plant helps to volatilize the contaminant; and phytotransformation, in which the plant root and its enzymes actively transform the contaminant. For example, horseradish peroxidase is a plant enzyme that is used to oxidize and polymerize organic contaminants.

The polymerized contaminants become insoluble and relatively unavailable.

Plants such as Indian mustard (*Brassica juncea*) and loco weed (*Astragalus*) are heavy metal accumulators and remove selenium and lead from soil. The above ground plant parts are harvested to dispose of the metals. Algae are used to accumulate dissolved selenium in some treatments. Poplar trees have even been genetically engineered to contain a bacterial methyl reductase that lets them methylate and volatilize arsenic, mercury, and selenium absorbed by their roots.

Examples

A 1992 U.S. Environmental Protection Agency (EPA) survey indicated that of 132 well-documented bioremediation studies, 75 involved petroleum or related compounds, 13 involved wood preservatives such as creosote, 7 involved agricultural chemicals, 5 examined tars, 4 treated munitions such as trinitrotoluene (TNT), and the rest involved miscellaneous compounds. As this list suggests, bioremediation of oil spills has been the single best example of successful bioremediation in practice.

In March, 1989, the *Exxon Valdez* oil tanker spilled millions of gallons of crude oil in Prince William Sound, Alaska. On many beaches, the EPA authorized the use of simple bioremediation techniques, such as stimulating the growth of indigenous oil-degrading bacteria by adding common inorganic fertilizers. Beaches cleaned by this method did as well as beaches cleaned by mechanical methods. In another instance of successful bioremediation, selenium-contaminated soil in the Kesterson National Wildlife Refuge in California was partially decontaminated in the 1980s through the method of supplying indigenous fungi with organic substrates such as casein and waste orange peels. This promoted as much as 60 percent selenium volatilization in less than two months.

A great deal of research into biodegradation and bioremediation of oil spills was conducted following the British Petroleum (BP) Deepwater Horizon oil spill in the Gulf of Mexico. Because the oil flowed from an offshore wellhead, affecting deepwater, surface water, and coastal areas alike, the cleanup conditions differed from those experienced in previous spills. Moreover, oil-degrading bacteria were already prevalent at the spill location, feeding on naturally occurring oil seeps along the seafloor. Researchers proposed enhancing anaerobic degradation in affected marshes and introducing genetically modified bacteria. They also learned that the indigenous bacteria were not consuming polycyclic aromatic hydrocarbons (PAHs) and that certain microorganisms naturally inhabit water trapped within oil and feed off it, which may lead to improved methods of bioremediation in future.

Mark Coyne

Further Reading

Alexander, Martin. *Biodegradation and Bioremediation.* 2nd ed. Academic Press, 1999.

Atlas, Ronald M., and Jim Philp, eds. *Bioremediation: Applied Microbial Solutions for Real-World Environmental Cleanup.* ASM Press, 2005.

Boopathy, Raj, Sara Shields, and Siva Nunna. "Biodegradation of Crude Oil from the BP Oil Spill in the Marsh Sediments of Southeast Louisiana, USA." *Applied Biochemistry And Biotechnology* 167, no. 6 (July 2012): 1560–1568.

"A Citizen's Guide to Bioremediation." *EPA*, Sept. 2012. Accessed from https://clu-in.org/download/Citizens/a_citizens_guide_to_bioremediation.pdf.

Fingas, Merv. *The Basics of Oil Spill Cleanup.* 2nd ed. CRC Press, 2001.

Frankenberger, William, and Sally Benson, eds. *Selenium in the Environment.* CRC Press, 1994.

Singh, V. P., and R. D. Stapleton, Jr., eds. *Biotransformations: Bioremediation Technology for Health and Environmental Protection.* Elsevier Science, 2002.

Skipper, H. D., and R. F. Turco, eds. *Bioremediation: Science and Applications.* American Society of Agronomy, 1995.

Stallard, Brian. "Oil Eaters: How Nature Cleans Up the Deepwater Horizon Spill." *Nature World News*, August 11, 2014.

■ Biosphere

FIELDS OF STUDY: Biology; Ecology; Ecosystem Management;

DEFINITION: The zone within which all life on earth exists

The conceptualization of all life on earth as part of one large, integrated system, the biosphere, helps to encourage understanding of the interrelatedness of all ecosystems and biotic communities.

Overview

The concept of the biosphere was introduced in the nineteenth century by Austrian geologist Eduard Suess. The biosphere is the zone, approximately 20 kilometers (12 miles) thick, that extends from the floors of the earth's oceans to the tops of the mountains, within which all life on the planet exists. It is thought to be more than 3.5 billion years old, and it supports nearly one dozen biomes, regions of similar climatic conditions within which distinct biotic communities reside.

Compounds of hydrogen, oxygen, carbon, nitrogen, potassium, and sulfur are cycled among the four major spheres—biosphere, lithosphere, hydrosphere, and atmosphere—to make the materials that are essential to the existence of life. The most critical of these compounds is water, and its movement between the spheres is called thewater cycle. Dissolved water in the atmosphere condenses to form clouds, rain, and snow. The annual precipitation for a region is one of the major controlling factors in determining the terrestrial biome that can exist. The water cycle follows the precipitation through various paths leading to the formation of lakes and rivers. These flowing waters interact with the lithosphere to dissolve chemicals as they flow to the oceans, where about one-half of the biomes on earth occur. Evaporation of water from the oceans resupplies the vast majority of the moisture existing in the atmosphere. This cycle supplies water continuously for the needs of both the terrestrial and the oceanic biomes.

The biosphere is also dependent on the energy that is transferred from the various spheres. The incoming solar energy is the basis for all life. Light enters the life cycle as an essential ingredient in the photosynthesis reaction. Plants take in carbon dioxide, water, and light energy, which is converted into chemical energy in the form of sugar, with oxygen generated as a by-product. Most animal life reverses this process during the respiration reaction, where chemical energy is released to do work by the oxidation of sugar to produce carbon dioxide and water.

The incoming solar energy also has a ramatic interaction with the water cycle and the worldwide distribution of biomes. Because of the earth's curvature, the equatorial regions receive a greater amount of solar heat than do the polar regions. Convective movements in the atmosphere (such as winds, high- and low-pressure systems, and weather fronts) and the hydrosphere (such as water currents) are generated during the redistribution of this heat. The weather patterns and general climates of earth are responses to these energy shifts. The seven types of climates are defined by mean annual temperature and mean annual precipitation, and there is a strong correspondence between the climate at a given location and the biome that will flourish.

Desert Biome

The major deserts of the world are located between 20 to 30 degrees latitude north and south of the equator. The annual precipitation in a desert biome

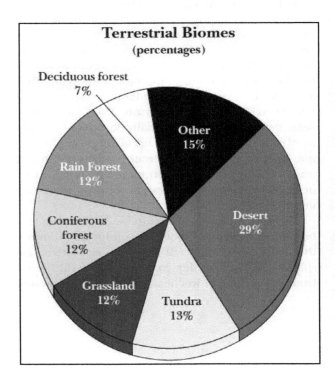

Terrestrial Biomes
(percentages)

- Deciduous forest 7%
- Other 15%
- Rain Forest 12%
- Desert 29%
- Coniferous forest 12%
- Grassland 12%
- Tundra 13%

is less than 25 centimeters (10 inches) per year. Deserts are located in northern and southwestern Africa, parts of the Middle East and Asia, Australia, the southwestern United States, and northern Mexico.

Deserts are characterized by life that is unique in its ability to capture and conserve water. Deserts show the greatest extreme in temperature fluctuations of all biomes: Daytime temperatures can exceed 49 degrees Celsius (120 degrees Fahrenheit), and night temperatures can drop to 0 degrees Celsius (32 degrees Fahrenheit). Most of the animals that live in desert biomes are active at night and retreat to underground burrows or crevices during the day to escape the heat. The water cycle in deserts rarely provides surface water, so plant life usually finds water through a wide distribution of shallow roots to capture the near-surface infiltration or a deep taproot system that finds groundwater located below the surface of dry streambeds. The plant life is characterized by scattered thorny bushes, shrubs, and occasional cacti. Animal life consists of an abundance of reptiles (mostly lizards and snakes), rodents, birds (many predatory types such as owls and hawks), and a wide variety of insects.

Deserts and semideserts cover approximately one-third of the land surface on earth. They continue to grow in size because of human influences such as deforestation and overgrazing.

Grassland Biome

Grasslands are found in a wide belt of latitudes higher than those in which desert biomes exist. Large grassland regions occur in central North America, central Russia and Siberia, subequatorial Africa and South America, northern India, and Australia. This biome flourishes in moderately dry conditions, having an annual rainfall between 25 and 150 centimeters (10 and 60 inches). Precipitation and solar heating are unevenly divided throughout the year, providing a wet, warm growing season and a cool, dry dormant season.

The animal life in grassland regions is characterized by large grazing mammals, such as wild horses, bison, antelopes, giraffes, zebras, and rhinoceroses, as well as smaller herbivores, such as rabbits, prairie dogs, mongooses, kangaroos, and warthogs. This abundance of herbivores allows for a large development of secondary and tertiary consumers in the food chain, such as lions, leopards, cheetahs, wolves, and coyotes. Grasslands have rich soils that provide the fertile growing conditions for a wide variety of tall and short grasses. Within a single square meter of this healthy soil, several hundred thousand living organisms can be found, from microbes to insects, beetles, and worms. The profusion of these smaller lifeforms fosters an abundance of small birds.

Grasslands have been environmentally stressed as humans have converted them to farmland because of their rich soils and to rangeland because of the grass supply. It is estimated that only 25 percent of the world's original grasslands remain undisturbed by human development. Worldwide, overgrazing and mismanagement of rangeland have caused large tracts of fertile grassland to become desert or semidesert.

Tropical Rain-Forest Biome

Rain forests receive heavy rainfall almost daily, with an annual average of more than 240 centimeters (95 inches). Temperatures in these areas are fairly constant from day to day and season to season, with an annual mean value of about 28 degrees Celsius (82 degrees Fahrenheit). The combination of plentiful rain and high temperatures causes high humidity, allowing some plants to utilize the atmosphere for their water supply via "air roots." This biome is also

Composite image of the earth's biosphere shows the planet's heaviest vegetative biomass in the dark sections, known to be rain forests. (NASA)

unique because the chemical nutrients needed to sustain life within it are almost entirely contained in the lush vegetation of the biosphere itself and not in the upper layers of soil of the lithosphere. The soils are thin and poor in nutrients.

The tropical rain forests contain a wider diversity of plant and animal species per unit area than any other biome. It is estimated that nearly two-thirds of all the plants and insects found on earth are contained in tropical rain forests. This enormous biodiversity is accommodated in part because each form of plant or animal occupies a specialized niche based on its ability to thrive with a particular level of sunlight that corresponds to a given height above the forest floor within the forest canopy. Numerous exotic insects, amphibians, reptiles, birds, and small mammals can coexist within a single canopy level. The plants growing in tropical rain forests currently provide ingredients found in 25 percent of the world's prescription and nonprescription drugs. It is estimated that at least three thousand tropical plants contain cancer-fighting chemicals.

Tropical rain forests are being destroyed at a fast rate for farmland, timber operations, mining, and grazing. It has been estimated that most of the animal and plant diversity of the rain forests will be lost by the year 2050. Further, if the high rate of destruction continues, the release of carbon dioxide into the atmosphere from the burning of biomass and fossil fuels may no longer be offset by plant consumption, and the balance of the carbon cycle will shift toward a higher concentration of carbon dioxide in the atmosphere.

Temperate Forest Biome

Temperate forests exist in areas where temperatures change dramatically during the four distinct seasons. Temperatures fall below freezing during the winter, with warmer, more humid conditions during the summer. Rainfall averages between 75 and 200 centimeters (30 and 80 inches) per year. This biome is often divided into forests with broad-leaved deciduous (leaf-shedding) trees and those with coniferous (cone-bearing) trees. Deciduous forests develop in regions with higher precipitation values, whereas the needle-like evergreen leaves of conifers have scales and thick, waxy coatings that allow them to flourish at the lower end of the precipitation range.

Deciduous forests develop more solid canopies with widely branching trees such as elm, oak, maple,

ash, beech, and other hardwood varieties. The forest floor often contains an abundance of ferns, shrubs, and mosses. Coniferous forests are usually dominated by pine, spruce, fir, cedar, and hemlock trees. Some deciduous trees, such as aspen and birch, often occur with the conifers. The coniferous forest floor is so acidic from decomposing evergreen needles that often only lichens and mosses can grow.

Temperate forests are home to diverse animal life. Common mammals of deciduous forests include squirrels, chipmunks, porcupines, raccoons, opossums, deer, foxes, black bears, and mice. Snakes, toads, frogs, and salamanders exist alongside a large bird population of thrushes, warblers, woodpeckers, owls, and hawks. The larger animals of the coniferous forests include moose, elk, wolves, lynx, grouse, jays, and migratory birds.

Forests have traditionally been viewed as a limitless timber resource by the lumber industry. The vast forests of Europe were cleared one thousand years ago. This liquidation of temperate forest continues in Siberia, where 25 percent of the world's timber reserves exist.

Tundra Biome

Tundras occur in areas near the Arctic ice cap and extend southward across the far northern parts of North America, Europe, and Asia. During the majority of the year, these largely treeless plains are covered with ice and snow and are battered by bitterly cold winds. Tundras are covered with thick mats of mosses, lichens, and sedges (grasslike plants). Because the winters are long and dark, tundra vegetation grows during the three months of summer, when there is almost constant sunlight.

Bogs, marshes, and ponds are common on the summer landscape because permafrost, a thick layer of ice that remains beneath the soil all year long, prevents drainage of melted waters. These wet areas provide perfect breeding grounds for mosquitoes, deerflies, and blackflies during the brief summer. These insects in turn serve as a source of food for migrating birds. Larger mammals, such as caribou, reindeer, musk ox, and mountain sheep, migrate in and out of the tundra. Some animals, such as lemmings, arctic hares, grizzly bears, and snowy owls, can be found in the tundra during all times of the year.

The tundra is the earth's most fragile terrestrial biome. Vegetation disturbed by human activity can take decades to replenish itself. Roads and pipelines must be constructed on bedrock or layers of added gravel; otherwise, they will melt the upper layers of the permafrost.

Oceanic Biomes

Oceans cover 70 percent of the earth's surface and contain 97.6 percent of the water of the hydrosphere. They play a primary role in regulating the earth's distribution of heat, and they are central to the water cycle. Oceans are instrumental in the survival of all life on earth. In addition, oceans house more than 250,000 species of marine plants and animals that occur as six common biomes.

Coral reefs are coastal biomes that develop on continental shelves in regions of clear, tropical waters. Collectively, coastal biomes make up only 10 percent of the world's ocean area but contain 90 percent of all ocean species. These are the regions where most commercial fishing is done. The vast open oceans contain only 10 percent of all oceanic species. Vegetation is mostly limited to free-floating plankton. Exotic bottom fauna exist on deep hydrothermal vents. Animal life includes whales, dolphins, tuna, sharks, flying fish, and squids.

A number of transitional biomes also exist at the ocean-land interface. The intertidal biome can be composed of sandy beaches or more rocky zones that are covered by water only during periods of high tide. A variety of crustaceans and mollusks are found on wet sandy beaches, whereas rock tidal pools contain kelp, Irish moss, and rockweed, all of which compete for space with snails, barnacles, sea urchins, and starfish.

Toby Stewart and Dion Stewart

Further Reading

Butz, Stephen D. *Science of Earth Systems.* 2nd ed. Thomson, 2008.
Ehrlich, Paul R., and Anne H. Ehrlich. *Extinction: The Causes and Consequences of the Disappearance of Species.* Ballantine, 1981.
Krebs, Robert E. "Biosphere: Envelope of Life." In *The Basics of Earth Science.* Greenwood, 2003.
McNeely, Jeffrey A., et al. *Conserving the World's Biological Diversity.* Island, 1990.
Smil, Vaclav. *The Earth's Biosphere: Evolution, Dynamics, and Change.* MIT Press, 2002.
Weiner, Jonathan. *The Next One Hundred Years.* Bantam, 1990.
Wilson, E. O., ed. *Biodiversity.* National Academy, 1990.
Woodward, Susan L. *Introduction to Biomes.* Greenwood, 2009.

■ Biosphere 2

FIELDS OF STUDY: Biology, Life Sciences, Ecosystems; Ecology, Environment, Environmentalism; History/Biography; Scientific Equipment, Tools, Techniques, and Methods; Technology and Applied Science

IDENTIFICATION: An environmental research facility in Arizona originally constructed as a self-sustaining, closed ecological system

Two Biosphere 2 missions during the 1990s explored the viability of maintaining and inhabiting a closed, human-made ecological system for prolonged periods. In the period since such colonization experiments ended, the facility has been a useful site for university-run environmental research.

Located on a 16-hectare (40-acre) campus near Oracle, Arizona, Biosphere 2 is a 1.27-hectare (3.14-acre) glass-and-steel structure that resembles a series of connected greenhouses. A basement "technosphere" of electrical, mechanical, and plumbing systems maintains Biosphere 2's temperature, humidity, and airborne particulate levels. Space Biospheres and Ventures, a private, for-profit firm founded by Biosphere 2 inventor John Allen and bankrolled by philanthropist Edward Bass, began constructing the facility in 1986 as a prototype for a self-sustaining space colony. Biosphere 2 was designed to mimic the earth—Biosphere 1—by being closed to exchanges of material or organisms from the outside environment but open to energy and information exchanges.

On September 26, 1991, Biosphere 2 was sealed with a team of four men and four women inside; the mission ended exactly two years later. A second, seven-person mission was conducted between March 6 and September 6, 1994. One month into the second mission, Bass dissolved his business partnership with Allen, citing project mismanagement. Federal marshals served a restraining order that ousted on-site management, and Bass's Decisions Investments Corporation took over the property.

Biosphere 2 near Tucson, Arizona, USA. By Daderot (Own work)

Biosphere 2 was intended as a century-long experiment to determine whether it is possible to maintain a self-sustaining human colony in a hostile environment. Crew members had to grow their own food, recycle the water they drank, and produce the oxygen they breathed. They were responsible for the health of the plant and animal species inside the sealed structure, and they had to maintain the complex apparatus that kept Biosphere 2 functioning.

The biomes of earth were represented within Biosphere 2 by a tropical rain forest, a desert, a savanna grassland, mangrove wetlands, and an ocean with a coral reef, plus an area of intensive agriculture. It proved to be impossible to keep the biomes separate: The desert, for example, was too wet. Also, the structure shut out 40 percent of the sun's light, and the ceiling was sometimes so hot that the treetops burned. Nineteen out of twenty-five vertebrate species inside the structure died, while others (such as ants and cockroaches) swarmed out of control.

Among the difficulties encountered during the first two-year experiment was a lack of oxygen: The integrity of the sealed environment had to be broken when it became apparent that the organically rich soil had consumed more oxygen than predicted. The biospherians produced about 80 percent of the food they needed but suffered crop failures because of unanticipated depredation by mites and other insects. One crew member had to be taken out of Biosphere 2 for emergency surgery on a wounded finger. Upon her return, she brought some supplies with her. Such incidents drew criticism that the giant terrarium was not as self-sufficient as intended, but the project

directors maintained that they had never expected perfection in this first model and that finding flaws in the design was precisely the purpose of the experiment.

Inevitably, crew members also experienced interpersonal friction. While the professionalism of the biospherians saw them through their differences, conflicts nevertheless had the potential to cause serious disruption of the mission. By the end of their two-year stay, three of the biospherians were taking part in therapy sessions by telephone.

Biosphere 2 attracted nationwide attention. The structure's thousands of windows allowed spectators to view almost everything going on inside. This public exposure made Biosphere 2 an excellent tool for generating interest in ecological concerns as well as in the human potential in space.

Columbia University assumed management of Biosphere 2 in 1996 and operated it as a research and education facility, conducting ecosystems studies focused on the effects of elevated carbon dioxide concentrations on plants, fish, and coral reefs. Columbia ended its association with the facility in 2003. In 2007, the Biosphere 2 campus and surrounding property were sold to a development company, which leased the core complex to the University of Arizona. The university continued use of Biosphere 2 as a center for environmental research and education and officially took control of the facility in 2011, thanks in part to a $20 million donation from the Philecology Foundation. Biosphere 2 is now a permanent part of the University of Arizona. Within the facility, scientists can manipulate environmental variables and obtain high-resolution measurements, making Biosphere 2 a unique laboratory for large-scale experiments in earth systems and environmental change and for experiments that examine climate change and sustainable development.

Robert B. Bechtel; updated by Karen N. Kähler

Further Reading

Alling, Abigail, and Mark Nelson. Life under Glass: The Inside Story of Biosphere 2. Oracle: Biosphere, 1993. Print.

Marino, B. D. V., and Howard T. Odum, eds. *Biosphere 2: Research Past and Present.* Amsterdam: Elsevier Science, 1999. Print.

Molles, Manuel C., Jr. *Ecology: Concepts and Applications.* New York: McGraw, 2013. Print.

Poynter, Jane. *The Human Experiment: Two Years and Twenty Minutes Inside Biosphere 2.* New York: Thunder's Mouth, 2006. Print.

Reider, Rebecca. *Dreaming the Biosphere: The Theater of All Possibilities.* Albuquerque: U of New Mexico P, 2009. Print.

■ Biosphere reserves & wilderness issues

FIELDS OF STUDY: Conservation Biology; Ecology; Ecosystem Management; Environmental Studies;

IDENTIFICATION: UNESCO-designated sites where the preservation of natural resources is integrated with research and the sustainable management of those resources

The worldwide network of biosphere reserves is the only international network of protected areas that also emphasizes sustainable development and wise use of natural resources; thus these sites enable the examination and testing of the objective of integrating conservation and development.

Overview

Through discussions that started in 1970, the United Nations Educational, Scientific, and Cultural Organization (UNESCO) initiated the Man and the Biosphere Programme to establish sites where the preservation of natural resources would be integrated with research and the sustainable management of those resources. The first biosphere reserve was designated in 1976, and by May, 2009, 553 such sites existed across 107 countries. In 1995 UNESCO convened a conference in Spain and developed the Seville Strategy for Biosphere Reserves, which was designed to strengthen the international network and encourage the use of the sites for research, monitoring, education, and training. In the early years of the program, preservation was stressed. The adoption of the Seville Strategy by UNESCO emphasized the role of people in the use of their natural resources.

Each biosphere reserve contains a legally protected core area where there has been minimal disturbance by people. Only uses that are compatible with the preservation of biological diversity are permitted in the protected core. Surrounding the core is a managed-use or buffer zone; research and environmental education are examples of activities suitable for the buffer zone. Surrounding the buffer zone is a zone of cooperation or transition zone. The boundaries of the transition zone are loosely defined and often include local towns and communities. Economic activities such as farming, logging, mining, and recreation occur within the transition zone and are not restricted by the biosphere reserve.

Only the boundaries of the core area are legally defined. The designation of a biosphere reserve does not alter the legal ownership of the land or water that is included within its zones. UNESCO does not have jurisdiction over any nation's biosphere reserves. In many cases the areas within reserves reflect a mosaic of landownership, including federal, state, local, and private ownership. Even the core area may be privately owned, as long as it is managed for its preservation.

In the United States, the core areas of some biosphere reserves are within national parks, such as Glacier and Yellowstone, whereas other biosphere reserves are composed of clusters of core areas, such as the ten units within the California Coastal Range Biosphere Reserve. The management and administration of a biosphere reserve often involves a number of interested citizens, government agencies, and owners.

The worldwide network of biosphere reserves represents the only international network of protected areas that also emphasizes sustainable development and wise use of natural resources. Hence they are sites where the objective of integrating conservation and development can be examined, demonstrated, and tested. Research at these sites serves to solve practical problems in resource management.

William R. Teska

Further Reading

Hanna, Kevin S., Douglas A. Clark, and D. Scott Slocombe, eds. *Transforming Parks and Protected Areas: Policy and Governance in a Changing World.* Routledge, 2008.

Sourd, Christine. *Explaining Biosphere Reserves.* UNESCO, 2004.

■ Biotechnology & genetic engineering

FIELDS OF STUDY: Biology, Life Sciences, Ecosystems; Inventions; Public Policy, Debates, Controversies; Science; Scientific Equipment, Tools, Techniques, and Methods; Technology and Applied Science

DEFINITIONS: Biotechnology is the use of living organisms, or substances obtained from such organisms, to produce products or processes of value to humankind; genetic engineering is the manipulation of deoxyribonucleic acid (DNA) and the transfer of genes or gene components from one species to another.

Biotechnology has made tremendous advances possible in human and veterinary medicine, agriculture, food production, and other fields. However, debates continue regarding the potential of biotechnology, in particular genetic engineering, to produce organisms that may disrupt ecosystems, negatively affect human health, or be used in ethically inappropriate ways.

The term "biotechnology" is relatively new, but the practice of biotechnology is as old as civilization. Civilization did not evolve until humans learned to produce food crops and domestic livestock through the controlled breeding of selected plants and animals. The pace of modifying organisms accelerated during the twentieth century. Through carefully controlled breeding programs, plant architecture and fruit characteristics of crops were modified to facilitate mechanical harvesting. Plants were developed to produce specific drugs or spices, and microorganisms were selected to produce antibiotics such as

penicillin and other useful medicinal and food products.

The ability to utilize artificial media to propagate plants led to the development of a technology called tissue culture. In some plant tissue culture, the tissue is treated with the proper plant hormones to produce masses of undifferentiated cells called callus tissue, which can also be separated into single cells to establish a cell suspension culture. Specific drugs or other chemicals can be produced with callus tissue and cell suspensions, or this tissue can be used to regenerate entire plants. Tissue culture technology is used as a propagation tool in commercial-scale plant production.

Numerous advances have also occurred in animal biotechnology. Artificial insemination, the process in which semen is collected from the male animal and deposited into the female reproductive tract through artificial techniques rather than natural mating, emerged as a practical procedure roughly a century ago, although as early as 1784 Italian biologist Lazzaro Spallanzani successfully inseminated a dog. Males in species such as cattle can sire hundreds of thousands of offspring through artificial insemination, whereas they could sire only fifty or fewer through natural means.

Embryo transfer is a technique used in humans to facilitate conception after in vitro fertilization, a procedure in which eggs are surgically removed from the ovaries and manually combined with sperm in a laboratory. Once fertilization and cell division are confirmed, the embryos are placed in the uterus. The eggs may be supplied by a woman who is unable to conceive naturally but who can carry a child to term. They may also be provided by an egg donor to a woman who cannot otherwise get pregnant; or a woman who cannot carry a child to term may supply eggs to be fertilized in vitro and implanted in a surrogate mother. Superovulation is the process in which females that are to provide eggs are injected with hormones to stimulate increased egg production. Embryo splitting is the mechanical division of an embryo into identical twins, quadruplets, sextuplets, and so on. Both superovulation and embryo splitting have made routine embryo transfers possible. In livestock, embryo transfer technology is used to combine the sperm from a superior male animal and several eggs, each of which can then be split into several offspring, from a superior female. The

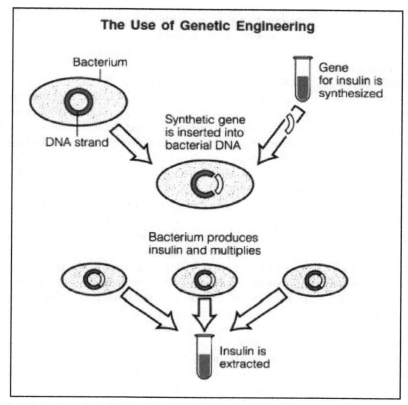

The Use of Genetic Engineering

Bacterium

DNA strand

Gene for insulin is synthesized

Synthetic gene is inserted into bacterial DNA

Bacterium produces insulin and multiplies

Insulin is extracted

Genetic engineering, the manipulation of genetic material, can be used to synthesize large quantities of drugs or hormones, such as insulin.

chemical, deoxyribonucleic acid, or DNA. The DNA of all cells, whether from bacteria, plants, lower animals, or humans, is very similar, and when DNA from a foreign species is transferred into a different cell, it functions exactly as the native DNA functions; that is, it codes for protein.

The simplest protocol for this transfer involves the use of a vector, usually a piece of circular DNA called a plasmid, which is removed from a microorganism such as a bacterium and cut open by an enzyme called a restriction endonuclease or restriction enzyme. A section of DNA from the donor cell that contains a previously identified gene of interest is cut out from the donor cell DNA by the same restriction endonuclease. The section of donor cell DNA with the gene of interest is then combined with the open plasmid DNA, and the plasmid closes with the new gene as part of its structure. The recombinant plasmid (DNA from two sources) is placed back into the bacterium, where it will replicate and code for protein just as it did in the donor cell. The bacterium can be cultured and the gene product (protein) harvested, or the bacterium can be used as a vector to transfer the gene to another species, where it will also be expressed. This transfer of genes, and therefore of inherited traits, between different species has revolutionized biotechnology and provides the potential for genetic changes in plants and animals that have not yet been envisioned.

Biotechnology and Agriculture

Biotechnology has had a tremendous impact on agriculture. Traditional breeding programs may be too slow to keep pace with the needs of a rapidly expanding human population. Biotechnology provides a means of developing higher-yielding crops in one-third of the time it takes to develop them though traditional plant breeding programs because the genes for desired characteristics can be inserted directly into a plant without having to go through several generations to establish the trait. Also, there is often a need or desire to diversify agricultural production

resulting embryos can then be transferred to the reproductive tracts of inferior surrogate females.

Recombinant DNA Technology

Biotechnological advances have enabled scientists to tap into the world gene pool. This technology has great potential, and its full magnitude is far from being fully realized. Theoretically, it is possible to transfer one or more genes or gene segments from any organism in the world into any other organism. Because genes ultimately control how an organism functions, gene transfer can have a dramatic impact on agricultural resources and human health.

Research has provided the means by which genes can be identified and manipulated at the molecular and cellular levels. This identification and manipulation depend primarily on recombinant DNA technology. In concept, recombinant DNA methodology is fairly easy to comprehend, but in practice it is rather complex. The genes in all living cells are very similar in that they are all composed of the same in a given area, but soil or climate conditions may severely limit the amount of diversification that can take place. Biotechnology can provide the tools to help solve this problem: Crops with high cash value can be developed to grow in areas that would not support unmodified versions of such crops. In addition, biotechnology can be used to increase the cash value of crops, as plants can be developed that can produce new and novel products such as antibiotics, hormones, and other pharmaceuticals.

As public pressure has grown for crop production to be more friendly to the environment, biotechnology has been touted as an important tool for the development of a long-term, sustainable, environmentally friendly agricultural system. Biotechnology is already being used to develop crops with improved resistance to pests. For example, a gene from the bacterium *Bacillus thuringiensis* (*B.t.*) codes for an insecticidal protein that kills insects but is harmless to other organisms. When this gene is transferred from the bacterium to a plant, insect larvae are killed if they eat from the leaves or roots of the plant. A number of *B.t.* plants have been developed, including cotton and potatoes. Crop varieties engineered for improved pest resistance have the potential to reduce reliance on pesticides; however, insect pests have developed resistance to some of these crops.

Biotechnology also plays an important role in the livestock industry. Bovine somatotropin, a hormone that stimulates growth in cattle, is harvested from recombinant bacteria and injected in dairy cattle to enhance milk production. However, questions have arisen as to whether overstimulating milk production is humane or healthy for cows, and fears regarding the health implications for humans consuming milk that contains bovine hormone residues have made many people seek organic dairy products free from artificial hormones. Some countries do not allow the use of these hormones in milk intended for human consumption.

Researchers are exploring the possibilities of genetically engineering animals that can resist disease or produce novel and interesting products such as pharmaceuticals. The cloning of Dolly the sheep in Scotland in 1996 opened a whole new avenue in the use of biotechnology for livestock production. The use of cloning technology in conjunction with surrogate mothers provides the means to produce a whole herd of genetically superior animals in a short period of time. However, reproductive cloning is expensive, its success rate is low, and many cloned animals have been found to be unhealthy and short-lived.

Biotechnology and Medicine

DNA technology also has a direct impact on human health and is used to manufacture a variety of gene products that are utilized in the clinical treatment of diseases. Several human hormones produced by this methodology are already in use. The hormone insulin, for instance, which is used to treat insulin-dependent diabetics, was the first major success in using a product of recombinant technology. Recombinant DNA-produced insulin has been used to treat diabetic patients since 1982. Genetic engineering has also been used to synthesize protropin, a human growth hormone (HGH) employed in the treatment of growth failure conditions such as hyposomatotropism. Without treatment with HGH, people suffering from these conditions do not produce enough growth hormone to achieve a typical adult height.

Somatostatin, another pituitary hormone, has also been produced through recombinant DNA techniques. This hormone controls the release of insulin and HGH. Small proteins called interferons normally produced by cells to combat viral infections have been produced using recombinant DNA methodology, as have some vaccines against viral diseases. Recombivax HB, the first of these vaccines, is used in vaccinating against hepatitis B, an incurable and sometimes fatal liver disease.

The potential for the future application of gene therapy has also been enhanced by advances in biotechnology. Among the forms of gene therapy currently being considered are gene surgery, in which a mutant gene that may or may not be replaced by its normal counterpart is excised from the DNA; gene repair, in which defective DNA is repaired within the cell to restore the genetic code; and gene insertion, in which a normal gene complement is inserted in cells that carry a defective gene.

Gene surgery and gene repair techniques are extremely complex and remain in the experimental stages. Gene insertion can potentially be done in germ-line cells such as the egg or sperm, the fertilized ovum or zygote, the fetus, or the somatic cells (nonreproductive cells) of children or adults. Although zygote therapy holds the most promise, as this technique could eliminate genetic disease, gene insertion in zygotes also represents a means by which traits such as strength or intelligence might be enhanced and the genetic traits of future generations artificially selected, a possibility that raises a host of ethical questions. Germ-line genetic modification has been performed successfully in laboratory animals, but unwanted mutations with serious or lethal consequences have also sometimes resulted.

Gene insertion into somatic cells does not make changes that are passed on to subsequent generations, so it does not present the ethical dilemma that germ-line manipulation does. In this technique, a gene or gene segment is inserted into specific organs or tissues as a treatment for an existing condition. In human clinical trials, somatic gene therapy has shown success in treating advanced melanoma, myeloid disorders, inherited childhood blindness, and severe combined immunodeficiency. However, the carrier molecules used to deliver the therapeutic gene to the target cells have the potential to provoke a serious or fatal immune response in the patient.

Environmental Issues

The potential benefits of biotechnology for human health, agriculture, and the environment are accompanied by potential drawbacks. Since the first recombinant DNA experiments in 1973, numerous social, ethical, and scientific questions have been raised about the possible detrimental effects of genetically engineered organisms on public health and the environment. The major environmental concerns are related to containment, or how to prevent genetically engineered organisms from escaping into the environment.

In the mid-1970's U.S. scientists invoked a self-imposed moratorium on genetic engineering experiments until the government could establish committees to develop safety guidelines that would apply to all recombinant DNA experimentation in the United States. This resulted in the formulation of guidelines specifying the degree of containment required for various types of genetic engineering experiments. Two types of containment, biological and physical, are addressed by the guidelines. "Physical containment" refers to the methods required to prevent an engineered organism from escaping from the laboratory; "biological containment" refers to the techniques used to ensure that an engineered organism cannot survive outside the laboratory. The guidelines associated with containment, particularly physical

containment, are sometimes difficult to monitor and enforce.

Some observers have noted that despite the rigors of the containment guidelines, the possibility remains that an engineered organism will eventually escape into the environment. Should this occur, the organism could cause environmental damage as great as or greater than that caused in the past by the introduction of foreign species to new habitats. For example, the introduction of rabbits to Australia dramatically upset the ecological balance on that continent. Hence field experiments with genetically engineered organisms must be strenuously controlled and monitored.

Although numerous safe field trials have been conducted with genetically engineered organisms, such as *B.t.* plants, widespread opposition to such practices remains. There appear to be few risks that cannot be ascertained within the laboratory associated with the release of genetically engineered higher plants, but opponents have expressed the fear that engineered genes could possibly be transferred by cross-pollination to other species of plants. Such a transfer could, for example, produce a highly vigorous species of weed. In addition, such gene transfers could potentially result in a plant that produces a toxin that would be detrimental to other plants, animals, or humans.

Because viruses and bacteria are major components of numerous natural biochemical cycles and readily exchange genetic information in a variety of ways, it is even more difficult to envision all the ramifications associated with releasing these genetically altered organisms into the environment. Field testing of genetically engineered organisms will always involve some element of risk, and assessment of the risks of such testing is easier for some species, such as higher plants, than for other species, such as bacteria.

A clear need exists for rigid controls, and minimizing the risks also requires integral cooperation among industry, governments, and regulatory organizations. Under the Cartagena Protocol on Biosafety, which entered into force in 2003, before an importing nation may release living modified organisms (LMOs) into the environment, the country into which the LMO is to be imported must first give its informed consent. The importer must clearly identify the LMO, detail its traits and characteristics, and explain its proper handling, storage, transport, and use.

With advances in the cloning of plants and animals, environmentalists and others have expressed concerns about losses in genetic variability. In nature, species survival is dependent on the genetic variability, or diversity, of the population. Genetic variability obtained through normal sexual reproduction provides a species with the ability to adapt to changes in the environment; because the environment is continually changing, loss of genetic variability usually leads to extinction of the species. Because cloning results in genetically identical individuals, the cloning of large numbers of animals or plants of particular species at the expense of those produced through sexual reproduction can lead to the loss of genetic variability and thus to eventual extinction of those species.

D. R. Gossett; updated by Karen N. Kähler

Further Reading

Chrispeels, Maarten J., and David E. Sadava, eds. *Plants, Genes, and Crop Biotechnology.* 2d ed. Sudbury, Mass.: Jones and Bartlett, 2003.

Drlica, Karl. *Understanding DNA and Gene Cloning: A Guide for the Curious.* 4th ed. Hoboken, N.J.: John Wiley & Sons, 2004.

Field, Thomas G., and Robert E. Taylor. *Scientific Farm Animal Production: An Introduction to Animal Science.* 10th ed. Upper Saddle River, N.J.: Prentice Hall, 2011.

Grace, Eric S. *Biotechnology Unzipped: Promises and Realities.* Rev. 2d ed. Washington, D.C.: National Academies Press, 2006.

Groves, M. J., ed. *Pharmaceutical Biotechnology.* 2d ed. Boca Raton, Fla.: Taylor & Francis, 2006.

Hill, Walter E. *Genetic Engineering: A Primer.* London: Taylor & Francis, 2002.

■ Black lung

FIELDS OF STUDY: Biology, Life Sciences, Ecosystems; Ecology, Environment, Environmentalism; Energy and Energy Resources; Health, Medicine, Disease, Illness; Science

DEFINITION: Chronic respiratory disease caused by long-term inhalation of coal and mineral dusts in closed coal-mining environments

Improvements of conditions for workers in coal mines have helped to reduce the incidence of coal workers' pneumoconi-osis, commonly known as black lung, but the disease has not been eradicated.

Since the Industrial Revolution, coal has provided energy for industrialized societies. With escalating demand, coal mining developed into a prevalent industry in many regions, such as Wales in Great Britain and the Appalachian Mountains of the United States. By the nineteenth century, the economies of such regions were dependent on coal.

The burning of coal produces gaseous and particulate (soot) pollution, and cities in the nineteenth century were characterized by black, soot-coated buildings and coal residue on other surfaces. Explosions caused by coal dust became common in coal mines and storage facilities. Slower to appear from the use of coal for energy were the greenhouse effect, acid rain, and coal workers' pneumoconiosis, also called black lung, caused by chronic inhalation of coal dust. This particle-induced fibrosis-emphysema produces lesions in respiratory bronchioles that interfere with the absorption and transport of oxygen in the lungs. Its symptoms are consistent with similar lung diseases: weakness and poor health, shortness of breath and oxygen starvation, heart disease, immune system irregularities, and lung cancers. It resembles diseases caused by fine airborne, respirable particles of asbestos (asbestosis); cotton, wood, and other plant-based dusts (farmers' lung); and silicas such as quartz, glass, and sand (silicosis).

The greatest incidence of black lung occurs in underground mining. Drilling, pulverizing, loading, and transporting coal generate large dust concentrations, which are breathed into the workers' lungs. Numerous safeguards have been instituted in coal mining to minimize the risks of workers' developing black lung. Mine passages are ventilated by fans and baffles, and sophisticated routing produces multi-region flows that keep the air at face level fresh. Mines also utilize wetting and scrubber systems to keep coal wet and water mists to remove dust from the air.

More recent developments include ventilation and filtering systems worn on the body—for example, helmets that provide continuous streams of filtered air across workers' faces. Research is ongoing in the development of drill bits and other components that can minimize the dust produced. The replacement of steel bits with bits coated with tungsten carbide, polycrystalline diamond, or other hard questionnaires, providing insight into the overall risks in a given operation. Emphasis has been placed on education regarding black lung and the regulatory infrastructure that now addresses it. Numerous government agencies offer information and services related to the disease, its prevention, its control, and compensation or support for those affected.

The MSHA's PEL for coal dust is 2 milligrams per cubic meter (mg/m^3) for unaffected workers and 1 mg/m^3 for workers with any signs of black lung. The National Institute for Occupational Safety and Health (NIOSH) recommends an exposure level no greater than 1 mg/m^3 for all workers. The Occupational Safety and Health Administration (OSHA) has set a slightly different PEL of 2.4 mg/m^3 for coal dust with less than 5 percent silica. In 1968-1969 the average dust concentration in underground coal mines was 6 mg/m^3, but since the Coal Act and the Mine Act, these averages have dropped to below 2 mg/m^3.

The silica content of coal dust affects the epidemiology of black lung as well as permissible exposure limits. Less than 1 mg/m^3 of silica can cause silicosis, and the current PEL for silicon is 0.1 mg/m^3, with reduction to 0.05 mg/m^3 being considered. Silica and mineral dusts are generated during initial drilling through rock to reach the coal in coal deposits that are interspersed with bedrock.

Significant progress was made over the last three to four decades of the twentieth century in fighting black lung and associated problems in coal mines. Government intervention, technological developments, and education should further improve the health, safety, and environmental status of the coal mining industry.

Robert D. Engelken

ceramic or metallic films has received attention, as has optimization of thread geometry and bit speed.

Since the Federal Coal Mine Health and Safety Act of 1969 and the Mine Act amendments of 1977, federal and state agencies (for example, the Mine Safety and Health Administration, or MSHA) have mandated that mine operators undertake efforts aimed at preventing black lung. Operators are required to sample mine air for deviations from permissible exposure limits (PELs) of coal and silica dusts, methane, carbon monoxide, sulfur dioxide, and hydrogen sulfide; to report these deviations; and to take appropriate measures to correct them.

Operators are also required to provide medical screenings for employees over time. Periodic chest X rays, measurements of lung capacity, cardiovascular checkups, and general blood, urine, and endocrine analyses warn of early signs of black lung. Worker health data are gathered through periodic

Further Reading

Goodell, Jeff. *Big Coal: The Dirty Secret Behind America's Energy Future.* New York: Houghton Mifflin, 2006.

Levine, Linda. *Coal Mine Safety and Health.* Washington, D.C.: Congressional Research Service, 2008.

Meyers, Robert A., ed. *Coal Handbook.* New York: Marcel Dekker, 1981.

Ripley, Earle, Robert Redmann, and Adele Crowder. *Environmental Effects of Mining.* Boca Raton, Fla.: CRC Press, 1996.

Witschi, Hanspeter, and Paul Nettesheim, eds. *Mechanisms in Respiratory Toxicology*. London: Chapman & Hall, 1982.

■ Black Sea & pollution

FIELDS OF STUDY: Biology, Life Sciences, Ecosystems; Ecology, Environment, Environmentalism; Oceans, Seas, Lakes, Bodies of Water; Places, Peoples, Societies; Pollution, Emissions, Toxic Waste, Hazardous Materials; Science

IDENTIFICATION: Large inland sea bounded by the Eurasian nations of Turkey, Bulgaria, Romania, Ukraine, Russia, and Georgia

Because of a lack of oxygen, the lower levels of the Black Sea are virtually lifeless, and the abundant life of the sea's upper levels has been gravely endangered by pollution, overharvesting, and the introduction of destructive nonnative species. Progress has been made in addressing these problems, however, as the result of dedicated international efforts.

It is believed that the Black Sea was formed when the rising waters of the Mediterranean Sea swamped a freshwater lake about 7,500 years ago. The sea has a surface area of approximately 448,000 square kilometers (173,000 square miles) and reaches a maximum depth of approximately 2,200 meters (7,200 feet). Five important rivers—the Kuban, Don, Dnieper, Dniester, and Danube—flow into it, and in turn its brackish surface water flows out into the Mediterranean through the Bosporus strait, the Sea of Marmara, and the Dardanelles strait. Colder, saltier water flows in beneath this current from the Mediterranean to fill the Black Sea's depths. Within the Black Sea itself, circulation between the two layers is poor.

Because the Black Sea's lower levels do not contain enough dissolved oxygen to enable bacteria to decompose the organic matter carried into the sea by the rivers, the water has grown increasingly eutrophied (saturated with nutrients) and anoxic (oxygen-depleted), creating the one of the largest "dead zones" of virtually lifeless water on the planet. Bacteria have evolved under these conditions, to react with naturally occurring sulfate ions in the seawater to produce the world's largest concentration of deadly hydrogen sulfide gas. Significant deposits of ammonia and methane are also present.

Fish and shellfish such as anchovy, mullet, tuna, mussels, and oysters were once found in abundance in the upper levels of the Black Sea, but in the latter decades of the twentieth century their numbers fell dramatically. This decline was caused in part by overfishing, but pollution from agriculture, industry, and shipping (particularly of crude oil) played a more important role. Cultural (human-caused) eutrophication of the sea's shallower waters contributed to a precipitous decline in fields of *Cystoseira* and *Phyllophora* algae, species essential to the survival of the food chain. In 1982 the alien carnivorous sea jelly *Mnemiopsis leidyi* was found for the first time in the Black Sea, and within a few years its rapidly growing numbers had destroyed a large proportion of the native species' eggs and larvae. During the 1990's radioactive substances resulting from nuclear power generation and the Chernobyl nuclear accident of 1986 began to enter the Black Sea as well.

By the end of the twentieth century, however, the Black Sea's ecology began to show a partial recovery owing to the region's economic slowdown and a resulting decrease in pollution. The sea had been recognized as a major environmental disaster area, and the six nations on its shores had drafted the Convention for the Protection of the Black Sea Against Pollution in 1992. This convention was succeeded by a number of other international efforts focusing on specific environmental problems, including the

Sunset in Black Sea, Gelendzhik, Russia. Sergio zevs at Russian Wikipedia.

Black Sea Ecosystem Recovery Project of 2004–7, which dealt primarily with eutrophication and hazardous waste. Nonetheless, as of a 2016 survey, the Black Sea contained 145 different pollutants and the hydrogen sulfide layer had expanded.

In the future the Black Sea's deposits of ammonia and methane may be utilized to produce fertilizer and to generate electricity, and its hydrogen sulfide may be tapped as a source of hydrogen gas for fuel. The extraction technologies involved are expected to have the added advantage of returning purified water to the sea.

Grove Koger

Further Reading

Ascherson, Neal. *Black Sea*. New York: Hill & Wang, 1995.

"Black Sea Region Briefing—The European Environment—State and Outlook 2015." *European Environment Agency*, European Union, 27 Sept. 2017, www.eea.europa.eu/soer-2015/countries/black-sea. Accessed 28 Mar. 2018.

Kostianoy, Andrey G., and Aleksey N. Kosarev, eds. *The Black Sea Environment*. Berlin: Springer, 2008.

Land, Thomas. "The Black Sea: Economic Developments and Environmental Dangers." *Contemporary Review* 278 (March, 2001): 144-151.

"Survey Finds Proliferation of Black Sea Pollutants." *UNDP*, United Nations Development Programme, 30 May 2017, www.undp.org/content/undp/en/home/presscenter/pressreleases/2017/05/30/survey-finds-proliferation-of-black-sea-pollutants.html. Accessed 28 Mar. 2018.

■ Black Wednesday

FIELDS OF STUDY: Disasters; Ecology, Environment, Environmentalism; History/Biography; Pollution, Emissions, Toxic Waste, Hazardous Materials

THE EVENT: Severe episode of photochemical smog in Los Angeles

DATE: September 8, 1943

After the Black Wednesday incident helped to demonstrate the extent of the health dangers posed by smog, government actions aimed at addressing the problem were undertaken.

The Los Angeles, California, basin is prototypical of a smog-producing area, with mountains rising on the east and north and persistent high-pressure weather systems during summer and early fall. Subsidence in upper levels of the high-pressure atmosphere results in air being compressed and heated. Westerly winds blowing over a cold ocean current carry cool, moist air in beneath the subsiding air, forming a temperature inversion at an altitude lower than the mountain peaks. With cool, moist air beneath hot, dry air, rising currents can ascend only to the inversion level. They then spread laterally and descend when they run into the natural barrier of the mountains. This situation places a lid over rising air, which causes pollutants to remain at low elevations for several days.

When Los Angeles experienced a severe episode of photochemical smog on September 8, 1943, the *Los Angeles Times* dubbed the day Black Wednesday. The human-made origins of Black Wednesday included increased industrialization and population growth in the Los Angeles area as a result of World War II. These factors led to a rise in the number of automobiles, with an accompanying increase in automotive emissions, as well as a higher yield of effluent from industrial smokestacks. In addition, a shortage of natural rubber led to the manufacture of synthetic rubber. A plant in the Los Angeles neighborhood of Boyle Heights produced a synthetic called butadiene, which appeared to be a significant source of air pollution. Other minor sources contributing to the photochemical smog were backyard incinerators used to burn refuse and the smudge pots, or orchard heaters, used by citrus growers.

The consequences for humans of exposure to photochemical smog can vary. Carbon monoxide (CO) from automotive exhaust can result in a change in physiology: Exposure to low levels of CO can produce impaired functions, whereas exposure to high concentrations may end in death. There seems to be a positive correlation between polyaromatic hydrocarbons and lung, skin, and scrotal cancers. The main complaints of those exposed to smog, however, are burning eyes and irritated throats. Peroxyacetyl nitrates (PAN) are the primary eye irritants, although acrolein and formaldehyde also contribute to the problem. Finally, reduced visibility is a product of aerosols contained in smog.

Vegetation is distressed by several components of photochemical smog. Ozone assaults leaf palisades, resulting in destruction of chlorophyll, lowered photosynthesis and respiration rates, and development of dark spots on leaf surfaces. Plant exposure to sulfur dioxide causes gas to combine with water to form sulfite ions, which cause leaves to darken, grow flaccid, and become dry. This condition eventually induces death of tissue. The effects of photochemical smog on animals were not studied or recorded during the Black Wednesday event, but animals are believed to experience impacts of exposure to smog that are similar to those experienced by humans.

Photochemical smog also alters inanimate objects. Rapid cracking and eventual deterioration of stretched rubber can result from exposure to smog. Likewise, breakdowns of natural and synthetic fabrics and fading of dyes can be traced to smog elements.

In the years following the Black Wednesday incident, government and civic organizations began to take steps aimed at curbing air pollution in Southern California. The use of backyard incinerators was banned, and increasingly strict laws were passed concerning automobile emissions.

Ralph D. Cross

Further Reading

Carle, David. *Introduction to Air in California.* Berkeley: University of California Press, 2006.

Jacobs, Chip, and William J. Kelly. *Smogtown: The Lung-Burning History of Pollution in Los Angeles.* Woodstock, N.Y.: Overlook Press, 2008.

Vallero, Daniel. *Fundamentals of Air Pollution.* 4th ed. Boston: Elsevier, 2008.

■ Bonn Convention on the Conservation of Migratory Species of Wild Animals (CMS)

FIELDS OF STUDY: Government, Politics, International Relations; International Relations, Agreements, Treaties; Ecology, Environment, Environmentalism; Biology, Life Sciences, Ecosystems; Animals, Zoology, Marine Biology.

THE CONVENTION: International agreement protecting animal species that migrate across national borders

DATE: Opened for signature on June 23, 1979

The Convention on the Conservation of Migratory Species of Wild Animals encourages the protection of migratory species by nations around the world. Most of the convention's success has been in fostering regional daughter agreements that protect particular migratory species of concern.

The Convention on the Conservation of Migratory Species of Wild Animals (also known as CMS or the Bonn Convention) arose as the result of recommendations made at the 1972 United Nations Conference on the Human Environment held in Stockholm, Sweden. Opened for signing in Bonn, Germany, in 1979, the treaty entered into force in 1983. By 2010 the convention had been signed by 113 nations, and many other nonsignatory nations were participating in CMS-sponsored agreements. The United Nations Environment Programme provides the CMS Secretariat.

The convention recognizes that the conservation status of a migratory species is vulnerable to threats in any states that species occupies or passes through. Appendix I to the convention lists endangered species for which concerted conservation action is required to ensure their survival. Parties to the convention (that is, signatory nations) are encouraged to forbid the taking of these species, to take steps to enhance their welfare, to remove obstacles to their migration, and to manage uses of the species by indigenous cultures. Appendix II lists migratory species that are not necessarily endangered but would benefit from conservation action.

CMS encourages states whose territories include the biogeographic ranges of migratory species to enter into one of four types of daughter agreements. In order of formality from least to most, these are designated as Action Plans, Memoranda of Understanding (MOUs), agreements (all lowercase in the CMS text), and AGREEMENTS (all capitals in the convention text).

Action Plans require the least of signatories and generally affirm that species of concern would benefit from research and conservation action and that parties will endeavor to engage in such action. Action Plans are also negotiated as components of the other kinds of agreements. Of the few stand-alone Action Plans that have been developed, one protects birds that use the migration routes within the Central Asian Flyway and another protects several species of African antelope.

MOUs are typically nonenforceable and do not require obligatory actions by parties, but they can help draw official and public attention to species of concern and result in conservation efforts on the species' behalf. The MOUs that have been negotiated under the auspices of CMS cover a range of species, from West African elephants to flamingoes in the

Andes to marine turtles in the Indian Ocean and off Southeast Asia.

Lowercase agreements tend to require action by their signatories that may or may not be obligatory, depending on the agreement. Agreements have been negotiated to protect gorillas in Central Africa, birds that migrate between Africa and Eurasia, European bats, and whales in European waters. Uppercase AGREEMENTS necessitate adequate *a priori* knowledge of migratory patterns and population status and require signatories to follow strict guidelines outlined in the CMS text. By the early years of the twenty-first century no AGREEMENTS had been negotiated.

The main criticism of CMS has been that its area of responsibility is too large for a single treaty, with most progress made by agreements negotiated under the convention but not by the main convention itself. It has also been criticized for fostering weak, nonenforceable agreements, but supporters of the convention note that the range of formalities with which agreements can be made encourages participation by states that perhaps would otherwise be hesitant to engage in conservation. The effectiveness of CMS is limited by the absence of several large states important to migratory species, including the United States, Canada, China, Russia, and Brazil, although several of these do participate in daughter agreements.

Adam B. Smith

Further Reading

Cioc, Mark. *The Game of Conservation: International Treaties to Protect the World Migratory Animals.* Ohio University Press, 2009.

DeSombre, Elizabeth R. *Global Environmental Institutions.* Routledge, 2006.

■ Bookchin, Murray

FIELDS OF STUDY: Ecology; Environmental Studies; Sociology;

Bookchin, the creator of the concept of social ecology, suggested in the 1960's that the prosperity of the post–World War II United States had been bought at the price of serious harm to the environment.

Overview

Like German socialist philosopher Karl Marx, Murray Bookchin argued that the human race cannot survive in a civilization based on life in the modern city, bureaucratic decision-making structures, and industrialized labor. Bookchin, however, built on Marx's insights to argue further that both socialism and capitalism are heedless of modern industry's impacts on the environment, and so neither socialism nor capitalism can be the basis for a sustainable society. He posited a close interconnection between human domination over nature and human beings' domination over one another, arguing that since the propensities to dominate nature and to dominate other humans sprang up together, they must be eliminated together.

Bookchin published his first two books, *Our Synthetic Environment* (1962) and *Crisis in Our Cities* (1965), under the pseudonym Lewis Herber. In these works he argued that it would not be an uprising of the proletariat but rather an uprising of an antiauthoritarian younger generation that would resolve the environmental crisis by dissolving all social hierarchies. This did not come to pass, of course, and some criticized Bookchin's faith in the younger generation as naïve. His insight concerning the connection between social problems and Earth's environment, however—that the existence of hierarchy, in addition to the misuse of technology, has brought humankind to the brink of disaster—is seen as a valuable contribution to environmental thought.

Throughout his career, Bookchin developed and refined his argument that a link exists between the "destructive logic behind a hierarchical social structure" and environmental crisis. He strongly criticized environmentalists who are satisfied to save endangered species or ban harmful chemicals yet support underlying social structures that produce new toxins and similar problems. He called for a return to life as it was before the Industrial Revolution, in particular citing what he saw as the organic and harmonious way of life of past societies such as the Plains Indians in North America. Some critics also deemed this notion naïve.

In addition to his writing, Bookchin served as professor of social ecology at Ramapo College in New Jersey and as director of the Institute for Social Ecology at Goddard College in Rochester, Vermont. Among his books are *Toward an Ecological Society*

(1980), *The Ecology of Freedom: The Emergence and Dissolution of Hierarchy* (1982), *Remaking Society* (1989), *The Philosophy of Social Ecology* (1990), *The Rise of Urbanization and the Decline of Citizenship* (1987), and *Social Ecology and Communalism* (2007).

Anne Statham

Further Reading

Barry, John. "Murray Bookchin, 1921-." In *Fifty Key Thinkers on the Environment*, edited by Joy A. Palmer. Routledge, 2001.

Bookchin, Murray. "What Is Social Ecology?" In *Earth Ethics: Introductory Readings on Animal Rights and Environmental Ethics*, edited by James P. Sterba. 2nd ed. Prentice Hall, 2000.

White, Damian. *Bookchin: A Critical Appraisal.* Pluto Press, 2008.

■ Boreal forests & climate change

FIELDS OF STUDY: Biology; Ecology; Ecosystem Management; Forestry; Environmental Studies;

IDENTIFICATION: Coniferous forests within the Subarctic land biome, existing in a nearly continuous band throughout the northern regions of North America, Europe, and Asia

Boreal forests play an important role in the cultural identities of people living in many parts of the world, particularly Canada and Siberia. These forests, which store large amounts of carbon and thus are a crucial element in the global carbon cycle, are threatened by resource development and climate change.

Overview

Boreal forests, or taiga, make up the world's largest land biome, covering vast parts of the Northern Hemisphere near 50 degrees of latitude and forming an ecologically sensitive habitat between the Arctic tundra and the temperate forest. Boreal forests extend through most of inland Canada, parts of Scandinavia, Russia (particularly Siberia), northern Mongolia and parts of central Asia, and northern Japan. They extend southward to parts of the Scottish highlands and the northern continental United States. Boreal forests are characterized by the dominance of conifers, such as firs, pines, spruces, hemlocks, and larches, and by a mean annual temperature between –5 and 5 degrees Celsius (23 and 41 degrees Fahrenheit).

Boreal forests typically have short, cool summers and long, cold winters. Precipitation can vary from 20 to 200 centimeters (approximately 8 to 79 inches) per year and falls mostly as snow. Because there is little evaporation, the ground remains moist during the summer growing season. Owing to the high latitude, summer days are very long and winter days are very short.

In addition to conifers, mosses and lichens form an important part of the boreal forest ecosystem. Some broad-leaved deciduous trees, such as birch, aspen, and willow, are also present in boreal forests. While low in biodiversity when compared with other biomes, boreal forests are home to a variety of animals as well as plants, many of them endangered. Animals found in boreal forests include reindeer or caribou; carnivores such as bear, wolverine, lynx, fox, weasel, and wolf; and more than three hundred species of birds.

Boreal forests rely on natural cycles of fire and insect damage followed by new tree growth; in North American boreal forests, these cycles are typically seventy to one hundred years long. Boreal forests store

Arctic bush along The Campbell Highway. By David Adamec (Own work)

large amounts of carbon, perhaps more than the world's tropical and temperate forests combined.

The primary threats to boreal forests are logging, development of oil and natural gas reserves, and climate change. Large areas of Siberian and Canadian boreal forests have been logged, often by clear-cutting. Substantial reserves of oil and natural gas exist under boreal forests in Alaska, Canada, and Russia. As world oil demand and prices rise and technologies for working in very cold climates improve, these reserves become possible candidates for development. It is unclear whether slow-growing boreal forests would be able to recover from the environmental impacts that accompany oil and natural gas extraction.

Although boreal forests require fire and insect infestations for their natural cycle of death and renewal, the increased frequency of both that is associated with climate change may have negative effects. Also, as temperatures rise, deciduous broad-leaved trees can outcompete conifers in more southerly parts of the boreal forest range.

Several countries have enacted measures to protect boreal forests through improved management of resource development and conservation. For example, Canadian logging companies are generally required to replant or encourage natural forest renewal, and in 2010 the Canadian federal government enlarged the areas of boreal forests to be protected from development.

Melissa A. Barton

Further Reading

Elliot-Fisk, Deborah L. "The Taiga and Boreal Forest." In *North American Terrestrial Vegetation*, edited by Michael G. Barbour and William Dwight Billings. Cambridge University Press, 2000.

Hari, Pertti, and Liisa Kulmala, eds. *Boreal Forest and Climate Change*. Springer, 2008.

Henry, J. David. *Canada's Boreal Forest*. Smithsonian Institution Press, 2001.

■ Borlaug, Norman

FIELDS OF STUDY: Agriculture, Farming, Animal Husbandry; Biology, Life Sciences, Ecosystems; Ecology, Environment, Environmentalism; Food, Hunger; History/Biography; Scientists, Engineers

CATEGORIES: Activism and advocacy; agriculture and food

IDENTIFICATION: American plant pathologist and environmental activist

Borlaug, who became known as the father of the Green Revolution, pioneered efforts to develop high-yield crops to increase food production throughout the world.

Norman Borlaug credited his childhood experiences on his family's farm with providing him with a practical approach to agriculture. In the 1930's Borlaug studied forest management and plant pathology at the University of Minnesota, earning a doctorate by 1942. In 1943 the Rockefeller Foundation, which U.S. secretary of agriculture Henry Wallace had convinced to fund agricultural aid for Mexican farmers, hired Borlaug to breed disease-immune crops that could be grown in varied climates. He perfected a strain of high-yield dwarf spring wheat.

While Borlaug was experimenting with plant breeding, the post-World War II global population rapidly increased. Some environmentalists, such as Paul R. Ehrlich, predicted that not enough food could be produced and mass starvation would occur. Borlaug believed that his wheat could prevent such a disaster. In 1963 the Rockefeller Foundation and the Mexican government established the International Maize and Wheat Improvement Center (known as CIMMYT, for its name in Spanish, Centro Internacional de Mejoramiento de Maíz y Trigo) and named Borlaug director of the Wheat Improvement Program. He traveled to India and other developing nations to share his high-yield agricultural techniques. Critics thought that Borlaug should plant indigenous crops rather than Western grains, but he emphasized that wheat provides necessary calories and nutrients.

The Indian and Pakistani governments resisted Borlaug's efforts until famine in their countries became extreme. Delayed seed shipments and the outbreak of war between India and Pakistan also hindered Borlaug's work. He persisted, however, and yields increased approximately 70 percent during the first season. By 1968 Pakistan was agriculturally self-sufficient and increased its yields from 3.4 million tons of wheat in 1963 to 18 million by 1997. India boosted its yields from 11 million tons to 60 million tons, even briefly exporting wheat.

The expansion of food production spearheaded by Borlaug, which saved hundreds of millions of people from starvation, was called the Green Revolution. Borlaug was awarded the Nobel Peace Prize in

1970 for his humanitarian efforts to secure the basic human right of freedom from hunger. This honor did not ensure continued support of his work, however. When he expressed interest in using his techniques to assist African agriculture, Borlaug's CIMMYT patrons stopped his funding because of a backlash among environmentalists that protested high-yield agriculture, claiming that its use of inorganic fertilizers and irrigation damages the environment. Borlaug countered with the argument that high-yield agriculture preserves habitats from slash-and-burn techniques used to create farmland. He criticized theorists who, in his opinion, do not comprehend the reality of what is economically and politically possible in developing countries. With colleagues Haldore Hanson and R. Glenn Anderson, he wrote *Wheat in the Third World* (1982).

Borlaug's projects in African nations were funded by Sasakawa-Global 2000, which was financed by former U.S. president Jimmy Carter and Japanese industrialist Ryoichi Sasakawa. Continuing the development of high-yield crop strains at CIMMYT in the 1990's, Borlaug wrote articles, lectured, and testified before the U.S. Congress about the opposition to his work posed by environmental lobbyists. After receiving government support in Ethiopia and Poland, he planned similar agricultural programs in the former Soviet Union and Latin America. Warning that arable land is finite, Borlaug stressed that uncontrolled population growth could result in starvation in the twenty-first century and demanded the storage of food reserves.

Elizabeth D. Schafer

Further Reading

Borlaug, Norman. "Are We Going Mad?" In *The Ethics of Food: A Reader for the Twenty-first Century*, edited by Gregory E. Pence. Lanham, Md.: Rowman & Littlefield, 2002.

Hesser, Leon. *The Man Who Fed the World: Nobel Peace Prize Laureate Norman Borlaug and His Battle to End World Hunger*. Dallas: Durban House, 2006.

Paarlberg, Robert. *Starved for Science: How Biotechnology Is Being Kept out of Africa*. Cambridge, Mass.: Harvard University Press, 2008.

See also: Agricultural revolution; Alternative grains; Green Revolution; High-yield wheat; Population growth; Slash-and-burn agriculture

■ Bovine growth hormone

FIELDS OF STUDY: Agriculture, Farming, Animal Husbandry; Elements, Substances, Chemicals, Compounds; Food, Hunger; Science; Technology and Applied Science

DEFINITION: Protein secreted by the anterior pituitary gland in cattle that controls the rate of skeletal and visceral growth

The administration of growth hormone to dairy cattle to increase milk production is controversial because of unsubstantiated allegations about the safety of the milk produced. It is also argued, however, that increasing the efficiency of milk production would benefit the environment by reducing the amount of feed needed and the waste produced per unit of production.

Growth hormone is produced by all vertebrate animals to control their rate of growth. Prior to the development of biotechnology, acquiring growth hormone was a laborious process, involving extraction from the pituitary glands of cadavers or slaughterhouse animals. All early studies of the hormone were dependent on these sources. Advances in biotechnology, however, now permit the efficient production of synthetic growth hormone, referred to as recombinant growth hormone. Recombinant human growth hormone is used to treat growth retardation conditions in children.

Recombinant bovine growth hormone, also known as recombinant bovine somatotropin, or rBST, is administered to beef cattle to increase their growth rate and administered to dairy cattle to increase their milk production. The Monsanto Company developed and tested the first such product, which it called Posilac. In 1993, the U.S. Food and Drug Administration (FDA) approved the use of Posilac, which increases milk production by at least 10 percent and has not been found to be harmful to cattle or human consumers of the milk so produced. Over the intervening years, the FDA has continued to affirm the safety of the product, despite continuing controversy about it and bans on its use by European, Canadian, and other governments.

To be effective, rBST must be injected because, as a protein, it would be degraded by the digestive system if administered orally. The milk of injected cows is indistinguishable from that of noninjected

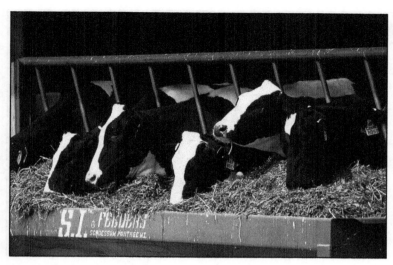
Holstein dairy cows.

cows, with the exception of slightly elevated insulin-like growth factor (IGF-1), although the latter remains within the physiological range of human breast milk. In any event, as a protein, IGF-1 is degraded in the human digestive system. Nevertheless, concerns have been raised about the health risks to consumers of milk from treated cows. None of these have been substantiated by any reputable scientific review in the United States or elsewhere. It has been argued that the bans by the European Union and Canada are based on political and economic considerations, with the governments protecting quota-based milk-production systems that would be disrupted by this product. From an environmental perspective, the ability to have fewer cows (using less land, consuming less feed, and generating less waste, including the greenhouse gas methane) producing the same amount of milk that would be produced by larger numbers of untreated cows is a definitive benefit.

The cattle injected with rBST are metabolically equivalent to genetically improved cattle and must be fed and treated as such. Like any high-producing cows, they have a slightly increased incidence of mastitis, an infection of the mammary gland, although it remains lower per gallon of milk produced. Mastitis is treated with antibiotics, and any milk with antibiotic residue must be withheld from the market. The assertion that rBST-treated cows are increasing the antibiotic content of the milk supply is unsupported by any evidence. Nevertheless, a number of American grocery chains and food companies have indicated that they will not sell dairy products from cows injected with rBST. However, given that the milk of rBST-treated cows is virtually indistinguishable from that of untreated cows, it is difficult, if not impossible, to verify the compliance of their suppliers.

James L. Robinson

Further Reading

Grace, Eric S. *Biotechnology Unzipped: Promises and Realities.* Rev. 2nd ed. Washington, DC: Joseph Henry, 2006. Print.

Hammond, Bruce G. "The Food Safety Assessment of Bovine Somatotropin (bST)." *Food Safety of Proteins in Agricultural Biotechnology.* Boca Raton: CRC, 2008. Print.

Schacter, Bernice. *Issues and Dilemmas of Biotechnology: A Reference Guide.* Westport: Greenwood, 1999. Print.

■ BP *Deepwater Horizon* oil spill

FIELDS OF STUDY: Disasters; Ecology, Environment, Environmentalism; History/Biography; Oceans, Seas, Lakes, Bodies of Water; Pollution, Emissions, Toxic Waste, Hazardous Materials

THE EVENT: Explosion and fire on the *Deepwater Horizon* drilling platform in the Gulf of Mexico that claimed eleven lives and triggered the largest accidental marine oil spill in history and the largest oil spill of any kind in the United States

DATES: April 20–July 15, 2010

The oil spill that began with an explosion on British Petroleum's Deepwater Horizon *drilling platform raised questions about the safety of deepwater drilling, the adequacy of the corporate response to the disaster and of governmental regulation of offshore oil drilling, and the possibility of long-term damage to the Gulf of Mexico's ecosystem.*

The *Deepwater Horizon* was a semisubmersible drilling platform owned by Transocean and under lease to British Petroleum (BP). In April 2010, it was located in the Gulf of Mexico approximately 84 kilometers (52 miles) southeast of Venice, Louisiana, where it was completing work on the exploratory Macondo 252 well. Oil had been found 5.5 kilometers (18,000

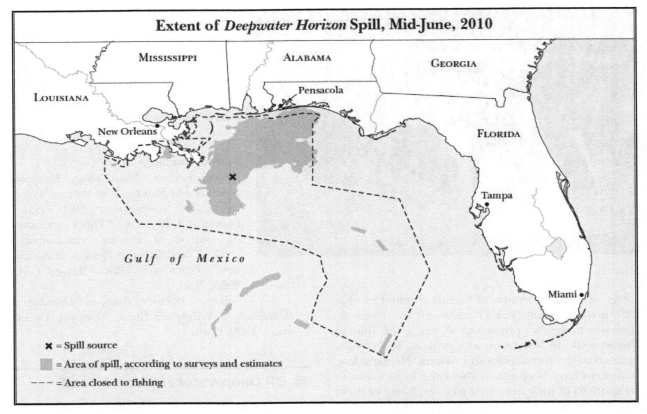

Extent of *Deepwater Horizon* Spill, Mid-June, 2010

✕ = Spill source

▪ = Area of spill, according to surveys and estimates

- - - = Area closed to fishing

feet) below the seafloor and 7 kilometers (23,000 feet) below the drilling platform. The drill hole had been—or was being—cemented to seal the well so that the drill pipe could be removed and the *Deepwater Horizon* could be moved to a new location. The cement failed, allowing gas and oil under high pressure to escape the reservoir and rise through the drill pipe casing and up the riser pipe to the drilling platform. A blowout preventer located on top of the wellhead was designed to cut through the drill casing and seal the wellhead in cased of an emergency. The blowout preventer also failed, and about 11:00 p.m. central daylight time on April 20 the escaping gas reached the surface and exploded, setting the *Deepwater Horizon* on fire. Most of the workers on the platform were evacuated without serious injury, but eleven who had been in close proximity to the explosion died and seventeen were injured.

Without any mechanism to stop the flow of oil to the platform, fireboats were unable to extinguish the flames. The drilling platform burned for about thirty-six hours and then sank, twisting and breaking the riser pipe that had connected the platform to the wellhead some 1.5 kilometers (5,000 feet) beneath the sea surface.

Magnitude of the Spill

On April 24, unmanned submarines working for BP detected oil flow from the wellhead and the collapsed riser pipe. The magnitude of the flow was estimated to be about 1,000 barrels per day (BPD), a figure repeated by both company and governmental officials. (One barrel of oil equals 42 gallons, or approximately 159 liters.) On April 26 a scientist with the National Oceanic and Atmospheric Administration (NOAA) estimated the flow at roughly 5,000 BPD based on satellite imagery of the oil slick. Nongovernmental scientists using similar methodologies provided estimates as high as 26,500 BPD.

After BP released video images of the underwater leak on May 12, independent experts reported estimates of up to 50,000 BPD. Despite the existence of potentially better methodologies, government officials adhered to their estimate of 5,000 BPD until May 27, when a government task force, the Flow Rate Group (FRG), released its first estimate: 12,000 to

25,000 BPD. FRG estimates were increased to 20,000 to 40,000 BPD on June 12 and to 35,000 to 60,000 BPD on June 15. By that time oil was being washed up on the shores of the coasts of Louisiana, Mississippi, Alabama, and Florida.

In the aftermath of the spill, both government and independent scientists appeared to agree that the actual flow rate was approximately 60,000 BPD and that the total release of oil into the Gulf was approximately 5 million barrels, roughly twenty times the volume of the 1989 *Exxon Valdez* oil spill in Prince William Sound. This was the largest oil spill in the history of the Gulf of Mexico, exceeding the 3 million gallons discharged into the Gulf after the 1979 PEMEX oil spill off the coast of Mexico.

Emergency Response

Within one week of the initial explosion, oil had reached the Mississippi Delta, and the nation became aware that the Gulf oil spill threatened serious economic and environmental damage. The event was better described as a discharge, a blowout, a flow, or a leak, but the term "spill" was almost universally adopted. In the space of a few days, President Barack Obama announced that the United States would use all available resources to contain the spill. Fishing was prohibited in the affected areas, and a moratorium was declared on further deepwater drilling in the Gulf of Mexico pending an investigation. President Obama announced that British Petroleum was responsible for the spill and that it would be held responsible for the cleanup. The U.S. Coast Guard commandant, Admiral Thad Allen, was named incident commander for the federal response, and it was announced that a national commission would be formed to study the disaster and make recommendations. BP chief executive officer Tony Hayward declared that BP would take full responsibility; he pledged to stop the leak, repair the damage to the Gulf, and pay all legitimate claims for damages.

From the beginning experts agreed that the permanent solution would be a relief well that would intersect the drill hole below the lowest level of drill pipe casing and above the top of the petroleum reservoir. Cement pumped through the relief well would seal the reservoir permanently. BP began drilling such a relief well on May 2. It was anticipated that the relief well would be completed in August,

but waiting that long to stop the flow of oil was not a viable option.

BP pursued multiple strategies to stanch the flow. Several attempted quick fixes were relatively unsuccessful. Remotely controlled underwater vehicles working for the company failed to close valves on the blowout preventer. Surface oil slicks were burned on several occasions, but the volume of oil consumed was relatively small. U.S. Air Force planes were enlisted to spray chemical dispersants on surface slicks while BP injected dispersants underwater in an effort to break up the oil flow at the source. More than 1.8 million gallons of dispersants were used—almost 800,000 gallons near the wellhead. Local fishing boats were hired to skim floating oil, and miles of booms were deployed in an effort to prevent slicks from contaminating ecologically sensitive coastlines. In many areas wind and waves rendered these strategies ineffective. Efforts were also undertaken to construct artificial barrier islands to protect fragile coastlines. Every strategy was controversial, and some worked at cross-purposes. Chemical dispersants, for example, made the use of booms and skimming less effective but also arguably less necessary. At the height of the crisis thousands of people and hundreds of vessels were employed in efforts to mitigate the environmental damage of the spill.

By early May it was apparent that at least three significant leaks were coming from a section of broken riser pipe that lay crumpled on the ocean floor still attached to the failed blowout preventer on the wellhead. On May 4 remotely controlled underwater vehicles successfully sawed off the free end of the leaking riser pipe and installed a shutoff valve, reducing the number of leaks to two, but without significantly diminishing the flow of oil. On May 7 and 8 one of three custom-built coffer dams was lowered over the largest leak on the ocean floor. This concrete and metal box, 12 meters (40 feet) high, was designed to capture the plume of escaping oil so that it could be pumped to the surface. The coffer dam failed, however, when a frozen mixture of gas and water clogged the system. A smaller version, dubbed "top hat," was lowered on May 11 but never deployed. Instead, BP chose to insert a 15.2-centimeter (6-inch) pipe directly into the leaking 53.3-centimeter (21-inch) riser pipe.

On May 16 BP announced that it was capturing most of the leaking oil, but the following day the estimate of oil captured was reduced to 1,000 BPD, approximately one-fifth of BP's estimated leak rate. Plans were announced for a "junk shot" to plug the leak by injecting the well with a high-pressure mixture of cement and solids such as shredded tires. It was never executed, however; instead BP chose the "top kill," which was designed to stop the flow by pumping drilling mud into the blowout preventer. This procedure failed to stop the flow, even after "junk shot" solids were added to the mixture.

By June 1, BP was working to saw off the broken riser pipe just above the blowout preventer and attach a cap connected to a new riser pipe. This strategy entailed significant risk because cutting off the bent riser pipe would increase the flow of oil into the Gulf. The cap was connected, but the fit was loose. Over time the fraction of escaping oil that was recovered slowly increased, approaching 50 percent. A significant fraction of the captured oil was burned at the surface. After about a month, while efforts continued to drill relief wells, BP removed the cap and replaced it with what amounted to a blowout preventer on top of the previous blowout preventer. After eighty-seven days, the flow of oil was stopped on July 15.

In August, as work on the relief wells continued, BP announced a successful "static kill." Tons of drilling mud followed by cement were pumped into the wellhead, providing increased assurance that the flow would not resume. The first relief well intersected Macondo 252 on September 16, and crews cemented the blown-out well from the bottom. The federal incident commander declared Macondo 252 officially sealed on September 19.

Consequences

The economic damages associated with the BP oil spill were dire. One study estimated just the short-term damage to the Gulf fishing industry at $115 to $172 million. Severe economic impacts were also associated with the deepwater drilling moratorium and the spill's damage to the "Louisiana brand." Perhaps the clearest economic indicator of damage done was reduced investor confidence in BP. Between April 21 and June 25, 2010, the value of BP stock declined by 55 percent, representing a reduction of $67 billion in market capitalization. By the time the well was sealed, BP had reportedly spent more than $11 billion on the capping and cleanup operations, and it had

created a $20 billion escrow account for payment of damages, which was depleted by 2013. In the autumn of 2010, BP announced that it had taken a pretax charge of $32.2 billion and had plans to sell up to $30 billion in assets. It had canceled its stock dividend.

In 2012, BP signed a settlement agreement to compensate businesses that suffered financial losses due to the spill. BP later attempted to challenge this settlement agreement in court, although the U.S. Supreme Court rejected the challenge in December 2014. Also in 2012, BP reached an agreement with the U.S. Department of Justice, in which the company pleaded guilty to fourteen criminal charges, including violations of the Clean Water Act and the Migratory Bird Treaty Act, which carried more than $4.5 billion in penalties and fines. In November 2012, the U.S. Environmental Protection Agency (EPA) suspended BP from entering into any new federal contracts, a ban that lasted until March 2014. In April 2016, courts approved a settlement with BP for natural-resource damages caused by the spill, allocating up to $8.8 billion for the restoration of damaged wildlife, habitats, and ecosystems.

BP's long-term liability will depend in part on the environmental and medical damage caused by the spill, which may be even more difficult to measure than economic damage. Studies are expected to continue for years if not decades. The fate of the spilled oil remains the subject of scientific controversy. No one knows with any degree of certainty what fraction evaporated, sank to the bottom of the Gulf, or remained suspended in the water column. The environmental consequences of the unprecedented intensive use of chemical dispersants remain unclear, but preliminary analyses by the EPA indicated that the environmental benefits of dispersant use outweighed the environmental cost.

The totality of environmental damage to the Gulf of Mexico from the *Deepwater Horizon* spill will certainly be significant, but the ecological significance of a major oil spill may depend significantly on the location. The ecological damage done by the *Exxon Valdez* grounding in Prince William Sound was disproportionate to the size of the spill. By contrast, the vastly larger PEMEX spill in the Gulf of Mexico is generally regarded as having caused relatively little environmental damage. Despite the attention given to the acute BP spill, the chronic damage from agricultural runoff throughout the Mississippi River basin probably remains the most significant ecological threat to the Gulf.

The BP oil spill raised important questions about the safety of deepwater drilling, the industry's preparedness for spills, and the government's supervision of industry behavior. Early reports by the national commission studying the spill indicated that the industry and the government were both poorly prepared for a spill of such magnitude. BP and its contractors had bypassed safety measures, and government agencies had routinely approved work that did not meet legal standards.

Craig W. Allin

Further Reading

Barstow, David, et al. "Between Blast and Spill, One Last, Flawed Hope." *The New York Times*, 21 June 2010, query.nytimes.com/gst/fullpage.html?res= 990CE2D91730F932A15755C0A9669D8B63&pag ewanted=all.

"Deepwater Horizon Oil Spill." *Office of Response and Restoration*, National Oceanic and Atmospheric Administration, US Dept. of Commerce, 23 Nov. 2016,response.restoration.noaa.gov/oil-and-chemical-spills/significant-incidents/ deepwater-horizon-oil-spill.

Hurley, Lawrence. "U.S. Supreme Court Rejects BP Challenge to Gulf Spill Settlement." *Reuters*, 8 Dec. 2014, www.reuters.com/article/ us-usa-court-bp-idUSKBN0JM1KR20141208.

Jernelöv, Arne. "The Threats from Oil Spills: Now, Then, and in the Future." *AMBIO: A Journal of the Human Environment*, vol. 39, no. 6, 2010, pp. 353–66.

Jonsson, Patrik. "Gulf Oil Spill: Where Has the Oil Gone?" *The Christian Science Monitor*, 27 July 2010, www.csmonitor.com/Environment/2010/0727/ Gulf-oil-spill-Where-has-the-oil-gone.

Ornitz, Barbara E., and Michael A. Champ. *Oil Spills First Principles: Prevention and Best Response*. Elsevier, 2002.

■ *Braer* oil spill

Fields of study: Disasters; Ecology, Environment, Environmentalism; History/Biography; Oceans, Seas, Lakes, Bodies of Water; Pollution, Emissions,

Toxic Waste, Hazardous Materials

The Event: Grounding of the oil tanker *Braer* at the Shetland Islands, resulting in the spilling of its cargo of crude oil into the sea

Date: January 5, 1993

The oil spilled when the Braer ran aground, killed or sickened thousands of shellfish, and led to severe economic setbacks for the local fishing industry.

When the oil tanker *Braer* ran aground at the southern tip of the Shetland Islands, located about 210 kilometers (130 miles) north of the Scottish mainland, more than one million barrels of crude oil were spilled into the Atlantic Ocean. Under the severe wind and wave conditions that prevailed around the Shetland Islands at the time, the spilled oil thoroughly mixed into the turbulent seawater and rapidly dispersed. Ten days after the spill, the concentrations in the vicinity of the wreck had fallen from several hundred parts per million (ppm) to 4 ppm, still about two thousand times the normal level.

Being less dense than water, most of the oil floated. The lightest, most volatile hydrocarbons started to evaporate, decreasing the volume of the spill but polluting the air. Subsequently, a slow decomposition process occurred, caused by sunlight and bacterial action. After several months, the oil mass was reduced by approximately 80 percent.

Shortly after the *Braer* oil spill, all fishing activities were prohibited in the surrounding areas. For most shellfish species, this ban remained in effect for more than two years, until the spring of 1995, when they were judged to be free of any significant levels of oil contamination. Shortly after fishing resumed, however, the catches of lobsters and queen scallops were found to be very poor, and the proportion of young lobsters and scallops was abnormally low.

Supported by the Shetland Fishermen's Association, the North Atlantic Fisheries College carried out a number of laboratory trials in 1996 and 1997 to determine what effects crude oil may have on lobsters and scallops and to investigate whether the *Braer* oil spill could have had adverse effects on these stocks. During the experiments, researchers used Norwegian Gullfaks crude oil, the same type as the *Braer*'s cargo, to simulate the spill conditions. Results of the study showed that in the short term, adult scallops

Braer Disaster Site

Norwegian Sea

Unst

Yell

Fetlar

Papa Stour

Whalsay

Mainland

Bressay　North Sea

Foula

SHETLAND ISLANDS

Lerwick

Garths Ness

Sumburgh Head

Quendale Bay

Fair Isle

---

the *Braer* oil spill, particularly by the large quantities of oil that had become incorporated into subtidal sediments.

Alvin K. Benson

Further Reading

Burger, Joanna. *Oil Spills.* New Brunswick, N.J.: Rutgers University Press, 1997.

Clark, R. B. *Marine Pollution.* 5th ed. New York: Oxford University Press, 2001.

National Research Council. *Oil in the Sea III: Inputs, Fates, and Effects.* Washington, D.C.: National Academies Press, 2003.

■ Brazilian radioactive powder release

FIELDS OF STUDY: Disasters; Ecology, Environment, Environmentalism; Health, Medicine, Disease, Illness; History/Biography; Nuclear Power, Nuclear Weapons, Radioactive Waste

THE EVENT: Accidental release of radioactive powder in Goiania, Brazil

DATES: September-October, 1987

When radioactive powder was released accidentally in Goiania, hundreds of people were contaminated, four of whom died. The incident raised the issue of responsibility for the disposal of radioactive waste.

On September 13, 1987, two men found an old radiation-therapy machine in an abandoned medical clinic in Goiania, a Brazilian state capital with a population of one million people. When they took the machine apart, they found a cylindrical lead container inside, which they sold to a local junk dealer. Unaware that the canister contained radioactive cesium 137, an isotope of cesium used in the treatment of cancer, the junk dealer opened the canister to investigate the curious blue light visible inside. He shared his discovery with friends, who were fascinated by the blue powder and the shimmer it made on their skin. The powder was rapidly distributed throughout the community as people gave samples to friends as gifts. Children played with it as if it were a new toy. Symptoms of radiation poisoning began days later.

Radiation destroys the reproductive mechanisms of cells, affecting to the greatest extent those cells that divide the most rapidly. These include bone

---

and lobsters could survive exposure to relatively high concentrations of oil, but lobster eggs and larvae suffered high mortality rates. Although the oil did not kill the adult lobsters, it did cause major behavioral abnormalities, including significant reductions in feeding, movement, responsiveness to stimuli, and aggression.

In May, 1997, the Scottish Office Fisheries Department released a document indicating that the *Braer* oil spill polluted a much wider area than previously thought. The report showed that levels of oil in prawns and mussels from a 1,036-square-kilometer (400-square-mile) zone of excluded fishing were still rising in 1996, and there were indications that the tides had spread the oil underwater all around the Shetland Islands' 1,450-kilometer (900-mile) coastline. Fishermen reported that their fishing grounds were ruined, with nothing replacing what was being caught. Into the late 1990's, considerable work was still being undertaken to rectify the damage done by

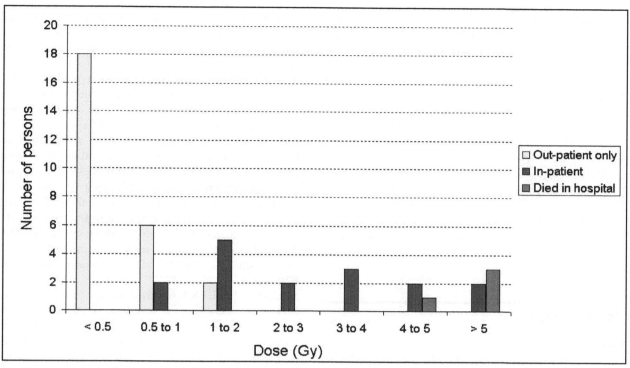

Health outcomes for the 46 most contaminated persons in the Goiânia accident, I took data from a IAEA report and used this for making the bar chart. By Cadmium

marrow, gastrointestinal tract, skin, and hair cells. Effects include burns, hemorrhaging, and, because bone marrow cells are involved in the immune response of the body, decreased white blood cell count, with consequent susceptibility to infections.

A team of doctors was dispatched to the area, and helicopters equipped with radiation detection equipment determined the "hot spots" in the city. Tons of materials were found to have traces of the powder, including furniture, buses, money, and animals. The doctors found that 244 people had been contaminated with doses up to 600 rads (1 rad is roughly equivalent to seven chest X rays) and immediately hospitalized 54 people. The patients were thoroughly washed to remove any excess cesium that may still have been on their skin, and they were fed Prussian blue, a compound known to complex with cesium and block its further absorption into the body. The doctors treated infections with antibiotics and hemorrhaging with blood-clotting factors. The Brazilian government enlisted the aid of the International Atomic Energy Agency (IAEA) and the Radiation Emergency Center Training Sites (REACTS), a World Health Organization unit that responds to radiation incidents in the Western Hemisphere.

Some controversy arose over the use of an experimental treatment involving granulocyte-macrophage colony-stimulating factor (GM-CSF) on severely ill patients. GM-CSF is one of five hormones that increase the production of white blood cells in bone marrow. The treatment is used in cancer patients because it offsets the effects of radiation and chemotherapy, allowing the use of larger doses. The six patients treated with GM-CSF in Brazil represented the worst cases of contamination. Four of them died, but the other two seemed to respond well to the treatment. By the end of the year, twenty-eight people remained hospitalized with radiation sickness, but there were no further fatalities.

The Brazilian Nuclear Energy Commission came under strong criticism for the accident, which caused widespread panic among the citizens of Goiania and other cities in Brazil. There was confusion regarding which government agency had the responsibility to license, monitor, and ensure proper disposal of radioactive waste in the country. The Brazilian Ministry of Health and the Ministry of Labor were also implicated as negligent of their responsibilities with regard to the monitoring of radioactive materials.

Suzanne Jones and Massimo D. Bezoari

Further Reading

Friis, Robert H. "Ionizing and Nonionizing Radiation." In Essentials of Environmental Health. Sudbury, Mass.: Jones and Bartlett, 2007.

Gusev, Igor A., Angelina K. Guskova, and Fred A. Mettler. Medical Management of Radiation Accidents. 2d ed. Boca Raton, Fla.: CRC Press, 2001.

Yard, Charles Richard. "Lost Radiation Sources: Raising Public Awareness About the Hazards Associated with Industrial and Medical Radiography Sources." Journal of Environmental Health 58, no. 10 (1996).

■ Breeder reactors

FIELDS OF STUDY: Energy and Energy Resources; Inventions; Nuclear Power, Nuclear Weapons, Radioactive Waste; Physics; Science; Technology and Applied Science

CATEGORIES: Energy and energy use; nuclear power and radiation

DEFINITION: Nuclear reactors designed to create more fuel than they use in the production of energy

Properly managed and maintained breeder reactors produce useful energy, generate less waste than conventional lightwater fission reactors, and reduce greenhouse gas emissions by reducing the use of fossil fuels.

As opposed to normal nuclear fission reactors that use uranium 235 as their energy source, breeder reactors can make use of the much more abundant uranium 238 or thorium 232. Whereas a typical fission reactor uses only about 1 percent of the natural uranium 235 that starts its fuel cycle, a breeder reactor consumes a much larger percentage of the initial fissionable material. In addition, if the price of uranium is more than two hundred dollars per kilogram, it is cost-efficient to reprocess the fuel so that almost all of the original fissionable material produces useful energy. Breeder reactors are designed to produce from 1 percent to more than 20 percent more fuel than they consume. The time required for a

breeder reactor to generate enough material to fuel a second nuclear reactor is referred to as the doubling time; the typical doubling time targeted in power plant design is ten years.

Scientists have proposed two main types of breeder reactors: fast-breeder reactors and thermal breeder reactors. The fast-breeder reactor uses fast neutrons given off by fission reactions to breed more fuel from nonfissionable isotopes. The most common fast-breeding reaction produces fissionable plutonium 239 from nonfissionable uranium 238. The liquid metal fast-breeder reactor (LMFBR) breeds plutonium 239 and uses liquid metal, typically sodium, for cooling and for heat transfer to water to generate steam that turns a turbine to produce electricity. The thermal breeder reactor uses thorium 232 to produce fissile uranium 233 after neutron capture and beta decay.

Unlike fossil-fuel-powered plants, breeder reactors do not generate carbon dioxide or other greenhouse gas pollutants. Environmental concerns related to any type of breeder reactor include nuclear accidents that could emit radiation into the atmosphere and the difficulty of safely disposing of radioactive waste by-products. In addition, for plutonium-based breeders a major concern is the possibility of the diversion of bred plutonium for nuclear weapon production. This concern can be addressed through the intermixing of actinide impurities with the plutonium; such impurities make little difference to reactor operation, but they make it extremely difficult for anyone to use the bred plutonium to manufacture a nuclear weapon.

France has been the most prominent nation in the implementation of breeder reactors. The Superphénix breeder reactor built on the Caspian Sea was used for power generation and desalination of seawater from 1985 to 1996. India has plans to build a large fleet of breeder reactors, including a large prototype LMFBR that uses a plutonium-uranium oxide mixture in the fuel rods. Russia, China, and Japan are also developing breeders. The Russian BN-600 fast-breeder reactor has experienced several sodium leaks and fires. If the sodium coolant in the central part of an LMFBR core were to overheat and bubble, core melting could accelerate in the event of an accident and release radioactive material into the environment. A strong reactor containment building and a reactor core designed so that the fuel rod bundles are interspersed within a depleted uranium blanket that surrounds the core could greatly decrease this effect.

Alvin K. Benson

Further Reading

Bodansky, David. *Nuclear Energy: Principles, Practices, and Prospects*. 2d ed. New York: Springer, 2004.

Mosey, David. *Reactor Accidents: Institutional Failure in the Nuclear Industry*. Sidcup, England: Nuclear Engineering International, 2006.

Muller, Richard A. *Physics for Future Presidents: The Science Behind the Headlines*. New York: W. W. Norton, 2008.

See also: Alternative energy sources; Nuclear accidents; Nuclear and radioactive waste; Nuclear power; Nuclear weapons production; Power plants; Radioactive pollution and fallout; Superphénix

---

■ Brent Spar occupation

Fields of study: Ecology, Environment, Environmentalism; Ethics, Advocacy, Policy, Protest; History/Biography; Oceans, Seas, Lakes, Bodies of Water; Pollution, Emissions, Toxic Waste, Hazardous Materials; Public Policy, Debates, Controversies

The Event: Occupation of an abandoned oil storage platform by Greenpeace protesters

Dates: April 30-May 23, 1995

As the result of their occupation of the Brent Spar, which Royal Dutch Shell had planned to sink, Greenpeace protesters were able to influence the company to adopt alternative disposal methods.

On April 30, 1995, fourteen Greenpeace volunteers boarded the abandoned oil storage platform Brent Spar, which was anchored off the western coast of Norway in the North Sea. The Brent Spar, a floating cylinder moored to the sea bottom, had been built in 1976, but it had been taken out of commission in 1991. Its owner, Royal

Dutch Shell, intended to lower the platform into the Atlantic Ocean and then sink it under more than six thousand feet of water.

Greenpeace had engaged in months of negotiations with Shell prior to the occupation. Representatives of the environmental activist group had urged Shell officials to develop a plan for dismantling the platform on land, citing studies that had concluded that on-land disposal and recycling of oil rigs is environmentally preferable to sea dumping. Shell replied with studies of its own asserting that deep-sea disposal is the more environmentally sound option.

When it became clear that Shell planned to proceed with the ocean dumping, Greenpeace sent fourteen volunteers to the platform. It also stepped up its publicity campaign, drawing support from the European Union (EU) commissioner for the environment, Denmark's minister for environment and energy, and other important sources. In May, the European Parliament passed a resolution opposing the dumping of the *Brent Spar*.

On May 22, Shell dispatched a team to the *Brent Spar* to remove the protesters, but bad weather delayed the evacuation. The volunteers ended their occupation the next day but vowed to continue the fight in the courts. However, an English judge refused to hear the Greenpeace case, stating that the English courts had no jurisdiction over the North Sea matter.

The Shell / ESSO Brent Spar, still under construction in the Netherlands. Photo scanned from a dia by my late father, in or around 1975. By Quistnix (Own work)

In June, German chancellor Helmut Kohl raised the question of the *Brent Spar* with British prime minister John Major. By then, Germany had joined the list of nations opposing the dumping of oil platforms in the sea. Shell nevertheless proceeded with its plan. In late June, therefore, Greenpeace activists again boarded the platform by helicopter. Meanwhile, demonstrations against Shell took place in Great Britain, Denmark, the Netherlands, Germany, and Switzerland. In Germany, a Shell gas station was firebombed, and the company's sales fell more than 15 percent.

On June 20, Shell announced that it would not dump the *Brent Spar* in the sea. Nine days later, the member nations of the Oslo Paris Commission (OSPAR), in a vote of eleven to two (Norway and the United Kingdom opposing), decided to impose a moratorium on sea disposal of oil platforms. The following month, Shell received permission from the Norwegian government to store the *Brent Spar* in an inlet on Norway's west coast while working out plans for its dismantling. The platform was finally dismantled in 1999, with parts of it repurposed as the foundation for a new ferry terminal at Mekjarvik, Norway.

Christopher Kent

Further Reading

Chasek, Pamela S., et al. *Global Environmental Politics.* 4th ed. Boulder, Colo.: Westview Press, 2006.

Entine, Jon. "Shell, Greenpeace, and *Brent Spar:* The Politics of Dialogue." *Case Histories in Business Ethics,* edited by Chris Megone and Simon J. Robinson. New York: Routledge, 2002.

Jordan, Grant. *Shell, Greenpeace, and the Brent Spar.* New York: Palgrave, 2001.

■ Brockovich, Erin

FIELDS OF STUDY: Biochemistry; Chemistry; Environmental Law; Environmental Studies; Law;

IDENTIFICATION: Legal clerk and environmental activist

DEFINITION: Chromium-6: Cr(VI); atoms of the element chromium in the highly reactive +6 oxidation state, generally in the form of inorganic ions in which Cr is the central atom; such compounds are highly dangerous due to the ease with which they damage and destroy carbon-based materials such as biochemicals within the human body

Erin Brockovich helped construct a legal case against the Pacific Gas and Electric Company for its role in polluting the drinking water of Hinkley, California, with chromium-6. The clients in the case received the largest settlement ever awarded in the United States in a direct-action lawsuit.

Overview

Erin Brockovich was born Erin Pattee; her mother, Betty Jo O'Neal-Pattee, was a journalist, and her father, Frank Pattee, was an industrial engineer. She graduated from Lawrence High School in 1978 and earned an associate in applied arts degree from Wade Business College in Dallas, Texas, in 1980. She then became a management trainee for the Kmart retail chain and moved to California. After a period in which she married and divorced twice (Steve Brockovich was her second husband), had three children, and held a variety of jobs, she became a secretary for the law firm of Masry & Vititoe of Northridge, California, in 1991.

Brockovich was assigned to work on a pro bono case for a home owner in Hinkley, California, and quickly developed a rapport with the client who was

Erin Brockovich, legal eagle and environmentalist, speaks at University of Sydney. By Eva Rinaldi from Sydney Australia

bringing a lawsuit that alleged contamination of the town's drinking water with chromium-6. Residents of the area, it was alleged, were experiencing above-average numbers of miscarriages and cancers. Brockovich discovered that from 1952 to 1966, the Pacific Gas and Electric Company (PG&E) used chromium-6 to fight corrosion in the cooling tower of its natural gas pumping station in Hinkley. Wastewater containing chromium-6 was then pumped into unlined ponds, from which it leached into the aquifer that supplied Hinkley's drinking water. Brockovich pursued the case tenaciously and signed up more than six hundred additional persons to participate in the lawsuit. In 1996, after winning an initial round in court, the clients agreed to PG&E's offer to settle all their claims against the company for $333 million—a record high settlement for a direct-action lawsuit in the United States.

The film *Erin Brockovich* was released in 2000 and starred Julia Roberts as the title character. It chronicled Brockovich's fight against PG&E. Throughout the first two decades of the twenty-first century, Brockovich remained an environmental activist and educator.

Thomas R. Feller

Further Reading

Bamberger, M., and R. E. Oswald. "Unconventional Oil and Gas Extraction and Animal Health." *Environmental Science: Processes & Impacts*, vol. 16, no. 8, 2014, pp. 1860–5.

Gates, Alexander E., and Robert P. Blauvelt. *Encyclopedia of Pollution*. Facts on File, 2011.

Goodman, Michael, et al. "Cancer Clusters in the USA: What Do the Last Twenty Years of State and Federal Investigations Tell Us?." *Critical Reviews in Toxicology*, vol. 42, no. 6, 2012, pp. 474–90.

Morgan, John W., and Mark E. Reeves. "Abstract A78: Cancer in Hinkley: What Was the Real Problem?." *Cancer Epidemiology Biomarkers & Prevention*, vol. 20, no. 10, 2011, p. A78.

Murphy, Patrick D. "Putting the Earth into Global Media Studies." *Communication Theory*, vol. 21, no. 3, 2011, pp. 217–38.

■ Brower, David

FIELDS OF STUDY: Ethics, Advocacy, Policy, Protest; Ecology, Environment, Environmentalism; Public Policy, Debates, Controversies; Authors, Writers.

IDENTIFICATION: Activism and advocacy; preservation and wilderness issues

Brower, who was vigorously involved in battles concerning environmental issues for more than fifty years, was one of the twentieth century's most influential and controversial environmental activists and writers.

David Ross Brower served as the first executive director of the Sierra Club from 1952 to 1969. He is credited by many with helping the San Francisco-based organization grow from two thousand to seventy-seven thousand members and developing it into a powerful national organization. He led the club in aggressive campaigns against U.S. government projects to develop wild areas, most notably fights that successfully stopped the construction of the Echo Park Dam, which would have flooded part of Dinosaur National Monument in Utah in the 1950's, and two different dams across the Colorado River in the Grand Canyon in the 1960's and 1970's. His enterprising tactics included full-page advertisements in *The New York Times* and the *San Francisco Chronicle*, which resulted in the Internal Revenue Service reclassifying the nonprofit Sierra Club as a lobbying organization and removing its tax-deductible status.

For more than twenty-five years, Brower focused much of his passion and energy on the Glen Canyon Dam in northeastern Arizona. "Glen Canyon died, and I was partly responsible for its needless death," Brower wrote in Eliot Porter's *The Place No One Knew: Glen Canyon on the Colorado* (1963). In the mid-1950's the U.S. Bureau of Reclamation was planning to construct dams across the Colorado River in the Grand Canyon and Glen Canyon, Arizona, and across the Green and Yampa rivers in Utah. Following the directives of the Sierra Club board of directors, Brower agreed to drop the club's opposition to the Colorado River dams if the Bureau of Reclamation would discontinue plans to build the two dams in Utah. The bureau agreed to the deal and moved forward to build the Glen Canyon Dam.

Before the construction was completed, Brower and the Sierra Club decided the compromise had been a mistake. They blamed their decision on a lack of familiarity with the spectacular beauty of Glen Canyon. (In 1996 the Sierra Club directors unanimously passed a motion by Brower to support draining Lake Powell, the behind the Glen Canyon Dam, and return the Colorado River flow to the most natural state possible. Brower did not advocate dismantling the dam; rather, he stated, it should be left "as a tourist attraction, like the Pyramids, with passersby wondering how humanity ever built it, and why.")

In the mid-1960's Brower and the Sierra Club successfully led an effort to prevent construction of the Bureau of Reclamation's proposed Marble Canyon Dam in the Grand Canyon and helped cripple the bureau's effort to build Bridge Canyon Dam farther downstream in the Grand Canyon. By 1969, however, the majority of the Sierra Club's board of directors found Brower's tactics too reckless, both financially and politically, and they removed him as executive director. He then formed the preservation-oriented Friends of the Earth and the League of Conservation Voters, both of which flourished under his leadership. He also facilitated the establishment of independent Friends of the Earth organizations in other countries. In 1982, after conflicts with members of the Friends of the Earth's professional staff and its directors, Brower moved on to form another group, Earth Island Institute, the stated mission of which was to globalize the environmental movement. He returned to the Sierra Club as a director in 1983 and was reelected in 1986 and 1995. In the fall of 1994 Brower helped develop the Ecological Council of Americas to improve cooperation among organizations in the Western Hemisphere that were attempting to integrate environmental and economic needs.

In the 1990's Brower called on the federal government to replace the U.S. Bureau of Land Management with a new agency called the National Land Service. Its mission would be to protect and restore private and public land in the United States. He also strongly advocated the creation of a national reserve system.

Throughout his life, Brower pushed the edges of environmental thought of the day. He pioneered ideas and methods to preserve the environment and create a global approach to issues. For many years Brower advocated the establishment of international natural reserves in areas of rich and ecosystems. The United Nations Educational, Scientific, and Cultural Organization (UNESCO) has established such a system of World Heritage Sites.

Brower also advocated a method known as CPR to guard against the destruction of natural areas and biodiversity: "C" is for *conservation,* or the rational use of resources: "P" represents the *preservation* of threatened, endangered, and yet undiscovered species; and "R" stands for *restoration* of lands already damaged by human activities. Many of his tactics and ideas seemed radical when he introduced them but later became standard practice among mainstream environmentalists. Russell Train, chairman of the Council on Environmental Quality during President Richard Nixon's administration, once said, "Thank God for Dave Brower; he makes it so easy for the rest of us to be reasonable."

Louise D. Hose

Further Reading

Brower, David. *Let the Mountains Talk, Let the Rivers Run: A Call to Save the Earth.* New ed. Sierra Club Books, 2007.

_____. "The Sermon." In *Speaking of Earth: Environmental Speeches That Moved the World,* edited by Alon Tal. Rutgers University Press, 2006.

McPhee, John. *Encounters with the Archdruid.* 1971. Reprint. Farrar, Straus and Giroux, 2000.

Porter, Eliot. *The Place No One Knew: Glen Canyon on the Colorado.* Edited by David Brower. Commemorative ed. Gibbs Smith, 2000.

Stoll, Steven. *U.S. Environmentalism Since 1945: A Brief History with Documents.* Palgrave Macmillan, 2007.

■ Brown, Lester

FIELDS OF STUDY: Agriculture; Ecology; Ecosystem Management; Environmental Studies;

Brown founded the Worldwatch Institute, an environmental think tank the mission of which is to analyze the state of the earth and to act as "a global early warning system."

Environmentalist Lester Brown. By Victor Soares/ABr

Overview

Lester Brown was raised on a small tomato farm in Bridgeton, New Jersey. He joined the 4-H Club and the Future Farmers of America at his local school. When he was fourteen, he and his brother purchased a used tractor and a small plot of land to grow tomatoes. Within a brief time, they became two of the most successful tomato farmers on the East Coast. Brown graduated from Rutgers University in 1955 with a degree in agricultural science and immediately put his education to practical use. He worked for six months in a small farming community in India, becoming intimately acquainted with hunger problems created by population growth and unsustainable agricultural practices.

In 1959 Brown earned a master's degree in agricultural economics and soon after joined the US Department of Agriculture as an international agricultural analyst. After leaving that post in 1969, he helped organize the Overseas Development Council, a private group devoted to analyzing issues relevant to relations between the United States and developing countries.

Brown's educational and career background prepared him well for his work and leadership in the Worldwatch Institute. While living and working in developing nations, he became acutely aware of such problems as the extensive poverty caused by economic systems dependent on cash crops for export to wealthy industrial countries and the use of agricultural practices that cause deforestation and desertification. He realized that food security could replace military security as the major concern of governments in the twenty-first century.

Shortly after Brown established the Worldwatch Institute in 1974, he and other staff members initiated the Worldwatch Papers, which focus on population growth and the resulting stress on natural resources, transportation trends, and the human and environmental impact of urbanization. In 1984 Brown established the institute's annual report, *State of the World*, a comprehensive overview of specific global environmental issues. This publication, eventually available in more than twenty-five languages, is used by political leaders, educators, and citizens as a resource for information on environmental problems and ways to address them. In 1992 Brown inaugurated the publication of *Vital Signs: The Trends That Are Shaping Our Future*. This annual handbook features environmental, economic, and social statistical indicators on trends likely to influence the world's future.

In Brown's view, global environmental problems should be addressed through international efforts funded by taxes on currency exchanges, taxes for pollution emissions, and a greater involvement by the United Nations. He has advocated a shift away from national spending on unsustainable economic growth and toward investing in research and development that enhances environmental quality and protection of natural resources.

Brown published numerous books, some in partnership with the Worldwatch Institute and some published by the Earth Policy Institute, which Brown founded in 2001 to raise awareness of environmental issues. His books include *In the Human Interest: A Strategy to Stabilize World Population* (1974), *Building a Sustainable Society* (1981), *Who Will Feed China? Wake-Up Call for a Small Planet* (1995), and *Plan B: Rescuing a Planet Under Stress and a Civilization in Trouble* (2003). In these and other writings, Brown warns about the ecological dangers of over-exploiting the earth's resources and urges those in the world's developed nations to change their lifestyles. He also advised governments and scientists to cooperate in finding solutions to environmental problems. In 2012 Brown was inducted into the Earth Hall of Fame, located in Kyoto, Japan. His autobiography, *Breaking New Ground: A Personal History,* was released in 2013.

In 2015 Brown published another book, *The Great Transition: Shifting from Fossil Fuels to Solar and Wind Energy.* Brown officially retired in June of that year, at the age of eighty-one. The Earth Policy Institute also closed upon his stepping down as president.

Ruth Bamberger

Further Reading

"Biography of Lester Brown." *Earth Policy Institute,* Rutgers University, 2015, www.earth-policy.org/about_epi/C32. Accessed 22 Mar. 2018.

Brown, Lester. *Breaking New Ground: A Personal History.* W. W. Norton, 2013.

Brown, Lester. "Worldwatch." In *Life Stories: World-Renowned Scientists Reflect on Their Lives and on the Future of Life on Earth,* edited by Heather Newbold. University of California Press, 2000.

Nelson, David E. "In Praise of Lester Brown." *Futurist* 42, no. 6 (2008).

Wallis, Victor. "Lester Brown, the Worldwatch Institute, and the Dilemmas of Technocratic Revolution." *Organization and Environment* 10, no. 2 (1997): 109-125.

■ Brownfields

FIELDS OF STUDY: Biochemistry; Biology; Chemistry; Civil Engineering; Ecosystem Management; Urban Planning; Waste Management;

IDENTIFICATION: Abandoned lots or other properties that were once used for commercial or industrial purposes and have the potential to contain harmful contaminants or pollutants

Governments have increasingly encouraged the redevelopment of brownfields, requiring that such redevelopment be preceded by the cleanup of any potentially hazardous substances in the soil and water on these abandoned industrial sites. In addition to the benefits of such cleanup for the environment, brownfield redevelopment reduces urban sprawl and improves property values.

Overview

Brownfields are found in cities and towns throughout the world, usually located in industrial areas. The potential hazards and liability issues associated with such sites' past uses become important when these areas are targeted for redevelopment. In order for municipalities to redevelop brownfields, they must determine liability for any problems on the sites and take any cleanup measures required by law. In the United States, the Comprehensive Environmental Response, Compensation, and Liability Act, widely known as Superfund, mandates liability laws in regard to the cleanup and redevelopment of brownfields and also sets cleanup and development standards. The redevelopment of brownfields can be beneficial to cities, promoting urban and community revitalization through sustainable reuse of land, reducing sprawl, increasing local property taxes, promoting jobs and economic development, and protecting the environment from harmful substances and pollutants.

Barriers to Redevelopment

In the United States, when redevelopment of a brownfield is being considered, the U.S. Environmental Protection Agency (EPA), a state agency, or both must determine the kind and extent of cleanup required and help to determine the liability for the cleanup. Cleanup efforts for brownfield redevelopment are often costly, and it can be difficult for developers to obtain loans to develop potentially hazardous land. Because this is the case, federal, state, and municipal governments may offer some financial contributions under the EPA's Brownfields Initiative, the U.S. Department of Housing and Urban Development (HUD)'s Brownfields Economic Development Initiative, or state and municipal funding programs.

The potential presence of harmful substances and pollutants can increase the difficulty of assessing and cleaning up a brownfield site. Depending on their previous uses, brownfields may contain many hazardous substances, such as petroleum, lead, asbestos, hydrocarbon, pesticides, tributyltin compounds, solvents, and diesel fuels; cleanup is thus imperative before such sites are developed. Sites that are determined to be harmful enough to be hazardous to individuals living and working around them are not

Maine Central Railroad Depot, East Brownfield, Maine.

considered brownfields; rather, these are designated as Superfund sites and are placed on either the Superfund National Priority List or a state priority list for cleanup.

Laws and Regulations

The term "brownfields" was first introduced in 1992 during a congressional hearing. The first legislation concerning brownfields was passed in 1995 when the EPA created its Brownfields Program. Through this program, the EPA seeks to motivate communities, states, and organizations to work together to improve local brownfield sites and use them as resources for redevelopment. Since the 1990's U.S. states and municipalities, along with the federal government, have created programs to provide tax incentives and grants for developers, organizations, and governments to redevelop brownfield sites.

The Small Business Liability Relief and Brownfields Revitalization Act, enacted in 2002, provides support for small businesses to redevelop brownfields through financial assistance and state and local program promotion. HUD's Brownfields Economic Development Initiative provides grants to cities to promote economic and community development; this program is directed toward development in low- and moderate-income neighborhoods, with the aim of promoting economic stability, job creation or retention, business improvement, and increased property taxes.

Benefits of Brownfield Redevelopment

As land pressures and urban sprawl have become increasingly problematic, brownfield redevelopment has grown in importance. The redevelopment of brownfields allows developers to use existing properties within cities rather than create developments that sprawl outward from urban centers, possibly disrupting functioning ecosystems. Additionally, brownfield redevelopment projects often increase the property values in their surrounding areas because of the improvements made to the previously abandoned sites. Brownfield redevelopment also reduces the potential for harm to humans and other forms of life from environmental hazards and pollution, as cleanup of all hazardous substances is a requirement of redevelopment of any brownfield site.

Courtney A. Smith

Further Reading

Davis, Todd S. *Brownfields: A Comprehensive Guide to Redeveloping Contaminated Property.* 2nd ed. American Bar Association, 2002.

De Sousa, Christopher. *Brownfields Redevelopment and the Quest for Sustainability.* Elsevier, 2008.

Dixon, Tim, et al., eds. *Sustainable Brownfield Regeneration: Liveable Places from Problem Spaces.* Blackwell, 2007.

Witkin, James B. *Environmental Aspects of Real Estate and Commercial Transactions: From Brownfields to Green Buildings.* 3rd ed. American Bar Association, 2005.

■ Brucellosis

FIELDS OF STUDY: Biology, Life Sciences, Ecosystems; Ecology, Environment, Environmentalism; Health, Medicine, Disease, Illness; Science

CATEGORY: Human health and the environment

DEFINITION: Infectious disease transmitted from animals to humans by gram-negative bacteria belonging to the genus *Brucella*

Brucellosis is uncommon in the United States and other in-dustrialized countries, but it is found frequently in many geographic regions of the world, including the Mediterra-nean basin, Eastern Europe, the Middle East, Asia, Africa, the Caribbean, South America, and Central America.

Bacteria belonging to the genus *Brucella* are nonmo-tile, exist as non-spore-forming short rods, and live inside their host cells. Different species tend to asso-ciate and infect specific hosts: *Brucella abortus* in cattle, bison, and buffalo; *B. canis* in dogs; *B. melitensis* in sheep, goats, and camels; *B. suis* in pigs, with its other bacterial strains found in European hares, rein-deer, caribou, and rodents. Four species are known to cause infections in humans: *B. abortus, B. canis, B. suis,* and *B. melitensis* (the most common infectious agent in humans).

Animal infection is transmitted through contact with infected animal parts and body fluids, including venereal transmission. Human infection occurs through direct inoculation on skin wounds; inhala-tion of aerosolized bacteria (classified as a class B bio-terrorism agent); occupational exposure in laborato-ries; exposure to fomites (contaminated objects); ingestion of raw meat, unpasteurized milk, and other dairy products; and possibly venereal transmission.

Brucellosis causes premature births in all animal species. In humans it also causes acute, nonspecific symptoms that include undulating fever, chills, weak-ness, headaches, depression, weight loss, and joint and muscle pains. Chronic complications include sacroiliitis, meningitis, endocarditis, and liver ab-scess; in men, epididymo-orchitis may occur.

Brucellosis is diagnosed through isolation and characterization in specialized growth cultures and through various serologic tests. The usual treatment regimen for human infection involves administra-tion of the antibiotics doxycycline and rifampin for six weeks to prevent relapse. No treatment has been developed for infected cattle or pigs. Antibiotic treat-ment has been used with some success in infected dogs and rams.

Prevention of human brucellosis can be achieved through the control of the infection in animals, pas-teurization of milk and related products, and avoid-ance of raw meat ingestion. Animal brucellosis can be prevented through disinfection of contaminated farms and implementation of effective animal health and sanitation programs, which should include steps to ensure that any animals introduced into existing herds, kennels, or other animal groupings are brucellosis-free.

Miriam E. Schwartz

See also: Antibiotics; Mad cow disease

■ Brundtland Commission

FIELDS OF STUDY: Biology, Life Sciences, Ecosystems; Ecology, Environment, Environmentalism; Gov-ernment, Politics, International Relations; His-tory/Biography; Organizations, Agencies, Com-missions, Centers; Renewable Resources

IDENTIFICATION: Body formed by the United Nations to propose long-term environmental strategies for achieving sustainable development through inter-national cooperation

DATE: Established in 1983

The work of the Brundtland Commission raised global awareness of the concept of sustainable development and thus led to the Earth Summit in 1992, which produced the Rio Declaration on Environment and Development as well as conventions on biological diversity and on climate change.

The Brundtland Commission's Report

The report of the Brundtland Commission, published as Our Common Future, *includes the following summary statement of the status of the relationship between nature and humanity near the end of the twentieth century.*

Over the course of this century, the relationship between the human world and the planet that sustains it has undergone a profound change.

When the century began, neither human numbers nor technology had the power radi-cally to alter planetary systems. As the century closes, not only do vastly increased human num-bers and their activities have that power, but major, unintended changes are occurring in the atmosphere, in soils, in water, among plants and animals, and in the relationships among all of these. The rate of change is outstripping the ability of scientific disciplines and our current capabilities to assess and advise.

Robin Attfield

A/42/427
English
Page 225

The most explosive development in the establishment of
chemical and pollutive industry has come in developing
countries. This is an outright danger. The last accidents are
but a few of those that may come. However, we recognize that
considerable responsibility rests on the trade union movement
in the individual countries in pressing for influence on
authorities and managements to avoid both such accidents and
investments from companies that do not follow acceptable
standards.

Technology development has improved environment in the
industrial parts of the world. The new production and
information systems make it more difficult, then, for the
developing countries to use cheap labour as a means to attract
industry to their countries. The future for these countries
does not look very bright, unless the international society
takes it upon itself to affect a sharing of production
technology and resources. This is politically difficult indeed.

> Juul Bjerke
> International Confederation of
> Free Trade Unions, WCED Public
> Hearing, Oslo, 24-25 June 1985

the adoption and enforcement of regulations on the packaging and
labelling of chemicals whose use may be potentially harmful, to
ensure that clear directions are provided in common local
languages. Consumer unions and other non-governmental
organizations should take the lead in collecting and distributing
comparative risk information on ingredients in consumer products
such as cleaning agents and pesticides.

74.   The chemical producer and user industries, as the source of
the risks associated with chemicals and as the greatest
beneficiary of their use should bear the responsibility for
ensuring (and the liability for not ensuring) that their products
meet the highest standards of safety, have the fewest adverse
side effects on health and the environment, and are handled with
appropriate care by workers and users. This will require the
fullest possible disclosure of information about the properties
and production processes of chemical substances and on
comparative risks, not only to the regulatory authorities but
also to the workers, consumers, and residents of the community in
which a chemical industry operates.

5.2 Hazardous Wastes

75.   Industrialized countries generate about 90 per cent of the
world's hazardous wastes. Although all estimates have a wide
margin of error, given considerable differences in definition of
'hazardous waste', in 1984 some 325 million to 375 million tons
were generated worldwide,[36] around 5 million tons of which
were in the newly industrialized and developing areas of the
world.[37]

Scans from the Brundtland Report.

The World Commission on Environment and Development—commonly known as the Brundtland Commission, for its chair, Gro Harlem Brundtland—was established because of growing worldwide recognition of the impacts of human development on the environment. Publication of the commission's 1987 report, titled *Our Common Future* (often referred to as the Brundtland Report), propelled issues of sustainable development to the forefront of international policy debates and decision making.

Our Common Future defines "sustainable development" as "development that meets the needs of the present without compromising the ability of future generations to meet their own needs." The report emphasizes that such development is sustainable socially and environmentally as well as economically, and it urges support for efforts to inaugurate sustainable systems of agriculture, industry, and energy generation that satisfy these requirements. A central theme of the report is the importance of maintaining sustainable levels of population. The report also explicitly states that living creatures have intrinsic value as well as instrumental value (a biocentric stance); the international community, however, replaced this biocentric approach with an anthropocentric one in the Rio Declaration on Environment and Development, which was produced by the 1992 Earth Summit.

Robin Attfield

■ Brundtland, Gro Harlem

FIELDS OF STUDY: Ecology, Environment, Environmentalism; Ethics, Advocacy, Policy, Protest; Government, Politics, International Relations; History/Biography; Politicians, Diplomats; Public Policy, Debates, Controversies

CATEGORIES: Activism and advocacy; ecology and ecosystems

IDENTIFICATION: Norwegian politician, physician, and environmental advocate

Brundtland has been called the "Green Goddess" because of the innovative environmental programs she initiated during her career as prime minister of Norway.

Gro Harlem Brundtland grew up in a politically active family. She graduated from Oslo University Medical School in 1963 and completed a master's degree in public health at Harvard University two years later. She served as a medical officer in Norwegian public health offices and participated in party politics.

In 1974, Brundtland was appointed Norway's minister of the environment. One year later she was named deputy leader of the Norwegian Labor Party. Elected to the Storting, Norway's parliament, in 1977, Brundtland became prime minister and leader of the Norwegian Labor Party from February to October, 1981. She was the youngest person and the first woman to achieve that office. Brundtland was also the first environmental minister to become a country's leader, contemplating political and environmental problems together. A popular prime minister, Brundtland was reelected three times, serving from 1986 to 1989, 1990 to 1993, and 1993 to 1996.

In 1983 Brundtland was chosen to chair the World Commission on Environment and Development sponsored by the United Nations. The twenty-three-member commission worked for three years devising a global agenda for environmental protection, enhancement, and management. Brundtland traveled around the world to assess environmental conditions. The 1987 report *Our Common Future*, also known as the Brundtland Report, explained that environmental deterioration is caused by poverty. It supported the idea of sustainable development—that is, development that does not destroy resources to attain economic growth. Brundtland emphasized that citizens of the world's nations should be active in decision making and accountable for environmental quality. The report raised public awareness of the environment but was criticized by some for being overly optimistic and for offering simplistic solutions.

Brundtland spoke at diplomatic gatherings to convince the world community to accept the report's proposals. She criticized economic development that depletes nonrenewable resources crucial for future generations and urged countries to stop such practices. In an address to the United Nations in 1988, Brundtland stressed the need for international environmental cooperation by citing the example of industrial pollution, which crosses national borders and causes acid rain in other countries. "The environment is where we all live," she said, "and development is what we all do in attempting to improve our lot within that abode. The two are inseparable." Brundtland urged coordinated political support of environmental issues because of her belief that the world shares one economy and environment and thus politicians should adopt global solutions to environmental problems, such as formulating environmentally sound energy policies.

Considered a champion of human rights and environmental quality in Norway and elsewhere, Brundtland has been the recipient of such awards as the Third World Prize. She has been praised for providing opportunities for women in her cabinet and other government positions during her time as prime minister. Despite her environmental rhetoric, Brundtland was criticized for her controversial support of Norwegian whaling in 1993. She resigned as prime minister in October, 1996. In July, 1998, she was named director general of the World Health Organization, a position in which she served until 2003, focusing on the worldwide prevention of disease, especially the improvement of children's health care. In 2007, she was appointed by Secretary-General Ban Ki-moon to serve as one of three United Nations special envoys on climate change.

Elizabeth D. Schafer

Further Reading

Brundtland, Gro Harlem. *Madam Prime Minister: A Life in Power and Politics.* New York: Farrar, Straus and Giroux, 2002.

Palmer, Joy A. "Gro Harlem Brundtland, 1939-   ." In *Fifty Key Thinkers on the Environment,* edited by Joy A. Palmer. New York: Routledge, 2001.

See also: Environmental economics; International Whaling Commission; *Our Common Future;* Sustainable development; United Nations Commission on Sustainable Development; United Nations Conference on the Human Environment

---

■ Burroughs, John

FIELDS OF STUDY: History/Biography; Popular Culture, Media, Publishing; Authors, Writers; Ecology, Environment, Environmentalism

CATEGORIES: Activism and advocacy; preservation and wilderness issues

IDENTIFICATION: American nature writer

Through his best-selling books, Burroughs raised Americans' awareness of the beauty of nature and the importance of preserving it.

John Burroughs grew up on a farm in the Catskill Mountains in New York, spending as much time as he could outdoors. Around the age of twenty, he decided that he would try to earn his living as a writer. After a brief teaching career, he spent ten years as a clerk in the U.S. Treasury Department in Washington, D.C. As a sideline, he published magazine essays about natural history and philosophy, always working to sharpen his writing skills. During these years he published his first book, *Notes on Walt Whitman as Poet and Person* (1867), the first biography of the great poet, who had also been a government clerk and who was Burroughs's personal friend.

Burroughs's first volume of essays, *Wake-Robin* (1871), was representative of the twenty-two collections that would follow: It featured close observations of natural history and commentary about simple country life, was made up mostly of essays (including such titles as "Birds' Nests" and "In the Hemlocks") that had been previously published in magazines, and won immediate acclaim. To Burroughs's first readers, the genre of nature writing was new and captivating, and Burroughs soon became its most popular practitioner. Sure now that he could live by his pen, he left his government job and moved back to New York, establishing a small fruit farm on the banks of the Hudson River in 1873. He continued to publish essays in some of the most popular magazines of his day and collected them into new books approximately every two years. His titles reveal something of the simple wonder that informs these books: *Fresh Fields* (1885), *Bird and Bough* (1906), and *Under the Apple-Trees* (1916).

Burroughs's work remained popular throughout his lifetime—a rare achievement for a writer. He formed lasting friendships with many of his admirers, including John Muir, Thomas Edison, and Henry Ford. Two more friendships led to books: *John James Audubon* (1902), an appreciation and biography, and *Camping with President Roosevelt* (1906).

After Burroughs's death in 1921, the John Burroughs Association was founded and the John Burroughs Sanctuary was established to preserve his property and many of his books in West Park, New York. Burroughs continues to be acknowledged as a pioneer and a master of the genre of nature writing,

John Burroughs, right, poses in Alaska in 1899 with naturalist and preservationist John Muir, one of the many admirers of Burroughs's nature writings. (Library of Congress)

and many of his books remain in print. The John Burroughs Association presents two annual awards for nature writing published in the preceding year: one to the author of an outstanding natural history essay and one to the author of a distinguished book of natural history. In 1997 Burroughs was named a charter member of the Ecology Hall of Fame in Santa Cruz, California.

Cynthia A. Bily

Further Reading

Walker, Charlotte Zoë, ed. *Sharp Eyes: John Burroughs and American Nature Writing.* Syracuse, N.Y.: Syracuse University Press, 2000.

Warren, James Perrin. *John Burroughs and the Place of Nature.* Athens: University of Georgia Press, 2006.

See also: Audubon, John James; Muir, John; Roosevelt, Theodore; Thoreau, Henry David

C

■ Captive breeding

FIELDS OF STUDY: Biology, Life Sciences, Ecosystems;
Animals, Zoology, Marine Biology; Ecology, Environment, Environmentalism
DEFINITION: Selective breeding of an endangered or
threatened species in captivity

*Captive breeding is sometimes the only way to save a species
from extinction. Captive-bred animals are often returned to
their native habitats once their populations have sufficiently
recovered and the animals have been properly conditioned to
survive in the wild.*

As conditions in zoos steadily improved throughout
the twentieth century and captive animals began
breeding, scientists realized that the breeding of
threatened and endangered species in captivity could
save some species that would otherwise become extinct. Many zoos began to shift their priorities from
entertainment to wildlife conservation in the late
1970s.

Initially, zoo animals were allowed to breed
without consideration of their genetic or health
status—the only guiding principle involved was
"more is better." Zoo populations, however, are far
too small to sustain healthy breeding; depending on
the species, a healthy breeding population might
range from seventy-five to four hundred animals.
The inbreeding that resulted from early zoo policies
led to fewer offspring, increased rates of birth defects, and susceptibility to disease. In response, the
Association of Zoos and Aquariums established the
Species Survival Plan (SSP) in 1981 to increase the
number of animals in the breeding pool. A computerized mating system, the SSP maintains genetic records of all captive animals of particular species, allowing zoos to exchange animals without fear of
inbreeding. By 2014 there were 450 SSP programs
covering hundreds of species.

In the 1990s captive breeding began to lose some
of its appeal as the costs began to outweigh the benefits. In vitro fertilization of gorillas can cost up to
$75,000, and the cost of the California Condor Recovery Plan was an estimated $20 million between
1974 and the late 1990s. Critics of captive-breeding
programs—and zoos in general—argue that such
large amounts of money could be better spent preserving animals' natural habitats. Opponents of the
US Endangered Species Act (1973) have also used
the existence of captive-breeding programs as an argument against habitat protection laws.

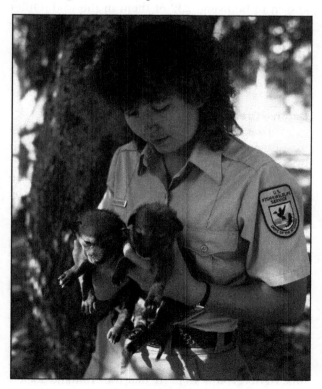

*FWS staff with two red wolf pups bred in captivity. The red wolf is
an endangered species that is currently found in the wild only as
experimental populations in Tennessee and North Carolina. By
George Gentry/U.S. Fish and Wildlife Service.*

Another drawback of SSPs and captive breeding in general is the problem of surplus animals. Breeding endangered species may be a good public relations tactic, but the culling of surplus animals is definitely not. One large issue faced by captive-breeding programs is what is to be done with animals that are genetically inferior or past breeding age, or those that have been hybridized in ways that would contaminate the gene pool. Contraceptive implants and separation are two common solutions, but some surplus animals end up in game parks and hunting preserves.

Despite its drawbacks, captive breeding remains the only option for some species, the most famous of which is the California condor. In an extraordinary measure of intervention, the last nine known condors in the wild were captured in 1985, bringing the total number in captivity to twenty-seven. By 1992 captive breeding had brought the population up to 134, and scientists gradually began returning birds to their natural habitat. By 2014, 432 condors were known to be living, 232 of them in the wild. Other species that have been saved by captive breeding include the black-footed ferret, the Arabian oryx, Przewalski's horse, and Père David's deer; the first three of these have been reintroduced, in limited numbers, into their original habitats.

Captive Breeding in Amusement Parks

Zoos are not the only amusement venues that breed in captivity or that have come under fire for their practices. Most aquariums, for example, breed their freshwater fish in captivity. saltwater fish have proven more difficult to breed in captivity. As of 2011, the vast majority of saltwater fish were still caught in the wild, with grave effects on the coral reefs where many of them lived. In the cases of these species, breeding in captivity could ultimately have positive environmental effects.

There is, however, a very famous and controversial case of breeding marine life in captivity is that of SeaWorld and orca whales. SeaWorld has bred these animals in captivity for decades and trained them for performance in their shows. The group of theme parks had long been the target of criticism from animal rights groups, in particular the Humane Society of the United States (HSUS) for their treatment of their animals. On February 24, 2010, SeaWorld trainer Dawn Brancheau was killed by an orca named Tilikum. Tilikum was involved in two previous trainer

deaths. While Tilikum was not born in captivity, he was caught at the age of two and raised in captivity for over thirty years. Following the 2010 incident, a documentary was released in 2013, called *Blackfish*, that addressed the event and SeaWorld's treatment of their captive animals, the aggression of the animals against each other in captivity, and the appropriateness of keeping orcas at all. In March 2016, following the backlash of those concerned for the life of the whales and safety of their trainers, as well as decreased park attendance, SeaWorld announced that it would stop its breeding of orcas and phase out the theatrical performances using them.

P. S. Ramsey

Further Reading

"California Condor." *National Park Service*. US Dept. of the Interior, 17 Nov. 2014. Web. 26 Jan. 2015.

Jamieson, Amber. "SeaWorld Decides to Stop Killer Whale Breeding Program." *Guardian*. Guardian News and Media, 17 Mar. 2016. Web. 19 Apr. 2016.

Loftin, Robert W. "Captive Breeding of Endangered Species." *Preserving Wildlife: An International Perspective*. Ed. Mark A. Michael. Amherst: Humanity, 2000. Print.

Moir, John. *Return of the Condor: The Race to Save Our Largest Bird from Extinction*. Guilford: Lyons, 2006. Print.

Zimmerman, Tim. "Killer in the Pool." *Outside*. Mariah Media, 30 July 2010. Web. 19 Apr. 2016.

■ Carbon dioxide air capture

FIELDS OF STUDY: Technology and Applied Science; Industries, Commercial Products; Inventions; Pollution, Emissions, Toxic Waste, Hazardous Materials

DEFINITION: The trapping or elimination of carbon dioxide emitted from industrial or commercial sources before it can enter the atmosphere

Carbon dioxide capture and sequestration or storage is anticipated to play a bridging role between carbon dependence and a sustainable low-carbon energy future by serving as the critical enabling technology that will lead to a significant reduction in CO_2 release into the air while allowing industrial processes such as the burning of coal for power generation to continue to meet global energy needs.

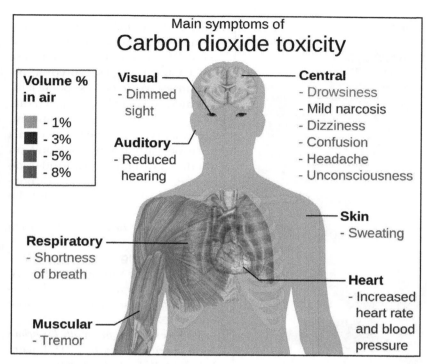

Main symptoms of
Carbon dioxide toxicity

**Volume %
in air**

- 1%
- 3%
- 5%
- 8%

Visual
- Dimmed
  sight

Auditory
- Reduced
  hearing

Central
- Drowsiness
- Mild narcosis
- Dizziness
- Confusion
- Headache
- Unconsciousness

Skin
- Sweating

Heart
- Increased
  heart rate
  and blood
  pressure

Respiratory
- Shortness
  of breath

Muscular
- Tremor

Main symptoms of carbon dioxide toxicity. Häggström, Mikael. "Medical gallery of Mikael Häggström 2014". Wikiversity Journal of Medicine

The term "carbon dioxide air capture" is used to describe a set of technologies aimed at preventing the carbon dioxide (CO_2) emitted from industrial or commercial sources from entering the atmosphere. The processes involved are also commonly referred to as carbon dioxide capture and sequestration or carbon capture and storage (CCS). The geoengineering technique of scrubbing (absorbing) CO_2 from ambient air is also sometimes referred to as CSS, as are biological techniques that employ organisms (such as plankton) and organic matter to capture CO_2 from the air.

In CCS, the process of capturing CO_2 from a large emissions source is often coupled with the subsequent compression of the gas, storage of the gas (for example, by injecting it into deep underground geological formations or into deep ocean masses called saline aquifers, or by converting it into the form of mineral carbonate), and recycling of the gas to enhance industrial processes, such as that seen in CO_2-assisted enhanced oil recovery (EOR), in which CO_2 gas is injected into an oil-bearing stratum under high pressure to cause oil to be displaced upward.

The CCS process begins with the capture of CO_2 generated by a power station or other industrial facility, such as a cement factory, steelworks, or oil refinery. The CO_2 can be captured before, during, or after the source's combustion (burning) of fossil fuels. Precombustion capture involves the separation of fossil fuels into hydrogen and CO_2 before they are burned. For example, in the instance of coal, the process involves the conversion of coal into a synthetic gas (syngas) made up of carbon monoxide and hydrogen. The syngas is reacted further with steam to produce a CO_2-hydrogen mix. Further processing produces a mix with a high concentration of CO_2, which is separated out. The remaining hydrogen is then utilized as a CO_2-free energy source that produces only heat and water vapor when combusted. Precombustion capture technology has been widely implemented in the fertilizer industry as well as in natural gas forming.

In oxy-fuel combustion, burning of the fossil fuel in oxygen instead of air results in an exhaust gas that is CO_2-free. This technology is commonly used in the glass furnace industry. In postcombustion capture, the CO_2 is separated from flue (exhaust) gases after the combustion of fossil fuels. The CO_2 content is usually much lower than in the gas that is separated during oxy-fuel combustion or precombustion capture, with the volume of CO_2 in the range of 3 percent to 15 percent by volume.

Challenges to Implementation
One challenge facing CCS is the demonstration of its efficacy and safety on an industrial scale at competitive cost. While CCS is known to be safe and is well understood in terms of the fundamental science and technical requirements, no evidence has been gathered regarding the process's long-term impacts on the environment (for example, the safety of storing CO_2 in geological formations) or possible danger to humans (for instance, if CO_2 leaks from storage).

CCS applied to a modern power plant could reduce CO_2 emissions by up to 90 percent compared to an equivalent plant with no CCS devices, but the

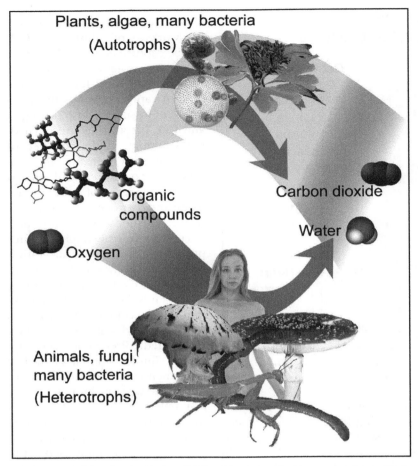

Autotrophs can use carbon dioxide (CO2) and water to form oxygen and complex organic compounds, mainly through the process of photosynthesis. All organisms can use such compounds to again form CO2 and water through cellular respiration. Derivative by Mikael Häggström, using originals by Laghi l, BorgQueen, Benjah-bmm27, Rkitko, Bobisbob, Jacek FH, Laghi L and Jynto.

and international levels the long-term rights, liabilities, and technical requirements associated with the use of CCS technologies. Moreover, before investors, scientists, politicians, and industries can be persuaded that CCS is a worthwhile investment, agreements need to be reached on a price on carbon emissions and on whether a carbon tax, cap-and-trade regime, or other carbon-trading/taxation framework will be implemented.

Rena Christina Tabata

Further Reading

Hanjalić, K., R. van de Krol, and A. Lekić, eds. *Sustainable Energy Technologies: Options and Prospects.* London: Springer, 2008.

Kutz, Myer. *Environmentally Conscious Fossil Energy Production.* Hoboken, N.J.: John Wiley & Sons, 2009.

Rackley, Steve. *Carbon Capture and Storage.* Boston: Butterworth-Heinemann, 2009.

Rojey, Alexandre. *Energy and Climate: How to Achieve a Successful Energy Transition.* Chichester, England: John Wiley & Sons, 2009.

Shiosani, Fereidoon P. *Generating Electricity in a Carbon-Constrained World.* Burlington, Mass.: Academic Press, 2009.

implementation of CO_2 capture is significantly more expensive than the use of traditional systems of emissions control. For example, capturing and compressing CO_2 increases the fuel requirement of a coal-fired plant by as much as 25-40 percent. It is estimated that the cost of energy produced by a new power plant with CCS is from 21 percent to 91 percent higher than that produced by a non-CCS power plant.

Aside from the cost and technical challenges of CCS, a regulatory framework needs to be established to support CCS and to clarify at regional, national,

■ Carbon footprint

FIELDS OF STUDY: Biology, Life Sciences, Ecosystems; Ecology, Environment, Environmentalism; Energy and Energy Resources; Pollution, Emissions, Toxic Waste, Hazardous Materials; Mathematics, Measurement, Mapping, Logic; Climate and Climate Change; Mathematics, Measurement, Mapping, Logic; Climate and Climate Change; Ecology, Environment, Environmentalism; Energy and Energy Resources; Pollution, Emissions, Toxic Waste, Hazardous Materials

CATEGORIES: Resources and resource management; energy and energy use

DEFINITION: Total amount of greenhouse gases produced to directly and indirectly support a certain human activity or a representative lifestyle, usually expressed in equivalent tons of carbon dioxide

The use of carbon footprint estimates allows individuals, organizations, and nations to understand their relative contribution to emissions of greenhouse gases, which have been linked to global warming. In turn, these estimates are used in the purchase of carbon offsets and in gauging progress toward goals set under international agreements such as the Kyoto Protocol.

The concept of the carbon footprint provides a useful way for individuals and organizations to understand their impact in contributing to global warming. The calculation of a carbon footprint has been extended to include assessment of the greenhouse gas contributions made by the production and shipment of individual products. The general concept is that once the magnitude of a carbon footprint is known, a strategy can be devised to reduce that footprint. Examples of reduction methods include technological developments, carbon capture, and improved process and product management. Additionally, carbon offsetting through the development of alternative projects, such as solar or wind power, is a common way to reduce carbon footprints.

The concept and name of the carbon footprint originate from the concept of the ecological footprint. The carbon footprint is related to both the ecological footprint and the overarching life-cycle assessment (LCA) approach. A carbon footprint is composed of two elements: the primary, or direct, footprint and the secondary, or indirect, footprint. The primary footprint is the amount of direct carbon dioxide (CO_2) emissions stemming from the burning of fuels—that is, for domestic energy consumption and transportation. The secondary footprint is the amount of indirect CO_2 emissions caused over the whole life cycle of

products, including the manufacture and eventual breakdown of the products.

Calculation of a carbon footprint generally begins with CO_2 emissions based on fuel consumption. Greenhouse gases other than CO_2 are typically translated to CO_2 equivalents through conversion rates, based on mass. Common greenhouse gases include methane, nitrous oxide, and chlorofluorocarbons (CFCs). To allow comparisons among the varied effects of different gases on the environment, scientists have developed methods of determining the greenhouse potency (global warming potential) of gases relative to that of carbon dioxide.

The calculation of carbon footprints for products is becoming mainstream in people's understanding of products and lifestyle adjustments to reduce greenhouse gas emissions. These carbon footprint analyses are also useful in guiding regulation. For example, the U.S. Environmental Protection Agency has calculated carbon footprints for paper, plastic, glass, cans, computers, and tires, among other materials. Researchers in Australia, Korea, and the United States have addressed the carbon footprints of paved roads. The United Kingdom Carbon Trust has

Average Carbon Footprints Around the World

NATION	AVERAGE CARBON FOOTPRINT PER CAPITA, 2004 (METRIC TONS)
Kuwait	38.00
United States	20.40
Australia	16.30
Russia	10.50
Germany	9.79
United Kingdom	9.79
Japan	9.84
Italy	7.69
China	3.84
India	1.21

Source: Data from U.S. Department of Energy.

worked with manufacturers on assessing foods, shirts, and detergents.

The ready availability of carbon footprint calculators on the Internet has led many individuals to analyze their own carbon footprints. These calculators ask questions concerning lifestyle (such as how many times a year an individual takes airline flights) to arrive at an approximate carbon footprint.

On an international scale, the 1997 Kyoto Protocol defines targets and timetables for reductions in greenhouse gas emissions. An understanding of carbon footprints is necessary to the implementation of the flexible mechanisms defined under this international agreement (certified emission reduction, joint implementation, and emissions trading), which require nations to determine necessary levels of reduction and to maintain benchmarking activities.

Jennifer F. Helgeson

Further Reading

Brown, Marilyn A., Frank Southworth, and Andrea Sarzynski. *Shrinking the Carbon Footprint of Metropolitan America.* Washington, D.C.: Brookings Institution Press, 2008.

Sim, Stuart. *The Carbon Footprint Wars: What Might Happen If We Retreat from Globalization?* Edinburgh: Edinburgh University Press, 2009.

Weber, Christopher L., and H. Scott Matthews. "Quantifying the Global and Distributional Aspects of American Household Carbon Footprint." *Ecological Economics* 66 (June, 2008): 379-391.

Wiedmann, Thomas, and Jan Minx. "A Definition of 'Carbon Footprint.'" In *Ecological Economics Research Trends*, edited by Carolyn C. Pertsova. Hauppauge, N.Y.: Nova Science, 2007.

See also: Carbon dioxide; Ecological footprint; Fossil fuels; Global warming; Life-cycle assessment

---

■ Carbon monoxide

FIELDS OF STUDY: Chemistry; Elements, Substances, Chemicals, Compounds; Pollution, Emissions, Toxic Waste, Hazardous Materials

CATEGORIES: Pollutants and toxins; atmosphere and air pollution

DEFINITION: Odorless and colorless toxic gas in which molecules consist of one carbon atom and one oxygen atom

The air pollutant carbon monoxide is a component of automobile exhaust emissions, but the gas is perhaps most dangerous indoors, where it can cause accidental death by asphyxiation.

Carbon monoxide (CO), an indoor and outdoor air pollutant, is formed by incomplete combustion of fossil fuels when insufficient oxygen is present to convert carbon compounds to nontoxic carbon dioxide. Indoors, CO may come from unvented kerosene and gas space heaters; leaking or improperly vented chimneys, furnaces, gas water heaters, wood stoves, gas stoves, and fireplaces; generators and other gasoline-powered equipment; automobile exhaust from attached garages; and tobacco smoke. Outdoors, CO is present in small amounts naturally in the atmosphere, chiefly as a product of volcanic activity, but also from naturally occurring fires.

Motor vehicle exhaust contributes about 56 percent of all CO emissions in the United States. The highest levels of CO occur in areas with heavy traffic congestion, and in cities, 85-95 percent of all CO emissions may come from motor vehicle exhaust. Other nonroad engines and vehicles (such as construction equipment and boats) contribute about 22 percent of CO emissions nationwide. Additional sources of CO emissions include industrial processes (metals processing and chemical manufacturing) and residential wood burning. The highest levels of outdoor CO typically occur during the winter months, for three primary reasons: Motor vehicles need more fuel to start at cold temperatures, some emissions-control devices (oxygen sensors and catalytic converters) operate less efficiently in the cold, and temperature inversion conditions, which trap CO near the ground beneath a layer of warm air, are more frequent.

CO enters the bloodstream through the lungs and binds to the blood protein hemoglobin, the main function of which is to transport oxygen to body tissues, including vital organs such as the heart and brain. The CO and hemoglobin combine to form the compound carboxyhemoglobin, and the hemoglobin is no longer available for transporting oxygen. In closed indoor environments, the level of carboxyhemoglobin in the body can rise to toxic levels and eventually result in asphyxiation.

People with heart disease are especially sensitive to CO poisoning because of its reduction of oxygen transport through the blood; they may experience

Fusarium ear rot, caused by the fungi Fusarium verticillioides and F. proliferatum, may typically be a more common ear rot of corn. By UIUC

chest pain if they breathe the gas. Infants, elderly persons, and individuals with respiratory diseases are also particularly sensitive to CO. CO can affect healthy individuals by impairing exercise capacity, visual perception, manual dexterity, learning ability, and the ability to perform complex tasks.

During the early 1970's, the U.S. Environmental Protection Agency (EPA) set two national air-quality standards for CO in motor vehicle emissions: a one-hour standard of 35 parts per million (the highest allowable level of CO measured in ambient air over a one-hour period) and an eight-hour standard of 9 parts per million. The EPA also mandated reductions in emissions from large industrial facilities. Advances in vehicle technologies and the development of cleaner fuels have resulted in reductions in CO emissions. Across the United States, air-quality stations measure the levels of CO (and other pollutants) in the air on a regular basis. The measurements are compared with the EPA standards, and areas that

have CO levels that exceed the standards are required to develop and carry out plans to reduce their CO emissions. As a result of these steps, CO emissions from automobiles, motorcycles, and light- and heavy-duty trucks have been reduced by more than 40 percent since 1970. The greatest reduction has been the nearly 60 percent decrease in automobile emissions of CO.

Bernard Jacobson

Further Reading

Kleinman, Michael T. "Carbon Monoxide." In *Environmental Toxicants: Human Exposures and Their Health Effects*, edited by Morton Lippmann. 3d ed. Hoboken, N.J.: John Wiley & Sons, 2009.

Penney, David G., ed. *Carbon Monoxide Poisoning.* Boca Raton, Fla.: CRC Press, 2008.

See also: Air pollution; Automobile emissions; Catalytic converters; Indoor air pollution; Smog

---

■ Carpooling

FIELDS OF STUDY: Economics, Business, Production, Commerce; Energy and Energy Resources; Ethics, Advocacy, Policy, Protest; Ecology, Environment, Environmentalism

DEFINITION: Shared use of vehicles for private journeys

A popular method of reducing commuting costs for individuals, carpooling offers substantial benefits to communities and to the environment by reducing traffic congestion, fuel consumption, and pollution of the atmosphere.

Carpooling is often an informal practice in which friends, neighbors, or colleagues ride together in their daily commutes. It can also involve extensive formal networks of drivers and riders. The forming of a car pool typically starts with the assembly of a list of people, such as employees of a given company or people living in the same area, interested in sharing rides to work or other destinations. The individuals on the list then contact one another and make arrangements. Fixed and recurring journeys, such as a shared commuting route, are the most common framework for organizing carpooling. Alternatively, in some cities certain roadside locations are popular sites where drivers riding alone in their vehicles can

American poster promoting carpooling during WWII. Features Uncle Sam saying "Fill those empty seats. Car sharing is a must."

pick up passengers and thus take advantage of high-occupancy vehicle (HOV) highway lanes. The costs of carpooling journeys are usually shared among drivers and riders in various ways; participants may rotate the cars used, split rental or fuel charges, or pay the owner of the car.

Proponents of the wider adoption of carpooling schemes note that the practice of carpooling has several benefits. Among these are cost savings for carpoolers in terms of reduced fuel usage and car wear; carpooling is also generally cheaper than public transport because salaried drivers are not required. Most participants are relieved of the stresses of driving, and many carpoolers share driving duties, so all participants receive this benefit over time; the problem of finding parking spaces is also greatly reduced. From the community perspective, traffic congestion is reduced, as is the strain on parking

services. Environmental benefits include reduced fuel consumption and an accompanying reduction in exhaust emissions. Other benefits connected with carpooling include increased mobility for nondrivers and for those in rural areas who lack access to public transport.

Local communities, including private companies and government authorities, support carpooling in various ways. The most visible of these is the provision of HOV lanes on busy routes; these specially marked lanes on freeways and other roads are reserved for public transportation vehicles and for private automobiles and trucks carrying multiple occupants. Preferential parking is also assigned to carpooling vehicles in some cities, and some employers offer financial incentives to encourage their employees to carpool. To support carpooling further, some employers provide guaranteed ride services—often in the form of prepaid taxi services—for occasions when carpooling arrangements break down and individual passengers are left without drivers.

An important development in carpooling is the transition from relatively static and prearranged carpooling to what has been called dynamic carpooling. Unlike habitual ride sharing, dynamic carpooling enables individuals to find drivers for one-time journeys at short notice. Such real-time and flexible matching of riders and drivers has become possible through technological innovations such as the widespread use of smartphones and the development of apps. Other technologies that play a role in the expansion and viability of dynamic carpooling are the ability to utilize global positioning systems (GPS) for drivers to navigate routes, and social networking to coordinate and vet drivers with passengers. Mobile-pay technologies also have the potential to simplify recordkeeping in dynamic carpooling transactions. Positive impacts of GPS and social networking might include efficiency and convenience for commuters, resulting in less environmental impact. Utilization of social networking allows the potential of a wider rider pool. Negatives might include compromised privacy or personal data, which could create passenger safety issues. Since the beginning of the twenty-first century, several pilot schemes in Europe and the United States have examined the feasibility of large-scale real-time matching. The aim is to establish dynamic carpooling as a flexible and convenient mode of transportation. An example is the Covoiturage carpooling scheme operating in France.

The success of carpooling schemes depends on the attainment of "critical mass"—a sufficiently large number of participants to ensure that both riders and drivers have confidence in the program. Carpooling schemes might struggle in this regard for several reasons. These include individual drivers' unwillingness to surrender the flexibility and freedom of a personal car, attachment to the personal space and privacy provided by a private car, fears about a possible lack of safety, and the perception of marginal utility—that is, once a car has been purchased and taxed, individual journeys seem to be inexpensive.

Andrew Lambert

Further Reading

Balbus, John, and Dushana Yoganathan Triola. "Transportation and Health." In *Environmental Health: From Global to Local,* edited by Howard Frumkin. 2d ed. Hoboken, N.J.: John Wiley & Sons, 2010. Print.

Deakin, Elizabeth, et al. "Dynamic Ridesharing." *Access,* no. 40, Spring 2012, pp. 23–28, www.access-magazine.org/wp-content/uploads/sites/7/2016/01/access40_dynamicridesharing.pdf. Accessed 22 Mar. 2018.

Friginal, Jesús, et al. "Towards Privacy-Driven Design of a Dynamic Carpooling System." *Pervasive and Mobile Computing,* vol. 14, Oct. 2014, pp. 71–82, doi.org/10.1016/j.pmcj.2014.05.009. Accessed 22 Mar. 2018.

Kemp, Roger L., ed. *Cities and Cars: A Handbook of Best Practices.* Jefferson, N.C.: McFarland, 2007. Print.

Marzotto, Toni, Vicky Moshier Burnor, and Gordon Scott Bonham. *The Evolution of Public Policy: Cars and the Environment.* Boulder, Colo.: Lynne Rienner, 2000. Print.

Moavenzadeh, F., and M. J. Markow. "Transportation Policy and Environmental Sustainability." In *Moving Millions: Transport Strategies for Sustainable Development in Megacities.* New York: Springer, 2007. Print.

Turnbell, Nancy. *Casual Carpooling: An Analysis of Its Mechanics and Merits.* Hauppauge: Nova Science, 2014. Print.

■ Carter, Jimmy

FIELDS OF STUDY: Government, Politics, International Relations; Politicians, Diplomats; Public Policy, Debates, Controversies; Ecology, Environment, Environmentalism; Energy and Energy Resources

CATEGORY: Preservation and wilderness issues

IDENTIFICATION: American politician who served as governor of Georgia and as president of the United States

During his political career, Carter made many decisions that demonstrated an environmentalist agenda.

Jimmy Carter was born into a family that owned a general store and farm in the small community of Plains, Georgia. He was appointed to the U.S. Naval Academy, graduating in 1946, and served in the Navy until his father's death in 1953, when he assumed his father's business responsibilities.

Carter expanded his family's businesses and successfully ran for local political office. He was elected to the Georgia Senate in 1962 and 1964. He was elected governor of Georgia in 1970 and served in the office from 1971 to 1975. Governor Carter reorganized the state government, consolidating many functions and putting all environmental agencies under the Department of Natural Resources. He rejected a U.S. Army Corps of Engineers plan to dam the Flint River, the last free-flowing large river in western Georgia. This was apparently the first such action ever taken by a governor of a U.S. state. He helped to arrange for the greater part of Cumberland Island to be given to the state of Georgia; it would later become Cumberland Island National Seashore. He also began acquiring land along the Chattahoochee River in Atlanta for state parks; these later became parts of the Chattahoochee River National Recreation Area.

Carter ran for the U.S. presidency in 1976 and won the election by a narrow margin over incumbent Gerald Ford. Early in his term, President Carter vetoed a public works bill that included nineteen water projects that he considered economically unjustified and environmentally unsound. Under intense political pressure he later signed a compromise bill that included nine of the projects. He also issued executive orders that directed federal agencies to protect or restore wetlands and floodplains wherever possible as a matter of government policy.

During the Carter administration a large number of important environmental acts were passed and signed into law by the president. These included the Alaska National Interest Lands Conservation Act (1980), the Fish and Wildlife Conservation Act (1980), and the Comprehensive Environmental Response, Compensation, and Liability Act, commonly referred to as Superfund (1980). It is remarkable that all of this was accomplished in the midst of a very difficult single term in office. President Carter's term began with a worldwide economic recession and instability in the international petroleum market, resulting in large national budget deficits, severe inflation, and high interest rates; it ended with the overthrow of the shah of Iran and the seizure of the U.S. embassy in Iran by the revolutionary Islamic government.

In response to the petroleum market problem, President Carter requested the creation of a cabinet-level Department of Energy. The mission of this department included research on reducing American dependence on fossil fuels and the development of alternative energy resources. Over the decades since, this research has had very desirable environmental effects.

Robert E. Carver

Further Reading

Horowitz, Daniel. *Jimmy Carter and the Energy Crisis of the 1970s: A Brief History with Documents.* Boston: Bedford/St. Martin's Press, 2005.

Stine, Jeffrey K. "Environmental Policy During the Carter Presidency." In *The Carter Presidency: Policy Choices in the Post-New Deal Era,* edited by Gary M. Fink and Hugh Davis Graham. Lawrence: University Press of Kansas, 1998.

See also: Alaska National Interest Lands Conservation Act; Department of Energy, U.S.; Environmental law, U.S.; Nuclear regulatory policy; Superfund

■ Cash for Clunkers

FIELDS OF STUDY: Government, Politics, International Relations; Laws, Acts, Resolutions; Economics, Business, Production, Commerce; Energy and Energy Resources; Pollution, Emissions, Toxic Waste, Hazardous Materials; Economics, Business, Production, Commerce; Energy and Energy Resources; Laws, Acts, Resolutions; Pollution, Emissions, Toxic Waste, Hazardous Materials

IDENTIFICATION: US federal government program that briefly subsidized purchases of cleaner-running and more fuel-efficient vehicles

DATES: June 24–August 24, 2009

The three goals of the Cash for Clunkers program were to help reduce American dependence on foreign oil, help reduce carbon emissions from passenger vehicles, and provide a stimulus to the American automobile industry. It at least partly achieved the first two goals, but most critics, backed by two studies, assert that it was essentially a failed program.

Enacted on June 24, 2009, and officially known as the Car Allowance Rebate System (CARS), the popularly called Cash for Clunkers program made a total of $3 billion available to subsidize the private purchase of more fuel-efficient automobiles, trucks, sport utility vehicles (SUVs), and vans before it was terminated ahead of schedule on August 24 because its funding had been exhausted by popular demand. The subsidies were disbursed as credits toward the purchase of only new vehicles and, depending on the magnitude of the improvement in miles per gallon (mpg) offered by the new vehicle, the individual credits were either $4,500 (for major mpg gains) or $3,500 (for lesser gains). New purchases had to cost less than $45,000, trade-ins generally had to have combined city and highway mileage ratings of 18 mpg or less, and all trade-ins were to be scrapped, not resold.

A similar program had been pursued previously by the Slovak Republic in Europe, and other countries were considering adopting such programs when the US Congress enacted Cash for Clunkers. The program's goals were to stimulate sales in the sagging American auto industry, to reduce American

"Death Row" of CFC cars. By 293.xx.xxx.xx (Own work)

Further Reading

Bergman, Garry D. *Cash for Clunkers and the Auto Industry: Background, Lessons, and Results.* Hauppauge: Nova Science, 2010. Print.

Foster, Ben, and Therese Langer. *Cash for Clunkers: A Missed Opportunity for Fuel Economy Gains.* Washington, DC: Amer. Council for an Energy-Efficient Economy, 2011. Digital file.

Gayer, Ted, and Emily Parker. "Cash for Clunkers: An Evaluation of the Car Allowance Rebate System." *Brookings.* Brookings Inst., 30 Oct. 2013. Web. 29 Jan. 2015.

Grabell, Michael. *Money Well Spent? The Truth behind the Trillion Dollar Stimulus, the Biggest Economic Recovery Plan in History.* New York: PublicAffairs, 2012. Print.

Plumer, Brad. "Almost Anything Would Have Been Better Stimulus than 'Cash for Clunkers.'" *Washington Post.* Washington Post, 31 Oct. 2013. Web. 29 Jan. 2015.

dependence on foreign energy by replacing "gas guzzlers" with more fuel-efficient vehicles, and to reduce carbon emissions emanating from older, fossil-fuel-burning vehicle engines.

The program had some success in achieving the second and third of these goals. By definition, replacing low-mileage vehicles with higher-mileage vehicles, all else (such as driving distances) remaining even, reduced the US demand for gasoline and resulted in lower carbon emissions per car on the road. To the extent that some of those cars were also hybrids, which run part of the time on their self-charging batteries, the benefit was enhanced. However, critics, backed by a 2013 study by the Brookings Institute and another by Texas A&M researchers, correctly noted that the program only subsidized at most slightly more than 690,000 dealer transactions involving more fuel-efficient vehicles—a proverbial drop in the ocean for a country with more than 250 million registered passenger vehicles. Morever, many American drivers were already being motivated to acquire more fuel-efficient vehicles by steep rises in gasoline prices in the months preceding initiation of the program.

Joseph R. Rudolph, Jr.

Catalytic converters

FIELDS OF STUDY: Technology and Applied Science; Inventions; Pollution, Emissions, Toxic Waste, Hazardous Materials

CATEGORY: Atmosphere and air pollution

DEFINITION: Devices that convert carbon monoxide, hydrocarbons, and nitrogen oxides in automobile exhaust gases into less harmful substances

The use of catalytic converters has significantly reduced air pollution caused by automobile exhaust.

Since their invention in the late nineteenth century, automobiles have revolutionized society. However, automobiles represented a significant new source of air pollution, particularly in urban areas. As early as 1943, the effects of automobile exhaust emissions on air quality were noted in the Los Angeles area. In 1952 A. J. Haagen-Smit showed that the interaction of nitrogen oxides and hydrocarbons from automobile exhaust with sunlight results in the formation of secondary pollutants, such as peroxyacetyl nitrates (PAN) and ozone. This new form of air pollution, termed photochemical or Los Angeles smog, was soon recognized as a major pollution problem in urban atmospheres.

In 1961 the state of California began regulating the release of pollutants from automobiles. Two years later, the first federal emission standards were imposed as part of the 1963 Clean Air Act. As further restrictions on automobile emissions were introduced in the 1960's and early 1970's, new devices were developed to aid in reducing emissions. Of these, the catalytic converter was the most important.

The first type of catalytic converter consisted of an inert ceramic support material coated with a thin layer of platinum or palladium metal. Carbon monoxide and hydrocarbons from the exhaust gases attached themselves to the metal surface, where they reacted with molecular oxygen and were converted into carbon dioxide and water. The use of a metal catalyst lowered the temperature and increased the rate at which reaction occurred, making possible the removal of almost all of these two pollutants from the exhaust gases.

Because lead, phosphorus, and other substances can coat the metal surfaces in catalytic converters and prevent them from functioning, the Environmental Protection Agency (EPA) was granted the authority to regulate gasoline composition and fuel additives as part of the 1970 Clean Air Act amendments. A consequence of the introduction of catalytic converters in new automobiles in the mid-1970's was the gradual switch from leaded to unleaded gasoline. As a result, emission of lead from transportation, the major source of lead as an air pollutant, decreased by 97 percent between 1978 and 1987.

While the first-generation catalytic converters dramatically reduced emission of carbon monoxide and hydrocarbons from automobiles, they had no effect on nitrogen oxide emissions. Dual-bed catalytic converters, developed in the early 1980's, use a two-step process to reduce emission of nitrogen oxides, carbon monoxide, and hydrocarbons. Dual-bed catalytic converters were followed by three-way converters, which use platinum and rhodium as the metal catalyst. A feedback system with an oxygen sensor is used to adjust the mixture of air and gasoline sent to the automobile engine to ensure maximum removal of pollutants.

The introduction of catalytic converters significantly reduced the release of pollutants by automobiles. In the United States, emission of carbon monoxide and hydrocarbons from transportation sources decreased by more than 50 percent between 1970 and 1995, even though the number of cars and trucks more than doubled. Similar reductions in automobile pollution have occurred in other countries where catalytic converters have been introduced.

Jeffrey A. Joens

Further Reading

Halderman, James D., and Jim Linder. *Automotive Fuel and Emissions Control Systems*. Upper Saddle River, N.J.: Pearson/Prentice Hall, 2006.

Yamagata, Hiroshi. *The Science and Technology of Materials in Automotive Engines*. Boca Raton, Fla.: CRC Press, 2005.

See also: Air pollution; Air-pollution policy; Automobile emissions; Black Wednesday; Clean Air Act and amendments; Smog

---

■ Center for Health, Environment, and Justice (CHEJ)

FIELDS OF STUDY: Ethics, Advocacy, Policy, Protest; Ecology, Environment, Environmentalism; Organizations, Agencies, Commissions, Centers; Public Policy, Debates, Controversies

IDENTIFICATION: American nonprofit organization established to assist local communities with environmental issues

DATE: Founded in 1981

When it was founded in 1981 as the Citizens Clearinghouse for Hazardous Waste, the organization that became the Center for Health, Environment, and Justice was part of an emerging grassroots movement among people concerned about protecting their local communities from the harmful consequences of environmental hazards.

During the late 1970's Lois Gibbs discovered that her child's school in the Love Canal neighborhood of Niagara Falls, New York, was built on thousands of tons of toxic chemicals. At the time no national organization existed to help communities with environmental issues. With no one to turn to for help, Gibbs organized the Love Canal Homeowners Association in 1978 to protest the situation in her neighborhood. This experience and the legal battles that followed led Gibbs to found the Citizens Clearinghouse for Hazardous Waste in 1981; the organization would later change its name to the Center for Health, Environment, and Justice (CHEJ). CHEJ subsequently grew into a national organization with Gibbs serving as executive director. Its main office is located in Falls Church, Virginia.

Since its establishment, CHEJ has remained a grassroots organization that focuses on helping communities coordinate their responses to environmental hazards. CHEJ seeks to assist local neighborhoods by providing necessary aid, information, resources, training, and strategic or technical assistance. In this way, the organization encourages individuals and communities to take social and political action.

CHEJ's stated mission is to "build healthy communities, with social justice, economic well-being, and democratic governance." This includes protecting consumers from hazardous or toxic products. CHEJ addresses its objectives through various campaigns and programs. Its BE SAFE campaign is a precautionary effort to prevent pollution, and its Child Proofing Our Communities campaign helps to educate communities about strategies for protecting children from environmental hazards. CHEJ's Green Flag Schools Program for Environmental Leadership works with schools to educate students about how they can engage in environmental advocacy. PVC: The Poison Plastic is an example of a CHEJ campaign for safe and healthy consumer products. This ongoing national campaign is aimed at moving major corporations away from using PVC plastic, a substance that is harmful for both the environment and human health.

Jeff Cervantez

■ Centers for Disease Control and Prevention

FIELDS OF STUDY: Government, Politics, International Relations; Organizations, Agencies, Commissions, Centers; Ecology, Environment, Environmentalism; Health, Medicine, Disease, Illness

CATEGORIES: Organizations and agencies; human health and the environment

IDENTIFICATION: U.S. federal agency that oversees all areas of public health

DATE: Founded on July 1, 1946, as the Communicable Disease Center

The Centers for Disease Control and Prevention monitors, diagnoses, and works to control outbreaks of disease in the United States. The agency also collects and analyzes data concerning public health and works to educate industries as well as the public regarding possible environmental causes of illness.

The Centers for Disease Control and Prevention has undergone significant changes, both in its primary function and in its name. The agency from which it would eventually arise was founded in 1942 as the Office of National Defense Malaria Control Activities, which was established in Atlanta, Georgia, with the goal of controlling or eliminating malaria in the southern United States. That agency's name was altered several times during the World War II years, reflecting its growing functions: It was absorbed into the Office of Typhus Fever Control (1942-1943), which became the Office of Malaria Control in War Areas (1944). On July 1, 1946, it became the Communicable Disease Center (CDC), the name it carried for some twenty years. Between 1967 and 1973 the CDC was incorporated into the Public Health Service, with a concomitant evolution in its function as well as its title as the Public Health Service became an agency within the Department of Health, Education, and Welfare and then its successor, the Department of Health and Human Services. The agency took on the more familiar name of Center for Disease Control until 1980, and from 1980 to 1992 it was known as the Centers for Disease Control; it was renamed the Centers for Disease Control and Prevention in 1992.

The original functions of the agency, reflected in its early titles, were the control and eradication of infectious diseases such as malaria and typhus. Using the newly developed insecticide dichloro-diphenyltrichloroethane, popularly known as DDT, the agency directed a spraying/eradication program between 1947 and 1949 for control of the mosquito vector throughout the South; millions of homes were treated, and the program proved successful. The number of reported cases of malaria was reduced by nearly 90 percent by 1949, and the disease was considered eradicated in the United States by 1951.

During the 1950's, the purview of the agency was broadened significantly, with a division devoted to venereal diseases incorporated in 1957 and a tuberculosis unit established in 1960. From the 1950's through the 1970's, the agency became increasingly involved in monitoring bacterial (cholera, salmonellosis) outbreaks as well as those associated with viral diseases (polio, hepatitis, mumps, rubella, influenza). The CDC sponsored frequent conferences and workshops with the aim of addressing problems of infectious disease as well as educating the public in these areas.

By the 1990's most major infectious diseases were under control in the United States, and the CDC moved to target other threats to the public health, such as chronic diseases and conditions associated at least in part with lifestyle: cancer, heart disease, workplace injuries, and environmental hazards. The agency also began to address the modern threat of bioterrorism. In order to carry out research on biological threats, the CDC maintains one of the few Biosafety Level 4 laboratories in the United States, used to study the most dangerous of biological agents. The CDC routinely interacts with equivalent agencies in other nations, as well as with the World Health Organization, to address public health threats around the world.

Richard Adler

Further Reading

Meyerson, Beth E., Fred A. Martich, and Gerald P. Naeh. *Ready to Go: The History and Contributions of U.S. Public Health Advisors.* Research Triangle Park, N.C.: American Social Health Association, 2008.

Tulchinsky, Theodore H., and Elena A. Varavikova. *The New Public Health.* 2d ed. Burlington, Mass.: Elsevier, 2009.

See also: Antibiotics; Asbestosis; Bacterial resistance; Birth defects, environmental; Brucellosis; Cancer clusters; Carcinogens; Chloramphenicol; Cloning; Environmental health; Environmental illnesses; Pandemics; Times Beach, Missouri, evacuation; World Health Organization

■ Ceres

FIELDS OF STUDY: Ethics, Advocacy, Policy, Protest; Business, Labor; Ecology, Environment, Environmentalism; Organizations, Agencies, Commissions, Centers

IDENTIFICATION: American nonprofit organization dedicated to injecting environmental considerations into investment decisions

DATE: Established in 1989

Ceres promotes the well-being of the environment and human society by uniting investors and key stakeholders, environmental organizations, and public interest groups to work with corporations and capital markets to integrate sustainability and environmentally responsible practices into their day-to-day operations.

The 1989 *Exxon Valdez* oil spill in Prince William Sound was the catalyst for the formation of Ceres. Meeting in Chapel Hill, North Carolina, fifteen major environmental groups joined with investors and public pension fund managers to encourage greater corporate consideration of the environmental consequences of their actions. With participation by the New York and California state pension funds, the Social Investment Forum, and a coalition of more than two hundred Protestant and Roman Catholic groups, the initial members of that group represented more than $150 billion in invested capital. The group was originally known by the acronym CERES (for Ceres, the Roman goddess of agriculture), which stood for the Coalition for Environmentally Responsible Economies; it eventually dropped the longer name altogether and became simply Ceres.

Ceres was founded on the notion that government regulation alone is not sufficient to effect material improvements in the environment. Rather, progress requires fundamental changes in corporate behavior and more responsible attitudes toward the environment. According to Ceres, investors can influence this shift in beneficial ways if their investment decisions include consideration of corporations' environmental track records. Ceres's first project was the development of a corporate code of environmental ethics. Originally called the Valdez Principles as a reminder of the oil spill, the code later become known as the Ceres Principles. This ten-point code of conduct calls for corporations to protect the biosphere,

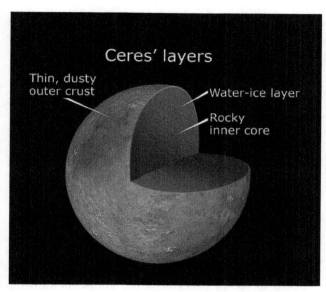

An artist's conception of the interior of Ceres, the only dwarf planet in the inner solar system. (NASA/ESA/A. Field, STScI)

use natural resources sustainably, reduce and responsibly dispose of wastes, conserve energy, reduce environmental and health risks to employees and communities, offer safe products and services, restore the environment, inform the public of hazards, ensure management commitment to environmental responsibility, and issue audit reports.

Ceres uses shareholder resolutions to initiate discussions of environmental responsibility at the highest corporate levels. In some corporations, such resolutions eventually lead to formal endorsement of the ten Ceres Principles. By endorsing the principles, companies acknowledge their environmental responsibility, actively commit to an ongoing process of continuous improvement, and agree to initiate comprehensive public reporting of environmental issues.

Initially, the Ceres Principles were adopted by companies that already had strong "green" reputations. In 1993, following lengthy negotiations, Sunoco became the first *Fortune* 500 company to endorse the principles. Several other large companies, including BankBoston, Bethlehem Steel, Coca-Cola, General Motors, and Polaroid, soon followed Sunoco's example. By 2010 more than fifty companies had endorsed the Ceres Principles, including thirteen *Fortune* 500 companies that had adopted their own equivalent environmental codes of conduct.

In 1997 Ceres launched the Global Reporting Initiative (GRI), which standardizes corporate environmental reporting to generate the equivalent of a financial report. Just as an official corporate financial report includes required information on expenses, revenue, and profitability, each company's GRI report includes required information on sustainability, environmental and social impacts, technological innovation, and other pertinent issues. GRI reports improve corporate accountability by ensuring that all stakeholders—investors, fund managers, community groups, environmentalists, and labor organizations—have access to standardized and consistent information. Armed with these data, environmentally conscious investors can measure corporate compliance with the Ceres Principles and thus use capital markets effectively to promote sustainable business practices.

Ceres partnered with the United Nations Environment Programme to issue draft GRI sustainability reporting guidelines in 1999. Finalized guidelines were released in 2000, and fifty organizations responded with their reports. In 2002 the GRI was established as an independent international body based in the Netherlands, and in 2009 more than twelve hundred organizations issued GRI reports.

Allan Jenkins;
Updated by Karen N. Kähler

Further Reading

Ceres. *Twenty-first Century Corporation: The Ceres Roadmap for Sustainability.* Boston: Author, 2010.

Friedman, Frank B. *Practical Guide to Environmental Management.* 10th ed. Washington, D.C.: Environmental Law Institute, 2006.

Leipziger, Deborah. *The Corporate Responsibility Code Book.* Sheffield, England: Greenleaf, 2003.

■ Certified wood

FIELDS OF STUDY: Economics, Business, Production, Commerce; Ethics, Advocacy, Policy, Protest; Ecology, Environment, Environmentalism; Industries, Commercial Products; Forests, Forestry; Renewable Resources; Ethics, Advocacy, Policy, Protest; Economics, Business, Production, Commerce; Ecology, Environment, Environmentalism; Industries, Commercial Products; Forests, Forestry; Renewable Resources

DEFINITION: Wood that has been harvested from a forest that has been audited by an independent agency to ensure that the forest is managed responsibly and sustainably

The movement toward forest certification has raised public awareness regarding the environmental benefits of sustainable forest management and has been credited with helping to slow the rate of deforestation around the world.

The Forestry Department of the United Nations Food and Agriculture Organization has estimated that more than half of the world's forests have been harmed or erased through overuse. During the early 1990's concerns about the rapid overlogging of forests—particularly tropical forests—led to the formation of a set of principles describing the sustainable growing and harvesting of timber. Several independent groups were established that offered to conduct objective studies of commercial forests to determine whether or not the forests were being managed responsibly. Although each group set its own standards, all of the groups adhered to several common principles: In a sustainable forest, the diversity of plants and animals, including threatened and endangered species, is protected; wood is not harvested faster than it can be regenerated; chemical fertilizers and pesticides are used minimally, if at all; rivers and streams are protected from erosion and pollution. In addition, a forest can be certified as sustainable only if the logging workers are treated fairly and any indigenous peoples who inhabit the land receive a share of the profits. The managers of certified forests must develop and continually update scientifically based management plans and continually monitor their operations for compliance.

The various certified wood programs are run separately—no United Nations body or other international oversight group has been established to ensure conformity, and most programs are run by scientific, environmental, or consumer groups, not by government agencies. By 2010, nearly 12 percent of the world's forests had been certified and more than fifty organizations offered wood certification, including two large umbrella groups. The larger of these is the Programme for the Endorsement of Forest Certification (PEFC), based in Geneva, Switzerland, and comprising thirty-five smaller bodies. PEFC certification has protected more than 210 million hectares (519 million acres) of forestland. Smaller but more influential in North America is the Forest Stewardship Council (FSC), based in Bonn, Germany, which certifies more than 105 million hectares (260 million acres). North America has three other important certifying bodies: the American Tree Farm System (ATFS), the Canadian Standards Association (CSA), and the Sustainable Forestry Initiative (SFI) Program.

All of the programs encourage consumers to investigate the wood products they purchase to ensure that they are made of certified wood. Products certified by the FSC carry labels identifying them as being made from "pure," "missed," or "recycled" materials, and each label bears a certificate number that the consumer can verify by referring to an online database. Some retailers have refurbished their stores with FSC-certified flooring or have made commitments to use FSC-certified paper pulp in their catalogs and other paper goods. At least one major home-improvement chain in the United States carries FSC-certified lumber in limited quantities. The demand for certified wood has grown steadily in the years since the process of certification was first introduced.

Cynthia A. Bily

A forest on San Juan Island.

Further Reading

Arabas, Karen, and Joe Bowersox. *Forest Futures: Science, Politics, and Policy for the Next Century.* Lanham, Md.: Rowman & Littlefield, 2004.

Berger, John J. *Forests Forever: Their Ecology, Restoration, and Protection.* Chicago: University of Chicago Press, 2008.

McEvoy, Thomas J. *Positive Impact Forestry: A Sustainable Approach to Maintaining Woodlands.* Washington, D.C.: Island Press, 2004.

■ Chalk River nuclear reactor explosion

FIELDS OF STUDY: Disasters; Ecology, Environment, Environmentalism; Nuclear Power, Nuclear Weapons, Radioactive Waste

THE EVENT: The world's first serious nuclear reactor accident

DATE: December 12, 1952

After an experimental nuclear reactor at Chalk River, Ontario, overheated, resulting in a hydrogen-oxygen explosion and release of more than one million gallons of radioactive water, a pipeline had to be constructed to divert the radioactive water and avoid contamination of the Ottawa River.

The experimental NRX reactor, run by the National Research Council of Canada, began operation at Chalk River, Ontario, in 1947. It was operating at low power on December 12, 1952, when a technician mistakenly opened four air valves in the system used to insert the control rods that slowed the rate of reaction. This action caused the control rods to move out of the reactor core, increasing the reaction rate and the amount of heat produced in the core. In the effort to return these control rods to their proper position, miscommunication resulted in the removal of additional control rods, causing the power generated in the reactor core to double every two seconds.

When the operator realized that the power was rapidly increasing, he "scrammed" the reactor, a process that forced the control rods into place, thus halting the nuclear reaction. However, the earlier error of opening the air valves kept some of the control rods from being pushed into place, and the temperature in the reactor continued to increase. To stop the reaction, operators dumped water rich in deuterium (heavy water) from the reactor core. Without this water, which slows the neutrons to a point where they can induce fission in the uranium core, the reaction ceased and the core began to cool. However, more than one million gallons of highly radioactive water flooded the basement of the reactor building. The reactor dome, a 4-ton lid on the reactor vessel, rose upward to release pressure from a hydrogen-oxygen explosion, and more radioactive water escaped, flooding the main floor of the building. The reactor operators were forced to evacuate the building, and eventually the entire reactor site, as radioactivity rose above safe levels.

The small size of the experimental NRX reactor minimized the radiation release. Since the Chalk River site was remote, the exposure of the general population to radioactivity was minimal. Nonetheless, a pipeline had to be constructed to divert the radioactive water and avoid contamination of the Ottawa River. The high levels of radioactivity made decontamination and cleanup of the NRX reactor difficult. In some parts of the reactor, workers participating in the cleanup effort could spend only

Chalk River Laboratories, run by Atomic Energy of Canada Limited, near Chalk River, Ontario, Canada. Photo take from Ottawa River.

minutes at work before accumulating the maximum permissible annual radiation dose for reactor workers. About three hundred military personnel from the United States and Canada, including future U.S. president Jimmy Carter, volunteered to participate in the cleanup of the NRX reactor. A 1982 study of the health of more than seven hundred workers who participated in the cleanup showed no increase in their death rate from cancer when compared to the general population.

George J. Flynn

Further Reading

Bodansky, David. "Nuclear Reactor Accidents." In *Nuclear Energy: Principles, Practices, and Prospects.* 2d ed. New York: Springer, 2004.

Krenz, Kim. *Deep Waters: The Ottawa River and Canada's Nuclear Adventure.* Montreal: McGill-Queen's University Press, 2004.

■ Chelyabinsk nuclear waste explosion

FIELDS OF STUDY: Disasters; Ecology, Environment, Environmentalism; Nuclear Power, Nuclear Weapons, Radioactive Waste; Pollution, Emissions, Toxic Waste, Hazardous Materials

THE EVENT: Nuclear explosion at a weapons production facility in the Chelyabinsk province of the Soviet Union

DATE: September 29, 1957

The nuclear explosion that took place at Mayak, a weapons production facility in Russia's Chelyabinsk province (then part of the Soviet Union), exposed 270,000 people to high levels of radiation.

The Mayak industrial complex began producing weapons-grade plutonium in 1948. For years after production began, workers dumped the complex's radioactive waste into the nearby Techa River. A waste storage facility was constructed in 1953 after people living near the Techa suffered from radiation poisoning. On September 29, 1957, one waste tank at the facility exploded. Although the exact cause of the explosion remains unknown, it is known that a cooling system failure contributed to the disaster.

A radioactive cloud consisting of between 70 and 90 tons of waste released an estimated 20 million curies of radiation into the environment. Of the waste material that was released, 90 percent fell back on the blast site and 10 percent drifted through the atmosphere, contaminating 2,000 square kilometers (772 square miles) of territory and exposing 270,000 people to radiation. Eyewitnesses later recalled seeing red dust settle everywhere, and the waters of the Techa River turned black for two weeks. Soon thereafter, plants died and leaves fell off the trees in the area. In less than two years, all the pine trees in a 28-square-kilometer (11-square-mile) area around the Mayak complex were dead.

Kirova Street, the central pedestrian street in Chelyabinsk, Russia. By Anthony Ivanoff (Own work)

The Soviet government closed all the stores in the area and shipped in food for the local population. Some ten thousand people were evacuated from the area, and the government burned houses and demolished entire towns to ensure that the residents could not return. However, many smaller communities continued to use local water sources, and later anecdotal accounts indicated that not all the contaminated crops in the region were destroyed. A dairy farm near the Techa River was allowed to operate until 1959.

The Chelyabinsk accident was kept secret, and for almost twenty years few people outside the region knew the extent of the disaster. The U.S. Central Intelligence Agency (CIA) learned of the incident but did not make the information public. Zhores Medvedev, a Soviet émigré, published the first account of the accident in 1976.

Evaluating the impact of the explosion proved difficult for two reasons: The Soviet government consistently denied the magnitude of the event, and the region was heavily polluted by other sources, especially the dumping of waste into the Techa River. In 1989 a U.S. official who visited the Mayak complex declared it to be the "most polluted spot on earth." By 1992 nearly one thousand area residents had been diagnosed with chronic radiation sickness. Rates for cancer were higher near Mayak than anywhere else in the Soviet Union, and the general health of the population, especially children, was poor by any standard.

Cleanup efforts were hampered by the secrecy that surrounded the event for nearly three decades, limited funds, and the high levels of contamination. Lake Karachay, located near Mayak, was so radioactive that a person standing on its shore for more than one hour would be exposed to a lethal dose of radioactivity. In the early twenty-first century the area remained a pressing environmental problem.

Thomas Clarkin

Further Reading

Garb, Paula, and Galina Komarova. "Victims of 'Friendly Fire' at Russia's Nuclear Weapons Sites." In *Violent Environments*, edited by Nancy Lee Peluso and Michael Watts. Ithaca, N.Y.: Cornell University Press, 2001.

Hoffman, David E. *The Dead Hand: The Untold Story of the Cold War Arms Race and Its Dangerous Legacy.* New York: Doubleday, 2009.

Makhijani, Arjun, Howard Hu, and Katherine Yih, eds. *Nuclear Wastelands: A Global Guide to Nuclear Weapons Production and Its Health and Environmental Effects.* 1995. Reprint. Cambridge, Mass.: MIT Press, 2000.

■ Chernobyl nuclear accident

FIELDS OF STUDY: Disasters; Ecology, Environment, Environmentalism; Nuclear Power, Nuclear Weapons, Radioactive Waste; Pollution, Emissions, Toxic Waste, Hazardous Materials

THE EVENT: Explosion of a nuclear power reactor at the Chernobyl power plant in the Soviet Union

DATE: April 26, 1986

The accident at the Chernobyl nuclear power plant drastically changed the lives of thousands of residents in northern Ukraine and southern Belarus. It also raised questions about the future of the plant itself; the ecological, human health, economic, and political repercussions of the incident; and the future of nuclear power programs worldwide.

On April 26, 1986, nuclear power reactor number 4 exploded at the Chernobyl Nuclear Power Plant, located about 15 kilometers (9 miles) from the small town of Chernobyl in the republic of Ukraine. As the core of the reactor began to melt, an explosion occurred that blew the top off the reactor and sent a wide trail of radioactive material across large parts of what was then the Soviet Union as well as much of Eastern and Western Europe. More than 116,000 people were evacuated within a 30-kilometer (19-mile) radius, and more than two dozen people died due to acute radiation syndrome (also known as radiation sickness).

In addition to the political, social, and economic aftermath of the explosion, the consequences of human inability to prevent or contain widespread damage were evident in the environment in the years following the Chernobyl disaster. A major release of radioactive materials into the atmosphere occurred during the first ten days following the explosion. Radioactive plumes reached many European countries within a few days, increasing radiation levels to between ten and one hundred times normal levels. Over time, the contaminated lithosphere created a new biogeographical province characterized by irregular and complicated patterns of radioactivity in

Chernobyl, Ukraine, 1986

Belarus, Ukraine, and Russia, the countries most affected. In spite of some success in efforts to slow the flow of certain soluble radionuclides into the Black and Baltic seas, as well as into the Pripet, Dnieper, and Sozh Rivers (all of which contribute water to the Kiev water reservoir), much contamination occurred that only the passage of time could resolve.

Contamination Effects

The effects of the radioactive contamination on vegetation have varied depending on the species. Damage to coniferous forests was more than ten times greater than that to oak forests and grass communities, and more than one hundred times greater than the damage to lichen communities. Ten years after the explosion, pine forests still had high levels of radionuclides in the uppermost layer of the forest floor, while birch forests had considerably lower levels. Large numbers of highly contaminated trees were felled, and restrictions were placed on cutting and using the wood in industry and for fuel.

Likewise, the degrees of radiation damage and the doses absorbed varied among plant communities. In addition to killing or damaging plant life, the radiation disturbed the functioning of plant reproductive systems, resulting in sterility or decreases in both seed production and fertility. Other effects involved changes in plant chlorophyll, necessary for removing carbon dioxide from the air.

Among animals, lower life-forms have been found to have higher radiosensitivity levels; that is, mammals are less sensitive to radioactivity than are birds, reptiles, and insects. The severity of damage also depends on whether it is external or internal. The impact of environmental contamination may be less severe for animals than for plants because of the ability of animals to move from place to place and make selective contact with the environment. Irradiation can have a wide range of effects among animal species, including death, reproductive disturbances, decrease in the viability of progeny, and abnormalities in development and morphology.

The contamination of aquatic ecosystems by Chernobyl radiation was considerable. The contamination of freshwater ecosystems has fallen with time, but continuing contamination has been evidenced by factors such as a transfer of radionuclides from bottom sediments and erosion of contaminated soil into water sources. Some restrictions have been placed on fishing in contaminated aquatic ecosystems.

The consequences of the Chernobyl accident for agriculture were severe. Drastic changes in land-use and farming practices became necessary as a result of contamination. As with other life-forms affected by radiation, the degree of contamination varies; in the case of agriculturally related contamination, damage depends on such things as the type of soil and the biological peculiarities of different plant species. As Ukraine produced 20 percent of the grain, 60 percent of the industrial sugar beets, 45 percent of the sunflower seeds, 25 percent of the potatoes, and about 33 percent of all the vegetables used in the former Soviet Union, the problem of soil contamination following the accident was serious. Furthermore, the problems extended beyond the borders of Ukraine: The contamination affected the reindeer herds of Scandinavia and sheep breeding in mountainous regions of the British Isles.

The scale of the contamination of the environment by the Chernobyl accident was so enormous that the task of protecting the population was not entirely successful. The long-term health effects of environmental contamination are caused only in part by external radiation. Scientists studying the problem believe that the majority of health problems in affected areas will be caused by the consumption of contaminated agricultural products, particularly dairy products.

Chernobyl Today

Construction of the Chernobyl New Safe Confinement (NSC), which was designed to replace the previous steel and concrete sarcophagus that was constructed around the destroyed nuclear reactor in 1986, began in 2010 and is expected to be completed in 2015. The Chernobyl NSC is designed to prevent radioactive materials from leaking into the environment from the reactor complex. Twenty-five years after the Chernobyl accident, in 2011, concentrations of cesium-137 in food products produced in areas surrounding the Chernobyl nuclear power plant were generally below international standards for action. However, some areas in the region continue to suffer from radionuclide contamination, and radiation levels can vary widely.

Three groups of people faced the highest exposure to radiation due to the Chernobyl accident: the clean-up crew, known as liquidators, who worked in the immediate vicinity of the reactor in the two years following the accident; the approximately 160,000 individuals who were living in and evacuated from the area surrounding the Chernobyl reactor in 1986; and the approximately 270,000 residents of strictly controlled zones (SCZs), areas with high levels of radioactive cesium. More than one hundred liquidators were diagnosed with acute radiation sickness; twenty-eight liquidators died in 1986 due to the effects of radiation exposure and an additional nineteen died by 2005. In the long term, there was a significant increase in the incidence of thyroid cancer among residents of the area who were children and adolescents at the time of the accident, and nearly five thousand cases of thyroid cancer have been attributed to radiation exposure due to the Chernobyl accident. Most of these thyroid cancer cases are due to the consumption of milk that was contaminated with iodine-131 in the weeks following the accident. A significantly increased risk of leukemia among the most highly exposed liquidators has also been reported. According to the World Health Organization, there may be up to four thousand additional cancer deaths among the liquidators, evacuees, and residents of the SCZs over their lifetime, representing a 3 to 4 percent increase over the normal incidence of cancers from all causes. Additional health effects related to the Chernobyl accident include an elevated risk of cataracts and cardiovascular disease. A 2005 study by the United Nations attributed fifty-six deaths to radiation exposure from Chernobyl.

The Chernobyl accident galvanized the antinuclear movement and prompted significant changes to reactor designs, nuclear regulations, and emergency response measures worldwide. Public access to the Chernobyl Exclusion Zone, which covers more than one thousand square miles surrounding the Chernobyl Nuclear Power Plant, continues to be restricted due to the elevated levels of radiation detected there, although the site remains a place of interest to scientists and, increasingly, to tourists.

Victoria Price

Further Reading

Alexievich, Svetlana. *Voices from Chernobyl: The Oral History of a Nuclear Disaster.* Trans. Keith Gessen. New York: Picador, 2006. Print.

Bailey, C. C. *The Aftermath of Chernobyl.* Dubuque: Kendall Hunt, 1993. Print.

Burlakova, Elena B., and Valeria I. Naydich, eds. *The Lessons of Chernobyl: 25 Years Later.* New York: Nova Science, 2012. Print.

Marples, David R. *Chernobyl and Nuclear Power in the USSR.* New York: St. Martin's, 1986. Print.

Marples, David R. *The Social Impact of the Chernobyl Disaster.* New York: St. Martin's, 1988. Print.

Medvedev, Zhores A. *The Legacy of Chernobyl.* New York: Norton, 1990. Print.

Nuclear Energy Institute. "Chernobyl Accident and Its Consequences." *Nuclear Energy Institute.* Nuclear Energy Inst., July 2011. Web. 28 Jan. 2015.

Savchenko, V. K. *The Ecology of the Chernobyl Catastrophe.* New York: Informa Healthcare, 1995. Print.

World Health Organization. "Health Effects of the Chernobyl Accident: An Overview." *World Health Organization.* WHO, Apr. 2006. Web. 28 Jan. 2015.

Yaroshinskaya, Alla. *Chernobyl: The Forbidden Truth.* Lincoln: Bison, 1995. Print.

■ Chipko Andolan movement

FIELDS OF STUDY: Ethics, Advocacy, Policy, Protest; Ecology, Environment, Environmentalism; Organizations, Agencies, Commissions, Centers; Forests, Forestry; Biology, Life Sciences, Ecosystems; Ecology, Environment, Environmentalism; Forests, Forestry

IDENTIFICATION: Movement started by villagers in northern India to stop lumber companies from clear-cutting mountain slopes

DATE: Originated in April, 1973

Through nonviolent protest, the Chipko Andolan movement put pressure on the Indian government to develop policies concerning natural resources that would be sensitive to the environment and to the needs of all the Indian people.

The forests of India are a critical resource for the subsistence of rural people throughout the country, especially in the hill and mountain areas. Mountain villagers depend on the forests for firewood, for fodder for their cattle, for wood for their houses and farm tools, and as a means to stabilize their water and soil resources. During the 1960's and 1970's the Indian government restricted villagers from huge areas of forestland, then auctioned off the trees to lumber companies and industries located in the plains. Large lots of trees were sold to the highest bidders by the Forest Department, with the purchase payments going to the Indian government.

Because of government restrictions and an ever-growing population, women who lived in mountain villages were forced to walk for hours each day just to gather firewood and fodder. In addition, when mountain slopes were cleared of trees, rains washed away the topsoil, leaving the soil and rocks underneath to crumble and fall in landslides. Much of the soil from the mountain slopes was deposited in the rivers below, raising water levels. At the same time, the bare slopes allowed much more rain to run off directly into the rivers, which resulted in flooding.

As trees were being felled for commerce and industry at increasing rates during the early 1970's, Indian villagers finally sought to protect their lands and livelihoods through a method of nonviolent resistance inspired by Indian leader Mohandas Gandhi. In 1973 this resistance spread and became organized into the Chipko Andolan movement, commonly referred to as the Chipko movement. The word *chipko* comes from a Hindi word meaning "to embrace," while *andolan* refers to a protest against harmful practices. Together the words literally mean "movement to hug trees."

The movement originated in April, 1973, as a spontaneous protest by mountain villagers against logging abuses in Uttar Pradesh, an Indian province in the Himalayas. When contractors sent their workers in to fell the trees, the villagers embraced the trees, saving them by interposing their bodies between the trees and the workers' axes. The movement was largely organized and orchestrated by village women, who became leaders and activists in order to save their means of subsistence and their communities.

After many Chipko protests in Uttar Pradesh, victory was finally achieved in 1980 when the Indian government placed a fifteen-year ban on felling live trees in the Himalayan forests. The Chipko movement soon spread to other parts of India, and

Birthplace of the Chipko Movement

clear-cutting was stopped in the Western Ghats and the Vindhya Range.

The Chipko protesters staged a socioeconomic revolution in India by gaining control of forest resources from the hands of a distant government bureaucracy that was concerned only with selling the forest in order to make urban-oriented products. The movement generated pressure for the Indian government to develop a natural resources policy that was more sensitive to the environment and the needs of all people.

Alvin K. Benson

Further Reading

Guha, Ramachandra. "Chipko: Social History of an 'Environmental' Movement." In *Social Movements and the State*, edited by Ghanshyam Shah. Thousand Oaks, Calif.: Sage, 2003.

Hill, Christopher V. *South Asia: An Environmental History*. Santa Barbara, Calif.: ABC-CLIO, 2008.

■ Chloracne

FIELDS OF STUDY: Biology, Life Sciences, Ecosystems; Chemistry; Elements, Substances, Chemicals, Compounds; Health, Medicine, Disease, Illness; Ecology, Environment, Environmentalism

DEFINITION: Skin disease resembling acne that results from exposure to chlorine and chlorine-containing compounds

Environmentalists have grown increasingly concerned about the negative impacts, including chloracne, that exposure to chlorinated compounds can have on human life.

Chloracne involves an increase of dry skin and a reduction in the ability to produce sebum, which moistens and protects skin. This condition has been linked to exposure to polychlorinated biphenyls (PCBs) and polychlorinated dioxins (PCDDs). PCBs, which are used in industry as lubricants, vacuum pump fluids, and electrical insulating fluids, harm the environment because they evaporate slowly and do not mix well with water. They are therefore widely dispersed in watercourses and in the atmosphere. Because they strongly resist degra-

dation, PCBs remain and accumulate in the environment.

Dioxins are a group of chlorinated aromatic hydrocarbons that are formed in trace amounts during production of the many chlorinated compounds used throughout industry. They are highly persistent in the environment. One dioxin commonly linked to chloracne is 2,3,7,8-tetrachlorodibenzodioxin (TCDD), which is a known human carcinogen. The primary source of dioxin in the environment is the burning of chlorine-containing compounds. Since dioxins are also formed in the production of chlorinated compounds used as herbicides, chlorine-compound exposure occurs in workplaces and in the environment.

Concern about the health risks posed to humans and wildlife by dioxin and related chlorine compounds in the environment was brought to public

Chloracne in this herbicide production worker involved almost every follicular orifice on his face and neck with comedones, papules and cystlike lesions. By NIOSH.

attention in 1962 with the publication of Rachel Carson's *Silent Spring*, which condemns the widespread use of chlorinated pesticides. Direct skin contact, inhalation, or ingestion of such compounds can result in chloracne, which produces skin lesions on the face, with more severe cases involving lesions on the shoulders, chest, and back. Symptoms may include small, colored, blisterlike pimples (pustules) and straw-colored cysts. Chloracne can develop from three to four weeks after exposure and can last up to fifteen years. Also related to the disease are nausea, bronchitis, and liver disease. It can also have a poisoning effect on the nervous system, which results in extended symptoms such as headache, fatigue, sweaty palms, and numbness in the legs. Chloracne does not respond well to antibiotics. Derivatives of vitamin A (such as gels) and retinoic acid creams may help, and isotretinoin (sold under such trade names as Roaccutane and Claravis) may also be an effective treatment.

In October, 1993, the American Health Association approved a resolution for the gradual phaseout of chlorine. The issue is not a simple one, however, because chlorine is used to benefit humans in disinfecting drinking water and making many medicines. Regardless, environmentalists are worried that chlorinated compounds are slowly poisoning the earth by working their way through the air, groundwater, and the food chain, as well as destroying wildlife and causing many diseases such as chloracne in humans.

Beth Ann Parker and Massimo D. Bezoari

Further Reading

Friis, Robert H. "Pesticides and Other Organic Chemicals." In *Essentials of Environmental Health.* Sudbury, Mass.: Jones and Bartlett, 2007.

Hill, Marquita K. "Pesticides." In *Understanding Environmental Pollution*. 3d ed. New York: Cambridge University Press, 2010.

■ Chloramphenicol

FIELDS OF STUDY: Chemistry; Elements, Substances, Chemicals, Compounds; Ecology, Environment, Environmentalism; Health, Medicine, Disease, Illness

DEFINITION: Broad-spectrum antibiotic used to combat harmful bacteria and organisms in humans and animals

Because of chloramphenicol's potential to cause very serious side effects, the US Food and Drug Administration has restricted the drug's use for humans and does not approve its use at all for animal feed or food-producing animals.

Chloramphenicol (CHPC) is known by many other names, including the trade name Chloromycetin. CHPC is an effective antibiotic, particularly in those cases that require penetration through purulent material (which either contains or discharges pus) to reach the infecting bacteria, as occurs in infections of pneumonia. It is also a good choice for otherwise intractable infections involving the eye, the nervous system, and the prostate gland. The more efficient penetration of CHPC into cells compared to other antibiotics increases its advantage in killing intracellular parasites, such as chlamydia, mycoplasma, and rickettsia.

The high acidity of CHPC is believed to contribute to its ability to penetrate necrotic material and cellular membranes. It kills bacteria by interfering with the protein-manufacturing systems occurring in the ribosomes of organisms. The mode of attack is unique in that reptilian, mammalian, and avian ribosomes are unaffected. In addition, the antibiotic does not destroy all the bacteria in infected tissue.

3D Chemical structure of the molecule Chloramphenicol. Made with Corina Software. By GarciaGerry (Own work)

Only highly susceptible bacteria are destroyed, with the remainder merely being inhibited from reproducing. This is an advantage because the inactive residual bacteria allow B cells in the immune system to develop an immune response to the bacteria. The result is akin to the use of inactive bacterial vaccinations in fighting disease.

Discovered in 1947, CHPC was released for public use in 1949. In 1959 researchers reported cardiovascular collapse and death in three infants after they were treated with CHPC. All exhibited a gray pallor (called gray syndrome) prior to death. A more complete study found that of thirty-one premature infants treated with the drug, 45 percent died exhibiting gray syndrome, while only 2.5 percent of a group of untreated infants died. The common feature among the fatal cases was the high level of the drug used in their treatment: 230 to 280 milligrams of CHPC per kilogram of body weight per day, five to ten times what later became the recommended dose.

CHPC was subsequently found to interfere with the energy-producing capacity of mitochondria in those organs with a high rate of oxygen consumption; the heart, liver, and kidneys are at particular risk. People who are unable to detoxify the drug efficiently—such as infants—are particularly susceptible to the accumulation of toxic levels in the blood.

CHPC is known to have other negative side effects, including nausea, diarrhea, and loss of appetite. In more severe cases, blood dyscrasias may result. This is a condition in which abnormal blood cells are produced while normal blood cell production is blocked because of interaction of CHPC with the patient's bone marrow. Patients who take CHPC orally may develop fatal anemia. Those who recover from such blood abnormalities resulting from the antibiotic have a high incidence of leukemia. Unfavorable interactions with other drugs—including phenytoin (used to treat heart disease), primidone (used for seizures), and cyclophosphamide (used in chemotherapy)—have also been noted. In addition, the antibiotic can interfere with vaccinations and is a potential carcinogen.

These side effects occur not only in humans but also in other animals. CHPC may build up to toxic levels in young animals because their liver detoxification mechanisms are not as well developed or efficient as those of adults. The antibiotic therefore is not approved for administration to food animals in the United States, as these animals may be ingested

by the young. Ingestion of CHPC by pregnant or lactating creatures must be avoided for similar reasons. Loss of appetite in dolphins, whales, and California sea lions has also been a noted side effect. Environmentalists and others have raised concerns that the antibiotic may be used in some agricultural settings outside the United States, putting humans at risk. In 2010, for example, the US Food and Drug Administration seized a shipment of honey from China that was found to be contaminated by CHPC; the bees that produced the honey had been fed the antibiotic as a measure to control certain diseases in the bee population.

Although the serious side effects of CHPC are rare, a study by the California Medical Association in 1967 found the occurrence of cases in humans to be as high as one per twenty-four thousand applications, depending on dose. The accumulation of such data was sufficient for the use of CHPC to be restricted, in the 1960s, to life-threatening cases for which there is little alternative treatment.

Jacqueline J. Robinson and Massimo D. Bezoari

Further Reading

"Chloramphenicol." *Merck Manuals*. Merck, Aug. 2013. Web. 22 Jan. 2015.

Forrest, Graeme N., and David W. Oldach. "Chloramphenicol." *Infectious Diseases*. Ed. Sherwood L. Gorbach, John G. Bartlett, and Neil R. Blacklow. 3rd ed. Philadelphia: Lippincott, 2004. Print.

Hilts, Philip J. "New Drugs, New Problems." *Protecting America's Health: The FDA, Business, and One Hundred Years of Regulation*. New York: Knopf, 2003. Print.

■ Chlorination

FIELDS OF STUDY: Biology, Life Sciences, Ecosystems; Ecology, Environment, Environmentalism; Water Resources; Pollution, Emissions, Toxic Waste, Hazardous Materials; Elements, Substances, Chemicals, Compounds

DEFINITION: Practice of disinfecting water by the addition of chlorine

Although the chlorination of public water in the United States has helped reduce outbreaks of waterborne disease, it has raised concerns about the possible formation of chloroorganic compounds in treated water.

By LaconicLight (Own work)

Drinking water, wastewater, and water in swimming pools are the most common water sources where chlorination is used to kill bacteria and prevent the spread of diseases. Viruses are generally more resistant to chlorination than are bacteria, but they can be eliminated with an increase in the chlorine levels needed to kill bacteria. Common chlorinating agents include elemental chlorine gas and sodium or calcium hypochlorite. In water these substances generate hypochlorous acid, which is the chemical agent responsible for killing microorganisms by inactivating bacteria proteins or viral nucleoproteins.

Public drinking water was chlorinated in most large U.S. cities by 1914. The effectiveness of chlorination in reducing outbreaks of waterborne diseases in the early twentieth century was clearly illustrated by the drop in typhoid deaths: 36 per 100,000 in 1920 to 5 per 100,000 by 1928. Chlorination has remained the most economical method of purifying public water, although it is not without potential risks. Chlorination has also been widely used to prevent the spread of bacteria in the food industry.

In its elemental form, high concentrations of chlorine are very toxic, and solutions containing more than 1,000 milligrams per liter (mg/l) are lethal to humans. Chlorine has a characteristic odor that is detectable at levels of 2-3 mg/l of water. Most public water supplies contain chlorine levels of 1-2 mg/l, although the actual concentration of water reaching consumer faucets fluctuates and is usually around 0.5 mg/l. Consumption of water containing 50 mg/l has produced no immediate adverse effects.

The greatest environmental concern regarding chlorination has less to do with the chlorine itself than it does with the potential toxic compounds that may form when chlorine reacts with organic compounds present in water. Chlorine, which is an extremely reactive element, reacts with organic material associated with decaying vegetation (humic acids), forming chloro-organic compounds. Trihalomethanes (THMs) are one of the most common chloro-organic compounds. At least a dozen THMs have been identified in drinking water since the 1970's, when health authorities in the United States came under pressure to issue standards for the identification and reduction of THM levels in drinking water.

Major concern has focused on levels of chloroform because of this compound's known carcinogenic properties in animal studies. Once used in cough syrups, mouthwashes, and toothpastes, chloroform in consumer products is now severely restricted. A 1975 study of chloroform concentrations in drinking water found levels of more than 300 micrograms per liter (µg/l) in some water, with 10 percent of the water systems surveyed having levels of more than 105 µg/l. In 1984 the World Health Organization set a guideline value of 30 µg/l for chloroform in drinking water.

Although there are risks associated with drinking chlorinated water, it has been estimated that the risk of death from cigarette smoking is two thousand times greater than that of drinking chloroform-contaminated water from most public sources. However, as water sources become more polluted and require higher levels of chlorination to maintain purity, continual monitoring of chloro-organic compounds will be needed.

Nicholas C. Thomas

Further Reading

Bull, Richard J. "Drinking Water Disinfection." In *Environmental Toxicants: Human Exposures and Their Health Effects*, edited by Morton Lippmann. New York: John Wiley & Sons, 2000.

Gray, N. F. *Drinking Water Quality: Problems and Solutions*. 2d ed. New York: Cambridge University Press, 2008.

■ Climax communities

FIELDS OF STUDY: Biology, Life Sciences, Ecosystems; Animals, Zoology, Marine Biology; Ecology, Environment, Environmentalism; Forests, Forestry; Plants, Vegetation, Botany, Horticulture

DEFINITION: Assemblages of plants and animals representing the end point in a successional sequence; mature communities in equilibrium with their environment

Climax communities are reservoirs of biological diversity. As levels of human disturbance increase, climax communities contract in area and begin to disappear. Efforts to preserve endangered species that focus on entire communities are more likely to be successful, especially at preserving unrecognized threatened species, than efforts that focus on one species alone.

The concept of a climax community was first proposed in 1916 by forestry biologist Frederic E. Clements in a monograph on the vegetation of Washington State. Clements postulated that there is a unique, discrete vegetation type for a given climate and topography, and that type will occur if succession is allowed to proceed to its end point. This concept has fallen into disfavor among theoretical ecologists and conservationists since World War II. A more modern view, based on numerous detailed studies, views communities as being in a state of constant flux that decreases in amplitude with time. The terms "mature," "late successional," and "old-growth" are used to describe what formerly was called a climax community.

Subtypes of climax communities sometimes recognized include polyclimax, where several different assemblages of plants and animals can represent a stable end point for a given area; subclimax, where the usual vegetation remains in a late stage of succession because of regular, infrequent disturbance; and plagioclimax, where the stable vegetation of a region has been shaped by human activity over a long period of time. An example of a plagioclimax is the species-rich oak savanna of Oregon and northern California, which was maintained by periodic burning in prehistoric times and grazing after European settlement. Excluding both fire and cattle results in overgrowth by conifers and a precipitous decline in diversity of herbaceous plants and insects.

Following massive disturbance, whether natural or caused by humans, the vegetation of an area experiences succession as early colonizing species modify the environment in ways that allow other species to colonize. Over time, the spatial complexity, species diversity, primary productivity, and stored biomass of the vegetation increases, as do the species diversity and food-web complexity of animals. In addition to being much richer biologically, mature communities are more resistant to external disruption than are early successional ones.

Climax communities include prairie and savanna vegetation as well as forest, but these and other vegetation types ideally suited to human exploitation persist mainly as small tracts deliberately preserved from development. Such preservation of fragments of an originally more extensive ecosystem is typically only partially successful in preserving stability and species diversity, because the complexity of an ecosystem depends on its size as well as lack of disturbance. Preserving small, widely separated tracts of virgin rain forest in the Amazon basin has, for example, led to the loss of larger predators from much of their original range, and this in turn has disrupted populations of prey species. Extensive areas of mature climax communities relatively free of human disturbance still extant in the early years of the twenty-first century include the rain forest of the Amazon basin, coniferous forests of North America and Siberia, and the Arctic tundra.

Martha A. Sherwood

Further Reading

During, H. T., M. J. A. Werger, and H. J. Willems, eds. *Diversity and Pattern in Plant Communities*. The Hague: SPB Academic Publishing, 1988.

Pynn, Larry. *Last Stands: A Journey Through North America's Vanishing Ancient Rainforests*. Corvallis: Oregon State University Press, 2000.

Van der Maarel, Eddy, ed. *Vegetation Ecology*. Malden, Mass.: Blackwell, 2005.

Verhoef, Herman A., and Peter J. Morin, eds. *Community Ecology: Processes, Models, and Applications*. New York: Oxford University Press, 2010.

■ Cloning

FIELDS OF STUDY: Technology and Applied Science; Inventions; Biology, Life Sciences, Ecosystems; Scientific Equipment, Tools, Techniques, and Methods; Public Policy, Debates, Controversies

CATEGORY: Biotechnology and genetic engineering

DEFINITION: Production of a population of genetically identical cells or organisms derived from a single ancestor, or the production and amplification of identical deoxyribonucleic acid molecules

Gene cloning is commonly used to produce genetically modified organisms and genetically engineered crops. Reproductive cloning has the potential to be used to mass-reproduce animals with special qualities, or to expand the population of an endangered species. With further development, therapeutic cloning might someday be employed to produce whole organs from single cells or replace disease-damaged cells with healthy ones.

The molecular cloning and engineering of deoxyribonucleic acid (DNA) molecules were first made possible with the discoveries of DNA ligase (enzymes that join DNA molecules) in 1967 and restriction endonucleases (enzymes that cut DNA molecules at specific nucleotide sequences) in 1970 by Hamilton Smith and Daniel Nathans. These enzymes allow scientists to cut and join DNA molecules from different species to produce recombinant DNA. For example, the DNA encoding human insulin can be combined with a plasmid, a small piece of DNA often found in bacteria such as Escherichia coli (E. coli). After the recombinant human-insulin-DNA/plasmid-DNA molecule is constructed, it can be inserted into a host cell such as E. coli. The recombinant DNA molecule will then replicate one or more times each time the E. coli DNA replicates. Thus a clone of identical recombinant human-insulin-DNA/plasmid-DNA molecules will result. If the recombinant molecule has been engineered with the requisite signals, the E. coli will produce copious amounts of human insulin. In 1972 the first recombinant DNA molecules were made at Stanford University, and in 1973 such molecules were inserted via plasmids into E. coli. The first successful synthesis of a human protein by E. coli was somatostatin, reported in 1977 by Keiichi Itakura and coworkers. In 1984 insulin was the first human protein made by E. coli to become commercially available.

The production of cloned recombinant DNA has been an indispensable tool in biological research and has increased the knowledge and understanding of the structure and function of DNA and the control of gene activity. Cloned DNA has led to the manufacture of important products of medical interest, the production of DNA for gene transfer and genetic engineering experiments, and the identification of mutations and genetic disease. Several different vectors have been developed for the delivery of DNA to a variety of plant, animal, and protistan cells, resulting in the creation of many transgenic species. Transgenic plants have been produced that are resistant to certain herbicides, insects, and viruses, and a variety of animals have been engineered with the human growth factor gene. Transgenic plants, animals, and protistans now produce a variety of human proteins, including insulin, antithrombin, growth hormone, clotting factor, vaccines, and many other pharmaceuticals and therapeutic agents, as well as molecular probes for the diagnosis of human disease. As a result of this technology, the costs of treating many diseases have declined.

The first human gene transfer experiment using cloned DNA was performed in 1990 on a four-year-old girl with severe combined immune deficiency (SCID). SCID is caused by a mutation in the adenine deaminase (ADA) gene that results in white blood cells deficient in their immune response. These cells were removed from the girl, the normal gene was inserted, and the genetically altered white cells were returned to her body, where they repopulated and expressed normal defense mechanisms. The girl's white cell numbers normalized after repeated treatments. While she continued to require ADA enzyme injections for primary management of her condition, she did develop normal immunity over time.

Environmental Impact of DNA Cloning

The construction of recombinant DNA molecules and their subsequent cloning have not been without controversy. In 1971 researcher Paul Berg planned an experiment to combine DNA from simian virus 40 (SV40)—a virus that causes tumors in monkeys and transforms human cells in culture—with bacteriophage 1 and to incorporate the recombinant molecule into E. coli. However, several scientists warned of

Milestones in Cloning

YEAR	EVENT
1892	Hans Adolph Eduard Dreisch clones sea urchins by separating the first two and four blastomeres.
1902	Hans Spemann successfully repeats Dreisch's experiment using salamanders.
1952	Robert Briggs and Thomas J. King successfully clone frogs by nuclear transplantation of embryonic nuclei to enucleated eggs.
1967	Deoxyribonucleic acid (DNA) ligase, the enzyme that joins DNA molecules, is discovered.
1969-1970	Daniel Nathans, Hamilton Smith, and others discover restriction endonucleases.
1971	Paul Berg plans to combine DNA with a bacteriophage and insert the recombinant DNA molecule into *Escherichia coli* (*E. coli*).
1972	The first recombinant DNA molecules are constructed at Stanford University.
1973	Recombinant DNA is first inserted into *E. coli.*
1974	Scientists call for a moratorium on recombinant DNA research until the National Institutes of Health (NIH) can study the safety of recombinant DNA research and develop guidelines.
1976	The NIH issues its guidelines for recombinant DNA research.
1983	The NIH grants permission to the University of California at Berkeley to release genetically engineered bacteria designed to retard frost formation on plants.
1986	Steen Willadsen clones sheep using early embryonic nuclei.
1987	Randall Prather and Willard Eyestone clone cows using early embryonic nuclei.
1990	The first human gene transfer experiment is performed on a patient with severe combined immune deficiency (SCID).
1997	Ian Wilmut and Keith Campbell announce the successful cloning of Dolly the sheep, the first mammal cloned from an adult cell.
2001	The first endangered wild animal, an Asian ox (gaur) is cloned.
2002	A study finds that the genes in about 4 percent of cloned mice function abnormally.
2003	Dolly the sheep is euthanized after contracting lung disease.
2009	The first clone of an extinct animal, a Pyrenean ibex (a species of wild goat), is born but dies within minutes.

a potential biohazard. Because E. coli is a natural inhabitant of the human digestive system, it was feared that the engineered E. coli could escape from the laboratory, enter the environment, become ingested by humans, and cause cancer as a result of its newly acquired DNA. The scientific community imposed a moratorium on recombinant DNA work in 1974 until the National Institutes of Health (NIH) could study the safety of recombinant DNA research and develop guidelines under which such work could proceed. The guidelines, originally published in 1976, were eventually relaxed after it was clearly demonstrated

that the work was not nearly as dangerous as initially feared.

In 1983 the NIH granted permission to the University of California at Berkeley to release bacteria that had been engineered to protect plants from frost damage. This was the first experiment intentionally designed to introduce genetically engineered organisms into the environment. Various environmental and consumer protection groups were successful in persuading federal judge John J. Sirica to order the suspension of the planned trial. Environmentalists feared that the bacteria could spread to other plants, prolong the growing season, cause irreparable harm to the environment, or enter the atmosphere and decrease cloud formation or alter the climate. The NIH and the university eventually won approval for their experiment, and the field trials were carried out in 1987.

While many scientists believe that the introduction of tested and approved engineered species into the environment will prove harmless and that early concerns were unfounded, many environmentalists still have reservations because the long-term environmental effects of genetically altered organisms remain unknown. It is feared that the introduction of some organisms will have negative impacts on the environment and irreversible global effects. Many worry that a genetically engineered organism such as a bacterium or virus could spread throughout the environment, causing human disease or ecological destruction.

The use of genetically engineered organisms could have many adverse effects. The introduction of new genes into an organism could extend the range of that species, causing it to infringe on the natural habitats of closely related or more distant species and thus disrupt the balance of nature. Many examples already exist of ecological disruption that has occurred as a result of the introduction of plant and animal species into areas where they have no natural predators. Some environmentalists believe that the use of herbicide-resistant crops will serve to prolong, extend, and even increase the use of toxic herbicides. Others fear that herbicide-resistant genes could be transferred to related plants, producing a population of herbicide-resistant weeds.

On the other hand, the introduction of organisms engineered through the cloning of recombinant DNA into the environment could have significant positive environmental impacts and increase world food production. Genetically altered plants could reduce the input of toxic chemicals into the environment. Genetic modification can create crops with larger yields; resistance to pests, pesticides, drought, and disease; higher tolerance to cold, heat, and drought; longer shelf life; and greater photosynthetic and nitrogen-fixing activity. Plants genetically engineered to produce a natural insecticide that is nontoxic to humans ideally alleviate the need for insecticide application; with the toxin produced by and confined to the plants themselves, there is no need to contaminate the entire area where they are grown. Bioremediation of toxic waste dumps, chemical spills, and oil spills could be enhanced by genetically engineered microorganisms.

Animal and Plant Cloning

The cloning of plants from cuttings has been successfully practiced for thousands of years and is commonly used for many important food crops. Successful animal cloning was first reported in 1892 by Hans Adolph Eduard Dreisch. Dreisch separated the first two and four embryonic cells (blastomeres) of the sea urchin and allowed them to develop into complete, genetically identical embryos.

The first report of successful animal cloning by nuclear transplantation was published in 1952 by Robert Briggs and Thomas J. King, who removed nuclei from embryonic frog cells and transplanted them into eggs from which their nuclei had been removed. By pricking the eggs with a glass needle the scientists induced them to divide and often develop into complete tadpoles. The first reliable reports of successful animal cloning by nuclear transplantation in mammals came in 1986 from Steen Willadsen in Cambridge, England. Willadsen cloned sheep from the nucleus of an early blastula cell. In 1987 Randall Prather and Willard Eyestone cloned cows while working in Neal First's laboratory at the University of Wisconsin.

In 1997 Ian Wilmut and Keith Campbell announced that they had successfully cloned a sheep named Dolly in Edinburgh, Scotland, the year before. Dolly was a milestone in cloning research because she was the first mammal cloned from an adult cell. Such animal cloning makes genetic engineering more efficient, because an animal would have to be engineered only once and then could be used to donate nuclei for cloning. The use of adult cells in cloning is advantageous in that the donor animal's physical characteristics are known before the animal is cloned. However, clones created from adult cells share those cells' shortened telomeres (the sequences at the ends of chromosomes that grow shorter with each generation of cell replication). Telomere shortening is associated with the aging and death of cells and of the entire organism, which means that the cloned animal is likely to have a greater susceptibility to degenerative conditions and a shortened life expectancy. Dolly, who was cloned from a six-year-old sheep, lived only six years before she had to be euthanized in 2003 because of a progressive lung disease. (Her breed typically lives about twelve years.) She had developed arthritis the year before. Whether her illnesses stemmed from premature aging is unclear; however, her telomeres were found to be short.

Although inbred stocks have been used for centuries in agriculture, it is feared that the extensive use of animal and plant clones could severely reduce the genetic variability of various important crop, forestry, and livestock species, making them more susceptible to disease and extreme environmental factors. On the other hand, the development of successful cloning techniques could rescue endangered species from the brink of extinction or allow for the creation of a population of genetically identical animals, which would be valuable in medical research. Moreover, cloning could be used to create an entire population of animals from one individual that has been genetically altered to produce a valuable pharmaceutical or organs suitable for human transplant. However, controversy would undoubtedly arise regarding the ethics of mass-producing animals through cloning for this purpose.

Reproductive cloning is costly, and more than 90 percent of cloning attempts do not result in viable offspring. Cloned mammals have tended to have immune function problems, increased infection rates, susceptibility to tumors, and short lives. A 2002 study of cloned mice found that about 4 percent of their genes functioned abnormally. Members of the American Medical Association and the American Association for the Advancement of Science have issued formal public statements advising against reproductive cloning in humans.

Charles L. Vigue;
Updated by Karen N. Kähler

Further Reading

Drlica, Karl. *Understanding DNA and Gene Cloning: A Guide for the Curious.* 4th ed. Hoboken, N.J.: John Wiley & Sons, 2004.

Fritz, Sandy, ed. *Understanding Cloning.* New York: Warner Books, 2002.

Klotzko, Arlene Judith. *A Clone of Your Own? The Science and Ethics of Cloning.* New York: Cambridge University Press, 2006.

Kolata, Gina Bari. *Clone: The Road to Dolly, and the Path Ahead.* New York: HarperCollins, 1998.

Williams, J. G., A. Ceccarelli, and A. Wallace. *Genetic Engineering.* 2d ed. Oxford, England: Bios, 2001.

Wilmut, Ian, Keith Campbell, and Colin Tudge. *The Second Creation: Dolly and the Age of Biological Control.* Cambridge, Mass.: Harvard University Press, 2001.

Wilmut, Ian, and Roger Highfield. After Dolly: The Uses and Misuses of Human Cloning. New York: W. W. Norton, 2006.

See also: Biotechnology and genetic engineering; Dolly the sheep; Genetically altered bacteria; Genetically engineered pharmaceuticals; Genetically modified foods; Genetically modified organisms; Wilmut, Ian

---

■ Cloud seeding

FIELDS OF STUDY: Meteorology, Atmospheric Sciences, Climatology; Weather; Technology and Applied Science; Scientific Equipment, Tools, Techniques, and Methods; Water Resources

DEFINITION: Practice of introducing agents into clouds for the purpose of intentionally modifying the weather

Because cloud and atmospheric processes are not completely understood, some doubt exists regarding whether cloud seeding actually works. In addition, some environmentalists are concerned that encouraging precipitation in one area may result in less precipitation in another.

Cloud seeding, which is relatively inexpensive and easily conducted, has long been the main technique used in weather modification. The seeding of clouds is undertaken for many purposes, including increasing rainfall for agriculture, increasing snowfall for winter recreational areas, dispersal of fog and clouds, and suppression of hail.

Most cloud seeding is directed at clouds with temperatures below freezing. These cold clouds consist of ice crystals and supercooled droplets (water droplets with subfreezing temperatures). Initially, supercooled droplets far outnumber ice crystals; however, the ice crystals quickly grow larger at the expense of the droplets and, after reaching sufficient size, fall as precipitation. The objective of seeding cold clouds is to stimulate this process in clouds that are deficient in ice crystals. The seeding agent is either silver iodide (AgI) or dry ice—solid carbon dioxide (CO_2) with a temperature of −80 degrees Celsius (−112

Line art drawing of cloud seeding. By Pearson Scott Foresman.

degrees Fahrenheit). Silver iodide pellets act as nuclei on which water droplets freeze to form precipitation, while dry ice pellets are so cold that they cause the surrounding supercooled droplets to freeze and grow into snowflakes. Warm clouds with temperatures above freezing can also be seeded through injection with salt crystals, which triggers the development of large liquid cloud drops that fall as precipitation.

Clouds must already be present for such weather modification techniques to work, since clouds cannot be generated by seeding. Most cloud seeding is done from aircraft, although silver iodide crystals can be injected into clouds from ground-based generators. One environmental concern is that seeding may only redistribute the supply of precipitation, so that an increase in precipitation in one area might mean a compensating reduction in another.

Since World War II, considerable research has gone into cloud seeding. However, scientists still cannot conclusively answer the question of whether cloud seeding actually works. One of the first large-scale experiments, conducted over south-central Missouri for five years during the 1950s, actually decreased rainfall. Apparently the clouds were overseeded, resulting in too many ice crystals competing for too few water droplets to form precipitation. In the 1970s and early 1980s, the National Oceanic and Atmospheric Administration (NOAA)

conducted a major experiment over southern Florida to test the effectiveness of seeding cumulus clouds. The initial results showed that under some conditions seeding increases rainfall, but a second, more statistically rigorous set of experiments failed to confirm the earlier results. Of the many experiments in cloud seeding that have been undertaken, only one, conducted in Israel in the 1960s and 1970s, has yielded statistically convincing confirmation of an increase in precipitation.

The conflicting results of the Florida and Israel studies point out the uncertainties of cloud seeding and the need for more basic knowledge of cloud and atmospheric processes. A major result of the many decades of investigating cloud seeding is the realization that weather events are quite complex and not yet fully understood. Without further basic understanding of atmospheric processes, large-scale weather modification through cloud seeding cannot be carried out with scientifically predictable results.

Craig S. Gilman

Further Reading

Ahrens, C. Donald. "Cloud Development and Precipitation." *Essentials of Meteorology: An Invitation to the Atmosphere.* 5th ed. Belmont: Thomson Learning, 2008. Print.

Cotton, William R., and Roger A. Pielke. *Human Impacts on Weather and Climate.* 2nd ed. New York: Cambridge UP, 2007. Print.

■ Club of Rome

FIELDS OF STUDY: Ethics, Advocacy, Policy, Protest; Ecology, Environment, Environmentalism; Organizations, Agencies, Commissions, Centers; Public Policy, Debates, Controversies

IDENTIFICATION: International think tank devoted to the study of the complex interrelationships of global problems

DATE: Established in April, 1968

The Club of Rome's influence in solving environmental problems surpasses the organization's low profile. From sponsoring the best-selling Limits to Growth *study in 1972 to promoting the benefits of energy efficiency, the Club of Rome has worked steadfastly for the betterment of humankind.*

In April, 1968, thirty-six prominent European scientists, businessmen, and statesmen gathered at the Accademia dei Lincei in Rome and formed the Club of Rome. Since its founding, the organization has focused on the *world problematique*, which is characterized by the complex interrelationships of global problems: environmental degradation, poverty, overpopulation, militarism, ineffective governmental institutions, and a global loss of human values. The Club of Rome commissions studies on important aspects of the *world problematique*, and the resulting reports become springboards for behind-the-scenes meetings with decision makers and for the initiation of projects recommended in the reports. Funding for Club of Rome reports and activities comes through arrangements with government agencies, academic research centers, and foundations.

By all accounts, Aurelio Peccei has been the most influential member of the Club of Rome. From the organization's founding in 1968 until his death in 1984, Peccei was instrumental in bringing people together, developing ideas into projects, finding funding, and providing logistic support for projects. In addition to Peccei's personal influence, the success of the club has relied on the contributions of its one hundred members from more than fifty countries. Many of the reports to the Club of Rome have been made possible by or have been directly authored by members.

The first report to the Club of Rome is also its best known. Club members obtained funding from the Volkswagen Foundation to commission a computer modeling team to forecast the future global system. The researchers' results were published in 1972 in *The Limits to Growth,* by Donella H. Meadows, Dennis L. Meadows, Jørgen Randers, and William W. Behrens III. This alarming report predicted that the human race would collapse by the year 2100 if current trends continued. The book became an international sensation, in large part through the publicity efforts of Peccei. Despite widespread criticism of the team's methodology and results, *The Limits to Growth* succeeded in sparking debate about the fate of humankind. It also generated greater interest in global modeling, including several follow-up studies commissioned by the club.

More than forty other reports to the Club of Rome have been published, with topics ranging from education to microelectronics. Reports with specifically environmental themes include *The Oceanic Circle: Governing the Seas as a Global Resource* (1998), by Elisabeth Mann-Borgese; *Factor Four: Doubling Wealth—Halving Resource Use* (1997), by Ernst von Weizsäcker, Amory B. Lovins, and Hunter L. Lovins; *The Future of the Oceans* (1986), by Elisabeth Mann-Borgese; *Energy: The Countdown* (1978), by Thierry de Montbrial; and *Beyond the Age of Waste* (1978), by Dennis Gabor and Umberto Colombo. Although these reports have not

Club of Rome Logo. By Jmortier (Own work)

achieved the visibility of *The Limits to Growth,* the club has used them as platforms for quiet environmental protection campaigns. In 2004, Meadows, Randers, and Meadows published a follow-up to their first report titled *Limits to Growth: The Thirty-Year Update.*

Andrew P. Duncan

Further Reading

Kula, E. *History of Environmental Economic Thought.* 1998. Reprint. New York: Routledge, 2003.

Meadows, Donella H., Jørgen Randers, and Dennis L. Meadows. *Limits to Growth: The Thirty-Year Update.* White River Junction, Vt.: Chelsea Green, 2004.

■ Coal ash storage

FIELDS OF STUDY: Geology, Geosciences; Energy and Energy Resources; Mineral Resources; Pollution, Emissions, Toxic Waste, Hazardous Materials

DEFINITION: Storage of the waste products of coal burning

Recycling the ash that results from coal burning provides a way to remove a waste product. Coal ash contains several environmental toxins, however, and unregulated storage of coal ash allows these toxins to leach into groundwater and pollute local water sources.

Many power plants burn coal to generate energy. The by-products of coal burning are called coal combustion by-products (CCBs) or coal ash. In 2007, coal-burning power plants in the United States generated approximately 131 million tons of coal ash.

Coal ash is generally divided into four types. Fly ash, the finest form of coal ash, forms from noncombustible matter in coal. Bottom ash, a coarse and granular material, comes from the bottom of coal-burning furnaces. Coal burned in a cyclone boiler produces a molten ash that, once cooled with water, forms a black material called boiler slag. Gases generated by coal burning, if passed through air-pollution-control systems called scrubbers that remove sulfur, generate flue gas desulfurization (FGD) gypsum.

Recycling and disposal represent the two options for managing coal ash. All four types of coal ash have several beneficial uses. Fly ash can substitute for Portland cement in concrete and produce stronger, less porous, and cheaper forms of concrete. Bottom ash and boiler slag contribute to road base, asphalt paving, and fill material, and engineers have used boiler slag for blasting grit, roofing-shingle aggregate, and snow and ice control. Farmers use FGD gypsum as a soil amendment, and builders use it to make wallboard. About one-third of coal ash and one-fourth of scrubber waste are recycled.

Methods of disposing of coal ash are divided into dry disposal, in which unwanted CCBs are transported to landfills, and wet disposal, in which coal ash is sluiced to storage lagoons. Combined coal ash in storage lagoons, known as ponded ash, accounts for approximately 30 percent of all disposed coal ash.

Coal ash often contains poisonous materials, such as arsenic, cadmium, chromium, lead, selenium, and other toxins that can cause cancer, liver damage, and neurological problems in humans and can kill fish and other wildlife. Toxins from coal ash storage lagoons can leach into groundwater. Studies by the U.S. Environmental Protection Agency (EPA) have shown that coal ash dumps can significantly increase the concentration of toxic metals in local drinking water. Worse still, coal ash used as fill-in material can ooze poisons into groundwater.

The retaining walls that enclose coal ash storage lagoons can also fail and produce environmental disasters. For example, on December 22, 2008, the ash dike enclosing a containment pond at the Tennessee Valley Authority's Kingston Fossil coal-burning plant, near Harriman, Tennessee, broke. Approximately one billion gallons of coal fly ash slurry flowed into tributaries of the Tennessee River, which supplies the drinking water for Chattanooga, Tennessee, and those who live downstream in Alabama, Tennessee, and Kentucky.

Because coal ash can be reused, it is not classified as a hazardous waste in the United States, nor is its reuse subject to federal oversight. The EPA moved to close this loophole in 2009, but the draft rule was held up by the Office of Management and Budget. The EPA's stated purpose was to prevent environmental damage from coal ash ponds by requiring such ponds to have synthetic liners and leachate collections systems and by phasing out leak-prone ash ponds.

Michael A. Buratovich

Further Reading

Freese, Barbara. *Coal: A Human History.* Cambridge, Mass.: Perseus, 2003.

Goodell, Jeff. *Big Coal: The Dirty Secret Behind America's Energy Future.* New York: Houghton Mifflin, 2006.

Greb, Stephen F., et al. *Coal and the Environment.* Alexandria, Va.: American Geological Institute, 2006.

■ Coastal Zone Management Act

FIELDS OF STUDY: Government, Politics, International Relations; Laws, Acts, Resolutions; Biology, Life Sciences, Ecosystems; Continents, Regions, Areas, Islands; Ecology, Environment, Environmentalism; Oceans, Seas, Lakes, Bodies of Water; Water Resources

CATEGORIES: Treaties, laws, and court cases; land and land use; water and water pollution

THE LAW: U.S. federal law providing for the management of land and water uses in coastal areas, including the Great Lakes

DATE: Enacted on October 27, 1972

The Coastal Zone Management Act has provided coastal zones with funding and research to create effective management programs to guide development. More than 153,000 kilometers (95,000 miles) of oceanic and Great Lakes coastlines are managed through these programs.

In 1970 the National Oceanic and Atmospheric Administration (NOAA) was created as an agency of the U.S. Department of Commerce. One of its charges was to develop a comprehensive plan to help guarantee the appropriate balance between the economic development of coastal and marine ecosystems and the protection of such ecosystems from pollution, overfishing, erosion, and invasive species. In 1972 the U.S. Congress passed the Coastal Zone Management Act (CZMA), creating a framework for local and federal partnerships to protect marine life and maintain clean water resources while permitting coastal economies to grow.

Under the CZMA, two new programs were created. The National Coastal Zone Management Program provides matching funds to coastal states that voluntarily submit management plans for conservation. More than half of the thirty-five eligible U.S. states and territories submitted approved plans by the end of 1979; by early 2010, Illinois was the only

eligible state that had not yet joined the program. The National Estuarine Research Reserve System studies and protects the coastal zones where freshwater and saltwater bodies intersect. By early 2010, twenty-seven estuaries had been designated as sanctuaries.

Cynthia A. Bily

See also: Beaches; Chesapeake Bay; Commercial fishing; Coral reefs; Environmental law, U.S.; Fisheries; Habitat destruction; Introduced and exotic species; Land-use policy; Sea-level changes; Water conservation

■ Cogeneration power systems

FIELDS OF STUDY: Technology and Applied Science; Inventions; Energy and Energy Resources

DEFINITION: Power generation that produces useful electricity and heat simultaneously

Since the mid-twentieth century cogeneration power systems have become increasingly attractive for the on-site industrial production of energy because of their cost-effectiveness and their efficiency.

Cogeneration is an energy recycling process. The cogeneration process puts to work the heat produced by the generation of electricity, energy which when produced off-site at conventional power stations is routinely lost, vented into the atmosphere largely through cooling towers. In conventional energy production, public utilities produce electricity at power plants and transmit thermal energy through miles of insulated piping to distant industrial and commercial complexes, most often factories, a process that routinely works at a tremendous inefficiency, roughly 25 percent (that is, nearly 75 percent of the energy is lost). Factories that rely on that energy must thus pay high rates for electricity that reflect the inefficiency of the system. In contrast, when a factory opts for a cogeneration plant on-site, a primary fuel source (most often natural gas, wood, or fossil fuel) is used to generate electricity, in this case a secondary fuel, and the heat that is naturally and simultaneously produced in that process is retained and used on-site, most prominently in space heating (and cooling) and in heating water. In utilizing the heat that is a by-product of electricity production, cogeneration (also

Fairbanks industrial section. The municipal cogeneration plant provides electricity and district heating. By D. Sikes

known as CHP, for "combined heat and power") offers a nearly 90 percent efficiency. Because it uses significantly lower amounts of fuel to produce usable energy, cogeneration production is often cited for its potential to save industry jobs.

Cogeneration, although attractive in an era of energy conservation, is hardly new—in fact, the original commercial electrical power plant designed by Thomas Edison more than a century ago was a cogeneration plant, largely for practical reasons: No network grid existed to move energy across distances. As power networks became established and government regulations sought to protect public utilities from unlicensed competition, public utilities gradually became the dominant providers of energy in return for government control of pricing and rates. When fuel prices were relatively stable and low, industries had little incentive to develop cogeneration technology. Since the major energy crisis of the mid-1970's, however, industries have increasingly looked toward cogeneration. In addition, in light of emerging scientific knowledge regarding global warming, a process that increases energy efficiency and recycles heat offers an environmentally friendly alternative to traditional power generation.

Given that the cogeneration process involves the burning of fossil fuels, it has the potential to contribute to air and water pollution, but most established environmental groups, most prominently the Sierra Club, have long backed cogeneration as part of any responsible comprehensive domestic energy agenda. Cogeneration is far better established in Europe than in the United States; in 2010 only about 10 percent of U.S. electricity needs were being met through cogeneration facilities, but the figure was rising. The kinds of facilities that most often use cogeneration are those in various process industries (breweries, food-processing plants, paper mills, brick and cement factories, textile plants, mineral refineries); some commercial and public buildings (hospitals, hotels, large universities, airports, military facilities) also use cogeneration. Given its potential to secure at least some short-term constraints on carbon dioxide emissions and its ability to maintain power supplies despite whatever interruption might affect the larger power grid, cogeneration has emerged as a significant element of environmentally conscious energy production.

Joseph Dewey

Further Reading

Flin, David. *Cogeneration: A User's Guide.* Stevenage, Hertfordshire, England: Institution of Engineering and Technology, 2009.

Jonnes, Jill. *Empires of Light: Edison, Tesla, Westinghouse, and the Race to Electrify the World.* New York: Random House, 2003.

Kolanowski, Bernard F. *Small-Scale Cogeneration Handbook.* Lilburn, Ga.: Fairmont Press, 2008.

Kutz, Myer. *Environmentally Conscious Alternative Energy Production.* Hoboken, N.J.: John Wiley & Sons, 2007.

■ Colorado River

FIELDS OF STUDY: Biology, Life Sciences, Ecosystems; Oceans, Seas, Lakes, Bodies of Water; Water Resources

CATEGORIES: Places; water and water pollution

IDENTIFICATION: Large river that flows through the southwestern United States and northwestern Mexico

The Colorado River is located in an arid region, and numerous disputes regarding rights to the river's water have arisen among the political entities that have land within the river basin: seven U.S. states and Mexico. All of these parties want to ensure that they will have continued access to the river's water for agricultural irrigation and urban-suburban expansion.

The Colorado River watershed has a drainage area of 637,000 square kilometers (246,000 square miles) and includes parts of seven western states (Colorado, Wyoming, Utah, Nevada, New Mexico, Arizona, and California) and parts of northwestern Mexico. The river begins in the Rocky Mountains of Colorado and flows for 2,330 kilometers (1,450 miles), to the Gulf of California.

Many dams were built on the Colorado River during the twentieth century for hydroelectricity and flood control, creating bodies of water that are also used for recreation. Together, these dams have the capacity to store more than 85 billion cubic meters (3,000 billion cubic feet) of water, a volume that is

roughly four times the average annual flow of the entire river. The two largest dams are Hoover Dam, on the border between Nevada and Arizona, and Glen Canyon Dam, in north-central Arizona. These dams represent 80 percent of the total water-storage capacity in the watershed. Irrigation accounts for two-thirds of the water use, with much of the remaining portion going to cities (such as Phoenix, Tucson, and Las Vegas) and evaporation. Withdrawals from the river include not only water use within the Colorado River watershed basin but also major deliveries to areas outside the basin, such as the Los Angeles metropolitan area, the farms of the Imperial Valley in southeastern California, portions of Baja California, the Central Utah Project, and the Colorado-Big Thompson Project to bring water to Denver and other areas east of the Rockies.

Over the years, numerous disputes have arisen over the rights to the water of the Colorado River. One attempt to resolve such disputes was the Colorado River Compact of 1922. That agreement made water allocations among states based on the water

Colorado River Storage Project Act

The Colorado River Storage Project Act of 1956 was passed after a bitter battle between environmental groups and the U.S. government to prevent the construction of Echo Park Dam. The act's main points follow:

The Act authorizes the Secretary of the Interior to construct a variety of dams, reservoirs, powerplants, transmission facilities and related works in the Upper Colorado River Basin. The Act also authorizes and directs the Secretary to investigate, plan, construct and operate facilities to mitigate losses of, and improve conditions for, fish and wildlife and public recreational facilities. The Act provides authority to acquire lands and to lease and convey lands and facilities to state and other agencies. . . .

The Act provides for the comprehensive development of the water resources of the Upper Colorado River Basin to: regulate the flow of the Colorado River; store water for beneficial consumptive use; make it possible for states of the Upper Basin to use the apportionments made to and among them in the Colorado River Compact and the Upper Colorado River Basin Compact, respectively; provide for the reclamation of arid and semiarid land, the control of floods, and the generation of hydroelectric power. . . .

By authorizing construction and prioritizing planning of specified projects, Congress does not intend to interfere with comprehensive development providing for consumptive water use apportioned to and among the Upper Colorado River Basin states or preclude consideration and authorization by Congress of additional projects. No dam or reservoir authorized by the Act shall be constructed within a national park or monument. . . .

Recreational, Fish and Wildlife Facilities. The Secretary is authorized and directed to investigate, plan, construct, operate and maintain: public recreational facilities on project lands to conserve scenery, the natural, historic and archaeologic objects, wildlife and public use and enjoyment; facilities to mitigate losses and improve conditions for the propagation of fish and wildlife. . . .

Robert M. Hordon

that had been available during the relatively limited period from 1896 to 1922, even though the river had been in existence for at least five million years. It was later understood that the period chosen was actually one of above-normal precipitation, as indicated by tree-ring analysis, which enabled scientists to extend the record back several centuries. The ten-year running mean for the annual flow of the Colorado River at Lee's Ferry below Glen Canyon Dam showed a downward trend from 1987 to 2007.

Problems with water quality in the Colorado River include high salinity levels that reflect the combination of an arid climate, the presence of saline soils, and the impacts of large amounts of surface-water runoff from irrigation return flows. Continuing population growth in the region is likely to add to problems of water demand and water quality. Environmentalists and others have suggested that those living in the region should take steps to conserve the water of the Colorado River through such practices as using native drought-resistant vegetation in landscaping (xeriscaping) and using lower-quality water for irrigating certain kinds of properties, such as golf courses.

Climate change could be another important factor in the future of the Colorado River. According to estimates by the Intergovernmental Panel on Climate Change, global warming could result in a 20 percent reduction in runoff in the Colorado River watershed by the middle of the twenty-first century. The resultant environmental impacts on the river system would be substantial.

Robert M. Hordon

Further Reading

Cech, Thomas V. *Principles of Water Resources: History, Development, Management, and Policy.* 3d ed. Hoboken, N.J.: John Wiley & Sons, 2010.

Powell, James L. *Dead Pool: Lake Powell, Global Warming, and the Future of Water in the West.* Berkeley: University of California Press, 2008.

See also: Droughts; Echo Park Dam opposition; Glen Canyon Dam; Global warming; Grand Canyon; Hoover Dam; Hydroelectricity; Irrigation; Riparian rights; Runoff, agricultural; Water conservation; Water rights; Watershed management

■ Commercial fishing

FIELDS OF STUDY: Economics, Business, Production, Commerce; Biology, Life Sciences, Ecosystems; Animals, Zoology, Marine Biology; Ecology, Environment, Environmentalism; Food, Hunger; Biology, Life Sciences, Ecosystems; Animals, Zoology, Marine Biology; Ecology, Environment, Environmentalism; Food, Hunger; Economics, Business, Production, Commerce

DEFINITION: Large-scale, mostly oceanic, fishing operations undertaken for profit

Beginning during the mid-twentieth century, larger, more efficient fishing fleets began exhausting coastal fishing areas and moving farther from port in their effort to meet growing demand. By the end of the century, such fleets had reached nearly every area of the world's oceans. Overfishing has depleted marine populations and in some cases has precipitated political crises.

Hooks, nets, and traps had little effect on populations of marine life until Europeans began operating fishing fleets during the late Middle Ages. Mechanization of fishing started in the nineteenth century, but world fishing production was still only around 3 million tons at the beginning of the twentieth century and 20 million tons during the 1950s. The subsequent development of better transportation allowed rapid shipment of premium catches, and the fishing industry reacted to the growing market by investing in larger boats and new technologies and techniques, including sonar, aerial spotting, and nylon nets.

Even more important was the introduction of factory ships. Such ships process and store the catch at sea, so a fishing fleet can work far from its home port. In one hour, a factory ship can harvest more fish than a sixteenth century fishing boat could harvest in one season. According to a 2018 study, over 70,000 industrialized fishing vessels were operational between 2012 and 2016. These large-scale operations often specialize in a single species and throw back nontarget fish. However, the nontarget bycatch fish that are returned to the water are usually dead or dying after being netted, dropped in a hold, and sorted.

Although fishing became industrialized, the old ideas of a limitless supply of fish and an uncontrolled sea remained. The stage was therefore set for a series

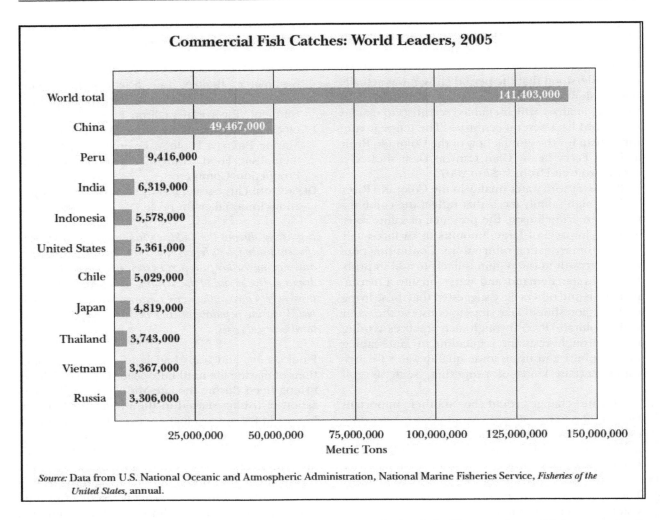

Commercial Fish Catches: World Leaders, 2005

	Metric Tons
World total	141,403,000
China	49,467,000
Peru	9,416,000
India	6,319,000
Indonesia	5,578,000
United States	5,361,000
Chile	5,029,000
Japan	4,819,000
Thailand	3,743,000
Vietnam	3,367,000
Russia	3,306,000

Source: Data from U.S. National Oceanic and Atmospheric Administration, National Marine Fisheries Service, *Fisheries of the United States,* annual.

of environmental disasters and political crises. One problem with fishing is that it is a hunter-gatherer operation rather than an agricultural one. Fishers do not nurture and protect schools of fish as farmers protect herds of cattle. This alone limits productivity. For example, there is little investment in habitat for fish, such as wetlands or rivers.

In addition, fish are considered a common property for which each hunter competes against the others. Any fishers who hold back in catching fish to save breeding stock for the future lose their catch to other boats. American ecologist Garrett Hardin referred to this phenomenon as the "tragedy of the commons," a concept he originally applied to publicly owned grazing lands. However, cattle on land can be counted, while fish populations are often gauged only by catch. Thus fishers working feverishly

to catch the dwindling numbers of fish create the illusion of a stable population. An entire fish species may ultimately be fished to near extinction, and the fishery may collapse, but the worst offenders will gain the most profit until disaster occurs. According to the United Nations Food and Agriculture Organization (FAO) in 2018, almost 90 percent of the world's fish stocks were overfished.

Meanwhile, ocean pollution has reduced productivity in some areas. Shallow waters close to land are naturally the most productive, but these areas are the first to be affected by pollution. Areas such as the Black Sea, the North Sea, and the Chesapeake Bay in the United States have experienced serious declines in fish production. In the Gulf of Mexico, the Sea of Japan, and other waters, excess nutrients, largely

from agricultural runoff, have been blamed for red tides (blooms of a poisonous species of algae).

Another form of environmental degradation is bottom destruction. Powerful boats use "rockhopper"-equipped trawl nets that drag across rough areas of the ocean floor to catch bottom fish such as cod, flounder, and turbot. This practice destroys habitat and food for the young of many species.

Consequences of Unsustainable Fishing Practices

Despite the environmental impacts of overfishing and destructive fishing practices, governments continue to subsidize bigger and more advanced boats that travel farther and deeper to catch dwindling fish stocks. According to the World Wildlife Fund and the World Economic Forum, the world's commercial fishing industry receives tens of billions of dollars in subsidies every year—support that has helped keep more fishing vessels in business than the oceans can sustainably support.

History shows many examples of unsustainable fishing spurred by economic factors. During the 1950s Icelandic gunboats and British warships threatened each other during the so-called Cod War to control fishing access in the North Atlantic. Peru had a similar contest of wills with the United States to control foreign production of anchovies caught off the Peruvian coast. However, the Peruvians did not limit their own production, and, as anchovy stocks dwindled, the fishery collapsed in 1972. Similarly, Canada and the United States misjudged the carrying capacity of the Grand Banks shoals southeast of Newfoundland, and by 1992 cod fishing in the area was halted. Despite this moratorium, the cod population has not recovered—in large part because excessive bycatch of this banned nontarget fish has continued to deplete its numbers.

Total fish production would probably have declined during the 1990s had aquaculture not rapidly increased during the same period. In 2006 fish farming supplied about half of all fishery products for human consumption, and its output was growing faster than any other animal-based food sector. Farm fisheries can produce indefinitely if they limit catches to practical levels. Even devastated farm fisheries can eventually recover. Doing the same for the open ocean, however, would require major diplomatic efforts. Voluntary bans on whaling and drift nets have been routinely ignored by some countries. Beyond management of wild stocks, fish farming has the potential for great production increases. However, aquaculture raises environmental concerns regarding pollution and genetic weakening of wild stocks if large numbers of domestic stocks escape.

According to the FAO, about 90 percent of global marine stocks were fully fished, overfished, or depleted by 2018. Scientists have noted that if marine fisheries are to recover and be used sustainably, a number of measures must be imposed and enforced worldwide, including the prohibition of destructive and unsustainable fishing practices, the limitation of access rights, and the establishment of protected marine areas. Some researchers maintain that if fishing practices continue unaltered, populations of all fish species caught for food in the early twenty-first century will collapse within fifty years.

Roger V. Carlson; updated by Karen N. Kähler

Further Reading

Chandran, Nyshka. "More Than Half the World's Oceans Are Being Hit By 'Industrial Fishing.'" CNBC, 22 Feb. 2018, https://www.cnbc.com/2018/02/22/commercial-fishing-covers-half-of-global-oceans-study.html. Accessed 27 Mar. 2018.

Clover, Charles. The End of the Line: How Overfishing Is Changing the World and What We Eat. U of California P, 2008.

"Commercial Fishing." NOAA Fisheries, National Oceanic and Atmospheric Administration, www.fisheries.noaa.gov/topic/commercial-fishing. Accessed 27 Mar. 2018.

Helfman, Gene S. Fish Conservation: A Guide to Understanding and Restoring Global Aquatic Biodiversity and Fishery Resources. Island, 2007.

Roberts, Callum M. The Unnatural History of the Sea. Island, 2007.

Rogers, Raymond A. The Oceans Are Emptying: Fish Wars and Sustainability. Black Rose, 1995.

State of World Fisheries and Aquaculture 2014. Food and Agriculture Org., 2014.

■ Commoner, Barry

FIELDS OF STUDY: Ethics, Advocacy, Policy, Protest; Ecology, Environment, Environmentalism; Public Policy, Debates, Controversies; Authors, Writers; Scientists, Engineers

CATEGORIES: Activism and advocacy; nuclear power and radiation; energy and energy use

IDENTIFICATION: American biologist and antinuclear activist

Commoner has raised public awareness of a number of important environmental issues, particularly regarding the use of energy resources, organic farming and pesticides, waste management, and toxic chemicals.

Barry Commoner graduated from Columbia University in 1937 and received an M.A. (1938) and a Ph.D. (1941) from Harvard University. He has been awarded a number of honorary degrees from prominent institutions, and his biography has appeared in *Who's Who in Science and Engineering*. His interest in becoming an environmental activist was sparked in the 1950's by the testing of nuclear weapons. In 1965 Commoner was president of the St. Louis Commission on Nuclear Information, and in 1966 he founded the Center for the Biology of Natural Systems (CBNS) at Washington University in St. Louis, Missouri. In 1981 the CBNS moved to Queens College, in the City University of New York (CUNY) system. The CBNS program has continually informed the public and government on environmental issues, including waste recycling and energy resources; it has provided extensive analysis of the generation and fate of dioxins.

Commoner is the author of several books on the environment, including *Science and Survival* (1966), *The Closing Circle: Nature, Man, and Technology* (1971), *Ecology and Social Action* (1973), *The Politics of Energy* (1979), and *Making Peace with the Planet* (1990). He publicizes environmental problems and relates them to modern technology. Commoner claims that modern methods of production cause human illness and that modern technologies that have resulted in environmental crises have safer alternatives. He believes that to restore the environment, humans need to adopt more benign ways of accomplishing tasks, such as eliminating the use of plastic wrap and recycling instead of incineration. He has promoted the view that there is economic value and profitability in the replacement technologies. He has drawn attention to the affiliations of some environmental scientists and has questioned their opinions, stating that environmental hazards are reliably recognized only through studies done by independent scientists. He has encouraged the public to become more informed, to achieve a greater understanding of the effects of particular technologies on the environment before using those technologies.

In recognition of his contributions to public awareness of environmental concerns, Commoner has been hailed by *Time* magazine as the "Paul Revere of Ecology" and by the *Earth Times* as "the dean of the environmental movement, who has influenced two generations." In 1980 Commoner was the presidential candidate of the Citizens Party, a liberal political party he helped found; the party's interests included an end to nuclear power, a switch to solar energy, and public control of the energy industry.

Commoner continues to lead the movement to eliminate pollution at its source. He asserts that prevention works while controls do not, and he publicly advocates the abandonment of fossil fuels as a primary source of energy. Having served society and the environment since the 1950's, he has succeeded in elevating the importance of considering environmental issues in all aspects of life.

Marcie L. Wingfield and Massimo D. Bezoari

Further Reading

Egan, Michael. *Barry Commoner and the Science of Survival: The Remaking of American Environmentalism.* Cambridge, Mass.: MIT Press, 2007.

Kriebel, David, ed. *Barry Commoner's Contribution to the Environmental Movement: Science and Social Action.* Amityville, N.Y.: Baywood, 2002.

See also: Alternative energy sources; Antinuclear movement; Renewable energy; Solar energy

■ Community gardens

FIELDS OF STUDY: Places, Peoples, Societies; Agriculture, Farming, Animal Husbandry; Cities, Urbanization, Urban Planning

DEFINITION: Plots of land, donated or rented by the bodies that hold the titles or leases, that are cultivated by local community members

Phoenix, AZ. By Angelica Phoenix from Phoenix, Arizona, USA

Community gardens provide recreation and education for participants, and for many, such spaces offer respite from the stresses of urban living. In some low-income areas, community gardens are important contributors to residents' basic food supplies.

Community gardens vary greatly in nature in different parts of the world. In North America, community gardens are generally small plots of land dedicated to "greening" projects in urban areas. The common image of a community garden in the United States is of a formerly vacant plot in a low-income urban area transformed into a green, productive garden. In Europe, community gardens are generally larger and more organized, and a garden may be rented by a single family for many generations. In developing nations, it is very common for small gardens to be open to public farming.

Matters such as assignment of plots and other organizational issues in community gardens are most often decided by the gardeners involved. Some gardens are organized so that all participants garden collectively; others are split up into divided plots and managed by individual gardeners or families. The land that becomes a community garden may be either publicly or privately owned.

One goal of community gardening for many participants is to achieve food security while creating a stronger relationship between individuals and their food. Community gardens generally promote organic cultivation methods. Many community gardeners state that, in addition to seeking healthy food alternatives, they are involved in the gardening because of the value of community building they derive from their participation.

In 2001 the American Community Gardening Association (ACGA) estimated that some 150,000 community gardens were in operation in the United States. At that time the South Central Farm in Los Angeles, California, established in 1994, was considered the largest community garden in the nation, at 5.7 hectares (14 acres). The garden was shut down in 2006, when the city of Los Angeles sold the land. By 2015, the ACGA's estimate had dropped to 18,000 community gardens in the United States and Canada.

Many organizations offer assistance in the creation of community gardens. The American Community Gardening Association provides advice—on everything from training to insurance policies—to groups seeking to establish gardens, so that they can do so sustainably and effectively. The American Horticultural Society runs a rapidly growing program that focuses on youth gardening, a form of community gardening aimed specifically at connecting children with nature.

In addition to being resources for those involved, community gardens are commonly believed to provide tangible improvements to the areas that surround them. Some research, however, appears to indicate that this belief may be more a matter of perception than of reality. A study conducted by Texas A&M and Texas State universities looked at the impact of community gardens on the numbers of property crimes in urban Houston and found that there was no statistically significant difference between crime rates in the areas surrounding the gardens and other areas. Interviewed residents, however, stated that community gardens created a positive influence in their neighborhoods. They commented on revitalization of neighborhood development and a changing tone toward illegal activity, including drug dealing. The members of the communities surrounding the gardens thus felt safer, despite the fact that the areas' crime rates were no lower than those in other areas.

Kara Kaminski

Further Reading

Amer. Community Garden Assn. *CommunityGarden. org.* ACGA, 2015. Web. 15 Jan. 2015.

Henderson, Elizabeth, with Robyn Van En. *Sharing the Harvest: A Citizen's Guide to Community Supported Agriculture.* Rev. ed. White River Junction, Vt.: Chelsea Green, 2007.

Lawson, Laura. *City Bountiful: A Century of Community Gardening in America.* Berkeley: University of California Press, 2005.

Lyson, Thomas A. *Civic Agriculture: Reconnecting Farm, Food, and Community.* Lebanon, N.H.: Tufts University Press, 2004.

Smith, Jeremy N., Sepp Jannotta, and Chad Harder. *The Urban Garden: How One Community Turned Idle Land into a Garden City and How You Can, Too.* New York: Skyhorse, 2014. Digital file.

■ Compact fluorescent lightbulbs

FIELDS OF STUDY: Technology and Applied Science; Industries, Commercial Products; Inventions; Energy and Energy Resources

DEFINITION: Lightbulbs that consume less energy and radiate a different light spectrum than incandescent bulbs and are designed to replace them

Compact fluorescent lightbulbs can have positive impacts on the environment in that they last longer than traditional incandescent lightbulbs and use significantly less energy than incandescents, so they create less waste and aid in energy conservation. Because compact fluorescent bulbs contain mercury, however, care must be taken in their disposal to avoid doing environmental harm.

Compact fluorescent lightbulbs (CFLs) were first introduced as an energy-saving alternative to traditional incandescent lightbulbs during the mid-1990's. They use less energy and have longer life spans than incandescent lightbulbs, which they are designed to replace. CFLs can use up to 75 percent less energy and last up to ten times longer than incandescents. CFLs can be used in most of the same lighting fixtures as incandescent bulbs, but different types of CFLs have been created for compatibility with various types of lighting fixtures, including those that use dimmer switches, three-way lamps, and outdoor fixtures.

Several kinds of fixtures and circumstances can reduce the overall efficiency of CFLs; enclosed light fixtures, for example, can create high temperatures that can shorten CFLs' life, and CFLs cannot withstand extremely low temperatures. Additionally, CFLs should not be used in fixtures that vibrate, including ceiling fans and garage door openers. The efficiency of CFLs is greatly reduced when they are turned on and off frequently, as most CFLs take at least three minutes to warm up and emit their maximum light.

CFLs and incandescent lightbulbs use different methods to produce light, which accounts for the different amounts of energy they use. An incandescent bulb produces light by running an electrical current through a wire to heat a filament. A CFL produces light by using electricity to ignite a gas within the bulb to produce invisible ultraviolet light, which then produces visible light by exciting a fluorescent white coating (phosphor) inside the bulb. A ballast regulates the electrical current within the bulb. After the gas within the CFL is ignited, the amount of electricity needed to keep the bulb lighted is significantly less than that used to heat the filament in an incandescent bulb.

State and local governments in the United States have set rules regulating the disposal and recycling of

Livin' green aka EU Light-Bulb Ban! By Levente Fulop from Brno, Czech Republic

broken and intact CFLs because these bulbs, like all fluorescent bulbs, contain small amounts of mercury; on average, each CFL contains about 4 milligrams (0.00014 ounce) of mercury. When a CFL is intact no amount of mercury is released, but mercury may be released from a broken CFL. The U.S. Environmental Protection Agency advises that the following special precautions should be taken when a CFL breaks, to avoid the possibility of mercury exposure. All people and animals should leave the room in which the bulb was broken, and the room should be allowed to air out for at least fifteen minutes. Disposable materials should then be used to clean up the remnants of the bulb, and all the cleanup materials should be disposed of immediately, along with the broken bulb and its remnants, in a glass jar or plastic bag that can then be sealed. The jar or bag should then be disposed of according to guidelines for disposal of toxic materials set by the local government.

Courtney A. Smith

Further Reading

Chiras, Daniel D. "Foundations of a Sustainable Energy System: Conservation and Renewable Energy." In *Environmental Science*. 8th ed. Sudbury, Mass.: Jones and Bartlett, 2010.

Goldblatt, David L. *Sustainable Energy Consumption and Society: Personal, Technological, or Social Change?* Norwell, Mass.: Springer, 2005.

Krigger, John, and Chris Dorsi. *The Homeowner's Handbook to Energy Efficiency: A Guide to Big and Small Improvements*. Helena, Mont.: Saturn Resource Management, 2008.

■ Composting

FIELDS OF STUDY: Biology, Life Sciences, Ecosystems; Agriculture, Farming, Animal Husbandry; Ecology, Environment, Environmentalism; Chemistry

CATEGORY: Waste and waste management

DEFINITION: Recycling of organic waste in a fashion that breaks down the matter into mulch, a rich soil conditioner

Composting has gained attention as an environmentally responsible way to reduce the amount of waste that goes to landfills.

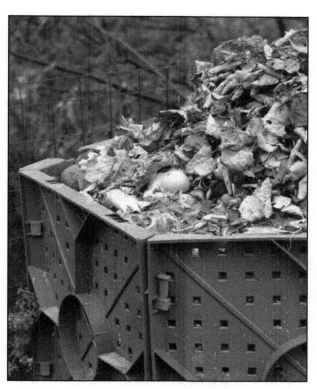

A backyard composting bin filled with yard and kitchen waste. (©Dreamstime.com)

All living things are part of a natural recycling process. For example, dead trees in a forest slowly break down into a soil-like substance that nurtures the growth of new forest plants. Composting is the same process in a slightly controlled environment.

A backyard or garden compost bin is basically a box with holes or slats, to let in air, that is filled with yard and kitchen waste. A fifty-fifty balance of items containing nitrogen and items containing carbon is needed. Items containing nitrogen include grass clippings, eggshells, coffee grounds, and vegetable and fruit peelings. Items containing carbon include dead leaves, evergreen needles, bark chips, and dryer lint. The various items are added in layers and topped with dirt to hold in moisture. As the waste decays, the bacteria present thrive. They feast on the waste, generating energy and more bacteria. The decomposing pile is occasionally turned with a shovel, and more yard or kitchen waste is added. The waste products from the bacteria, together with what is left after they feast on scraps, form a dry mulch that can be used as a natural garden fertilizer.

Trash and garbage collected from the public by sanitation workers is sometimes composted in municipal processing plants. Decomposable materials are sorted from glass, metal, and other inorganic materials, and the organic items are then shredded or broken down into smaller pieces. In this way, local governments can reduce the amount of waste that is added to landfills or burned.

Two methods are used for mechanical composting. An open-window facility requires a large area of land. It is similar to backyard compost bins but on a large scale. Mounds of organic waste are piled in long, low rows called windows. They are turned or mixed every few days so the aerobic (oxygen-requiring) bacteria that are digesting the waste have adequate oxygen. The aerobic bacteria may take up to eight weeks to digest the organic waste completely. The activity of the microbes creates temperatures in the piles of up to 65 degrees Celsius (150 degrees Fahrenheit). Any bacteria or organisms carrying disease die at this temperature. The odor produced as the material decomposes makes the siting of open-window facilities difficult, as most people object to having such facilities operating near where they live.

The other type of mechanical composting facility encloses the waste in tanks. Paddles mix the material, adding air at the same time. Tank composting facilities use 85 percent less space than do open-window facilities, and the compost is fully digested in about one week. The digested compost is dried, screened, and made into pellets before it is used as a soil conditioner or fertilizer. Mechanically processed compost has low marketability, however, because of the cost of transport and because of competition from the chemical fertilizers readily available to commercial farmers.

Lisa A. Wroble

Further Reading

Nardi, James B. "Composting as an Antidote to Soil Abuse." In *Life in the Soil: A Guide for Naturalists and Gardeners.* Chicago: University of Chicago Press, 2007.
Scott, Nicky. *Composting: An Easy Household Guide.* White River Junction, Vt.: Chelsea Green, 2007.

See also: Agricultural chemicals; Biofertilizers; Landfills; Organic gardening and farming; Waste treatment

■ Comprehensive Nuclear-Test-Ban Treaty (CTBT)

FIELDS OF STUDY: Government, Politics, International Relations; International Relations, Agreements, Treaties; Nuclear Power, Nuclear Weapons, Radioactive Waste
THE TREATY: International agreement banning nuclear weapons testing
DATE: Opened for signature on September 10, 1996

Although not in force, the Comprehensive Nuclear-Test-Ban Treaty serves as an international voice against nuclear testing. The treaty seeks to end all supercritical weapons tests without inhibiting the continued development and refinement of nuclear weapons by those nations that already possess test data.

Since 1945, at least 2,080 nuclear weapons test explosions have been conducted—most by the United States (1,054), followed by the Soviet Union (715), France (210), the United Kingdom (45), China (45), India (6), Pakistan (2), North Korea (2), and an unconfirmed entity (1). The Partial Test Ban Treaty of 1963 and the Outer Space Treaty of 1967 banned atmospheric and space-based tests, but France and China continued atmospheric testing until 1974 and 1976, respectively. Despite the provisions of the Nuclear Non-Proliferation Treaty of 1968, Pakistani and North Korean tests are reported to have originated in Chinese fuel and designs. The Strategic Arms Limitation Treaty (SALT) and the Strategic Arms Reduction Treaty (START) between the United States and the Soviet Union limited and reduced the numbers of strategic nuclear warheads held by the two nations, but not their thousands of tactical nuclear weapons.

The Comprehensive Nuclear-Test-Ban Treaty, also known as the Comprehensive Test Ban Treaty, or CTBT, would require nations to agree not to conduct supercritical nuclear tests, to allow their territory to be used for such tests, or to encourage other nations to conduct such tests. A global verification regime would have four elements: an international monitoring system, a consultation and clarification process for suspected violations, on-site inspections, and confidence-building measures. The treaty was signed by seventy-four nations and passed by United Nations General Assembly resolution in September, 1996, but it cannot go into force until 180 days after ratification by the forty-four nations possessing nuclear reactors.

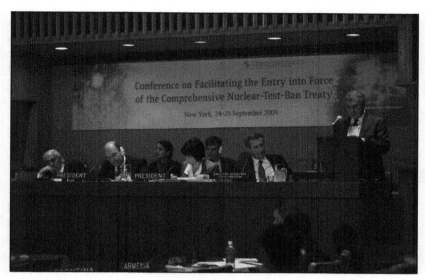

25 September 2009 - New York. Deputy Undersecretary, Minister of Foreign Affairs of Turkey Unal Cevikoz makes a statement during the Conference on Facilitating the Entry Into Force of the Comprehensive Nuclear-Test-Ban Treaty.

Egypt, North Korea, India, Iran, Israel, Indonesia, Pakistan, China, and the United States have all cited supreme national security compulsions in declining to sign or ratify the treaty.

The CTBT is seen as devoid of intent toward universal nuclear disarmament. Its timing coincided with the advent of ACI Red, the U.S. Department of Energy's teraFLOPS computer developed to simulate numerically the physical processes in a nuclear explosion reliably enough to predict weapon performance using the large test database. China and France completed several tests in 1992-1996 before signing the CTBT, and France set off twelve thermonuclear tests in the pristine islands of the South Pacific Mururoa and Fangataufa atolls in 1996.

Although not in force, the CTBT serves as an international voice against nuclear testing. In 2009 the debate among nuclear powers appeared to shift toward the amount of testing required to ensure a validated prediction capability in order to maintain the "minimum credible deterrent" for national security.

Narayanan M. Komerath and Padma P. Komerath

Further Reading

Dahlman, O., S. Mykkeltveit, and H. Haak. *Nuclear Test Ban: Converting Political Visions to Reality.* New York: Springer, 2009.

Hansen, Keith A. *The Comprehensive Test Ban Treaty: An Insider's Perspective.* Stanford, Calif.: Stanford University Press, 2006.

Malik, Mohan. "A. Q. Khan's China Connection." *China Brief* (Jamestown Foundation), May 22, 2004.

Tetiarhi, G. "French Nuclear Testing in the South Pacific." *Contemporary Pacific* 17, no. 2 (2005): 378-381.

Wittner, Lawrence S. *Confronting the Bomb: A Short History of the World Nuclear Disarmament Movement.* Stanford, Calif.: Stanford University Press, 2009.

■ Congo River basin

FIELDS OF STUDY: Places, Peoples, Societies; Continents, Regions, Areas, Islands; Oceans, Seas, Lakes, Bodies of Water; Biology, Life Sciences, Ecosystems; Ecology, Environment, Environmentalism; Forests, Forestry; Mineral Resources

IDENTIFICATION: Central African watershed that drains into the Congo River in its passage to the Atlantic Ocean

The Congo River basin contains rich biodiversity and considerable mineral wealth, but because the area is shared by a number of countries, the exploitation of the basin's resources is often uncontrolled. As a result, the habitats of many species native to the basin have been disturbed or destroyed, and several species have become endangered.

The Congo River basin covers an area of 3.7 million square kilometers (1.4 million square miles) that includes all of the Democratic Republic of the Congo

Lindi river, a tributary of the Congo river, near Kisangani, RDC. By Piet Clement (Own work)

(DRC; formerly known as Zaire) and the Republic of the Congo (ROC), most of the Central African Republic, and sections of Angola, Rwanda, Burundi, Tanzania, and Zambia. It includes the Lake Tanganyika basin to the east, which is best seen as a subbasin, the lake itself being in a separate rift valley. In the north, the Ubangi River is the main tributary to the Congo River. The Congo River itself is 4,700 kilometers (2,920 miles) long, having its source in Zambia. It is the deepest river in the world and the second-longest river in Africa, after the Nile.

The river basin contains one-fourth of the world's remaining tropical rain forests; in addition to the forest ecosystems, areas of savanna are found in the northeast and south, and high mountains to the east contain alpine meadow. Transport through the basin is achieved mainly by water, along the extensive system of rivers. Roads and railroads are linked to river ports, many of which are connected to various mining and quarrying activities; all such transportation routes are generally in poor states of repair. Since the late twentieth century, increasing numbers of logging roads have been opened into the rain forests. Few large towns and cities are located in the basin; those that have been established are situated mainly on the River Congo itself.

The river has not been harnessed for hydroelectric purposes to any great extent, but ambitious plans have been proposed to add two much larger dams to two existing small dams at Inga Falls, southwest of the capital cities of Kinshasa (DRC) and Brazzaville (ROC); it is estimated that by 2030 these dams could supply some 20 percent of Africa's electricity.

In the past, extensive mining operations in the DRC, mainly in the south of the country along the Zambia border, have brought little benefit to the country. In the early twenty-first century, China negotiated an extensive deal to build roads, railways, hospitals, and schools for the DRC and the ROC in return for mining copper, nickel, and cobalt at certain concessions. The DRC is estimated to hold one-third of the world's cobalt and 10 percent of its copper.

The main ecological threat to the Congo River basin comes from deforestation caused by uncontrolled logging and agricultural clearance, and the subsequent destruction of animal habitats. Many endangered species are native to the basin, foremost among them the mountain gorillas in the Virunga National Park in the east. The civil war that was fought in the DRC between 1998 and 2003, along with later turmoil, did great damage to the park. Also at risk are forest elephants, hippopotamuses, pygmy chimpanzees, western lowland gorillas, and the primates drills and mandrills. The chimpanzee population is estimated to have declined from 2 million to 200,000 from 1990 to 2010. Many of these species have been killed for food or have been killed or captured for sale on the black market.

David Barratt

Further Reading

Gondola, Ch. Didier. *The History of Congo.* Westport, Conn.: Greenwood Press, 2002.

Renton, David, David Seddon, and Leo Zeilig. *The Congo: Plunder and Resistance.* London: Zed Books, 2007.

Ruiz Pérez, M., et al. "Logging in the Congo Basin: A Multi-country Characterization of Timber Companies." *Forest Ecology and Management* 214 (August, 2005): 221-236.

Surhone, Lambert M., Miriam Timpledom, and Susan Marseken, eds. *Tropical and Subtropical Forests: Congo Basin, Amazon Basin.* Beau Bassin, Mauritius: Betascript, 2010.

■ Coniferous forests

FIELDS OF STUDY: Biology, Life Sciences, Ecosystems; Ecology, Environment, Environmentalism; Forests, Forestry; Plants, Vegetation, Botany, Horticulture

CATEGORIES: Forests and plants; ecology and ecosystems

DEFINITION: Forests constituted primarily of evergreen trees that are species of conifers

Boreal coniferous forests form the largest single forest system on earth and thereby are a major part of the world ecosystem. Human exploitation, population pressures, pollution, and climate change have had negative impacts on the range and variety of conifers.

Coniferous forests constitute a vast biome that lies primarily in the high latitudes of the Northern Hemisphere but also occurs throughout the world. Conifers are evergreens that have compound seed cones, needle- or scale-shaped leaves, distinctive water-transporting tissue and pollen grain structure, and compact wood. They are thought to date back to the Carboniferous period, about 300 million years ago. In the twenty-first century, 546 conifer species, in 67 genera, are known to exist. Of these, the most common species are as follows: in the Northern Hemisphere, pines (*Pinus*), firs (*Abies*), spruces (*Picea*), and junipers (*Juniperus*); in the Southern Hemisphere, yellowwoods (*Podocarpus*). Although not as abundant in plant and animal species as tropical forests, coniferous forests form a major segment of the world ecosystem.

Conifers grow on every continent except Antarctica and on many coastal and oceanic islands. Although many species are native to tropical and subtropical biomes, the majority are in the boreal forest biome, also called taiga. This is a belt of forest that extends across Canada into Alaska in North America and across northern Europe and Russia in Eurasia, reaching as much as 73 degrees north latitude in Siberia. In the Southern Hemisphere, coniferous forests extend as far as 55 degrees south latitude on Chile's Tierra del Fuego. About 60 percent of species are found in a range of altitude between 500 and 1,500 meters (1,600 and 5,000 feet), although there are sea-level species and one that survives at altitudes up to 4,800 meters (15,800 feet). Additionally, conifers have been cultivated for some two hundred years, and introduced or exotic species of conifers have entered ecosystems as they have been planted in gardens and parks.

Conifers are hardy and typically grow larger and live longer than hardwood species of trees. In fact, the world's oldest known tree, a Great Basin bristlecone pine in eastern California, is nearly five thousand years old, and the tallest tree is a sequoia at 115.56 meters (379.1 feet), also in California. Most conifer species occur in temperate, moist climates. For instance, the taiga in general has an average minimum temperature of about 6.6 degrees Celsius (44 degrees Fahrenheit) and receives about 50 centimeters (20 inches) of rain yearly.

The variety of conifer species and the variety of flora and fauna among them are generally low in coniferous forests; in the taiga spruce, tamarack (or larch), and balsam fir dominate as climax species. Nonetheless, the sheer number of trees affords an immense natural resource. Among the wildlife in the taiga alone are wolves, coyotes, bears, foxes, lynx, deer, moose, rabbits, and many species of raptors and songbirds. Coniferous forests have long been sources of raw materials for humans as well, principally timber for construction and pulp for paper.

About one-third of conifer species are imperiled within their natural range; twenty are critically endangered. The expanding human population is the greatest stressor because of losses of forestland to settlement and agriculture, increased frequency and intensity of fires near settlements, air and water pollution from agriculture and industry, and the introduction of exotic pests and diseases. Moreover, human-accelerated climate change may force the migration of some species northward, where it is not blocked by agriculture or cities.

Roger Smith

Further Reading

Andersson, Folke, ed. *Coniferous Forests.* San Diego, Calif.: Elsevier, 2005.

Eckenwalder, James E. *Conifers of the World: The Complete Reference.* Portland, Oreg.: Timber Press, 2009.

Powell, Graham R. *Lives of Conifers.* Baltimore: The Johns Hopkins University Press, 2009.

See also: Boreal forests; Climax communities; Deciduous forests; Forest and range policy; Forest management; Old-growth forests; Rain forests; Sustainable forestry

■ Conservation biology

FIELDS OF STUDY: Biology, Life Sciences, Ecosystems; Animals, Zoology, Marine Biology; Ecology, Environment, Environmentalism; Forests, Forestry; Plants, Vegetation, Botany, Horticulture; Ethics, Advocacy, Policy, Protest; Ethics, Advocacy, Policy, Protest; Ecology, Environment, Environmentalism; Biology, Life Sciences, Ecosystems; Animals, Zoology, Marine Biology; Ecology, Environment, Environmentalism; Forests, Forestry; Plants, Vegetation, Botany, Horticulture

CATEGORIES: Ecology and ecosystems; animals and endangered species

DEFINITION: Applied science concerned with the preservation of biological diversity at different levels

Conservation biologists, who actively promote the protection of biodiversity, argue that the prevention of the further loss of any plant and animal species is crucial to the future of humankind.

The field of conservation biology emerged during the 1970's as many scientists became concerned about the loss of various species of plants and animals and the destruction of ecosystems, especially tropical forests, as the result of human activities. Conservation biologists are concerned with protecting biological diversity on three levels: species diversity, genetic diversity, and ecosystem diversity. The interdisciplinary science of conservation biology involves input from such varied fields of knowledge as genetics, biogeography, ecology, philosophy, and policy development. Conservation biologists conduct research and disseminate their findings through publications and other presentations; many also serve as advisers to policy makers, and some work directly with local groups toward conservation projects.

Conservation biologists generally focus on five major threats to biodiversity: habitat degradation and loss, habitat fragmentation, species overexploitation, species invasion, and climate change. It has been estimated that habitat degradation and habitat fragmentation account for more than 70 percent of species endangerment and extinction; these threats to biodiversity are caused by agriculture, mining, fires, urbanization, and other human activities. Efforts to preserve habitats have focused mainly on preserving areas with relatively high biodiversity.

Species overexploitation, or the unsustainable use of given species for food or other purposes, is believed to be the next most serious threat to biodiversity, followed by species invasion, or the introduction of nonnative species to an ecosystem. Throughout history, humans have moved plant and animal species out of their native habitats and into other places, both intentionally and unintentionally. It is estimated that more than three thousand plant species have been introduced in California alone. The introduction of new species can have devastating effects on native species, such as by crowding them out or by changing the relationships between native predators and prey. Conservation biologists recognize that it is unrealistic to try to prevent species invasion, so they concentrate on minimizing the damage caused by species introduction.

The threat that global climate change poses to biodiversity was not fully recognized until the late twentieth century. It has been estimated that more than half of all the world's species are sensitive to climate change, with some more severely affected than others.

Conservation biologists and other environmentalists have undertaken efforts to protect biodiversity on several different levels, including the genetic, species, population, habitat, landscape, and ecosystem levels. Most conservation efforts in the past focused on protecting endangered species, but ecosystem-level efforts have increasingly been undertaken. Many of the world's national governments have passed laws to protect endangered or threatened species, such as the U.S. Endangered Species Act, and have developed plans to protect these species.

Other strategies for protecting biodiversity include the captive-breeding programs conducted by many zoos and the storage of seeds from wild plants in seed banks. Although such strategies are useful with some species, the conservation of other species requires the maintenance of their natural habitats. Conservation biologists and others have thus focused on preserving habitats, landscapes, and ecosystems. Many countries have set aside land in various types of reserves, which have proven to be very effective tools of conservation biology. Such reserves vary from those that are strictly protected (no human encroachment or use of the species within reserve boundaries) to those that allow sustainable exploitation of the resources—including plant and animal species—present.

No less important than the protection of habitats is the protection of species genetic diversity; without a diverse gene pool, a species population cannot evolve and adapt to environmental changes. One strategy for protecting genetic diversity involves the storage of species genes in gene banks.

Sergei A. Markov

Further Reading

Bush, Mark B. *Ecology of a Changing Planet.* Upper Saddle River, N.J.: Prentice Hall, 2000.

Chivian, Eric, and Aaron Bernstein, eds. *Sustaining Life: How Human Health Depends on Biodiversity.* New York: Oxford University Press, 2008.

Groom, Martha J., Gary K. Meffe, and Carl Ronald Carroll. *Principles of Conservation Biology.* 3d ed. Sunderland, Mass.: Sinauer, 2006.

Hunter, Malcolm L., Jr. *Fundamentals of Conservation Biology.* 3d ed. Hoboken, N.J.: Wiley-Blackwell, 2006.

Zeigler, David. *Understanding Biodiversity.* Westport, Conn.: Praeger, 2007.

See also: Biodiversity; Convention on Biological Diversity; Endangered Species Act; Endangered species and species protection policy; Extinctions and species loss; Habitat destruction; Wildlife refuges; Wilson, Edward O.

■ Conservation easements

FIELDS OF STUDY: Economics, Business, Production, Commerce; Ecology, Environment, Environmentalism

DEFINITION: Legal agreements limiting the kinds of uses permitted on private lands

Conservation easements encourage various forms of conservation on privately held lands while providing tax benefits to landowners.

An easement is a legal entitlement providing its holder certain privileges regarding the use of property owned by another. In the United States, a conservation easement is a legal agreement between a landowner and another party—generally a group such as a local or state land trust, a government agency, a nonprofit organization, or an environmental conservation group—for the purpose of limiting the uses of the property subject to the easement. The easement limits uses and development of the land that would disturb the condition of the aspect of the land that is valued. Some typical prohibitions concern the construction of roads and commercial buildings, mining of the land, and harvesting of its trees. Conservation easements usually last in perpetuity and are legally binding independent of who comes to own the land. The land is still usable by its owner, but the owner's use of it is limited by the terms of the easement.

Landowners can receive certain financial benefits for donating their land through conservation easements. Regarding income taxes, the donation of land constitutes a charitable gift and, as such, may be tax-deductible. Regarding estate taxes, lands that do not have easements may be subject to extremely high state and federal inheritance taxes. A conservation easement on the land reduces its value (since its economic uses are limited) and thus has a positive effect on the amount of inheritance taxes heirs must pay. Regarding gift taxes, again because an easement reduces the value of the land, more land may be given to a family member before it becomes subject to federal gift taxes. Regarding property taxes, having land protected by a conservation easement may qualify it for a reduction in property taxes (laws on this point vary from state to state).

Although conservation easements provide financial benefits, their intended purpose is to support conservation. The privately owned lands subject to conservation easements may serve as core habitats for species, or they may buffer and connect publicly owned lands such as nature reserves or national parks. These functions support the ecosystems found on the public lands. Buffer lands help provide cushions between lands that can be developed without restriction and lands that provide core habitats for flora and fauna. Lands that serve a connective function allow animals to move more freely from one publicly owned area to another, whether they are migrating, hunting, or establishing new territory.

Conservation Easement Boundary markers identify Neil Hanson's Emergency Watershed Protection (EWP) Flood Plain Easement located east of Bowesmont, in the Red River basin of ND, Wednesday May 1, 2013. By U.S. Department of Agriculture

Further, much of the land that provides habitat for federally listed endangered species is privately owned.

Conservation easements have not been without controversy. One area of conflict concerns the abuse of such easements for tax-shelter purposes. Critics have noted that some owners receive the tax breaks that come with easements but do not maintain their lands properly in accordance with their easement agreements. Additionally, controversies have arisen regarding changes to the terms of easements by successive owners of particular lands. For example, the National Trust for Historic Preservation approved substantial changes to the terms of the Myrtle Grove easement, which covered land on Maryland's eastern shore in the Chesapeake Bay watershed, raising objections from many environmentalists.

George Wrisley

Further Reading

Gustanski, Julie A., and Roderick H. Squires, eds. *Protecting the Land: Conservation Easements Past, Present, and Future*. Washington, D.C.: Island Press, 2000.

Journal of Forestry. "Focus on . . . Private Forest Landowners: FAQs about Conservation Easements." 100, no. 3 (2002): 4.

Keske, Catherine. *The Emerging Market for Private Land Preservation and Conservation Easements*. Saarbrücken, Germany: VDM Verlag, 2008.

Rissman, Adena R., et al. "Conservation Easements: Biodiversity Protection and Private Use." *Conservation Biology* 21, no. 3 (2007): 709-718.

■ Conservation movement

FIELDS OF STUDY: Ethics, Advocacy, Policy, Protest; Ecology, Environment, Environmentalism; Public Policy, Debates, Controversies; Biology, Life Sciences, Ecosystems; Animals, Zoology, Marine Biology; Renewable Resources

IDENTIFICATION: Activities of individuals, private organizations, and government agencies to preserve natural resources or establish policies for using them wisely

The early conservation movement focused attention on the perilous state of natural resources as human societies moved toward increasing commercialization and urbanization in the nineteenth and twentieth centuries. Proponents of conservation continue to work to convey the importance of resource sustainability.

The roots of the conservation movement can be traced to Europe during the late eighteenth century. Individuals repulsed by the growing commercialization and dehumanization brought on the by the Industrial Revolution promoted a return to nature. While some areas had been preserved in their natural state for centuries, either as hunting grounds or as refuges for the upper classes, during the nineteenth century governments in Europe and in North America began setting aside green space, even in urban areas, for recreation and relaxation. In some countries, notably Germany, government control over forests and rivers was used not only to conserve natural resources but also to generate revenues from the harvest of renewable resources such as trees and wildlife. Coordinated efforts to preserve wilderness areas, however, emerged first in the United States. The initiatives of individuals and organizations involved in these efforts grew into the modern conservation movement.

Beginnings of the Movement

From its inception, the conservation movement in the United States was highly decentralized, but people who became involved shared an overarching goal: to preserve some aspect of the natural world from the ravages of rampant commercial development and urbanization. Efforts to save some of America's wilderness areas from the encroachment of civilization led to the creation of Yellowstone National Park in 1872, and some states had taken steps to set aside particularly beautiful areas (many of them difficult to reach). On the other hand, the first true conservation bill passed by the U.S. Congress in 1876 was vetoed by President Ulysses Grant.

Although American writers such as Henry David Thoreau had celebrated the value of the natural landscape, the first true conservationist to emerge on the national scene was John Muir. A Scotsman who had settled in California, Muir spent most of his adult life writing about the beauties of the wilderness, particularly the Yosemite Valley, a preserve set aside by the state in 1864. At that time many people looked upon the wilderness as a place of escape from the grime of city life. Powerful commercial interests, however, saw unsettled areas as opportunities for profit. The mining and timber industries coveted the natural resources there, farmers and ranchers sought lands for grazing, and railroads saw possibilities in

creating tourist destinations or shorter routes between population centers.

Muir was one of dozens of amateurs who made their livings by other means but devoted their lives to saving the country's wilderness for future generations. Many were responsible for creating new national parks or monuments, saving sites that had been commercialized (such as Niagara Falls), or establishing wildlife sanctuaries to preserve dwindling numbers of birds, fish, and mammals. Muir lobbied to preserve Yosemite and additional wilderness sites. Eventually he found a strong ally in President Theodore Roosevelt, a lifelong sportsman and conservationist who used his political power to establish numerous national monuments to save lands from mining, timbering, and settlement. Muir was a preservationist. His goal was to have lands set aside, protected from all development or use.

A second important figure in the conservation movement, Gifford Pinchot, could best be described as a utilitarian. Pinchot earned a degree in forestry and eventually became head of the U.S. Forest Service, making him one of the first professional conservationists. He argued that natural resources should be managed carefully, but renewable resources should be available for commercial purposes. These two views came to dominate the debate among conservationists for nearly a century as groups struggling to preserve sites intact clashed with those who saw responsible use as a viable alternative to saving lands from outright, wholesale exploitation.

Over the next century the conservation movement would be advanced by both amateurs and professionals. A few crossed from one group to the other. Notable among them was Stephen T. Mather, who made a fortune in business and then turned his talents to creating the National Park Service in 1916, for which he served as the first director. Intent on preserving the national parks for future generations, Mather often found himself pitted against Pinchot and the Forest Service in debates concerning the proper balance between preservation and commercial use of national lands.

Spurred by Muir's leadership, in 1892 a group of Californians formed the Sierra Club, which would become a driving force in promoting conservation throughout the United States. Similar organizations sprang up in the East, many modeled on the first such club, the Appalachian Mountain Club, established in 1876.

Henry David Thoreau, in 1861. By Geo. F. Parlow

Eventually the idea of conservation grew to include wildlife as well as landscape. Ironically, some of the most avid conservationists were sportsmen. They recognized that careful management of game populations would ensure that hunters could enjoy their sport for decades to come. Aware of what wanton slaughter had done to the American bison population during the nineteenth century, they often lobbied for limits on the numbers of animals that individual hunters could kill.

Conservationist groups were not always successful, however. Despite the protests of the Sierra Club and others, the U.S. government agreed to the creation of the Hetch Hetchy Dam in the Yosemite area to provide water for San Francisco, causing the loss of millions of hectares of natural landscape. Lobbying did push several presidents to create wildlife refuges, setting aside lands where game animals lived or that they used as migratory routes. Eventually these

sanctuaries became part of the National Wildlife Refuge System.

Between the World Wars

By the end of World War I a number of conservation groups were active in the United States. Individual organizations, however, tended to focus on single aspects of conservation. For example, the Audubon Society, founded in 1905, limited its interest to the plight of birds, while the Izaak Walton League, established in 1922, was concerned with the condition of rivers and lakes because its members were involved in sportfishing. In fact, during this period many conservation organizations were underwritten by firearms companies and sports businesses. As a result, the utilitarian view of conservation tended to be favored in political decisions.

Concurrently, preservationists such as the National Park Service's Mather tried to have more lands set aside; on occasion these efforts were supported by financiers such as John D. Rockefeller, Jr., who purchased properties to expand or create parks. Some narrow-minded conservation efforts led to ecological disasters, however. For example, by the 1920's the gray wolf population in Yellowstone National Park was eliminated, ostensibly to make the park safer for tourists (and for the livestock of nearby ranchers). The absence of these predators led to an explosion of the ruminant population, which then overgrazed the available vegetation; eventually thousands of elk and deer starved.

The election of Franklin D. Roosevelt as president in 1932 brought one of the most active proponents of the conservationist movement into the White House. Roosevelt had a genuine love of the outdoors and was a conservationist at heart. He was a utilitarian when it came to conservation, however, and above all a politician. He believed that a government-controlled program of land retirement, soil and forest restoration, flood control, and hydroelectric power generation would serve two aims simultaneously: The nation's natural landscapes could be preserved or put to good use at the same time people could be given meaningful employment.

Combining his zeal for conservation with the need to revitalize the American economy during the Great Depression, Roosevelt created numerous programs to further the improvement of the nation's natural resources. Notable among these were the Civilian Conservation Corps and the Works Progress

Administration, agencies that put people to work improving national parks and other wilderness areas, making them accessible to the public, and restoring many of the renewable resources that had been lost over the years to commercial development. Among his principal successes, Roosevelt oversaw the opening of Great Smoky Mountains National Park in 1934.

Not all of the projects Roosevelt promoted under the banner of conservation were beneficial to the natural environment, however. The Tennessee Valley Authority oversaw the erection of numerous dams to provide hydroelectric power to rural communities, in the process destroying millions of hectares of forestlands and valleys. Politically, the most significant change in the conservation movement under Roosevelt was the affiliation of environmental causes with the Democrats rather than the Republicans, who had been leaders in conservation in previous years.

Conservation after World War II

After World War II ended, the United States entered a period of economic prosperity that saw the population grow and industry expand to meet worldwide demand for American goods. As a result, individuals and corporations interested in development lobbied for relaxation of conservation rules that had been put in place during the previous six decades. Many argued for a return to commercial operations in government-protected areas. Conservation groups, which by then numbered in the dozens, fought back with mixed success to maintain and expand the protections in place.

Organizations such as the Sierra Club and the Wilderness Society developed activist tactics to bring attention to the long-term dangers of development in wilderness areas. These groups were successful in defeating a plan to create a dam on the Green River at Echo Park, on the Utah-Colorado border, during the 1950's. Most notably, under the leadership of the Wilderness Society's executive secretary Howard Zahniser, conservationists prodded Congress to pass the Wilderness Act in 1964. That law set aside more than 3.6 million hectares (9 million acres) of land, restricting even minimal development or human use.

The publication of Rachel Carson's *Silent Spring* in 1962, detailing the environmental dangers of toxic waste, gave new impetus to the conservationists and sparked the larger environmental movement. As a consequence, during the 1960's conservation groups began to unite with those interested in larger environmental issues. Sierra Club executive director David Brower became a leading spokesman for environmental causes. The most significant success achieved by these groups in lobbying governmental agencies was the passage of the National Environmental Policy Act of 1969, which established the government's role in protecting humans and the natural environment from damage caused by human development or technology. In December, 1970, the Environmental Protection Agency was established to enforce environmental policies throughout the United States.

International Conservation Efforts

By the middle of the twentieth century, the modern conservation movement had become international. The record of conservation groups in Europe was strong; many had been successful in continuing and strengthening already existing laws to preserve natural resources. Beginning during the 1960's conservationists in Australia led highly organized campaigns to reverse the effects of human contamination on the natural environment, specifically targeting problems with the quality of soils and the eradication of several species of animals. In Africa, Asia, and South America, however, conservationists had mixed success. Often conservation efforts conflicted with the needs of the people for resources to support life. This was especially true in Africa, where native peoples relied on wildlife for sustenance, and in South America, where lands covered by rain forests were needed for farming. Some successes were achieved when native populations were convinced that conservation would provide long-term economic stability.

At the same time, however, commercial interests continued to harvest animals and timber far in excess of the population's needs, ignoring the environmental catastrophes caused by their actions. Often, government-sponsored programs wreaked havoc on natural resources. Nowhere was this more apparent than in China, where the need for energy to fuel the country's growing population and expanding industrial base led to construction of the massive Three Gorges Dam on the Yangtze River, flooding millions of hectares, destroying or seriously affecting land and riverine populations. From 1970 onward, however, China began to take an active approach to wildlife preservation, as did several other Asian nations.

One of the most successful conservation initiatives

undertaken outside the United States has been that of the Central American nation of Costa Rica. Beginning in 1970 the Costa Rican government worked to create a highly developed national park system where conservation practices would be strictly enforced. By 2000 nearly 25 percent of Costa Rica's landmass had been set aside for preservation.

Laurence W. Mazzeno

Further Reading

Chester, Charles A. *Conservation Across Borders: Biodiversity in an Interdependent World.* Washington, D.C.: Island Press, 2006.

Coggins, Chris. *The Tiger and the Pangolin: Nature, Culture, and Conservation in China.* Honolulu: University of Hawaii Press, 2003.

Evans, Sterling. *The Green Republic: A Conservation History of Costa Rica.* Austin: University of Texas Press, 1999.

Fox, Stephen. *John Muir and His Legacy: The American Conservation Movement.* Boston: Little, Brown, 1981.

Gibson, Clark L. *Politicians and Poachers: The Political Economy and Wildlife Policy in Africa.* New York: Cambridge University Press, 1999.

Maher, Neil M. *Nature's New Deal: The Civilian Conservation Corps and the Roots of the American Environmental Movement.* New York: Oxford University Press, 2008.

Markus, Nicola. *On Our Watch: The Race to Save Australia's Environment.* Melbourne: University of Melbourne Press, 2009.

Minteer, Ben and Robert Manning, eds. *Reconstructing Conservation: Finding Common Ground.* Washington, D.C.: Island Press, 2003.

Phillips, Sarah T. *This Land, This Nation: Conservation, Rural America, and the New Deal.* New York: Cambridge University Press, 2007.

Runte, Alfred. *National Parks: The American Experience.* 4th ed. Lanham, Md.: Taylor Trade, 2010.

■ Conservation of natural resources

FIELDS OF STUDY: Ethics, Advocacy, Policy, Protest; Ecology, Environment, Environmentalism; Public Policy, Debates, Controversies

DEFINITION: Planned use of natural resources to benefit the maximum number of people for as long as possible

The goals of conservation often conflict with the drive toward the exploitation of natural resources for immediate economic gain and also with the ethic of preservation, which promotes the indefinite preservation of natural resources in their undisturbed state.

For centuries few people recognized that nature's resources are finite. Only since the mid-nineteenth century has the issue of conserving resources been taken seriously. In North America, the eighteenth and nineteenth centuries were largely devoted to conquering the wilderness. As pioneers cleared forests, little or no thought was given to the idea that they could ever be exhausted. Bison and other animals were hunted nearly to extinction, and bounties were placed on wolves and other predators. In the seas, millions of seals were killed, and whales were hunted relentlessly.

Almost too late, it became apparent to many people that soils were being depleted by erosion and that once-plentiful native plant and wildlife populations were in decline. Even the quality of air, surface water, and groundwater deteriorated. An increasing number of people began calling for an end to environmentally destructive practices. An important influence was that of diplomat and naturalist George Perkins Marsh, whose travels had made him keenly aware of the results of centuries of land abuse in Europe. Marsh's book

Man and Nature: Or, Physical Geography as Modified by Human Action (1864) defined the connections among soil, water, and vegetation. From such influences came the public park movement, including the establishment of Yellowstone National Park.

Emergence of the Modern Conservation Movement

During the early twentieth century, the living standards of most Americans generally improved, but at the same time it was recognized that consumption of natural resources had to be controlled. Out of this realization emerged a human-centered conservation philosophy known as wise use, which dictated that human beings should use nature in such a way that its resources could continue to be used over long periods of time.

Among the conservationists of the era were U.S. president Theodore Roosevelt and forester Gifford Pinchot. Roosevelt increased the extent of the national forests in the United States and created many

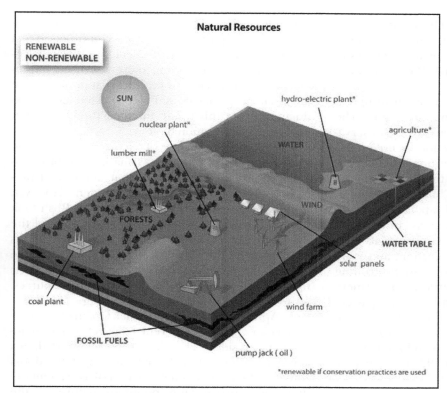

Natural Resources

RENEWABLE
NON-RENEWABLE

SUN

nuclear plant*

hydro-electric plant*

agriculture*

lumber mill*

WATER

FORESTS

WIND

WATER TABLE

solar panels

coal plant

wind farm

FOSSIL FUELS

pump jack (oil)

*renewable if conservation practices are used

The earth has many natural resources, some are renewable and others are not. Conservation practices will ensure that resources do not become depleted. © EBSCO

influential textbook *Game Management* (1933), although he is better known today for his collection of essays

A Sand County Almanac, and Sketches Here and There, which was published in 1949, soon after Leopold's death. Paul B. Sears achieved prominence with *Deserts on the March* (1935), which vividly dramatized the problems of the Dust Bowl of the 1930's.

The conservation legacy of President Franklin D. Roosevelt includes his attempts to restore the depressed U.S. economy by creating various work programs, including the Civilian Conservation Corps (CCC). Many of these programs were aimed at soil conservation, reforestation, and flood control.

Postwar Developments

In the two decades following World War II, concerns about the Cold War and economic expansion kept conservation far from the forefront of American thought. As the population rapidly expanded, air and water pollution worsened, grasslands became overgrazed, and agricultural chemicals were used in increasing quantities. The complacency of the times was shattered by the publication of Rachel Carson's *Silent Spring* (1962), which warned that dichloro-diphenyl-trichloroethane (DDT) and other pesticides were threatening the lives of animals and humans. The book caused widespread public concern, and laws were ultimately passed that outlawed DDT in the United States.

Under President John F. Kennedy's administration, attention was given once more to environmental issues in general and to conservation. Funds were appropriated to improve air quality, and new land was acquired for parks. Stewart Udall, secretary of the interior under Kennedy and his successor, Lyndon B. Johnson, advocated a new positive attitude toward protection of the environment. During the 1960's, a time of great scientific activity and social ferment,

wildlife refuges. Pinchot, a friend and associate of Roosevelt, became chief forester of the U.S. Department of Agriculture and greatly influenced the conservation movement. He applied European methods of managing forests that were consistent with the wise-use philosophy. This put him in conflict with naturalist John Muir and others who wished to preserve wilderness areas in their natural state. Two opposing camps developed: On one side were preservationists, who argued that nature deserves to be protected for its own sake; on the other were conservationists, who believed in regulated exploitation.

During the 1920's and 1930's, scientific advances and economic problems influenced conservation views and policies. The ecosystem concept, the principle that nature is composed of local units with interacting living and nonliving components, developed. It was to become the cornerstone of the science of ecology and an important tool of conservation. During this same period a new, scientific approach to wildlife management emerged. Aldo Leopold, regarded as the father of the new science, wrote the ecologists employed advanced technologies in conducting ecosystem analyses. Among the social movements of the decade was a new environmentalism, which culminated in the first Earth Day celebration in 1970.

The 1970's saw the expansion of environmentalism, and the term "environmentalism" came to be understood as almost synonymous with "conservation." The former clear distinction between the terms "conservation" and "preservation" was blurred. Environmental organizations continued to elaborate their views and increase their visibility. More action-oriented alternative groups used sabotage tactics to stop development in wilderness areas. In contrast, the Nature Conservancy became known for its businesslike policy of acquisition, protection, and management of natural areas. In response to the growing awareness of environmental issues among Americans, a new round of federal legislation was passed. Under President Richard Nixon, the Environmental Protection Agency (EPA) was created in 1970. The revised Clean Air Act of 1970 was followed by the Clean Water Act of 1972, and in 1973 Congress enacted the Endangered Species Act.

Policy and Politics

The 1980's were marked by new conservation problems and a general indifference at the federal level in the United States. Among the global problems identified were stratospheric ozone depletion and global warming.Reversals of environmental protections occurred during the administration of President Ronald Reagan after he appointed James Watt as secretary of the interior. Watt attempted to dismantle many of the environmental protection programs that had been put in place during the previous decades.

The 1990's had their own environmental challenges and successes. After twelve years of apathy, conservationists were reinvigorated by the election of Bill Clinton as president and high-profile environmentalist Al Gore as vice president. Despite continued optimism among environmentalists and significant gains in environmental protections, however, an antienvironmental movement also developed. Many politically conservative individuals and organizations began to assert that environmentalism had gone too far. Business leaders and property owners complained of overregulation, and even some religious authorities expressed concerns that nature had been elevated in importance above humans. Nevertheless, the majority of Americans continued to feel that nature deserves to be protected. The late twentieth century saw a growing awareness of the importance of biodiversity and increasing support for the idea that all species should be protected against extinction. From this trend emerged the value-laden science of conservation biology.

Under the presidency of George W. Bush, the early twenty-first century was marked by business- and industry-friendly policies that diminished protections for wildlife and the environment. However, in the final month of his administration, Bush took the historic action of designating three areas of the Pacific Ocean as marine national monuments. This status protects the Marianas Trench, Pacific Remote Islands, and Rose Atoll marine national monuments from destruction or extraction of their resources, waste dumping, and commercial fishing.

In April, 2010, President Barack Obama held a national conservation conference that echoed one convened by President Theodore Roosevelt more than a century earlier. Dubbed America's Great Outdoors Initiative, Obama's conference took into account the developed, urban, and populous nature of the country. The twenty-first century strategy for the nation that came out of the conference proposed partnerships among government, nonprofit organizations, and private landowners for land preservation efforts that would be smaller in scale than national parks and designated wilderness areas and thus less likely to encounter heated political opposition.

Thomas E. Hemmerly; updated by Karen N. Kähler

Further Reading

Adams, Jonathan S. *The Future of the Wild: Radical Conservation for a Crowded World.* Boston: Beacon Press, 2006.

Carroll, Scott P., and Charles W. Fox, eds. *Conservation Biology: Evolution in Action.* New York: Oxford University Press, 2008.

Chiras, Daniel D., and John P. Reganold. *Natural Resource Conservation: Management for a Sustainable Future.* 10th ed. Upper Saddle River, N.J.: Benjamin Cummings/Pearson, 2010.

Cox, George W. *Conservation Biology: Concepts and Applications.* 2d ed. Dubuque, Iowa: Wm. C. Brown, 1997.

Groom, Martha J., Gary K. Meffe, and Carl Ronald Carroll. *Principles of Conservation Biology*. 3d ed. Sunderland, Mass.: Sinauer, 2006.

Hambler, Clive. *Conservation*. New York: Cambridge University Press, 2004.

Kline, Benjamin. *First Along the River: A Brief History of the U.S. Environmental Movement*. 3d ed. Lanham, Md.: Rowman & Littlefield, 2007.

Macdonald, David W., and Katrina Service, eds. *Key Topics in Conservation Biology*. Malden, Mass.: Blackwell, 2008.

Pullin, Andrew S. *Conservation Biology*. New York: Cambridge University Press, 2002.

■ Conservation of polar bears

FIELDS OF STUDY: Biology, Life Sciences, Ecosystems; Animals, Zoology, Marine Biology; Ecology, Environment, Environmentalism

DEFINITION: Large white bear species native to the Arctic Circle

Polar bears face several threats as a species, including the loss of habitat, some the result of global warming and some caused by human activities related to mineral extraction in the Arctic. Governments, environmental organizations, and individuals have been involved in efforts to preserve the species.

The polar bear (*Ursus maritimus*) is one of the earth's largest land-roving animals. Mature male polar bears may weigh as much as 770 kilograms (1,700 pounds). Polar bears live principally in the Arctic, in about twenty different locations. Their thick fur and blubber beneath their skin enable them to survive in the frigid climate of their habitat. Their principal food source is seals, which they hunt in the icy Arctic waters, but they also eat whale meat, vegetation, and kelp. Polar bears depend on the pack ice of the Arctic as they travel far from land while hunting for food; they also depend on soft snow, in which they prepare their dens for birthing.

Polar bears have been hunted for their white fur in Russia since the fourteenth century. The commercial trade in the fur increased over the centuries as more people moved into Arctic regions and firearms made killing the bears easier. However, in comparison to the hunting of other Arctic species, such as the arctic fox, the commercial hunting of polar bears has never been important for the fur industry. The hunting of polar bears reached a peak during the early twentieth century, when perhaps 1,500 bears were killed annually, and then fell off as the population of bears declined. Later in the century the use of mechanized hunting and hunting from snowmobiles, icebreakers, and airplanes increased the number of bears killed to a new peak of 1,200 to 1,300 during the late 1960s.

Although hunting and poaching pose problems for the survival of the polar bear as a species, the main threat to the polar bear is global warming. As pack ice has disappeared and snowfall has decreased, the bears have found it increasingly difficult to hunt seals. This problem is compounded by reductions in the seal population, which may also be linked to global warming. The habitat destruction caused by the processes associated with the extraction of oil and coal from Arctic lands has also contributed to the decline of polar bears. In 2015 the International Union for Conservation of Nature estimated the

Polar bears. By Atwell Gerry, U.S. Fish and Wildlife Service

total population of polar bears in the Arctic to be 22,000 to 30,000. The U.S. Geological Survey has projected that if the trends seen in the early twenty-first century continue, two-thirds of the polar bear population will disappear by 2050, and by 2080 only a few will remain in the Arctic Circle.

In 1973 the five nations having the most land in the polar bears' feeding range—the United States, Canada, the Soviet Union, Denmark (in Greenland), and Norway—signed the International Agreement for the Conservation of Polar Bears, which established rules that allowed for the capturing and killing of polar bears only for scientific research purposes or to preserve the ecology of the Arctic. An exception was made for native peoples hunting bears in a traditional manner. The agreement also specified that skins and other objects of value taken from polar bears could not be sold commercially, and it outlawed the hunting of the bears from planes and icebreakers. Norway later banned all hunting of polar bears.

Polar bears are listed in Appendix II of the Convention on International Trade in Endangered Species (CITES), which means that CITES signatory nations are allowed to conduct limited commercial hunting of the animals. Concerned environmental groups have petitioned to have the bears listed instead in Appendix I of the convention, which would prohibit signatory nations from all commercial hunting of polar bears. These groups' efforts to protect polar bears have put them in conflict with some of the indigenous peoples of the Arctic, who want to retain the right to hunt polar bears as part of their traditional cultural practices.

Frederick B. Chary

Further Reading

Ellis, Richard. *On Thin Ice: The Changing World of the Polar Bear.* New York: Alfred A. Knopf, 2009.

Kazlowski, Steven. *The Last Polar Bear: Facing the Truth of a Warming World.* Seattle: Mountaineers Books, 2008.

"Polar Bear Status, Distribution & Population." *WWF*, 2017, wwf.panda.org/what_we_do/where_we_work/arctic/wildlife/polar_bear/population/. Accessed 28 Mar. 2018.

Rosing, Norbert. *The World of the Polar Bear.* Tonawanda, N.Y.: Firefly Books, 2006.

■ Conservation of rhinoceros populations

FIELDS OF STUDY: Biology, Life Sciences, Ecosystems; Animals, Zoology, Marine Biology; Ecology, Environment, Environmentalism

DEFINITION: Large herbivorous mammals native to Africa and southern Asia

Efforts are ongoing to conserve and protect the world's remaining populations of rhinoceros, several species of which have been hunted to near extinction.

The term "rhinoceros" is used to refer to a group of five species in the family Rhinocerotidae, one of the largest remaining megafauna. The rhinoceros has a thick, protective, armorlike skin and can grow to weigh more than one ton. The most distinctive physical characteristic of the rhinoceros is the large horn on its nose. Unlike the horns of other mammalian species, the horn of the rhinoceros lacks a bony center and is composed only of keratin, the same protein that makes up human hair and fingernails. Some rhinoceros species, the Indian and Javan rhinoceros, have a single horn, while the African and Sumatran species have two horns.

Of the five existing species of rhinoceros, two are native to Africa and three are native to southern Asia. The two African species are the black rhinoceros (*Diceros bicornis*) and the white rhinoceros (*Ceratotherium simum*). The three Asian species are the Indian rhinoceros, also known as the greater one-horned rhinoceros (*Rhinoceros unicornis*); the Javan rhinoceros (*Rhinoceros sondaicus*); and the Sumatra, or Asian two-horned, rhinoceros (*Dicerorhinus sumatrensis*). Three of the five species (Javan, Sumatran, and black) are listed as "critically endangered" on the International Union for Conservation of Nature's Red List of Threatened Species, with the Javan rhinoceros one of the most rare and endangered large mammals worldwide. The white rhino is Red Listed as "near threatened" and the Indian rhinoceros is listed as "vulnerable."

Despite their large size and fierce reputation, rhinoceroses are vulnerable to poaching, especially during their daily drink from a water hole. The rhinoceros horn is highly valued by practitioners of traditional Asian medicine, who use derivatives of the horn to treat fevers and convulsions. Rhinoceros horns are also used in making dagger handles.

BLACK RHINOCEROS
U.S. Fish and Wildlife Service/J&K Hollingsworth

There are several species of rhinoceros: black, white, Javan, Indian, and Sumatran. All are listed as endangered on the US Endangered and Threatened Wildlife and Plants List. Rhinos are killed illegally for their horns. US Fish and Wildlife Service.

Poaching levels in some African countries in the early twenty-first century threatened to jeopardize gains that had been made in rhinoceros populations, with poaching estimated to equal annual population growth. Poaching has caused a greater than 96 percent decrease in Africa's black rhino population, and it appears to be increasing in some countries, as the illegal horn trade has progressively worsened since 2006, while efforts to protect the rhinoceros have become increasingly ineffective.

Many plans for the conservation and recovery of rhinoceros species have been put in place and have been effective in increasing rhinoceros populations in certain areas. Although the Indian rhino was nearly extinct by the early twentieth century, the population of this species reached 3,500 in India and Nepal in 2015, according to the World Wide Fund for Nature, as a result of concentrated protection efforts. Conservation efforts directed toward the southern subspecies of white rhino, which had been nearly decimated at the end of the nineteenth century, have elevated this population so that it is the most abundant rhinoceros subspecies. Almost the entire population of the northern subspecies of white rhino was located within Garamba National Park in the Democratic Republic of the Congo, where the animals were protected by guards. However, after war broke out in the area, leading to unchecked poaching, the last few remaining northern white rhinos in Garamba were killed in the mid-2000s before they could be moved to another conservancy in Kenya. In 2009, the only three remaining northern white rhinos were transferred from a zoo in the Czech Republic to the conservancy in Kenya; after one of them, the last male northern white rhino, died in 2018, only two females remained. In addition to efforts to protect rhinoceros species in the wild, zoos have created species survival plans for rhinoceroses that include breeding programs, education programs, and plans for the introduction of captive-bred animals into secure habitats.

The installation of high-voltage fencing around some preserves has curbed the poaching of rhinoceroses somewhat, but the practice persists, in part because of poor enforcement of the laws against hunting these animals and in part because of the increasing availability of automatic weapons to potential poachers. In areas that have experienced the most poaching, efforts have been made to relocate rhinoceros populations to safer regions.

C. J. Walsh

Further Reading

Cunningham, Carol, and Joel Berger. *Horn of Darkness: Rhinos on the Edge.* Oxford UP, 1997.

Enright, Kelly. *Rhinoceros.* Reaktion Books, 2008.

"Greater One-Horned Rhino." *WWF,* wwf.panda.org/what_we_do/endangered_species/rhinoceros/asian_rhinos/indian_rhinoceros/. Accessed 27 Mar. 2018.

Hamilton, Garry. *Rhino Rescue: Changing the Future for Endangered Wildlife.* Firefly Books, 2006.

Nuwer, Rachel. "Do the World's Three Remaining Northern White Rhinos Have a Future?" *Nature,* PBS, 28 July 2016, www.pbs.org/wnet/nature/blog/can-science-save-northern-white-rhino-sudan-najin-fatu/. Accessed 27 Mar. 2018.

Nuwer, Rachel. "Sudan, the Last Male Northern White Rhino, Dies in Kenya." *The New York Times*, 20 Mar. 2018, www.nytimes.com/2018/03/20/science/rhino-sudan-extinct.html. Accessed 27 Mar. 2018.

■ Conservation of savannas

FIELDS OF STUDY: Places, Peoples, Societies; Continents, Regions, Areas, Islands; Biology, Life Sciences, Ecosystems; Ecology, Environment, Environmentalism; Plants, Vegetation, Botany, Horticulture; Animals, Zoology, Marine Biology; Biology, Life Sciences, Ecosystems; Animals, Zoology, Marine Biology; Continents, Regions, Areas, Islands; Ecology, Environment, Environmentalism; Plants, Vegetation, Botany, Horticulture

DEFINITION: Tropical or subtropical grassland environments with wet and dry seasons

Savanna environments host large populations of insects, birds, herbivorous grazing animals, and predatory animals. Many nations have established nature preserves to protect valuable savanna resources, as hunting and poaching have rapidly reduced the populations of some once-numerous savanna inhabitants and agricultural encroachment has shrunk the land area of savannas worldwide.

Savannas form in tropical or subtropical wet-dry climates, with moisture from the intertropical convergence zone dominant in wet months. Savannas have an average temperature of at least 16 degrees Celsius (64.4 degrees Fahrenheit) during the coolest months and receive between 50 and 255 centimeters (20 and 100 inches) of rain yearly. Savannas have poor drainage; the vegetation in savanna regions is dominated by drought-resistant grasses and a few trees. Fires, which occur during the dry season and prevent forests from developing, are essential in maintaining these grasslands.

Savannas form at the borders of tropical rain forests. In Africa, the savanna of the Sahel lies to the north of the rain forest, and northern and southern savannas meet in the East African savanna. The Colombian and Venezuelan llanos of the Orinoquía region are north of the Amazon rain forest, and the Argentine pampas and Brazilian *cerrado* are south of the rain forest. Almost the entire country of Uruguay is savanna. Savannas occupy roughly 25 percent of the continent of Australia, running across the northern tropics. South of the Himalaya Mountains, the Terai-Duar savanna in northern India, Nepal, and Bhutan is maintained by the yearly monsoon.

Savannas support large numbers of herbivorous and predator animals, birds, reptiles, and insects. Termites play an important role in savanna ecosystems; their mounds dot savannas worldwide. Termites consume cellulose and lignin from living grasses and trees, as well as vegetative litter. Primates (including human beings) exploit savanna termites as a high-protein source of food.

During the wet season (which may arise from monsoonal rains), large animal herds graze over the grasslands; during the dry season, herds move toward lakes and rivers. Predators follow the herbivores. Migratory birds from Asia, Europe, and North America winter in Southern Hemisphere savannas, joining large numbers of ground-living sedentary

Amazing native grasslands in the Missouri Coteau, Saskatchewan. The Canadian Prairies rolling hills of Missouri Coteau are filled with pothole wetlands making it one of the most important areas for waterfowl in North America. By Sarah Green (Missouri Coteau Uploaded by SriMesh)

birds. Historically, sleeping sickness in Africa, spread by the tsetse fly, and malaria, spread by mosquitoes, kept human populations from exploiting many savannas, but modern insecticides and modern medicines have mitigated these disease factors somewhat, and human occupation of savannas has climbed steadily since the mid-twentieth century.

Human activities are the major threat to savannas worldwide. Illegal trade in endangered species of savanna birds, such as South American parrots, and African and Asian animals, including tigers, lions, and primates, is a multibillion-dollar industry worldwide. Some endangered birds and animals are prized as pets; others are killed for their pelts or for use of their body parts in foods or medicines. Efforts to stop the trade in endangered species and their products have had limited results. For example, hunting of the endangered African bush elephant (also known as the Savanna elephant) was prohibited in 1989, but poachers continue to kill the elephants for their ivory tusks. The population of these elephants stood at only an estimated ten thousand in 2010.

It has been estimated that if conversion of the Brazilian *cerrado* savanna to croplands continues at the rates seen in the late twentieth century, the savanna will disappear by 2030. Oil production in the Venezuelan llanos and Brazilian *cerrado* may also alter the savanna biome. In Australia, pressure from the cattle industry to alter the natural savanna to provide for optimal beef production has changed the savanna ecosystem. Problems have arisen there from the introduction of nonnative plant species, land clearance, and pastoral grazing, which has changed the natural pattern of fires in the savanna.

Anita Baker-Blocker

Further Reading

Bassett, Thomas J., and Donald Crummey, eds. *African Savannas: Global Narratives and Local Knowledge of Environmental Change.* Portsmouth, N.H.: Heinemann, 2003.

Mistry, Jayalaxshmi, and Andrea Berardi, eds. *Savannas and Dry Forests: Linking People with Nature.* Burlington, Vt.: Ashgate, 2006.

Pennington, R. Toby, and James A. Ratter. *Neotropical Savannas and Seasonally Dry Forests: Plant Diversity, Biogeography, and Conservation.* Boca Raton, Fla.: CRC Press, 2006.

Roach, Mary. "Almost Human." *National Geographic*, April, 2008, 126-145.

■ Conservation of the whooping crane

FIELDS OF STUDY: Biology, Life Sciences, Ecosystems; Animals, Zoology, Marine Biology; Ecology, Environment, Environmentalism

DEFINITION: Migratory crane species native to North America

Efforts to prevent the extinction of the whooping crane have had some success, but the whooping crane population remains very small. This regal bird has become an important symbol for wildlife conservation.

Standing at a height of 1.5 meters (5 feet) or more, with a wingspan of up to 2 meters (7 feet), whooping cranes are the tallest birds in North America. Named for their loud, bugling call, they are white with black-tipped wings, black beaks, and bare patches of red skin on the tops of their black-banded heads. Marshes are vital to the survival of whooping cranes, which nest in tall marsh grasses and eat blue crabs and other foods found in wetland areas. Unlike other cranes, whoopers are slow to mature. After reaching the age of four years, a whooping crane chooses a mate for life; in the wild, these birds may live up to twenty-four years. Adult females produce only two eggs in a clutch, and often only one of the two chicks survives. For this reason, the whooping crane population has never been abundant.

In the nineteenth century, the total number of whooping cranes was estimated at 1,400. Two flocks were known to migrate to Canada from Louisiana and Texas. Their numbers rapidly dwindled as their wetland habitats were destroyed with the expansion of the human population. The magnificent look of adult whoopers also made them targets for sport hunting. Every death of a whooping crane also ended the reproductive life of the surviving mate. By 1900, only about 100 whooping cranes were left. Despite the fact that the Migratory Bird Treaty, signed by the United States and Canada in 1918, made the hunting of whooping cranes illegal, the number of whooping cranes dwindled to only 15 by the late 1930s because of the continuing loss of wetlands.

In 1937, the wintering grounds of the Texas flock were set aside as the Arkansas National Wildlife Refuge. By 1944, this flock had grown from 15 to 21 in number, but the last of 6 whoopers from the Louisiana flock died in 1948. Conservationists were delighted when it was discovered in 1954 that whooping

Patokah River National Wildlife Refuge, IN. By U.S. Fish and Wildlife Service Headquarters

cranes were breeding in a secluded section of Wood Buffalo National Park in Alberta, Canada. To help ensure the flock's survival, officials arranged for eggs to be taken from the nests so that the chicks could be raised safely in captivity. These birds were later returned to the flock, helping build the population. Another flock that does not migrate was established at Florida's Kissimmee Prairie Sanctuary using captive-bred whoopers.

Conservation efforts have increased the whooping crane population to around 750, according to the International Crane Foundation in 2018. Of this number, only about 430 are part of the wild flock in the Arkansas National Wildlife Refuge that migrates between Canada and the United States. The proximity of the refuge to shipping routes with barges carrying chemicals and fertilizers has raised fears among conservationists that an accidental spill could wipe out the whole flock. Since 1999, attempts have been made to establish a second migratory flock in the wild. Some success has been seen in a project run by the nonprofit group known as Operation Migration, which began in 2001; the project uses ultralight planes to teach whooping cranes a migration route from Wisconsin to Florida.

Lisa A. Wroble

Further Reading

Brulliard, Karin. "A 50-Year Effort to Raise Endangered Whooping Cranes Comes to an End." *The Washington Post*, 18 Sept. 2017, www.washington-post.com/news/animalia/wp/2017/09/18/a-50-year-effort-to-raise-endangered-whooping-cranes-comes-to-an-end/?utm_term=.d4c91e9795ff. Accessed 27 Mar. 2018.

Gibbons, Whit. "Birds and the Ecovoid." *Keeping All the Pieces: Perspectives on Natural History and the Environment.* 1993. U of Georgia P, 2010.

Roman, J. "A Whooping Success: The World's Most Endangered Crane Makes a Comeback." *Wildlife Conservation*, vol. 110, no. 3, 2007, pp. 38–45.

Scott, Chris. *Endangered and Threatened Animals of Florida and Their Habitats.* U of Texas P, 2004.

"Whooping Crane." *International Crane Foundation*, 2018, www.savingcranes.org/species-field-guide/whooping-crane/. Accessed 27 Mar. 2018.

◼ Conservation of wolves

FIELDS OF STUDY: Biology, Life Sciences, Ecosystems; Animals, Zoology, Marine Biology; Ecology, Environment, Environmentalism

DEFINITION: Predatory, carnivorous mammals of the family Canidae

The gray wolf, once the most widely distributed mammal in North America, inhabits a fraction of its former range, and the red wolf is the world's most endangered wild canid. Widespread habitat destruction, human infiltration, and predator-control programs resulted in considerable wolf population decline in the early twentieth century. Since the 1970s, however, recovery programs, combined with legislative changes, have allowed some wolf populations to increase.

Wolves, the largest members of the dog family (Canidae), were once abundant throughout North America, Europe, and Asia. Gray wolves are the most abundant wolves, with two species in North America: the gray wolf (*Canis lupus*) and the subspecies red

FWS biologist Alice Whitelaw carries a gray wolf to a health examination prior to transport to Yellowstone National Park. This gray wolf was part of a group of approximately 20 wolves captured in Alberta, Canada, during January 1996. US Fish and Wildlife Service.

wolf (*Canis rufus*). Both vary in color, ranging from gray to brown and black, with some gray wolves even being white in color. Although red wolves generally have a characteristic reddish tint to their fur, they are mostly brown in color. As the most dominant large carnivores in North America, wolves play an important role as predators in the ecosystems of which they are a part; they are considered a keystone species. Wolves generally hunt in packs and feed on large animals such as deer and elk; one of their primary functions within ecosystems is to remove sick or injured animals from these prey populations.

Although wolves rarely attack humans, they are widely regarded as being among the world's fiercest animals. A decline in native prey species for wolves occurred concurrently with an increase in domestic livestock animals during the settlement of North America, and over time, because of the tendency of wolves to prey on livestock, government agencies began to initiate intensive predator-control programs aimed at reducing wolf populations. In the lower forty-eight US states, except Minnesota, gray wolves were hunted nearly to extinction and ultimately were listed as endangered. Only several hundred gray wolves in Minnesota, an isolated wolf population on Michigan's Isle Royale, and a few red wolves remained. In 1926, the last gray wolf in Yellowstone National Park was killed during a time when Congress sanctioned predator control. Red wolf populations were decimated through habitat loss and predator control; the US Fish and Wildlife Service declared the subspecies extinct in the wild in 1980.

Shifts in land use and legislative changes eventually slowed declines in wolf populations in the United States. Recovery programs, natural migration of wolves from Canada, protection from unregulated hunting, and improved prey habitats resulted in growth in the gray wolf population in the lower forty-eight states to numbers exceeding five thousand by the early years of the twenty-first century. The National Park Service ended systematic killing of predators in 1933. The Endangered Species Act was passed in 1973, and in 1980 the US Fish and Wildlife Service established the Northern Rocky Mountain Wolf Recovery Plan. In 1995, after an absence of nearly seventy years, wolves were reintroduced into Yellowstone National Park. Because of the success of recovery programs, in 1996 the International Union for Conservation of Nature reduced the status of the gray wolf on the organization's Red List to that of "least concern"; it had maintained that status as of 2018. In 1970, a captive-breeding program was established to increase the red wolf population and reintroduce the subspecies to the wild; however, by 2017, the US Fish & Wildlife Service reported that the red wolf population in the wild was estimated to be between forty-five and sixty, with approximately two hundred in captive breeding areas. Restoration efforts for red wolves have included programs at the Alligator River National Wildlife Refuge in northeastern North Carolina and at other national wildlife refuges.

C. J. Walsh

Further Reading

Busch, Robert H. *The Wolf Almanac: A Celebration of Wolves and Their World.* New and revised ed., Lyons Press, 2007.

Fears, Darryl. "Can Red Wolves Be Saved Again?" *The Washington Post,* 5 Feb. 2018, www.washingtonpost. com/news/national/wp/2018/02/05/feature/ red-wolves-may-be-going-extinct-in-the-wild-again/?utm_term=.34991d5593a3. Accessed 26 Mar. 2018.

Mech, L. David, and Luigi Boitani, editors. *Wolves: Behavior, Ecology, and Conservation.* U of Chicago P, 2007.

Peterson, Rolf. *The Wolves of Isle Royale: A Broken Balance.* 1995. U of Michigan P, 2007.

"Red Wolf Recovery." *US Fish and Wildlife Service,* 25 May 2017, www.fws.gov/redwolf/. Accessed 26 Mar. 2018.

■ Conservation of Yosemite Valley

FIELDS OF STUDY: Places, Peoples, Societies; Parks, Monuments, Reserves; Ecology, Environment, Environmentalism; Forests, Forestry; Plants, Vegetation, Botany, Horticulture

IDENTIFICATION: Scenic valley of the Merced River located on the western slope of the Sierra Nevada in east-central California

The Yosemite Valley was part of the first reserve set aside by the United States as an area to be preserved for future generations, a concept that soon thereafter led to the establishment of a national park system.

Caucasians first entered Yosemite Valley in 1851 during conflicts between California gold miners and local Native Americans. In 1864, after lobbying by early conservationists, U.S. president Abraham Lincoln signed the Yosemite Land Grant, which gave Yosemite Valley and an area a few miles to the south called Mariposa Big Tree Grove—15,900 hectares (39,200 acres) of federal land in all—to the state of California as a reserve to be used for public enjoyment and recreation. The state-supervised reserve was the first area specifically set aside by the United States to be preserved for all future generations. Its inception planted the seed for the national park

Theodore Roosevelt; John Muir; Muir and Teddy Roosevelt at Glacier Point, Yosemite Valley. Library of Congress.

system, although Yellowstone, not Yosemite, was the first site officially designated a national park, in 1872.

Despite the protection provided by the 1864 land-grant legislation, the floor of Yosemite Valley was used for commercial purposes, including plowing and orchard planting, timber cutting, and grazing. The unprotected, high-mountain country surrounding the valley was also logged and grazed. American preservationist John Muir, while exploring the area in the late 1860's, became concerned about these disturbances to the natural landscape. For the next two decades, he publicized his concerns and worked to preserve the high country.

Muir's efforts paid off in 1890 when some 377,000 hectares (932,000 acres) of the high country surrounding Yosemite Valley gained federal protection through the establishment of Yosemite National Park. However, the valley itself and Mariposa Grove remained under California's jurisdiction. Muir and others then worked to get Yosemite Valley transferred from state to federal government jurisdiction in order to protect it and consolidate the public holdings into a single, unified national park. To help rally public support for Yosemite Valley and other land in the Sierra Nevada, Muir and others founded the Sierra Club in 1892.

In 1903 Muir persuaded President Theodore Roosevelt that the valley needed federal protection, and in 1906 California ceded the area back to the federal government. Yosemite Valley and Mariposa Grove thus became part of Yosemite National Park. There was a cost, however: The overall size of the park was reduced to about 308,000 hectares (761,000 acres), and private mining and timber holdings in the park were excluded from restrictions. In 1913, despite the opposition of Muir and other conservationists, the U.S. Congress approved a project to dam and flood Hetch Hetchy Valley in the northwest corner of Yosemite National Park to create a reservoir to supply water to the city of San Francisco.

Since its inception as a state park in 1864, Yosemite has been a magnet for tourists. By the early years of the twenty-first century, the national park was attracting millions of visitors—and their automobiles—each year. Minimizing the environmental damage that can be caused by such high numbers of visitors is an ongoing problem for Yosemite and for other national parks.

Jane F. Hill

Further Reading

Perrottet, Tony. "John Muir's Yosemite: The Father of the Conservation Movement Found His Calling on a Visit to the California Wilderness." *Smithsonian* 39, no. 4 (July, 2008): 48-55.

Radanovich, Leroy. *Yosemite Valley*. Charleston, S.C.: Arcadia, 2004.

■ Conservation policy

FIELDS OF STUDY: Government, Politics, International Relations; Laws, Acts, Resolutions; Public Policy, Debates, Controversies; Regulation, Standards and Practices; Ecology, Environment, Environmentalism

DEFINITION: Laws and regulations designed to limit the economic exploitation of natural resources in the public interest

Trends in conservation policy in the United States have varied in emphasis between allowing for limited exploitation of resources and prohibiting most economic uses of partic-

ular resources so that they can be preserved in an undeveloped state. Both approaches, however, have led to the protection and preservation of public lands and animal habitats.

The first use of the term "conservation" in relation to the natural environment was claimed by Progressive intellectuals in the early twentieth century. In his autobiography *Breaking New Ground* (1947), Gifford Pinchot, first chief of the U.S. Forest Service and a close friend of President Theodore Roosevelt, recalled realizing that all the natural resource problems are really one problem: the use of the earth for the permanent good of humans. The idea needed a name; presidential adviser Overton Price suggested "conservation," and the matter was settled.

Milestones in Conservation Policy

Year	Event
1864	Yosemite Valley is ceded to California to create a park.
1872	The Yellowstone National Park Act establishes the world's first national park.
1891	The Forest Reserve Act authorizes the U.S. president to establish national forests.
1894	The Yellowstone Game Protection Act closes parks to hunting and commercial fishing.
1897	The Forest Management Act mandates that national forests be managed to perpetuate water supplies and wood products.
1900	The Lacey Act prohibits interstate shipment of wildlife that has been killed illegally.
1902	The Newlands Act establishes a national reclamation policy.
1903	The first National Wildlife Refuge is created at Pelican Island, Florida.
1905	The U.S. Forest Service is created within the Department of Agriculture to manage national forests.
1906	The Antiquities Act authorizes the creation of national monuments by presidential proclamation.
1910	The Pickett Act authorizes presidential land withdrawals for any public purpose.

1911	The Weeks Act provides for governmental purchase of national forestlands.
1913	The Hetch Hetchy Dam is authorized in Yosemite National Park.
1916	The National Park Service is created in the Interior Department to manage national parks.
1918	The Migratory Bird Treaty Act restricts the hunting of migratory birds.
1933	The Civilian Conservation Corps Act is passed.
1933	The Tennessee Valley Authority is created.
1934	The Taylor Grazing Act regulates grazing on public lands.
1937	The Federal Aid in Wildlife Restoration (Pittman- Robinson) Act provides federal aid to states for wildlife management.
1946	The U.S. Bureau of Land Management is created.
1950	The Federal Aid in Fish Restoration (Dingell-Johnson) Act provides federal aid to states for sport fish management.
1956	The Fish and Wildlife Act creates the U.S. Fish and Wildlife Service in the Interior Department.
1956	A proposal to construct Echo Park Dam in Dinosaur National Monument is defeated.
1960	The Multiple Use-Sustained Yield Act clarifies the purposes of national forests.
1964	The Wilderness Act establishes the National Wilderness Preservation System.
1964	The Land and Water Conservation Fund Act provides a trust fund for parkland acquisition.
1968	The National Wild and Scenic Rivers Act establishes a national river conservation system.
1968	The National Trails System Act establishes a national system of recreational trails.
1970	The National Environmental Policy Act requires environmental impact statements for federal activities that affect the environment.

1970	The Environmental Protection Agency (EPA) is created.
1970	Clean Air Act amendments establish stricter air-quality standards.
1971	The United Nations Educational, Scientific, and Cultural Organization (UNESCO) Biosphere Reserve Program recognizes areas of global environmental significance.
1972	The Clean Water Act establishes stricter water-quality standards.
1972	The United Nations Environmental Conference in Stockholm, Sweden, is attended by 113 nations.
1972	Federal Water Pollution Control Act amendments provide protection for wetlands.
1972	The Federal Environmental Pesticides Control Act requires pesticide registration.
1972	The Marine Mammal Protection Act imposes a moratorium on hunting or harassing of marine mammals.
1973	The Convention on International Trade in Endangered Species of Wild Fauna and Flora (CITES) prohibits international trade in endangered species.
1973	The Endangered Species Act commits the United States to the preservation of biological diversity.
1974	The Safe Drinking Water Act sets federal standards for public water supplies.
1976	The Toxic Substances Control Act authorizes the EPA to ban substances that threaten human health or the environment.
1976	The Federal Land Policy and Management Act directs the Bureau of Land Management to retain public lands and manage them for multiple uses.
1976	The Resource Conservation and Recovery Act directs the EPA to regulate waste production, storage, and transportation.
1976	The National Forest Management Act gives statutory protection to national forests and sets standards for management.

1977	The Surface Mining Control and Reclamation Act establishes environmental standards for strip mining.
1977	Clean Air Act amendments set high standards for air quality in large national parks and wilderness areas.
1980	The Fish and Wildlife Conservation Act provides federal aid for the protection of nongame wildlife.
1980	The Alaska National Interest Lands Conservation Act establishes more than 40.5 million hectares (100 million acres) of national parks and wildlife refuges in Alaska.
1980	The Comprehensive Environmental Response, Compensation, and Liability Act (CERCLA) establishes the Superfund hazardous waste cleanup program.
1982	The Nuclear Waste Policy Act establishes a process for siting a permanent nuclear waste repository.
1985	The U.S. government establishes the Conservation Reserve Program (CRP) to reduce agricultural surpluses by encouraging farmers to reduce the amounts of land they devote to crops, thereby helping to prevent soil erosion and reduce carbon in the atmosphere.
1987	The Montreal Protocol limits the production and consumption of chlorofluorocarbons (CFCs).
1988	The Ocean Dumping Act prohibits the dumping of sewage sludge and industrial waste.
1990	Clean Air Act amendments strengthen the Clean Air Act.
1992	The Earth Summit in Rio de Janeiro, Brazil, is attended by 179 nations.
1997	The Kyoto Protocol on Climate Change encourages global reduction in greenhouse gas emissions.
2001	The Roadless Area Conservation Rule, a federal policy initiative designed to protect national forests from commercial development, is issued.
2005	More than 4,000 hectares (approximately 10,000 acres) of Puerto Rican rainforest are added to the U.S. national forest system.
2008	The Food, Conservation, and Energy Act extends CRP enrollment authority through 2012.
2009	The Omnibus Public Land Management Act adds 850,000 hectares (2.1 million acres) of new wilderness areas in nine U.S. states.

Origins of Conservation Policy

The antecedents of modern conservation policies go back centuries. Aboriginal cultures around the world developed taboos governing behavior on the hunt. Venetians established reserves for deer and wild boar in the eighth century. Hunting reserves were common in Europe and Asia, and in colonial America those trees thought best for ships' masts were preserved for that purpose by decree.

Conservation policy, as the term is now understood, is a product of the nineteenth century, when population growth, urbanization, and industrialization created unprecedented opportunities for people to influence the natural world in which they lived, both for good and for ill. By the end of the nineteenth century, more Americans lived in cities than on farms. The nation was connected from coast to coast by telegraph and rail, and economic growth was rapid.

Most natural resource policies of the nineteenth century were designed to facilitate economic development. Best known among these policies was the Homestead Act of 1862, which gave free land to settlers, but similar policies provided free land to railroads and states. Other laws stimulated growth by providing for free use of timber and minerals on public lands.

The economic progress of the nineteenth century came at high cost to the environment, typified by the profligate use of forests and the near extermination of North American buffalo, and some prominent Americans took notice. In 1832 the artist and journalist George Catlin wrote of the probable extinction of the buffalo and American Indians, and he advocated a large national park where both might be preserved. Henry David Thoreau echoed Catlin's concerns in 1858, calling for national preserves. In 1864 George Perkins Marsh published *Man and Nature: Or, Physical Geography as Modified by Human Action,* the earliest important text with an ecological perspective.

As economic exploitation diminished the supply of natural resources, public attitudes began to change, and with them governmental policies. Although many laws continued to encourage economic growth, others reflected the growing desire for conservation. In 1864 the U.S. Congress sought to preserve the Yosemite Valley and Mariposa Big Tree Grove by giving them to the state of California for a public park. Eight years later Congress established the world's first national park at Yellowstone. In 1884 additional legislation prohibited all hunting and commercial fishing within Yellowstone National Park. In 1891 Congress established what would eventually become the national forest system when it authorized the president to set aside forest reserves on public lands.

Preservation Versus Wise Use

These early conservation policies stressed resource preservation. Parks and forest reserves were simply set aside; none was effectively managed. The lack of management—especially forest management—displeased the advocates of scientific forestry, who also considered themselves conservationists. Early in its history, thus, the American conservation movement was divided, with some conservationists preaching "preservation" and others "wise use."

These contradictory tendencies were epitomized in the conflict between John Muir, founder of the Sierra Club, and Gifford Pinchot, principal architect and first chief of the U.S. Forest Service. Muir was the intellectual heir of Thoreau and Catlin. A perceptive scientist and popular author, he devoted his life to the exploration, enjoyment, and preservation of natural ecosystems worldwide. Pinchot had studied scientific forestry at its source in Germany. He was a gifted politician, and his passion was not for preservation but for wise use. Muir believed that people could not improve on nature; his conservation was aesthetic and spiritual. Pinchot was committed to maximizing the human benefits from resource use through science; his conservation was economic and utilitarian. Although friends for a time, Muir and Pinchot eventually parted ways, with Muir becoming an advocate for preservation and national parks and

Pinchot an advocate for wise use and national forests.

In the United States the legacy of Pinchot is alive and well in the multiple-use management principles of the Forest Service and the Bureau of Land Management and in organizations such as the Society of American Foresters, the International Society of Fish and Wildlife Managers, the National Rifle Association, and the Soil Conservation Society of America. Muir's emphasis on preservation has been institutionalized in the National Park Service and the Fish and Wildlife Service as well as in organizations such as the National Audubon Society, the Nature Conservancy, the Sierra Club, and the Wilderness Society.

Progressive Era

Many historians emphasize three eras of American conservation policy corresponding roughly to the Progressive Era, the New Deal, and the so-called environmental decade of the 1970's. The Progressive Era, epitomized by the presidency of Theodore Roosevelt, was the first golden age of American conservation policy. During this period Congress passed a number of pathbreaking conservation laws. The Lacey Act of 1900 put the power of federal enforcement behind state game laws, criminalizing the interstate transport of wildlife killed or captured in violation of state regulations. Another milestone of wildlife conservation was the ratification of a migratory bird treaty with Canada and passage of a law to enforce the treaty. With the Migratory Bird Treaty Act of 1918, the federal government asserted national authority to manage wildlife for conservation purposes, authority that was upheld by the U.S. Supreme Court in the case of *Missouri v. Holland* (1920).

Two critically important governmental agencies were created during this era: the

Forest Service and the Park Service. In 1905 advocates of wise use and scientific forestry were rewarded with a Forest Service in the Department of Agriculture. The new agency's first director was Gifford Pinchot, the nation's foremost advocate of multiple-use forest management based on scientific principles. Under Pinchot's leadership the concepts of multiple use and sustained yield were applied in the rapidly growing national forest system. When Theodore Roosevelt became president, the United States had 18.6 million hectares (46 million acres) of national forest. By the end of his term of office, Roosevelt had increased the total size of the national forest system to 78.5 million hectares (194 million acres).

During the Progressive Era, advocates of preservation were often unsuccessful in their opposition to the policies of wise-use conservationists, but in the end they also had a victory. The most painful loss came in Yosemite National Park, where advocates of wise use joined forces with the city of San Francisco to dam the Hetch Hetchy Valley for a municipal water supply, forever destroying a natural valley some regarded as comparable to Yosemite Valley itself. The public outcry over the damming of Hetch Hetchy contributed to pressure for better park protection, however, and in 1916 preservationists achieved a long-sought goal: creation of the National Park Service to manage the growing system of fourteen national parks, including Yellowstone (1872), Yosemite and Sequoia (1890), Mount Rainier (1899), Crater Lake (1902), Wind Cave (1903), Mesa Verde (1906), Glacier (1910), Rocky Mountain (1915), and Hawaii and Lassen Volcanic (1916).

Two new forms of conservation reserves made their debut during this era: national wildlife refuges and national monuments. Roosevelt regarded wildlife sanctuaries as critical to the survival of game species. In 1903 he acted on his belief, creating the nation's first national wildlife refuge on Pelican Island in Florida. He had no specific legal authority to create a national wildlife refuge, but his usurpation was accepted at the time and later approved in principle. In 1910 the Pickett Act authorized the president to set aside land for any public purpose. National monuments began on a firmer foundation, but here too Roosevelt pushed conservation to the limit. The Antiquities Act of 1906 authorized the president to establish national monuments. As the name suggests, the law anticipated relatively small reservations to protect archaeological sites, but the monuments Roosevelt designated included 34,400 hectares (85,000 acres) at Petrified Forest, 120,600 hectares (298,000 acres) at Mount Olympus, and 326,200 hectares (806,000 acres) at the Grand Canyon. All of these later became national parks.

New Deal Era
The New Deal was, for the most part, a response to disaster. The primary disaster was the Great Depression, but the decade of the 1930's also saw the Dust Bowl, a minor climatic change that produced disastrous results on the Great Plains. New Deal conservation policies were responsive to the economic and ecological crises of the era, and they stressed wise use through scientific management rather than preservation. The Tennessee Valley Authority was created in 1933 to stimulate employment and economic growth in Appalachia through scientific management of the area's natural resources. The Taylor Grazing Act of 1934 was designed to end overgrazing of western public lands by imposing a system of permits based on principles of scientific management. The Civilian Conservation Corps and the Soil Conservation Service were both established during this era, and each contributed to repairing environmental damage. Greater concern for the management rather than the disposal of western public lands was also reflected in the creation in 1946 of the Bureau of Land Management to replace the General Land Office.

Environmental Decade
The so-called environmental decade lasted almost twenty years. It began with the inauguration of President John F. Kennedy, persisted through the presidential administrations of Lyndon B. Johnson, Richard Nixon, Gerald Ford, and Jimmy Carter, and ended with the inauguration of President Ronald Reagan. The conservation policies of this era were responsive to post-World War II economic growth that seemed to ensure economic prosperity while threatening quality of life. Stewart Udall, U.S. secretary of the interior, warned of a *Quiet Crisis* (1963), Rachel Carson of a *Silent Spring* (1962), Barry Commoner of *The Closing Circle* (1971), and Paul R. Ehrlich of *The Population Bomb* (1968). Conservation policy matured into environmental policy during this era. Conservation was still about husbanding natural resources, but to the historic concerns of conservation—such as forests, wilderness, and wildlife—were added concerns regarding clean water and clean air, energy supplies, and the problems posed by hazardous and toxic wastes. During this era Congress passed most of the major laws that continue to shape conservation policy at the beginning of the twenty-first century.

Preservation policy was strengthened. In 1964 Congress passed the Wilderness Act and the Land and Water Conservation Fund Act. The former established the National Wilderness Preservation System, which has grown from more than 3.6 million hectares (9 million acres) to more than 40.5 million hectares (100 million acres). The latter facilitated acquisition of land for parks and open space. Four years later Congress established a national system of trails as well as a national system to protect wild and scenic rivers from certain kinds of development. Both the Forest Service and the Bureau of Land Management were given new statutory direction emphasizing planning and preservation, sometimes at the expense of economic development. At the end of the era Congress passed the Alaska National Interest Lands Conservation Act (1980), making conservation withdrawals of more than 40.5 million hectares of public lands and doubling the size of the national park and wildlife refuge systems nationwide.

Wise-use conservation was also well served as Congress radically increased federal regulation of resource use. President Johnson established a presidential commission on natural beauty and addressed world population and resource scarcity in his 1965 state of the union speech. Environmental management was nationalized through a series of far-reaching statutes addressing air pollution, water pollution, marine resources, noise pollution, biological diversity, toxic chemicals, and hazardous waste. New burdens were placed on government and private citizens. The National Environmental Policy Act of 1969 required all governmental agencies to study the probable environmental effects of their actions before moving forward. A large number of environmental enforcement programs were reorganized in 1970 into the newly created Environmental Protection Agency (EPA). The EPA is an independent agency, but presidents have routinely regarded its director as having cabinet status.

Conservation Policy for a New Millennium

At the policy level, the era following the environmental decade was one of consolidation rather than new initiatives. The Reagan administration was hostile to environmental policy and attempted to tilt public policy toward less environmental regulation. President Reagan was able to prevent the adoption of major new conservation policies, but his administrative efforts—led by Interior Secretary James Watt—to roll back environmental laws were successfully resisted by Congress. A major new air-pollution statute was passed during the presidential administration of George H. W. Bush, but this was exceptional for the era. Bill Clinton's presidential administration gave

greater attention to conservation policy, but in the years following the 1994 elections there was little cooperation between the president and Congress on environmental issues.

Americans have come to expect government to practice conservation and protect environmental quality. Doing so has become increasingly difficult. Beyond the policy gridlock of the 1980s, 1990's, and 2000s, the issues themselves became more difficult. The most pressing issues—such as stratospheric ozone depletion, climate change, and biological diversity—were beset by scientific uncertainty. Such concerns are also global in scope and thus beyond the ability of any single nation to address independently. The future of conservation policy appears to be in the international arena, where extant institutions lack the authority to govern. Treaties addressing the use of ozone-destroying chlorinated fluorocarbons, the preservation of biological diversity, and the limitation of heat-trapping greenhouse gas emissions demonstrate that nations are giving increasing attention to conservation issues, but international achievements remain modest.

Despite decades of government conservation efforts, a 2015 *Proceedings of the National Academy of Sciences* analysis indicated that the Wilderness Act and other existing US policies have favored scenic vistas, particularly in the West, and endangered mammals and birds at the expense of vulnerable reptiles, amphibians, and trees. Thus, the researchers found a mismatch between what has been protected and the species and geographical areas that most need it in order to preserve biodiversity.

In the late 2010s, the administration of President Donald Trump increasingly turned away from conservation in order to exploit natural resources. Soon after his inauguration in 2017, Trump announced the US withdrawal from the landmark international Paris Agreement on emissions reduction and, that December, shrank the Grand Staircase–Escalante and Bears Ears National Monuments, constituting the largest such reduction in land protection to date. The following year, the administration rewrote Interior Department guidance to facilitate public uses such as mining and oil and gas extraction, over and against habitat protection and mitigation of human activity. The future of US conservation policy, both at home and abroad, was thus called into question.

Craig W. Allin

Further Reading

Allin, Craig W. *The Politics of Wilderness Preservation.* 1982. Reprint. Fairbanks: University of Alaska Press, 2008.

Chiras, Daniel D., and John P. Reganold. *Natural Resource Conservation: Management for a Sustainable Future.* 10th ed. Upper Saddle River, N.J.: Benjamin Cummings/Pearson, 2010.

Davis, David Howard. *American Environmental Politics.* Belmont, Calif.: Wadsworth, 1998.

Dowie, Mark. *Conservation Refugees: The Hundred-Year Conflict Between Global Conservation and Native Peoples.* Cambridge, Mass.: MIT Press, 2009.

Eilperin, Juliet. "Energy and Environment Interior Rescinds Climate, Conservation Policies Because They're 'Inconsistent' with Trump's Energy Goals." *The Washington Post,* 5 Jan. 2018, www.washingtonpost.com/news/energy-environment/wp/2018/01/05/interior-rescinds-climate-conservation-policies-because-theyre-inconsistent-with-trumps-energy-goals. Accessed 4 Apr. 2018.

French, Hilary. *Vanishing Borders: Protecting the Planet in the Age of Globalization.* New York: W. W. Norton, 2000.

Hayes, Samuel P. *Conservation and the Gospel of Efficiency: The Progressive Conservation Movement, 1890-1920.* 1959. Reprint. Pittsburgh: University of Pittsburgh Press, 1999.

Jenkins, Clinton N., et al. "US Protected Lands Mismatch Biodiversity Priorities." *Proceedings of the National Academy of Sciences,* vol. 112, no. 16, 21 Apr. 2015, pp. 5081–86, doi: doi.org/10.1073/pnas.1418034112. Accessed 4 Apr. 2018.

Nash, Roderick. *Wilderness and the American Mind.* 4th ed. New Haven, Conn.: Yale University Press, 2001.

Rosenbaum, Walter A. *Environmental Politics and Policy.* 7th ed. Washington, D.C.: CQ Press, 2008.

■ Conservation Reserve Program (CRP)

FIELDS OF STUDY: Economics, Business, Production, Commerce; Agriculture, Farming, Animal Husbandry; Ecology, Environment, Environmentalism

IDENTIFICATION: Cropland reduction and conservation program of the US Department of Agriculture

DATE: Created on December 23, 1985

Initially established to reduce agricultural surpluses by encouraging farmers to reduce the amounts of land they devoted to crops, the Conservation Reserve Program has grown to become an environmental protection program as well, preventing soil erosion and reducing carbon in the atmosphere.

The history of agriculture in the United States reveals a pattern of crop production increasing faster than demand, resulting in downward pressure on crop prices and farm income. Improvements in equipment, chemicals, and seed genetics have increased yields. In 1982, farmers produced a surplus of 230 million metric tons (254 million US tons) of crops, swamping the available storage capacity. The government response, announced by President Ronald Reagan on January 11, 1983, was a payment-in-kind (PIK) program. Under this program, farmers were given certificates for crops in storage in return for taking land out of production.

The PIK program was generous, with wheat farmers getting up to 95 percent of the normal crop. Farmers responded by removing 33.3 million hectares (82.3 million acres) of cropland from the 1983 growing season. This steep reduction from the 170 million hectares (420 million acres) planted in 1982 had a devastating economic impact on small towns dependent on agriculture. Farmers bought less fuel and fertilizer, and they did not hire seasonal workers. The resulting stress on rural communities made it clear to policy makers that wide swings in the amounts of land planted were unacceptable. The US Congress responded to the overproduction issue with the Conservation Reserve Program (CRP), which was created under Title XII of the 1985 Food Security Act.

The twin goals of CRP were to decrease crop surpluses through reduction in land area planted and to prevent cropland erosion. Enrollment was voluntary, with farmers submitting bids for the amount of payment required to remove land from production for ten to fifteen years. Participants were paid a rental fee plus half the cost of establishing a permanent cover of trees or grasses. Enrollment increased rapidly, with approximately 13.8 million hectares (34 million acres) enrolled during the first nine sign-up periods from 1986 through 1989.

Over time Congress enhanced the environmental protection aspects of CRP. The Food, Agriculture, Conservation, and Trade Act of 1990 extended the enrollment period through 1995 and added water-quality protection as a criterion for land selected.

Switchgrass offers ground cover and wildlife habitat in a field put into the Conservation Reserve Program in southern Iowa. Photo by Lynn Betts, USDA Natural Resources Conservation Service

The Federal Agriculture Improvement and Reform Act of 1996 included an Environmental Benefits Index for selection of land suitable for enrollment.

The environmental impact of CRP is substantial—ground-cover plants on CRP lands annually remove an estimated 17 million metric tons (18.7 million U.S. tons) of carbon from the atmosphere and reduce soil erosion by more than 443 million metric tons (488 million U.S. tons). These lands also provide critical habitat for wildlife, including upland game birds, grassland songbirds, and prairie mammals. CRP lands are particularly important to migratory waterfowl. Duck species that had historically nested in the Prairie Pothole region of the northern plains were in serious trouble during the 1980s, with populations near their lowest level in the preceding fifty years. Habitat provided by CRP increased the ducks' nesting success, helping the population rebound from 25.6 million breeding ducks in 1985 to 42 million in 2009.

CRP continues as an important environmental and agricultural program. The Food, Conservation, and Energy Act of 2008 extended CRP enrollment authority to September 30, 2012. It set the enrollment authority at 15.8 million hectares (39 million acres) through 2009 but reduced enrollments to 13 million hectares (32 million acres) for fiscal years 2010 to 2012. In 2009 there were 14 million hectares (34.7 million acres) enrolled at an annual rental cost

of $1.76 billion per year, an average cost of about $125 per hectare ($50 per acre) per year. With considerable support for CRP from agricultural producers, organizations concerned with waterfowl, and the environmental community, the program is likely to continue to be included in future farm legislation.

Allan Jenkins

Further Reading

Hamilton, James T. *Conserving Data in the Conservation Reserve.* Washington, DC: RFF, 2010. Print.

Napier, Ted, Silvana M. Napier, and Jiri Tvrdon, eds. *Soil and Water Conservation Policies and Programs: Successes and Failures.* Boca Raton: CRC, 2000. Print.

■ Continental shelves and pollution

FIELDS OF STUDY: Biology, Life Sciences, Ecosystems; Animals, Zoology, Marine Biology; Continents, Regions, Areas, Islands; Ecology, Environment, Environmentalism; Oceans, Seas, Lakes, Bodies of Water

DEFINITION: Nearly flat platforms of land that extend into the seas at the margins of continents

Human activities have had many negative environmental impacts on the world's continental shelves, both directly and indirectly. These impacts include pollution of the waters of the shelves' ecosystems through runoff from land, the direct dumping of wastes, and oil extraction; the construction of artificial reefs and breakwaters; and the dredging of sand and gravel.

Continental shelves constitute the parts of the oceans most utilized by humans, but much of the environmental degradation that the shelves have undergone has resulted indirectly from human activities on land. The waters of the continental shelves in many parts of the world have become polluted by chemical fertilizers, industrial wastes, and sewage released into the seas from rivers and storm drains. Such pollution threatens the plants and animals present in coastal ecosystems.

During the early 1960's, for example, the brown pelican, a seabird species native to the coasts of the Americas, almost became extinct owing to coastal pollution. Scientists found that the brown pelican population was dying out because the birds were laying eggs with extremely thin shells that would break in the nest, so few hatchlings survived. The cause was determined to be the presence of the pesticide Dichloro-diphenyl-trichloroethane (DDT) in coastal waters, which came from agricultural runoff that was deposited in the Gulf of Mexico by the Mississippi River. DDT had accumulated in the bodies of the fish on which the pelicans fed. After the dangers of DDT were recognized, use of the pesticide was eventually banned in the United States.

Chemical pollution of coastal waters remains a problem, however. In some areas, pollution of the continental shelves by agricultural runoff containing fertilizers has led to the creation of hypoxic (oxygen-deprived) areas known as dead zones. The nitrogen and phosphorus in fertilizers are nutrients that cause algae to grow at accelerated rates. When the algae die and sink to the bottom, their decay depletes the dissolved oxygen in the water, and the fish and other marine life die. A seasonal hypoxic zone the size of the state of New Jersey forms during the summer months at the mouth of the Mississippi River in the Gulf of Mexico, and similar dead zones are found on continental shelves around the world.

Coral reefs, many of which develop along the edges of continental shelves, have been increasingly damaged by human activities, both indirectly and directly. Chemical pollution is thought to contribute to the discoloration of these reefs known as bleaching and white-band disease, and serious damage to reefs can result from the dragging of anchors across them and from shipwrecks. Other damaging human activities include the use of harmful chemicals and even dynamite to drive reef organisms out of their hiding places and the mining of reefs to collect coral for ornamental purposes. Policy makers and legislators have responded to increasing recognition among scientists that the ecosystems of coral reefs need to be protected. In the United States, for instance, the National Marine Sanctuaries Program protects the reefs of the Florida Keys as well as thirteen other pristine marine sites around North America, Hawaii, and American Samoa.

Dumping of Wastes

Various kinds of environmental damage to the continental shelves have resulted directly from human actions. For example, humans have intentionally changed coastal seabeds—and thus destroyed marine habitats and disrupted ecosystems—by building breakwaters, pilings for bridges, artificial reefs, and wind farms; in addition, in some cases, these areas have been used for the disposal of construction debris, municipal solid waste, and outdated military hardware.

An extreme example of the dumping of waste on a continental shelf is provided by New York City, which has always faced difficulty in the disposal of construction debris. Manhattan Island is only 21.6 kilometers (13.4 miles) long and 3.7 kilometers (2.3 miles) wide, and it represents some of the most expensive real estate in the world. In 1890 builders in Manhattan began the practice of dumping construction debris and other waste in the New York Bight, an indentation in the coastline between New York State and New Jersey. The mound formed on the continental shelf in this area was soon so large that it was jokingly called an underwater Mount Everest. Amendments made in 1986 to the Marine Protection, Research, and Sanctuaries Act of 1972 (also known as the Ocean Dumping Act) prohibited dumping in this area, and a new dump site was opened 170 kilometers (106 miles) offshore. Since that time, an even larger mound of waste materials has been accumulating on the seabed at a depth of 2,500 meters (8,200 feet).

The dumping of obsolete military hardware in coastal waters creates special problems because such hardware may contain materials that are hazardous. Two crewmen on a clam boat off the shore of Massachusetts had to be hospitalized in June, 2010, for example, after they hauled up World War I-era military shells filled with mustard gas along with a load of clams. It turned out that the U.S. military had been using the area as a dumping ground for munitions from after World War II through 1970.

Dredging and Oil Spills

In addition to building and dumping things on continental shelves, humans also take things out. Sand is routinely dredged from the continental shelf off southern Florida, for example, to "nourish" beaches that have lost their sand due to erosion, and some cities that are heavily dependent on tourist revenue, such as Delray Beach and Palm Beach, have had their beaches rebuilt several times. In countries that are highly industrialized and densely populated, continental shelves may be mined for the sand and gravel required for construction. It has been estimated that 25 percent of the sand and gravel needed for construction in southeastern England comes from offshore; the proportion is believed to be even higher for Japan. In addition to exploiting continental shelves for sand and gravel, humans also mine deposits of valuable minerals, such as diamonds and gold, on some of the world's continental shelves.

Oil spills represent another way in which humans degrade the shelves. Production platforms and drilling rigs jut up offshore in areas where oil and gas deposits are found, and the oil that can leak or spill from these rigs has the potential to foul the ocean and seabed for hundreds of miles around. Two examples of disastrous spills that resulted from such offshore oil extraction have taken place in the Gulf of Mexico.

In 1979 a blowout in an exploratory well drilled by Petróleos Mexicanos (PEMEX), the Mexican state-owned oil company, in 50 meters (164 feet) of water off the coast of Mexico caused a spillage of oil that fouled the seabed and beaches as far away as Texas.

An even greater tragedy was the blowout of BP's *Deepwater Horizon* rig off the coast of Louisiana in 2010. Heavy reddish-brown oil from this spill fouled the continental shelf and beaches as far away as Florida, even though the well was drilled 72 kilometers (45 miles) offshore in water 1,524 meters (5,000 feet) deep.

Donald W. Lovejoy

Further Reading

Ketchum, Bostwick H., ed. *The Water's Edge: Critical Problems of the Coastal Zone.* Cambridge, Mass.: MIT Press, 1972.

Porter, James W., and Karen G. Porter, eds. *The Everglades, Florida Bay, and Coral Reefs of the Florida Keys: An Ecosystem Sourcebook.* Boca Raton, Fla.: CRC Press, 2002.

Sverdrup, Keith A., and E. Virginia Armbrust. *An Introduction to the World's Oceans.* New York: McGraw-Hill, 2009.

Viles, Heather A., and Tom Spencer. *Coastal Problems: Geomorphology, Ecology, and Society at the Coast.* London: Arnold, 1995.

Walsh, John J. *On the Nature of the Continental Shelves.* San Diego, Calif.: Academic Press, 1988.

■ Controversy over wild horses and burros

FIELDS OF STUDY: Biology, Life Sciences, Ecosystems; Animals, Zoology, Marine Biology; Ethics, Advocacy, Policy, Protest

DEFINITION: Feral horses and burros living in the rangelands of the western United States

What should be done with the wild horses and burros of the United States has long been the subject of debates, primarily between ranchers who want to protect rangeland for their livestock and animal activists, environmentalists, historians, and others who want to preserve and protect the animals in their wild state.

Bands of untamed horses and burros can be found on the publicly owned rangelands of the western United States. The largest herds live on the public lands of eleven states: Nevada, Wyoming, Utah, Oregon, California, Colorado, Idaho, Arizona, Montana, North Dakota, and New Mexico. Feral horses also can be found on islands off the eastern coast of the United States, including Assateague and Cumberland. The Bureau of Land Management (BLM) and the U.S. Fisheries and Wildlife Service are the primary custodians of these animals.

History

Horses are natural denizens of grasslands, but they have migrated beyond their original native territory owing to human migrations. During the nineteenth and early twentieth centuries, equines abandoned after mining collapses, for example, discovered bioniches in arid lands, where the hardiest survived. Such horses formed herds or joined herds that had been created earlier by horses descended from those originally brought to the New World during the Spanish Conquest in the sixteenth century. Other equines originated in the great horse cultures of the Native Americans that the U.S. Army destroyed in the nineteenth century. Thriving populations gradually

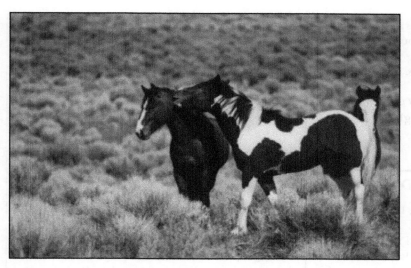

Wild horses on Steens Mountain in Oregon. (Bureau of Land Management (BLM))

became competitors with the ranching industry (chiefly cattle and sheep ranchers).

Environmental disruptions that resulted from the wild and domesticated beasts sharing unrestrained access to fragile desert ecosystems included overgrazing, soil compaction, degradation of riparian environments, and overpopulation owing to the lack of natural predators (ironically, natural predators such as wolves and mountain lions had been annihilated because they threatened livestock). Before passage of the Taylor Grazing Act of 1934, ranchers routinely grazed livestock on federal lands and their private holdings as well with no restrictions.

In 2010 it was estimated that some 37,000 feral horses and burros were living on millions of acres of public lands in the United States, half of them in Nevada. Another 34,000 that had been gathered in annual roundups were warehoused in government facilities around the country. At such facilities, the younger horses and burros await adoption or sale and the older and weaker animals receive care on an indefinite basis. Some wild horse advocacy groups have challenged the scientific methodology used in arriving at these figures; the BLM conducts only "rough counts." The formulas that the BLM uses to determine the numbers of animals—both wildlife and livestock—that shared rangeland can sustain with grazing are also a source of contention.

Debates

A lengthy legal history accompanies disputes over the fate of wild horses. Animal activists, wildlife biologists, environmental impact analysts, and historians often line up on one side to oppose ranchers, underfunded government agencies, and other vested economic interests. During the 1950's a Nevada woman, Velma Johnston, derisively dubbed "Wild Horse Annie," exposed the inhumane treatment of wild horses that were being corralled, shipped, and slaughtered to make pet foods. Her national campaign contributed to the eventual passage of groundbreaking national legislation in 1971 with the Wild Free-Roaming Horses and Burros Act. In 1978 that act was amended to "protect the range from wild horse overpopulation."

Debates surrounding the treatment of wild horses and burros often include examination of whether these animals can be classified as wildlife. Investigation of the genetic history of wild horses has demonstrated that they are indigenous to North America. Genus *Equus* migrated to Asia via the Bering land bridge in Paleolithic times, expanded into Europe, and then returned in the company of the Spanish conquistadores during the sixteenth century. This finding subverts a legal strategy to declare these equines invasive species, which would allow them to be disposed of as nuisances, as they would no longer be protected with native wildlife status.

Battles over the handling of wild horses and burros continue to be waged in the courts. Severe budget cuts have strained the caretaking capabilities of the BLM, and a sense of urgency surrounds the question of what to do with the horses collected in the annual roundups that are not adopted or sold. Debates continue, as advocates for wild horses and burros argue against euthanasia for healthy animals and many U.S. taxpayers express an increasing unwillingness to continue funding their care.

JoEllen Broome

Further Reading

Lindholdt, Paul, and Derrick Knowles, eds. *The Individual and Public Lands in the American West.* Spokane: Eastern Washington University Press, 2005.

Marshall, Julie Hoffman. *Making Burros Fly: Cleveland Amory, Animal Rescue Pioneer.* Boulder, Colo.: Johnson Books, 2006.

Ryden, Hope. *America's Last Wild Horses.* Rev. ed. New York: Lyons Press, 1999.

Stillman, Deanne. *Mustang: The Saga of the Wild Horse in the American West.* Boston: Houghton Mifflin Harcourt, 2008.

■ Convention on Biological Diversity

FIELDS OF STUDY: Government, Politics, International Relations; International Relations, Agreements, Treaties; Regulation, Standards and Practices; Animals, Zoology, Marine Biology; Ecology, Environment, Environmentalism; Biology, Life Sciences, Ecosystems; Plants, Vegetation, Botany, Horticulture

CATEGORIES: Treaties, laws, and court cases; ecology and ecosystems; resources and resource management

THE CONVENTION: International agreement that provides for the conservation of biological diversity, the sustainable use of biological resources, and the equitable distribution of the benefits of such resources

DATE: Opened for signature on June 5, 1992

The Convention on Biological Diversity is regarded as the first comprehensive international agreement to address the conservation and use of biological diversity across all levels of biological organization—from genetic resources to ecosystem services.

The objectives of this Convention, to be pursued in accordance with its relevant provisions, are the conservation of biological diversity, the sustainable use of its components and the fair and equitable sharing of the benefits arising out of the utilization of genetic resources, including by appropriate access to genetic resources and by appropriate transfer of relevant technologies, taking into account all rights over those resources and to technologies, and by appropriate funding.

The Convention on Biological Diversity is one of several historically important documents produced at the United Nations Conference on Environment and Development (UNCED), also known as the Earth Summit, held in Rio de Janeiro, Brazil, in June

---

Objectives of the Convention on Biological Diversity

Article 1 of the Convention on Biological Diversity sets out the convention's objectives, which guide all of its specific provisions and define the fundamental obligations of its signatories.

The objectives of this Convention, to be pursued in accordance with its relevant provisions, are the conservation of biological diversity, the sustainable use of its components and the fair and equitable sharing of the benefits arising out of the utilization of genetic resources, including by appropriate access to genetic resources and by appropriate transfer of relevant technologies, taking into account all rights over those resources and to technologies, and by appropriate funding.

Brian G. Wolff

---

of 1992. The convention, which entered into force on December 29, 1993, is closely linked to the principles of sustainable development and represents an international commitment to the conservation of biological diversity, its sustainable use, and the fair distribution of benefits arising from the utilization of genetic resources. The convention formally recognizes that the conservation of biological diversity is a common concern, an integral part of the development process, and the responsibility of all sovereign states.

Signatory nations—that is, the parties to the convention—are required to develop integrated national biodiversity strategies and action plans. Other key provisions require the establishment of protected areas for the conservation of biological diversity, the restoration of degraded ecosystems, the development of programs to promote the recovery of threatened species in collaboration with local residents, and the development of programs to control alien species and the risks posed by genetically modified organisms. The parties are obliged to report on their implementation of the provisions in the convention.

Several articles of the convention deserve special mention. Article 13 establishes the importance of public education and awareness and requires the parties to promote and encourage public understanding of the importance of conserving biological diversity while cooperating with other states and international organizations to develop educational and public-awareness programs. Article 15 addresses access to genetic resources and biopiracy by affirming state sovereignty over natural resources and prohibiting the exploitation of genetic resources without prior informed consent. Articles 20 stipulates that developed countries that are parties to the convention will provide financial resources to help developing country parties implement measures to fulfill their obligations under the convention; Article 21 establishes a mechanism for distributing that financial aid. Article 25 establishes the Subsidiary Body on Scientific, Technical, and Technological Advice, which provides the Conference of the Parties (COP) with advice relating to the implementation of the convention.

The COP, the governing body of the convention, implements the provisions of the convention through the decisions it makes at its meetings. The first COP was held in Nassau, Bahamas, in 1994. Since the third COP in 1996, ordinary meetings have been held biennially. A two-part extraordinary meeting in 1999-2000 produced the Cartagena Protocol on Biosafety, a supplement to the convention that regulates the international trade, handling, and use of genetically modified organisms that pose a potential threat to the conservation and sustainable use of biological diversity.

Brian G. Wolff

Further Reading

Andersen, Regine. "The Convention on Biological Diversity." In *Governing Agrobiodiversity: Plant Genetics and Developing Countries.* Burlington, Vt.: Ashgate, 2008.

Rosendal, Kristin G. *The Convention on Biological Diversity and Developing Countries.* Norwell, Mass.: Kluwer Academic, 2000.

United Nations. Secretariat of the Convention on Biological Diversity. *Handbook of the Convention on Biological Diversity Including Its Cartagena Protocol on Biosafety.* 3d ed. Montreal: Author, 2005.

See also: Agricultural chemicals; Balance of nature; Biodiversity; Biopiracy and bioprospecting; Biosphere reserves; Earth Summit; Sustainable development; United Nations Environment Programme

■ Convention on International Trade in Endangered Species

FIELDS OF STUDY: Government, Politics, International Relations; International Relations, Agreements, Treaties; Regulation, Standards and Practices; Animals, Zoology, Marine Biology

CATEGORIES: Treaties, laws, and court cases; animals and endangered species

THE CONVENTION: International agreement aimed at conserving endangered animal and plant species

DATE: Opened for signature on March 3, 1973

The Convention on International Trade in Endangered Species was the first international agreement concerning the conservation of wildlife that constituted a legal commitment by the parties to the convention and also included a means of enforcing its provisions.

Until the 1970's, international agreements that had been made to address the preservation of species did not include any binding legal commitment on the part of the countries signing them; thus they were ineffectual in protecting the species they were written to protect. In 1969, however, the United States passed the Endangered Species Conservation Act, which contained a provision that gave the secretaries of interior and commerce until June 30, 1971, to call for an international conference on endangered species. The resulting conference, which was held in Washington, D.C., in March, 1973, resulted in the Convention on International Trade in Endangered Species of Wild Fauna and Flora (CITES).

The United States was the first country to ratify the convention, which entered into effect on July 1, 1975; by 2010, 175 nations in total were parties to the agreement. CITES is intended to conserve species and does this by managing international trade in those species. It was the first international convention on the conservation of wildlife that constituted a legal commitment by the parties to the convention and also included a means of enforcing its provisions. This enforcement includes a system of trade sanctions and an international reporting network to stop trade in endangered species. The system established by CITES does, however, contain loopholes through which states with special interest in particular species can opt out of the global control for those species.

A major feature of CITES is its categorization of three levels of vulnerability of species. Appendix I

Species Protected by CITES

SPECIES TYPE	SPECIES	SUBSPECIES	POPULATIONS
Mammals	617	36	26
Birds	1,455	17	3
Reptiles	657	9	10
Amphibians	114	0	0
Fish	86	0	0
Invertebrates	2,179	5	0
Total fauna	5,108	67	39
Plants	28,977	7	3
Total	34,085	74	42

includes all species that are threatened with extinction and whose status may be affected by international trade. Appendix II includes species that are not yet threatened but might become endangered if trade in them is not regulated. It also includes other species that, if traded, might affect the vulnerability of the first group. Appendix III lists species that a signatory party identifies as subject to regulation in order to restrict exploitation of that species. The parties to the treaty agree not to allow any trade in the species on the three lists unless an exception is allowed in CITES.

The species listed in the appendixes may be moved from one list to another as their vulnerability increases or decreases. According to the convention, states may implement stricter measures of conservation than those specified in the convention or may ban trade in species not included in the appendixes. CITES also establishes a series of import and export trade permits within each of the categories. Each nation designates a management authority and a scientific authority to implement CITES. Exceptions to the ban on trade are made for scientific and museum specimens, exhibitions, and movement of species under permit by a national management authority.

The parties to CITES maintain records of trade in specimens of species that are listed in the appendixes and prepare periodic reports on their compliance with the convention. These reports are sent to the CITES secretariat in Switzerland, administered by the United Nations Environment Programme (UNEP), which issues notifications to all parties of

state actions and bans. The secretariat's functions are established by the convention and include interpreting the provisions of CITES and advising countries on implementing those provisions by providing assistance in writing their national legislation and organizing training seminars. The secretariat also studies the status of species being traded in order to ensure that the exploitation of such species is within sustainable limits.

The CITES Conference of Parties meets every two or three years in order to review implementation of the convention. The meetings are also attended by nonparty states, intergovernmental agencies of the United Nations, and nongovernmental organizations considered "technically qualified in protection, conservation or management of wild fauna and flora." The meetings are held in different signatories' countries: The first took place in Berne, Switzerland, on November 2-6, 1976. At the conference, the parties may adopt amendments to the convention and make recommendations to improve the effectiveness of CITES.

CITES has been incorporated into Caring for the Earth: A Strategy for Sustainable Living. This strategy was launched in 1991 by UNEP, the International Union for Conservation of Nature (IUCN), and the World Wide Fund for Nature (WWF). Other nongovernmental groups working to support CITES are Fauna and Flora International (FFI), Trade Records Analysis of Flora and Fauna in Commerce (TRAFFIC International), and the World Conservation Monitoring Centre (WCMC).

Some of the species protected by CITES have received additional protection under later agreements. In certain cases, however, states have allowed trade in listed species to continue for economic purposes or have refused to sign CITES because of the extent to which they trade in a species or species part, such as ivory. Others have signed because they needed help in stopping illegal trade and poaching of species within their borders. Whales have proven to be a difficult species to protect. Whales are given protection under CITES according to the status of specific species. The moratorium on commercial whaling instituted in 1986 by the International Whaling

Commission (IWC) was intended to strengthen the CITES protection by species, but the whaling states have disagreed on the numbers of whale populations, and some have withdrawn from the IWC and resumed their whaling activities.

Colleen M. Driscoll

Further Reading

Chasek, Pamela S., et al. *Global Environmental Politics.* 4th ed. Boulder, Colo.: Westview Press, 2006.

Hutton, Jon, and Barnabas Dickson, eds. *Endangered Species, Threatened Convention: The Past, Present, and Future of CITES.* Sterling, Va.: Earthscan, 2000.

International Union for Conservation of Nature. *Conserving the World's Biological Diversity.* Washington, D.C.: Island Press, 1990.

Van Dyke, Fred. "The Legal Foundations of Conservation Biology." In *Conservation Biology: Foundations, Concepts, Applications.* 2d ed. New York: Springer, 2008.

See also: Endangered Species Act; Endangered species and species protection policy; International Convention for the Regulation of Whaling; International whaling ban; Pets and the pet trade; Poaching; Whaling

■ Convention on Long-Range Transboundary Air Pollution

FIELDS OF STUDY: Government, Politics, International Relations; International Relations, Agreements, Treaties; Regulation, Standards and Practices; Pollution, Emissions, Toxic Waste, Hazardous Materials; Ecology, Environment, Environmentalism

CATEGORIES: Treaties, laws, and court cases; atmosphere and air pollution

THE CONVENTION: International agreement to limit air pollution, including pollution created in one country that affects the environment in another

DATE: Opened for signature on November 13, 1979

Although the Convention on Long-Range Transboundary Air Pollution has had little direct effect on air quality, it is important because it was the first agreement among nations of Eastern Europe, Western Europe, and North America regarding the environment.

Until the 1970's most local, regional, and national regulations regarding industrial air pollution were concerned only with pollution generated in the immediate area. For example, regulations in a particular community might call for taller industrial smokestacks to carry pollution farther away, but there was little official concern about where that pollution might eventually return to earth. Similarly, local assessments and treatments of pollution tended not to consider pollution that might come to an area from distant generators. The only exceptions were a small number of treaties between two countries, such as between the United States and Canada or between Germany and France.

In 1972 the United Nations Conference on the Human Environment, held in Stockholm, Sweden, drew attention to the harmful effects of acid rain, including damage to forests, crops, surface water, and buildings and monuments, especially in Europe. Data revealed that while all European nations were producing alarming levels of air pollution, several nations were receiving more pollution from beyond their borders than they were generating on their own. It became clear that pollution is both imported and exported, that sulfur and nitrogen compounds can travel through the air for thousands of miles, and that any serious attempt to deal with air pollution must reach beyond political boundaries. Two major studies of the long-range transport of air pollutants (LRTAP), conducted under United Nations sponsorship in 1972 and 1977, conclusively proved that air pollution is an international—even a global—problem caused primarily by fossil-fuel combustion and harming both industrial and nonindustrial nations around the world.

In 1979 the United Nations Environment Programme organized a convention in Geneva, Switzerland, for the thirty-four member countries of the United Nations Economic Commission for Europe (UNECE), a group that includes all European nations, the United States, and Canada. Significantly, the gathering had the participation of Eastern European nations under the Soviet Union, marking the first time these nations had collaborated with Western Europe to solve an international environmental problem. The Convention on Long-Range Transboundary Air Pollution was signed by thirty-two nations on November 13, 1979, and went into effect on March 16, 1983. It called upon signatory nations

Fundamental Principles of the Convention on Long-Range Transboundary Air Pollution

Articles 2 through 5 of the Convention on Long-Range Transboundary Air Pollution set out the fundamental principles of the agreement, by which all contracting parties agree to be bound.

Article 2:

The Contracting Parties, taking due account of the facts and problems involved, are determined to protect man and his environment against air pollution and shall endeavour to limit and, as far as possible, gradually reduce and prevent air pollution including long-range transboundary air pollution.

Article 3:

The Contracting Parties, within the framework of the present Convention, shall by means of exchanges of information, consultation, research and monitoring, develop without undue delay policies and strategies which shall serve as a means of combating the discharge of air pollutants, taking into account efforts already made at national and international levels.

Article 4:

The Contracting Parties shall exchange information on and review their policies, scientific activities and technical measures aimed at combating, as far as possible, the discharge of air pollutants which may have adverse effects, thereby contributing to the reduction of air pollution including long-range transboundary air pollution.

Article 5:

Consultations shall be held, upon request, at an early stage between, on the one hand, Contracting Parties which are actually affected by or exposed to a significant risk of long-range transboundary air pollution and, on the other hand, Contracting Parties within which and subject to whose jurisdiction a significant contribution to long-range transboundary air pollution originates, or could originate, in connection with activities carried on or contemplated therein.

Cynthia A. Bily

to limit and eventually reduce air pollution, in particular sulfur emissions, using the best and most economically feasible technology; to share scientific and technical information regarding air pollution and its reduction; to permit transboundary monitoring; and to collaborate in developing new antipollution policies. Under the terms of the convention, an international panel would undertake a comprehensive review every four years to determine whether goals were being met, and an executive body would meet each year.

The convention did not include any specific plan for the reduction of air pollution. It did not contain any language calling for particular amounts by which emissions would be reduced, nor did it include a schedule by which the reductions would occur. Scandinavian nations, which were among the countries most affected by acid rain, urged the other participants to adopt these kinds of policies, but other countries, led by the United States, the United Kingdom, and West Germany, defeated the proposal.

In the years after the convention went into force, however, several nations did make commitments to reduce emissions by specific amounts, including West Germany, which changed its position as further information was revealed about deforestation caused by acid rain. At the 1983 executive body meeting, eight nations, including Canada, West Germany, and the Scandinavian countries, made a formal commitment to reduce their emissions by 30 percent by 1993, using 1980 levels as the baseline. Over the next two years thirteen more nations announced similar goals, and in 1985 the commitment to a 30 percent reduction was formally adopted as an amendment to the convention that was signed by nineteen nations.

Neither the United States nor the United Kingdom agreed to the 30 percent reductions, and neither country signed the 1985 protocol. The United Kingdom informally agreed to attempt to reduce emissions by 30 percent but was unwilling to commit the financial resources to guarantee the reduction, especially since the benefits were uncertain. In fact, many scientists felt that a 30 percent reduction would not be enough to yield significant improvement. The United States argued that it had already taken major steps to reduce its emissions prior to 1980, so using 1980 data as a baseline would subject the United States to unrealistic and unfair demands for further reduction. This refusal to ratify the protocol caused tension between the United States and Canada, because much of the air pollution that affects eastern Canada comes from the Great Lakes industrial belt in the United States.

Cynthia A.Bily

Further Reading

Brunnee, Jutta. *Acid Rain and Ozone Layer Depletion: International Law and Regulation*. Boston: Hotei, 1988.

Elsom, Derek M. *Atmospheric Pollution: Causes, Effects, and Control Policies*. Malden, Mass.: Blackwell, 1987.

Fishman, Jack. *Global Alert: The Ozone Pollution Crisis*. New York: Plenum, 1990.

Sand, Peter H. "Air Pollution in Europe: International Policy Responses." *Environment* 29 (December 1987): 16-20, 28-29.

Visgilio, Gerald R., and Diana M. Whitelaw, eds. *Acid in the Environment: Lessons Learned and Future Prospects*. New York: Springer, 2007.

Wetstone, G. S., and A. Rosencranz. *Acid Rain in Europe and North America: National Responses to an International Problem*. Washington, D.C.: Environmental Law Institute, 1983.

See also: Acid deposition and acid rain; Air pollution; Air-pollution policy; United Nations Conference on the Human Environment; United Nations Environment Programme

---

■ Corporate average fuel economy standards

FIELDS OF STUDY: Government, Politics, International Relations; Laws, Acts, Resolutions; Public Policy, Debates, Controversies; Regulation, Standards and Practices

DEFINITION: Federal standards designed to improve automobile fuel efficiency in the United States

Vehicle fuel economy standards were imposed in the United States during the 1970s in an effort to reduce fuel consumption, but increased driving and use of larger vehicles led to higher per-capita consumption over the next three decades. During the early twenty-first century, however, rising gasoline prices revived interest in improving the standards.

In response to the energy crisis of the 1970s, the U.S. Congress enacted legislation intended to reduce American dependence on oil imports. The 1975 corporate average fuel economy (CAFE) standards mandated fuel-efficiency levels for automobile manufacturers. Each manufacturer's annual automobile output had to meet the assigned average for that model year. If a fleet exceeded the CAFE standards, the manufacturer faced a substantial fine. To ensure that manufacturers did not import fuel-efficient foreign cars to offset low averages in their domestic output, the legislation required that import and domestic fleets be evaluated separately.

The 1978 standard for passenger cars was 18 miles per gallon (mpg). Averages gradually increased over the years (with the exception of a rollback during the late 1980s, prompted by a petition from automakers). By the 1990s the passenger car standard had reached 27.5 mpg, while the standard for light trucks (which included vans and sport utility vehicles, or SUVs) was 20.7 mpg. Between 1996 and 2001, provisions in the Department of Transportation's appropriations bills prohibited changes in the standards.

During the late 1990s many environmentalists pressed for more stringent CAFE standards. They argued that improved fuel economy would reduce the introduction of greenhouse gases and other harmful automobile by-products into the atmosphere. In addition, it would serve to protect U.S. wilderness areas where the threat of oil drilling remained a possibility. Proponents of more stringent standards also pointed to the increased use of minivans and SUVs. When CAFE standards first were imposed, light-truck-class vehicles were used predominantly for business and agricultural purposes, and lower standards were set for light trucks in order to protect small businesses and farmers. SUVs, vans, and trucks weighing between 8,500 and 10,000 pounds were not subject to any fuel economy standards at all. During the 1990s, minivans and SUVs proliferated as means of personal transportation, meaning more fuel-hungry vehicles on the road and a rise in per-capita fuel consumption.

Critics argued that CAFE standards had no impact on foreign oil imports, which continued to rise after the regulations were enacted. After a period of concern during the Persian Gulf War in 1991, most consumers regarded the continuing decline in gasoline prices that marked the mid-1990s as evidence that

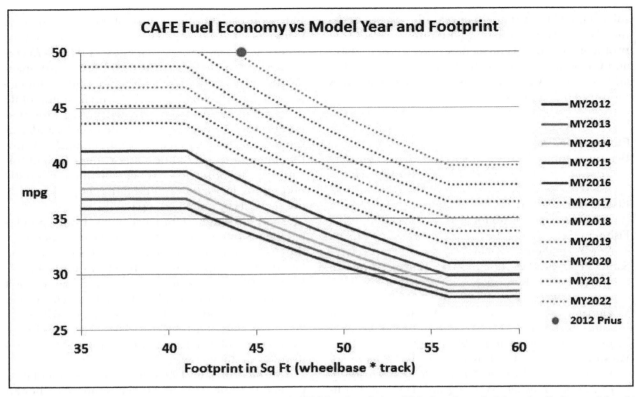

EPA/NHTSA Fuel Economy standards plus proposals through 2022 based on their published mathematical formulas. By James Adcock (Own work)

the issue was not critical. CAFE opponents also contended that the standards hurt the U.S. automobile industry and the country's economy in general. They claimed that the costs of manufacturing vehicles with increased fuel efficiency were passed on to consumers in the form of higher vehicle prices that unfairly affected not only individuals but also small businesses. More important, critics asserted, manufacturers achieved better performance by building smaller cars from lighter materials—vehicles that provided less protection to passengers in the event of accidents. This argument gained ground in 1991 when the U.S. Department of Transportation released a study indicating that higher CAFE standards were directly related to increases in traffic injuries and fatalities. (Later studies, however, suggested that the quality of a vehicle's engineering plays a greater role than its mass in determining how it fares in an accident.)

Environmentalists countered that higher vehicle costs were offset by savings in fuel expenses. As for the increase in traffic deaths, they maintained, automobile exhaust causes environmental damage that also results in deaths. They pointed to global warming and its consequences as proof that CAFE standards were necessary. However, as long as gasoline prices remained low, these arguments made little headway with most politicians and automobile manufacturers.

In 2003, with gas prices on the rise, new light-truck standards were issued: 21.0 mpg for model year (MY) 2005, 21.6 mpg for MY 2006, and 22.2 mpg for MY 2007. By 2007, per-capita fuel consumption in the United States had exceeded pre-1975 levels. That year, lawmakers increased CAFE standards to a combined level of efficiency for new cars and light trucks of 35 mpg by 2020. The legislation also subjected vehicles weighing between 8,500 and 10,000 pounds to

CAFE standards for the first time, effective in 2011. In 2009, following a spike in gas prices the previous year, President Barack Obama's administration accelerated the timetable, calling for a fleetwide average of 35.5 mpg (39 mpg for cars, 30 mpg for trucks) by 2016 in conjunction with a 30-percent reduction in tailpipe greenhouse gas emissions. An even more ambitious goal was announced in 2011: the Obama administration reached an agreement with thirteen automobile manufacturers to achieve an average fuel efficiency of 54.5 mpg by 2025.

Thomas Clarkin; updated by Karen N. Kähler

Further Reading

An, Feng, et al. *Passenger Vehicle Greenhouse Gas and Fuel Economy Standards: A Global Update.* Washington, D.C.: International Council on Clean Transportation, 2007.

Csere, Csaba. "Can We Hit the Target?" *Car & Driver* Nov. 2014: 54. Print.

Marks, Paul. "Fuel for the Road Ahead." *New Scientist* 8 Sept. 2012: 20. Print.

National Research Council. *Effectiveness and Impact of Corporate Average Fuel Economy (CAFE) Standards.* Washington, D.C.: National Academies Press, 2002.

Nivola, Pietro S. *The Long and Winding Road: Automotive Fuel Economy and American Politics.* Washington, D.C.: Brookings Institution Press, 2009.

■ Côte d'Ivoire toxic waste incident

FIELDS OF STUDY: Disasters; Ecology, Environment, Environmentalism; Health, Medicine, Disease, Illness; Pollution, Emissions, Toxic Waste, Hazardous Materials

THE EVENT: Illegal dumping of toxic petroleum wastes in and around the city of Abidjan in the West African nation of Côte d'Ivoire

DATE: August, 2006

One of the worst cases of intentional dumping of dangerous toxic wastes, the Côte d'Ivoire incident demonstrates how developing nations can be exploited by unscrupulous corporations based in developed nations.

In August, 2006, at least 400 tons of toxic waste products derived from the processing of petroleum were illegally dumped at night in sites in and around Abidjan, a port city that is the former capital of Côte d'Ivoire (Ivory Coast). The wastes came from the tanker *Probo Koala*, which was registered in Panama. Approximately 100,000 residents of the Abidjan region were adversely affected by the dumping. Local hospitals reported that at least 30,000 people sought medical attention, and 17 died from exposure to the toxic wastes. Hundreds of contaminated livestock around Abidjan had to be euthanized. Health problems stemming from the environmental contamination have continued among locals. Persistent physical complaints of those exposed include ailments from breathing difficulties and choking to body lesions, blisters, nosebleeds, headaches, and nervous system paralysis.

Trafigura, a transnational trading company based in Great Britain, Switzerland, and the Netherlands, had chartered the ship but denied any wrongdoing for several years after the incident, claiming that only "slops" (mere dirty water from the washing of the ship's tanks) had been dumped. Trafigura sued British newspapers for libel when they reported the company's involvement in the dumping and worked to restrain the British news media with gag orders. Although the Ivorian government prosecuted locals who had been bribed, some of the legal issues surrounding the case have remained unresolved.

Dutch chemical-cleanup teams that visited twelve of at least eighteen affected Abidjan waste sites verified that the tanker "slops" were, in fact, toxic. The dumped materials contained dangerous concentrations of hydrogen sulfide, a killer gas, several tons of which were found; among other caustic agents found were mercaptans (also known as thiols) and gasoline. Port records show that the ship had visited a port in Amsterdam to offload the wastes, but the company did not want to pay the high fee—$300,000—required to cover the expensive treatment and disposal of the waste. Instead a front company, named Compagnie Tommy, was immediately created in Abidjan. Local Ivorian personnel of the front company were apparently bribed to take the waste and surreptitiously dump it in poor urban regions.

Location map of the "zone de confiance" (ZDC, "buffer zone") created in Côte d'Ivoire, after the Civil War. By Hégésippe Cormier aka Hégésippe.

In the months following the incident, as national and international investigations began, many Ivorian government officials resigned. Even as lawyers for Trafigura tried to sue British news media companies for libel and worked to prevent the publishing of further news stories about the incident, an e-mail trail was exposed that showed the company's involvement in cover-ups and influence peddling in high places, including among British lords who served on Trafigura boards.

Patrick Norman Hunt

■ Council on Environmental Quality (CEQ)

FIELDS OF STUDY: Government, Politics, International Relations; Organizations, Agencies, Commissions, Centers; Regulation, Standards and Practices; Ecology, Environment, Environmentalism

IDENTIFICATION: Division of the executive office of the president of the United States responsible for co-ordinating federal environmental efforts and aiding in developing environmental policies and initiatives

DATE: Established in 1970

The Council on Environmental Quality is a major player in the U.S. government's environmental efforts. As the overseer of the National Environmental Policy Act and adviser to the president, the council plays an integral part in shaping and directing the federal government's environmental policies.

The Council on Environmental Quality (CEQ) was established as part of the National Environmental

Council on Environmental Quality building in Washington, D.C. By AgnosticPreachersKid (Own work)

Policy Act of 1969 (NEPA), sweeping legislation that requires U.S. federal agencies to consider the environmental impacts that could arise from any actions they plan to take before they act. Under NEPA, federal agencies must undertake environmental impact assessments whereby the environmental consequences of any planned actions are analyzed and alternatives are considered. The CEQ is charged with overseeing this general process and ensuring that federal agencies fulfill their duties under the act. Additionally, the CEQ acts as a mediator in cases in which an agency disagrees regarding the adequacy of another's assessment.

The CEQ also works to advance the president's agenda and to advise on issues related to the environment. The council's chair is chosen by the president and serves as the president's chief environmental policy adviser. As the environmental arm of the White House, the CEQ works with different agencies, scientists, and the public to balance environmental, economic, and social agendas. The council is also directed to collect and analyze the latest information related to the environment. As part of this role, the CEQ assists the president in preparing the Environmental Quality Report, an overview of the nation's environmental status submitted annually to Congress.

Daniel J. Connell

■ Cousteau, Jacques

FIELDS OF STUDY: Ethics, Advocacy, Policy, Protest; Biology, Life Sciences, Ecosystems; Animals, Zoology, Marine Biology; Ecology, Environment, Environmentalism; Oceans, Seas, Lakes, Bodies of Water; Media, Film, Television

CATEGORIES: Activism and advocacy; animals and endangered species

IDENTIFICATION: French explorer, conservationist, and filmmaker

Cousteau, one of the twentieth century's best-known explorers and conservationists, gained widespread attention for environmental issues, particularly those concerning the world's oceans.

Jacques Cousteau was, in his own mind, neither scientist nor adventurer. Rather, he considered himself a filmmaker. In 1971 Cousteau said, "I am not a

Explorer and conservationist Jacques Cousteau. (Library of Congress)

scientist, I am rather an impresario of scientists." Cousteau, however, probably did recognize the vital role he played in exciting public interest in the ocean and revealing the intricacies of humanity's relationship to it.

Cousteau's long career began in 1933 with a stint in the French navy. In 1943, during his military service, he developed, with Émile Gagnan, the Aqua-Lung, the first commercially available self-contained underwater breathing apparatus (scuba). In 1950 Cousteau bought the retired minesweeper *Calypso* for use as a research ship. The many films and books Cousteau authored in his lifetime helped finance the *Calypso*'s expeditions, which brought the wonders of the oceans to an international audience. He is perhaps best known to many Americans from his documentary television series *The Undersea World of Jacques Cousteau*, which aired from 1966 to 1976.

By 1956 Cousteau's research activities had become a full-time career, so he resigned from the navy. In 1957 Prince Rainier III named Cousteau director of the Oceanographic Museum of Monaco, a post he held for thirty-one years. During the 1950's and 1960's Cousteau sometimes explored the same sites several times. As a result of these trips, he eventually recognized that human activities were degrading the aquatic environment.

In 1958 Cousteau helped establish the world's first undersea marine reserve off the coast of Monaco. In 1960 he spoke out against France's plans to dispose of nuclear waste in the Mediterranean Sea. One decade later, he summed up his fears about ocean pollution by stating, "The oceans are in danger of dying."

In 1974 Cousteau founded the Cousteau Society, a nonprofit organization "dedicated to the protection and improvement of the quality of life for present and future generations." Among other achievements, this group has provided logistical support and facilities for hundreds of scientists, helped develop postgraduate environmental science and policy programs at universities worldwide, and worked toward the adoption by the United Nations of a "Bill of Rights for Future Generations"—all causes to which Cousteau himself was strongly committed. In addition to revealing the ocean's majesty through books, films, and television, Cousteau strove to alert the public to the dilemma he recognized during his explorations:

> The pursuit of technology and progress may today endanger the very survival of . . . practically all life on earth. . . . [However] the technology that we use to abuse the planet is the same technology that can help us to heal it/

Cousteau received numerous awards and honors for his environmental efforts, including the United Nations International Environmental Prize (1977) and a place on the United Nations Global 500 Roll of Honor (1988). He served as adviser for environmental sustainable development to the World Bank and was a member of the United Nations High-Level Board on Sustainable Development (1992). In 1992 France's president appointed Cousteau chairman of the newly created Council on the Rights of Future Generations. Three years later he resigned from the council in protest over the resumption of nuclear weapons testing in the South Pacific.

Clayton D. Harris

Further Reading

Kroll, Gary. *America's Ocean Wilderness: A Cultural History of Twentieth-Century Exploration.* Lawrence: University Press of Kansas, 2008.

Matsen, Brad. *Jacques Cousteau: The Sea King.* New York: Pantheon Books, 2009.

See also: Environmental education; Ocean dumping; Ocean pollution; Sustainable development

---

■ Cross-Florida Barge Canal

FIELDS OF STUDY: Biology, Life Sciences, Ecosystems; Continents, Regions, Areas, Islands; Ecology, Environment, Environmentalism; Oceans, Seas, Lakes, Bodies of Water; Plants, Vegetation, Botany, Horticulture; Economics, Business, Production, Commerce; Ethics, Advocacy, Policy, Protest; Ecology, Environment, Environmentalism; Oceans, Seas, Lakes, Bodies of Water

IDENTIFICATION: Intended shortcut for shipping across Florida that would have linked the Gulf of Mexico with the Atlantic Ocean

Efforts to build the Cross-Florida Barge Canal caused decades of controversy among environmentalists, government officials, and business interests until it was finally decommissioned in 1990 and the land was converted into a state recreation and conservation area.

Florida's unique peninsular shape and its 6,115 kilometers (3,800 miles) of tidal shoreline have long frustrated military, industry, and shipping interests. Since no river cuts across the state, ships and barges have had to travel around Florida's southern tip. In earlier times, this trip was often a perilous undertaking because of turbulent storms and the existence of many dangerous reefs and shoals.

Even before Florida became a state, various interest groups and individuals began calling for the creation of a transpeninsula waterway. Bowing to pressure, the Florida legislature created the Florida State Canal Commission in 1821 to explore the possibility of building such a canal. Five years later, the U.S. Congress adopted the cause and authorized the first of twenty-eight surveys that were carried out to find a convenient and safe route for an inland ship canal across the state. One proposal after another

either proved to be impractical or failed to gain political support.

Construction History

In 1935 President Franklin D. Roosevelt, intending to ease unemployment problems in Florida, used $5 million in federal relief money as start-up funds for the construction of a ship canal. The proposal called for a 9-meter (30-foot) sea-level ship canal that would stretch across the north-central part of the state from the Atlantic Ocean to the Gulf of Mexico. On September 19, 1935, Roosevelt pressed a telegraph key from his office in Washington, D.C., and set off an explosive blast in Florida that officially began the canal's construction.

Roosevelt's action received popular support across north-central Florida, a region where many communities welcomed the new jobs and economic boost the canal was expected to generate. Intense opposition to the canal also existed, however. Railroad interests, fearing competition from shipping interests, hotly objected to the canal construction and lobbied in Congress to end it. Many south Floridians, fearing that a ship canal would allow saltwater intrusion to jeopardize the state's downstream supply of underground water, joined the protest. Three years after the project began, Roosevelt yielded to political pressure and cut off funding; he called on Congress to help, but Congress failed to appropriate any money for the canal, and construction ground to a halt.

World War II rekindled interest in the canal. German submarine attacks against U.S. ships along the Florida coast prompted Congress to ask the Army Corps of Engineers to reexamine the issue of building a canal to meet the nation's wartime needs. The corps responded with scaled-back plans for a barge canal, but Congress again failed to provide funding, and the project stagnated for years. In 1964 Congress finally authorized $1 million to get construction under way and promised more funds later. The Army Corps of Engineers now had responsibility for the project. Its engineers came up with plans for a five-lock waterway that would stretch 296.8 kilometers (184.4 miles) from Port Inglis on Florida's west coast to the Intracoastal Waterway at the St. Johns River on the east.

Opposition from Environmentalists

Opposition to the project quickly developed. Environmentalists argued that the canal would disrupt

Cross Florida Barge Canal

build less than one-third of the canal. Great stretches of trees had been leveled, rivers and streams altered, two locks built, a dam constructed, and much earth moved.

In March, 1974, the Middle District Court of Florida overruled Nixon's action, but it upheld the injunction. Supporters of the canal received another blow in 1977 when both the Army Corps of Engineers and the Florida cabinet went on record calling for an end to construction. Despite these actions, canal proponents continued to lobby in Congress and succeeded in postponing a complete dismantling of the transwaterway project for years. Finally, in 1990, both the U.S. Congress and the Florida legislature officially and permanently deauthorized the barge canal.

Environmentalists hailed the defeat of the Cross-Florida Barge Canal as a major environmental victory, but they soon faced new problems. Debates arose over questions of what was to be done with completed sections of canal and the adjacent canal lands. In 1993 the Florida legislature resolved the issue when it authorized the conversion of 177 kilometers (110 miles) of the defunct canal zone into a huge nature preserve named the Cross-Florida Greenway State Recreation Area, or the Cross-Florida Greenway (renamed the Marjorie Harris Carr Cross-Florida Greenway in 1998, in honor of a leader of the movement to stop the canal). In addition to providing land that humans can use for outdoor recreation, the 28,300-hectare (70,000-acre) corridor also serves as a permanent wildlife refuge—one of the largest in the southern United States.

One controversial issue remained unresolved. It focused on the fate of the Rodman Dam, which was built in the center of the state on the Ocklawaha River prior to the final decommissioning of the canal.

the natural flow of rivers and creeks in the region, flood woodland areas, and destroy many endangered and threatened plants and animals. In 1969 the Environmental Defense Fund (EDF), along with the Florida Defenders of the Environment, sued in a U.S. district court to stop construction. Nearly two years later, on January 15, 1971, the court granted the plaintiffs an injunction. Four days later, President Richard Nixon, citing environmental and economic concerns, issued a presidential order that suspended construction. By now, $74 million had been spent to

Environmentalists argued that since the dam was no longer needed, it should be demolished so that the Ocklawaha River could be restored to its natural flow pattern. Supporters of the dam—including local merchants and the bass fishing enthusiasts and fish camp owners who used the reservoir created by the dam—wanted to keep it in place, citing the reservoir's economic benefits to the local community as a recreational area. Even though Florida governor Lawton Chiles, the state cabinet, and the Department of Environmental Protection expressed support for restoration efforts of the Ocklawaha River and elimination of the Rodman Dam, the state legislature withheld the necessary funds.

John M. Dunn

Further Reading

Buker, George E. *Sun, Sand, and Water: A History of the Jacksonville District U.S. Army Corps of Engineers, 1821-1975.* Jacksonville, Fla.: U.S. Army Corps of Engineers, 1980.

Flippen, J. Brooks. *Nixon and the Environment.* Albuquerque: University of New Mexico Press, 2000.

Florida Defenders of the Environment. *Environmental Impact of the Cross-Florida Barge Canal with Special Emphasis on the Ocklawaha Regional Ecosystem.* Gainesville: Author, 1970.

Irby, Lee. "A Passion for Wild Things: Marjorie Harris Carr and the Fight to Free a River." In *Making Waves: Female Activists in Twentieth-Century Florida,* edited by Jack E. Davis and Kari Frederickson. Gainesville: University Press of Florida, 2003.

Tebeau, Charlton W. *A History of Florida.* Miami: University of Miami Press, 1981.

■ Cultural eutrophication

FIELDS OF STUDY: Biology, Life Sciences, Ecosystems; Ecology, Environment, Environmentalism; Oceans, Seas, Lakes, Bodies of Water; Pollution, Emissions, Toxic Waste, Hazardous Materials; Water Resources

DEFINITION: Unwanted increase in nutrient concentrations in sensitive waters caused by human activities

Cultural eutrophication causes the degradation of productive aquatic environments, which has prompted state and federal governments to regulate point and nonpoint source pollution in surrounding watersheds.

Eutrophication (from the Greek term meaning "to nourish") is the sudden enrichment of natural waters with excess nutrients, such as nitrogen, phosphorus, and potassium, which can lead to the development of algae blooms and other vegetation. In addition to clouding otherwise clear water, some algae and protozoa (namely, *Pfiesteria*) release toxins that harm fish and other aquatic wildlife. When the algae die, their decomposition produces odorous compounds and depletes dissolved oxygen in these waters, which causes fish and other organisms to suffocate.

Eutrophication is a naturally occurring process as an environment evolves over time. Cultural eutrophication is a distinct form of eutrophication in which the process is accelerated by human activities, including wastewater treatment disposal, runoff from city streets and lawns, deforestation and development in watersheds, and agricultural activities such

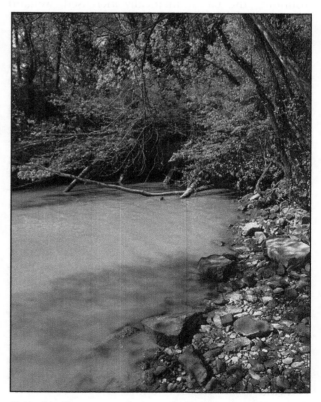

Eutrophication at a waste water outlet in the Potomac River, Washington, DC.

as farming and livestock production. These activities contribute excessive amounts of available nutrients to otherwise pristine waters and promote rapid and excessive plant growth.

Eutrophication of the Great Lakes, particularly Lake Erie, was one of the key factors that prompted passage of the Clean Water Act and various amendments during the 1970s. This act specifically addressed the disposal of sewage into public waters, a major contributor to cultural eutrophication. However, it did not specifically address nonpoint source pollution, which comes from sources that are not readily identifiable. Agricultural activities such as farming, logging, and concentrated livestock operations all contribute to nonpoint source pollution through fertilizer runoff, soil erosion, and poor waste disposal practices that supply readily available nutrients to surrounding watersheds and lead to eutrophication in these environments.

The Chesapeake Bay is an excellent case study in cultural eutrophication. As development surrounding the bay dramatically increased, wetland and riparian buffers that helped reduce some of the impact of additional nutrients were destroyed. Eutrophication in the bay during the 1980s threatened the crabbing and oyster industry. Consequently, in 1983 and 1987, Maryland, Pennsylvania, and Virginia, the three states bordering the Chesapeake Bay, agreed to a 40 percent reduction of nutrients by the year 2000 from point and nonpoint sources in all watersheds contributing to the bay. These reductions were to be accomplished through such actions as the banning of phosphate detergents, the implementation of management plans to control soil erosion, the protection of wetlands, and the institution of controls on production and management of animal wastes. Although these steps reduced phosphorus levels in the Chesapeake Bay and kept nitrogen levels constant, regulators remained unsure how much nutrient reduction must take place for the bay and its surroundings to resemble their original condition.

Mark Coyne

Further Reading

Grady, Wayne. *The Great Lakes: The Natural History of a Changing Region.* Vancouver: Greystone, 2007. Print.

Laws, Edward A. "Cultural Eutrophication: Case Studies." *Aquatic Pollution: An Introductory Text.* 3rd ed. New York: Wiley, 2000. Print.

McGucken, William. *Lake Erie Rehabilitated: Controlling Cultural Eutrophication, 1960's-1990's.* Akron: U of Akron P, 2000. Print.

■ Cuyahoga River fires

FIELDS OF STUDY: Disasters; Biology, Life Sciences, Ecosystems; Ecology, Environment, Environmentalism; Oceans, Seas, Lakes, Bodies of Water; Pollution, Emissions, Toxic Waste, Hazardous Materials; Water Resources

THE EVENT: Burning of oil slicks on the surface of the Cuyahoga River near Cleveland, Ohio

DATES: November, 1952, and June 22, 1969

The fire that occurred on the oil-slicked Cuyahoga River in 1969 demonstrated the poor environmental condition of the Great Lakes and sparked a major media event that served to sway public opinion toward supporting the cleanup of Lake Erie.

The Cuyahoga River divides the city of Cleveland into east and west sides. Originating on the Appalachian Plateau 56 kilometers (35 miles) east of Cleveland, the river meanders 166 kilometers (103 miles) to Lake Erie. About 8 kilometers (5 miles) from its mouth, it becomes a sharply twisting but navigable stream that forms part of Cleveland's harbor. Industrial development took place along the river in the early nineteenth century, and by 1860 docks and warehouses lined the ship channel. Industry had claimed virtually all of Cleveland's riverfront by 1881, when, according to Cleveland mayor Rensselaer R. Herrick, the discharge from factories and oil refineries made it an open sewer running through the center of the city.

In 1951 the Ohio Department of Natural Resources reported that the Cuyahoga River was heavily polluted with industrial effluents at its mouth, creating conditions that were unsatisfactory for the existence of aquatic life. In September of that year, thousands of dead fish were washed ashore just west of the river's mouth, and observers noted that the area gave off strong river odors.

An oil slick burned on the Cuyahoga River for days in November, 1952, causing an estimated $1.5 million in damage, without attracting national attention. Almost seventeen years later, at approximately noon on Sunday, June 22, 1969, the Cuyahoga River

Cuyahoga River in the Cuyahoga Valley National Park

again caught fire. The fire was brought under control by approximately 12:20 P.M., but not before it had done some $50,000 worth of damage to two key railroad trestles over the river in the Flats area of Cleveland. An oil slick on the river had caught fire and floated under the wooden bridges, setting fire to both. Witnesses reported that the flames from the bridges reached as high as a five-story building. The fireboat *Anthony J. Celebrezze* rushed upstream and battled the blaze on the water while units from three fire battalions brought the flames on the trestles under control. Responsibility for the oil slick was placed on the waterfront industries, which used the river as a dumping ground for oil wastes instead of reclaiming the waste products.

The railroad trestles that burned were not all that sustained damage in the fire. Cleveland's reputation as "the best location in the nation" was severely damaged by the occurrence. The city became the brunt of numerous jokes, and the mass media across the country characterized it as the only city with a river so choked with pollution that it had burned. No river in the United States had a more notorious national reputation than the Cuyahoga River. Media coverage of the fire helped galvanize nationwide public support for efforts to clean up not only Lake Erie in particular but also the environment in general.

Charles E. Herdendorf

Further Reading

Adler, Jonathan A. "Fables of the Cuyahoga: Reconstructing a History of Environmental Protection." *Fordham Environmental Law Journal* 14 (2002): 89-146.

Grady, Wayne. *The Great Lakes: The Natural History of a Changing Region.* Vancouver: Greystone Books, 2007.

McGucken, William. *Lake Erie Rehabilitated: Controlling Cultural Eutrophication, 1960's-1990's.* Akron, Ohio: University of Akron Press, 2000.

D

■ Dams and reservoirs

FIELDS OF STUDY: Agriculture; Civil Engineering; Ecosystem Management; Environmental Studies; Hydrodynamics; Hydrology;

SIGNIFICANCE: Structures that obstruct the natural flow of water in rivers and streams, and the bodies of water created by the impoundment of water behind or upstream of such structures

Because dams obstruct the natural flow of water, they have significant effects on stream and river ecosystems. Although dams provide benefits such as flood control and hydroelectric power generation, they also have a number of negative environmental impacts.

Overview

Dams are designed for a number of purposes, including conservation, irrigation, flood control, hydroelectric power generation, navigation, and recreation. Not all dams create reservoirs of significant size. Low dams, or barrages, have been used to divert portions of stream flows into canals or aqueducts since human beings' first attempts at irrigation thousands of years ago. Canals, aqueducts, and pipelines are used to change the direction of water flow from a stream to agricultural fields or areas with high population concentrations.

Dams and reservoirs provide the chief, and in most cases the sole, means of storing stream flow over time. Small dams and reservoirs are capable of storing water for weeks or months, allowing water use during local dry seasons. Large dams and reservoirs have the capacity to store water for several years.

As urban populations in arid regions have grown and irrigation agriculture has dramatically expanded, dams and reservoirs have increased in size in response to demand. They are frequently located hundreds of kilometers from where the water is eventually used. The construction of larger dams and reservoirs has resulted in increasingly complex environmental and social problems that have affected large numbers of people. This has been particularly true in tropical and developing nations, where most of the large dam construction of the last three decades of the twentieth century was concentrated.

Sizes and Purposes of Dams

Early dams and their associated reservoirs were small, and dams remained small, for the most part, until the twentieth century. The first dams were simple barrages constructed across streams to divert water into irrigation canals. Water supply for humans and

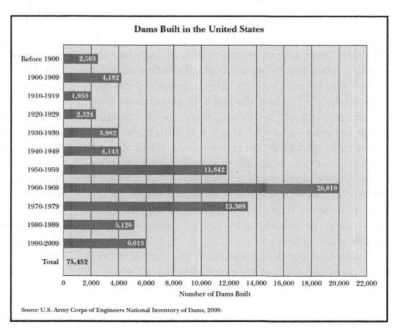

Dams Built in the United States

	Number of Dams Built
Before 1900	2,503
1900-1909	4,182
1910-1919	1,953
1920-1929	2,324
1930-1939	3,982
1940-1949	4,143
1950-1959	11,842
1960-1969	20,019
1970-1979	13,369
1980-1989	5,120
1990-2009	6,015
Total	75,452

Source: U.S. Army Corps of Engineers National Inventory of Dams, 2009.

animals undoubtedly benefited from these diversions, but the storage capacity of most dams was small, reflecting the limited technology of the period. The earliest dams were constructed some five thousand years ago in the Middle East, and dams became common two thousand years ago in the Mediterranean region, China, Central America, and South Asia.

The energy of falling water can be converted by water wheels into mechanical energy to perform a variety of tasks, including the grinding of grain. Dams create a higher "head" or water level, increasing the potential energy, and thus served as the earliest energy source for the beginnings of the Industrial Revolution during the nineteenth century. The most significant contribution of dams to industrialization occurred in 1882 with the development of hydroelectricity, which permitted energy to be transferred to wherever electric power lines were built rather than being confined to river banks.

During the nineteenth century, large-scale settlement of the arid regions of western North America and Asia soon exhausted the meager local supplies of water and prompted demands for both exotic supplies from distant watersheds and storage for dry years. Big dams for storage and big projects for transportation of the water were thought to be the answer. Small dam projects could be financed locally; grander schemes required the assistance of federal or national governments. To justify expenditures on larger dams, promoters of these projects touted the multiple uses for reservoir water as benefits that would offset the projects' costs. Benefit-cost ratios thus became the tool by which potential projects were judged. To raise the ratio of benefits to costs, promoters placed increasing importance on intangible benefits—those to which it is difficult to assign universally agreeable currency values. While dams in arid regions were originally justified chiefly for irrigation, public water supply, and power, decisions to build dams in wetter areas were usually based on projected benefits from flood control, navigation, and recreation in addition to power generation and public water supply.

Complicating the equation is the fact that multiple uses are frequently conflicting uses. While all dams are built to even out the uneven flow of streams over time, flood control requires an empty reservoir to handle the largest floods; conversely, power generation requires a high level of water in the reservoir to provide the highest head. Public water supply and navigation benefit most from supplies that are manipulated in response to variable demand. Recreation, fishing, and the increasingly important factor of environmental concerns focus on in-stream uses of the water.

By the last two decades of the twentieth century, environmental costs and benefits and the issue of Native American water rights in the American West dominated decisions concerning dam projects in the United States, and few dams were constructed. Most of the best sites for the construction of large dams in the developed nations had been utilized, and the industry turned its attention to the developing nations. Most of the large dam projects of the last quarter of the twentieth century were constructed in or proposed for developing nations and the area of the former Soviet Union.

Human Impacts

Small dams have small impacts on the environment; they affect small watersheds and minor tributaries and usually have only a single purpose. Farm ponds and tanks, as they are known in many parts of the world, generally cover a fraction of 1 hectare (2.47 acres) in area and are only a few meters in height. These tiny ponds are designed to store water for livestock, crop irrigation and occasionally for human supply. They frequently serve recreational purposes as well, such as fishing. During dry spells they become stagnant and subject to contamination by algae and other noxious organisms, which can threaten the health of humans and livestock. Otherwise, they have little negative impact on the environment or on nearby people and animals.

Large dams and reservoirs are responsible for environmental and social impacts that often appear to be roughly related to their size: The larger the dam or reservoir, the greater the impact. Geographical location is also important in assessing a project's impact. Scenic areas in particular, or those with endangered species of plants or animals or irreplaceable cultural or archaeological features, raise more controversy and litigation if they are chosen as potential sites for dam and reservoir projects.

People in tropical regions suffer proportionately greater health-related impacts from dams than do those in corresponding nontropical areas. The large numbers of workers required for the construction of big dams and associated irrigation projects can carry diseases into unprotected populations. Stagnant or slow-moving waters in reservoirs and irrigation canals, as well as fast-moving waters downstream of dams, are associated with particularly vicious tropical health risks. Snails in slow-moving water carry schistosomiasis, a parasitic disease that infects intestinal and urinary tracts, causing general listlessness and more serious consequences, including failure of internal organs and cancer. Estimates of the numbers of people infected range into the hundreds of millions. Malaria, lymphatic filariasis (including elephantiasis), and other diseases are carried by mosquitoes that breed and thrive where there is standing water; the incidence of such insect-borne diseases dramatically expands near irrigation projects and reservoirs. River blindness, which results from the bite of black flies, is associated with fast-flowing water downstream of dams and affects hundreds of thousands of humans.

The flooding of densely populated river valleys by reservoirs displaces greater numbers of people, with attendant health problems and social impacts, than similar projects in sparsely populated areas. Population displacement in developing countries, especially those in the Tropics, causes greater health and social problems than in developed nations, where remedial measures and compensation are more likely to assuage the loss of homestead and community.

Environmental Impacts

Many of the environmental problems created by large dams are associated with rapid changes in water level below the dams or with the ponding of stream flow in the reservoirs, which replaces fast-flowing, oxygenated water with relatively stagnant conditions. Indigenous animal species, as well as some plant life, are adapted to seasonal changes in the natural stream flow and cannot adjust to the postdam regime of the stream. Consequently, the survival of these species may be threatened. In 1973 the Tennessee Valley Authority—the worldwide model for builders of many large, integrated river basin projects—found that the potential demise of a small fish, the snail darter, stood in the way of the completion of the Tellico Dam. After considerable controversy and litigation, the dam was completed in 1979, but few large projects have been proposed in the United States since then, particularly in the humid East. Since the early 1970's, the arguments for abandoning dam projects have

been more likely to be backed up by laws, regulations, and court decisions.

Construction of the Hetch Hetchy Dam in the Sierra Nevada mountain range of California in the early twentieth century sparked vigorous dissent, which is said to have led to the growth of the Sierra Club and organized environmental opposition to dam building. This opposition successfully challenged the construction of the Echo Park Dam on the Green River in Colorado in the early 1950's but was unsuccessful in stopping the construction of the Glen Canyon Dam on the Colorado River, which was completed in 1963. Glen Canyon, however, was the last of the big dams constructed in the American West. The preservationists, whose arguments chiefly concerned scenic and wilderness values, with attendant benefits to endangered species, lost the Glen Canyon battle but won the war against big dams. The controversy surrounding the Glen Canyon Dam continued for more than three decades after its completion, pitting wilderness and scenic preservationists against powerboat recreationists, who benefit from the access accorded by the dam's reservoir to the upstream canyonlands.

All reservoirs eventually fill with silt from upstream erosion; deltas form on their upstream ends. Heavier sediments, mainly sands, are trapped behind the dam and cannot progress downstream to the ocean. The Atlantic coastline of the southeastern United States suffers from beach erosion and retreat because the sands are no longer replenished by the natural flow of nearby rivers. The Aswan High Dam on the Nile River in Egypt has had a similar impact on the Nile Delta. Moreover, the natural flow of sediments downstream has historically replenished the fertility of floodplain soils during floods. To the extent that the flood-control function of a dam is successful, new fertile sediment never reaches downstream agricultural fields. While irrigation water provided by the dam may permit the expansion of cropland, this water in arid regions is often charged with higher-than-normal amounts of salts, which then accumulate in the soils and eventually become toxic to plant life.

Reservoir waters release methane from decaying organic matter into the atmosphere. Methane is a greenhouse gas that promotes global warming, and some estimates suggest that the effect of large reservoirs is roughly equal to the greenhouse gas pollution of large thermal-powered electrical generation plants. The weight of the water in large reservoirs has also been implicated in causing earthquakes, which may lead to the failure of a dam. Dam failure may also occur because of poor construction or poor design, or because the builders had inadequate knowledge of the geology of the site. Tens of thousands of lives have been lost as a consequence of such failures.

Neil E. Salisbury

Further Reading

Berga, L., et al., eds. *Dams and Reservoirs, Societies, and Environment in the Twenty-first Century.* Taylor & Francis, 2006.

Billington, David P., and Donald C. Jackson. *Big Dams of the New Deal Era: A Confluence of Engineering and Politics.* University of Oklahoma Press, 2006.

Cech, Thomas V. "Dams." In *Principles of Water Resources: History, Development, Management, and Policy.* 3rd ed. John Wiley & Sons, 2010.

Goldsmith, Edward, and Nicholas Hildyard. *The Social and Environmental Effects of Large Dams.* Random House, 1984.

Leslie, Jacques. *Deep Water: The Epic Struggle over Dams, Displaced People, and the Environment.* Farrar, Straus and Giroux, 2005.

McCully, Patrick. *Silenced Rivers: The Ecology and Politics of Large Dams.* Enlarged ed. Zed Books, 2001.

Stevens, Joseph E. *Hoover Dam: An American Adventure.* University of Oklahoma Press, 1988.

■ Darling, Jay

FIELDS OF STUDY: Popular Culture, Media, Publishing; Journalism, Publishing, Literature; Ethics, Advocacy, Policy, Protest; Parks, Monuments, Reserves; Government, Politics, International Relations; Laws, Acts, Resolutions; Parks, Monuments, Reserves; Regulation, Standards and Practices

CATEGORIES: Activism and advocacy; animals and endangered species

IDENTIFICATION: American cartoonist and wildlife conservationist

Darling was instrumental in starting the federal duck stamp program, which generated revenue to buy new lands to serve as waterfowl refuges, as authorized by the Migratory Bird Conservation Act.

Jay Darling was an editorial cartoonist by profession. He was known among his peers as Ding, the name with which he signed his drawings. His biting cartoons, which won him two Pulitzer Prizes and national recognition, often depicted the destruction of America's waterfowl and their habitat by overhunting and periodic drought—particularly during the Dust Bowl of the 1930's, which dried the wetlands that the birds required.

The passage of the Migratory Bird Conservation Act by the U.S. Congress in 1929 laid the groundwork for Darling's major contribution to waterfowl conservation. That act authorized the U.S. Department of Agriculture to acquire wetlands and preserve them as waterfowl habitat, but it provided no permanent source of funding for the purpose. In 1934 President Franklin D. Roosevelt appointed a committee to look into the need for waterfowl refuges. Among its members were Darling, who had been a fierce critic of Roosevelt's wildlife policies, wildlife conservationist Aldo Leopold, and publisher Thomas Beck. The committee's recommendation that $50 million be spent for new refuges rekindled an idea that had lain dormant for years: to require waterfowl hunters to pay fees for the privilege of hunting each year by buying stamps known as duck stamps. The revenue generated from the stamps would be used to buy new refuge lands authorized by the Migratory Bird Conservation Act.

In March, 1934, Congress passed the Migratory Bird Hunting and Conservation Stamp Act, which required waterfowl hunters sixteen years or older to buy an annual duck stamp. That same month, Roosevelt appointed Darling chief of the Department of Agriculture's Bureau of Biological Survey, forerunner of the U.S. Fish and Wildlife Service. While serving as chief, Darling carried out the 1934 act's mandate by initiating the federal duck stamp program; Darling also designed the first duck stamp.

The first Duck Stamp, featuring art by Jay Darling. (USFWS)

It took some time for money from the sale of the duck stamps to start flowing, however, so Darling began raising money from other programs within the Department of Agriculture to purchase refuge land. He is credited with obtaining $20 million for wildlife conservation and setting aside 1.8 million hectares (4.5 million acres) as refuge land during his twenty-month tenure at the Bureau of Biological Survey. He resigned in November, 1935, dismayed by conservationists' lack of collective strength in focusing attention on wildlife issues.

At the first government-sponsored North American Wildlife Conference in 1936, Darling helped to organize the 36,000 wildlife societies then in existence across the United States into a national body called the General Wildlife Federation. Darling was unanimously chosen president of the federation. Two years later, the group's name was changed to the National Wildlife Federation, and Darling was re-elected its president.

In 1942 Darling was awarded the Theodore Roosevelt Medal for distinguished service in wildlife conservation; in 1960 he received a National Audubon Society medal for distinguished service in natural resource conservation. A 2,013-hectare (4,975-acre)

wildlife refuge established on Sanibel Island, Florida, in 1945 was dedicated to Darling in 1978. Now known as the J. N. "Ding" Darling National Wildlife Refuge, it supports a wide diversity of birds and other animals.

Jane F. Hill

Further Reading

Darling, Jay N. *J. N. "Ding" Darling's Conservation and Wildlife Cartoons.* Des Moines, Iowa: J. N. "Ding" Darling Foundation, 1991.

Jonson, Laurence F. *Federal Duck Stamp Story: Fifty Years of Excellence.* Davenport, Iowa: Alexander, 1984.

Lendt, David L. *Ding: The Life of Jay Norwood Darling.* 4th ed. Mt. Pleasant, S.C.: Maecenas Press, 2001.

See also: Conservation; Fish and Wildlife Service, U.S.; Hunting; Leopold, Aldo; Migratory Bird Act; Wildlife management; Wildlife refuges

---

■ Darwin, Charles

FIELDS OF STUDY: Biology, Life Sciences, Ecosystems; Animals, Zoology, Marine Biology; Ecology, Environment, Environmentalism; Philosophy and History of Science; Authors, Writers; Journalism, Publishing, Literature

CATEGORY: Ecology and ecosystems
IDENTIFICATION: English naturalist

Darwin's theory of evolution through natural selection, the dominant paradigm of the biological sciences, underlies the study of ecosystems.

Darwin: Beaks and Evolution

During its voyage around the world, the HMS *Beagle* visited the Galápagos Islands in 1835. It was there that Charles Darwin was able to observe the interesting variety of plants and animals. The Galápagos are removed from any large land mass, being situated about six hundred miles west of the coast of Ecuador. Darwin's observations of the islands' fauna contributed to the development of his ideas about evolution and the origin of species. The different animal species living in the islands were quite different from species anywhere else in the world. Of particular interest to him were the thirteen species of finches that he collected. Finches are small, sparrow-sized birds, and the thirteen species were similar to one another except for features related to their feeding habits, especially their beaks. Darwin noted striking differences in the size and shape of the beaks and observed that their structure was related to the type of food the birds ate. Short, thick beaks were suitable for crushing seeds. Long, thin beaks were useful for feeding on insects. Large beaks were effective in opening hard fruits. Each species appeared to be adapted to its own local food supply. Darwin reasoned that the finches in the Galápagos had descended from a single ancestral species that had come to the island from South America. The adaptive radiation of the finches was one of the cornerstones of his reasoning that adaptation to the local food supply was related to the origin of new species by the process of natural selection.

Charles Darwin was born on February 12, 1809, the fifth of six children. His mother died when he was eight, leaving him in the care of his elder sisters. His father was a country doctor with a wide practice.

In 1825, Darwin went to Edinburgh, Scotland, to study medicine. He proved to be a poor student of anatomy, however, and he was sent to Christ's College, Cambridge, to prepare for the ministry. Though not a distinguished student, Darwin took an interest in natural science. At Cambridge, he met John Stevens Henslow, a botany professor, who encouraged his interest in natural history and helped to secure for him a position as naturalist aboard HMS *Beagle*, soon to depart on a five-year scientific expedition around the world. Darwin's experiences during the voyage from 1831 to 1836 were instrumental in shaping his theory of evolution.

As the voyage took the ship along the coast of South America, Darwin kept detailed journals in which he carefully observed differences among the South American flora and fauna, particularly on the Galápagos Islands. He would later draw on these extensive field observations to formulate his theory of natural selection.

After his return to London, Darwin began a study of coral reefs, and he became secretary to the Geological Society and a member of the Royal Society. He married his first cousin, Emma Wedgwood, in January, 1839.

Darwin worked for the next twenty years on his journals from the *Beagle*'s voyage, gathering information to support his theory of evolution through natural selection. His preliminary work might have continued indefinitely if he had not received, on June 18, 1854, an essay from Alfred Russel Wallace, a field naturalist in the Malay archipelago, outlining a theory of evolution and natural selection similar to Darwin's own. Darwin immediately wrote to his friends Sir Charles Lyell and Sir Joseph Dalton Hooker, explaining his dilemma and including an abstract of his own theory of evolution. Lyell and Hooker proposed that in order to avoid the question of precedence, the two papers should be presented simultaneously. Both were read before a meeting of the Linnean Society in Dublin on July 1, 1858, and they were published together in the society's journal that year.

Darwin then began writing an abstract of his theory, which he entitled *On the Origin of Species by Means of Natural Selection: Or, The Preservation of Favoured Races in the Struggle for Life*. All 1,250 copies sold out on the first day of publication in London on November 24, 1859. Darwin argued that since all species produce more offspring than can possibly survive, and since species populations remain relatively constant, there must be some mechanism working in nature to eliminate the unfit. Variations are randomly introduced in nature, some of which will permit a species to adapt better to its environment. These advantageous adaptations are passed on to the offspring, giving them an advantage for survival. Darwin did not understand the genetic mechanisms by which offspring inherit adaptations. It would take another seventy years before the forgotten work of the Austrian geneticist Gregor Mendel was rediscovered and integrated with Darwin's theories to provide a fuller view of the evolutionary process.

Darwin was surrounded by a storm of controversy after the publication of his work. Objections came both from orthodox clergy and from unconvinced scientists. For the rest of his life, Darwin worked at home on successive editions of *On the Origin of Species*, further studies on plants and animals, and his famous

The Descent of Man, and Selection in Relation to Sex (1871). He died on April 19, 1882, and was buried with full honors in the scientists' corner at Westminster Abbey, next to Sir Isaac Newton.

Darwin's work had an immeasurable influence on the development of modern biology, ecology, morphology, embryology, and paleontology. His theory of evolution established a natural history of the earth and enabled humans to see themselves for the first time as part of the natural order of life. A lively debate continues among scientists about revisionist theories of evolution, including Stephen Jay Gould's notion of "punctuated equilibria," or sudden and dramatic evolutionary changes followed by long periods of relative stability. While they disagree about details, however, modern biologists agree that neoevolutionary theory remains the only viable scientific explanation for the diversity of life on earth.

Alexander Scott

Further Reading

Berra, Tim M. *Charles Darwin: The Concise Story of an Extraordinary Man.* Baltimore: The Johns Hopkins University Press, 2009.

Eldredge, Niles. *Darwin: Discovering the Tree of Life.* New York: W. W. Norton, 2005.

Quammen, David. *The Reluctant Mr. Darwin: An Intimate Portrait of Charles Darwin and the Making of His Theory of Evolution.* New York: Atlas Books, 2006.

See also: Biodiversity; Ecosystems; Extinctions and species loss

■ Dead zones

FIELDS OF STUDY: Ecology; Ecosystem Management; Environmental Studies; Hydrology; Oceanography;

SIGNIFICANCE: Aquatic environments incapable of sustaining life

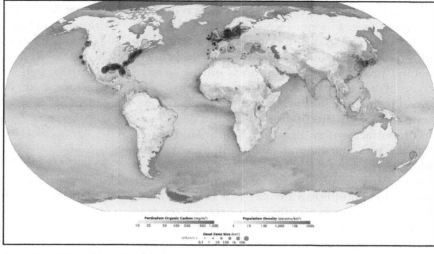

Data from Robert Diaz, Virginia Institute of Marine Science (dead zones); the GSFC Ocean Color team (particulate organic carbon); and the Socioeconomic Data and Applications Center (SEDAC) (population density). By Robert Simmon & Jesse Allen (NASA Earth Observatory).

The occurrence of dead zones in waters along heavily inhabited lakeshores and coastlines has increased drastically since the end of the twentieth century. Human nutrient inputs into these ecosystems from fertilizer use and pollution have contributed to more frequent eutrophication events, fueling this source of economic and ecological devastation.

Overview

In aquatic ecosystems, just as in all others, there are certain nutrients whose limited presence or availability prevents the unrestrained growth of particular species. In nearshore marine waters and lakes these so-called limiting nutrients are nitrogen and phosphorus. Their restricted availability keeps microscopic organisms called algae from reaching unsustainable and destructive levels.

Normally these algae form the base of the food web, utilizing the sun's energy to convert carbon dioxide into oxygen and food. However, in the presence of excess nitrogen and phosphorus, the algae can reproduce uncontrollably in a process called eutrophication, resulting in an algal bloom. As the algae population peaks and begins its decline, microbes begin decomposing the dead algae, consuming oxygen in the process. Eventually the dissolved oxygen in the aquatic environment is depleted, resulting in the death of all organisms in the ecosystem. At this stage, the environment is deemed a hypoxic or dead zone.

In some cases, an influx of nitrogen and phosphorus into an aquatic ecosystem can be the result of natural processes. In certain areas on the western coasts of the continents, for example, a process called upwelling occurs, in which prevailing winds and currents bring nutrients up from the ocean depths and to the surface, where algae live. Humankind's interference with the natural cycling of nitrogen and phosphorus, however, has led to significant inputs of these nutrients into aquatic ecosystems as well. Nitrogen and phosphorus are mass-produced for use as fertilizers. After the fertilizers are spread on crop fields, rainwater and irrigation runoff carries these nutrients into rivers and streams, which in turn feed estuarine and marine habitats. Likewise, inadequately treated sewage and wastewater laden with nutrients from cities and towns is often pumped into aquatic habitats.

More than 140 dead zones have been documented around the world, and the number continues to rise. The largest known dead zone is located in the Baltic Sea, where agricultural runoff and poorly treated sewage contribute to a dead zone tens of thousands of square kilometers in size. Similarly, in the United States a seasonal hypoxic zone the size of New Jersey forms during the summer months at the mouth of the Mississippi River in the Gulf of Mexico. Fishery yields there and in other locations affected by dead zones have sharply declined, sapping the lifeblood of coastal economies and cutting into marine food production.

While ominous, dead zones are not necessarily permanent. The infamous Black Sea dead zone was once the largest in the world, covering an area of approximately 40,000 square kilometers (15,000 square miles). When the Soviet Union collapsed in 1991, the industrialized agricultural economy of the region also collapsed, and the resulting drop in fertilizer use cut nitrogen and phosphorus input into the Black Sea by more than half. Within about a decade, the dead zone virtually disappeared. Although this example provides hope, the ecosystem of the Black Sea has yet to recover fully, as it supports limited marine life. To combat dead zones efficiently, political action through management of fertilizer use and pollution will be needed, not only to rein in current dead zones but also to prevent future outbreaks entirely.

Daniel J. Connell

Further Reading

Erisman, Jan Willem, et al. "Consequences of Human Modification of the Global Nitrogen Cycle." *Philosophical Transactions: Biological Sciences* 368.1621 (2013): 1–9.

Nassauer, Joan Iverson, Mary V. Santelmann, and Donald Scavia, eds. *From the Corn Belt to the Gulf: Societal and Environmental Implications of Alternative Agricultural Futures.* Resources for the Future, 2007.

Sielen, Alan B. "The Devolution of the Seas." *Foreign Affairs* 92.6 (2013): 124–32. Print.

Vernberg, F. John, and Winona B. Vernberg. *The Coastal Zone: Past, Present, and Future.* University of South Carolina Press, 2001.

■ Debt-for-nature swaps

FIELDS OF STUDY: Agriculture; Agronomy; Business; Conservation Biology; Economics; Ecosystem Management; Forest Management; Forestry;

SIGNIFICANCE: Strategy for reducing foreign debt in developing nations by trading debt forgiveness or debt reduction for guarantees of environmental activities by debtor nations

Although some critics view debt-for-nature swaps as a form of cultural imperialism, these arrangements offer a way for environmental organizations to encourage developing nations to preserve ecosystems, conserve natural resources, and protect significant cultural sites.

Overview

An international finance crisis began during the late 1980's when many developing nations found that they had borrowed more from international lending institutions, mostly private banks, than they could repay. To recover some of the principal on the loans, banks began to sell the loans in financial markets, usually discounted to a fraction of their original value because of the threat of default. Several options to relieve this debt burden on developing nations were explored. One option was to refinance the debt to lower the interest rates and extend the time for repayment. Another strategy was to encourage domestic financial reforms in debtor nations by increasing domestic investment, expanding the domestic economy, raising taxes, reducing

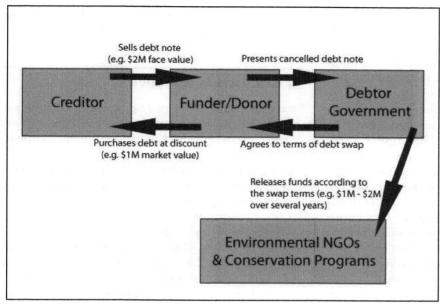

Process diagram of a debt-for-nature swap

non-debt-related expenditures, or inflating the currency in order to pay the debt eventually. Finally, creditor nations and institutions could partially forgive the debt. Debt-for-nature swaps combine elements of all three of these options.

How Debt-for-Nature Swaps Work

In debt-for-nature swaps, environmental organizations buy discounted debt in the financial markets from the banks. Instead of collecting the full amount of interest and principal from the debtor nations, the environmental organizations agree to forgive all or a portion of the debt if the debtor nations invest amounts up to the principal value of the debt in local preservation efforts, often the purchase of land for national parks or investment in skilled staff and improvements for existing parks. In these arrangements, conservation organizations benefit through an increase in local funding for conservation, and banks benefit because they have a new market for the debt. The debtor nations benefit in several ways: They are able to invest their funds in their own nations rather than transferring funds to the lending nations; they use inflated local currency rather than high-value, scarce, dollar-based foreign exchange; and they reduce their outstanding debt and interest payments on that debt, which allows them to

continue making payments on the remaining debt and maintain their international credit ratings.

Debt-for-nature swaps erase the "debt overhang," that portion of debt that, if forgiven, allows the remaining debt to continue to be assumed by creditor nations or institutions with satisfactory levels of burden on the debtor nations and satisfactory debt payment risks for the creditor nations. Because environmental organizations purchase the debt at a discount, they are able to multiply their impacts on the environment. For example, in the first debt-for-nature swap in 1987, Conservation International purchased $650,000 in Bolivian debt for $100,000, then required the Bolivian government to establish a $250,000 endowment fund in local Bolivian currency to pay operating costs for a biosphere reserve in the Bolivian Amazon before erasing the debt.

In debt-for-nature swaps, debtor nations buy back a portion of their outstanding debt with an investment in a portion of their own natural capital. Natural capital includes caches of nonrenewable resources such as mineral or oil reserves, natural resources such as old-growth forests or endangered species habitat, historical artifacts such as prehistoric ruins or fossil deposits, and cultural resources such as the homelands of primitive indigenous peoples or significant architectural sites. The preservation of this natural capital has positive benefits for the ecology, sustainable development, and biodiversity. A swap is also likely to improve the debtor nation's economic ability to repay the remaining debt, because the preserved cultural and natural resources often serve as tourist attractions, cultural centers, and locations for academic and commercial research.

Participation of Financial Institutions

Because some private lending institutions will not voluntarily participate in debt-relief processes that reduce the financial institutions' capital or potential profit from loans, governments in creditor nations either mandate financial institutions' participation or provide financial incentives, such as tax deductions and tax credits, to encourage participation. Creditor governments justify these actions as a component of their foreign economic development programs, as a component of their environmental programs, as philanthropic support for preservation of the earth's cultural and natural heritage, or as economically justifiable domestic self-interest. For example, encouraging nations in tropical zones to protect rain forests helps to reassure nations in the northern temperate zones that existing climate patterns supported by those rain forests will be maintained. Maintaining these climate patterns is necessary to prevent natural and human-made disasters, reduce the demands on industrialized nations to provide humanitarian relief from increased numbers of natural disasters, ensure continued rainfall in agricultural zones in temperate regions, prevent desertification, maintain good air quality and reduce the greenhouse effect, ensure global biodiversity, and improve the living conditions for every person on the planet.

Some nations, among them Costa Rica, welcome the opportunities presented by debt-for-nature swaps. Other nations—Brazil is an example—see the swaps as a form of environmental imperialism in which foreign environmental organizations shape domestic government policy. They argue that restricting large areas of land for parks and nature reserves reduces the amount of land available for economic production and access by poor subsistence farmers.

Gordon Neal Diem

Further Reading

Mahony, Rhona. "Debt-for-Nature Swaps: Who Really Benefits?" 1992. In *Tropical Rainforests: Latin American Nature and Society in Transition*, edited by Susan E. Place. Rev. ed. Scholarly Resources, 2001.

Meier, Gerald M. *The International Environment of Business: Competition and Governance in the Global Economy.* Oxford University Press, 1998.

Mulder, Monique Borgerhoff, and Peter Coppolillo. "Global Issues, Economics, and Policy." In *Conservation: Linking Ecology, Economics, and Culture.* Princeton University Press, 2005.

Page, Diana. "Debt-for-Nature Swaps: Experience Gained, Lessons Learned." *International Environmental Affairs* 1 (Fall, 1989): 275-288.

Sachs, Jeffrey. "Making the Brady Plan Work." *Foreign Affairs* 68 (Summer, 1989): 87-104.

■ Deciduous forests

FIELDS OF STUDY: Biology, Life Sciences, Ecosystems; Ecology, Environment, Environmentalism; Forests, Forestry; Plants, Vegetation, Botany, Horticulture

DEFINITION: Natural areas consisting of diverse plant species that lose their leaves annually at the end of each growing season

Deciduous forests are important ecosystems that support multiple life cycles and provide habitat for native populations and wildlife. Located in the most heavily populated areas throughout the globe, these forests are declining because of human activity, including overuse and environmental pollution.

Deciduous forests did not exist until the end of the last ice age, which was some 20,000 years ago, as the plant species associated with this forest type were unable to adapt to the glacial climate. The word "deciduous" is derived from the Latin word *decidere*, which means "fall off." Deciduous forests are located mainly in the temperate forest biome, which has very seasonal weather patterns consisting of four seasons with warm summers and cold winters and precipitation in the form of rain and snow throughout the year.

In the fall season the leaves of deciduous trees change from green to brilliant yellow, orange, red, and brown because of a lack of the green pigment chlorophyll, which they can no longer produce as daylight wanes. Eventually the leaves fall off as they go into dormancy at the end of the growing cycle, and most trees in the temperate deciduous forests remain bare during the winter months.

The temperate forest biome is located in the middle latitudes of the earth, and temperate or deciduous forests can be found in eastern North America, eastern Asia, and western Europe. Parts of Australia and New Zealand also contain deciduous forests. Less prominent are the tropical and subtropical deciduous forest biomes that exist in South America and Southern Africa. Plants in these biomes are dependent on seasonal temperatures and

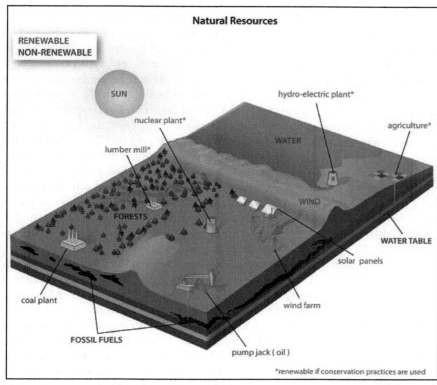

Natural Resources

RENEWABLE
NON-RENEWABLE

SUN

nuclear plant*

hydro-electric plant*

lumber mill*

agriculture*

WATER

FORESTS

WIND

WATER TABLE

solar panels

coal plant

wind farm

FOSSIL FUELS

pump jack (oil)

*renewable if conservation practices are used

The earth has many natural resources, some are renewable and others are not. Conservation practices will ensure that resources do not become depleted. © EBSCO

rainfall. Most of the trees in these forests, such as teak and ebony, drop their leaves in the dry season in order to conserve water, but new leaves sprout once the rainy season begins.

Forest Zones and Plant Associations
Temperate deciduous forests consist of five distinct zones or strata. The first is the tree stratum. Trees in this zone, including maple, oak, beech, hickory, walnut, chestnut, basswood, linden, elm, and sweet gum species, average from 18 to 30 meters (60 to 100 feet) in height. The second stratum, the small tree and sapling zone, is made up of younger trees found in the tree stratum. The third stratum consists of shrubs, including such species as azaleas, rhododendrons, mountain laurels, and huckleberries. The herbal or fourth zone consists of short herbal plants, and the rich soils of the forest floor make up the ground stratum, the fifth zone, which includes lichens, mushrooms, and mosses.

E. Lucy Braun, an important botanist and plant ecologist of the early twentieth century, spent much

of her life studying and cataloging the deciduous forests of eastern North America in order to preserve them at a time when humans were involved in random deforestation and logging. Braun and others created deciduous forest subcategories known as forest regions based mainly on the regions' natural vegetation composition, but also on physiognomy. These regions vary from ones that are made up mainly of deciduous plants, such as the oak-hickory and beech-maple regions, to forest communities that include coniferous species, which do not shed their leaves in the winter, including the oak-pine and hemlock-white pine-northern hardwood regions. Braun named one of the major deciduous forest communities in eastern North America the "mixed mesophytic." Unlike most forest communities, which have only two or three dominant species, the mixed mesophytic deciduous forest community is made up of more than eighty plant species.

Animal Species
Temperate deciduous forests flourish with a variety of fauna. Mammals include deer, elk, bears, squirrels, skunks, raccoons, rabbits, opossums, foxes, and porcupines. Other diverse species found in these forests include many varieties of salamanders, frogs, snakes, and spiders. Small and large birds, such as wild turkeys, owls, hawks, and the bald eagle, depend on deciduous forests for habitat. During winter months some of the deciduous forest animals, especially birds, migrate to warmer climates where food is plentiful, while animals such as squirrels slow their metabolisms and store nuts and seeds in the hollows of trees to survive the winter months. Bears are among the animals that hibernate during winters in temperate deciduous forests.

Many animals associated with temperate deciduous forests have long been on the decline, such as bobcats, mountain lions, and timber wolves. Loss of habitat and human slaughter have led to decreases in the populations of several of these species to the extent that they have been recognized as endangered or threatened and in need of protection from extinction. The continual loss of deciduous forests caused by logging, blights, plagues, nutrient depletion owing to pollution, and climate change has exacerbated negative effects on all of the species that make their homes in these forests.

Carol A. Rolf

Further Reading

Braun, E. Lucy. *Deciduous Forests of Eastern North America.* 1950. Reprint. Caldwell, N.J.: Blackburn Press, 2001.

Delcourt, Hazel R. *Forests in Peril: Tracking Deciduous Trees from Ice-Age Refuges into the Greenhouse World.* Blacksburg, Va.: McDonald & Woodward, 2002.

Frelich, Lee E. *Forest Dynamics and Disturbance Regimes: Studies from Temperate Evergreen-Deciduous Forests.* New York: Cambridge University Press, 2008.

Yetman, David A. *A Tropical Deciduous Forest of Alamos: Biodiversity of a Threatened Ecosystem in Mexico.* Tucson: University of Arizona Press, 2000.

■ Decline of the ozone layer

FIELDS OF STUDY: Meteorology, Atmospheric Sciences, Climatology; Atmospheric Structure and Dynamics; Climate and Climate Change; Pollution, Emissions, Toxic Waste, Hazardous Materials.

SIGNIFICANCE: Region of the lower stratosphere in which most of the earth's ozone is found

Earth's ozone layer protects life on the planet from exposure to dangerous levels of ultraviolet light. Because of the introduction of certain human-made chemicals into the atmosphere, the amount of stratospheric ozone steadily declined during the second half of the twentieth century.

Summary

Ozone (O_3) is a molecule made of three atoms of oxygen. It is considered a trace gas because it accounts for only .000007 percent of the earth's atmosphere. Ozone concentrations are measured in terms of Dobson units, which represent the thickness of all the ozone in a column of the atmosphere if it were compressed—on average only 3 millimeters (0.118 inch) thick. Depending on where it is found in the atmosphere, ozone may have either a positive or a negative impact on life. When ozone is near Earth's surface, it is a major air pollutant, a chief constituent of smog, and a greenhouse gas. Fuel combustion and other human activities increase the quantities of ozone in this atmospheric region. Ozone that resides in the stratosphere protects Earth's organisms from lethal intensities of solar ultraviolet (UV) radiation. Without this shield of ozone, which is created through naturally occurring processes, life on Earth as it is now known would probably cease to exist. Approximately 90 percent of Earth's ozone is found in the stratosphere.

Ozone concentration peaks in the lower stratosphere, between the altitudes of 20 and 25 kilometers (12 and 16 miles). Within this "ozone layer," two sets of chemical reactions, both powered by UV radiation, continuously occur. In one reaction, ozone is produced; in the other, ozone is broken down into oxygen molecules and ions. Slightly more ozone is produced than is destroyed by these reactions, so that stratospheric ozone is constantly maintained by nature. Because UV radiation is a catalyst for both reactions, most of this radiation is used up and prevented from ever reaching earth's surface.

UV radiation is categorized as UVA, UVB, or UVC, depending on wavelength. UVC rays readily kill living cells with which they come into contact. UVB rays, although less energetic than UVC rays, also damage cells. The ozone shield prevents all UVC rays from reaching the surface; however, some UVB radiation does pass through the ozone layer. It is contact with this radiation that causes sunburns, accelerates the natural aging of the skin, and has been shown to increase rates of skin cancer and cataracts. In 2018, the American Cancer Society estimated that more than five million new cases of skin cancer occur each year in the United States, mainly as a result of UV radiation. Some researchers estimate that every 1 percent decline in ozone concentration causes a 2 percent increase in UV intensity at Earth's surface, resulting in a greater risk of skin cancer, cataracts, and immune deficiencies.

Increased UV radiation also harms plant and animal life. Some studies have suggested that yields from crops such as corn, wheat, rice, and soybeans

Antarctic Ozone Hole as at Sept. 22, 2012. By NASA

drop by 1 percent for each 3 percent decrease in ozone concentration. Increased UV radiation in polar regions impairs and destroys phytoplankton, which makes up the base of the food chain. A decrease in phytoplankton would likely cause population reductions at all levels of the ecosystem. Fewer than 1 in every 100,000 molecules in the atmosphere is ozone, a ratio that both underscores and belies the critical role ozone plays in protecting human health and the global environment.

Discovery of the Antarctic Ozone Hole

Satellites placed in orbit during the late 1970's allowed scientists to observe concentrations of stratospheric ozone. Observations showed that during the Southern Hemisphere's spring (primarily September and October), the ozone layer above Antarctica thinned dramatically, then recovered during November. These findings were initially dismissed as being caused by instrument error; however, the measurements were confirmed by the British Antarctic Survey in 1985. During that spring, the loss of ozone exceeded 50 percent of normal concentrations. Alarmingly, continued satellite measurements indicated that each year throughout the 1980's and 1990's, the ozone concentration over Antarctica

dropped to record lows, and the size of the ozone-depleted area (dubbed the "ozone hole") increased. In 1986 the size of the ozone hole grew larger than the size of the Antarctic continent, and in 1993 the hole was larger than all of North America.

During an intensive Antarctic field program in 1987, extremely high levels of chlorine monoxide (ClO) were found in the stratosphere. This finding was seen by many scientists as evidence that the cause of ozone depletion was chlorofluorocarbons (CFCs), anthropogenic chemicals that make excellent refrigerants, cooling fluids, and cleaning solvents. Since the 1950's, millions of tons of CFCs had been produced in the United States alone. CFC leakage from old refrigerators and automobile air conditioners, combined with a lack of chemical recycling efforts, allowed huge quantities of CFCs to make their way into the atmosphere. Also, one of the CFCs, CFC-11, was used for decades as a propellant in aerosol spray cans until it was banned during the late 1970's.

In the stratosphere, UV radiation breaks down CFCs, causing them to release chlorine (Cl), a gas that readily reacts with ozone. The reaction produces oxygen (O_2) and ClO, which then combine to produce O_2 and Cl. Thus, at the end of these reactions, the chlorine atom is again free to destroy another ozone molecule. It is estimated that a single chlorine atom may reside in the stratosphere for fifty years or longer and destroy hundreds of thousands of ozone molecules.

Most scientists believed the detection of stratospheric ClO was the "smoking gun" that proved that human-made CFCs were the cause of ozone depletion. However, many industrialists and others opposed to what they perceived as overzealous environmental regulations asserted that the chlorine in the atmosphere was a result of natural processes such as volcanic eruptions or sea spray. This theory was finally debunked in 1995 when scientists also found hydrogen fluoride in the stratosphere. Hydrogen fluoride is not produced by any natural process; however, fluoride would be liberated from a CFC molecule when it is broken down by UV radiation. Scientifically, there is no longer any debate that ozone destruction is a direct result of CFCs. Other chlorine-containing compounds have also been implicated in ozone destruction, as have some bromine-containing compounds. While bromine is less abundant in the stratosphere than chlorine, atom for atom it is more effective than chlorine in destroying ozone.

Global Ozone Depletion

Since the initial satellite observations of the 1970's and 1980's, the understanding of the complex science of the formation of the Antarctic ozone hole has greatly improved. Most ozone-destroying compounds are released in the Northern Hemisphere; however, they mix throughout the lower atmosphere in about one year and then mix into the stratosphere in two to five years. A key element that enhances ozone depletion is the presence of polar stratospheric clouds. These clouds form only in the polar regions where temperatures in the stratosphere drop to below –80 degrees Celsius (–112 degrees Fahrenheit). The surfaces of these clouds are sites on which inactive chlorine and bromine are converted into the reactive forms that destroy ozone. The dark Antarctic stratosphere becomes so frigid during winter that these clouds are produced in abundance. As spring begins, the stratosphere is hit with solar UV radiation, accelerating the ozone depletion process. A strong vortex of winds circles the South Pole every winter, keeping the Antarctic stratosphere isolated from neighboring air masses. This allows the ozone-destroying reactions to act on a limited amount of ozone that cannot be replenished by ozone from other latitudes. The result is the appearance of the ozone hole each spring. In late spring the winds weaken, allowing comparatively ozone-rich air from other latitudes to mix into the Antarctic atmosphere.

Ozone concentrations declined globally during the second half of the twentieth century as a result of rising levels of atmospheric chlorine and bromine. It was discovered that an ozone hole also forms over the Arctic in the Northern Hemisphere during the spring, although the hole is smaller in size and higher in ozone concentrations than its Antarctic counterpart. The main reason for the difference between the Arctic and Antarctic is that the winds encircling the Arctic are typically not as strong as those in the Antarctic, thus allowing ozone-rich air to mix constantly into the Arctic. Still, significant ozone depletion occurred throughout the 1990's as Arctic spring concentrations dropped about 30 percent below average levels.

Ozone levels in other parts of the world also declined. Ground stations measured decreasing stratospheric ozone levels at midlatitudes. Satellites indicated a negative trend in ozone concentrations in both hemispheres, with a net decrease of about 3 percent per decade. The depletion increased with latitude and was somewhat larger in the Southern Hemisphere. Over the United States, Europe, and Australia, 4 percent per decade was typical. A new threat to ozone followed the eruption of Mount Pinatubo in the Philippines in 1991, the century's second most violent volcanic eruption and the largest one to occur since ozone monitoring began. Massive amounts of sulfur aerosols were injected into the stratosphere. Volcanic aerosols function like the ice crystals in the Antarctic stratosphere by helping convert chlorine and bromine from their inactive state to a reactive one. During the two years following the eruption, record low levels of annual ozone concentrations were recorded: 9 percent below normal between 30 and 60 degrees north latitude.

As expected, measurements also indicated increased UV radiation reaching Earth's surface. During the 1990's, summer levels of UVB increased 7 percent annually over Canada, while winter levels increased 5 percent per year. At the same time, the incidence of skin cancer grew faster than that of any other form of cancer, with reported cases doubling between 1980 and 1998.

International Response

As evidence grew during the 1980's that CFC production was responsible for ozone depletion, the international community decided to act through a series of treaties and amendments. The multilateral Vienna Convention for the Protection of the Ozone Layer of 1985 outlined the responsibilities of states to prevent human-driven ozone depletion. The Vienna Convention laid the groundwork for the Montreal Protocol on Substances That Deplete the Ozone Layer, which was adopted in 1987. The Montreal Protocol put into place a framework for the phaseout of CFC production in developed countries beginning in 1993. In the following years, as ozone levels kept falling, amendments added more chemicals to the phaseout, accelerated the phaseout timetable, and called for the developing world's participation. By 2018 the Montreal Protocol had been ratified by 197 countries, although not all of them had ratified all the subsequent amendments. Under the amended protocol, hydrobromofluorocarbons, CFCs, halons, and carbon tetrachloride have already been phased out;

methyl chloroform and methyl bromide have been phased out in developed countries and were generally phased out in developing countries by 2015; and hydrochlorofluorocarbons were scheduled to be phased out by 2020 in developed countries and 2040 in developing countries. Certain essential-use exemptions have been made for those countries beyond the official phaseout dates.

Since the beginning of the twenty-first century, concentrations of ozone-depleting substances in the stratosphere have been on the decline as a result of the Montreal Protocol. These substances have such a long residence time in the atmosphere, however, that even with a ban on production, their concentrations in the stratosphere are not expected to return to pre-1980 levels until 2050 at the earliest. According to the U.S. Environmental Protection Agency (EPA), Antarctic ozone is projected to return to pre-1980 levels between 2060 and 2075. Factors including volcanic eruptions, solar activity, and changes in atmospheric temperature, composition, and air motion could affect the ozone layer's rate of recovery.

Some studies have predicted that maximum ozone depletion will occur between 2000 and 2020, followed by a slow recovery. UV radiation levels at Earth's surface are also expected to increase during the early part of the twenty-first century, bringing with them negative health and ecological effects. The largest ozone hole ever recorded occurred in September, 2006. However, according to an EPA report, over most of the world the ozone layer remained relatively stable between 1998 and 2007.

The story of the ozone layer contains both positive and negative lessons regarding human interaction with the environment. Human production of CFCs and other compounds during the latter half of the twentieth century caused significant, long-term harm to the earth's protective barrier against deadly UV radiation. Human health has been affected, and immeasurable damage has been inflicted on many ecosystems. With Earth in the balance, however, the international community decided to act, and did so forcefully. Without the Montreal Protocol, the fate of the ozone layer and life on earth would have been sealed. It is known that human activity has the power to destroy the global environment, but perhaps human activity may have the power to save it as well. That this hopeful outcome may be in jeopardy was underscored in 2018 by the report of an observed rise in atmospheric concentrations of at least one banned CFC over the previous decade, indicating that the Montreal Protocol is not being upheld as it should be.

Craig S. Gilman; updated by Karen N. Kähler

Further Reading

Bakker, Sem H., ed. *Ozone Depletion, Chemistry, and Impacts.* Nova Science, 2009.

Cagin, Seth, and Philip Dray. *Between Earth and Sky: How CFCs Changed Our World and Endangered the Ozone Layer.* Pantheon Books, 1993.

Cancer Facts & Figures 2018. American Cancer Society, 2018, www.cancer.org/content/dam/cancer-org/research/cancer-facts-and-statistics/annual-cancer-facts-and-figures/2018/cancer-facts-and-figures-2018.pdf. Accessed 27 Mar. 2018.

Joesten, Melvin D., John L. Hogg, and Mary E. Castellion. "Chlorofluorocarbons and the Ozone Layer." In *The World of Chemistry: Essentials.* 4th ed. Thomson Brooks/Cole, 2007.

Mackenzie, Rob. "Stratospheric Chemistry and Ozone Depletion." In *Atmospheric Science for Environmental Scientists,* edited by C. Nicholas Hewitt and Andrea V. Jackson. Wiley-Blackwell, 2009.

Parson, Edward A. *Protecting the Ozone Layer: Science and Strategy.* Oxford University Press, 2003.

Somerville, Richard C. J. *The Forgiving Air: Understanding Environmental Change.* 2d ed. American Meteorological Society, 2008.

Turco, Richard P. *Earth Under Siege: From Air Pollution to Global Change.* 2nd ed. Oxford University Press, 2002.

United Nations Environment Programme. *Environmental Effects of Ozone Depletion and the Interaction with Climate Change: 2006 Assessment.* Author, 2006.

■ Deep ecology

FIELDS OF STUDY: Anthropology; Biology; Ecology; Environmental Studies; Ethics; Philosophy;

SIGNIFICANCE: School of environmental philosophy based on environmental activism and ecological spirituality

The thinking of deep ecologists has attracted criticism from some quarters at the same time it has expanded approaches to environmental ethics.

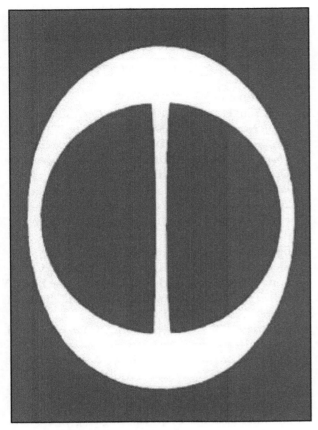

Deep ecology. By Xvegandettax (Own work)

Overview

The term "deep ecology" was first used by Norwegian philosopher Arne Naess in 1972 to suggest the need to go beyond the anthropocentric view that nature is merely a resource for human use. Since that time, the term has been used in three major ways. First, it has been used to refer to a commitment to deep questioning about environmental ethics and the causes of environmental problems; such questioning leads to critical reflection on the fundamental worldviews that underlie specific environmental ideas and practices. Second, the term has been used to refer to a platform of generally agreed-upon values that a variety of environmental activists share; these values include an affirmation of the intrinsic value of nature, the recognition of the importance of biodiversity, a call for a reduction of human impact on the natural world, greater concern with quality of life than with material affluence, and a commitment to changing economic policies and the dominant view of nature.

Third, "deep ecology" has been used to refer to particular philosophies of nature that tend to emphasize the value of nature as a whole (ecocentrism), an identification of the self with the natural world, and an intuitive and sensuous communion with the earth.

Because of its emphasis on fundamental worldviews, deep ecology is often associated with non-Western spiritual traditions, such as Buddhism and Native American cultures, as well as with radical Western philosophers such as Baruch Spinoza and Martin Heidegger. It has also drawn on the nature writing of Henry David Thoreau, John Muir, Robinson Jeffers, and Gary Snyder. Deep ecology's holistic tendencies have led to associations with the Gaia hypothesis, and its emphasis on diversity and intimacy with nature has linked it to bioregionalism. Deep ecological views have also had a strong impact on environmental activism, including the Earth First! movement.

Deep ecologists have sometimes criticized the animal rights perspective for continuing the traditional Western emphasis on individuals while neglecting whole systems, as well as for a revised speciesism that still values certain parts of nature (animals) over others. Some deep ecologists have also been critical of mainstream environmental organizations such as the Sierra Club for not confronting the root causes of environmental degradation.

Ecofeminists have criticized deep ecology for failing to consider gender differences in the experience of the self and nature, for failing to examine the connection between the oppression of women and human treatment of nature, and for promoting a holism that, the ecofeminists assert, disregards the reality and value of individuals and their relationships. Social ecologists have criticized deep ecology for failing to critique the relationship between environmental destruction on the one hand and social structure and political ideology on the other. In addition, a distrust of human interference with nature has led some deep ecology thinkers to present pristine wilderness, with no human presence, as the ideal. In rare and extreme cases, deep ecologists have implied a misanthropic attitude. In some instances, especially in early writings by deep ecologists, such criticisms have had considerable force. However, these problematic views are not essential to deep ecology, and a number of deep ecologists have developed a broadened view that overlaps with ecofeminism and social ecology.

David Landis Barnhill

Further Reading

Bender, Frederic L. *The Culture of Extinction: Toward a Philosophy of Deep Ecology.* Humanity Books, 2003.

Devall, Bill. *Simple in Means, Rich in Ends: Practicing Deep Ecology.* Peregrine Smith, 1988.

Diehm, Christian. "Darwin and Deep Ecology." *Ethics and the Environment* 19.1 (2014): 73–93.

Katz, Eric, Andrew Light, and David Rothenberg, eds. *Beneath the Surface: Critical Essays in the Philosophy of Deep Ecology.* MIT Press, 2000.

Kober, Gal. "For They Do Not Agree in Nature: Spinoza and Deep Ecology." *Ethics and the Environment* 18.1 (2013): 43–63.

■ Deforestation

FIELDS OF STUDY: Biology, Life Sciences, Ecosystems; Agriculture, Farming, Animal Husbandry; Ecology, Environment, Environmentalism; Forests, Forestry; Plants, Vegetation, Botany, Horticulture.

SIGNIFICANCE: Loss of forestlands through encroachment by agriculture, industrial development, or nonsustainable commercial forestry

Deforestation, particularly in tropical regions, has given rise to concerns among environmentalists and scientists, in large part because of the role that tropical forests play in moderating global climate.

Toward the end of the twentieth century, environmentalists became active in decrying the apparent accelerating pace of deforestation because of the loss of wildlife and plant habitats caused by the practice as well as its negative effects on biodiversity. By the 1990's research by mainstream scientists had confirmed that deforestation was indeed occurring on a global scale and that it posed a serious threat to global ecology. Although steps were taken to slow rates of deforestation in the early years of the twenty-first century, the loss of forestlands continued.

Deforestation as a result of expansion of agricultural lands or nonsustainable timber harvesting has occurred in many regions of the world at different periods in history. The Bible, for example, refers to the cedars of Lebanon. Lebanon, like many of the countries bordering the Mediterranean Sea, was thickly forested several thousand years ago. A growing population, overharvesting, and the introduction of grazing animals such as sheep and goats decimated the forests, which never recovered.

Similarly, the forests of Europe and North America have shifted in total area as human populations have changed over the centuries. When the European colonists arrived in the New World, they immediately began clearing the forests. Trees were harvested for building materials and export back to Europe or were simply felled and burned to clear space for farming. In North America, however, as agriculture became increasingly mechanized and farming shifted to the prairies, abandoned farms reverted to woodland. Environmental historians believe, in fact, that a greater percentage of land area in North America is now forested than was covered with trees prior to the arrival of European colonists. A similar phenomenon has taken place in many northern European countries as their populations have become increasingly urbanized.

As the European industrialized nations have gained forestland, however, the less developed countries in Latin America, Asia, and Africa have lost woodlands. While some of this deforestation has been caused by a demand for tropical hardwoods for lumber or pulp, the leading cause of deforestation in the twentieth and twenty-first centuries, as it was several hundred years ago, has been the expansion of agriculture. Growing demand by the industrialized world for agricultural products such as beef has led to millions of hectares of forestland being bulldozed or burned to create pastures for cattle. Researchers in Central America have watched with dismay as large beef-raising operations have expanded into fragile ecosystems in countries such as Costa Rica, Guatemala, and Mexico.

A tragic irony in this expansion of agriculture into tropical rain forests is that the soil underlying the trees is often unsuited to use as pastureland or raising other crops. Exposed to sunlight, the soil is quickly depleted of nutrients and often hardens. The once-verdant land becomes an arid desert prone to erosion that may never return to forest. As the soil becomes less fertile, thorny weeds begin to choke out the desirable forage plants, and the cattle ranchers move on to clear fresh tracts.

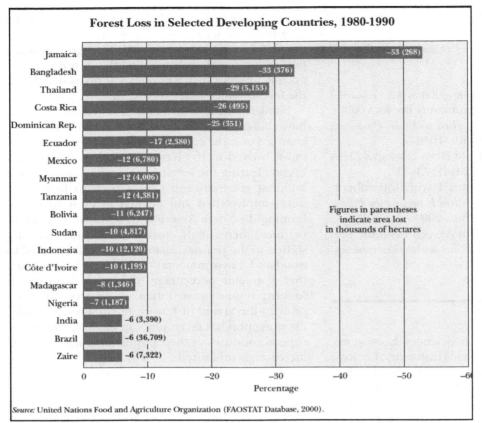

Forest Loss in Selected Developing Countries, 1980-1990

Jamaica −53 (268)
Bangladesh −33 (376)
Thailand −29 (5,153)
Costa Rica −26 (495)
Dominican Rep. −25 (351)
Ecuador −17 (2,380)
Mexico −12 (6,780)
Myanmar −12 (4,006)
Tanzania −12 (4,381)
Bolivia −11 (6,247)
Sudan −10 (4,817)
Indonesia −10 (12,120)
Côte d'Ivoire −10 (1,193)
Madagascar −8 (1,346)
Nigeria −7 (1,187)
India −6 (3,390)
Brazil −6 (36,709)
Zaire −6 (7,322)

Figures in parentheses indicate area lost in thousands of hectares

Percentage

Source: United Nations Food and Agriculture Organization (FAOSTAT Database, 2000).

Slash-and-Burn Agriculture and Logging

Apologists for the beef industry often argue that their ranching practices are simply a form of slash-and-burn agriculture and do no permanent harm. It is true that many of the indigenous peoples in tropical regions have practiced slash-and-burn agriculture for millennia with only minimal impact on the environment. These farmers burn the understory, or low-growing shrubs and trees, to clear small plots of land. Any large trees that survive their fires are cut down with axes and then burned.

Anthropological studies have shown that the small plots these peasant farmers clear can usually be measured in square meters or feet, not in hectares or acres like cattle ranches, and are used for five to ten years. As fertility of the soil declines in one plot, the farmer clears a small plot next to the depleted one. The farmer's family or village gradually rotates through the forest, clearing small plots and using them for a few years, and then shifting to new ground, until they eventually come back to where they began

one hundred or more years before. As long as the size of the plots cleared by peasant farmers remains small in proportion to the forest overall, slash-and-burn agriculture does not contribute significantly to deforestation. If the population of farmers grows, however, and more land must be cleared with each succeeding generation, as has been happening in many tropical countries, then even traditional slash-and-burn agriculture can be as ecologically devastating as the more mechanized cattle ranching operations.

Although logging is not the leading cause of deforestation, it remains a significant factor. Tropical forests are rarely clear-cut, as they typically contain hundreds of different species of trees, most of which may have no commercial value. Loggers may select only a few trees for harvesting from each stand. Selective harvesting is a standard practice in sustainable forestry, but just as loggers engaged in the disreputable practice of high-grading across North America in the nineteenth century, so loggers have high-graded in the late twentieth and early twenty-first centuries in Malaysia, Indonesia, and other tropical forests. High-grading is a practice in which loggers cut over a tract to remove the most valuable timber while ignoring the damage being done to the residual stand. The assumption is that, having logged over the tract once, the timber company will not be coming back. This practice stopped in North America not because the timber companies voluntarily recognized the ecological damage they were doing but because they ran out of easily accessible, old-growth timber to cut. Fear of a timber famine caused logging companies to create forest plantations and to undertake the practice of sustainable forestry. While global satellite photos indicate significant deforestation has occurred in tropical areas, enough easily harvested old-growth forest remains in some areas that there is no economic incentive for timber companies to switch to sustainable forestry.

Logging may also contribute to deforestation by making it easier for agriculture to encroach on forestlands. Logging companies build roads for their own use while harvesting trees, and farmers and ranchers later use these roads to move into the logged tracts, where they clear whatever trees the loggers have left.

Environmental Impacts

The extent of the problem of deforestation has long been a subject of

Results of Deforestation

Source: Adapted from A. K. Biswas, "Environmental Concerns in Pakistan, with Special Reference to Water and Forests," in *Environmental Conservation,* 1987.

debate. The United Nations Food and Agriculture Organization (FAO), which monitors deforestation worldwide, bases its statistics on measurements taken from satellite images. These data indicate that between 2000 and 2005 the net loss of forest area globally was 7.3 million hectares (18 million acres) per year, a reduction from 8.9 million hectares (22 million acres) per year in the decade between 1990 and 2000. In the period 2000-2005, South America and Africa had the greatest losses: South America lost 4.3 million hectares (10.6 million acres) of forest per year, and Africa lost 4 million hectares (9.9 million acres) per year. Environmental activists have been particularly concerned about forest losses in Indonesia and Malaysia, two countries where timber companies have been accused of abusing or exploiting native peoples in addition to engaging in environmentally damaging harvesting methods.

Researchers outside the United Nations have challenged FAO's data, with some scientists claiming the numbers are much too high and others providing convincing evidence that, if anything, FAO's

numbers are too low. Few researchers, however, have tried to claim that deforestation on a global scale is not happening. In the 1990's the reforestation of the Northern Hemisphere, while providing an encouraging example that it is possible to reverse deforestation, was not enough to offset the depletion of forestland in tropical areas.

Deforestation affects the environment in a multitude of ways. The most obvious is in a loss of biodiversity. When an ecosystem is radically altered through deforestation, the trees are not the only thing to disappear. Wildlife decreases in number and in variety, and other plants also die. As forest habitat shrinks through deforestation, various plants and animals become vulnerable to extinction. Many biologists believe that numerous animals and plants native to tropical forests will become extinct as the result of deforestation before humans ever have a chance to become aware of their existence.

Other effects of deforestation may be less obvious. Deforestation can lead to increased flooding during rainy seasons. Rainwater that once would have been slowed or absorbed by trees instead runs off denuded hillsides, pushing rivers over their banks and causing devastating floods downstream. The role of forests in regulating water has long been recognized by both engineers and foresters. Flood control was, in fact, one of the motivations behind the creation of the federal forest reserves in the United States during the nineteenth century. More recently, disastrous floods in Bangladesh have been blamed on the logging of tropical hardwoods in the mountains of Nepal and India.

Conversely, trees can also help to mitigate drought. Like all plants, trees release water into the atmosphere through the process of transpiration. As the world's forests shrink, fewer greenhouse gases such as carbon dioxide will be removed from the atmosphere, less oxygen and water will be released into it, and the world will become a hotter, dryer place. Scientists and policy analysts alike are in agreement that deforestation is a major threat to the environment. The question is whether effective policies can be developed to reverse it.

Männikkö

Further Reading

Chew, Sing C. *World Ecological Degradation: Accumulation, Urbanization, and Deforestation, 3000 B.C.-A.D. 2000.* AltaMira Press, 2001.

Dean, Warren. *With Broadax and Firebrand: The Destruction of the Brazilian Atlantic Forest.* University of California Press, 1997.

Geist, Helmut J., and Eric F. Lambin. "Proximate Causes and Underlying Driving Forces of Tropical Deforestation." *BioScience* 52, no. 2 (2002): 143-150.

Humphreys, David. *Logjam: Deforestation and the Crisis of Global Governance.* Earthscan, 2006.

Palmer, Charles, and Stefanie Engel, eds. *Avoided Deforestation: Prospects for Mitigating Climate Change.* Routledge, 2009.

Richards, John F., and Richard P. Tucker, eds. *World Deforestation in the Twentieth Century.* Duke University Press, 1990.

Rudel, Thomas K., and Bruce Horowitz. *Tropical Deforestation: Small Farmers and Land Clearing in the Ecuadorian Amazon.* Columbia University Press, 1994.

Sanchez, Ilya B., and Carl L. Alonso, eds. *Deforestation Research Progress.* Nova Science, 2008.

Sponsel, Leslie E., Robert Converse Bailey, and Thomas N. Headland, eds. *Tropical Deforestation: The Human Dimension.* Columbia University Press, 1996.

See also: Logging and clear-cutting; Old-growth forests; Rain forests; Rainforest Action Network; Slash-and-burn agriculture; Sustainable forestry.

■ Department of Energy, U.S.

FIELDS OF STUDY: Government, Politics, International Relations; Organizations, Agencies, Commissions, Centers; Regulation, Standards and Practices; Energy and Energy Resources

CATEGORIES: Organizations and agencies; energy and energy use

IDENTIFICATION: Cabinet-level division of the executive branch of the U.S. government that oversees energy matters

DATE: Created on August 4, 1977

In addition to maintaining standards for the regulation of production and distribution of energy within the United States, the U.S. Department of Energy oversees and supports energy-related research, promotes energy conservation, and supports public education and information dissemination about energy.

The U.S. Department of Energy (DOE) began operations October 1, 1977, having been created by legislation signed into law by President Jimmy Carter on August 4, 1977. That legislation merged a number of existing federal agencies into a single cabinet department answering to the president. This action was taken during a time of energy shortages in the United States; it was believed that a single governmental body would be more effective than a variety of independent agencies in implementing a national energy policy.

During the early twentieth century, the U.S. government was little involved in making policy concerning energy use other than its role in implementing daylight saving time during the world wars. After World War II, the Atomic Energy Commission (AEC) was established to oversee nuclear energy technology. In 1974 the AEC was dissolved, and two new agencies, the Nuclear Regulatory Commission (NRC) and the Energy Research and Development

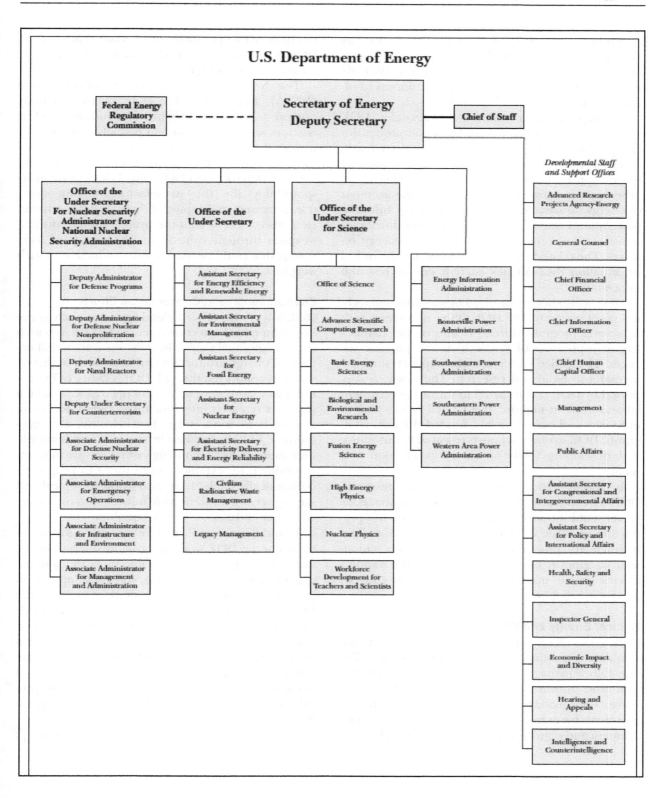

U.S. Department of Energy

Federal Energy Regulatory Commission

Secretary of Energy
Deputy Secretary

Chief of Staff

Developmental Staff and Support Offices

Office of the Under Secretary For Nuclear Security/ Administrator for National Nuclear Security Administration

Office of the Under Secretary

Office of the Under Secretary for Science

Advanced Research Projects Agency-Energy

General Counsel

Deputy Administrator for Defense Programs

Assistant Secretary for Energy Efficiency and Renewable Energy

Office of Science

Energy Information Administration

Chief Financial Officer

Deputy Administrator for Defense Nuclear Nonproliferation

Assistant Secretary for Environmental Management

Advance Scientific Computing Research

Bonneville Power Administration

Chief Information Officer

Deputy Administrator for Naval Reactors

Assistant Secretary for Fossil Energy

Basic Energy Sciences

Southwestern Power Administration

Chief Human Capital Officer

Deputy Under Secretary for Counterterrorism

Assistant Secretary for Nuclear Energy

Biological and Environmental Research

Southeastern Power Administration

Management

Associate Administrator for Defense Nuclear Security

Assistant Secretary for Electricity Delivery and Energy Reliability

Fusion Energy Science

Western Area Power Administration

Public Affairs

Associate Administrator for Emergency Operations

Civilian Radioactive Waste Management

High Energy Physics

Assistant Secretary for Congressional and Intergovernmental Affairs

Associate Administrator for Infrastructure and Environment

Legacy Management

Nuclear Physics

Assistant Secretary for Policy and International Affairs

Associate Administrator for Management and Administration

Workforce Development for Teachers and Scientists

Health, Safety and Security

Inspector General

Economic Impact and Diversity

Hearing and Appeals

Intelligence and Counterintelligence

Administration (ERDA) were created by the Energy Reorganization Act. ERDA, along with other agencies, became the Department of Energy in 1977. By the twenty-first century DOE included dozens of offices, agencies, and administrations.

Through its various offices and agencies, DOE seeks to provide a framework for a comprehensive energy policy for the United States. The department is responsible for the regulation of various parts of the energy industry within the United States. Another important function of DOE is the management of energy information; through its Energy Information Administration, DOE collects and distributes statistics about energy usage and U.S. energy reserves. The related Office of Scientific and Technical Information disseminates current energy research information.

DOE is also heavily involved in scientific and technological research. The DOE Office of Science, with its several program offices, is one of the nation's largest supporters of research in the physical sciences. The Office of Science also supports environmental and biological research. The research supported by DOE is conducted in various government laboratories throughout the United States and in university and corporate labs funded through DOE grants. DOE strongly supports research in innovative and developing fields of energy production and usage.

In addition to energy regulation and research, DOE is heavily involved in hydroelectric power. Four power administrations within DOE oversee the production and sale of electricity produced in federal hydroelectric power plants. DOE also works nationwide to support the modernization of the nation's electric grid to make electric energy more efficient and more reliable.

Nuclear Energy and Weapons

DOE works closely with the NRC to oversee the nation's nuclear energy industry. DOE's Nuclear Energy Office manages research programs for both fission and fusion energy systems. Naval nuclear reactors are managed directly by DOE, but the department shares responsibility with the NRC for management and regulation of civilian reactors. Through

its Office of Civilian Radioactive Waste Management, DOE is responsible for both civilian and military radioactive waste storage and disposal.

The National Nuclear Security Administration (NNSA), an agency within DOE, oversees military nuclear technology. This includes military nuclear reactors, such as naval nuclear propulsion systems, as well as the nation's nuclear arsenal. American nuclear weapons are technically on loan to the Department of Defense from DOE. The NNSA assumes responsibility for the manufacture, maintenance, transport, and safekeeping of these nuclear weapons. DOE also works to limit the proliferation of nuclear weapons through controls on the export of technology that could be used in the production of such weapons.

Environmental and Conservation Efforts

DOE works with other federal agencies, such as the Environmental Protection Agency (EPA), to research technologies that may reduce the environmental impacts of energy production and use. Much of this research is conducted through DOE's Office of Energy Efficiency and Renewable Energy (EERE), which supports research into renewable energy technologies such as wind, solar, hydroelectric, and geothermal. EERE is involved in research into high-risk, high-value energy technologies that private industry is unwilling to investigate until they can be proven economically viable. DOE also works with local and state governments to provide information on energy efficiency and clean energy technology.

In addition to its role in developing new sources of clean energy, DOE works to promote energy conservation and supports research into more efficient energy production, transmission, and consumption. As part of this work, DOE is involved, along with the EPA, in supporting the Energy Star program, which promotes efficiency in a wide variety of home and office products. The Weatherization Assistance Program, administered by EERE, assists low-income home owners with weatherproofing their homes and making them more energy-efficient. EERE also provides information to the public regarding energy-efficient construction.

Raymond D. Benge, Jr.

Further Reading

Consumer's Union of the United States. "Energy Star Has Lost Some Luster." *Consumer Reports*, October, 2008, 24-26.

Dietz, Thomas, and Paul C. Stern, eds. *Public Participation in Environmental Assessment and Decision Making.* Washington, D.C.: National Academies Press, 2008.

Holl, Jack. *The United States Department of Energy: A History.* Washington, D.C.: Government Printing Office, 1982.

See also: Atomic Energy Commission; Energy conservation; Energy-efficiency labeling; Environmental Protection Agency; Nuclear Regulatory Commission

---

■ Department of the Interior, U.S.

FIELDS OF STUDY: Government, Politics, International Relations; Organizations, Agencies, Commissions, Centers; Regulation, Standards and Practices; Energy and Energy Resources; Renewable Resources; Mineral Resources

CATEGORIES: Organizations and agencies; land and land use; resources and resource management

IDENTIFICATION: Cabinet-level division of the executive branch of the U.S. government responsible for the management of federally owned lands and underground natural resources

DATE: Created on March 3, 1849

Because vast sections of the U.S. territorial landmass fall outside the realm of private ownership, a separate body of laws and special administrative arrangements are required to guard the common material and ecological interests of the American people. The U.S. Department of the Interior is charged with overseeing those interests.

The idea of a federal administration responsible for internal, or domestic, affairs came in the first stages of the United States' independence, but it was not until James Polk's presidency that a bill creating the Department of the Interior was passed by Congress. Proponents of the new federal department argued that a number of essential governmental activities had for many years been placed under executive branch administrations that had no logical connection with them. Two examples (in the first half of the nineteenth century) were the General Land Office under the secretary of the treasury and the Indian Affairs Office under the Department of War.

By the twenty-first century eleven major administrative subsections were operating within the Department of the Interior. Of these the most important, or at least most widely recognized by the public at large, are the Bureau of Land Management (BLM), the National Park Service (NPS), the Bureau of Indian Affairs (BIA), and the U.S. Geological Survey (USGS).

The National Park Service is the most publicly visible agency under the secretary of the interior. The NPS is responsible for the administration of more than fifty national parks (the first of which, Yellowstone National Park, was established in 1872) as well as more than three hundred other sites that together receive millions of visitors yearly. Each national park is overseen by highly trained and professional NPS staff with the goal of maintaining the highest levels of ecological responsibility while at the same time offering public access to extraordinary natural sites.

BLM activities cover a wide range of concerns related to the management of more than 101 million hectares (250 million acres) of federal land and some 283 million hectares (700 million acres) of underground mineral deposits. Beyond overall supervision of this public domain, the BLM is charged with a number of specific responsibilities, ranging from support for private implementation of large-scale renewable energy projects to the management of populations of wild horses and burros on BLM lands. Within the vast extent of BLM lands are several categories of land use and infrastructure that require special administration. These include 64,000 kilometers (40,000 miles) of roads, 850 bridges, and more than 29,000 kilometers (18,000 miles) of recreational trails.

An important responsibility of the BLM—acting in cooperation with its sister branch the USGS—is to lease out land-use rights to private investors engaged in productive exploitation of government-owned lands. A large part of such leasing involves seasonal grazing rights for ranchers. Even more productive in terms of BLM revenues (but controversial from the viewpoint of some environmentalists) is the leasing out of a variety of mining rights. Companies operating under agreements with the BLM pay royalties

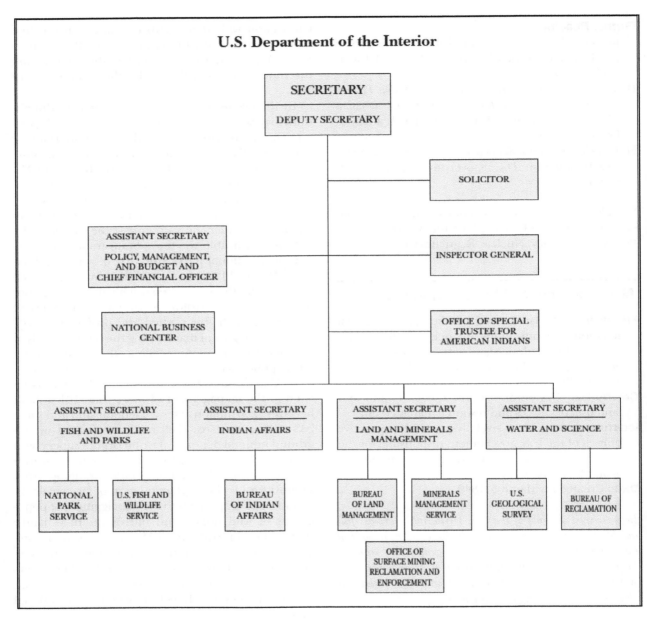

U.S. Department of the Interior

to the government according to the value of (for example) energy resources they extract and market from BLM lands. An example of this process is found in the area of oil and gas production. In 2008 the BLM collected a total of $5.5 billion from companies engaged in oil and gas extraction on BLM lands. Such funds are shared equally between the states where the lands are located and the U.S. Treasury, usually with the assumption that the revenues will be invested in some form of energy development, with increasing emphasis on renewable energy sources.

The Bureau of Indian Affairs, which evolved out of the original 1824 Indian Affairs Office, is overseen by the Department of the Interior's assistant secretary for Indian affairs. The BIA is responsible for administering more than 20.2 million hectares (50 million acres) of land held in trust by the federal government for 564 Native American tribes. Three major offices work within the BIA through twelve regional offices and more than eighty local agencies. The most general office is the Office of Indian Services, which oversees general assistance (Indian child welfare, tribal government organization, and so on) and services connected with reservation road maintenance and assistance following natural disasters.

The Office of Justice Services of the BIA oversees all issues relating to local law enforcement in coordination with tribal police (more than two hundred law-enforcement agencies are involved, including a police academy) and a network of local tribal courts. A third key office of the BIA is the Office of Trust Services, which assists in administering specific tribal trust lands, assets, and natural resources.

The role of the U.S. Geological Survey (created in 1879) dovetails, in one way or another, with the work of all other branches of the Department of the Interior. The USGS, which is headquartered in Reston, Virginia, and operates branch offices in Colorado and California, carries out extensive mapping operations as part of its general responsibility to classify public lands according to their geological structure and mineral resources. It also works in cooperation with international scientific agencies to monitor earthquake and volcanic activity throughout the world.

Byron Cannon

Further Reading

Andrews, Richard N. L. *Managing the Environment, Managing Ourselves: A History of American Environmental Policy.* 2d ed. New Haven, Conn.: Yale University Press, 2006.

Merchant, Carolyn. *American Environmental History: An Introduction.* New York: Columbia University Press, 2007.

Platt, Rutherford H. *Land Use and Society: Geography, Law, and Public Policy.* Rev. ed. Washington, D.C.: Island Press, 2004.

See also: Bureau of Land Management, U.S.; Fish and Wildlife Service, U.S.; National Park Service, U.S.; National parks; Overgrazing of livestock; Sagebrush Rebellion; Watt, James; Wild horses and burros

■ Desertification

FIELDS OF STUDY: Biology, Life Sciences, Ecosystems; Ecology, Environment, Environmentalism

CATEGORIES: Land and land use; resources and resource management

DEFINITION: Land degradation in arid, semiarid, and dry subhumid regions brought about by human activities and climatic variations, such as prolonged droughts

Desertification is recognized by scientists and policy makers as a major economic, social, and environmental problem that occurs in roughly two-thirds of the world's countries and threatens one-fifth of the world's population. Coupled with climate effects, humankind's misuse and overuse of the land can render it unproductive.

Deserts are climatic regions that receive less than 25 centimeters (10 inches) of precipitation per year. They constitute the most widespread of all climates of the world and occupy 25 percent of the world's land area. Most deserts are surrounded by semiarid climates referred to as steppes, which occupy 8 percent of the world's lands. Deserts occur in the interiors of continents, on the leeward sides of mountains, and along the west sides of continents in subtropical regions. All of the world's deserts risk further desertification.

Scientists use various methods to determine the historical climatic conditions of a region. These methods include studies of the historical distribution of trees and shrubs as determined from deposit patterns in lakes and bogs, patterns of ancient sand dunes, changes in lake levels through time, archaeological records, and tree rings (dendrochronology).

The largest deserts occur in North Africa, Asia, Australia, and North America. Four thousand to six thousand years ago, these desert areas were less extensive and were occupied by prairie or savanna grasslands. Rock paintings found in the Sahara show that humans during an earlier era in that region hunted buffalo and raised cattle on grasslands where giraffes browsed. The region near the Tigris and Euphrates rivers was also fertile. In the desert of northwest India, cattle and goats were grazed, and people lived in cities that have long since been abandoned. The deserts in the southwestern region of North America appear to have been wetter, according to studies of tree rings from this area. Ancient Palestine, which includes the Negev Desert of present-day Israel, was a lush area occupied by three million people.

The United Nations has predicted that future desertification will claim an area the size of the United States, the former Soviet Union, and Australia combined. As of 2006 the world's deserts were estimated to support more than 500 million inhabitants. It has been stated that "the forests came before civilization, the deserts after." Climate created the deserts, but humankind has aided their growth across the grasslands of the steppe and savanna climatic boundaries.

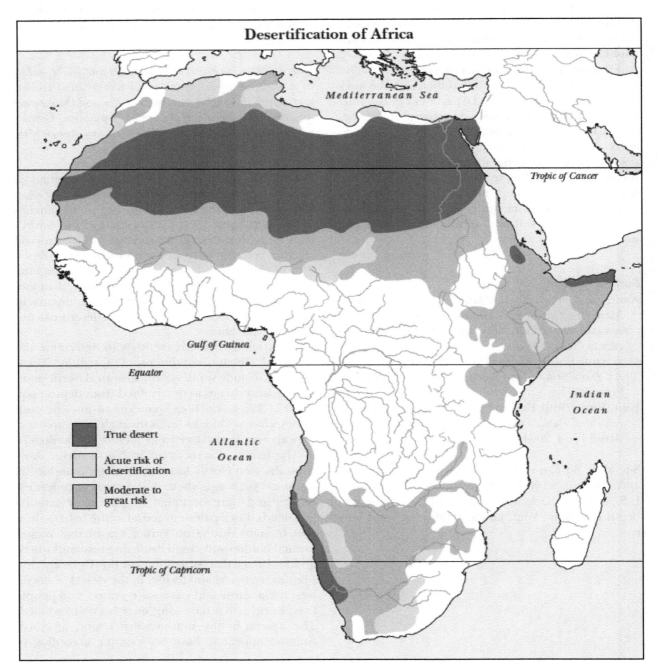

Desertification of Africa

Legend:
- True desert
- Acute risk of desertification
- Moderate to great risk

According to the United Nations, the world's hyperarid or extreme deserts are the Atacama and Peruvian deserts (located along the west coast of South America), the Sonoran Desert of North America, the Takla Makan Desert of central Asia, the Arabian Desert of Saudi Arabia, and the Sahara of North Africa, which is the largest nonpolar desert in the world. The arid zones surround the extreme desert zones, and the semiarid zones surround the arid zones. Areas having a high risk of becoming desert surround the semiarid zones. By the late 1980's the expanding deserts were claiming about 6.1 million hectares (15 million acres) of land per year, or an area approximately the size of the state of West Virginia. The total area threatened by desertification equaled about 37.5 million square kilometers (14.5 million square miles). According to a 2004 United Nations estimate, roughly 6 million hectares (14.8 million acres) of productive land have been lost to desertification every year since 1990.

Causes

Two main factors influence the process of desertification: climatic variations and human activities. The major deserts of the world are located in areas of high atmospheric pressure, which experience subsiding dry air unfavorable to precipitation. Since the late 1960's subtropical deserts have been experiencing prolonged periods of drought that have caused these areas to be dryer than usual.

The problem of desertification came to the attention of the world during the late 1960's and early 1970's as a result of severe drought in the Sahel, a region that extends in an east-west direction along the southern margin of the Sahara in West Africa. Rainfall declined an average of 30 percent in the Sahel, and scientific research was conducted to examine the natural mechanisms causing the drought. One set of studies was related to changes in global circulation patterns associated with changes in heat distribution in the oceans. A correlation was found between sea surface temperatures and the reduction of rainfall in the Sahel. It was determined that the Atlantic Ocean's higher surface temperatures south of the equator and lower temperatures north of the equator west of Africa are associated with lower precipitation in northern tropical Africa. However, the exact cause of the change in sea surface temperature patterns remained undetermined.

Land-cover changes play a major role in desertification. A lack of rain causes the ground and soils to become extremely dry, which allows the thin soil to blow or wash away. As the water table drops from the lack of natural recharge of aquifers and the withdrawal of water by the desert's inhabitants, the people who live on the land are forced to migrate to the grasslands and forests at the fringes of the desert. Overgrazing, overcultivation, misuse of pesticides and fertilizers, deforestation, and poor irrigation practices (which can cause salinization of soils) eventually lead to a repetition of the process, and the desert begins to encroach on its surroundings. Changes in population size, climate, and social and economic conditions can speed the desertification process.

The fundamental cause of desertification, therefore, is human activity. Anthropogenic change is intensified when factors such as seasonal dryness, drought, and high winds stress an already fragile dryland ecosystem. Many different forms of social, economic, and political pressure can cause the overutilization of these arid environments. People may be pushed onto unsuitable agricultural land because of land shortages, poverty, and other uncontrollable forces, while farmers overcultivate the fields in the few remaining fertile land areas.

Consequences

A reduction in vegetation cover and soil quality may affect the local climate by causing a rise in temperatures and a reduction in moisture. This can, in turn, have impacts on the area beyond the desert by causing changes in the climate and atmospheric patterns of the region. Substantial vegetation cover changes in humid and subhumid areas have the potential to cause significant regional climatic changes. Desertification is a global problem because it can cause the loss of vegetation and animal diversity, as well as the pollution of rivers, lakes, and oceans. As a result of excessive rainfall and flooding in subhumid areas, fields lacking sufficient vegetation may be eroded by runoff.

Desertification can also lead to food shortages, which are often accompanied by social unrest. Unless food production, distribution, and costs can meet the needs of the world's expanding population, hunger and other untenable conditions associated with desertification could cause millions of refugees and emigrants to flee the developing and the least developed countries. The ongoing loss of productive land to desertification, however, affects the world's ability to keep up with global requirements for food production.

Studies have been conducted to determine how rising levels of greenhouse gases are likely to affect the rate of desertification. Rising temperatures and changes in rainfall patterns influence desertification; desertification and even the efforts to combat it may in turn affect climatic change because they influence the emission and absorption of greenhouse gases. Desert soils hold more than one-fourth of the world's organic carbon stores and almost all of its inorganic carbon. Declines in vegetation and soil quality can result in the release of carbon, while revegetation can influence the absorption of carbon from the atmosphere. The use of fertilizers to reclaim drylands may cause an increase in nitrous oxide emissions. Conclusive evidence to support such theories has not yet been gathered, however.

Combating Desertification

In response to the 1968-1974 drought in Sahelian West Africa, representatives from various countries met in Nairobi, Kenya, in 1977 for a United Nations conference on desertification. The conference resulted in the Plan of Action to Combat Desertification, which listed twenty-eight measures that national, regional, and international organizations could take to combat land degradation. A lack of adequate funding and commitment by governments caused the plan to fail, however; when the United Nations Environment Programme (UNEP) assessed the plan in 1991, it found that little had been accomplished and that the desertification problem had worsened.

As a result of the 1977 United Nations conference, several countries developed national plans of action to combat desertification. In Kenya, local organizations worked with primary schools to plant five thousand to ten thousand seedlings per year. One U.S.-based organization promoted reforestation by providing materials to establish nurseries, training programs, and extension services. Community-level efforts to combat desertification yielded promising results, and UNEP recognized that such projects tend to have a greater success rate than top-down projects. Participants at the Earth Summit, held in

Rio de Janeiro, Brazil, in 1992, supported the concept of sustainable development at the community level to combat the problem of desertification.

In 1994, the United Nations Convention to Combat Desertification (UNCCD) was adopted. A direct result of the Earth Summit, this legally binding international instrument is an agreement between developing and developed countries to address desertification as a global coalition. Of all the multilateral environmental agreements, the UNCCD has the largest membership (193 parties as of 2008).

The UNCCD prioritizes Africa, where desertification processes have affected about 46 percent of the continent. The convention's stated principles include the need for the populations and communities who suffer desertification's effects to be involved in designing and implementing the programs intended to combat the problem. Cooperative exchange is encouraged not only between developed and developing countries but also among those countries, regions, and communities affected by desertification. Sustainable development and an integrative approach to the physical, biological, and socioeconomic aspects of desertification are also emphasized, as is poverty eradication as a key component of effective antidesertification efforts.

Roberto Garza; updated by Karen N. Kähler

Further Reading

Chiras, Daniel D. "Creating a Sustainable System of Agriculture to Feed the World's People." In Environmental Science. 8th ed. Sudbury, Mass.: Jones and Bartlett, 2010.

Geist, Helmut. The Causes and Progression of Desertification. Burlington, Vt.: Ashgate, 2005.

Glantz, Michael H., ed. Desertification: Environmental Degradation in and Around Arid Lands. Boulder, Colo.: Westview Press, 1977.

Gore, Rick. "The Desert: An Age-Old Challenge Grows." National Geographic, November, 1979, 594-639.

Goudie, Andrew. "The Human Impact on Vegetation." In The Human Impact on the Natural Environment: Past, Present, and Future. 6th ed. Malden, Mass.: Blackwell, 2005.

Hulme, Mike, and Mick Kelly. "Exploring the Links Between Desertification and Climate Change." Environment 35, no. 6 (July/August, 1993): 4-1.

United Nations. Convention to Combat Desertification Secretariat. Desertification: Coping with Today's Global Challenges. Eschborn, Germany: Author, 2008.

See also: Aral Sea destruction; Deforestation; Environmental justice and environmental racism; Grazing and grasslands; Kalahari Desert; Nile River; Soil salinization; Sustainable development; United Nations Convention to Combat Desertification

---

■ Deserts & dunes

FIELDS OF STUDY: Ecology; Ecosystem Management; Environmental Studies; Physical Geography;

KEY CONCEPTS:

ARIDISOL: a type of soil that contains little or no organic matter; typically alkaline and composed mostly of salts such as chlorides, sulfates, and carbonates

DEFLATION: the removal of particles of clay, dust, sand, and rock from dry soil by strong winds

DESERT PAVEMENT: a surface covered by a thin layer of small, round, stones that are closely packed together; the residual deposits left behind after the process of deflation

DESERT VARNISH: a smooth, dark, hard, shiny coating that forms on exposed rock in desert environments; usually the film is composed of manganese or iron oxides

EOLIAN: of a deposit, arising from or carried by the action of the wind

ERG: any vast, flat area of desert covered in sand; applied especially to the sand dunes of the Sahara Desert

FLUVIAL: of a deposit, arising from, carried by, or occurring in a river

PLAYA: a flat, dry lake-bed usually characterized by clay or salt deposits, where rainwater accumulates temporarily but eventually evaporates or moves underground; also called a pan or a dry lake

RAIN SHADOW: a dry region that forms on the side of a mountainous area protected from the prevailing winds and, therefore, the moisture they carry

SALTATION: a bouncing, jumping motion in which small, hard particles such as sand move over an uneven surface as a result of the flow of air or water

SLIP FACE: the sloping side of a dune that faces away from the prevailing wind; also called lee slope

WASH: a narrow channel or streambed that is dry through most of the year but that can become partly or totally submerged during flash floods that occur during sudden heavy rains; also called wadi

Deserts are arid or semiarid regions, defined as areas that receive an extremely small quantity of precipitation each year. Deserts and semideserts cover approximately one-third of the earth's total surface area and are found on every continent. Deserts and semideserts are characterized by unique geological and ecological features that are not present in more humid environments. These features include dunes, which are landforms of loose, shifting mounds or ridges made of sand or other sedimentation.

Desert Characteristics

Although the word "desert" immediately conjures an unmistakable image of a hot, sandy expanse, starkly empty of life, a great deal of variation makes up desert environments. While many are hot, some are freezing cold. Some border the ocean and others have annual rainy seasons. Three-fourths of desert surfaces are covered not by sand but rather by some other material, such as clay, rock, ice, or aridisol, a type of soil that contains little or no organic matter. (Aridisols are typically alkaline and composed mostly of salts such as chlorides, sulfates, and carbonates.)

Multiple definitions of deserts and systems for classifying them exist. One of the most widely used desert classification systems was developed by American scholar and field geographer Peveril Meigs, in the 1950's. Meigs sorted the earth's dry regions based on the amount of precipitation each receives in a year. Regions with twelve or more months in a row with no rainfall are known as extremely arid; regions that receive less than 250 millimeters (10 inches), of rainfall per year are known as arid; regions that receive between 250 and 500 millimeters (10–20 inches) of rainfall per year are known as semiarid. Only extremely arid and arid regions qualify as true deserts; semiarid regions, which are often unforested grasslands that border deserts, are sometimes known as steppes. Another way of defining a desert draws on a system developed by Russian-born German climatologist Wladimir Köppen, who proposed that a desert be identified as a region that loses more water each year through evaporation than it gains through precipitation.

Many deserts, despite being arid most of the year, do have some surface water. Ponds, lakes, and streams may form temporarily during brief heavy rainstorms, causing flash floods. Some deserts, however, are also crossed by permanent bodies of water, such as Egypt's Nile River or the Rio Grande in the Chihuahuan Desert; both of these rivers have their sources in high mountainous areas and traverse the desert on their way to the coast. In other deserts, subsurface water exists in the form of underground aquifers, or reservoirs of water, that sometimes rise to the surface and create oases, or isolated regions of fertile land.

Major Deserts of the World

The majority of the world's desert regions are located within two bands, or belts, each of which is within 25 degrees of the equator. In these belts, dry trade winds cause cloud cover to disperse, letting sunlight quickly heat the earth's surface. The Sahara Desert in North Africa is an example of a trade wind desert. The Sahara, which stretches from the Atlantic Ocean to the Red Sea, is the largest hot desert in the world. The central Sahara region, which occupies an area of about 9.1 million square kilometers (sq km), or about 3.5 million square miles, is the driest; its regions to the north and south receive more precipitation and are more vegetated. The central Sahara is recorded as receiving less than 25 millimeters (1 inch) of rainfall per year, although precipitation patterns are extremely erratic there. There may be some years when this region receives no rainfall at all, but it is also possible that brief, intense thunderstorms may occur.

Much of the central Sahara is covered in ergs, or vast, flat, sandy areas. However, the region also is marked by a variety of surface landforms, including large dunes (such as Chech dune and Raoui dune); flat, high, stone plateaus; wide plains covered in gravel; dry riverbeds or wadis; low-lying salt flats; and the occasional oasis. A few mountain ranges, such as the Ahaggar (also known as the Hoggar) and the Tibesti mountains, also occur in this area. The Sahara is an extremely windy place, where temperatures of higher than 50 degrees Celsius (122 degrees Fahrenheit) have been recorded; winter and nighttime temperatures, though, may dip to below freezing.

The equatorial belt region also is home to a type of desert known as a rain shadow desert. These are dry areas that form between two mountain ranges that each block moist air currents from being blown toward the valley they enclose. The Gobi Desert is a rain shadow desert kept arid by the vast mountain ranges of the Himalayas; it spans northern China and southern Mongolia (*gobi* is the Mongolian word for "desert") and is bounded by, among other mountains, the Altai and Hangayn (or Khangai) to the north and the Yin and Qilian to the south.

Much of the Gobi, which occupies an area of about 1.3 million square kilometers (about 500,000 square miles), is not covered in sand, but dry sedimentary rock such as chalk and gypsum. These rock plains were formed 65 million or more years ago, and the Gobi has been the source of dinosaur and other fossils and of the remains of Stone Age societies. The climate in this region is marked by bitterly cold winters and warm summers. The total yearly rainfall in the Gobi ranges from about 200 millimeters (about 8 inches) in the northeast, which receives summer monsoons, to less than 50 millimeters (about 2 inches) in the extremely arid west.

Not all of the world's deserts, however, have formed near the equator. In cold environments like at the earth's poles, the air can no longer hold much moisture and there is little or no precipitation; any water that exists on the surface is not found in rivers or lakes, but is locked in the form of ice. The inland plateau of the Antarctic receives little snow, and it is considered the world's largest desert at more than 14.2 million square kilometers (about 5.5 million square miles). Although the rest of the continent is marked by such varied surface features as mountains, glaciers, and coral reefs, the Antarctic desert is relatively featureless. The snow is packed into flat, firm plains marked only by small dune-like formations known as sastrugi (or zastrugi).

Dune Formation Processes

For a dune to form, a handful of key environmental factors must first be met. First, an abundant supply of dry sediment, usually sand, must exist. Second, there must be a way to transport that material, such as winds or moving water. These winds or water must be moving quickly enough to move the sediment, but not so powerfully as to destroy the mounds that are formed. Finally, there must be a place for the accumulated sediment to be deposited. The sand that makes up a dune may come from the eolian processes that erode mineral particles from the surface of rocks, or may be composed of biological materials like the calcium-carbonate-rich crumbled shells or skeletons of marine organisms.

In a dune formed by eolian, or wind-driven, processes, sand particles may be transported in several different ways. Extremely tiny or light particles may be held in place vertically while they move long distances horizontally; their weight is fully supported by upward currents of air, while turbulent eddies of wind push them forward. This process is known as suspension. In saltation, particles move downwind in a continuous series of hops, skips, and jumps. Each time a particle jumps, it moves a short distance only, but as it moves it hits other particles and triggers them to hop forward as well. In the process of creep, saltating particles that hit large, heavy grains may push those grains slowly downwind.

All of these processes cause sand particlesto build up, though they do not necessarily create dunes. They may form sand sheets, or flat sandy plots of land, or ripples, which are low crests and troughs on the surface of a sandy surface (with the biggest particles at the crests). Ripples can grow into dunes under the continued action of the wind, which keeps moving particles up to the crest of the pile by saltation and creep, until the slip face becomes steep enough to collapse in a tiny avalanche. This collapsing sand becomes stabilized at a particular angle, known as the angle of repose. As this cycle of build up and collapse repeats, the dune inches forward in the direction of the wind.

The process by which underwater or riverbed dunes are formed through fluvial, or water-driven, processes, is similar. However, fluvial processes can carry larger particles in suspension than can be carried by eolian processes. In addition, saltation is less common underwater than it is in air, and suspension is more common. Finally, some particles are carried by rivers as dissolved sediments, which later recrystallize.

Types of Dunes

A minimum of five primary types of dunes—crescentic, linear, dome, parabolic, and star—have been identified by geologists, although many additional subtypes and variations exist. The basic category a dune falls into depends on its geometric shape, which is determined by factors such as wind direction and strength, sediment type and quantity, and the presence or absence of vegetation.

Crescentic dunes, as their name implies, roughly resemble a crescent moon in shape. Narrow curved tips form at the edges of the dune, pointing downwind; the dune's concave slip face (a slip face is a slope on the opposite side of the prevailing wind) is between these tips. Crescentic dunes are also known as barchans and are the most common dune shape on Earth. Typically, they form in areas where the land is flat and, the wind blows consistently from a single direction. These fast-moving dunes have been known to travel as quickly as 100 meters (about 328 feet) per year across a desert.

Sand ridges that are either long and straight or sinuous—curving back and forth—are called linear, or longitudinal, dunes. Particularly, sinuous dunes are sometimes known as seifs, from the Arabic word for "sword." (Ancient Eastern swords had curving blades.) Linear dunes often form when there are winds that blow from two directions; each wind forms ridges that are parallel to the direction in which it blows. Rare dome dunes are roughly oval or circular in shape and do not have a clear slip face; parabolic dunes are shaped like the letter *U* and often form in deserts that are near a coast. The long arms of such dunes point upwind and are stabilized by the presence of vegetation growing in the sand, while the convex curve of a parabolic dune is pushed forward by the wind. Finally, star dunes are composed of a tall central mound from which several long arms—a minimum of three—radiate outward. Each arm has its own slip face and is formed by a wind that blows in a different direction. Star dunes are common in certain parts of the Sahara Desert.

Any of these types of dunes may be further described as either simple, compound, or complex. Simple dunes have the minimum number of slip faces required to fall into a particular category; they usually form when the prevailing wind or winds remain relatively stable in strength and direction. Compound dunes, which tend to be large, comprise two or more smaller dunes with the same geometric shape, forming one atop the next. Complex dunes are similar to compound dunes, but they are formed of multiple smaller dunes with different geometric shapes. For complex dunes to form, the strength and direction of the wind or winds must change after the formation of the first dune.

Desertification

Desertification is defined as the degradation of formerly fertile land—that is, the decrease in the ability of what was once productive land to support the continued growth of vegetation. Desertification can be attributed to a variety of complex environmental factors, including the loss of nutrients and moisture in the soil, increased salinization of soil, and an increase in wind and water erosion. In the course of Earth's history, desert regions have formed, enlarged, and shrunk in size because of natural processes that had nothing to do with human activities. Desertification, however, is accelerating because of anthropogenic causes.

An estimated 70 percent of the world's dryland regions are experiencing either moderate or severe desertification. This phenomenon is caused by droughts and changes in temperature, cloud cover, and wind patterns from global warming, overgrazing, deforestation, irrigation, and other effects of unsustainable human land use. For example, livestock grazing on already semiarid land can remove vegetation that would otherwise prevent the erosion of soil by wind or water, and repeated cultivation of crops on the same land may deplete the supply of nutrients contained in the soil or make it harder for it to absorb water. Proximity to an existing desert is not necessary for desertification to occur.

M. Lee

Further Reading

Abraham, Athol D., and Anthony J. Parsons. *Geomorphology of Desert Environments*. Springer, 2009.

Aleshire, Peter. *Deserts*. Chelsea House, 2008.

Doran, Peter T., W. Berry Lyons, and Diane M. McKnight, eds. *Life in Antarctic Deserts and Other Cold, Dry Environments*. Oxford University Press, 2010.

Laity, Julie. *Deserts and Desert Environments*. Wiley-Blackwell, 2008.

Mather, Anne. "Arid Environments." In *Environmental Sedimentology*, edited by Chris Perry and Kevin Taylor. Blackwell, 2007.

Maun, Anwar M. *The Biology of Coastal Sand Dunes*. Oxford University Press, 2009.

Pye, Kenneth, and Haim Tsoar. *Aeolian Sand and Sand Dunes*. Springer, 2008.

Verstraete, Michel M., Robert J. Scholes, and Mark Stafford Smith. "Climate Change and Desertification: Looking at an Old Problem Through New Lenses." *Frontiers in Ecology and the Environment* 7, no. 8 (October 2009): 421–428.

■ Destruction of the northern spotted owl's habitat

FIELDS OF STUDY: Biology, Life Sciences, Ecosystems; Animals, Zoology, Marine Biology; Ecology, Environment, Environmentalism; Forests, Forestry; Public Policy, Debates, Controversies

IDENTIFICATION: Medium-sized, dark brown owl native to the coniferous forests of southwestern Canada and the northwestern United States

Destruction of northern spotted owl habitats by timber companies has led to intense conflict between loggers trying to earn a living and environmentalists striving to save this threatened species and the old-growth forests it inhabits. A 1995 U.S. Supreme Court decision regarding the owl upheld the government's authority to conserve habitat as part of its efforts to protect a threatened or endangered species.

The northern spotted owl (*Strix occidentalis caurina*) favors a habitat of old-growth trees for foraging, roosting, and nesting. The survival of the species has been threatened by the commercial harvesting of old-growth timber in California, Oregon, Washington, and British Columbia. During the 1880's the owl's habitat totaled about 6.1 million hectares (15 million acres); one century later it had dwindled to fewer than 2 million hectares (5 million acres), almost entirely on federal lands.

In 1984 four conservation groups appealed the U.S. Forest Service's regional plans for timber harvesting within the owl's range. Four years later, federal regulators proposed setting aside up to 890 hectares (2,200 acres) of suitable habitat for each nesting pair of owls. While timber companies argued that such a policy would lead to dire economic consequences in the region, environmentalists insisted that more habitat was needed. In 1990 the northern spotted owl was listed as a threatened species under the 1973 Endangered Species Act. The next year, environmental groups sued the U.S. Department of the Interior for failing to protect the owl, and a federal district court in Seattle, Washington, ordered the cessation of logging operations in the region's old-growth federal forests. In 1992 the U.S. Fish and

Northern Spotted Owl. By Bureau of Land Management (Northern Spotted Owl)

Wildlife Service (FWS) designated critical habitat for the owl on almost 2.8 million hectares (6.9 million acres) of federal lands in the Pacific Northwest. During that year's presidential campaign, candidate Bill Clinton promised that if elected he would convene a summit to consider the spotted owl controversy.

At the resulting Forest Summit in 1993, President Clinton and members of his cabinet met in Portland, Oregon, with representatives from environmental groups, the timber industry, and the salmon fishery industry. Thousands of timber workers gathered in Portland to demonstrate their concerns about the recent loss of between thirteen thousand and twenty thousand jobs in the industry. Clinton subsequently announced a compromise plan that allowed the logging industry to cut about 1.2 billion board feet of timber each year, down from about 5 billion board feet each year during the preceding decade. The administration estimated that only six thousand jobs would be lost as a result of the logging cutback. To compensate for the loss, the president asked Congress to create the Northwest Economic Adjustment Fund, which would provide $1.2 billion in aid over the next five years. The district court of Seattle upheld the legality of the Clinton plan.

The timber industry went to court to challenge the Clinton administration's broad interpretation of the Endangered Species Act. At issue was whether the government might restrict activities, such as logging, that only indirectly limit the habitat of the northern spotted owl. In *Babbitt v. Sweet Home Chapter of Communities for a Great Oregon* (1995), the U.S. Supreme Court ruled that the government has the discretionary authority to protect any habitat required by an endangered species.

No affected group was entirely happy with the Clinton compromise. In 1997 the U.S. Forest Service released the results of a study that found the spotted owl population was dropping by 4.5 percent per year and that the rate was accelerating. While environmentalists worried about the owl's fate, the timber industry claimed that the settlement would lead to a total of about eighty-five thousand job losses. Numerous lumber mills were forced to close, and many workers either moved elsewhere or retrained for other jobs, which often paid minimum wage. In 1996 the timber industry of Linn County, Oregon, generated only $2.1 million, about 17 percent of what it had generated eight years earlier.

In early 2003 the FWS made an agreement with logging interests to conduct a status review of the northern spotted owl and consider revisions to its critical habitat. The FWS concluded in 2004 that the owl should remain listed as a threatened species. Spotted owl populations were found to be in decline in Canada, Washington, and northern Oregon, despite habitat protection and restoration; in southern Oregon and California, populations were generally stable or experiencing only slight declines or increases.

The FWS status review also led to revision of the owl's critical habitat—a reduction of approximately 647,500 hectares (1.6 million acres), effective in September, 2008. A 2008 FWS plan for the owl's recovery proposed a network of managed habitat blocks on federal land. The FWS noted that securing habitat alone will not be sufficient to effect recovery, citing a larger, more aggressive competing species, the barred owl (*Strix varia*), that threatens to displace the northern spotted owl. The barred owl, an eastern North America native, expanded its range westward during the twentieth century. Some interbreeding and hybridization of the spotted and barred owl species have been noted.

Environmental groups lashed out at the FWS cutback in habitat area. They accused George W. Bush's presidential administration of political interference with the recovery plan and challenged the plan in court. In 2009, under the administration of President Barack Obama, the plan and revised habitat designation were remanded for reevaluation.

Thomas T. Lewis; updated by Karen N. Kähler

Further Reading

Bevington, Douglas. *The Rebirth of Environmentalism: Grassroots Activism from the Spotted Owl to the Polar Bear.* Washington, D.C.: Island Press, 2009.

Courtney, Steven P., et al. *Scientific Evaluation of the Status of the Northern Spotted Owl.* Portland, Oreg.: Sustainable Ecosystems Institute, 2004.

Johnsgard, Paul A. *North American Owls: Biology and Natural History.* Washington, D.C.: Smithsonian Institution Press, 2002.

Keiter, Robert B. "Ecology Triumphant? Spotted Owls and Ecosystem Management." In *Keeping Faith with Nature: Ecosystems, Democracy, and America's Public Lands.* New Haven, Conn.: Yale University Press, 2003.

Stout, Benjamin B. *The Northern Spotted Owl: An Oregon View, 1975-2002.* Victoria, B.C.: Trafford, 2006.

U.S. Fish and Wildlife Service. *Final Recovery Plan for the Northern Spotted Owl (Strix Occidentalis Caurina).* Portland, Oreg.: Author, 2008.

■ Destruction of the rain forests

FIELDS OF STUDY: Biology, Life Sciences, Ecosystems; Ecology, Environment, Environmentalism; Forests, Forestry; Plants, Vegetation, Botany, Horticulture.

SIGNIFICANCE: Ecosystems of diverse plant and animal species that develop in regions receiving average annual rainfall of 50 to 800 centimeters (20 to 315 inches)

Rain forests are the world's most biologically diverse terrestrial ecosystems. They also play an indispensable role in the preservation and maintenance of global climate. Logging, mining, agriculture, urbanization, and a host of other pressures related to human activity have drastically reduced the extent of rain forests, and their area continues to decline dangerously.

Overview

The world's largest rain forest, located mostly in Brazil, covers most of the Amazon River basin. Other countries with large rain forests include Indonesia, Cameroon, and Malaysia. Countries with smaller rain forests include Australia, China, Côte d'Ivoire, and Nigeria and countries of the Caribbean Islands, northern South America, and the Pacific Islands. Biodiversity in these forests is very high for both plants and animals. In the tropical rain forests, a few hundred species of plants may be found within a hectare of land. Many scientists believe that the tropical rain forests, which cover only 6 to 7 percent of the earth's surface, may house more than half of the earth's plant and animal species. Because of this, tropical rain forests constitute important laboratories for scientists worldwide. Many chemicals with important pharmaceutical properties have been found in rain-forest plants. These include quinine, long used in the treatment of malaria, and vincristine and vinblastine, used against pediatric leukemia and Hodgkin's disease.

Trees in tropical rain forests may grow to more than 90 meters (300 feet) in height. These tall trees, along with their middle-layered or middle-storied plants, have leaves that spread like a sea to form what is generally called the forest canopy. Large buttress roots such as those of the kapok trees of Brazil and the fig trees in Sabah, Malaysia, anchor the large trees while at the same time functioning to absorb essential nutrients and moisture from the soil. Nutrient recycling is critical to the luxuriant growth of plants in tropical rain forests. It is also essential for the numerous epiphytes (plants that grow nonparasitically on trees) present in the lower to middle stories of the rain forests.

Although temperate rain forests have not received the same level of media attention as tropical rain forests, they are just as fascinating and are similarly threatened with regard to loss of biodiversity. These forests, which occur in places such as the Pacific Northwest and southeastern United States, are characterized by deciduous tree species (species that shed their leaves during the winter months) or by evergreen pine tree species. Among the many important species of trees are the large redwoods (sequoias) of Northern California. These giant trees can grow to heights of more than 90 meters and are among the oldest trees in the world. Other temperate rain

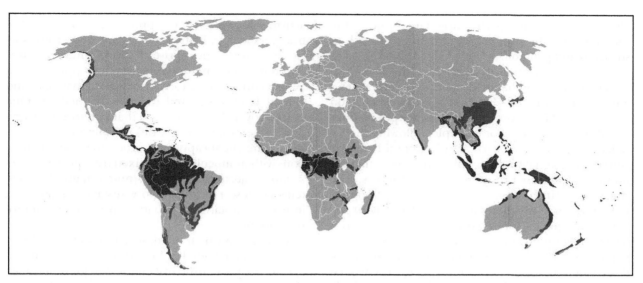

Location of tropical (dark green) and temperate/subtropical (light green) rainforests in the world. By Ville Koistinen

forests may be found in central and northern Europe, temperate South America, and New Zealand.

Importance and Destruction

The luxuriant growth of the plants in tropical rain forests gives the impression that rich and fertile soils underlie them. However, as slash-and-burn agriculture and other production techniques have demonstrated, the soils are generally infertile. The luxuriant growth is the result of the tremendous amount of nutrient recycling that takes place among species in a humid environment. Thus the removal of native plants to clear space for agriculture depletes necessary biomass for recycling and eventually exposes the soils to rapid erosional forces. After a few years of high crop productivity, yields decline dramatically, leading to further clearing of more forests.

Despite this productivity problem, the tropical rain forests play significant roles in the lives of the people who inhabit them, and they are a source of important materials for economic development. Indigenous peoples have developed the means to cohabit with other living organisms in these unique environments. However, civilization, industrialization, and population growth are gradually threatening the homelands and the very existence of these native peoples.

Rain forests exert a major influence on rainfall patterns, so that land clearance in such forests causes these areas to become drier. Perhaps most important, the abundant plant life in rain forests enhances the global environment through photosynthesis, an ongoing biological process that removes carbon dioxide from the atmosphere and produces oxygen. This process is an important factor in the prevention of global warming.

Rain-forest destruction has been occurring for many centuries. The process, which first started in the temperate rain forests of Europe and North America, greatly intensified in tropical areas during the latter half of the twentieth century. Rain forests are believed to have covered more than 14 percent of the earth's surface at one time, but they are now vanishing at such an alarming rate that countries such as Thailand, Nigeria, Indonesia, Côte d'Ivoire, and Malaysia have already lost more than half of their original forestland. Between August, 2006, and July, 2007—during a period of declining deforestation rates—Brazil lost 1.1 million hectares (2.7 million acres) of rain forest in the Amazon. In the Congo basin, rain-forest losses have threatened the very existence of several indigenous peoples. In Indonesia, which is second only to Brazil in the amount of tropical rain forest land it contains, the deforestation rate in the period 2000-2005 was 1.8 million hectares (4.4 million acres) each year.

Factors Contributing to Destruction

Many factors are responsible for the loss of tropical rain forests. These include population growth and associated development, fuelwood collection, industrialization, and mineral exploitation. Agriculture has also taken its toll, particularly large-scale cattle ranching and the production of cash crops such as soybeans and palm oil.

Human population growth—and the accompanying demand for habitable and agricultural land and other resources—has had a major impact on rain forests. Migration of large human populations has also taken its toll. For example, following the Sahelian drought of the early 1980's, Côte d'Ivoire received an estimated 1.5 million refugees, thereby putting significant pressures on its resources. The situation in Nigeria, with one of the highest population densities in Africa, is similar. By 2010 only 10 percent of Nigeria's forest cover remained, the rest having fallen to logging, agriculture, and petroleum exploration. It has been estimated that at the rate of destruction seen in the first decade of the twenty-first century, Nigeria may be without rain forests by 2020. Meanwhile, as cities expand and new megalopolises are created in industrialized countries, temperate rain forests also continue to lose ground.

Related to population growth is the growing need for energy. Many countries that still have abundant rain forests use wood as their main source of energy. Therefore, along with intensive logging for export, cutting wood as biomass for fuel has accelerated the destruction of the rain forests and led to severe erosional problems.

Another important factor contributing to rain forest destruction is slash-and-burn agriculture, in which land is cleared, burned, and subjected to crop and livestock production for a few years, followed by new slashing and burning of previously undisturbed forestlands. While crop yields are initially high, they rapidly decline after the second and third years. Subsistence agriculture, upon which slash-and-burn agriculture is based, was originally associated with small populations. Land could be allowed to go fallow for many years, leading to full regeneration of secondary forests under natural conditions. Increased population, along with other factors, has greatly reduced the length of time land can be allowed to go fallow, and more forests have been destroyed to keep up with demand.

Halting Destruction

Reforestation efforts have been under way for many years in Europe and North America to restore lost temperate rain forests. However, such reforestation

activities have often been approached from an industrial perspective. Plantations of only one or two species are grown, giving rise to monocultures. This is different from a natural regeneration approach that aims eventually to restore an area's original plant and animal biodiversity and watershed functions. One 2010 study in Australia found that rain-forest restoration projects involving a diverse mix of trees were more efficient at capturing carbon than were plantations with monocultures or mixed tree species. Restoration projects that strive to mimic natural ecosystems are also more likely to withstand diseases and insect infestations than are monoculture plantations.

One way in which the destruction of tropical rain forests is being halted or slowed is through the use of agroforestry systems—sustainable integrations of agriculture and forestry—to complement and reduce slash-and-burn agriculture. The collection of fuelwood can be decreased during sunny months through the use of inexpensive solar cookers, which are nonpolluting and cost nothing to operate. Another approach is the establishment of nature preserves, national parks, and large botanical gardens, as has been done successfully in Costa Rica. Promoting rain forests as destinations for sustainable tourism creates an economic incentive against deforestation. Nature preserves have also been established for a number of temperate rain forests in the United States and elsewhere. Yet another strategy is the debt-for-nature swap, in which a national debt is forgiven in exchange for environmental preservation efforts. The United States has forgiven billions of dollars in loans to a number of Central and South American countries, with the condition that these countries set aside large tracts of forestland as nature preserves.

The research organization Bioversity International, which began as an agricultural agency of the United Nations Food and Agriculture Organization, works to preserve the genetic resources of forest plants in addition to those of traditional crop resources. Facilities such as the Kew Royal Botanic Gardens in Great Britain participate in the Millennium Seed Bank, a partnership that conserves seeds for plants outside their native habitats. This program has successfully banked some 10 percent of the planet's wild plant species, focusing its efforts on plants and regions, such as rain forests, that are most at risk of being obliterated by human activity and climate change.

Participants in the 1992 Earth Summit in Rio de Janeiro, Brazil, adopted a set of principles regarding sustainable forestry, and in 2007 the United Nations General Assembly adopted the Non-legally Binding Instrument on All Types of Forests to bring all stakeholders together in sustainable forest management efforts. The first international instrument devoted to sustainable forest management, its purpose is to strengthen and provide a framework for political commitment, action, and cooperation. In 2008 the United Nations launched the United Nations Collaborative Initiative on Reducing Emissions from Deforestation and Forest Degradation, or UN-REDD. This program provides developing forested countries with financial incentives to protect and better manage their forests, thereby contributing to the fight against global climate change.

Oghenekome U. Onokpise; updated by Karen N. Kähler

Further Reading

Bush, Mark B., and John Flenley. *Tropical Rainforest Responses to Climatic Change.* Springer, 2007.

Forsyth, Adrian, Michael Fogden, and Patricia Fogden. *Nature of the Rainforest: Costa Rica and Beyond.* Comstock, 2008.

Kirk, Ruth, Jerry F. Franklin, and Louis Kirk. *The Olympic Rain Forest: An Ecological Web.* Updated ed. University of Washington Press, 2001.

London, Mark, and Brian Kelly. *The Last Forest: The Amazon in the Age of Globalization.* Random House, 2007.

Marent, Thomas, with Trent Morgan. *Rainforest.* Dorling Kindersley, 2006.

Primack, Richard B., and Richard Corlett. *Tropical Rain Forests: An Ecological and Biogeographical Comparison.* Blackwell, 2005.

Weber, William, et al., eds. *African Rain Forest Ecology and Conservation: An Interdisciplinary Perspective.* Yale University Press, 2001.

■ Detoxification (environmental)

FIELDS OF STUDY: Chemistry; Elements, Substances, Chemicals, Compounds; Pollution, Emissions, Toxic Waste, Hazardous Materials

DEFINITION: Reduction or elimination of the toxic properties of a substance to make it less harmful to or more compatible with the environment

Hazardous substances often enter the environment as the result of various manufacturing processes and other human activities. The detoxification of air, water, and soil that have been negatively affected by such substances can help to minimize environmental damage.

Increasing industrialization during the twentieth century led to the release of large amounts of hazardous waste and by-products into the environment. Pesticides were another source of toxins, as agriculture worked to maintain the crop yields necessary to feed the growing population of the world. Some toxins are analogues of harmful substances that occur naturally and may degrade rapidly by natural means. Others are more persistent in the environment and produce unwanted effects. "Detoxification" is the general term applied to the various processes by which toxins are removed from the environment or are rendered less harmful.

Toxic Substances

A substance is considered hazardous if it poses a threat to human health or the environment when it is spread, treated, disposed of, or transported. Toxic and hazardous substances often occur as a result of the manufacture of materials designed to protect humans and improve quality of life. Sources of hazardous waste include the manufacture of chemicals and allied products, the manufacture of petroleum and coal products, the primary metals industry, and the metals fabrication industry. Environmental releases of toxic chemicals may occur unintentionally through emissions from compressors, pump seals, valves, spills, pipelines, and storage tanks, or intentionally through discharges of wastes into air or water or through inappropriate disposal in landfills. The Environmental Protection Agency (EPA) has reported that Americans generate 1.6 million tons of household hazardous wastes each year.

The disposal of hazardous substances is not a simple matter. Many toxic substances are not suitable for disposal in regular landfills used for trash. Some hazardous substances are water-soluble and can leach through the soil into rivers, lakes, and groundwater supplies to pollute sources of potable water. Some wastes have a significant vapor pressure and can be spread over wide areas by wind and air currents. Corrosive wastes must be disposed of in containers that will not decompose.

Public concerns regarding toxic substances in the environment have elicited different approaches to solving these problems. Environmental activists have advocated the use of natural pesticides and nonpolluting agricultural chemicals. The U.S. Congress has addressed the issue of toxic substances in the environment with regulations that specify detoxification procedures for wastewater, contaminated soil, and landfills. These regulations include the Federal Water Pollution Control Act (1974), the Safe Drinking Water Act (1974), and the Federal Environmental Pesticide Control Act (1972).

Methods of Detoxification

Many natural processes cause detoxification of harmful substances in the environment. Gaseous pollutants or toxins that are exposed to sunlight are subject to photochemical decomposition, in which ultraviolet light causes bonds within the compounds to break. The resulting fragments react with oxygen (oxidation) or water (hydration) to form less toxic compounds. These may undergo repeated degradation in the same manner. Microbial degradation, in which organisms metabolize a wide variety of organic compounds to carbon dioxide and water or convert them into less harmful substances, promotes detoxification of many organic toxins. Some newer pesticides, such as organophosphates, are designed to degrade on repeated exposure to water, forming relatively harmless products. Earlier pesticides, such as polychlorinated biphenyls (PCBs), were found to degrade slowly in the environment. Toxins with slow detoxification pathways bioaccumulate in organisms, causing harmful effects on fish and wildlife. Such effects may be magnified in the food chain.

Efforts to supplement natural detoxification processes include enzymatic (biological) and other chemical methods. Many microorganisms capable of metabolizing toxins have been isolated and cultured in order to treat hazardous wastes. Such treatments are usually carried out at regional waste management centers. One type of chemical treatment involves chelation or precipitation. This is useful for eliminating metals, either in ionic or elemental form, from water and soil. In this method, an organic compound forms an insoluble precipitate with the metal. Filtration removes the precipitate, which can then be subjected to further disposal methods in concentrated form. Composting, or land farming, involves spreading waste materials over a large land area,

where they decompose. Pesticides and wastes from paper mills have been detoxified this way. Land farming requires monitoring to ensure that toxins in the wastes do not leach into groundwater.

Thermal treatment is considered a safer process. An example of this type of detoxification method is incineration, during which high temperatures oxidize the solid and liquid organic wastes to carbon dioxide and water in the presence of oxygen. However, people living in communities near incinerators often fear ill effects from possible emissions or leaks. One solution to this concern is the incineration of wastes on ships. *Vulcanus,* a Dutch ship, was used to incinerate large quantities of Agent Orange, a hazardous herbicide contaminated with toxic dioxins.

Another method of detoxification is vitrification, in which toxic materials are converted to glass. Vitrification has been used to dispose of asbestos, which is considered to be a highly hazardous material. It has been reported that vitrification can work with almost any kind of waste, including industrial sludges, soil contaminated by lead, and medical wastes.

Beth Ann Parker and Massimo D. Bezoari

Further Reading

Brooks, Adrienne C. "A Glass Melange: New Options for Hazardous Wastes." *Science News* 147 (January 21, 1995).

Häggblom, Max M., and Ingeborg D. Bossert, eds. *Dehalogenation: Microbial Processes and Environmental Applications.* Norwell, Mass.: Kluwer Academic, 2003.

Lave, Lester B., and Arthur C. Upton. *Toxic Chemicals, Health, and the Environment.* Baltimore: The Johns Hopkins University Press, 1987.

Newman, Michael C. *Fundamentals of Ecotoxicology.* 3d ed. Boca Raton, Fla.: CRC Press, 2010.

Shen, Samuel K., and Patrick F. Dowd. "Detoxifying Enzymes and Insect Symbionts." *Journal of Chemical Education* 69 (October, 1992): 796-780.

■ Detrimental health effects of smog

FIELDS OF STUDY: Atmospheric Chemistry; Chemical Engineering; Environmental Science; Photochemistry; Waste Management;

SIGNIFICANCE: Air pollution resulting from the combination of smoke with fog or from sunlight acting on unburned hydrocarbons emitted from automobiles

Severe smog episodes have been responsible for many deaths and widespread illness in cities around the world. Growing recognition of the detrimental health effects of smog have led many governments to pass laws designed to reduce chemical pollutants in the air.

Overview

Originally a blend of the words "smoke" and "fog," the term "smog" was coined to describe the severe air pollution that results when smoke from factories combines with fog during a temperature inversion. As one ascends upward from the earth's surface, the air temperature drops by about 3 degrees Celsius (5.5 degrees Fahrenheit) every 300 meters (1,000 feet). Temperature inversions occur when this normal condition is reversed so that a blanket of warm air is sandwiched between two cooler layers. A temperature inversion restricts the normal rise of surface air to the cooler upper layers, in effect placing a lid over a region. When the air above a city cannot rise, the air currents that carry pollutants away from their sources stagnate, causing pollution levels to increase drastically. A combination of severe air pollution, prolonged temperature inversion, and moisture-laden air may result in what has been termed "killer fog."

Photographed under the Enviromental Protection Agency's (EPA) program to document subjects of environmental concern, a plane is photographed monitoring smog over Los Angeles, c. 1972. NARA

Killer Fogs

Several acute episodes of killer fog occurred during the twentieth century. One was in the Meuse Valley of Belgium. During the first week of December, 1930, a thick fog and stagnant air from a temperature inversion concentrated pollutants spewing forth from a variety of factories in this heavily industrialized river valley. After three days of such abnormal conditions, thousands of residents became ill with nausea, shortness of breath, and coughing. Approximately sixty people died, primarily elderly people and persons with chronic heart and lung diseases. The detrimental effects on health were later attributed to sulfur oxide gases emitted by combusting fossil fuels; the gases were concentrated to lethal levels by the abnormal weather. The presence of coal soot, combined with moisture from the fog, exacerbated the effect.

A second episode occurred in Donora, Pennsylvania, during the last week of October, 1948. Donora is situated in a highly industrialized river valley south of Pittsburgh. A five-day temperature inversion with fog concentrated the gaseous effluents from steel mills with the sulfur oxides released by burning fossil fuels. Severe respiratory tract infections began to occur, especially in the elderly, and 50 percent of the population became ill. Twenty people died, a tenfold increase in the normal death rate.

A third major episode occurred in London, England, in early December, 1952. At that time, many residents burned soft coal in open grates to heat their homes. When a strong temperature inversion and fog enveloped the city for five consecutive days, Londoners began complaining of respiratory ailments. By the time the inversion had lifted, four thousand excess deaths had been recorded. In this case it was not only the elderly who were affected—deaths occurred in all age categories. During the next decade London experienced two additional episodes: one in 1956, which claimed the lives of one thousand people, and one in 1962, which caused seven hundred deaths. The decline in mortality rates resulted from the restriction of the use of soft coal, with its high sulfur content, as a source of fuel. Sulfur oxide compounds are responsible for causing lung problems during such episodes; therefore, the term "killer fog" has come to be replaced by the more accurate "sulfurous smog."

Photochemical Smog

Photochemical smog, first noticed in the Los Angeles basin in the late 1940's, has been an increasingly serious problem in cities around the world. Moisture is not part of the equation in this type of air pollution, and smoke-belching factories dumping tons of sulfur oxide compounds into the atmosphere are not required. Rather, photochemical smog results when unburned hydrocarbon fuel, emitted in automobile exhaust, is acted upon by sunlight. The Los Angeles basin, hemmed in by mountains to the east and ocean to the west, has a high density of automotive traffic and plenty of sunshine. Varying driving conditions mean that gasoline is never completely consumed by automobile engines; instead, it is often changed into other highly reactive substances. Sunlight acts as an energy catalyst that changes these compounds into the variety of powerful oxidizing agents that constitute photochemical smog. This type of smog has a faint bluish-brown tint and typically contains several powerful eye irritants. The chemical reactions also produce aldehydes, a class of organic chemical best typified by an unpleasant odor.

The complicated chemistry of photochemical smog also produces ozone, which is extremely reactive; it damages plants and irritates human lungs. Because ozone production is stimulated by sunlight and high temperatures, it becomes a particularly pernicious problem during the summer, especially during morning rush hours. Under temperature inversion conditions, the ozone created in photochemical smog can increase to dangerous levels. Ozone is highly toxic. It irritates the eyes, causes chest irritation and coughing, exacerbates asthma, and damages the lungs.

Photochemical smog and ozone are now common ingredients in urban air. Although acute episodes of ozone-induced mortality are rare, concerns have grown about the detrimental long-term consequences of the brief but repetitive exposures to ozone consistently inflicted on commuters. It appears as though no curtailment of the problem will be possible in urban areas in the United States without significant changes in transportation systems, strict limits on growth, and radical alterations in lifestyle, including automobile use.

George R. Plitnik

Further Reading

Elsom, Derek M. *Smog Alert: Managing Urban Air Quality*. Earthscan Publications, 1996.

Grant, Wyn. *Autos, Smog, and Pollution Control: The Politics of Air Quality Management in California*. Edward Elgar, 1995.

Hinrichs, Roger A., and Merlin Kleinbach. *Energy: Its Use and the Environment*. 4th ed. Thomson Brooks/Cole, 2006.

Jacobs, Chip, and William J. Kelly. *Smogtown: The Lung-Burning History of Pollution in Los Angeles*. Overlook Press, 2008.

Vallero, Daniel. *Fundamentals of Air Pollution*. 4th ed. Elsevier, 2008.

■ Development gap

FIELDS OF STUDY: Government, Politics, International Relations; International Relations, Agreements, Treaties; Nations, States, Governments; Ecology, Environment, Environmentalism

DEFINITION: Inequalities of wealth, health, and educational opportunities between rich, developed countries and poor, developing countries

The development gap highlights the interdependence of developed and developing countries. When billions of people in poor nations suffer from socioeconomic deprivation and environmental degradation, developed countries are affected by massive cross-border migration, political instability, and terrorism. The existence of the development gap makes clear the need for global cooperation and swift action to address issues that affect the environment, such as poverty and climate change.

The United Nations uses the Human Development Index to measure the progress of development of each country annually in terms of gross domestic product, educational attainment, health outcomes, and gender equality. The findings of this measurement in 2009 indicated that global disparities between rich, developed nations (often conventionally referred to as the North) and poor, developing nations (the South) were widening. While the richest 20 percent of population consumes 80 percent of global resources, 1.4 billion people in developing countries were living in extreme poverty in 2005. One in four children under the age of five years was undernourished. More than 100 million children had no access to basic education.

Poverty in developing countries is often perceived to be the result of an inadequacy of resources, but in reality the opposite is the case: Many poor countries actually possess abundant natural resources, such as dense forest in Congo, rich oil reserves in Nigeria, and gold mines in Ghana. The concept of "resource curse" has been used to explain the ironic outcomes of abundant resources leading to poverty. Scholars suggest that the abundant reserves of minerals in poor regions of the South resulted in colonialism in the eighteenth and nineteenth centuries in which rich nations of the North took advantage of the indigenous populations of those areas. These and other abundant resources also led to armed conflicts and corruption within developing countries in the postindependence era. Other factors, such as high population growth rates, weak governments, and poor infrastructure, also explain the fragile state of many poor nations.

High levels of poverty have significant impacts on the environment. Poor countries are prone to crop failure and famine because of deforestation, land degradation, desertification, and loss of biodiversity. They are less prepared than richer nations to handle the aftermath of natural disasters and are particularly vulnerable to the effects of climate change.

The lack of development in poor countries has reciprocally affected rich countries. Wars and other conflicts lead to regional instability, which often triggers massive cross-border migration; an example is the flight of Haitian refugees to the United States during the 1980's. Rapid environmental degradation in developing countries has also been linked to the acceleration of global warming.

Bridging the Gap

A wide gap between developed and developing countries is not inevitable, however. The so-called economic miracle that took place in the Far East during the 1980's and the emergence of the BRIC countries (Brazil, Russia, India, and China) during the 1990's have shown that high economic growth in a nation helps to alleviate poverty among that nation's citizens. Between 1981 and 2004, for example, some 500 million people in China climbed out of poverty

thanks to an influx of direct foreign investment, massive job opportunities, and consequently huge foreign reserves.

Since the end of the twentieth century, developed countries have increased their role in addressing global poverty. The abolition of external debt by some of the developed countries has helped to lessen the financial burdens of developing countries. Developed nations have also increased the amount of foreign aid they provide to assist poor countries in buying food and medicines and in building basic infrastructure. For example, the member countries of the Organization for Economic Cooperation and Development (OECD) alone paid out $120 billion in foreign aid in 2008.

In an attempt to deal with the complex problems associated with development, the United Nations held the Millennium Summit in September, 2000. The summit produced a set of goals, known as the Millennium Development Goals, that included halving the number of the world's total population living in extreme poverty by 2015, achieving universal primary education, and achieving environmental sustainability. Efforts to reach the goal of environmental sustainability have included the investment of increased resources in conservation, reforestation, projects to ensure clean water supplies, and improved sanitation. The 1997 Kyoto Protocol's Clean Development Mechanism assists poor countries with exploiting clean energy resources, such as solar cooking, wind farms, and biofuels. Technology transfers from developed nations have helped developing countries to adapt to environmental changes associated with climate change. Drought-resistant crops, for example, have been introduced in poor nations to help farmers cope with increasingly long dry seasons.

Obstacles and Controversies

The narrow focus on the gap between developed and developing countries—the so-called North-South divide—has been criticized as playing down the socioeconomic disparities found even within developed countries. In the United Kingdom, for example, a 2003 parliamentary report stated that 3.6 million of the nation's children were living in poverty. Other forms of disparities, such as urban-rural differences and gender gaps, both in developed and developing countries, are also deserving of attention.

The politics of development is complicated. Many scholars and nongovernmental organizations argue that the persistence of the development gap is related to the unequal global structures of agricultural and trading policies. Heavy farming subsidies in the United States and France have placed poor farmers at a disadvantage. Fluctuating commodity price levels also interfere with farmers' ability to make long-term investments and plans. Scholars have pointed out that the unsuccessful outcomes of the 2009 United Nations Climate Change Conference in Copenhagen, Denmark, demonstrate a strong sense of skepticism on the part of both developed countries (led by the United States) and developing countries (led by China) regarding the "right" path to a low-carbon economy.

Sam Wong

Further Reading

Collier, Paul. *The Bottom Billion: Why the Poorest Countries Are Failing and What Can Be Done About It.* New York: Oxford University Press, 2007.

Sen, Amartya. *Development as Freedom.* 1999. Reprint. New York: Oxford University Press, 2009.

United Nations. *Millennium Development Goals Report 2009.* New York: Author, 2009.

Whalley, John, and Sean Walsh. *Bridging the North-South Divide on Climate Post-Copenhagen.* Waterloo, Ont.: Centre for International Governance Innovation, 2009.

World Bank. *World Development Report 2000/2001: Attacking Poverty.* Washington D.C.: Author, 2000.

■ Diamond v. Chakrabarty

FIELDS OF STUDY: Government, Politics, International Relations; Trials, Court Decisions, Mediations, Adjudications; Technology and Applied Science; Inventions; Scientific Equipment, Tools, Techniques, and Methods

THE CASE: U.S. Supreme Court ruling on genetic engineering

DATE: Decided on June 16, 1980

The Supreme Court's decision in the case of Diamond v. Chakrabarty was pivotal, as the Court determined that genetically engineered microorganisms are patentable products of human ingenuity.

In 1972 Ananda Chakrabarty, a microbiologist at the General Electric Research and Development Center in Schenectady, New York, attempted to patent a genetically engineered bacterium that could decompose compounds such as camphor and octane in crude oil. Chakrabarty's patent application was initially rejected because the patent office had a long history of excluding living organisms from patent protection. Chakrabarty, through General Electric, successfully appealed this decision. In 1979 the acting commissioner of patents and trademarks appealed the reversal. The case was argued before the U.S. Supreme Court on March 17, 1980.

In a five-to-four decision, the Supreme Court ruled that living things are patentable if they represent novel, genetically altered variants of naturally occurring organisms. The majority decision held that Chakrabarty's organism is manufactured since he had inserted new genetic information into it and that the organism is new because a similar organism is unlikely to occur in nature without human intervention. The organism thus falls within the meaning of the patent statute: It is a product of human ingenuity with a distinctive name, character, and use. The minority opinion held that previous congressional acts that specifically excluded living organisms from patent protection were clearly intended to apply in this case.

This decision let emerging biotechnology companies get patent protection for their living products and allowed them potentially to capitalize on the revolution in genetic engineering. The justices of the Supreme Court realized the ramifications of their decision in terms of its impact on the ethics of patenting living things and its potential to accelerate the release of possibly harmful genetically engineered organisms. However, the basis of their decision was fundamentally narrow: Did Chakrabarty's work constitute patentable material? The Court held that the further development of biotechnology or its restrictions is a congressional and executive concern, not a judicial one.

Diamond v. Chakrabarty did not greatly influence the extent to which genetically altered organisms have been released into the environment; rather, public opposition to the release of genetically engineered organisms has played the dominant role in this area. Instead, the lasting impact of the Court's decision in *Diamond v. Chakrabarty* lies in its extension of the definition of patentable products to compounds or organisms that exist in nature but can be further manipulated by biotechnological means. This had been true only for certain hybrid plants developed through the use of conventional breeding techniques. Furthermore, the decision became the judicial basis for later decisions regarding attempts to patent genetic sequences that may be common to living organisms but require human ingenuity if they are to be extracted, sequenced, replicated, and reinserted into new organisms with their properties intact.

Mark Coyne

Further Reading

Resnik, David B. *Owning the Genome: A Moral Analysis of DNA Patenting.* Albany: State University of New York Press, 2004.

Rimmer, Matthew. *Intellectual Property and Biotechnology: Biological Inventions.* Northampton, Mass.: Edward Elgar, 2008.

■ Dichloro-diphenyl-trichloroethane (DDT)

FIELDS OF STUDY: Agriculture; Biochemistry; Chemistry; Ecosystem Management; Environmental Science; Public Health;

SIGNIFICANCE: Synthetic organochlorine insecticide

Dichloro-diphenyl-trichloroethane, better known as DDT, has been used extensively in agriculture and for control of insect-borne diseases worldwide. However, its persistence in the environment and ability to accumulate in the food chain have resulted in devastating consequences to wildlife. The harmful effects of DDT became a major focus for the emerging environmental movement during the 1960's.

Overview

During the 1930's scientists began searching for organic (carbon-based) insecticides. Prior to that time, insecticides were mainly derived from toxic metals, such as arsenic and mercury. In 1939, while experimenting with chlorinated hydrocarbons, Swiss chemist Paul Hermann Müller discovered the insecticidal properties of DDT, a chemical that had first been synthesized more than half a century earlier. His findings led to the development of the first synthetic, organic insecticide, which was introduced commercially by the Swiss chemical company J. R. Geigy A.G. in 1942. DDT was initially used to provide protection against typhus to civilians and Allied troops during World War II by killing body lice. Before that, pyrethrum powder was a common means for combating body lice; however, Japan was the chief exporter of this chrysanthemum-derived repellent, and hostilities had left the Allies with insufficient pyrethrum supplies. DDT's key role in suppressing a typhus epidemic in Italy in 1943 led to Müller's receiving the Nobel Prize in Physiology or Medicine in 1948.

When news of DDT's effectiveness was released by the British government in 1944, the U.S. Department of Agriculture (USDA) concluded that before DDT could be recommended for use by farmers, more information about its toxicity was needed. By the 1946 crop year, limited use was permitted even though evidence suggested that DDT might have some acute toxic effects on birds and that it could be stored in animal fat and excreted in milk. Commercial demand for DDT was fueled in large part by accounts of how well it had performed during wartime. The success of DDT served as an impetus for chemical companies to begin an intensive search for other organic pesticides.

Between 1940 and 1980, at least 1.8 billion kilograms (4 billion pounds) of DDT were used. More than 1,200 different formulations were developed for industrial, agricultural, and public health applications in the United States alone. Annual worldwide production peaked in 1964 at 90 million kilograms (198 million pounds).

Milestones in DDT History

Year	Event
1874	The first synthesis of DDT is reported.
1939	Paul Müller discovers DDT's insecticidal properties.
1942	The first commercial DDT formulations are introduced by the Swiss company J. R. Geigy.
1943-1945	DDT is used on civilians and military troops in Europe for the control of lice and typhus.
1946	The limited use of DDT on crops is permitted by the U.S. Department of Agriculture.
1948	Müller receives the Nobel Prize in Physiology or Medicine for the development of DDT as an insecticide. The first insects to develop resistance to DDT are observed.
1950's	DDT is used widely for agriculture, public health, and domestic pest control. Laboratory and field studies reveal the negative effects of DDT.
1957	The Clear Lake study shows the bioaccumulation of DDT in aquatic life and birds; citizens on Long Island, New York, file a suit in an attempt to halt aerial DDT spraying.
1958	Robert Barker publishes the results of studies that link DDT to declines in robin populations.
1961	Annual production levels of DDT in the United States peak at 160 million pounds.
1962	Rachel Carson publishes *Silent Spring,* which explains the dangers of DDT to a broad audience.
1963	The President's Science Advisory Committee releases a report on pesticide use that becomes the keystone of the drive to ban DDT.
1964	The U.S. Federal Commission on Pest Control is established.
1967	The Environmental Defense Fund (EDF) is formed.
1968	Joseph Hickey and Daniel Anderson publish a report on DDT's impact on declining raptor populations.
1968	The Wisconsin Hearings, the first major legal challenge to the use of DDT, begin.
1969	Malaria is virtually eliminated in China, largely as a result of DDT use.
1969	Michigan and Arizona become the first states to ban DDT use.
1969	The EDF files petitions with U.S. federal agencies seeking the elimination of the use of DDT.
1969	The use of DDT in residential areas is banned in the United States.
1970	The Environmental Protection Agency (EPA) is established.
1972	The EPA bans DDT use in the United States.
1990's	Studies suggest that DDT acts as an endocrine disrupter.
1993	Reports in the *Journal of the National Cancer Institute* claim that DDT may increase the risk of breast cancer.
1998	International negotiations to phase out the production and use of DDT and other persistent organic pollutants begin in Montreal, Canada.
2000	South Africa reintroduces the use of DDT to combat the spread of malaria by mosquitoes.
2004	DDT is among the chemicals covered by the Stockholm Convention on Persistent Organic Pollutants, an international treaty designed to eliminate or reduce the release of toxic, bioaccumulative chemicals.
2008	Twelve nations, including India and several Southern African countries, are reported to be using DDT to combat malaria.

Cloud spraying for mosquitos at Norman Park, 1947 City Council workers are cloud spraying DDT (Dichloro-Diphenyl-Trichloroethane) to a mosquito breeding swamp at Norman Park.

A New Pollutant

The insecticidal properties of DDT are related to its ability to act as a nerve poison and to pass freely through insect cuticles. In addition to causing convulsions, paralysis, and death, DDT can also interfere with calcium-dependent processes. Because DDT in crystalline form is not readily absorbed through animal skin (unlike DDT mixed in solution), the compound was initially regarded as a safe alternative to metal-based insecticides.

Although effective, DDT does have undesirable characteristics. As a broad-spectrum insecticide, DDT kills a wide variety of organisms, including beneficial insects such as bees. Also, development of resistance to DDT among pest insects was observed as early as 1948. Because of its chemical composition, DDT is preferentially stored in animal fat and is therefore not readily excreted by animals that ingest it. This fat solubility and DDT's persistence in the environment cause the pesticide to accumulate in the food chain.

The first clear evidence of the bioaccumulation of DDT came from a case study in Clear Lake, California. Between 1949 and 1957 DDT was used to control gnats on the lake. By the mid-1950's, the health of fish-eating birds in the area began to decline; several bird species, especially grebes, were dying in large numbers. Because no infectious agent was found, scientists used new analytical methods developed to measure compounds in tissues. High levels of DDT were detected in plankton, fish, and birds in and around Clear Lake. The studies also clearly showed biomagnification: Levels of pesticide residues were found to be sequentially higher at each step in the food chain, with concentrations in grebes and gulls up to 100,000 times greater than in the formulations of DDT that were sprayed.

By the mid-1950's DDT's toxicity was becoming evident throughout the United States. DDT was used in the Midwest and New England to control the elm bark beetle, an insect that spreads the fungus that causes Dutch elm disease. Several studies between 1954 and 1958 noted sharp declines in robin populations—in some areas by as much as 70 to 90 percent. Extensive aerial spraying for gypsy moths during the 1950's from Michigan to New England coincided with significant declines in many species of songbirds and bees. Ironically, this affected populations of some of the natural predators of the intended target pests.

The DDT spraying also had a negative impact on agriculture. In addition to reduced pollination caused by the loss of bees, farmers were discovering that cows' milk and farm produce were contaminated with pesticide residues. In the Pacific Northwest, DDT used to control the spruce budworm devastated salmon populations. Coastal spraying along the Atlantic Ocean to control the salt marsh mosquito took a heavy toll on migrating birds, marine life, and raptors.

The effect of DDT on raptor populations is well known. In 1968 an article in *Science* magazine by wildlife ecologists Joseph Hickey and Daniel Anderson reported that the decline in populations of birds of prey was largely caused by eggshell breakage caused by chlorinated hydrocarbons. Calcium processes were altered in birds containing high DDT levels in their fatty tissues, resulting in the production of eggs with dangerously thin shells. The young did not hatch because the eggs were crushed during incubation. The American eagle and the osprey ended up on the brink of extinction largely as a result of widespread DDT use.

Ban on DDT

During the late 1950's the first DDT-related lawsuits were filed over losses to farmers and beekeepers and in attempts to stop further aerial spraying. The most notable case of the time was filed in 1957 by a group of citizens led by well-known ornithologist Robert Cushman Murphy in order to gain an injunction to stop the spraying of DDT over Long Island, New York. The injunction was not granted, but the case went all the way to the U.S. Supreme Court, which declined to hear it.

Perhaps one of the most significant events leading to the ban of DDT was the publication of Rachel Carson's book *Silent Spring* in 1962. The author described the negative environmental impact of pesticides such as DDT, and the subsequent public outcry led to a dramatic decline in DDT use. Production of DDT in the United States peaked in 1961, and global production began to decline around 1964. As a result of the controversy spawned by Carson's book, the President's Science Advisory Committee was charged with reviewing pesticide use. The committee's report, published in 1963, called for legislative measures to safeguard the health of the land and people against pesticides. The Federal Commission on Pest Control was established in 1964, and four governmental committees studied DDT in depth between 1963 and 1969. Ultimately, these investigations led to the establishment of the Environmental Protection Agency (EPA) in 1970.

DDT was also a major impetus for the formation of associations whose missions were aimed at protecting the environment and public health. The newly formed Environmental Defense Fund (EDF) initiated a series of court hearings and lawsuits related to DDT during the late 1960's. In October, 1969, it filed petitions with the USDA and the Department of Health, Education, and Welfare seeking elimination of the use of DDT. When no effective action resulted, EDF, along with other environmental groups and individuals, took the case to court. On May 28, 1970, the U.S. Court of Appeals for the District of Columbia rendered two major rulings on DDT in response to EDF's litigation. In addition to leading to the eventual ban of DDT, these rulings set important environmental law precedents: They provided power to membership associations (environmental groups) and served to protect public interests.

In 1972 the EPA banned the use of DDT in the United States except in cases of pest-control emergencies (for example, to avoid outbreaks of typhus, bubonic plague, and rabies) and highly restricted the use of other chlorinated hydrocarbons. However, the ban applied only to DDT use within U.S. borders; it still allowed American companies to produce DDT for export, which they continued to do for several years. Many other countries also banned or severely restricted DDT manufacture and use.

Persistence of DDT

Even decades after the ban on DDT in the United States and several other countries, the pesticide continues to be found in significant concentrations in marine animals and other wildlife. DDT can be detected in the tissues of almost every person on earth, especially indigenous peoples living in the Arctic and workers from insecticide production plants and agriculture. DDT is present in human breast milk, and it can pass through the placenta from mother to fetus to impair brain development and increase the risk of birth defects.

New concerns about DDT's toxicity arose as a result of studies published beginning during the early 1990's. Data suggest that DDT and its metabolites can act as endocrine disrupters—compounds that mimic naturally occurring hormones in animals. Evidence indicates that such compounds can decrease sperm count and fertility, affect the onset of puberty, alter male and female characteristics in wildlife, increase the risk of cancer of reproductive organs, and otherwise affect growth, development, metabolism, and reproduction.

In 2004 an international treaty restricting production and use of DDT entered into force. This treaty, the Stockholm Convention on Persistent Organic Pollutants, is intended to eliminate or reduce the release of several toxic, bioaccumulative chemicals. DDT is among the initial twelve persistent organic pollutants (POPs) specified in the treaty. Unlike most of the other POPs, DDT may be used for disease vector control under the Stockholm Convention until other effective and affordable control methods are available. The convention allows the spraying of indoor walls with DDT, notably as a weapon against malaria and other mosquito-borne tropical diseases, and many countries in Africa and Asia employ DDT in this way. South Africa credits much of its success in controlling malaria in the early twenty-first century to its reintroduction of DDT use in 2000. The World Health Organization recommends that if indoor DDT spraying for mosquito control is conducted, it should be part of an integrated vector management approach—that is, one that uses insecticide-treated mosquito nets, drainage of mosquito-breeding bodies of water, and other methods to discourage overdependence on DDT and development of DDT-resistant mosquito species.

Diane White Husic; updated by Karen N. Kähler

Further Reading

Carson, Rachel. Silent Spring. 40th anniversary ed. Houghton Mifflin, 2002.

Colborn, Theo, Dianne Dumanoski, and John P. Myers. Our Stolen Future: Are We Threatening Our Fertility, Intelligence, and Survival? Plume, 1996.

Dunlap, Thomas R., ed. DDT, "Silent Spring," and the Rise of Environmentalism: Classic Texts. University of Washington Press, 2008.

Glausiusz, Josie. "Can A Maligned Pesticide Save Lives?" Discover, November, 2007, 34-36.

Karasov, William H., and Carlos Martínez del Rio. Physiological Ecology: How Animals Process Energy, Nutrients, and Toxins. Princeton University Press, 2007.

Schapira, Allan. "DDT: A Polluted Debate in Malaria Control." The Lancet 368, no. 9553 (2006): 2111-2113.

World Health Organization. DDT and Its Derivatives: Environmental Aspects. Author, 1989.

■ Dioxin

FIELDS OF STUDY: Biology, Life Sciences, Ecosystems; Ecology, Environment, Environmentalism; Pollution, Emissions, Toxic Waste, Hazardous Materials; Elements, Substances, Chemicals, Compounds; Chemistry; Elements, Substances, Chemicals, Compounds; Pollution, Emissions, Toxic Waste, Hazardous Materials

DEFINITION: Toxic chemical that is a by-product of certain manufacturing processes

Dioxin has become an environmental concern because exposure to the chemical, even in trace amounts, can cause severe health problems in humans and other organisms.

Approximately seventy-five different types of dioxins exist, but the term "dioxin" is commonly used to refer to a variety known as 2,3,7,8-tetrachlorodibenzo-p-dioxin (TCDD), a highly toxic chemical that has caused great concern among environmentalists. Dioxin can be destroyed by exposure to direct sunlight in the presence of hydrogen, but the chemical can remain under the surface of the ground for ten years or longer.

One of the earliest documented cases of dioxin exposure occurred in West Germany in 1957, when thirty-one workers at a chemical plant developed chloracne, a skin disease that is one of the characteristic effects of exposure. In 1977 investigators in the Netherlands discovered dioxin in fly ash from a municipal incinerator. By 1980 scientists had determined that dioxin is produced when practically any organic substance is burned.

At first it was thought that chloracne was the only effect of exposure to dioxin. As time went on, however, experiments with animals revealed that dioxin is highly toxic. Researchers found that guinea pigs could be killed by as little as 1 microgram of dioxin per kilogram of body weight, but hamsters could take a dose of 5,000 micrograms per kilogram. Further experimentation showed that the organs within different animals were also affected differently by the chemical. Such differences among animal species and organs had never been found with any previously tested substance, and they invalidated the usual methods used in testing on animals. Because of this, dioxin became known as the first environmental hormone. That is, it acts like a hormone in animals and plants in that it has strange effects on various organs.

Scientists also began to suspect that dioxin could be involved in causing various cancers. The most famous exposure incident occurred between January, 1965, and April, 1970, when the US military used the defoliant Agent Orange during the Vietnam War to kill trees and plants that provided hiding places and food for North Vietnamese soldiers. One of the herbicides used was contaminated with dioxin during the manufacturing process. After the war, the National Academy of Sciences reviewed more than six thousand studies of dioxin exposure and came to the conclusion that four kinds of cancer could be linked to the chemical.

Other studies of dioxin exposure have produced mixed results. Thirty-seven thousand people were exposed to dioxin in Seveso, Italy, in 1976 after a factory explosion. Although no immediate human fatalities

Chemical structures of Dioxin isomers. Small blue numbers show numbering of atoms in hetero-cycle. By H Padleckas (Own work)

were traceable to the accident, a significant number of male births in the region were interrupted before term during the four months following exposure. Dioxin was therefore suspected of being a factor in the decline of male births worldwide. Two hundred workers were exposed to dioxin in 1949 at Nitro, West Virginia, and several died from cancer. Sweden reported six times the normal cancer rate in people exposed to dioxin, but Finland traced nineteen hundred cases of exposure and found no harmful effects. A Veterans Administration study of eighty-five thousand Vietnam veterans found lower-than-normal rates of cancer. Many researchers have explained such disparate findings by noting that dioxin does not seem to cause cancer itself; rather, it acts as an influence on other cancer-causing chemicals.

Another well-publicized dioxin incident occurred in 1983 in Times Beach, Missouri, when a local resident tried to settle the dust on the town's roads by wetting the roads with a spray of recycled oil that was unknowingly contaminated with dioxin. The federal government bought the entire town and moved everyone out to prevent any further exposure to the chemical, even though at the time it was not known that dioxin could cause any of the cancers later linked to exposure.

In a September, 1994, report, the Environmental Protection Agency (EPA) stated that perhaps no more than 14 kilograms (30 pounds) of dioxin are released into the US environment annually. Even this trace amount is unacceptable, however, given that dioxin is suspected of being an endocrine disrupter, which means that trace amounts can disrupt the effects of other hormones and cause numerous disorders. An EPA lab worker was quoted as saying, "I don't know a hormone system that dioxin doesn't like to disrupt." To make matters worse, approximately seventy other chemicals in the environment are also suspected of being disrupters, including dichloro-diphenyl-trichloro-ethane (DDT) and other insecticides that were used for many years. The 1994 EPA report also stated that dioxin may be responsible for damaging immune systems and creating other hormone-related diseases, such as diabetes. For example, mice treated with dioxin readily die after exposure to viruses that ordinarily would have no effect on them.

Scientific investigation of dioxin has expanded the view of environmental chemicals to include environmental hormones and hormone disrupters. These seventy or more substances are like no other chemicals known in the past, raising the critical question of how they are to be regulated when so little is known about their effects. All previous ways of measuring are invalid because these substances do not have uniform effects. One animal is killed by a tiny exposure and another is seemingly unharmed, while both may have internal effects that remain undiscovered.

Robert B. Bechtel

Further Reading

Friis, Robert H. "Pesticides and Other Organic Chemicals." *Essentials of Environmental Health.* Sudbury: Jones, 2007. Print.

Schecter, Arnold, and Thomas Gasiewicz, eds. *Dioxins and Health.* 2nd ed. New York: Taylor, 2002. Print.

Young, Alvin Lee. *The History, Use, Disposition, and Environmental Fate of Agent Orange.* New York: Springer, 2009. Print.

■ Diquat

FIELDS OF STUDY: Chemistry; Elements, Substances, Chemicals, Compounds; Industries, Commercial Products; Pollution, Emissions, Toxic Waste, Hazardous Materials; Ecology, Environment, Environmentalism

DEFINITION: Contact herbicide

As is the case for many herbicides, diquat has the potential to contaminate supplies of drinking water if it is released into wastewater and subsequently absorbed into soil.

The herbicide diquat, which has been used in the United States since the 1950's, is potentially toxic if swallowed or inhaled. It is not produced in the United States, but nearly one million pounds of the compound are imported each year. Approximately two-thirds of this amount is utilized as desiccant or defoliant, with another one-third used for aquatic weed control. Diquat is readily adsorbed into clay particles in the soil, sediment in water, and the surfaces of weeds. While it is biodegradable, if it is adsorbed into plant life and subject to photodegradation by sunlight, when bound to sediment diquat remains stable for weeks or even months. Ultimately, however, the herbicide undergoes degradation through the action of soil flora.

The extensive overgrowth of weeds affecting both crops and waterways has created significant problems in management. Regulations pertaining to use of herbicides remain under the auspices of the Environmental Protection Agency (EPA) and its various offices. Cutbacks in funding, however, have hampered research into the short- and long-term effects of using herbicides in the control of weed problems; therefore, the long-term effects of diquat are unclear.

Since diquat is a nonselective herbicide, its use is limited. It is used as a growth regulator in suppressing the flowering of sugarcane and to control aquatic weeds in the absence of endangered plant species. However, the most important use of diquat is in the desiccation of potato haulm or seed crops such as clover and alfalfa. Such practices are generally carried out to prepare crops for harvest. Application of diquat results in loss of moisture from the leaf, usually killing the plant. Desiccation may also be utilized in prevention of seed loss resulting from scattering of seed upon opening of the pod. The application of diquat prior to harvest of crops such as alfalfa greatly reduces seed loss.

The primary metabolic effect of diquat seems to be its ability to divert electrons activated during photosynthesis into the production of toxic compounds such as hydrogen peroxide. Peroxide production in turn results in membrane damage to those parts of the plant in contact with the herbicide. Human exposure to diquat is primarily occupational, with agricultural workers who use the chemical at highest risk. Most actual poisonings have been intentional, with diquat used as a means of suicide. Nevertheless, though diquat is not as toxic as some herbicides, the level of its toxicity is mainly a function of degree. Exposure to significant levels of the chemical may cause damage to the central nervous system and kidneys, while cataract formation is the most common effect of chronic exposure.

Richard Adler

Chemical structure of diquat. By Edgar181 (Own work)

Further Reading

Manahan, Stanley E. "Water Pollution." In *Fundamentals of Environmental Chemistry*. 2d ed. Boca Raton, Fla.: CRC Press, 2001.

Udeh, Patrick J. "Organic Contaminants in Drinking Water." In *A Guide to Healthy Drinking Water: All You Need to Know About the Water You Drink*. Lincoln, Nebr.: iUniverse, 2004.

■ Disposable diapers in landfills

FIELDS OF STUDY: Technology and Applied Science; Industries, Commercial Products; Ecology, Environment, Environmentalism; Pollution, Emissions, Toxic Waste, Hazardous Materials

DEFINITION: Single-use diapers made from paper and plastic products

Every year an estimated 27 billion or more soiled diapers end up in landfills in the United States alone. Since the 1970's, environmentalists have debated whether reusable cloth diapers are more earth-friendly than disposables. The convenience of disposables has led to their gaining and holding market dominance in the United States, and their use has spread even to developing nations.

The modern disposable diaper typically consists of a plastic layer treated with a surfactant that wicks moisture into the diaper and away from the skin; an absorbent layer of wood pulp mixed with sodium polyacrylate, a polymer that assumes a gel-like form when it is exposed to liquid; and a backing layer made from a plastic such as polyethylene. Leg cuffs and the top of the diaper are made from polypropylene or another water-resistant material to minimize leakage. Petroleum- and wood-derived adhesives are applied as a hot melt to hold the layers together. Some disposable diapers feature a reusable outer cover and a disposable or flushable liner. Other disposable absorbent goods, such as adult incontinence products and feminine sanitary products, have a composition similar to that of disposable diapers.

Although the wood pulp and human waste contained in disposable diapers are biodegradable, in conventional disposables these materials are sealed within the diapers' nonbiodegradable plastic backing. Furthermore, landfills do not contain the oxygen and water needed for the biodegradable components of disposable diapers to break down. It has been estimated that a disposable diaper would take 550 years to decompose in a landfill and 450 years to disintegrate in the ocean.

A 2005 industry report estimated that, on average, a baby uses a total of 3,700 to 4,200 diapers before toilet training is completed. Economic and cultural factors influence how many diapers a baby goes through before toilet training. In Japan, for example, diapers are changed more frequently than they are in the United States. However, babies in the United States take longer to toilet train, in part because of fears that rushing this phase of a child's development will cause psychological stress. The United States consumes more diapers per baby than do other countries. Some 96 percent of American babies wear disposable diapers. In a 2015 report, the Environmental Protection Agency estimated that in 2013 disposable diapers (for both infants and adults) accounted for 3.6 million tons of waste in municipal waste streams.

History

Disposable diapers began to appear on the market during the 1940's. The earliest disposables were high-cost, low-performance items intended for use primarily during travel. The diaper brand Pampers, which offered improved performance, was first marketed in 1961 but did not catch on quickly. The only convenience the disposables offered then was that they could be thrown away; caregivers still had to fold and pin them, just as they had to fold and pin cloth diapers. As the popularity of Pampers gained momentum, more brands were marketed, and the competition prompted improvements, such as prefolded and shaped diapers, greater absorbency, leak guards, resealable closures, different designs for boys and girls, and decorative plastic backings. By 1980 disposable diapers accounted for 1.4 percent of the discarded material in municipal waste streams.

While manufacturers worked on improving the convenience of the product for consumers, they also strove to address environmental concerns. They experimented with "green" disposables, which were made from plastic films that eventually broke down in water. Others had backings made from a cornstarch-polyethylene blend to promote degradation after they were discarded.

Procter & Gamble, the maker of Pampers, conducted two separate pilot programs during the late 1980's and early 1990's. One was intended to create a

Disposable diapers at Kroger. By ParentingPatch (Own work)

considerations but also because of concerns regarding infant health. A 1999 study had found that rats exposed to disposable diapers suffered eye, nose, and throat irritation. A study published the following year linked disposables with high testicular temperatures in boys and subsequent low sperm production.

Improved design also helped boost cloth diaper sales. Borrowing features from their disposable counterparts, modern cloth diapers included Velcro, button, and snap closures, elasticized legs, and liquid-resistant covers. "Hybrid" diapers were developed that combined reusability and disposability, featuring washable coverings fitted with flushable or compostable inserts.

Meanwhile, the disposable diaper industry made its own advances. Some manufacturers employed a new plastics additive technology to enable diapers to break down after sufficient exposure to light, heat, and mechanical stress. In some brands, chlorine bleaching was eliminated. By 2010 high-temperature composting methods, advanced plastics recycling technologies, and waste-to-energy schemes fueled by diapers were being explored.

partially flushable diaper. This was partly in response to complaints that fecal matter should enter the sewage system, not landfills. The program was discontinued after only three years, however, because consumers did not want to bother with removing the flushable inner section and discarding the plastic cover. Some municipal officials also claimed that diapers would overtax sewage treatment systems. Finally, the diaper was not compatible with water-saving, low-flush toilets.

In another program, Procter & Gamble set up centers to recycle diapers. The centers separated organic materials from the plastics, which were processed and recycled into other products. The company found that products made from recycled diapers had low marketability, however. The project was deemed a technical success but an economic failure.

In early 2008 *Time* magazine reported that cloth diapers had experienced sales increases of 25 to 50 percent in the preceding years. In some communities—including Westmount, Quebec; Vienna, Austria; and Munich, Germany—municipal solid waste departments had begun subsidizing cloth-diaper purchases to minimize the number of diapers discarded in landfills. The increasing appeal of reusables arose not only because of environmental

Disposable Versus Cloth

Proponents of disposable diapers argue that diapers in landfills are not the real issue; rather, the problem is garbage in general and the limited space for landfills. They maintain that the amount of garbage going into landfills during a baby's diapering life is minimal when compared with the total amount of garbage adults send to landfills each day. They assert that human urine and feces that travel to landfills with diapers are not really an issue, either, given that pet fecal matter also ends up in landfills, as does medical waste containing fecal matter and urine.

Those who object to disposable diapers because they contribute to the volume of solid waste sent to landfills argue that cloth diapers are the better alternative. They cite the potential for human fecal matter in landfills to contaminate groundwater with bacteria and viruses. Proponents of disposables counter that, whether parents launder their own cloth diapers or have a diaper service perform this chore, energy is burned and pollution is added to the environment. Hot water, bleach, and energy are used in washing and drying diapers. Diaper services consume additional energy by transporting soiled and cleaned diapers in fossil-fuel-burning motor vehicles, not to mention adding to traffic congestion; however, services have been shown to consume less wash water per diaper than does home laundering.

In regard to the energy and resources used to manufacture both types of diapers, neither appears to be an ideal option from the standpoint of the environment. Cloth diapers are typically made from cotton (although diapers made from other renewable resources, such as hemp and bamboo fiber, have become increasingly popular), and growing cotton consumes huge amounts of resources. Cotton is one of the most water-intensive crops grown, and vast quantities of pesticides are used on cotton unless it is grown organically. In addition, harvesting and transporting plant fiber consumes energy, and the chlorine bleach used in processing cotton produces toxic by-products. Spinning the fiber into cloth and fashioning it into diapers uses still more energy.

Conventional disposable diapers are made from wood pulp; although this is a renewable resource derived from trees, it does not replenish itself as quickly as cotton. Disposables also contain plastics, which are derived from nonrenewable petrochemical resources. Their manufacture consumes water and energy and involves chemical bleaching agents. Effluents from the pulp, paper, and plastics industries have a toxicity that rivals that of cotton-growing and -processing effluents.

The ways in which cloth diapers are washed and dried have a major influence on the environmental impacts of reusables. Home laundering tends to consume more water than do the laundering processes used by diaper services, but home launderers can minimize the environmental impacts of the use of cloth diapers by washing the diapers at lower temperatures and by line drying them instead of tumble drying them.

Lisa A. Wroble; updated by Karen N. Kähler

Further Reading

Aumônier, Simon, Michael Collins, and Peter Garrett. An Updated Lifecycle Assessment Study for Disposable and Reusable Nappies. Bristol, England: Environment Agency, 2008.

Brower, Michael, and Warren Leon. The Consumer's Guide to Effective Environmental Choices: Practical Advice from the Union of Concerned Scientists. New York: Three Rivers Press, 1999.

Management Institute for Environment and Business. "Procter & Gamble Inc.: Disposable and Reusable Diapers—A Life-Cycle Analysis." In Environmental Management: Readings and Cases, edited by Michael V. Russo. 2d ed. Thousand Oaks, Calif.: Sage, 2008.

US Environmental Protection Agency. "Advancing Sustainable Materials Management: Facts and Figures 2013." The United States Environmental Protection Agency, June 2015, p. 71, www.epa.gov/sites/production/files/2015-09/documents/2013_advncng_smm_rpt.pdf. Accessed 22 Mar. 2018.

■ Dolly the sheep

FIELDS OF STUDY: Technology and Applied Science; Inventions; Biology, Life Sciences, Ecosystems; Animals, Zoology, Marine Biology; Public Policy, Debates, Controversies

CATEGORY: Biotechnology and genetic engineering

IDENTIFICATION: First mammal successfully cloned from adult cells

DATES: Born July 5, 1996; died February 14, 2003

The birth of Dolly and subsequently cloned animals raised a host of ethical issues and opened the door to possible means of improving human health and the environment. Dolly's comparatively short life span, about half that of the typical sheep of her breed, may have been related to her clone origins.

On February 5, 1997, Ian Wilmut of the Roslin Institute in Edinburgh, Scotland, announced the birth of Dolly the sheep, the first clone produced from a cell taken from an adult mammal. Scientists and the general public were shocked at this announcement, because it was believed that cloning a mammal from an adult cell was, at the time, technically impossible.

Dolly was seven months old before her birth was made public. Because she was cloned from mammary cells, the research team named her after well-endowed country-western singer Dolly Parton.

How Dolly Was Created

A clone is an organism developed from a single cell isolated from another organism. The cell donor and the clone are genetically identical. Prior to the creation of Dolly, no attempts at cloning a mammal from adult cells had been unequivocally successful. In the early 1980's scientists had created clones of mammals by using donor cells from young embryos. The research team that cloned Dolly first cloned a pair of sheep, Megan and Morag, from embryonic cells grown in the laboratory. Adult cells and embryonic cells have identical genetic material, or deoxyribonucleic acid (DNA); however, adult cells produce proteins specific to the type of cell they become. For example, brain cells produce neurotransmitters and do not produce hemoglobin, even though they possess the hemoglobin gene. Scientists believed that the structure of the DNA in an adult cell was irreversibly altered during the process of maturation to gain this specificity and therefore could not be used to produce a clone.

Wilmut and his colleagues at the Roslin Institute used a novel approach to clone Dolly. The donor cells were sheep udder cells from a six-year-old pregnant ewe. The cells had been frozen for about three years, and the donor was long deceased. The researchers believed that prior attempts at cloning mammals from adult cells had failed because the cells were too active or in the wrong phase of their life. To make the cells quiescent, the research team starved them for several days. Meanwhile, the researchers removed genetic material of eggs from a different breed of sheep, a process called enucleation. They then fused the starved cells with the enucleated donor eggs and implanted them into surrogate mother sheep of a third breed. Of 277 attempts, only a single egg went full-term, resulting in the birth of Dolly. Dolly looked strikingly different from the breed of the egg donor or the surrogate mother but identical to the breed that donated the adult DNA, an observation that provides suggestive evidence that she developed from the donor DNA.

Initially many questions surrounded the validity of the experiment that produced Dolly. Some scientists believed that she could have been the result of a contaminating fetal cell, and the results of the experiment were not easily replicated by other researchers. However, in July, 1998, Japanese scientists announced the birth of two calves cloned from adult cow uterus cells, and researchers in Hawaii successfully produced more than fifty mouse clones from adult mouse ovarian cells. Also, DNA analysis of Dolly confirmed that she was indeed the first clone of an adult mammal. After reaching sexual maturity, Dolly mated naturally and on April 13, 1998, gave birth to a lamb, showing that she was a healthy young adult whose ability to reproduce was not compromised by her unusual origin. She would have two more pregnancies and bear five more lambs during her life.

Implications

In May, 1999, researchers found that the telomeres in Dolly's cells were shorter than those in other mammals of similar age, a finding borne out in other cloning research. Telomeres, which are sequences at the ends of chromosomes, become progressively shorter as an organism ages, but it was not clear whether Dolly's life span would be shorter than usual. By January, 2002, Dolly was showing signs of arthritis; whether the condition was the result of premature aging or the amount of time she had spent indoors on a hard floor was unclear. She subsequently developed a progressive lung disease.

The ailing Dolly was euthanized in February, 2003, at the age of six and a half. Sheep of her breed typically live to be about twelve. A postmortem examination confirmed that she had arthritis in her hind legs and that her lung ailment was sheep pulmonary adenomatosis (a lung tumor associated with a retrovirus), a fatal disease common in older sheep, particularly those living indoors. The examination revealed no other abnormalities. During her lifetime, she had tended toward stoutness, but her keepers attributed Dolly's weight problem not to her clone origins but to her living mostly indoors and being fed treats by her many visitors. Dolly's remains were donated to the National Museum of Scotland in Edinburgh, where her preserved body was placed on exhibit.

There are numerous potential applications for the cloning technology that produced Dolly. Scientists envision using cloning in tandem with genetic engineering to create animals with organs suitable for transplant into humans, or ones that produce human proteins for use in pharmaceuticals. In fact, Wilmut's research was sponsored by the Scottish pharmaceutical company PPL Therapeutics, Ltd. His subsequent research involved sheep cloned from fetal cells that had been genetically altered to carry a human gene that caused the animals' milk to contain a blood-clotting protein with the potential for use in treating human hemophilia.

Some researchers envision entire herds of genetically identical cattle. Because it is very difficult to produce prize milk- or meat-producing animals consistently with traditional breeding methods, repeated cloning of one prize breeding animal would greatly speed the process. A potentially serious problem with genetically identical herds, however, is that genetic diversity allows species to survive changes in their environment and attacks by disease. Diseases affecting only a few individuals of a genetically diverse species may become rampant in a genetically identical one. If genetic diversity is lost, it could lead to the extinction of that species.

Cloning has long been regarded as a possible means of bringing endangered animal species back from the brink of extinction, particularly those species that do not breed well in captivity. However, the expense and failure rate of the technique may be too great for it to be practicable. The year 2001 saw the birth of the world's first cloned endangered wild animals. A cloned gaur (a type of Southeast Asian ox) was successfully brought to term by a domestic cow that served as its surrogate mother, but the newborn succumbed to common dysentery two days after its birth. A cloned European mouflon, one of the world's smallest wild sheep species, fared better. Born to a domestic sheep, the mouflon was raised at a wildlife center in Sardinia. Other endangered species that have since been successfully cloned include the Javan banteng (a type of wild cattle) and the African wildcat. The first clone of an extinct animal was born in 2009. Cloned from the frozen skin of a bucardo, or Pyrenean ibex, a subspecies of wild goat that went extinct in 2000, the animal died minutes after birth.

Karen E. Kalumuck; updated by Karen N. Kähler

Further Reading

Einsiedel, Edna. "Brave New Sheep: The Clone Named Dolly." In *Biotechnology: The Making of a Global Controversy,* edited by Martin W. Bauer and George Gaskell. New York: Cambridge University Press, 2002.

Franklin, Sarah. *Dolly Mixtures: The Remaking of Genealogy.* Durham, N.C.: Duke University Press, 2007.

Kolata, Gina Bari. *Clone: The Road to Dolly, and the Path Ahead.* New York: HarperCollins, 1998.

Morgan, Rose M. *The Genetics Revolution: History, Fears, and Future of a Life-Altering Science.* Westport, Conn.: Greenwood Press, 2006.

Wilmut, Ian, Keith Campbell, and Colin Tudge. *The Second Creation: Dolly and the Age of Biological Control.* Cambridge, Mass.: Harvard University Press, 2001.

Wilmut, Ian, and Roger Highfield. *After Dolly: The Uses and Misuses of Human Cloning.* New York: W. W. Norton & Company, 2006.

See also: Biotechnology and genetic engineering; Cloning; Genetically modified organisms; Wilmut, Ian

---

■ Dolphin-safe tuna

FIELDS OF STUDY: Biology; Ecosystem Management; Fishing; Fisheries Management;

SIGNIFICANCE: Commercially produced food products containing tuna fish caught using methods that minimize dolphin mortality

In the mid-twentieth century, massive numbers of dolphins died in tuna nets. Concerns regarding the magnitude of the dolphin mortality led to the concept of dolphin-safe tuna, and laws, standards, and industry practices were established with the intent of protecting dolphins during tuna fishing.

Overview

The eastern tropical Pacific tuna fishery covers the ocean from California to Hawaii and south to the equator and Chile. Dolphins and yellowfin tuna frequently feed in the same areas within this region. During the mid-twentieth century, the tuna fishing industry adopted the practice of locating schools of tuna by spotting associated dolphin populations. Dolphins are mammals and must remain near the surface in order to breathe. The tuna fishing industry exploited this knowledge, using dolphins to locate yellowfin tuna swimming below the surface. During the late 1950's technological developments enabled fishing boats that had been limited to catching individual tuna with poles and lines to capture entire schools of the fish in purse-seine nets. It became

Dolphin safe tuna logo from the US Department of Commerce. By United States Department of Commerce (Source: NOAA website)

common industry practice to encircle dolphin schools with huge purse seines in order to capture the associated tuna schools. Dolphins and tuna together were herded with speedboats and helicopters into the nets. The dolphins, of no commercial value to the tuna fishing industry, were sometimes released alive, but often they became entangled in the nets and drowned.

By the early 1970's the number of dolphins killed annually in the eastern Pacific Ocean had risen to more than 300,000. A 2008 estimate by the U.S. National Oceanic and Atmospheric Administration (NOAA) Fisheries Service placed the number of dolphins killed by tuna fishing since the 1950's at more than 6 million.

Public awareness of the plight of the dolphins began as early as the mid-1960's, leading to the 1972 passage of the U.S. Marine Mammal Protection Act (MMPA). Intended to prevent exploitation of dolphins and related aquatic animals, the act limited the number of dolphins that could be killed annually to 20,500. Unsatisfied, conservationists and animal rights activists pushed for a tuna boycott, a move that succeeded largely because of the widespread popularity of dolphins. By 1977 annual dolphin deaths in

purse seines had declined to about 25,450. The respite was brief, however: As U.S. fishing fleets declined during the early 1980's, foreign vessels began to enter the eastern Pacific fishery. This led to an increase in dolphin mortality; by 1986, the numbers had risen to 133,000 deaths per year.

In 1990 declining sales and concern about public opinion led the three major canners of tuna sold in the United States to stop buying tuna that had been caught through the intentional setting of nets around dolphins. At the same time, much of the U.S. tuna fishing fleet moved into the western tropical Pacific Ocean, where tuna and dolphin do not habitually swim in the same waters. In November, 1990, the United States enacted the Dolphin Protection Consumer Information Act (DPCIA), which set conditions for protecting dolphins during purse-seine tuna fishing but included few provisions for enforcement. In 1994 provisions of the 1992 U.S. International Dolphin Conservation Act went into effect. Under the act, only dolphin-safe tuna—tuna caught using methods that do not involve chasing, encircling, or killing dolphins—could be sold in the United States, the country constituting the largest market for canned tuna.

Critics of the legislation claimed that canneries were simply using the term "dolphin-safe" as a marketing tool and that use of the term was no true guarantee of dolphin-friendly fishing practices. Criticism escalated after the MMPA was amended by the 1997 International Dolphin Conservation Act (IDCA), which redefined the dolphin-safe label. Under the new, looser guidelines, dolphins could be caught in nets as long as they were not physically harmed. An individual dolphin could thus legally be chased, captured, and released many times during its life.

In 1999, by which time reported dolphin mortality had fallen to fewer than 3,000 per year, the Agreement on the International Dolphin Conservation Program (AIDCP) went into effect. This binding document, which replaced a voluntary international program established during the early 1990's, adopted most of the IDCA's provisions. Over the next decade the United States, the European Union, and eleven other major fishing countries ratified or acceded to the AIDCP.

A 2004 decision in a lawsuit filed by the Earth Island Institute, the U.S. Humane Society, and other organizations restored the original definition of "dolphin-safe" for tuna sold in the United States. Tuna caught through methods that involve chasing, encircling, and capturing dolphins without physically harming them can legally be sold in the United States but cannot be labeled dolphin-safe. By 2008, according to figures from the NOAA Fisheries Service, the number of dolphins captured unintentionally by the tuna industry had been reduced to an estimated 1,000 per year.

P. S. Ramsey; updated by Karen N. Kähler

Further Reading

Bonanno, Alessandro, and Douglas Constance. *Caught in the Net: The Global Tuna Industry, Environmentalism, and the State.* University Press of Kansas, 1996.

Kennelly, Steven J., and Matt K. Broadhurst. "By-Catch Begone: Changes in the Philosophy of Fishing Technology." *Fish and Fisheries* 3, no. 4 (2002): 340-355.

White, Thomas I. *In Defense of Dolphins: The New Moral Frontier.* Blackwell, 2007.

■ Dredging

FIELDS OF STUDY: Biology, Life Sciences, Ecosystems; Ecology, Environment, Environmentalism; Oceans, Seas, Lakes, Bodies of Water; Mineral Resources

CATEGORY: Water and water pollution

DEFINITION: Removal by excavation or suction of sedimentary materials from the bottoms of lakes, rivers, estuaries, and coastal areas

Dredging is performed to maintain navigation systems, exploit mineral resources, or remove polluted bottom sediments. The activity of dredging disturbs bottom-dwelling organisms and has negative impacts on water quality. It also generates waste sediment, which must be used or disposed of in an environmentally responsible manner.

Natural erosion processes, sometimes enhanced or exacerbated by human activity, break down rock and soil into sediments that ultimately migrate downstream. When suspended sediments eventually sink to the bottom of a lake, river, estuary, or bay, they form deposits that can impede navigable waterways or increase the likelihood of flooding. Dredging, or removing underwater sediments with digging or suction equipment, keeps ports, harbors, and waterways open for commerce, security, flood-control, and recreational purposes.

Dredging also serves as a mining method. Where suspended sediments contain ore minerals, the dense ore particles sink more readily than nonore materials and form concentrated deposits. Diamonds, cassiterite (a major tin mineral), ilmenite (a titanium ore mineral), and gold are among the minerals mined by dredging. Other resources obtained through dredging include sand and gravel, which are used in construction. In areas where land is expensive, dredging river bottoms for these materials is an alternative to quarrying them on land. For example, dredging along the Kansas River in the Kansas City, Missouri, metropolitan area has provided a local source of sand and gravel for many years.

Another reason for dredging is to remove polluted bottom sediments from a body of water. Contaminant removal by dredging generates its own problems, as disturbing the sediments allows toxic materials that have settled out of suspension to reenter the overlying water, where they can affect aquatic life or be transported to another location. Maintenance dredging for navigation purposes is similarly problematic when it occurs in bodies of water where sewage or industrial pollutants have contaminated bottom sediments.

Large quantities of sediment are displaced during dredging operations. In the United States alone, maintenance dredging of navigable waters generates several hundred million cubic yards of sediment per year. In Southeast Asia, large dredges used to mine tin deposits handle more than 5 million cubic meters (177 million cubic feet) of sediment annually.

Dredging can mobilize existing contaminants but is not in itself a significant source of pollutants. However, dredging disrupts the habitats of bottom-dwelling organisms and can kill them outright. In addition, the dredging process and associated dumping of waste sediments in open waters causes turbidity (water cloudiness caused by suspended particles), which can harm or kill organisms that need clear water to survive. Oysters, for example, are detrimentally affected by turbid waters. Dredging can also affect erosion patterns, river flow, and ocean currents. In the Kansas River, dredging has removed far more sediment than can be replenished naturally. This has resulted in increased riverbank erosion, a wider and deeper river channel, a lowered water surface, a steeper bed gradient, and loss of vegetation and farmland along the river.

Clean dredged sediments can be employed for beneficial purposes, among them replenishing beaches and creating wetlands habitat. They can also be dried and used in construction materials or as fill dirt. Heavily polluted waste sediment must be sent to a secure disposal facility equipped to handle the contaminants in question.

In the United States, concerns about environmental degradation and watershed management issues related to dredging led to the adoption of a national dredging policy in 1995. The National Dredging Team (NDT), a multidisciplinary group made up of representatives from several governmental agencies and cochaired by the Environmental Protection Agency and the Army Corps of Engineers, serves as a forum for implementation of the policy. The NDT works to ensure that timely dredging operations keep navigable waterways open while protecting, conserving, and restoring the coastal environment. A priority of the NDT is the beneficial use of waste sediments.

Robert L. Cullers; updated by Karen N. Kähler

Further Reading

Bray, R. N., ed. *Environmental Aspects of Dredging.* London: Taylor & Francis, 2008.

National Dredging Team. *Dredged Material Management: Action Agenda for the Next Decade.* Washington, D.C.: U.S. Environmental Protection Agency, 2003.

Palermo, Michael R., et al. *Technical Guidelines for Environmental Dredging of Contaminated Sediments.* Vicksburg, Miss.: U.S. Army Corps of Engineers, Environmental Laboratory, 2008.

See also: Clean Water Act and amendments; Coastal Zone Management Act; Ocean dumping; Ocean pollution; Sedimentation; Water pollution

■ Drinking water

FIELDS OF STUDY: Biology; Biochemistry; Environmental Sciences; Hydrology;

SIGNIFICANCE: Water supplies that are safe for human consumption

Many areas of the world lack sufficient safe drinking water to support their populations. International, national, and local efforts have been undertaken to conserve existing water supplies, to clean up polluted water supplies with appropriate treatment, and to find new ways of distributing safe drinking water to those who need it.

Overview

In many parts of the world human beings lack access to safe drinking water. Millions of people die each year because of a lack of drinking water or because their water supplies are contaminated owing to unsanitary conditions. Even in developed countries where water supplies are sufficient, drinking water may contain dangerous contaminants, including such toxic chemicals as lead and arsenic, harmful microorganisms, and even radioactive compounds such as radon. In 2010, the United Nations declared clean water a universal human right, but as of 2017, according to a report by the World Health Organization and United Nations Children's Fund, 2.1 billion people still lacked access to safe drinking water at home and 4.5 billion did not have safely managed water sanitation services.

In June 2018, the United Nations released a report emphasizing the dire state of the world's safe water supply. The agency identified several elements that have continued to thwart the goal of ensuring access to safe water and sanitation for all people in the world by 2030. According to the report, urbanization, pollution, climate change, and population growth are just some of the factors causing the limitation of access to safe water due to environmental degredation and strain on natural resources such as water. The United Nations subsequently estimated that, based on trends at that point, between 4.8 and 5.7 billion people could be living in areas that are water-scarce for at least one month per year by 2050.

Quality, Accessibility, and Regulation

Most problems with water quality involve contamination with disease-causing (pathogenic)

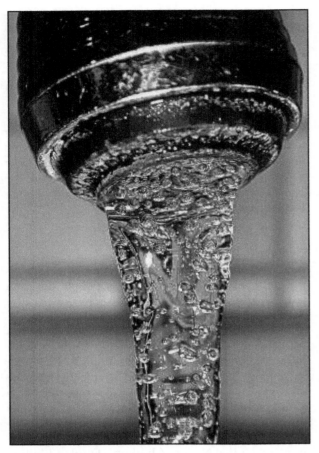

Photo taken by Alex Anlicker

drinking-water resources, even in regions with large supplies of water. In many developing countries people have no choice but to use water that is polluted with various wastes—including human sewage, animal excrement, and a variety of pathogenic microorganisms—because no water treatment systems are in place.

In many locations, drinking water is obtained from groundwater sources. Groundwater—water found beneath the ground surface in soil and rock spaces—can generally be used for drinking with minimal treatment because it has already been purified by passing through soil. Wells must be dug, drilled or bored in order to reach this water. A 2014 US Geological Survey report showed that in 2010, an estimated 63 percent of US public supply water (which includes drinking water for most households) came from rivers and lakes and about 37 percent from groundwater sources. According to the US Geological Survey, over 20 percent of total national water withdrawals in the United States came from groundwater sources in 2015. In many parts of the world, groundwater usage is increasingly outpacing the rate of groundwater replacement.

Several countries have introduced regulations intended to ensure the good quality of drinking water. In the United States, the Environmental Protection Agency (EPA) sets standards for drinking water under the 1974 Safe Drinking Water Act. These standards cover some ninety-four possible contaminants, including biological and chemical substances. For example, the EPA sets the acceptable number of microorganisms per 1 milliliter (0.034 ounce) of water at fewer than 10, and water that is considered drinkable can contain no coliform bacteria. However, many pharmaceutical contaminants are not covered by the EPA's regulations.

microorganisms. Safe, clean drinking water is free of all pathogenic microbes. A number of dangerous microorganisms can be transmitted by water, including viruses (for example, hepatitis A), bacteria (*Salmonella* and *Vibrio cholera*), protozoa (*Giardia, Cryptosporidium,* and *Entamoeba*), and parasitic worms, or helminths (*Ascaris lumbricoides*). Pollution and microbial contamination make the waters of most rivers, lakes, and ponds (surface water) unfit for human consumption without prior purifying treatment. The most common method of treating surface water to produce safe drinking water is disinfection by chlorination. Chloramines and ultraviolet light are also used for treatment.

A sufficient quantity of good-quality drinking water exists to satisfy the needs of all human beings on the planet, but the water is not distributed in such a way that it reaches populations in all parts of the world. Population growth also has impacts on

Desalination and Conservation

The need to obtain more drinking water in some regions has led to increased use of desalination technologies as well as increasing emphasis on the conservation of existing water supplies. The desalination of ocean water produces billions of gallons of drinking water per day around the world, but this process can have some negative environmental impacts, such as thermal pollution and damage to shoreline ecosystems.

Water conservation is the most cost-effective way to reduce demand for drinking water. Both local and national governments in many nations have introduced regulations and programs aimed at encouraging water conservation on the level of individual households; among the areas targeted for reduced usage of drinking-water supplies have been lawn maintenance and toilet flushing. The practice of rainwater harvesting is encouraged in some areas, and some governments have instituted strict compulsory water metering to raise awareness of the need to conserve water.

Another option for increasing supplies of drinking water is the restoration of municipal and industrial wastewater to drinkable quality. Using technologies such as membrane bioreactor treatment (which involves treating wastewater with certain types of microorganisms and then putting it through microfiltration, followed by disinfection with ultraviolet light), communities can turn their own wastewater into drinking water.

Sergei A. Markov

Further Reading

"Global Water, Sanitation, & Hygiene (WASH)." *Centers for Disease Control and Prevention.*, 8 Nov. 2013, www.cdc.gov/healthywater/global/index.html. Accessed 30 Jan. 2015.

"Goal 6: Ensure Access to Water and Sanitation for All." *Sustainable Development Goals: 17 Goals to Transform Our World,* United Nations, www.un.org/sustainabledevelopment/water-and-sanitation. Accessed 28 Mar. 2018.

Bakker, Karen, ed. *Eau Canada: The Future of Canada's Water* UBC Press, 2007.

de Villiers, Marq *Water* Stoddart, 2000.

Hammer, Mark J. *Water and Wastewater Technology.* Pearson, 2004.

Shannon, Mark A., et al. "Science and Technology for Water Purification in the Coming Decades." *Nature,* vol. 452, 2008, pp. 301–10.

Sigee, David. *Freshwater Microbiology.* Wiley, 2005.

Watts, Jonathan. "Water Shortages Could Affect 5bn People by 2050, UN Report Warns." *The Guardian,* www.theguardian.com/environment/2018/mar/19/water-shortages-could-affect-5bn-people-by-2050-un-report-warns. Accessed 20 Sept. 2018.

Wright, Richard T. *Environmental Science: Toward a Sustainable Future.* 10th ed., Pearson, 2008.

■ Drought

FIELDS OF STUDY: Climatology; Meteorology; Environmental Sciences; Environmental Studies; Climate Modeling; Physical Geography; Hydrometeorology; Hydroclimatology; Atmospheric Science; Climate Zones; Climate Classification; Hydrology; Earth System Modeling;

KEY CONCEPTS:

ADIABATIC: a change of temperature within the atmosphere that is caused by compression or expansion without transfer of heat into or out of the system

DESERTIFICATION: the relatively slow, natural conversion of fertile land into arid land or desert

EVAPOTRANSPIRATION: the combined water loss to the atmosphere from both evaporation and plant transpiration

PALMER DROUGHT INDEX: a widely adopted quantitative measure of drought severity that was developed by W. C. Palmer in 1965

POTENTIAL EVAPOTRANSPIRATION: the water needed for growing plants, accounting for water loss by evaporation and transpiration

PRECIPITATION: any form of liquid water or ice that falls from the atmosphere to the ground

SAHEL: the semiarid southern fringe of the Sahara in West Africa that extends from Mauritania on the Atlantic coast to Chad in the interior

SOIL MOISTURE: water that is held in the soil and that is therefore available to plant roots

SUBSIDENCE: in meteorology, the slow descent of air that becomes increasingly dry in the process, usually due to an area of high pressure

Drought is an unusually long period of below-normal precipitation. It is a relative rather than an absolute condition, but the end result is a shortage of water for plant growth, affecting the people who live in that region and beyond. Drought is particularly disastrous for farmers and the practice of agriculture.

Impact of Drought

Droughts have had enormous impacts on human societies since ancient times. The most obvious effect is crop and livestock failure, which have caused famine and death through thousands of years of human

---

A Time Line of Historic Droughts

1270-1350 SOUTHWEST: A prolonged drought destroys Anasazi Indian culture.

1585-1587 NEW ENGLAND: A severe drought destroys the Roanoke colonies of English settlers in Virginia.

1887-1896 GREAT PLAINS: Droughts drive out many early settlers.

1899   INDIA: The lack of monsoons results in many deaths.

1910-1915 SAHEL, AFRICA: First in a series of recurring droughts.

1933-1936 GREAT PLAINS: Extensive droughts in the southern Great Plains destroy many farms and create the Dust Bowl during the worst U.S. drought in more than 300 years.

1968-1974 SAHEL, AFRICA: Intense period of drought; 22 million affected in four countries, 200,000-500,000 estimated dead, millions of livestock lost.

1977-1978 WESTERN UNITED STATES: Severe drought compromises agriculture.

1981-1986 AFRICA: Drought in 22 countries, including Angola, Botswana, Burkina Faso, Chad, Ethiopia, Kenya, Mali, Mauritania, Mozambique, Namibia, Niger, Somalia, South Africa, Sudan, Zambia, and Zimbabwe, results in 120 million people affected, several million forced to migrate, significant loss of life and of livestock.

1986-1988 MIDWEST: Many farmers are driven out of business by a drought.

1986-1992 SOUTHERN CALIFORNIA: Drought brings increased water prices, loss of water for agricultural production, water rationing.

1998   MIDWEST: Drought destroys crops in the southern part of the Midwest.

1999   LARGE PART OF UNITED STATES: Major drought strikes the Southeast, the Atlantic coast, and New England; billions of dollars in damage to crops.

Beg. 2006 WESTERN UNITED STATES: Drought-induced wildfires cause significant property and environmental damage in both urban and rural areas.

---

history. Drought has resulted in the demise of some ancient civilizations and, in some instances, the forced mass migration of large numbers of people. Water is so critical to all forms of life that a pronounced shortage could, and has, decimated whole populations.

The effects of drought are profound. The dry conditions in the Great Plains of North America in the early 1930's in conjunction with extensive and improper farming activities resulted in the creation of the Dust Bowl, which at one point covered more than 200,000 square kilometers, or an area about the size of Nebraska. During the early 1960's, a severe drought affected the Mid-Atlantic states. Parts of New Jersey experienced sixty consecutive months of below-normal precipitation, so depleting local water supplies that plans were actively considered to bring rail cars of water into Newark and other cities in the northern part of the state, as the reservoirs that usually supplied the region were practically dry. The

Sahel region south of the Sahara in West Africa had a severe drought beginning in the late 1960's and continuing into the early 1970's, creating an enormous negative impact on the local population, livestock, and vegetation. Hundreds of thousands of people starved, thousands of animals died, and many tribes were forced to migrate south to areas of more reliable precipitation. Large areas of eastern Africa in the Sudans and Ethiopia continue to experience an on-going state of drought.

Drought Characteristics

Almost all droughts occur when slow-moving air masses that are characterized by subsiding air movements dominate an area. Often, the air comes from continental interiors where the amount of moisture that is available for evaporation into the atmosphere is very limited. When these conditions occur, the potential for precipitation is low for a number of reasons. First, the humidity in the air is already low, as the continental air mass is distant from maritime (moist) influences. Second, air that subsides undergoes adiabatic heating at the rate of 10°C per 1,000 meters.

The term "adiabatic" refers to a change of temperature within a gas (such as the atmosphere) that occurs as a result of compression (descending air) or expansion (rising air), without any input or extraction of heat from external sources. For example, assume that air at a temperature of 0°C is passing over the Sierra Nevada in eastern California at an elevation of 3,500 meters. As the air descends and reaches Reno, Nevada, at an elevation of 1,200 meters, the higher atmospheric pressure found at lower elevations results in compression and heating at the dry adiabatic rate of 10°C per 1,000 meters, yielding a temperature in the Reno area of 23°C. Thus, adiabatic heating from subsiding air masses results in a decline in relative humidity and an increase in moisture-holding capacity. In addition, the movement of air under these conditions is usually unfavorable for vertical uplift and the beginning of the condensation process. The final factor that reduces precipitation potential is the decrease in cloudiness and corresponding increase in sunshine, which in turn leads to an increase in evapotranspiration demands that favor soil moisture loss.

Another characteristic associated with droughts is that once established, they appear to persist and even expand into nearby regions, resulting in desertification in extreme cases. This tendency is apparently related to positive feedback mechanisms. For example, the drying out of the soil influences air circulation and the amount of moisture that is then available for precipitation farther downwind. At the same time, the atmospheric interactions that lead to unusual wind systems associated with droughts can induce surface-temperature variations that, in turn, lead to further development of the unusual circulation pattern. Thus, the process builds on itself, causing the drought to both last longer and intensify. The situation persists until a major change occurs in the circulation pattern in the atmosphere.

Many climatologists concur with the concept that precipitation is not the only factor associated with drought. Other factors that demand consideration include moisture supply, the amount of water in storage, and the demand generated by evapotranspiration. Although the scientific literature is replete with information about the intensity, length, and environmental impacts of drought events, the role of individual climatological factors that can increase or decrease the severity of a drought is not fully understood.

Drought Identification

Research in drought identification has been changing over the years. Drought was once considered solely in terms of precipitation deficit. Although that lack of precipitation is still a key atmospheric component of drought, sophisticated techniques are now used to assess the deviation from normal levels of the total environmental moisture status. These techniques have enabled investigators to better understand the severity and length of drought events, as well as the extent of the affected area.

Drought has been defined in a number of ways. Some authorities consider it to be merely a period of below-normal precipitation, while others relate it to the likelihood of forest fires. Drought is also said to occur when the yield from a specific agricultural crop or pasture is significantly less than expected. It has also been defined as a period when soil moisture or groundwater decreases to a critical level.

Drought was identified early in the twentieth century by the U.S. Weather Bureau as any period of twenty-one or more days when precipitation was 30 percent or more below normal. Subsequent examination of drought events that were identified by this method revealed that soil moisture reserves were often elevated during these events to the extent that there was sufficient water to support vegetation. It was also determined that the amount of precipitation preceding the drought event was ample or even heavy. Thus, it became apparent that precipitation should not be used as the sole measure to identify drought. Subsequent research has shown that the moisture status of an area is affected by additional factors.

Further developments in drought identification during the middle decades of the twentieth century began to focus on the moisture demands that are associated with evapotranspiration in an area. Evaporation is primarily the process by which liquid water becomes water vapor at the surface and enters the atmosphere. To a lesser extent, this also includes the conversion of "solid water," as ice and snow, either directly by sublimation or through first melting into an intermediate liquid state. Transpiration refers to the loss of moisture by plants to the atmosphere. Although evaporation and transpiration can be studied and measured separately, it is convenient to consider them in applied climatological studies as the single process of evapotranspiration.

There are two ways to define evapotranspiration. The first is actual evapotranspiration, which is the actual or real rate of water-vapor return to the atmosphere from the earth and vegetation; this process could also be called "water use." The second is potential evapotranspiration, which is the theoretical rate of water loss to the atmosphere if one assumes continuous plant cover and an unlimited supply of water. This process could also be called "water need," as it indicates the amount of soil water needed if plant growth is to be maximized. Procedures have been developed that enable one to calculate the potential evapotranspiration for any area from monthly mean temperature and precipitation values.

Some drought-identification studies have focused on agricultural drought, looking at the adequacy of soil moisture in the root zone for plant growth. This procedure involved the evaluation of precipitation, evapotranspiration, available soil moisture, and the water needs of plants. The goal of this research was to determine drought probability based on the number of days when soil moisture storage is reduced to zero.

Evapotranspiration was also used by the Forest Service of the U.S. Department of Agriculture when it developed a drought index to be used by fire-control managers. The purpose of the index was to provide a measure of flammability that could create forest fires. This index has limited applicability to nonforestry users, as it is not effective for showing drought as an indication of total environmental stress.

Palmer Drought Index

One of the most widely adopted drought-identification techniques was developed by W. C. Palmer in 1965. The method, which became known as the Palmer Drought Index, defines drought as the period of time, usually measured in months or years, when the actual moisture supply at a given location is consistently less than the climatically anticipated or appropriate supply of moisture. The calculation of this index requires the determination of evapotranspiration, soil moisture loss, soil moisture recharge,

surface runoff, and precipitation. The Palmer Drought Index values range from approximately +4.0 for an extremely wet moisture status class to -4.0 for extreme drought. Normal conditions have a value close to 0. Positive values indicate varying stages of abundant moisture, whereas negative values indicate varying stages of drought.

Although the Palmer Drought Index is recognized as an acceptable procedure for incorporating the role of potential evapotranspiration and soil moisture in magnifying or alleviating drought status, there have been some criticisms of its use. For example, the method produces a dimensionless parameter of drought status that cannot be directly compared with other environmental moisture variables, such as precipitation, which are measured in units (centimeters, millimeters) that are immediately recognizable. In addition, the index is not especially sensitive to short drought periods, which can affect agricultural productivity.

In order to address these shortcomings, other researchers use water-budget analysis to identify deviations in environmental moisture status. The procedure is similar to the Palmer method inasmuch as it incorporates the environmental parameters of precipitation, potential evapotranspiration, and soil moisture. However, the moisture status departure values are expressed in the same units as precipitation and are therefore dimensional. Drought classification using this index method ranges from approximately 25 millimeters for an above-normal moisture status class to -100 millimeters for extreme drought. The index would be close to 0 for normal conditions.

Significance

Drought is invariably associated with some form of water shortage, yet many regions of the world have regularly occurring periods of dryness. Three different forms of dryness have a temporal dimension described as perennial, seasonal, and intermittent. Perennially dry areas include the major deserts of the world, such as the Sahara, Arabian, and Kalahari. Precipitation in these areas is not only very low but also very erratic. Seasonal dryness is associated with regions where the bulk of the annual precipitation comes during a few months of the year, leaving the rest of the year without rain or other precipitation. Intermittent dryness is associated with those instances where the overall precipitation is reduced in humid regions or where the rainy season in seasonally dry areas does not occur or is shortened.

The absence of precipitation when it is normally expected creates variable problems. For example, the absence of precipitation for one week in an area where daily precipitation is the norm would be considered a drought. In contrast, it would take two or more years without any rain in parts of Libya in North Africa for a drought to occur. In those areas that have one rainy season, a 50 percent reduction in precipitation would be considered a drought. In regions that have two rainy seasons, the failure of one could lead to drought conditions. Thus, the word "drought" is a relative term, as it has different meanings in different climatic regions.

User demands also influence drought definition. Distinctions are often made among climatological, agricultural, hydrologic, and socioeconomic drought. Climatological, or meteorological, drought occurs at irregular periods of time, usually lasting months or years, when the water supply in a region falls far below the levels that are typical for that particular climatic regime. The degree of dryness and the length of the dry period are used as the definition of drought. For example, drought in the United States has been defined as occurring when there is less than 2.5 millimeters of rain in a forty-eight hour period. In Great Britain, drought has been defined as occurring when there are fifteen consecutive days with less than 0.25 millimeter of rain for each day. In Bali, Indonesia, drought has been considered as occurring if there is no rain for six consecutive days.

Agricultural drought occurs when soil moisture becomes so low that plant growth is affected. Drought must be related to the water needs of the crops or animals in a particular place, since agricultural systems vary substantially. The degree of agricultural drought also depends on whether shallow-rooted or deep-rooted plants are affected. In addition, crops are more susceptible to the effects of drought at different stages of their development. For example, inadequate moisture in the subsoil in an early growth stage of a particular plant will have minimal impact on crop yield as long as there is adequate water available in the topsoil. However, if subsoil moisture deficits continue, then the yield loss could become substantial.

Hydrologic drought definitions are concerned with the effects of dry spells on surface flow and groundwater levels. The climatological factors associated with the drought are of lesser concern. Thus, a hydrological drought for a particular watershed is said to occur when the runoff falls below some arbitrary value. Hydrological droughts are often out of phase with climatological and agricultural droughts and are also basin-specific; that is, they pertain to the particular watersheds that they affect.

Socioeconomic drought includes features of climatological, agricultural, and hydrological drought and is generally associated with the supply and demand of some type of economic good. For example, the interaction between farming (demand) and naturally occurring events (supply) can result in inadequate water for both plant and animal needs. Human activities, such as poor land-use practices, can also create a drought or make an existing drought worse. The Dust Bowl in the Great Plains and the Sahelian drought in West Africa provide ready examples of the symbiotic relationship between drought and human activities.

In a sense, droughts differ from other major geophysical events such as volcanic eruptions, floods, and earthquakes because they are actually nonevents. They result from the absence of events (precipitation) that should normally occur. Droughts also differ from other geophysical events in that they often have no readily recognizable beginning and take some time to develop. In many instances, droughts are only recognized when plants start to wilt, wells and streams run dry, and reservoir shorelines recede.

There is wide variation in the duration and extent of droughts. The length of a drought cannot be predicted, as the irregular patterns of atmospheric circulation are not fully known and remain unpredictable. A drought ends when the area receives sufficient precipitation and water levels rise in the wells and streams. Because the severity and areal extent of a drought cannot be predicted, all that is really known is that they are an integral part of the overall natural system and that they will continue to occur.

Robert M. Hordon

Further Reading

Ahrens, C. Donald. *Meteorology Today: An Introduction to Weather, Climate and the Environment.* 8th ed. Thomson Brooks-Cole, 2007.

Bryson, Reid A., and Thomas J. Murray. *Climates of Hunger.* University of Wisconsin Press, 1977.

Climate, Drought, and Desertification. World Meteorological Organization, 1997.

Dixon, Lloyd S., Nancy Y. Moore, and Ellen M. Pint. *Drought Management Policies and Economic Effects in Urban Areas of California, 1987–92.* RAND, 1996.

Fisher, R. J. *If Rain Doesn't Come: An Anthropological Study of Drought and Human Ecology in Western Rajasthan.* Manohar, 1997.

Frederiksen, Harald D. *Drought Planning and Water Resources Implications in Water Resources Management.* World Bank, 1992.

Hidore, John, John E. Oliver, Mary Snow, and Richard Snow. *Climatology.* 3d ed. Merrill, 1984.

Knight, Gregory, Ivan Raev, and Marieta Staneva, eds. *Drought in Bulgaria.* Ashgate Publishing Limited, 2004.

Mainguet, Monique. *Aridity: Drought and Human Development.* Springer-Verlag, 2010.

Lutgens, Frederick K., Edward J. Tarbuck, and Dennis Tasa. *The Atmosphere: An Introduction to Meteorology.* 11th ed. Prentice Hall, 2009.

Wilhite, Donald A., ed. *Drought and Water Crises: Science, Technology, and Management Issues.* CRC Press, 2005.

Wilhite, Donald A., and William E. Easterling, with Deborah A. Wood, eds. *Planning for Drought: Toward a Reduction of Societal Vulnerability.* Westview Press, 1987.

Workman, James G. *Heart of Dryness: How the Last Bushmen Can Help Us Endure the Coming Age of Permanent Drought.* Walker Publishing Company, 2009.

■ Dubos, René

FIELDS OF STUDY: Ethics, Advocacy, Policy, Protest; Ecology, Environment, Environmentalism; Popular Culture, Media, Publishing; Authors, Writers; Journalism, Publishing, Literature; Scientists, Engineers

CATEGORIES: Activism and advocacy; ecology and ecosystems

IDENTIFICATION: French-born American bacteriologist and environmental writer

Through his writings, Dubos encouraged exploration of the manner in which humans interact with the environment.

René Dubos was born into a family of poor French shopkeepers. He excelled as a student in the Collège Chaptal in Paris and decided to pursue a career as a scientist. Later, inspired by the work of Louis Pasteur, about whom he wrote two books, Dubos determined to study bacteriology. In 1924 he settled in the United States, and he eventually became a U.S. citizen. From 1924 to 1927 Dubos undertook study and research at Rutgers University in New Jersey and then moved to Rockefeller University in New York City. Except for a brief period at Harvard (from 1942 to 1944), he remained associated with Rockefeller University until he became director of Environmental Studies at the State University of New York College at Purchase in 1971.

Dubos first achieved international recognition through his discovery of what would become the first commercially marketed antibiotic, tyrothricin, in 1939. The development of tyrothricin awakened medical researchers to the enormous possibilities for soil-produced antibacterial agents.

During the 1950's Dubos developed an interest in ecology, and over the next twenty-five years, he became one of the world's most outspoken and heralded environmentalists. Aided by his second wife, Letha Jean Porter, a former research associate, Dubos wrote prolifically about environmental issues and the way humans ought to relate to the natural world. He emphasized that the quality of human life (mental, physical, and spiritual) depends primarily on the establishment of a symbiotic relationship between humankind and nature. He rejected the claims made by more extreme environmentalists that human life is destined to become extinct on a planet filled with chemical waste.

Dubos's book *The Unseen World* (1962) gained him international recognition as an influential commentator on the environment. There followed a series of books over the next thirty years, including *So Human an Animal* (1968), *A God Within* (1972), and *The Wooing of Earth* (1980). In 1969 he was cowinner of the Pulitzer Prize in general nonfiction for *So Human an Animal.* In the 1960's and 1970's Dubos achieved a sort of celebrity status and was often featured in major newsmagazines and newspapers.

Dubos's most important contribution to the environmental dialogue was a report published in 1972 as *Only One Earth: The Care and Maintenance of a Small Planet.* Maurice Strong, general secretary for the United Nations Conference on the Human

Environment, commissioned Dubos to chair an international committee of experts that would prepare a commentary on the condition of the earth for the United Nations Conference on the Human Environment, held in Stockholm, Sweden, in 1972. Dubos then chose well-known British environmentalist Barbara Ward to assist in preparing and writing the final report. Much of the Ward-Dubos report focused on the need to maintain a balance in the earth's ecosystems—a balance that was in jeopardy. Although many of the experts consulted were displeased that *Only One Earth* did not predict doom, the report inspired the United Nations to focus attention on worldwide environmental problems. As a consequence, the Stockholm Conference established the United Nations Environment Programme to observe environmental issues and coordinate information about them on a worldwide basis.

Ronald K. Huch

Further Reading

Cooper, Jill E. "A Brief Romance with Magic Bullets: René Dubos at the Dawn of the Antibiotic Era." In *Silent Victories: The History and Practice of Public Health in Twentieth-Century America*, edited by John W. Ward and Christian Warren. New York: Oxford University Press, 2007.

Moberg, Carol L. *René Dubos, Friend of the Good Earth: Microbiologist, Medical Scientist, Environmentalist*. Washington, D.C.: ASM Press, 2005.

See also: Spaceship Earth metaphor; United Nations Conference on the Human Environment; United Nations Environment Programme

---

■ Ducktown, Tennessee

FIELDS OF STUDY: Biology, Life Sciences, Ecosystems; Ecology, Environment, Environmentalism; Pollution, Emissions, Toxic Waste, Hazardous Materials; Mineral Resources

IDENTIFICATION: Town in southeastern Tennessee

Copper mining operations that began in Ducktown, Tennessee, during the late nineteenth century led to the eradication of plant life and subsequent soil erosion in the region. The transformation of forestland into an artificial desert demonstrated the hazards of extracting natural resources without consideration for its effect on the surrounding area.

In 1843 a gold rush led prospectors to the southeastern corner of Tennessee, where, instead of gold, they found copper. This discovery led to the founding of several mining companies in 1850. The Copper Basin, an area of approximately 19,400 hectares (48,000 acres) surrounding the area where the city of Ducktown is located, was the only place in the eastern United States to produce significant amounts of copper, and by 1902 Tennessee was the sixth-largest copper-producing state in the nation.

After the copper ore was mined, it was put through a process called roasting to separate the copper from the rest of the ore, which included zinc, iron, and sulfur. Firewood was harvested from the surrounding forests and placed in heaps in roofed sheds with open sides. The ore was piled onto the heaps of firewood, which were then lit. These heaps, which covered vast areas of ground, were then allowed to roast for three months.

The smoke arising from the ores during the roasting was highly sulfuric. In addition to hindering vision, the smoke contained sulfuric gas, sulfuric dust, and sulfuric acid that descended onto the earth. The extent of the pollution was first acknowledged around 1895, when individual citizens filed lawsuits for damage to vegetation. The state of Georgia filed similar lawsuits in 1904 and 1905. The heap method was soon abandoned. Instead, raw ore was smelted in furnaces without being roasted first.

The ore-processing companies also built taller smokestacks to take advantage of higher air currents that would disperse the smoke, but that only spread the sulfuric vapors over a larger area. It was not until 1911 that the problem of sulfuric pollution was controlled to some extent by a process that captured the smoke for the valuable sulfuric acid that could be derived from it. By that time, the years of sulfuric pollution and systematic deforestation had turned the Ducktown area into the only desert east of the Mississippi River. Erosion washed away the topsoil, leaving a bare, rocky terrain that, at its greatest extent, covered about 130 square kilometers (50 square miles). Copper mining continued until 1986, when it became impossible for local producers to compete with the price of imported copper.

During the 1930's copper mining companies worked with the Tennessee Valley Authority (TVA) to reforest the area. More than fourteen million trees were planted over the next several decades, and grasses were also planted. Little resulted from the

The Ducktown Historic District in Ducktown, Tennessee, in the southeastern United States. By Brian Stansberry (Own work)

The Dust Bowl revealed the damage that mechanized agriculture could cause if not accompanied by a program of soil management.

Overview

Droughts periodically occur in the Great Plains of the United States. During such periods, winds pick up loose soil and create dust storms, especially during the spring months. Settlers reported numerous examples of this natural phenomenon during the nineteenth century. During the twentieth century, new agricultural practices and overgrazing by cattle sped soil erosion in the region. Tractors and other machines allowed farmers to plow larger areas for planting wheat. In the process, they destroyed the natural grasses, the root systems of which had stabilized the soil. Because the wheat replaced the grasses, most farmers remained unaware that they were contributing to a coming catastrophe.

In 1931 a severe drought struck the Great Plains; it centered on the Texas and Oklahoma panhandles, northeastern New Mexico, eastern Colorado, and southwestern Kansas. The wheat crop withered in the fields, and its root systems were no longer able to support the soil. As the drought continued, soil particles that normally clustered together within grass root networks separated into a fine dust. When the winds blew in early 1932, they lifted the dust into the air, marking the beginning of the environmental disaster that a newspaper reporter later dubbed the Dust Bowl.

Although their number and severity increased, dust storms remained an issue of local and regional concern for the first two years. However, as the drought continued into 1934, the storms grew so immense that they caused damage in areas far from the plains. A storm that emanated from Montana and Wyoming in May, 1934, deposited an estimated twelve million tons of dust on Chicago, Illinois. Ships that were some 480 kilometers (300 miles) offshore in the Atlantic Ocean reported that dust from the same storm landed on their decks. Incidents such as

plantings until the 1970's, when improved methods of fertilization and soil churning increased the plants' chances of survival. By the 1990's only about 405 hectares (1,000 acres) of land appeared to be bare, with large gullies and widely spaced trees. The restoration of the forest was not totally accepted by local residents, however, who believed that a small portion of the desert should be saved as an example of severe environmental degradation.

Rose Secrest

Further Reading

Davis, Donald Edward. *Where There Are Mountains: An Environmental History of the Southern Appalachians.* Athens: University of Georgia Press, 2000.

Pipkin, Bernard W., et al. *Geology and the Environment.* 5th ed. Belmont, Calif.: Thomson Brooks/Cole, 2008.

■ Dust Bowl ecological disaster

FIELDS OF STUDY: Agriculture; Climatology; Environmental Science; Environmental Studies; History; Hydrology; Meteorology;

THE EVENT: Environmental disaster marked by huge dust storms in the southern region of the Great Plains of the United States

DATE: 1930's

A farmer's son sits on a sand dune near his home in Liberal, Kansas, during the 1930's. (Library of Congress)

these provoked national concern over the growing crisis on the plains.

Scientists identified two types of dust storms: those caused by winds from the southwest and those resulting from air masses moving from the north. While no less damaging, the more frequent southwest storms tended to be milder than the terrifying northern storms, which came to be known as "black blizzards." Huge walls of dust, sometimes more than 1.6 kilometers (1 mile) high, rolled across the plains at 100 kilometers per hour (62 miles per hour) or faster, driving frightened birds before them. The sun would disappear, it would become as dark as night, and frightened people would huddle in their homes, their windows often taped shut. On occasion, people stranded outside during these severe storms suffocated. Some black blizzards lasted less than one hour; others reportedly continued for longer than three days.

Most historians argue that the Dust Bowl was one of the worst ecological disasters in the United States, one that could have been mitigated had farmers practiced soil conservation in the years before drought struck. Instead, farms were ruined, causing some 3.5 million people to abandon the land. Many of them moved into small towns on the plains, while others journeyed to California in search of

opportunity. Cattle and wildlife choked to death. Human respiratory illnesses increased markedly during the Dust Bowl era, and a number of people died from an ailment known as dust pneumonia. Anecdotal evidence indicates that many people grew depressed as the dust storms continued year after year.

The mid-1930's marked the peak of the Dust Bowl, with seventy-two storms that reduced visibility to less than 1.6 kilometers (1 mile) reported in 1937. The return of the rain in the late 1930's eased the crisis, and by 1941 the disaster was over. However, by that time ecologists and farmers had begun to undertake soil conservation measures in response to the crisis. The U.S. government provided expertise and financial support for many of these efforts. Farmers practiced listing, a plowing process that makes deep furrows to capture the soil and prevent it from blowing. Alternating strips of planted wheat with dense, drought-resistant feed crops such as sorghum slowed erosion by blocking wind and retaining moisture, which prevented the soil from separating into dust. On lands not farmed, natural grasses were planted to prevent erosion. The government also sponsored the Shelterbelt Project, a program that used rows of trees to form windbreaks. Millions of trees were planted throughout the Great Plains, with more than 4,828 kilometers (3,000 miles) of shelterbelts created in Kansas alone.

Despite the experiences of the 1930's, once the drought ended many farmers returned to the farming practices that had damaged their fields. Soil conservation experts worried that the region would suffer a return of Dust Bowl conditions when the rains stopped. Their predictions came to pass in 1952, when another drought led to a series of dust storms, including several storms with wind gusts clocked at 129 kilometers (80 miles) per hour. That drought ended in 1957, but in accord with a twenty-year cycle, the region again faced a shortage of rainfall in the early 1970's. At that time some analysts confidently predicted that dust storms such as those seen in the 1930's were a thing of the past. They claimed that irrigation with aquifer water from deep wells would prevent soil erosion. However, shrewd

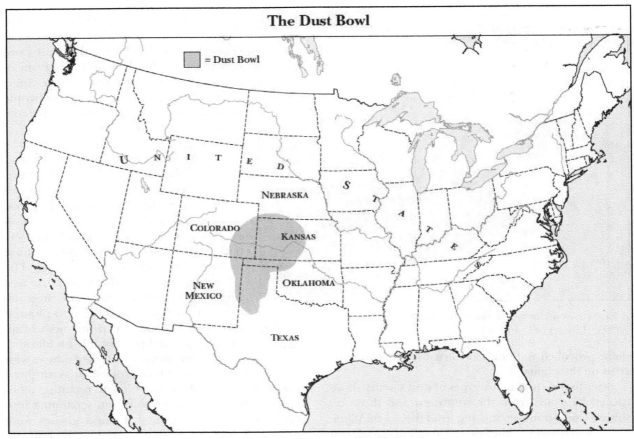

The Dust Bowl

□ = Dust Bowl

observers pointed out that the fate of the region was now tied to a resource, aquifer water, that would become increasingly precious in the coming years. The possibility that the Great Plains could again witness a devastating ecological catastrophe like that of the 1930's remains.

Thomas Clarkin

Further Reading

Bonnifield, Paul. *The Dust Bowl: Men, Dirt, and Depression.* University of New Mexico Press, 1979.

Cunfer, Geoff. *On the Great Plains: Agriculture and Environment.* Texas A&M University Press, 2005.

Hurt, R. Douglas. *The Dust Bowl: An Agricultural and Social History.* Burnham, 1981.

Lookingbill, Brad D. *Dust Bowl, USA: Depression America and the Ecological Imagination, 1929-1941.* Ohio University Press, 2001.

Worster, Donald. *Dust Bowl: The Southern Plains in the 1930s.* 25th anniversary ed. Oxford University Press, 2004.